IN DEFENCE
OF
NAVAL SUPREMACY

"For understanding the dreadnought revolution, Jon Sumida's *In Defence of Naval Supremacy* is as important as V.R. Berghahn's *Tirpitz-Plan* for the German naval buildup."

Professor Charles Fairbanks, *International History Review*

"This is one of those books that fundamentally change the way people think about a certain subject."

Professor Paul G. Halpern, *Albion*

"Sumida has offered a study that will profoundly influence our understanding of the Royal Navy before World War I and, in the widest sense, how we view the relationships between technology, finance, and government policy."

Commander (RAN) James Goldrick, *Naval War College Review*

"this monograph must surely remain one of the fundamental studies of the subject."

Professor C.J. Bartlett, *Times Higher Education Supplement*

"This book confirms Professor Sumida's reputation as a historian of exceptional quality."

Richard Ollard, *Financial Times*

"tightly argued, richly researched, and historically and technologically sophisticated . . . a beautifully presented case study of service politics in a matter of high-technology defense procurement – especially intriguing because the characteristic dilemmas, temptations and frustrations are observable in their infancy."

Professor Daniel A. Baugh, *Journal of Military History*

"By any standards this is a remarkable book."

Robert Gardiner, *Warship 1989*

IN DEFENCE
OF
NAVAL
SUPREMACY

FINANCE, TECHNOLOGY AND
BRITISH NAVAL POLICY, 1889-1914

Jon Tetsuro Sumida

London and New York

To the
Sumida and Washino families

First published in 1989
by Unwin Hyman Ltd

First published in paperback in 1993
by Routledge
11 New Fetter Lane, London EC4P 4EE

Simultaneously published in the USA and Canada
by Routledge
29 West 35th Street, New York, NY 10001

Printed in Great Britain at the University Press, Cambridge

British Library Cataloguing in Publication Data

Sumida, Jon Tetsuro
  In Defence of naval supremacy: financial
  limitation, technological innovation and
  British naval policy, 1889–1914.
  1. Great Britain. Royal Navy, 1884–1914
  I. Title
  359'.00941

Library of Congress Cataloging in Publication Data

Sumida, Jon Tetsuro
  In defence of naval supremacy: financial limitation,
  technological innovation, and British naval policy, 1889–1914/
Jon Tetsuro Sumida.
  p. cm.
  Bibliography: p.
  Includes index.
  1. Great Britain—Military policy. 2. Great Britain. Royal Navy-
  -History—19th century. 3. Great Britain. Royal Navy-
  -History—20th century. 4. Great Britain. Royal Navy-
  -Appropriations and expenditures. 5. Technology and state—
  Great Britain. I. Title.
  VA454.S86 1988
  359'.03'0941—dc19

ISBN 0-415-08674-4

Contents

List of Figures and Schematic Diagrams

"The Truth," replied Algernon Moncrieff, "is rarely pure and never simple."

Oscar Wilde, *The Importance of Being Earnest*

Preface

This book attempts to explain how the interaction of major structural factors such as economics, finance and technological change; lesser structural factors such as bureaucratic organization and service sociology; and random factors such as the personalities of individuals and, as will be seen, even the contents of a basket of oysters, influenced the course of British naval policy during the quarter century that preceded the outbreak of the First World War. In particular, this monograph tells the story of Admiral Sir John Fisher's efforts to build capital ships that were qualitatively superior to those of foreign rivals in response to financial difficulties that had made it impossible to build conventional units in adequate numbers; of the related attempts to develop Arthur Hungerford Pollen's system of fire control, which was to have given the Royal Navy a monopoly of long-range hitting; of the changes in British financial structure that made Fisher's radical strategy of techological innovation unnecessary; and of the disruption of the Admiralty by disagreements over Fisher's ideas on capital ship design and Pollen's gunnery instruments, which was to have disastrous consequences at the battle of Jutland in 1916.

This volume deals with a number of big issues: the relationship between economics, finance and national security policy; technology and strategy; the development of defence bureaucracy; the dynamics of strategic arms rivalry; the politics of defence and social welfare; and even the early history of the computer. It is primarily concerned, however, with certain key questions about British naval policy in the early 20th century: what caused the Admiralty to turn to a policy of radical technical innovation in capital ship design in 1905, what factors affected the development of this policy, and to what extent and why did the policy succeed or fail.

The present work offers an interpretation of the dreadnought period that differs fundamentally from previous accounts, provides much new information about British naval finance and naval gunnery, and is based upon the careful study of a wide range of secondary writing and documents, the latter including many papers that have never before been used by historians. The text has thus been thoroughly annotated and, in many instances, extended quotation has been preferred to more compact paraphrasing in order to give readers a direct impression of the form as well as the substance of a particular character's views. A clear understanding of naval finance, service politics and fire control technology was considered to be essential to the comprehension of the important historical processes with which this book is concerned; these subjects have, therefore, been explained in detail.

The financial chronology used in the first and last chapters requires some justification. The period 1889–1914 has been divided into three eight-year groups, with a two-year fragment left over at the end. Such a division not only greatly facilitated financial analysis, but also seemed to correspond almost exactly to phases in the development of large armoured British warships. Between 1889 and 1896, the characteristics and functions of battleships and first-class cruisers were distinct; between 1897 and 1904, the distinction became much less clear; between 1905 and 1912 attempts were made, by one means or another, to combine the two into a single type; and from 1913 this effort was abandoned. Each phase began with a change in British design policy; rivals would then attempt to match or even overmatch Britain's new construction, which in turn would prompt the Royal Navy to build even more units; the phase would end and a new one begin with either Britain or her rivals turning to a new warship type. In the late 19th and early 20th century, a large armoured warship took from two to three years to build, which may have been the reason why the cycle of action, reaction, counter-reaction, and change consistently required about eight years to be worked out.

Complete texts of Pollen's major writing on gunnery and detailed explanations of such technical matters as "danger space," range-finding by triangulation, range-finding by coincidence, reflecting surfaces in coincidence range-finders, cases of change of range, and the trigonometric computation of change of range and bearing rates (that is, the working of a dumaresq), can be found in the author's edition of the Pollen papers, published by the Navy Records Society in 1984.[1] The descriptions of the Argo Clocks and Dreyer Tables given in the *Pollen Papers*, however, were incomplete, or faulty in a number of respects and thus corrected versions have been offered in the present work.[2] Consideration for reader patience, as well as limitations of space, precluded the presentation of a full account of the important changes in naval gunnery that took place between 1919 and 1925. This subject will be covered, however, in a planned sequel to the present work, which will be entitled *In Defence of Naval Parity: Finance Technology, and British Naval Policy, 1919–1939*. The editing of a second volume of documents for the Navy Records Society on Royal Navy gunnery, tactics and warship design from 1899 to 1939 is currently under way, which together with the *Pollen Papers*, will constitute a companion set to the author's completed and planned monograph treatments of British naval affairs in the 20th century.

Notes to Preface

1 Jon Tetsuro Sumida, (ed.), *The Pollen Papers: The Privately Circulated Printed Works of Arthur Hungerford Pollen, 1901–1916* (London: George Allen & Unwin for the Navy Records Society, 1984).

2 The present volume also completely supersedes the author's preliminary report of his findings and doctoral dissertation, for which see Jon Tetsuro Sumida, "British Capital Ship Design and Fire Control in the *Dreadnought* Era: Sir John Fisher, Arthur Hungerford Pollen, and the Battle Cruiser," *Journal of Modern History*, Vol. 51 (Special Issue: *Technology and War*) (June, 1979), pp. 205–30, and Jon Tetsuro Sumida, "Financial Limitation, Technological Innovation, and British Naval Policy, 1904–1910, unpublished Ph.D. dissertation, University of Chicago (August, 1982).

Acknowledgements

I am indebted to my undergraduate adviser at the University of California, Santa Cruz, Professor George Baer, now of the United States Naval War College at Newport, Rhode Island, and my graduate supervisors at the University of Chicago, Professors Emmet Larkin and William McNeill. Professor Baer's fine teaching and wise counsel gave me a strong start on the road to becoming a professional historian. Professor Larkin's rigorous instruction in colloquium on the reading of historical monographs, and the setting of strict standards in writing seminars, provided historical training that greatly influenced the conception and writing of the present monograph. Professor McNeill has been a constant source of provocative suggestion, and academic and moral support; his acceptance in 1977 of my at that time highly speculative article on British capital ship design for the *Journal of Modern History*, of which he was then editor, was instrumental in my decision to abandon 19th century British university politics as a dissertation subject and to turn instead to the serious study of the Royal Navy.

The late Captain Stephen Roskill, the official historian of the Royal Navy during the Second World War, was a great friend and patron to the author and this project. A former naval gunnery officer, he immediately recognized the significance of the relationship between fire control and capital ship design, and from the first did everything in his power to forward my work. I regret that he did not live to see the outcome of the research in which he was so deeply interested. Professor Paul Kennedy has been a long-time influence, friend and advocate. His *Rise and Fall of British Naval Mastery*, in particular, turned my attention to the subject of naval finance, and provided much of the framework within which my ideas on British naval affairs have been developed.

Mr David Brown, the head of the Naval Historical Branch, was always very helpful during my many visits to the Naval Library, particularly with regard to the finding of obscure Admiralty technical documents that were crucial to my story. His good humor, and understanding of naval policy and the importance of technology have been much appreciated by the author. I must also express my thanks to the following archivists, whose cooperation contributed to the making of this book: Mr Correlli Barnett, Miss Marion Stewart and Miss Elizabeth Bennett of the Archive Center at Churchill College, Cambridge; Ms Helen Langley of the Bodleian Library, Oxford; Mr Rod Suddaby of the Imperial War Museum; Mr Alan Pearsall of the National Maritime Museum; and Dr N. A. M. Rodger of the Public Record Office.

I owe a great deal to the support and encouragement given to my work by Drs Jean-Francois Delpech, Norman Friedman, G. A. H. Gordon, Paul

Halpern, Sir Michael Howard, Barry Hunt, Ruddock F. Mackay, Stephen Roberts, David Rosenberg, Donald M. Schurman, David Trask and Sam Wells, and Mr Richard Ollard. Admiral Sir Desmond Dreyer, Admiral Sir Frank Twiss, Dr Charles Fairbanks, Mr Eric Groves, Lieutenant Commander James Goldrick and Professor Bryan Ranft read the manuscript in draft and offered many valuable corrections and suggestions. Mr. N. J. M. Campbell, Commander Michael Craig-Waller, Admiral Royer Dick, Dr Robert Friedel, Mr Hugh Lyon, Mr Anthony Nutbourne, Mr Scott Palmer, Mr Iain Russell, Mr Philip Wilton and Mr Christopher Wright assisted me from time to time with information about a number of technical matters. Two of my undergraduate history students at the University of Maryland, Mr Jeffrey Simpson and Mr Lawrence Tuohy, wrote research papers on British naval affairs that clarified my views on important subjects. Mr Constantine Symeonides-Tsatsos, my research assistant at the Wilson Center, was an intelligent, enthusiastic, and tireless associate, who collected much of the statistical data on British naval finance.

Some twenty years ago, Dr Alexander M. Saunders, then of the Department of Pathology, Stanford Medical School, for whom I worked as a laboratory assistant, suggested that I investigate the subject of computers, and underwrote the costs of acquiring books and taking programming courses at the university. As a result I learned, among other things, a good deal about analog computation, which when combined with later undergraduate instruction in calculus and physics, enabled me to deal with the technical aspects of gunnery that are a major subject of this book.

Over the past ten years Mr Anthony Pollen has given me complete access to his father's many papers, the freedom to draw my own conclusions, thorough-going intelligent criticism of my writing and generous hospitality. His writing on his father's work, which I was allowed to read in draft, greatly assisted my own inquiries, providing both new information and useful perspectives. No scholar could have asked for a better friend and colleague on what has proved to have been an extraordinarily rewarding voyage of academic discovery.

I have been fortunate enough to receive significant financial support for my research and writing from a number of institutions. The University of Chicago and the American Philosophical Society issued grants that covered the costs of photocopying many of the Pollen papers. The Department of History at the University of Maryland, College Park, paid for most of the expenditures on photographs. The Division of Arts and Humanities at the University of Maryland, College Park, gave me a full semester of research in Britain, while Churchill College, Cambridge, assisted my work during this period by making me an Archives Fellow Commoner. The Graduate School of the University of Maryland provided two summer research grants and travel support. And a six-month fellowship at the Wilson Center in Washington, D.C., under the auspices of the International Security Studies Program, enabled me to carry out a large proportion of the work of revising my doctoral dissertation into the present monograph.

The main burden of research and writing costs, however, were borne by my family. My parents, Mr and Mrs Theodore T. Sumida, financed nearly two years of research in Britain from November 1977 to August 1979, and a second short but highly productive research trip to Britain in May and June of 1982. My wife Janet has willingly accepted the necessity of heavy expenditure on books, photocopying, repeated travel to Britain, and first-class word-processing equipment. Without such help and cooperation, it is highly doubtful that the present work would have been started, let alone completed.

My thanks are due to the following for copyright permissions: Houghton Mifflin Company for the American edition of Randolph S. Churchill's *Winston S. Churchill, Companion Volume II, parts 2 and 3*, and Curtis Brown Ltd. for the British edition of the same; Jonathan Cape Ltd. for extracts of Fisher correspondence contained in *From the Dreadnought to Scapa Flow* edited by Arthur J. Marder; Methuen & Co. Ltd. for the passage from Sir William James's *The Sky was always Blue*; Oxford University Press for the extract of the Austrian naval attaché report quoted in Arthur J. Marder's *From the Dreadnought to Scapa Flow*, Volume 3, revised; the Controller of Her Majesty's Stationery Office for crown-copyright material; the Bodleian Library for extracts of letters in the Selborne papers; the British Library for materials in the Balfour papers; the Broadlands Archives Trust for material in the Battenberg papers at the Imperial War Museum; the Trustees of the National Maritime Museum for extracts from the diary of Admiral Sir E. W. Slade; Mr Mark Bonham-Carter for materials in the Asquith papers. Lieutenant Commander Henry Plunkett-Ernle-Erle Drax for material in the Drax papers at Churchill College; Miss Dorothy Bacon for the letters of Sir Reginald Bacon; Admiral Sir Desmond Dreyer for material in the Dreyer papers at Churchill College; the present Lord Fisher for the Fisher papers at Churchill College; Mrs Simon Fergusson for the papers of Constantine Hughes-Onslow; the present Lord Jellicoe for the Jellicoe papers in the British Library; Mr Anthony Pollen for material in the Pollen papers; and Lady Barbara Wilmer for materials from the Hurd papers at Churchill College.

The attempt was made where appropriate to contact the holders of copyright. I hope that, in those instances where communication did not take place, the complete form of the note citation will be considered adequate acknowledgement.

It remains to be stated that the full responsibility for the contents of this book is the author's.

Jon Tetsuro Sumida
College Park, Maryland
April 1988

List of Abbreviations

A.C.	Aim Correction
Adm.	Admiralty
Cab.	Cabinet
C.C.	Churchill College, Cambridge
CCB	*Claimants Correspondence Bundle* (Pollen Papers)
CFS	*Conway's [All the World's] Fighting Ships, 1860–1905* vol. 1
D.N.O.	Director of Naval Ordnance
FGDN	*Fear God and Dreadnought*, Arthur J. Marder, (ed.) (3 vols, Jonathan Cape)
FDSF	*From the Dreadnought to Scapa Flow*, (Arthur J. Marder) (5 vols, Oxford University Press)
FP	*Fisher Papers* (2 vols, Navy Records Society)
F.P.	Fisher Papers (Churchill College, Cambridge)
FS	*Fighting Ships*, Fred T. Jane (ed.)
IQ/DNO	*Important Questions dealt with by D.N.O.* (alternative title to *MRPQ/DNO*)
I.T.P.	Inspector of Target Practice
I.W.M.	Imperial War Museum (London)
MRPQ/DNO	*Monthly Record of Principal Questions dealt with by Director of Naval Ordnance* (N.L.M.D.)
NA	*The Naval Annual*
N.L.M.D.	Naval Library of the Ministry of Defence (London)
N.M.M.	National Maritime Museum (Greenwich)
P.O.L.	Patent Office Library (London)
PP	*Pollen Papers*, J. Sumida (ed.) (Navy Records Society)
P.P.	Pollen Papers (Pollen family)
P.R.O.	Public Record Office (Kew)
RCAI	Royal Commission on Awards to Inventors
R.M.A.	Royal Marine Artillery
R.N.	Royal Navy

Introduction to the Paperback Edition[1]

A great deal of military history has been concerned with strategy. A considerably smaller, though not insubstantial, proportion of the literature has been devoted to the study of military administration, which would include finance, procurement, and logistics. But although the importance of the relationship between military planning and resources has readily been acknowledged — and indeed should be obvious — the exact nature of the connection has rarely been the subject of systematic investigation. As a consequence, much of the writing on such matters as the influence of financial factors on military decision making, or the interplay of technological change and the formulation of military policy, amounts to, at best, relatively crude generalization and, at worst, unsubstantiated speculation. A brief examination of the basic nature of the military finance problem, particularly as it has been affected by innovation in military *matériel* over approximately the last 150 years, suggests that a radically different approach to the writing of serious military history may be in order.

During the industrial era, the three main factors governing the level of military spending in peacetime were capital investment, overhead, and depreciation — that is, purchases of new equipment, the ordinary costs of manning and upkeep, and the rate at which machinery already in service had to be replaced by new machinery in order to maintain state-of-the-art capability. The third was primarily a function of the speed of technological innovation. Improvement in weapons engineering might not only be expensive in its own right, but by rendering recently acquired capital goods obsolete, reduce their value to the point that wholesale replacement was essential in order to be able to field a combat-effective force. If repeated rapidly, and if the stock of military equipment that had to be superseded each time was large, weapons acquisition expenditure could be driven upwards to prohibitive levels. Borrowing could defer the day of reckoning, but ultimately the fiscal stability of the government would require either higher taxes or some form of retrenchment.

Radical developments in technology could, on the other hand, have positive as well as negative financial effects. The replacement of a large inventory of conventional equipment by fewer but more capable units could minimize the initial costs of replacement and over time lower operating expenses. The early adoption of novel material could also stop spending on obsolescent gear — whose value would shortly begin to decline rapidly — sooner than would otherwise have been the case. And the surprise introduction of new model weapons could disrupt seriously the armaments production programs of rival powers, allowing the initiator of change to cut procurement in proportion to the reductions in foreign

xvi

output. Thus a conscious policy of achieving substantial savings through the acceleration of technical innovation could be pursued as a response to rising military expenditure brought on by rapid technological change in a manner akin to fighting fire with fire.

Forcing the pace of invention in order to achieve strategic advantage, however, involved considerable risks. The introduction of a more capable but expensive weapons system might in the short run result in significant gain, but if the technological initiative was not maintained by further breakthroughs, the numerical competition in equivalent armaments was likely to resume at a more costly level. If technical circumstances were other than propitious, achieving meaningful increases in capability through innovation might require outlays on research, development, and production that exceeded the cost of deploying larger numbers of conventional units of equal or greater military value. There was always the possibility that unanticipated and insoluble technical problems would compromise the practicability of new armaments. And even if technical and financial factors were favorable, the difficulties attending the perfection of key components might lead to delays and spending overruns that would in turn precipitate personal, political, or administrative conflicts fatal to the completion of a weapons program.

The development of weapons systems of the most advanced type in any case was bound to generate a plethora of formidable engineering problems, demand heavy expenditure over a protracted period, and make necessary changes in military technique that divided service opinion. These difficulties, moreover, would have to be addressed by technicians, military leaders, civilian bureaucrats, and politicians whose efforts were generally ill-coordinated and immediate interests frequently opposed. Given the interactions of many forces in complicated, varying, and unpredictable ways, it was impossible for even the best-informed officials to follow all or comprehend exactly events as they transpired. The complexity of the process and the interdependence of its many parts, moreover, multiplied the opportunities for making crucial mistakes, so that misjudgments in what appeared to be minor matters could have major and perhaps decisive negative effects.

Because the vision of senior executives and their immediate staffs was incomplete, their official papers and memoirs do not contain the information required to describe the procurement process as a whole. High level memoranda, minutes, and official summaries, moreover, were as a rule written from a command perspective that distorts the appearance of policy implementation by obscuring the degree to which chaos and contingency prevailed over directives issued from the top. For these reasons, the records of military and political leaders, which have been the principal sources of most historical monographs on defence policy, cannot be considered an adequate basis for the study of an advanced weapons procurement program. The history of this subject must instead be painstakingly reconstructed piece by piece from a wider range of materials than has previously been customary, including especially those dealing with matters financial and technical.

Such an approach requires the historian to examine very large quantities of evidence, investigate much that is recondite, and present major findings about significantly related but nonetheless diverse topics. As a result, annotation of sources will be extensive, discussions of the arcane unavoidable, and narrative structure intricate. All of which is to say that properly executed, the history of the development of a sophisticated piece of military hardware will not make easy reading. Serious reflection on the character of the proof, coming to terms with centrally important but difficult to understand issues related to money and machinery, and comprehension of the interrelationship of disparate story lines are each in of themselves difficult tasks. The accomplishment of all three must constitute a daunting challenge, the hardships of which may be mitigated but by no means eliminated even under the best of circumstances by interesting material, artful arrangement, or attractive writing.

The present monograph on what has been called "the *Dreadnought* Revolution" of the early twentieth century deals with national security decision making as a multi-level process that was influenced heavily by budgetary pressure, technical uncertainty, flaws in bureaucratic organization, and the vagaries of chance. Such an approach differs sharply from previous treatments of British naval policy, which have for the most part focused on the actions of a few senior officers and politicians, paid scant attention to finance, greatly oversimplified the technical issues, ignored administrative context, and largely factored out the role of happenstance. This book, as a consequence, offers discussions of warship technology, the functioning of the Admiralty, the parliamentary politics of naval finance, and the operational consequences of pre–1914 failures in gunnery procurement that not only depart from established accounts, but taken collectively raise serious doubts about their fundamental narrative and interpretive integrity.[2]

The calling into question of long-held understandings about Britain's navy in the First World War era through the exploitation of new sources and methodology may have a more general significance. Nearly all studies of weapons procurement, and military policy and strategy as well, have been based on the same limited kinds of evidence and unsatisfactory historical techniques that have informed past treatments of dreadnought capital ships. The historical literature on these matters, therefore, may be equally unreliable, and require systematic reinvestigation, reconstruction, and reinterpretation.[3] In the late twentieth century, moreover, financial and technological considerations have loomed increasingly large in the making of public policy with regard to industrial development, social welfare, and health. The dynamics of government decision making on civilian questions have thus assumed many of the characteristics of military policy processes, the understanding of which are likely to require comparable instruments of analysis and investments of labor.

In an illuminating essay on the dilemmas of defence planning in the atomic age, David Alan Rosenberg observed that if the American public, its leaders in Congress, and, especially, its present and prospective policy-makers in the executive branch (including the military) were more aware of the realities of American nuclear strategy and the real options for change, if some of the historical myths were defused and the shrouds of secrecy parted, there might be a far better opportunity for clear-headed consideration of how to proceed in dealing with the central strategic and political problem of our time.[4]

Whatever power that historical writing may have to counter the pernicious play of ignorance in the making of nuclear or other forms of public policy, military and civilian, must be derived from its capacity to represent accurately the complex nature of governmental processes. As argued above, history of this sort will push the outer limits of what scholars can synthesize and readers assimilate. But in the words of Arthur Hungerford Pollen on the question of improving gunnery at sea through the adoption of more sophisticated methods of aiming naval artillery, such efforts ought perhaps to be regarded "as a thing no longer a luxury or even desirable, but as a plain necessity of the situation."[5]

Notes to Introduction

1   Changes in the paperback text have been restricted to minor text corrections. The following notes have been corrected or expanded: Ch. 2, n. 55; Ch. 6, n. 131, n. 347, n. 355; Epilogue, n. 127. I am indebted to Professors Sir Michael Howard, Paul Kennedy, William McNeill, and David Rosenberg for their support for the paperback edition of this work, and to Claire L'Enfant of Routledge, without whose conscientious efforts it would not have appeared. I also owe much to the following reviewers of the first edition (1989): C.J. Bartlett, Daniel A. Baugh, D.K. Brown, P.K. Crimmin, S. Mathwin Davis, Charles Fairbanks, Robert Gardiner, James Goldrick, Nancy Gordon, Paul Halpern, John McDermott, Peter Nailor, Richard Ollard, Sir Julian Oswald, Larry Owens, Stanley Sandler, Ronald Spector, David Stevenson, and Christopher Wright.

2   Charles Fairbanks, "The Origins of the *Dreadnought* Revolution: A Historiographical Essay," *International History Review*, 13 (May 1991).

3   For the extent to which existing views of such important matters as the early development of the submarine, the Allied shipping crisis of 1917, the battleship versus aircraft carrier controversy between the World Wars, and American nuclear strategy may be revised by the new historical techniques, see Nicholas A. Lambert, "The Influence of the Submarine upon Naval Strategy, 1898–1914," unpublished D. Phil. dissertation, Oxford University, 1992; Jon Tetsuro Sumida, "Forging the Trident: British Naval Industrial Logistics, 1914–1918," in John Lynn, ed., *Feeding Mars: Essays on Logistics and Resource Mobilization in Western Warfare from the Middle Ages to the Present* (Boulder: Westview, 1993) and "The Best Laid Plans . . . : The Development of British Battle Fleet Tactics, 1919–1942," *International History Review*, 14 (November 1992); and David Alan Rosenberg, "The Origins of Overkill: Nuclear Weapons and American Strategy, 1945–1960, " *International Security*, 7 (Spring 1983).

4 David Alan Rosenberg, "Reality and Responsibility: Power and Process in the Making of United States Nuclear Strategy, 1945–68," *The Journal of Strategic Studies*, 9 (March 1986), pp. 50–1.

5 Arthur Hungerford Pollen, untitled paper of 1916, in Jon Tetsuro Sumida, ed., *The Pollen Papers: The Privately Circulated Printed Works of Arthur Hungerford Pollen 1901–1916* (London: George Allen & Unwin for the Navy Records Society, 1984), p. 337.

Part I
1889–1906

"We distinguish trees by considering their general shape and their characteristic details, for instance, the leaf or the bark; while seemingly more prominent features, such as the circumference, the number of branches, etc., can be safely disregarded, as can so many things which lend themselves best to historical narrative."

Sir Lewis Namier,
The Structure of Politics at the Accession of George III

[1]

The Strategy of Numerical Superiority: Naval Rivalry and Financial Crisis, 1889-1904

1 State Finance and Pre-industrial British Naval Power

The early development of Britain as a major naval power was influenced strongly by geographical factors, which inclined her population to look to the sea for both economic gain and defence against invasion. But the naval ambitions of the English state were repeatedly checked by financial weakness. In the 15th century, the navy of Henry V dominated the channel, but upon his death, the bulk of the fleet was sold in order to liquidate royal debts. In the 16th century, the sale of confiscated church properties enabled Henry VIII to support military operations in France with a powerful navy, while in the time of his daughter Elizabeth I, a large proportion of England's considerable naval strength consisted of private vessels that were supported in large part by plunder from raids on Spanish treasure. The early Stuarts, however, lacked the windfall income or the backing of free enterprise of their predecessors, and England's naval power thus diminished. Heavy borrowing that was secured by high taxation and the expropriation of Royalist estates, enabled the Commonwealth government to build the largest fleet that England had ever known, which achieved great success in wars with the Netherlands and Spain. But political considerations prevented the restored Stuarts from resorting to the fiscal expedients of the Interregnum, and in the wars with the Dutch during the late 17th century, a weakened Royal Navy suffered serious reverses.[1]

During the Stuart period, naval costs were increased significantly by technological change. The gun armament of Tudor warships had been relatively ineffective because large caliber pieces were slow firing and few in number. Decisive results could only be achieved by boarding, which meant that in a fleet action ships fought either individually or, at best, in cooperation with a few other vessels against a single opponent. During the 17th century, however, the rate of fire of heavy naval ordnance was improved significantly by an increase in the number of men that served each gun and through the adoption of more effective loading equipment.[2] Advances in hull construction, sail plan and rigging allowed the construction of larger warships that could carry more heavy guns and bigger crews.[3] Unlike earlier vessels, the new model warships possessed sufficient fire power along their broadsides to shatter the hulls of their opponents although not across the bow or stern where few guns could be brought to bear. European navies thus sought to cover the vulnerable ends of each vessel and to present a wall of powerful broadsides to the enemy by the adoption of close-order and the line-ahead formation, which required the elements of a fleet to cooperate in battle as never before.[4]

The growth in the number of large guns, crew size and warship dimensions resulted in substantial increases in expenditure.[5] The new tactics, which required skillful leadership and a hierarchy of command, forced states to create a professional naval officer corps at great expense.[6] Because even the most heavily armed commercial vessels were incapable of maintaining the integrity of the line formation—upon which the security of the fleet depended—when confronted by a first-class warship, armed merchantmen could no longer be used as an economical means of providing a battle fleet with significant reinforcement in wartime.[7] And beginning in the 17th century, powers with extensive maritime commercial interests to protect found it necessary to build and maintain specialized cruising warships in some numbers at considerable cost, in response to the advent of purpose-built commerce raiders that were too swift to be overtaken by armed merchantmen.[8] Thus in spite of the great expansion of England's economy that took place following the Restoration, which increased tax revenue,[9] and the reforms of Samuel Pepys in the 1680s, which reduced the corruption of naval administration,[10] the English state continued to lack the fiscal resources that were required to maintain a navy of sufficient strength in wartime. A French force heavily defeated the main English battle fleet in 1690, and the containment of French naval power during the next few years was achieved only by the combined efforts of England and the Netherlands.

By the 18th century, however, England's naval position had been transformed by fundamental changes in her system of state finance. The close control of revenue and expenditure by the Treasury, which provided the foundations of an efficient financial administration, was established between the restoration of the Stuarts in 1660 and the accession of the Hanoverians in 1714.[11] The expansion of England's agrarian and mercantile economies after the Restoration produced capital that could be invested in long-term government securities. And the revolution of 1688–89 removed sources of disagreement that had forestalled cooperation between King and Parliament, which opened the way to the creation of a permanent funded debt. From 1689, the exigencies of a major European war in which England was a leading participant generated fiscal obligations that could only be met through heavy borrowing. In 1693, after serious military and naval reverses that were attributable to the inadequate financing of England's war effort, the crown for the first time resorted to long-term borrowing through an act of Parliament. By this means, the financial commitments of the state were secured by statutory provisions for the punishment of royal officials who violated the terms of the act, and by the power of the legislature to increase taxes if necessary to enable the government to meet its authorized financial responsibilities. The Bank of England was created in 1694 to facilitate parliamentary approved borrowing, which became a permanent fixture of English state finance, and over the course of the next half century, the interest-rate paid on state loans was substantially reduced by changes in terms that reflected growing confidence in the solvency of the crown.[12]

The British state thus acquired the capacity to raise immense sums on short notice and at relatively low rates of interest. France and Spain, on the other hand, who were to be Britain's chief maritime rivals in the 18th century, were burdened with inefficient financial administrations, lacked national banks that were capable of managing the supply of credit to the state, and, in the absence of parliamentary institutions that controlled the national budget, were incapable of gaining the confidence of monied interests at home or abroad that would have enabled them to constitute a scheme of public debt comparable to that of Britain. Thus while the combined economic resources of both powers were substantially greater than that of Britain, their capacity to borrow in time of war was far less.[13]

Britain's "financial revolution" not only enabled her to mobilize large naval forces on the outbreak of war and to keep them active over the course of hostilities, but also meant that she could subsidize the military operations of allied continental powers and to field not inconsiderable armies of her own, which forced France, in particular, to spend money on land forces that might otherwise have been used to strengthen her navy. The financial inefficiency of France and Spain, on the other hand, prevented them from sustaining large scale naval operations for extended periods without compromising their military position on the continent, which was of primary importance. In strategic terms, this allowed Britain to maintain continuous control of home waters and to defend her far-flung commercial and colonial interests, while her two main opponents were reduced to commerce raiding with cruising warships and privateers, and occasional forays with battle fleets in pursuit of limited objectives.[14] The Royal Navy's overall numerical superiority and greater activity may have had important tactical consequences as well. Daniel Baugh has suggested that the aggressiveness of British naval officers in battle was attributable both to their willingness to take risks in the knowledge that naval losses could be replaced, and to their superior seamanship, which could be explained by the longer time that they spent at sea.[15]

The superiority of Britain's system of state finance was thus the basis of strategic and perhaps tactical advantages that were major contributors to her emergence as Europe's preeminent naval power during the 18th and early 19th centuries. In the wars of Spanish and Austrian Succession, the Seven Years War and the American Revolution, the Royal Navy was opposed by the combined naval might of France and Spain. During these conflicts British battle fleets rarely achieved conclusive results, but their limited successes were none the less sufficient to prevent invasion. And while losses of merchant ships to enemy raiders were often considerable, the Royal Navy's cruising warships were effective enough to keep trade routes open, with the result that British overseas commerce continued to expand even in time of war. Britain's naval ascendancy reached its apex during the 23 years of conflict from 1792 to 1815 against revolutionary and imperial France, and its allies. British battle fleets won an unprecedented succession of decisive victories over the navies of the Netherlands, Denmark, Spain and France. British squadrons and flotillas imposed a close blockade of the continental European seaboard. And the British convoy system, as in previous years, minimized losses of merchant shipping in the face of a vigorous privateering offensive. In 1815, there could be little doubt of the Royal Navy's capacity to guarantee the security of both the home territory and the maritime commercial interests upon which Britain's economic prosperity depended.[16]

2   The Industrial Revolution and British Naval Supremacy

During the 18th century, advances in British manufacturing techniques and organization resulted in the establishment of the world's first industrial system. Other countries were at first slow to adopt the new methods of production, and Britain, as a consequence, enjoyed a commanding economic lead for the greater part of the 19th century. In 1880, Britain's output of coal, pig iron and crude steel was more than twice that of any continental great power, while her margin of superiority in the manufacture of cotton textiles was even larger. Much of this production was exported, and carried in British merchant vessels. Between 1815 and 1880, the value of British domestic exports more than quadrupled, while merchant tonnage nearly tripled.[17] In 1880, Britain's share of world trade was 23 per cent, or more than double that of France, her nearest rival.[18] As a result of the development of industrial and commercial advantages of this magnitude, Britain possessed not only the wealth to spend more on naval armaments than any opponent or likely coalition of opponents, but also the industrial plant that was required to build warships more quickly and in greater quantity.

From the 1880s, however, Britain's economic lead was substantially reduced as the other European great powers, and the United States and Japan as well, industrialized. By the end of the first decade of the 20th century, the German Empire had overtaken Britain in the output of both pig iron and crude steel, and had made greater progress in the advancement of the important new chemical and electrical industries.[19] Britain's industrial growth slowed sharply as foreign competition reduced the demand for her domestic exports and by 1910 her share of world trade had fallen to little more than 14 per cent.[20] Although Britain retained enormous advantages in banking and shipping, her superiority in the production of wealth during the late 19th and early 20th centuries was no longer so absolute as to discourage France and Russia, and then Germany, from challenging her with substantial naval building programs, and for a time Germany even appeared to possess the capacity to build capital ships in greater numbers and at a faster rate.[21]

Britain's naval position was also undermined by the tremendous improvement in the financial capability of the continental great powers. During the 19th century, the German Empire and France reformed their state bureaucracies, which increased the efficiency of financial administration;[22] developed expanding industrial economies, which produced profits that could be invested in government securities; founded national banks, which provided an apparatus through which the state could borrow,[23] and constituted elected legislative bodies that controlled the state budget in the manner of the British parliament, which improved government credit because loans to the state were secured by the measure of control over taxation and spending that was held by the elected representatives of monied interests.[24] The German and French governments acquired the capacity, as a consequence, to borrow enormous amounts at rates of interest that were roughly comparable to those paid by the British crown, which meant that, in the event of war, they could not only support the operations of their own powerful navies, but also provide or secure loans to fiscally weaker great power allies that had significant naval forces to deploy. Britain remained Europe's strongest financial power, but she no longer possessed the overwhelming advantage in borrowing upon which her naval supremacy in wartime during the 18th and early 19th centuries had in large part been based.

The task of maintaining Britain's naval supremacy in the face of decreasing economic and financial advantage was made even more difficult by great increases in the pace of technological change. During the 18th and early 19th centuries, warship design had remained fundamentally unaltered, because the lack of practical alternatives to wood construction, wind power, and cast-iron, muzzle-loading smooth-bore guns that fired solid projectiles, had restricted development to matters of detail.[25] Industrialization, however, generated advances in metallurgy, steam power and ordnance design that opened the way to major changes in naval materiel. Over the course of the 19th century, the Admiralty's willingness to innovate in order to obtain increases in capability, and the necessity of matching the technical advances of foreign navies, resulted in the transformation of the Royal Navy's warships and associated equipment. Auxiliary steam propulsion was adopted for large warships in the 1830s, and by the 1860s, the Royal Navy had introduced iron construction, armour protection and built-up rifled artillery that fired shells as well as solid projectiles. By the 1880s, the development of technology had resulted in the complete abandonment of sails, the replacement of iron with steel hull construction, the further great improvement of naval ordnance and armour, and the advent of the torpedo.[26]

The adoption of steam propulsion, armour protection and the greater dimensions that were allowed by iron or steel construction, led to enormous growth in the cost of building a warship. H.M.S. *Warrior*, an iron-hull armoured steam-propelled battleship that was launched in 1860, was nearly six times the price of its 18th century counterpart, the first-rate wooden sailing ship-of-the-line. Improvements in ordnance, armour and steam engineering over the next quarter century resulted in further cost increases. Expenditure on the building of H.M.S. *Nile*, a battleship launched in 1888, was thus more than twice that of the *Warrior*.[27] While the slow pace of technological change during the age of sail meant that a ship-of-the-line that was kept in good condition could retain most, if not all, of its original fighting value for as long as half a century,[28] the rapid and continuous improvement of naval materiel in the 19th century reduced new battleships to obsolescence within a few years.[29] And although the replacement of wood with far more durable iron or steel construction substantially reduced expenditures on hull repairs,[30] the substitution of steam for wind power added the very considerable expenses of engine maintenance and fuel.[31]

In contrast, moreover, with the technically relatively simple and basically unchanging sailing warships of the 18th century, which could be made efficient within a fairly short time with crews that were for the most part made up of recent recruits or impressed men, the mechanically far more complex and rapidly evolving steam warships of the 19th century, could only be run efficiently with experienced crews that contained many technical specialists. By the late 19th century, in addition, the rising cost of domestic labor had prompted British shipowners to employ foreign seamen in such great numbers that the capacity of the merchant marine to serve as a reliable reserve of semi-trained manpower in war, as had previously been the case, was a matter of some doubt. The 18th century practices of hire-and-discharge and impressment, which had enabled the Royal Navy to keep peacetime manning levels at only a fraction of wartime requirements, were therefore replaced by continuous-service and a small naval reserve and, in addition, wages and serving conditions were improved in order to encourage enlistments and increase retention. Peacetime manning levels thus approached those of wartime while labor costs climbed, which resulted in a substantial rise in the expenditure that was devoted to the manning of the fleet.[32]

The increases in naval capital costs, rate of capital depreciation and overhead expenses did not pose serious financial problems during much of the 19th century, because the weakness of foreign navies enabled Britain to maintain her naval supremacy with a fleet that was neither large nor wholly up-to-date.[33] British naval expenditure, as a consequence, grew at a modest rate, and was more than matched by the rising state revenues that were produced by a rapidly developing industrial economy.[34] Beginning in the late 1880s, however, the expansion and improvement of the navies of great power rivals prompted Britain to increase the size and efficiency of her fleet. Warships of all types and of the most recent design were built

8

in large numbers, which in turn required the construction of additional docking and repair facilities. Units of recent vintage that had been rendered obsolescent by the latest technical advances were relegated to the second-line and replaced by new models. And by the end of the century, the number of seamen in service and in the reserve during peacetime, of which the former much predominated, exceeded the peak manning levels of the Napoleonic Wars.[35] Spending on the Royal Navy, as a consequence, increased rapidly.[36]

The transformation of materiel by technological change during the 19th century also deprived the Royal Navy of important tactical advantages that it had enjoyed before industrialization by virtue of the high quality of its personnel. During the age of sail, the superior ship-handling skills of the Royal Navy's officers and men had given British fleets and single warships the capacity to out-maneuver their opponents. British naval gunners had achieved significantly higher rates of fire than their less well trained and disciplined counterparts in opposing navies. And the high morale of the Royal Navy's crews, who kept their fighting spirit in spite of casualties suffered while approaching the enemy, had enabled British commanders to obtain decisive results by exploiting their fire-power superiority to maximum effect through close action.[37] The tactical significance of superior seamanship was greatly discounted, however, by the advent of steam propulsion. The equivalence of good gunnery with arduous training and discipline was reduced by the mechanical improvement of loading and gunlaying. And with the introduction of the torpedo, close action became impracticable regardless of the inclination of British commanders or the bravery of their crews.

The manifold effects of industrialization not only diminished Britain's naval power, but also magnified her national danger in other ways. By the mid-19th century the advent of machine tools and mass production methods had made it possible to produce breech-loading firearms in large quantity at relatively low cost and, simultaneously, progress in steam engineering and the iron industry had led to the construction of railroads. The more efficient firearms could be manipulated effectively with far less training than was required by the old pattern muzzle-loading musket or rifle, while railroads allowed the movement of large numbers of men, their associated equipment and supplies over great distances with unprecedented rapidity. Prussia, Austria, France and Russia, as a consequence, replaced their small long-service professional armies with much larger short-service conscript forces.[38] In Britain, however, the state lacked the power to impose, and society was unwilling to accept, compulsory military service. Britain thus continued to make do with a professional army that lacked the numbers that were required to provide an adequate military defence against invasion in the event of war with a continental European great power.[39]

The effect, on the other hand, of even a short interruption of Britain's overseas commerce became far more serious because of the great increase in her consumption of imported food. In 1750, Britain had exported nearly a quarter of her grain production, and although she had begun to import grain by the end of the century, domestic agriculture still satisfied the needs of the great bulk of her inhabitants in 1815.[40] Demand for food over the course of the 19th century, however, was increased greatly by the nearly four-fold expansion of Britain's population, who for the most part lived in towns and cities. From the 1870s, moreover, the absence of agricultural tariffs and the availability of cheap foreign supplies, which could be purchased with exports of manufactured goods, resulted in a sharp fall in British grain production. By 1895, as a consequence, nearly four-fifths of Britain's wheat came from abroad, a dependency that made the security of British maritime lines of communication a matter of vital necessity.[41] In the late 19th century, there was good reason to believe, therefore, that the maintenance of Britain's naval supremacy was more important to her survival as a great power than ever before.

3   Technology, Finance, and British Naval Expansion

During the 1840s and 1850s, the wooden ship-of-the-line, which had remained essentially unchanged for nearly two centuries, was superseded in the Royal Navy by a variant that was equipped with steam engines and a screw propeller as well as masts and sails. By 1860, the British battle fleet was for the most part composed of the new model screw ships-of-the-line.[42] During the following decade, however, the pace of technological change quickened to the point that capital ships were rendered obsolete by new developments before they could be completed. The iron-clad battleship introduced in 1859, which took approximately three years to build, had gone through seven distinct evolutionary stages by 1864.[43] The process of technological improvement continued, so that among the 30 vessels that were fit to take a place in the line of battle in 1870 there were to be found 3 types of steam engine, 4 screw arrangements, 16 schemes of armour protection, 18 hull models and no fewer than 20 scales of armament,[44] a situation that was exacerbated over the next decade by further technical advances and the emergency acquisition of odd vessels during the Russian war scare of 1878.[45]

In 1879, the Director of Naval Construction formulated the design of the *Collingwood*, a battleship whose speed, cruising radius and arrangement of armament were much superior to previous vessels of capital rank. During the early 1880s, the Admiralty ordered five additional units of similar design, the six vessels being referred to collectively as the "Admiral" class. The improvements in performance, however, were only achieved within the restrictions of size that were dictated by financial considerations through a reduction in the extent of the hull that was protected by heavy armour, and the new vessels were, as a consequence, severely criticized for their vulnerability to gunfire. The hull of the "Admirals" also lacked height above the waterline—which was known as freeboard—and thus were unable to maintain speed in rough seas. The next four British battleships, which were ordered in 1884 and 1885, reverted to the practice of providing heavy armour protection at the expense of other attributes, but were no more satisfactory with regard to freeboard. The Admiralty then suspended orders for new battleships after concluding in 1886 that the ineffectiveness of existing naval ordnance against the larger torpedo craft that had begun to come into service had made the type obsolete.[46]

During the 1870s, Britain had built relatively few new warships, while continental naval powers such as France had made considerable additions to their fleets.[47] The Carnarvon Committee of 1879, which had been formed in order to investigate naval deficiencies that had been revealed in the mobilization against Russia the year before, concluded, therefore, that the navy was far too small to carry out the tasks that would be required of it in war. But their call for immediate and substantial new warship construction, which was to be supported by a considerable increase in taxation, was not carried out.[48] In 1884, after two years of serious disagreement with France over imperial matters, Britain was confronted with the prospect—all be it faint—of a hostile Franco-German naval alliance that outnumbered her in battleships and practically equalled her in cruisers.[49] Public anxiety over Britain's naval vulnerability led to the announcement in 1884 of a five year scheme of greater expenditure on new warship construction, named the "Northbrook Program" after the First Lord. Increases in spending on naval building in 1885–86 and 1886–87 were followed, however, by reductions in 1887–88 and 1888–89.[50]

Britain's failure to build greater numbers of warships in the 1870s and 1880s in response to the growth of foreign fleets, and increasing international tension, had much to do with both the continued confidence of her political leadership in her overall naval, financial and economic strength, and uncertainty over the future viability of the battleship.[51] But problems with the budget must also have been an important factor. During this period, large amounts were expended annually to cover the costs of major colonial military operations in Afghanistan and in Africa. And while serious disagreements with Russia in 1878 and 1885 did not lead to war, considerable sums had to be spent upon the emergency expansion and precautionary mobilization of military and naval forces. Increases in government revenue that were due to the rising yield from existing taxes were not enough to cover the extraordinary military expenditure, and neither Liberal nor Conservative governments were prepared to press for significant increases in taxation to make up the difference. As a consequence, substantial deficits were incurred in the late 1870s and mid 1880s.[52]

During the late 1880s, the worsening international situation increased British anxiety about naval security. In early 1888, a war scare with France again led to public clamor for naval expansion, and by the end of the year there were ominous signs of an impending Franco-Russian alliance that would possess nearly as many battleships as Britain.[53] Demands for the enlargement of the Royal Navy coincided, moreover, with the completion of administrative reforms and technical improvements that had increased Britain's capacity to build warships efficiently. During the second half of the 1880s, the Royal Dockyards had been thoroughly reorganized and reequipped,[54] the Admiralty gained greater control over the production of naval armament and ammunition through the transfer of charges for naval ordnance from the army to the navy estimates, while defects in heavy gun design that had in the past resulted in serious delays in the completion of warships had been overcome.[55] In 1888, Parliament passed the Imperial Defence Act, which among other things provided funds in addition to monies approved under the navy estimates for a modest program of five third-class cruisers and two torpedo gunboats.[56] But the great expansion of the Royal Navy could not begin until the shortcomings of the battleship had been rectified and the financial circumstances of the government improved.

By the end of the 1880s, technical improvements in steam power, armour and armament had made it possible to build an effective ocean-going battleship at a reasonable cost. In 1885, the Royal Navy adopted triple-expansion machinery in place of the compound engines that had previously been standard, which increased fuel economy by about 15 per cent.[57] Experiments in 1886 with the obsolete ironclad *Resistance* led to the development of a more efficient arrangement of armour, while the advent of nickel-steel armour in 1888, which was superior to the compound armour that was then in service, allowed reductions in the thickness of plates, and thus in the weight of protection. The exploitation of triple-expansion engines and new armour arrangements, and the partial use of nickel-steel armour, together with an acceptable increase in displacement, enabled William White, the Director of Naval Ordnance, to raise the freeboard of the battleships that were to be ordered in 1889—and by so doing to improve seaworthiness—without undue sacrifice of armament, speed, range or protection. The development of the quick-firing gun during the 1880s, moreover, provided the new model battleships with a weapon that was effective against even the largest torpedo craft.[58]

In the meanwhile, reductions in non-naval spending had greatly improved the financial position of the government. Between 1880 and 1884, budgets had been burdened with the cost of paying off loans that had been required in the late 1870s to cover the expenditure on colonial wars, and military and naval preparations against Russia. The liquidation of these debts resulted in a sharp reduction in debt charges in 1885, and although additional borrowing had been required in 1884 to meet the expense of military operations in the Sudan and South Africa, and a second crisis with Russia, the debt charge did not rise to the heights of the earlier years of the decade. After 1885, moreover, Britain restricted her colonial military activity and was able to avoid further major confrontations with great powers. Large budget surpluses were thus achieved in the late 1880s in spite of a slight fall in the level of revenue. And in 1888, G. J. Goschen, the Chancellor of the Exchequer, put through a conversion scheme that achieved a considerable decrease in the cost of servicing the National Debt that was to become effective from April 1889.[59] By the end of the 1880s, it had thus become possible to spend much more on the navy without recourse to the politically dangerous alternatives of borrowing or greatly increased taxation.

4 The Naval Defence Act and Spencer Program

As late as in the summer of 1888, the naval members of the Board of Admiralty—who provided the First Lord, a civilian and politician, with professional advice—did not believe that a large program of new warship construction was necessary. In June, Admiral Sir Horace Hood, the First Naval Lord, testified to a select committee of the House of Commons on the navy estimates that, in general, he and the other naval lords were satisfied with the strength of the Royal Navy. Earlier in the year, however, William White, the Director of Naval Construction, had reported that 72 obsolete vessels should be retired by 1892 and replaced by an equal number of up-to-date units. And when pressed in July for a confidential report on the requirements of the navy in the event of war with France, the naval lords called for a five year program that provided for the building of no fewer than 10 battleships, 37 cruisers and 18 torpedo-gunboats, a total of 65 ships. The Cabinet considered papers related to this proposal in October and November, and on 1 December, Lord George Hamilton, the First Lord, supported the implementation of the program in a memorandum to the Cabinet on the navy estimate for 1889-90.[60]

In November 1888, George Goschen, the Chancellor of the Exchequer, had opposed increased spending on the navy on the grounds that large numbers of new warships were not required. The denial of naval necessity was, however, publicly controverted by expert naval opinion. Hamilton's proposals to the cabinet were followed in mid December by the sharp criticism of British naval weakness by Lord Charles Beresford, a late naval member of the Board of Admiralty and M.P., in the House of Commons, and in February 1889 by the presentation to both houses of Parliament of a report of a committee of admirals on the fleet maneuvers of the previous year that was highly critical of the state of the navy.[61] The case for economy was further weakened by the fact that Goschen's own conversion scheme would reduce the cost of servicing the national debt beginning in the next fiscal year, which would release funds that could be spent on fleet expansion. Popular support for increased naval expenditure, moreover, was strong.[62] The program outlined by Hamilton was thus not only accepted by the Cabinet, but augmented by the provision for five additional cruisers. The government's Naval Defence Bill was presented to Parliament in March 1889, and authorized the expenditure of £21,500,000 over a five year period for the building of 10 battleships, 42 cruisers and 18 torpedo gunboats.[63]

Six of the battleships, 20 of the cruisers, and 12 of the torpedo gunboats were to be built in the Royal Dockyards at a cost of £11,500,000, which was to be provided out of the shipbuilding and armaments votes of the navy estimate. The bill allocated an additional £4,750,000 for dockyard work under these votes over the five years of the program to complete vessels ordered before 1889 and, in order to prevent wide variations in the size of the estimates from year to year, stipulated that the total of £16,250,000 be supplied in five annual installments of £3,250,000. Funds unspent at the end of the year were not to be returned to the Treasury as was normally the case, but were to be placed into a special account for use in the remaining years of the program. In the event that spending in excess of the annual allocation and the balance in the special account was necessary in order to complete the program vessels within five years, the bill allowed for advances on the next year's allocation to be issued by the Treasury out of the Consolidated Fund or through borrowing.[64]

The remaining 4 battleships, 22 cruisers, and 6 torpedo gunboats were to be built under contract in private yards at a cost of £10 million. The bill stipulated that one-seventh of this amount was to be issued out of the Consolidated Fund each year over a seven year period into the same special account described beforehand, from which payments were to be made for work carried out on the specified contract vessels. The completion of all of the contract vessels within five years as called for under the legislation meant, of course, that spending would anticipate the sixth- and seventh-year deposits. For this reason, the Treasury was authorized to issue advances from either the Consolidated Fund or through loans to cover expenditure that exceeded the balance in the special account with the stipulation that the advances be repaid from the special account before the end of the seven year term.[65]

The Naval Defence Bill provided for an average annual increase in spending on warship construction of some £2,600,000. Of this amount, only 30 per cent—about £600,000—was covered under the navy estimates,[66] while the remaining 70 per cent—the £2,000,000 allocated to contract built vessels—came from monies appropriated from outside of the estimates. But through the expedient of amortizing five years of spending over seven, the latter sum was reduced to annual payments into the special account of £1,430,000, which was very little more than the £1,380,000 that would be saved annually as a consequence of the debt conversion scheme that was scheduled to come into effect from April 1889. The passage of the bill was thus strongly favored by the fact that the spending increase on warship construction for the Royal Navy was for the most part balanced by the reduction in debt service charges, which meant that substantial borrowing or increases in taxation during a period of economic uncertainty were unnecessary.[67]

On 7 March 1889, the First Lord associated the new naval program with a public declaration of fundamental strategic principle. "Our establishment," he maintained in the House of Commons, "should be on such a scale that it should at least be equal to the naval strength of any two other countries."[68] By "our establishment," Hamilton meant the number of battleships, it being understood that Britain required a substantial numerical superiority in cruisers for the defence of her extended lines of maritime supply,[69] and his description of what was to become known as the "two-power standard" was no more than a reiteration of a rule that had guided the naval policy of earlier governments.[70] He moved beyond what was accepted as given and departed from precedent, however, by asserting that the standard be measured in terms of warships "of the newest type and most approved design,"[71] which were to be larger than their foreign counterparts so as to allow them to be given a comparable armament and protection with more powerful engines for higher speed.[72]

Hamilton was probably not the first and certainly not the last politician to defend proposals for large increases in defence spending on the grounds of economy. In previous years, the building of warships had often been interrupted because the annual provision for funding new construction under the navy estimate was inadequate. The completion of warships was therefore delayed, and their overall cost thereby substantially increased. The provision that allowed unexpended balances from one year to be carried over to the next, however, meant that the underspending that would occur during the early years of the program, when building was just beginning, could be applied to the middle years when construction work was at its peak. The First Lord thus argued that the government's legislation would enable the vessels of the program to be completed in less time than foreign counterparts, which would result in a lower cost per unit and a longer effective service life.[73] He maintained, moreover, that the large building program would discourage the naval aspirations of rival powers, which would enable Britain to reduce her naval building in later years. The completed program, Hamilton believed, would be "adequate not only to our immediate, but also to our future wants"[74] because it was "one which I do not think all the Dockyards of Europe would complete in the time we propose; and if there are any nations abroad who do wish to compete with us in naval armaments, the mere enunciation of this scheme will show to them the utter futility of their desire."[75] The bill was passed after light opposition, and became the Naval Defence Act on 31 May 1889.[76]

A number of difficulties were encountered in the course of implementing the act. In practice, the parliamentary approval of funding in advance for a five year program led to disputes between the Treasury and the Admiralty over accounting, and in Parliament over the question of the carrying over of unexpended balances, and therefore this method of financing the navy was not repeated.[77] The orders for the large number of warships authorized by the act coincided with a great upsurge in the construction of merchant shipping in British private yards,[78] and as a consequence, the demand for labor and materials related to shipbuilding was increased suddenly and substantially, which resulted in a sharp rise in wages and prices.[79] The Admiralty, moreover, increased the size and otherwise improved the designs of the second-class battleships, second-class cruisers and torpedo gunboats, which raised the cost of these vessels,[80] while various other factors had resulted in spending that had not been anticipated by the act.[81] Parliament thus found it necessary to pass amending legislation in 1893, which authorized the expenditure of an additional £1,350,000, extended the time allowed to complete the program by one year and rectified several accounting problems.[82]

The Naval Defence Act was none the less a success from the standpoint of shipbuilding and finance. The continuous availability of funds, taken together with the administrative reforms and improvements in ordnance design of the late 1880s, resulted in the completion of most of the program on schedule, which minimized excess spending. By the end of 1893–94, the intended last year of the program, all but five second–class cruisers and four torpedo gunboats were in commission or ready for service, and these vessels were finished by the close of the following fiscal year. On average, expenditure above the original cost estimate for each warship ran to about 3 per cent, which was a great improvement over the figures of 20 to 30 per cent that had been the case between 1875 and 1885.[83] The vessels provided by the Naval Defence Act nearly doubled the number of effective battleships and cruisers available to the Royal Navy,[84] and while the second–class cruisers were criticized for being inadequately armed,[85] the seven first–class battleships of the *Royal Sovereign* class, which were the centerpiece of the program, were considered to be the finest vessels of capital rank in the world.[86]

The Naval Defence Act did not, however, have the restraining effect on the warship building of rival powers that Hamilton had predicted. Between 1889 and 1893, France and Russia, who were the two next largest naval powers after Britain and from August 1891 formal allies,[87] laid down 12 battleships, and by the end of 1893 had announced plans to lay down an additional five such vessels at the beginning of 1894. Britain, in comparison, had built 10 battleships under the Naval Defence Act, laid down one battleship under the estimates of 1892–93, and projected two battleships under the estimates of 1893–94, which left her two vessels short of a "two-power" standard measured in capital ships of the most recent design.[88] By 1893, moreover, relations between Britain, and France and Russia, had deteriorated seriously as a result of disagreements over Siam, Afghanistan, and Egypt.[89] A Liberal government had come to power in 1892, and for a time the Cabinet resisted demands in Parliament and the press for a large increase in warship building. These began in August 1893 in response to reports that Russia planned to establish a permanent naval force in the Mediterranean. But after bitter debate, the Cabinet formally agreed on 8 March 1894 to a five year program named after Lord Spencer, the First Lord, which authorized the construction of 7 battleships, 20 cruisers and over 100 flotilla craft at a cost of £21,263,000.[90]

William Ewart Gladstone, the venerable Liberal statesman and Prime Minister, had resigned from the government on 1 March 1894 when it became clear that an overwhelming majority of his Cabinet colleagues had accepted the necessity of large increases in naval spending, which he believed would lead to financial disaster.[91] Gladstone's serious concern with naval finance was not without some cause. The new construction program resulted in an increase in the navy estimate for 1894–95 of 20 per cent over the previous year, which compelled Sir William Harcourt, the Chancellor of the Exchequer, to make adjustments in the financial terms of the Imperial Defence and Naval Defence Act accounts, and to increase the yield of death duties through the introduction of a system of graduated rates.[92] Expenditure on the navy in 1895–96 was expected to be even higher than in the previous fiscal year because work on the nine battleships[93] and two large cruisers laid down the year before would reach its peak level, while the expansion of the fleet, the growth in the size of battleships and the threat of torpedo attacks against fleet anchorages required the deepening of harbors and the construction of additional docks, naval barracks and port defences.[94]

The increase in spending on warship construction could be covered by increased revenue from the death duties, the income from which was expected to be substantially greater in 1895-96 because the new graduated rates had been in force for only part of the previous year.[95] But in order to fund the building or improving of naval shore facilities, Spencer proposed that the navy estimate should be relieved of most of the burden of paying for what were known as naval works, which were to be taken up by a separate naval works account that could be financed out of a surplus in the Consolidated Fund or if necessary through borrowing.[96] The legislation that was presented to Parliament, provided £1 million to be spent on naval works in 1895-96 above the amount allocated for that purpose under the navy estimate, and the Treasury was authorized to borrow all or a part of this sum in the form of issuing terminable annuities, the principal and interest of which were to be repaid within thirty years out of the navy estimate.[97] This measure was passed by Parliament, and in July 1895 became the Naval Works Act of 1895.[98]

The Liberal government was replaced in June 1895 by a Conservative-Unionist administration, which ordered the construction of five battleships in addition to those sanctioned by their predecessors. Spending on warship construction, and naval works as well, was thus again expected to increase in 1896-97. But during the fiscal year 1895-96 the financial position of the government was transformed by a very great increase in the productivity of existing taxation. Income from death duties far exceeded expectations, while a sharp upturn in economic activity resulted in a commensurate rise in other tax receipts.[99] In spite of large supplementary estimates that were required to cover the costs of shipbuilding, the army and a military campaign in Africa, the surplus of income over expenditure at the end of the year was still one of the largest on record. Surpluses were customarily allocated to the reduction of the National Debt. The Conservative government, however, chose instead to devote most of the excess balance to cover both expenditure under the previously passed Naval Works Act of 1895, and to fund a second and even larger Naval Works Act[100] which, as a consequence, did not include provision for borrowing.[101]

It will be remembered, that during the 1880s the completion of warships had often been delayed by lack of funds, that the Naval Defence Act had provided a remedy in the form of allowing unexpended balances allocated to new construction to be carried over to the next fiscal year, and that this practice was not continued for administrative reasons. The absence of such a provision after 1894 did not, however, matter because the funding authorized by Parliament for the purposes of warship construction was never exceeded. This occurred because the productive capacity of Britain's building yards was insufficient to meet the combination of high naval and commercial demand for new vessels, a deficiency that was compounded by labor disputes. As a result, the delivery of warships was delayed, payments for completed units were in turn deferred, and thus in place of the financial shortages of the 1880s, the navy was confronted with the problem of large unexpended balances at the end of each fiscal year.[102]

Between fiscal years 1889-90 and 1896-97, expenditure on the navy, which included the sums provided by the Imperial Defence Act of 1888, the Naval Defence Acts of 1889 and 1893, and the Naval Works Acts of 1895 and 1896, minus interest payments, as well as the amounts spent under the navy estimates, increased from £15,888,502 to £23,790,835, a growth of no less than 65 per cent.[103] Conservative and Liberal governments were able to provide the funds required by naval expansion without serious financial difficulty for several reasons. The reduced level of colonial military activity and the avoidance of great power confrontations that required mobilization minimized spending on naval and military operations as compared with the 1870s and 1880s, the charge on the National Debt was reduced by Goschen's conversion scheme, revenue from the death duties was greatly increased by the introduction of graduated rates and the growth of economic prosperity, particularly with the end of the "great depression" of 1873-96, increased the yield from existing taxation. But during the next eight years, the rising cost of building battleships and first-class cruisers, and the expense of colonial warfare in Africa, were to precipitate a crisis in naval finance.

5 Technological Change, Colonial War, and Financial Retrenchment

During the period beginning with the Naval Defence Act and ending with the estimates of 1896-97, improvements in armour had been a major contributor to reductions in the building costs of British first-class battleships. The Harvey process of face-hardening, which was first tested in 1891, resulted in armour plates that were far more resistant to both penetration and cracking than those made of conventional nickel-steel.[104] The use of Harvey armour, together with the advent of lighter but more effective main battery guns and the adoption of a sloping armoured deck, made it possible to build first-class battleships under the 1893-94 estimates and Spencer program that were not only better protected but also less costly than their Naval Defence Act predecessors.[105] Krupp armour, which was produced by more sophisticated methods of face-hardening that made it considerably harder and tougher than even Harvey armour, appeared in 1894.[106] The use of Krupp in the place of Harvey armour, and the decision to accept a lower standard of protection to the hull amidships for the battleships ordered under the estimates of 1896-97, allowed a greater area of the hull to be covered by armour and a further decrease in the cost per unit.[107]

The trend of declining battleship construction costs was sharply reversed, however, by changes in design. The adoption of new model main battery guns, mountings of greater weight, and an increase in the thickness and extent of armour protection, which were made necessary

18

by the growth in the size of foreign battleships, resulted in the building of vessels under the estimates of 1897–98, 1898–99, 1899–1900 and 1900–01, that were considerably more expensive than those ordered previously.[108] By the turn of the century, moreover, France and Russia had begun to build battleships with Krupp armour that rendered large areas of their hulls proof against projectiles fired from the 6-inch quick-firing guns that composed the secondary batteries of British battleships. The eight first-class British battleships ordered under the estimates of 1901–02, 1902–03 and 1903–04, thus added an intermediate battery of fast-firing 9.2-inch guns to the main battery of 12-inch guns and secondary battery of 6-inch guns that had been standard since the vessels of the Spencer program.[109] These vessels were, as a consequence, 10 per cent greater in displacement and no less than 20 per cent greater in cost than their immediate predecessors of the 1900–01 program. And with the two battleships authorized by the 1904–05 estimates, the 6-inch gun battery was eliminated altogether and replaced by additional 9.2-inch guns, which resulted in a further increase in size and expense.[110]

During the same period, the growth in the dimensions and cost of first-class cruisers greatly exceeded that of battleships. The first-class cruisers of the Naval Defence Act and Spencer program had not been provided with side armour because neither nickel-steel nor Harvey plates could be mounted in thicknesses that were sufficient to stop the projectiles of medium–caliber quick-firing guns over a great enough area of the hull to be effective without requiring prohibitively large increases in size and cost. These vessels instead relied upon an armoured deck that was located at the waterline, which shielded the vital machinery spaces and magazines from the explosions of hits on the hull or superstructure above, but left the armament largely unprotected.[111] With the advent of Krupp armour, however, it became possible to cover a considerable area of the side of a first-class cruiser with plates that were capable of stopping medium–caliber quick-firer projectiles without involving unacceptable increases in size and expense. In June 1897, White argued that such a vessel would be capable of engaging a battleship in close action with some prospect of success.[112] Large cruisers with side armour were required, moreover, to match the new construction of foreign rivals. In 1896, the French had begun building a large cruiser with vertical protection and the capacity to steam at very high speed. Although this vessel mounted Harvey rather than Krupp armour, it was nevertheless big and fast enough to outclass Britain's most powerful protected—that is, deck armoured—cruisers then built or building. And in 1897, the Russians began work on a similar vessel that was armoured with Krupp steel.[113]

The Royal Navy ordered its first six armoured—that is, side armoured-cruisers under the estimates of 1897–98. The displacement of these vessels was some nine per cent, and their cost no less than 36 per cent, greater than that of their immediate protected cruiser predecessors. The French, however, responded by cutting back new battleship construction in order to concentrate on building fast armoured cruisers in large numbers: her program of 1897–98 included no fewer than seven such vessels in addition to the one of 1896 and the Russian ship of 1897.[114] Britain was thus forced to order four armoured cruisers under the estimate of 1898–99, and an additional four vessels under a supplementary estimate later that same fiscal year. The displacement of the first four vessels was 18 per cent, and their cost some 32 per cent, greater than that of the armoured cruisers ordered under the previous year's estimate. The displacement and cost of the four vessels built under the supplementary estimate, on the other hand, were substantially reduced by eliminating the 9.2-inch guns of the main battery, but they nevertheless remained more expensive than any of the protected cruisers that had been built previously. Six more armoured cruisers of the smaller type introduced with the supplementary estimate of 1898–99, were ordered under the estimates of 1899–1900 and 1900–01.[115]

But the enormous British efforts of 1898–99, 1899–1900 and 1900–01, were countered by French and Russian programs, which during the same period added eight vessels to the nine already under way.[116] Britain was thus compelled to increase her slender margin of superiority with an order for six armoured cruisers in 1901–02. With these vessels, an attempt was again made to save money by restricting size, which was only slightly greater than that of the reduced designs of the preceding three years. Armoured cruisers of such small dimensions could not, however, mount the 9.2-inch guns that were required to smash the Krupp medium armour of foreign vessels, and thus the two armoured cruisers ordered under the 1902–03 estimates were increased in displacement by some 25 per cent and in cost by no less than 36 per cent over the vessels ordered the year before in order to accommodate a main battery of 9.2-inch guns. The four armoured cruisers of the 1903–04 program were only slightly more expensive than the vessels of 1902–03 in spite of the fact that the secondary battery was strengthened by the substitution of 7.5-inch guns for 6-inch guns, but the three armoured cruisers ordered under the estimate of 1904–05 were provided with additional 7.5-inch guns, which resulted in a rise in displacement of 8 per cent, and in cost of almost 18 per cent, over that of their immediate predecessors.[117]

During the eight fiscal years from 1897–98 to 1904–05, British expenditure on battleships and first-class cruisers was much greater than during the preceding eight fiscal years from 1889–90 to 1896–97. During the earlier period 25 battleships were ordered as compared with 27 during the later. But although there was little difference in the number of vessels, the growth in the cost-per-unit during the second period resulted in a substantial difference in spending: £16.8 million was spent on battleship construction during the years from 1889–90 to 1896–97, which rose to no less than £29.6 million during the years from 1897–98 to 1904–05. The increase in expenditure on first-class cruisers during the second period, however, was even greater. Only 19 first-class cruisers were ordered during the first period, while no fewer than 35 were ordered in the second. Increases in the cost-per-unit after 1897 were such, moreover, that the cost of the first-class cruisers authorized under the estimates of 1904–05 was more than triple that of the vessels built under the Naval Defence Act. The combined effect of greater numbers and increased cost-per-unit was

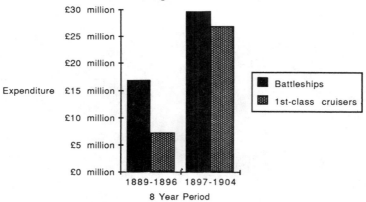

Figure 1   *Expenditure on battleships and first-class cruisers, 1889-1904*

a nearly four-fold rise in spending on first-class cruisers, from £7.3 million during the first period to £26.9 million during the second. And although much less was spent on second- and third-class cruiser construction during the later period, expenditure on all cruiser classes was none the less nearly double that spent between 1889-90 and 1896-97 (see Figure 1).[118]

Between 1897 and 1904, 26 battleships and 30 first-class cruisers were completed, as compared with 21 battleships and only 16 first-class cruisers between 1889 and 1896. The first-class cruisers of the later period, moreover, were considerably bigger than those of the earlier, and thus required commensurately larger crews. The manning requirements of the Royal Navy, as a consequence, grew at a much faster rate during the eight years after 1897 than the eight years before. The numbers of active naval personnel voted by Parliament rose from 65,400 in fiscal year 1889-90 to 93,750 in 1896-97, which in financial terms involved a growth in annual expenditure on manning [votes 1, 2, 13, and 14] over eight years of from £6,234,228 to £8,028,466, an increase of 29 per cent. Between fiscal years 1897-98 and 1904-05, on the other hand, the numbers of men voted rose from 100,050 to 131,100, which resulted in a growth in annual expenditure on manning over eight years of from £8,367,161 to £11,888,707, an increase of 42 per cent. The enormous rise in the number of active naval personnel was not matched by the commensurate expansion of the naval reserve, which fell from being nearly a quarter the size of the active manning level in 1889-90 to little more than a fifth by 1904-05.[119]

The growth in the number and size of battleships and first-class cruisers, and the increases in naval personnel, required the construction of additional barracks, docks and other port facilities. Expenditure on new works during the period from 1897-98 to 1904-05 was thus practically five times greater than that during the previous eight years, rising from some £5.1 million to £24.8 million. During the earlier period, nearly three-quarters of the spending on works had been covered by the navy estimates, with the balance of £1.4 million having been supplied out of the £3.8 million authorized by the Naval Works Acts of 1895 and 1896.

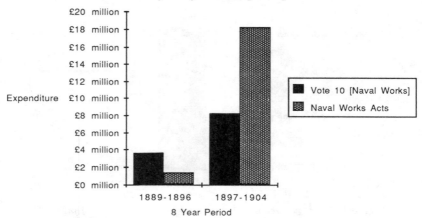

Figure 2   *Expenditure on naval works, 1889-1904*

During the second period, however, the main burden of paying for new works was shifted from the navy estimates to sums provided by Naval Works legislation. £2.4 million left over from the Naval Works Acts of 1895 and 1896 were available for spending after 1897, and Naval Works Acts that were passed in 1897, 1899, 1901 and 1903, sanctioned an additional £17.9 million. Of this authorized total of £19.3 million, £18.2 million was spent by the end of fiscal year 1904–05, which meant that expenditure on the navy in addition to the amounts provided under the navy estimates was over 50 per cent greater during the second period as compared with the first (see Figure 2).[120] Beginning with the Naval Works Act of 1899, provision was again made for borrowing through terminable annuities, which became necessary after the outbreak of the Boer War [see next paragraph].[121] Annuity payments out of the works vote of the navy estimates began in fiscal year 1901–02, and by the end of fiscal year 1904–05, £1.6 million had been so expended. This reduced effective spending on works under the works vote between fiscal years 1897–98 and 1904–05 from the nominal figure of £8.2 million to £6.6 million. The net relief to the estimates provided by the Naval Works Acts during this period—that is, the total amount spent under the Naval Works Acts minus the annuity paid out of the navy estimate—thus came to £16.6 million, a sum that was nearly equal to the amount spent on battleships during the previous eight fiscal years.[122]

Expenditure under the navy estimates during the second period never-theless greatly exceeded that of the first. The navy estimate rose from £21.8 million in 1897–98 to no less than £38.3 million in 1904–05 and, as a consequence, the total spent under the navy estimates during the second period was more than 78 per cent higher than the total spent during the first, increasing from £137.3 million to £245 million.[123] At first, increased spending under the navy estimates and Naval Works Acts caused little difficulty for the government because continued vigorous economic growth produced even larger increases in tax revenue. But between October 1899 and May 1902, the war in South Africa resulted in military expenditures that forced the government not only to raise taxes, but to resort to borrowing on such a scale that the size of the National Debt grew by nearly a quarter. The collapse of the inflated war economy in 1903, moreover, resulted in a £10 million decline in income from taxes in fiscal year 1903-04 as compared with 1902-03 and although income increased by £1.9 million in the next fiscal year, the financial situation remained serious.[124]

As early as in October 1901, Sir Michael Hicks Beach, the Chancellor of the Exchequer, had warned the Cabinet that the relentless growth in naval expenditure would lead "straight to financial ruin."[125] Any hopes that he might have entertained with regard to reductions in the navy estimate were, however, dashed by the reply several weeks later of Lord Selborne, the First Lord. "To me it seems that the expenditure of this country on maintaining its Credit and its Navy," he began,

> stands on a different plane to any other expenditure. Its Credit and its Navy seem to me to be the two main pillars on which the strength of this country rests, and each is essential to the other. Unless our financial position is strong, the Navy cannot be maintained. Unless the Navy is fully adequate for any call which may be made upon it, our national Credit must stand in jeopardy.[126]

"As regards new construction," Selborne thus continued,

> I can hold out no hopes of such a slackening of our efforts as the Chancellor of the Exchequer suggests. To do so would surely entail our falling into an inferiority of strength in respect of France and Russia, and would leave our mercantile marine inadequately defended—a responsibility which, I take it, no one would be ready to accept.[127]

As it was, he argued, Britain had run her "margin of naval strength to a finer point than prudence warrants."[128] Britain, the First Lord then maintained, required not merely an equality, but a superiority in numbers over the battleship fleets of France and Russia such "as will offer us the reasonable certainty of success in a war."[129] More armoured cruisers, he added, were required to overmatch the large programs of the French.[130]

Selborne's suggested policy of "equality plus a margin" was not formally considered by the Cabinet until a year later, in October 1902.[131] At this time he insisted that Britain should possess superiorities in vessels built and building of six battleships and 14 armoured cruisers over the combined strengths of France and Russia by December 1907.[132] Such a goal could only be achieved by laying down three battleships and four armoured cruisers in each of the four fiscal years from 1903-04 to 1906-07, which Selborne projected would entail an initial increase in the navy estimate of from £2.5 million to £3 million, though he expressed the hope that there would be no further increases on the same scale within the period named.[133] The Cabinet's approval of the scheme did not pass without a warning from Charles Ritchie, Hicks Beach's successor at the Exchequer. "I cannot help viewing with considerable concern the financial outlook," he cautioned, and one of the greatest dangers that I am afraid of is that, sooner or later, with a shilling income tax, and with bad times, entailing want of employment, and perhaps an appreciably increased price of bread, there will be a violent reaction, resulting in sweeping reductions of our army and navy.[134]

But Ritchie admitted that Britain could not "safely reduce the expenditure on the navy, at least for the present, while Russia, France and Germany are adding to their fleets."[135] "Our hands," he confessed, "are practically forced by the actions of others."[136]

Even Selborne recognized that increases in the navy estimates could not continue indefinitely. In February 1903, he warned the Admiralty that they were "*very near their possible maximum*," and that economies were, therefore, essential.[137] Instead of the anticipated maximum increase of £3 million, however, the expenditure under the estimates of 1903–04 exceeded that of the previous fiscal year by more than £4 million. Much of the overspending was attributable to Britain's purchase of two second-class battleships from Chile to prevent their acquisition by Russia for use against Japan, a British ally. In compensation, a battleship and an armoured cruiser were eliminated from the 1904–05 program, but the financial prospects for that year were nevertheless far worse than Selborne had predicted in 1902. In place of the promised minimal rise, the draft estimate showed an increase of £2.5 million over 1903–04.[138] "I am in despair," the First Lord thus lamented to Arthur J. Balfour, the Prime Minister, on 28 October 1903, "about the financial outlook."[139]

By this time there were signs from outside the government that the opposition to rising naval spending had become politically significant. "The large and continued increase in the Estimates for the Navy," the editor of the *Naval Annual* had noted in 1903,

> accompanied as it is by a heavy increase in the Army Estimates, will, we fear, produce a reaction which will have most serious consequences on the future safety of the Empire. The results of recent bye-elections may be taken as some indication that such a reaction has begun, and that the electorate does not approve the unchecked growth of public expenditure.[140]

In 1904, the Committee of Public Accounts of the House of Commons raised strong objections to the provision of funds for the navy outside the estimate by means of borrowing under the Naval Works Acts, a practice which they observed "tends to obscure the real expenditure." The committee thus recommended that "it would be more in accordance with sound rules of finance and would tend to simplify the national accounts and maintain an efficient control over expenditure if the bulk of these services were included as formerly in the annual Estimate."[141]

In January 1904, Selborne conceded the necessity of reducing the size of the increase in the estimate by striking six small vessels from the proposed building program.[142] This did not satisfy Austen Chamberlain, Ritchie's replacement at the Exchequer. "However reluctant we may be to face the fact," he insisted to the Cabinet on 28 April 1904, "the time has come when we must frankly admit that the financial resources of the United Kingdom are inadequate to do all that we should desire in the matter of Imperial defence."[143] Selborne was to be allowed an increase of more than £1 million in the navy estimate of 1904–05 over the previous year, but he was forced to agree to an unspecified large decrease in the estimate for 1905–06.[144] And although he was promised the passage of a Naval Works Act that would provide an additional £5.8 million over the next several years,[145] much of its effect would be vitiated by the annuity payments on the accumulated debt of earlier Naval Works legislation, which from 1905–06 would require that more than £1 million be paid out of the works vote of the navy estimate each year. The First Lord was none the less determined to complete the full program of battleship and armoured cruiser construction that had been outlined to the Cabinet in 1902. The designs of the two types of 1904–05 were, moreover, to be given a heavier armament than their predecessors, which meant that there would be substantial increases in the cost per unit.[146]

Considerable amounts were then being spent under the navy estimates that were either not strictly essential for purposes of war preparation, or capable of being spent with greater effect if allocated differently. But neither the Treasury nor the Admiralty, to whom Parliament had largely delegated the task of detailed financial control,[147] possessed the bureaucratic means that were required to impose the economies that would have allowed increased expenditure on new construction on the one hand, and lower naval spending overall on the other. Over the course of the second half of the 19th century and the early years of the 20th century, the funding of the Upper Establishment of the Treasury, which bore the brunt of the administrative burden of the department, had not been increased in the name of economy in government. Although naval expenditure during this period rose sharply and thus increased the work load, Treasury oversight of spending on the navy was left to three clerks, who were also responsible for the Foreign Office, the Colonial Office, the War Office, the Royal Woods and the Municipal Corporations.[148] Given understaffing of this degree, Treasury control was bound to be weak,[149] and in fact their scrutiny of the estimates did not include the shipbuilding program or an expert examination of contracts.[150]

The instruments of financial supervision within the Admiralty were no more effective. According to instructions promulgated in 1885, the Accountant General was responsible for the criticism of, and advice on, the estimates, the financial review of liabilities and expenditure; and the consideration of spending in the dockyards and on new works or repairs.[151] In a memorandum of 1910, the Admiralty Permanent Secretary maintained, however, that

one department of the Admiralty cannot act as a check on the financial operations of another Department: that a finance Department cannot legitimately criticize except in so far as it can say that higher authority is necessary to expenditure proposed, and can refuse to pass expenditure incurred until it is satisfied that the claim for payment is financially in order. In other words, the Accountant General's Department can secure financial regularity, but it cannot exercise financial control. [152]

The Admiralty Finance Committee, whose members included the Parliamentary and Financial Secretary, the Accountant General, and the Secretary to the Controller, was supposed to be the main instrument of financial control, [153] but in practice was concerned simply with "reviewing the progress of expenditure as compared with estimates." [154]

The situation with regard to policy formulation as a means of achieving greater financial efficiency was no better. The Treasury at this time left matters of major policy to the government department concerned. [155] The Board of Admiralty, for its part, was little more than an administrative body, largely unconcerned with policy and unassisted by a naval staff—in short possessing neither the habit of mind nor the bureaucratic machinery that was required to formulate and implement policy effectively. [156] The service members of the Board were, moreover, unaccustomed to thinking of even their administrative function in financial terms. The Sea Lords, Selborne warned on 16 February 1903,

> must take finance to their fireside to sit beside efficiency and not leave the derelict orphan to my sole charge. Further they must reverse their mental process. They must cease to say "This is the ideal plan; how can we get money enough to carry it out?" They must say instead "Here is a sovereign; how much can we squeeze out of it that will really count for victory in a Naval war?" [157]

These entreaties went unheeded, however, and when Lord Walter Kerr, the First Naval Lord, gave notice of his retirement in 1904, Selborne sought a replacement who he believed would be capable of coming up with the convincing measures of economy that were by now desperately required. He chose Admiral Sir John Arbuthnot Fisher.

Fisher had recently served with distinction as Commander-in-Chief of the Mediterranean Fleet, the Royal Navy's premier command, and as Second Naval Lord of the Admiralty, where he had been responsible for the introduction of major personnel changes. He was a man of quick intelligence, strong opinion, vigorous industry and unbending resolution, who possessed great personal charm, respected talent and delegated authority easily. Fisher was also devious, unforgiving and ruthless. Thus while he won politically influential patronage and the loyalty of capable subordinates, he was at the same time distrusted by many of his naval peers. Under ordinary circumstances, the First Lord might not have been disposed to favor Fisher, about whom he appears to have had some misgivings, [158] but he badly needed a man capable of preserving the integrity of the new warship construction program while simultaneously implementing changes in policy that would result in reductions in naval expenditure.

Fisher may have attracted Selborne's attention with claims that he was capable of carrying out measures that would result in considerable

26

decreases in naval spending without sacrifices in fighting capability. "We can't go on with such increasing Navy Estimates," Fisher had written to J. R. Thursfield, the journalist, on 5 July 1903, "and I see my way very clearly to a *very great reduction* WITH INCREASED EFFICIENCY!"[159] In any case, Selborne asked Fisher to become his service chief that autumn upon the retirement of Kerr. Selborne's brief to his candidate was unequivocal. "It is quite certain," he informed Fisher on 14 May,

> that the Navy Estimates have for the present reached their maximum in the present year. In 1905-06 not only can there be no possible increase, but it is necessary, for the influence of the Admiralty over the House of Commons and for the stability of the national finances, that we should show a substantial decrease.[160]

Following Fisher's acceptance of his offer on 16 May, Selborne extended the executive powers of his prospective service chief. The Orders in Council of 10 August 1904, and new instructions affecting the distribution of business of October 1904, not only changed the nomenclature of the service members of the board from "Naval Lords" to "Sea Lords,"[161] but assigned essentially administrative responsibilities to the Second, Third and Fourth Sea Lords while making the First Sea Lord accountable for "all large questions of Naval policy and maritime warfare" and also "the fighting and sea-going efficiency of the Fleet, its organization and mobilization; the distribution and movements of all Ships in Commission or in Fleet Reserve."[162] In combining the appointment of a man of strong ideas and character with the enhancement of the authority of his position, Selborne undoubtedly acted in the hope that the direction of a powerful individual might serve in the absence of an articulate bureaucratic mechanism of policy making.[163]

During the summer of 1904, Fisher had drafted a policy prospectus in which he described the actions which he intended to take upon assuming office.[164] He opened with strong remarks on the need both to maintain British naval supremacy and to reduce naval spending. "The British Empire," he declared,

> floats on the British Navy. We must have no doubt whatever about its fighting supremacy and its instant readiness for war! To ensure this and at the same time to effect the economy which the finances of the country render imperative there must be drastic changes! To carry these out we must have the three R's! We must be Ruthless, Relentless, Remorseless!

Fisher then proposed that great economies and increases in fighting efficiency could be achieved through administrative reform, the redistribution and concentration of the fleet, the sale of obsolete warships, changes in the manning of the active fleet, and the reconstitution of the naval reserve. Spending on non-essential items was to be drastically cut. Many warships that had been deployed on distant foreign stations were to be brought back to home waters, and ineffective units that had been serving abroad or languishing in reserve were to be sold for scrap. The concentration of the fleet at home would serve strategic requirements and allow the Admiralty to reduce or eliminate expensive dockyard establishments that had been maintained abroad. The sale of warships was to raise cash that could be spent for naval purposes, lower expenditure on repairs, and free port facilities for use by more modern units. This would in turn reduce requirements for additional naval works, and provide personnel that could be used to shorten the length of commissions in the interest of morale and to recast the reserve in such a way that the manning requirements of the fleet would be satisfied with fewer numbers. The centerpiece of Fisher's program, however, was to be the introduction of new model capital ships of unprecedented speed and fire power, which were to be built at a cost that Britain could afford through the exploitation of the latest technical developments.

Notes to Chapter 1

1 G. J. Marcus, *A Naval History of England*, Vol. 1: *The Formative Centuries* (Boston: Little, Brown, 1961) and D. B. Quinn and A. N. Ryan, *England's Sea Empire, 1550-1642* (London: George Allen & Unwin, 1983).
2 Brian Lavery, *The Ship of the Line*, Vol. 1: *The Development of the Battlefleet, 1650-1850* (London: Conway Maritime Press, 1983), pp. 22-3.
3 Frank Howard, *Sailing Ships of War, 1400-1860* (London: Conway Maritime Press, 1979), pp. 89-150.
4 Michael Lewis, *The Navy of Britain: A Historical Portrait* (London: George Allen & Unwin, 1948), pp. 449-54, and John Creswell, *British Admirals of the Eighteenth Century: Tactics in Battle* (London: George Allen & Unwin, 1972), pp. 15-26.
5 John Wolf, *The Emergence of the Great Powers, 1685-1715* (New York: Harper & Row, 1951; paperback edn 1962), pp. 171-2.
6 G. Teitler, *The Genesis of the Professional Officers' Corps* (Beverly Hills, California: Sage Publications, 1974), pp. 112-27.
7 Lavery, *Ship of the Line*, Vol. 1, pp. 26-7.
8 Howard, *Sailing Ships of War*, pp. 151-3.
9 Charles Wilson, *England's Apprenticeship, 1603-1763* (London: Longman, 1965), pp. 160-211.
10 Richard Ollard, *Pepys* (New York: Holt, Rinehart & Winston, 1974), pp. 278-95.
11 P. G. M. Dickson and John Sperling, "War Finance, 1689-1714," in *The New Cambridge Modern History*, 14 Vols (Cambridge: Cambridge University Press, 1970), Vol. 6, p. 285.
12 Sir John Clapham, *The Bank of England: A History*, 2 Vols (Cambridge: Cambridge University Press, 1944), Vol. 1, and P. G. M. Dickson, *The Financial Revolution in England: A Study in the Development of Public Credit, 1688-1756* (London: Macmillan, 1967).
13 J. F. Bosher, *French Finances, 1770-1795: From Business to Bureaucracy* (Cambridge: Cambridge University Press, 1970); Geoffrey Parker, "The Emergence of Modern Finance in Europe, 1500-1730," in *The Fontana Economic History of Europe*, Vol. 2: *The Sixteenth and Seventeenth Centuries* (London: Fontana, 1974) and James C. Riley, *International Government Finance and the Amsterdam Capital Market, 1740-1815* (Cambridge: Cambridge University Press, 1980),

especially pp. 165–85, and *The Seven Years War and the Old Regime in France: The Economic and Financial Toll* (Princeton: Princeton University Press, 1986).

14 Paul Kennedy, *The Rise and Fall of British Naval Mastery* (New York: Charles Scribner's Sons, 1976), pp. 69–147. For a general account of naval warfare in the 18th century from the French point of view, see E. H. Jenkins, *A History of the French Navy* (Annapolis, Md.: Naval Institute Press, 1973), pp. 69–200. For a detailed study of the French abandonment of a battle fleet strategy, see Geoffrey Symcox, *The Crisis of French Sea Power, 1688-1697: From the Guerre d'Escadre to the Guerre de Course* (The Hague: Martinus Nijhoff, 1974). For the effect of administrative and financial difficulties on French naval efficiency in the mid 18th century, see James Pritchard, *Louis XV's Navy, 1748-1762: A Study of Organization and Administration* (Kingston and Montreal: McGill–Queen's University Press, 1987).

15 Daniel A. Baugh, *British Naval Administration in the Age of Walpole* (Princeton: Princeton University Press, 1965), p. 146.

16 For the Royal Navy in the 18th and early 19th centuries, see Marcus, *Naval History*, Vol. 1, and [Vol. 2]: *The Age of Nelson: The Royal Navy, 1793-1815* (New York: Viking, 1971).

17 B. R. Mitchell, *European Historical Statistics, 1750-1970,* abridged edn (New York: Columbia University Press, 1978), pp. 186–9, 217–8, 223, 253, 298, 302, 347.

18 Kennedy, *British Naval Mastery*, p. 190.

19 Mitchell, *European Historical Statistics*, pp. 217, 223, 271, 290–1. See also A. L. Levine, *Industrial Retardation in Britain, 1880-1914* (New York: Basic Books, 1967).

20 Kennedy, *British Naval Mastery*, p. 190. See also Derek H. Aldcroft (ed.), *The Development of British Industry and Foreign Competition, 1875-1914* (London: George Allen & Unwin, 1968).

21 *FDSF*, Vol. 1, pp. 151–6.

22 J. F. Bosher, "French Administration and Public Finance in their European Setting," in *The New Cambridge Modern History*, 14 Vols (Cambridge: Cambridge University Press, 1965), Vol. 8, p. 591; W. H. Bruford, "German Constitutional and Social Development, 1795-1830," in *The New Cambridge Modern History*, Vol. 9, p. 379; and J. A. Hawgood, "Liberalism and Constitutional Developments," in *The New Cambridge Modern History*, Vol. 10, p. 206.

23 For the development of German and French national banks, see Salomon Flink, *The German Reichsbank and Economic Germany: A Study of the Policies of the Reichsbank in their Relation to the Economic Development of Germany, with Special Reference to the Period after 1923* (New York: Greenwood Press, 1969; first published in 1930), pp. 1–35, and Andre Liesse, *Evolution of Credit and Banks in France from the Founding of the Bank of France to the Present Time* (Washington, D.C.: Government Printing Office, 1909).

24 For the control of the state budget by the legislature in Prussia and France, see Hajo Holborn, *A History of Modern Germany, 1840-1945* (New York: Alfred A. Knopf, 1969), pp. 77–80, and Frank Maloy Anderson, *The Constitutions and other Select Documents Illustrative of the History of France, 1789-1907*, 2nd edn (New York: Russell & Russell, 1967; first published in 1904; 2nd edn, 1908), pp. 577–86, 635. For the control of the Prussian legislature by the wealthy, see Theodore S. Hamerow, *The Social Foundations of German Unification, 1858-1871: Ideas and Institutions* (Princeton: Princeton University Press, 1969), pp. 297–307. For the influence of financial interests in the legislature of the Third Republic, see Jean-Marie Mayeur and Madeleine Reberioux, *The Third Republic from its*

Origins to the Great War, 1871-1914, translated by J. R. Foster (Cambridge: Cambridge University Press, 1984; first published in France in 1973), pp. 90–4.

25 Howard, *Sailing Ships of War*.

26 Bernard Brodie, *Sea Power in the Machine Age* (Princeton: Princeton University Press, 1941).

27 For the cost of a first-rate ship-of-the-line, see Geoffrey Bennett, *The Battle of Trafalgar* (Annapolis: Naval Institute Press, 1977), p. 19. For the cost of the *Warrior*, see Oscar Parkes, *British Battleships: A History of Design, Construction and Armament*, new and revised edn (London: Seeley Service, 1957), p. 16. For the stability of wholesale price indices from the late 18th through the mid 19th centuries, see Mitchell, *European Historical Statistics*, pp. 388–9.

28 G. J. Marcus, *Heart of Oak: A Survey of British Sea Power in the Georgian Era* (London: Oxford University Press, 1975), pp. 4–5.

29 Brodie, *Sea Power in the Machine Age*, p. 213.

30 Sir Thomas Brassey, *The British Navy: Its Strength, Resources, and Administration*, 5 Vols (London: Longmans, Green, and Co., 1883), Vol. 4, pp. 114–6, and Robert Greenhalgh Albion, *Forests and Sea Power: The Timber Problem of the Royal Navy, 1652-1862* (Cambridge: Harvard University Press, 1926), pp. 84–6.

31 Brassey, *The British Navy*, Vol. 2, p. 402.

32 For the manning of the Royal Navy in the 18th century, see Marcus, *Heart of Oak*, pp. 99-114, and Baugh, *British Naval Administration*, pp. 147-240, 452-93. For the changes of the 19th century, see T. A. Brassey, "Manning," in *NA, 1896*, pp. 208-18; T. A. Brassey, "The Manning of the Navy in Time of War," in *NA, 1898*, pp. 102-17, and Eugene L. Rasor, *Reform in the Royal Navy: A Social History of the Lower Deck, 1850 to 1880* (Hamden, Conn.: Archon Books, 1976). For the creation of the naval reserve system, see Frank C. Bowen, *History of the Royal Naval Reserve* (London: Lloyd's, 1926).

33 For the composition and strength of European navies during the 19th century, see *CFS*.

34 B. R. Mitchell and Phyllis Deane, *Abstract of British Historical Statistics* (Cambridge: Cambridge University Press, 1971), pp. 392-3, 396-7.

35 T. A. Brassey, "Naval Reserves," in *NA, 1902*, pp. 65-6, and Intelligence Department, Admiralty, "Diagram Showing the Number of Ships in Commission and Engine Room Ratings, Seamen, and Marines voted each year from 1739 to 1903 Inclusive" (May 1904), Adm. 1/7663, P.R.O.

36 See Chapter 1, section 5.

37 For the superiority of the Royal Navy's personnel in the 18th and early 19th centuries, see Baugh, *British Naval Administration*, pp. 145-6; Creswell, *British Admirals*, pp. 255-6; Peter Padfield, *Guns at Sea* (London: Hugh Evelyn, 1973), pp. 119-33.

38 Dennis E. Showalter, *Railroads and Rifles: Soldiers, Technology, and the Unification of Germany* (Hamden, Connecticut: Archon Books, 1975), and John Gooch, *Armies in Europe* (London: Routledge & Kegan Paul, 1980), pp. 109-44.

39 W. S. Hamer, *The British Army: Civil-Military Relations, 1885-1905* (Oxford: Clarendon Press, 1970).

40 J. D. Chambers and G. E. Mingay, *The Agricultural Revolution, 1750-1880* (New York: Schocken Books, 1966), pp. 16, 148-9.

41 Ibid., pp. 179-81; Arthur J. Marder, *The Anatomy of British Sea Power: A History of British Naval Policy in the Pre-Dreadnought Era, 1880-1905* (Hamden, Conn.: Archon Books, 1964; first published in 1940), p. 85; and Paul Bairoch, "Agriculture and the Industrial Revolution, 1700-1914," in Carlo M. Cipolla

(ed.), *The Industrial Revolution, 1700-1914* (New York: Harper & Row, 1976), p. 477.

42 *CFS*, p. 3, and Andrew Lambert, *Battleships in Transition: The Creation of the Steam Battle Fleet, 1815-1860* (London: Conway Maritime Press, 1984).

43 Brodie, *Sea Power in the Machine Age*, p. 205, and Stanley Sandler, *The Emergence of the Modern Capital Ship* (Newark: University of Delaware Press, 1979).

44 Admiral G. A. Ballard, *The Black Battlefleet* (Annapolis: Naval Institute Press, 1980), p. 13.

45 Parkes, *British Battleships*, pp. 203–80.

46 Marder, *Anatomy*, pp. 123–6, and Parkes, *British Battleships*, pp. 316–36, 342.

47 *CFS*, p. 282.

48 Parkes, *British Battleships*, pp. 307, 324, and Bryan Ranft, "The protection of British seaborne trade and the development of systematic planning for war, 1860-1906," in Bryan Ranft (ed.), *Technical Change and British Naval Policy, 1860-1939* (London: Hodder & Stoughton, 1977), p. 3.

49 William L. Langer, *European Alliances and Alignments, 1871-1890*, 2nd edn, paperback (New York: Vintage, 1964; first published 1931; 2nd edn, 1950), pp. 297–318, and Brassey, *The British Navy*, Vol. 2, pp. 199–226.

50 Marder, *Anatomy*, p. 123, and Parkes, *British Battleships*, p. 328.

51 For British confidence in her overall naval position, see Brassey, *The British Navy*, Vol. 1, pp. xiii–xvi, and Parkes, *British Battleships*, p. 351. For the uncertainty over the battleship, see note 46.

52 Sidney Buxton, *Finance and Politics: An Historical Study, 1789-1885*, 2 Vols (New York: Augustus M. Kelley, 1966; first published 1888), Vol. 2, pp. 235–322, and Appendix, Tables 1 and 2.

53 Marder, *Anatomy*, pp. 126–31, and Langer, *European Alliances and Alignments*, pp. 491–2.

54 Parkes, *British Battleships*, p. 349, and D. K. Brown, *A Century of Naval Construction: The History of the Royal Corps of Naval Constructors, 1883-1983* (London: Conway Maritime Press, 1983), pp. 62–4.

55 Great Britain, Parliament, *Parliamentary Papers, 1889*, Vol. 50, "Statement of First Lord of the Admiralty, explanatory of the Navy Estimates, 1889-90," p. 8; and *Parliamentary Papers*, 1890, Vol. 44, "Statement of First Lord of the Admiralty, explanatory of the Navy Estimates, 1890-91," p. 10.

56 Great Britain, Laws, Statutes, etc. *Imperial Defence Act, 1888*. 51 & 52 Vict. c. 32.

57 William Hovgaard, *Modern History of Warships: Comprising a Discussion of Present Standpoint and Recent War Experiences* (London: Conway Maritime Press, 1971; first published 1920), p. 371.

58 Parkes, *British Battleships*, pp. 344–5, 349, 354–61.

59 Great Britain, Laws, Statutes, etc. *National Debt (Conversion) Act, 1888*. 51 Vict, chpt. 2, and idem, *National Debt Redemption Act, 1889*. 52 Vict. c. 4. For accounts of the Goschen debt conversion scheme, see Edward Walter Hamilton [Treasury], "Memorandum on National Debt Conversion" (28 February 1888) Cab. 37/21, 4, Cabinet Papers, P.R.O., and idem, *Conversion and Redemption: an account of the operations under the National Debt Conversion Act, 1888, and the National Debt Redemption Act, 1889* (London: Eyre & Spottiswoode, 1889), and Bernard Mallet, *British Budgets, 1887-88 to 1912-13* (London: Macmillan, 1913), pp. 10–23. For its effect, see Appendix, Tables 1 and 2.

60 Admiralty, "The Requirements of the British Navy" (9 August 1888) Cab. 37/22, 24; Admiralty, "Special programme for new construction, 1889-90 to

1893–94" (31 October 1888) Cab. 37/22, 28; Admiralty, "Special programme for new construction, 1889–90 to 1894–95" (1 November 1888) Cab. 37/22, 30; Lord George Hamilton, "Navy Estimates, 1889–90" (10 November 1888) Cab. 37/22, 36; Lord George Hamilton, "Naval Estimates: 1888–89 [*recte* 1889–90]" (1 December 1888) Cab. 37/22, 40; *Cabinet Papers*, P.R.O.; and Parkes, *British Battleships*, pp. 351–2.

61 Parkes, *British Battleships*, pp. 351–2
62 Ibid., p. 352.
63 Great Britain, Parliament, *Parliamentary Papers, 1889*, Vol. 5, "A Bill to Make further provision for Naval Defence and defray the expenses thereof."
64 Ibid.
65 Ibid.
66 Mallet, *British Budgets*, p. 65.
67 For the annual savings in debt charges, see note 59. For the uncertainty of economic conditions, see Mallet, *British Budgets*, p. 66.
68 Great Britain, Parliament, *Parliamentary Debates* (Commons) 4th series, Vol. 333 (1889), p. 1171.
69 Marder, *Anatomy*, pp. 88n., 106.
70 *Parliamentary Debates*, Vol. 333 (1889), p. 1171.
71 Ibid., p. 1173.
72 Ibid., p. 1185.
73 Ibid., pp. 1170, 1175; see also Mallet, *British Budgets*, pp. 29, 64–7.
74 *Parliamentary Debates*, Vol. 333 (1889), p. 1173.
75 Ibid., p. 1191.
76 Great Britain, Laws, Statutes, etc. *Naval Defence Act, 1889*, 52 Vict., c. 8.
77 Great Britain, Parliament, *Parliamentary Papers*, 1894, Vol. 54, "Statement of the First Lord of the Admiralty explanatory of the Navy Estimates for 1894–95"; "Further Notes on the Naval Defence Act 1889," undated memorandum by unknown author, N.L.M.D., London; and Mallet, *British Budgets*, pp. 49–52.
78 Sidney Pollard and Paul Robertson, *The British Shipbuilding Industry, 1870-1914* (Cambridge, Mass.: Harvard University Press, 1979), p. 32.
79 Great Britain, Parliament, *Parliamentary Papers, 1890*, Vol. 44, "Statement of First Lord of the Admiralty, explanatory of the Navy Estimates, 1890–91," p. 8.
80 Great Britain, Parliament, *Parliamentary Papers, 1893-94*, Vol. 6, "Memorandum. Explanatory of Naval Defence Amendment Bill," p. 1.
81 Ibid., and "Further Notes on the Naval Defence Act 1889," undated memorandum by unknown author, N.L.M.D..
82 Great Britain, Laws, Statutes, etc. *Naval Defence Act of 1893*, 56 & 57 Vict., c. 45.
83 Great Britain, Parliament, *Parliamentary Papers, 1890-91*, Vol. 51, "Statement of First Lord of the Admiralty, explanatory of the Navy Estimates, 1891–92," p. 11.
84 Effective battleships and cruisers are here taken to be vessels that had been laid down from 1880. Effective battleships thus include units beginning with the "Admiral" class, and effective cruisers of the first, second, and third class include units beginning with the "Imperieuse" class, "Leander" class, and "Surprise" class. Thus the pre-Naval Defence Act fleet was composed of 10 effective battleships and 46 effective cruisers. For the particulars of these vessels, see *CFS*, pp. 28–82.

85 Ibid., pp. 76-7.
86 Parkes, *British Battleships*, p. 356.
87 For the Franco-Russian entente, see William Leonard Langer, *The Franco-Russian Alliance, 1890-1894* (Cambridge, Massachusetts: Harvard University Press, 1929), and George F. Kennan, *The Fateful Alliance: France, Russia, and the Coming of the First World War* (New York: Pantheon Books, 1984).
88 *CFS*, and Marder, *Anatomy*, p. 191.
89 A. J. P. Taylor, *The Struggle for Mastery in Europe* (Oxford: Clarendon Press, 1954), pp. 325-45.
90 For a full account of the complex story behind the Spencer program, see Marder, *Anatomy*, pp. 174-205.
91 Ibid.
92 Mallet, *British Budgets*, pp. 79-94.
93 These were the two battleships of the 1893-94 program [*Majestic* and *Magnificent*] plus the seven vessels of the Spencer program [balance of the *Majestic* class].
94 Lord Spencer, "New Works for the Navy" (January 16, 1895) Cab. 37/38, 6, *Cabinet Papers*, P.R.O.
95 Mallet, *British Budgets*, pp. 97, 100.
96 "New Works for the Navy," Cab. 37/38, 6.
97 Great Britain, Parliament, *Parliamentary Papers*, 1895, Vol. 5, "A Bill to Make provision for the Construction of Works in the United Kingdom and elsewhere for the purpose of the Royal Navy, and to amend the Law relating to the Acquisition of Land for Naval Purposes." For an explanation and history of terminable annuities, see Buxton, *Finance and Politics*, Vol. 2, pp. 28-33.
98 Great Britain, Laws, Statutes, etc. *Naval Works Act, 1895*, 58 & 59 Vict., chpt. 35.
99 Mallet, *British Budgets*, pp. 102-3.
100 Ibid., p. 103 and n.
101 Great Britain, Laws, Statutes, etc. *Naval Works Act, 1896*, 59 Vict., c. 6. I am indebted to Mr. Jeffrey Simpson, a particularly able undergraduate history major at the University of Maryland, College Park, who brought the differences between the acts of 1895 and 1896 to my attention.
102 Great Britain, Parliament, *Parliamentary Papers*, 1902, Vol. 61 (*Accounts and Papers*, Vol. 7), Cmnd. 1055, 1902, "Report of the Committee Appointed to Inquire into the Arrears of Shipbuilding."
103 See Appendix, Table 3.
104 Edward L. Attwood, *War-Ships: A Text-book on the Construction, Protection, Stability, Turning, etc., of War Vessels*, 6th edn (London: Longmans, Green & Co., 1917; f. p. 1904), p. 155, and William Hovgaard, *Modern History of Warships*, pp. 464-7.
105 Parkes, *British Battleships*, pp. 381-5.
106 Attwood, *War-Ships*, pp. 158-60, and Hovgaard, *Modern History of Warships*, pp. 467-8.
107 Parkes, *British Battleships*, pp. 392-7.
108 Ibid., pp. 403, 416.
109 Ibid., pp. 421-9.
110 For the size and cost of British battleships, see Appendix, Table 16.
111 Director of Naval Construction [Sir William White], "Submission of the Director of Naval Construction with reference to the design of New First Class Cruisers ("Diadem" Class)" (13 July 1895), Adm. 116/878, P.R.O.

112 Director of Naval Construction [Sir William White], "Report on the Design of Armoured Cruisers by the Assistant Controller and Director of Naval Construction" (10 June 1897), Adm. 116/878.

113 *CFS*, pp. 190, 304.

114 Marder, *Anatomy*, p. 283.

115 For the size and cost of British armoured cruisers, see Appendix, Table 17. For the considerations that led to the reduction in the dimensions of British armoured cruisers, see Director of Naval Construction [Sir William White], "Report on the Design for New Cruisers, Supplemental Programme, 1898–99, by the Assistant Controller and Director of Naval Construction" (27 September 1898), with comments of the members of the Board of Admiralty, in Commander King-Hall, "The Evolution of the Cruiser" (1928), Adm. 1/8724/93, P.R.O.

116 *CFS*, pp. 190, 305–6.

117 See Appendix, Table 17. For the considerations that governed the design of the later large armoured cruisers, see undated memorandum, " 'Minotaur' Class" in King-Hall "The Evolution of the Cruiser," Adm. 1/8724/93, P.R.O.

118 For the numbers, cost-per-unit, and total expenditure by warship type per annum, see Appendix, Tables 8, 9, 16, and 17.

119 See Appendix, Tables 12, 13, and 22.

120 See Appendix, Table 7.

121 Great Britain, Laws, Statutes, etc., *Naval Works Act, 1899*, 62 & 63 Vict., c. 42.

122 See Appendix, Table 4.

123 See Appendix, Table 3.

124 Mallet, *British Budgets*, pp. 102–240.

125 Chancellor of the Exchequer [Sir Michael Hicks Beach], "Financial difficulties: Appeal for economy in estimates" (October 1901), p. 8, Cab. 37/58, 109, *Cabinet Papers*, P.R.O.

126 First Lord [Lord Selborne], "The Navy Estimates and the Chancellor of the Exchequer's Memorandum on the Growth of Expenditure" (16 November 1901), p. 2, Cab. 37/59, 118, *Cabinet Papers*, P.R.O.

127 Ibid., p. 5.

128 Ibid.

129 Ibid., p. 7.

130 Ibid., pp. 13–5.

131 First Lord [Lord Selborne], "Navy Estimates, 1903–1904" (10 October 1902), p. 2, Cab. 37/63, 142, *Cabinet Papers*, P.R.O.

132 Ibid.

133 Ibid., pp. 10–11.

134 Chancellor of the Exchequer [Charles Ritchie], "Public Finance" (23 December 1902), p. 4, Cab. 37/63, 170, *Cabinet Papers*, P.R.O.

135 Ibid.

136 Ibid.

137 First Lord [Lord Selborne] to the Admiralty Permanent Secretary [Sir Evan MacGregor], 16 February 1903, in "Distribution of Business, 1904," in Adm. 1/7737, P.R.O.

138 First Lord [Lord Selborne], "Memorandum on Navy Estimates, 1904–1905" (2 January 1904), Cab. 37/67, 90, *Cabinet Papers*, P.R.O.

139 Selborne to Balfour, 28 October 1903, Selborne Papers, Bodleian Library, from set of typescript letters collected by Arthur J. Marder read by the author in the summer of 1979, but as of now (April 1988) apparently no longer part of the collection.

140 *NA, 1903,* p. iii.
141 Great Britain, Parliament, *Parliamentary Papers* (Commons), 1904, Vol. 5 (Parliamentary Papers, nos. 152, 207, and 288) *First, Second and Third Reports from the Committee of Public Accounts; with the Proceedings of the Committee, "First Report," p. v, "Proceedings of the Committee, p. xxx.*
142 "Memorandum on Navy Estimates, 1904–1905," *Cabinet Papers.*
143 Chancellor of the Exchequer [Austen Chamberlain], "The financial position" (28 April 1904), Cab. 37/70, 61, *Cabinet Papers,* P.R.O.
144 FP, Vol. 1, p. xvii.
145 Ibid., and see also Great Britain, Laws, Statutes, etc., *Naval Works Act,* 1905, 5 Ed., c. 20.
146 *FP,* Vol. 1, p. xvii.
147 William F. Willoughby, Westel W. Willoughby, and Samuel McCune Lindsay, *The System of Financial Administration of Great Britain* (Washington, DC: The Brookings Institution, 1929), pp. 266–8.
148 Henry Roseveare, *The Treasury: The Evolution of a British Institution* (New York: Columbia University Press, 1969), pp. 210, 230.
149 For the larger size of the Upper Establishment division concerned with national defence required by the Treasury to assert effective control of rearmament before the Second World War, see ibid., p. 270. For a more complete description of the bureaucratic means by which the Treasury controlled defence spending in the 1930s, see G. C. Peden, *British Rearmament and the Treasury, 1932-1939* (Edinburgh: Scottish Academic Press, 1979), ch. 2.
150 Great Britain, Parliament, Commons, *Report from the Select Committee on Estimates; together with the Proceedings of the Committee, Minutes of Evidence and Appendices* (1912) [henceforward cited as the *Report from the Select Committee on Estimates*], pp. 6–10.
151 "Financial Responsibility—the Navy, 1524-1964," p. 11, an extremely informative unpublished history written under the auspices of N.L.M.D. (August, 1981), to the author courtesy of Mr. David Brown.
152 Admiralty Permanent Secretary to First Lord, "Memorandum on Financial Control, with special reference to the functions of the Accountant General under Order in Council of 18 Nov. 1885" (1 July 1910), p. 10, Adm. 1/8126, P.R.O.
153 "Financial Responsibility," p. 11.
154 Memorandum, "Re-constitution of the Admiralty Finance Committee" in "Finance Committee, 1902-1913," Case 3710, Adm. 116/865B, P.R.O.
155 *Report from the Select Committee on Estimates,* p. 10.
156 N. A. M. Rodger, *The Admiralty* (Lavenham, Suffolk: Terence Dalton, 1979), pp. 93–119.
157 Selborne to the Admiralty Permanent Secretary, 16 February 1903, in "Distribution of Business, 1904" (31 December 1904), Adm. 1/7737, P.R.O.
158 Ruddock F. Mackay, *Fisher of Kilverstone* (Oxford: Clarendon Press, 1973), pp. 245–52, 290–7, 305.
159 Quoted in Mackay, *Fisher of Kilverstone,* p. 285; see also Fisher to Viscount Esher, June 17, 1904, *FGDN,* Vol. 1, p. 318.
160 *FP,* Vol. 1, p. xvii.
161 Great Britain, Admiralty, *The Orders in Council for the Regulation of the Naval Service* (London: HMSO, 1908), Vol. 9, pp. 122–3.
162 Section IX, 'Distribution of Business,' in "Official Procedure and Rules" (20 October 1904), p. 42, Adm. 1/7814, P.R.O.

163 To a certain degree, the Orders in Council only formalized what had been custom, for which see Great Britain, Parliament, *Parliamentary Papers, 1890*, Vol. 19, Cmnd. 5979, 1890, "Preliminary and Further Reports (With Appendices) of the Royal Commissioners Appointed to Enquire into the Civil and Professional Administration of the Naval and Military Departments and the Relation of those Departments to Each other and to the Treasury," pp. ix-xiv, and Admiral Sir Vesey Hamilton, *Naval Administration: The Constitution, Character, and Functions of the Board of Admiralty, and of the Civil Departments it Directs* (London: George Bell, 1896), pp. 48-9. For the recognition by contemporaries, however, of the significance of the Orders in Council with regard to the extension of the authority of the First Sea Lord, see statement of the Admiralty and Parliamentary and Financial Secretary in the House of Commons, *Hansard's Parliamentary Debates*, Vol. 142 (6 March 1905), p. 437; "A Retrograde Admiralty" in *Blackwood's Edinburgh Magazine*, Vol. 177 (May 1905), reprinted in "Barfleur" [Admiral Sir Reginald Custance], *Naval Policy: A Plea for the Study of War* (Edinburgh and London: William Blackwood and Sons, 1907), pp. 9-13 and 'Civis' [Sir William White], *The State of the Navy in 1907: A Plea for Inquiry* (London: Smith, Elder, 1907), pp. 23-4, 34-43.

164 Print on "Admiralty House, Portsmouth" stationery (undated, but see Mackay, *Fisher of Kilverstone*, pp. 310-1), F.P. 4932, FISR 8/38, C.C.

[2]

The Strategy of Qualitative Superiority: Sir John Fisher and Technological Radicalism, 1904-1906

1 Introduction: Sir John Fisher and the Dreadnought

In early 1905, a special Admiralty committee, appointed at Fisher's initiative, investigated the feasibility of greatly increasing the fire power and speed of the battleship and armoured cruiser through the replacement of the mixed-caliber armaments and reciprocating engines that had previously been standard with uniform-caliber ("all-big-gun") armaments and turbine engines. Designs incorporating the novel systems of ordnance and propulsion were approved by the Admiralty in the spring of 1905. The first of the new model warships, the battleship *Dreadnought*, was laid down in the fall of 1905 and completed in a year. The three armoured cruisers of the *Invincible* class, which were to become known as battle cruisers, were laid down in the spring of 1906, and completed in 1908. In comparison with the battleship, the battle cruisers were much less heavily protected, but were nearly equal in armament and much faster. The successful trials of both new types led to the construction of additional battleships and battle cruisers of essentially similar design, which were referred to collectively as "dreadnoughts." By the outbreak of war in 1914, dreadnoughts and improved dreadnoughts had almost completely displaced pre-dreadnought battleships and armoured cruisers in the Royal Navy's first-line order of battle.

The completion of the *Dreadnought* some two years before the units of the *Invincible* class entered service meant that public attention was focused from the beginning on the battleship. Although the first dreadnought

37

program called for three battle cruisers and only one battleship, later programs provided for many more battleships than battle cruisers, with the result that by 1914, battle cruisers accounted for no more than a third of the British dreadnoughts in service. And the destruction of three battle cruisers in action at Jutland in 1916, which was attributed to their inadequate protection, largely discredited the type. For most likely these reasons, the major historical accounts of the "dreadnought revolution" have cast the battleship as the central character, while the battle cruiser has been relegated to a supporting role.[1] Fisher, however, had intended otherwise. He believed that British capital ships should be faster than any opponent and capable of hitting their targets at long range, which could only be achieved without exorbitant expense by reducing the scale of armour protection. Fisher had thus preferred the battle cruiser over the battleship, a position that he maintained throughout his tenure as First Sea Lord and thereafter to the end of his life.

2 Speed and Capital Ship Design

Fisher had favored a combination of superior speed and long-range hitting for British battleships as early as in 1882. In 1881, he had been given command of the *Inflexible*, the newest and most powerful battleship in the Royal Navy. Fisher was dissatisfied with her design, however, and on 12 September 1882 he wrote to Admiral Sir Beauchamp Seymour, the Commander-in-Chief of the Mediterranean Fleet, pointing out that his vessel was both slower and armed with smaller guns than the Italian battleship *Dandolo*.[2] "It is difficult," Fisher explained to Seymour,

> to exaggerate the importance of this excess of speed possessed by the *Dandolo*. As the Yankees say, it would enable her to do *'just what she darn pleases.'* She would have more than the advantages given in the olden time by possessing the weather gauge, and her guns being of far greater power than ours, she could remain out of our range and deliberately shell us . . .[3]

Enemy fleets, opposed by what were likely to be superior British forces, would almost certainly flee rather than suffer certain defeat, hence Fisher also observed that British battleships required a superiority in speed that would enable them to compel unwilling opponents to fight. "In Mrs. Somebody's Cookery Book," Fisher quipped to Seymour, "the receipt for Jugged Hare begins with, 'First catch your hare.'"[4]

But while high speed could be justified by the need to prevent an enemy fleet from escaping, a superiority in gun caliber did not confer a superiority in long-range hitting as Fisher supposed. Although, in theory, a gun of the largest caliber was capable of firing a projectile accurately to greater distances than a gun of the next largest size, in practice, any such superiority in ballistical performance would have been cancelled by the fact that existing methods of gunlaying did not fully compensate for the roll, pitch and yaw of a ship, which meant that naval guns could not be aimed with precision.[5] And without the ability to hit an opponent at ranges at which that opponent could not effectively reply, the ability to keep the range long through superior speed had no purpose. Fisher's views on naval gunnery were probably formed in the absence of experience with long-range firing at sea under battle conditions,[6] an error that he would later repeat. But though his argument with regard to the worth of superior speed and gun caliber lacked validity, battleships that were better armed and faster than the *Inflexible* were already under construction at the time of his letter to Seymour.

Between 1880 and 1883, the Royal Navy laid down five battleships of the "Admiral" class, which were armed with breech-loading guns that were more effective than the muzzle-loading pieces of the *Inflexible*, yet weighed much less. The reduction in the weight of armament allowed a decrease in the ship's displacement and finer lines that resulted in a significant increase in speed without requiring an increase in power.[7] Fisher deplored the Admiralty's decision to build five vessels to the same pattern, which departed from the established practice of rapidly developing battleship design through the building of a succession of ships that were each an improvement on its predecessor. In particular, he believed that further increases in speed were necessary. In late 1882 or early 1883, these views were expressed to Nathaniel Barnaby, the Director of Naval Construction, who disagreed with Fisher on the grounds that the building of British battleships with greater speed would provoke the construction by foreign powers of comparable vessels that would render the bulk of the existing British battle fleet obsolete.[8] "Isn't the principle right," Fisher argued in reply to Barnaby on 25 January 1883, "to make each succeeding iron-clad an improvement and as perfect as you can! There is no progress in uniformity!"[9] But in the absence of major advances in steam engineering, further significant increases in speed could only be obtained by adopting powerplants of much greater size and cost. Although Fisher insisted that additional expense should be no object,[10] the Admiralty had good reasons to doubt Parliament's willingness to come forward with the funds that would be required,[11] and Barnaby's position prevailed: the last two "Admirals" were laid down that year, and succeeding battleships had less rather than more speed—indeed, a faster class of British first-class battleships would not appear for more than a decade.[12]

Important technical advances in artillery, on the other hand, were about to produce a great change in battleship armament. The process had begun in December 1881, when the War Office had advertised for a single-barrelled gun capable of firing a six-pound projectile at a rate of twelve aimed rounds per minute, the need for such a weapon having arisen with the advent of French and Russian fast torpedo boats that were too large to be stopped by the small projectiles fired by the multi-barrelled machine guns then in service. By 1883, both the Hotchkiss and Nordenfeldt companies had been able to develop quick-firing guns of 2.2-inch caliber that satisfied the Admiralty's requirements, and in the same year, trials began of a 4.7-inch gun and accompanying mounting that had been developed by the Elswick Ordnance Company. When perfected after several years of development, the new model 4.7-inch gun was capable of firing ten aimed shots a minute, which was four to six times faster than a 5-inch gun with the old pattern breech and mounting, and no less than 20 times faster than the 13.5-inch guns that constituted the main armament of the latest battleships. The 4.7-inch gun was followed in turn by the substantially more powerful 6-inch gun, which could fire five aimed rounds per minute, and while this was half the rate of its smaller predecessor, it was still ten times that of a 13.5-inch gun.[13]

Sir John Fisher played a key role in the development of both the 4.7-inch and 6-inch quick-firing guns. In April 1883, he had assumed command of H.M.S. *Excellent*, the Royal Navy's gunnery school at Portsmouth, after several months convalescing from the dysentery that had forced him to give up his command of *Inflexible* the previous November; then three years later he was appointed Director of Naval Ordnance effective from November 1886. At *Excellent* and as D.N.O., Fisher was responsible for the experiments and trials that led to the adoption of the new guns, and he undoubtedly played a leading role in the Admiralty's decision to arm the first-class battleships of the Naval Defence Act, the *Royal Sovereign* class, with a secondary battery composed of quick-firing 6-inch guns.[14]

The four 13.5-inch guns of the main battery of a *Royal Sovereign* weighed more than three times as much as the ten 6-inch guns of the secondary battery.[15] A 6-inch gun was a better weapon than a 13.5-inch gun when ranges were long, however, because its much higher rate of fire significantly increased the probability of making hits. In view of the superior effective range of the 6-inch gun and the considerable power of its projectile, there was much to be said for the reduction of the main battery in exchange for a greater number of quick-firers, more protection, higher speed or a reduction in cost. By 1892, Fisher was in a position to formulate the requirements for a battleship designed along these lines. He had been promoted to Rear-Admiral in 1890, had left the Ordnance Department to become Admiral Superintendent of the Portsmouth Dockyard in May 1891, and in February 1892 was appointed to the post of Controller, which placed him in charge of, among other things, warship design. In August 1892, the assumption of office by a Liberal government devoted to economy forced the Admiralty to consider ways of reducing expenditure. For his part Fisher advocated the construction of six second-class battleships armed with a 6-inch quick-firing battery that was equal to that of a first-class battleship such as *Royal Sovereign*, but which substituted 10-inch guns for 13.5-inch guns in the main battery, with the displacement thus saved used to reduce size, which saved expenditure, and to increase engine power, which raised speed.[16] Fisher's colleagues on the Board of Admiralty, however, were not convinced of the wisdom of reducing the caliber of the main armament, and only one vessel of this design, which was named *Renown*, was approved.

Fisher then took steps in late 1893, again in his capacity as Controller, to increase the speed of warships through the replacement of the conventional shell boiler by the large water-tube Belleville type. Water-tube boilers eventually became standard, but not before technical shortcomings had caused considerable controversy.[17] Fisher continued, however, to rise in rank and responsibility. He was promoted to Vice-Admiral in May 1896 and, upon taking command of the North America and West Indies station in August 1897, he was given *Renown*, which had been completed the previous January, as his flagship. When in September 1899 Fisher assumed command of the Mediterranean Fleet, then the main force of the Royal Navy—following an interlude as the British representative at the Hague Conference during the summer—he continued to fly his flag from *Renown* until he returned to the Admiralty as Second Sea Lord in 1902. *Renown* was faster than any of the newer and more heavily armed first-class battleships of the Mediterranean Fleet,[18] and there can be little doubt that Fisher retained her as his flagship for this reason.

Fisher at this time valued high speed in battleships on several grounds. He believed, in the first place, that a fast battleship could be used to catch and destroy enemy cruisers. "I will give you my experience," Fisher wrote from the Mediterranean to Lord Selborne, the First Lord, on 19 December 1900,

> of the value of speed in battleships (an experience that impressed me immensely!) when I 'mopped up' all the cruisers one after another with my flagship the battleship *Renown*. The heavy swell and big seas had no corresponding effect on the big *Renown* as it had on the smaller *Talbot*, *Indefatigable*, and other cruisers . . .[19]

Secondly, Fisher was certain that a superiority in speed over enemy battleships was required if a British fleet were to be able to catch an opponent in retreat. "*It is clearly necessary,*" he wrote again to Selborne on 5 January 1901, "*to have superiority of speed in order to compel your opponent to accept battle . . .*"[20] Thirdly, Fisher was convinced that a superiority in speed could be used to keep the range long enough to avoid the danger of torpedoes. The torpedo threat, he warned his subordinate commanders in the Mediterranean in papers written between 1899 and 1902, meant that "we should never close the enemy within 2,000 yards or *3,000 yards if pursuing! This, however, infers [sic] superiority of speed, especially for battleships.*"[21] And finally, Fisher hoped that a superiority in speed could be used to control the range at which an action would be fought in order to exploit the capabilities of certain armaments. "If we have the advantage of speed," he argued,

> which is the first desideratum in every class of fighting vessel (Battleships included), then, and then only, we can choose our distance for fighting. If we can choose our distance for fighting, then we can choose our armament for fighting![22]

Also in his Mediterranean papers Fisher called for battle ranges of from 3,000 to 4,000 yards at a time when the annual prize firings were carried out at 1,400 to 1,600 yards.[23] At the longer ranges, the 6-inch quick-firing gun was superior to the big guns of the main battery, he maintained, because "the increased rapidity of firing . . . enables the range to be quickly obtained."[24] "The armament we require," he explained further,

is the greatest number of the largest quick-firing guns in *protected positions.*
They call it the *secondary armament*; it really is the primary armament!

In these days of very rapid movement the huge gun firing (comparatively)
slowly is as obsolete as the foot soldier in the Boer War!

Whoever hits soonest and oftenest will win![25]

Fisher expected that long range shooting with 6-inch quick-firers would
result in heavy damage to enemy vessels before British ships could be hit
in return. French battleships, he wrote to Selborne on 6 October 1901,
were to be knocked out at long range

> by one of the multitudes of quick-firing projectiles that will be flying about
> . . . even if all the rest are lost shots! We carry more ammunition than any
> foreign ship and can afford 'long bowls'. Also (I speak from experience) there
> is nothing more demoralizing than to be fired at without firing back.[26]

Fisher, in short, believed that superiority in speed could be used to
impose a long-range engagement upon an opponent which could be won
decisively with quick-firers. And with the commissioning in 1901 of the
Cressy, the first of the new type armoured cruisers,[27] the Royal Navy
began to be equipped with warships that were even better suited to Fisher's
vision of naval battle than the *Renown*. A *Cressy*, whose displacement
of 12,000 tons was practically the same as that of the *Renown*, lacked
heavy armour protection and carried a much weaker main battery, but
could steam as high as 21 knots, which was more than two knots faster
than *Renown*,[28] and was equipped with twelve 6-inch quick-firers in its
secondary battery, compared with the ten mounted by the battleship. At
the long ranges at which Fisher wished to fight, the weak main battery
was not likely to be a disadvantage because big-guns could not fire rapidly
enough to score a significant number of hits, which also meant that little
was lost through the sacrifice of thick armour given the unlikelihood of
being struck by enemy heavy-caliber projectiles. The *Cressy* class was
followed by the armoured cruisers of the *Drake* class, which were laid
down in 1899 and entered service in 1903. The "Drakes" displaced 2,000
tons more than the "Cressys," which was only 350 tons less than the
battleships of the same program year, steamed two knots faster, and
carried a secondary battery consisting of no fewer than sixteen 6-inch
quick-firers, or four more than the latest first-class battleship.[29]

"It is a cardinal mistake," Fisher maintained in his Mediterranean
papers, "to assume that Battleships and Armoured Cruisers have not
each of them a distinct mission."[30] But his attempt to distinguish the
two types on the basis of function was practically annihilated by his
simultaneous insistence that virtually no distinction could be made with
regard to form. Armoured cruisers, he argued on the same page, should
be as large as battleships.[31] And elsewhere within the same print, he
declared that

> the Armoured Cruiser of the first-class is a swift Battleship in disguise. It has
> been asked that the difference between a Battleship and an Armoured Cruiser

may be defined. It might as well be asked to define when a kitten becomes a cat.[32]

But in 1899, with the outbreak of war in South Africa against the Boers, the Admiralty concluded that vessels of the dimensions of the "Cressys," to say nothing of the even larger "Drakes," were too expensive to be built in the numbers that were required to protect British commerce, and the next several armoured cruiser classes were of smaller displacement, slower and less well-armed in order to reduce the cost per unit.[33] Fisher not only opposed this retreat,[34] but in February 1902 produced a paper that called for armoured cruisers that were even faster than the "Drakes."[35] And on 26 March 1902 he urged Selborne to build a hypothetical "H.M.S. 'Perfection'" whose speed and quick-firing armament were greater than that of any armoured cruiser then built, building or projected.[35]

"It is absurd," Fisher complained on 27 February 1902 to Rear-Admiral Lord Charles Beresford, then a Conservative Member of Parliament, "to say because our figure for new construction stands at 9 millions we can't spend more! *That is not true . . . . It is simple madness to underbuild.*"[37] But by 1902, the Admiralty's efforts to build armoured cruisers in large numbers that were practically the size and cost of battleships had already resulted in a great rise in expenditure on such vessels, and the weakness of British finance was such that further increases could not long continue. In 1903, the collapse of the economic boom created by heavy government expenditure during the Boer War, which had just ended, reduced the receipts from taxation, increasing the strain on a financial system already burdened by the repayment of large debts contracted during the conflict. Joseph Chamberlain's failure in 1903 to convince the Conservative-Unionist government to implement a policy of protective tariffs, moreover, ruled out the possibility of quickly providing new financial resources that might have been applied to naval construction.[38]

There was, however, an alternative to the expensive policy of building both battleships and armoured cruisers. The necessity of fighting at long range to avoid torpedoes, the big gun's inability to make hits at such ranges, the superfluity of heavy armour if big-gun projectiles did not pose a serious threat, and the fact that a superiority in speed conferred the ability to control the range of an action, suggested that armoured cruisers were capable of defeating battleships, while their superior speed would enable them to outpace a retreating fleet of battleships and compel it to engage. There were good reasons, therefore, to believe that an armoured cruiser could fulfill the function of a battleship even more effectively than a battleship could, and without the expense of big-guns and thick armour.

In the 1901 edition of the authoritative naval annual *Fighting Ships*, William Laird Clowes, a leading naval historian, insisted upon the superiority of the medium-caliber quick-firer over the slow-firing big-gun, and the necessity of having a superiority of speed that would enable a British fleet to "force the foe to fight."[39] He was thus convinced "very strongly, indeed, that a large, fast and well-armoured cruiser, mounting numerous protected guns of medium calibre, but having neither very thick armour nor very heavy guns, would be fair match for the largest and most costly battleship now afloat."[40] Fred T. Jane, the editor of *Fighting Ships*, agreed with Clowes. His arguments were presented to the Royal United Services Institution in a paper read on 6 June 1902. "It may be taken that any enemy," Jane maintained,

> save the three-Power one, will pursue a *guerre de course*,[41] simply because we are stronger, and he must do that or *nothing* with his armoured ships. Very good! Our duty is to smash him when he does. But to cook our hare we have to catch him. Whence it logically follows that speed is more essential to us than to any nation. We must have it at all costs, surely.[42]

"Is there anything outside 2,000 yards," he then asked,

> that the big guns [*sic*] in its hundreds of tons of mediaeval castle can effect, that its weight in 6-inch guns without the castle could not effect equally well? And inside 2,000, what, in these days of gyros, is there that the torpedo cannot effect with far more certainty?[43]

Jane thus suggested that British strategic interests might be better served by replacing the battleship with large armoured cruisers that exchanged big-guns and thick armour for high speed.[44]

Fisher considered the replacement of the battleship by the armoured cruiser seriously while in command of the Mediterranean Fleet. In his Mediterranean papers, he included a translation of a French article entitled "Wars of the Future," in which the anonymous author argued that battleships were unnecessary because coast defence could be entrusted to submarines, and the protection of maritime communications on the high seas could be left to "*Great Armoured Cruisers of 16,000 tons, steaming from 24 to 25 knots.*"[45] In June 1901, the Admiralty asked a number of senior naval officers to comment on proposals for a fast battleship that had been discussed at the United States Naval Institute. Fisher responded with a letter in which his endorsement of the fast battleship concept amounted to a call for the replacement of the conventional battleship by a more powerful type of armoured cruiser. He observed in his reply to the Admiralty on 25 June 1901, that if the assertion of an American naval architect that the speed of a battlship could be increased to 21 knots "without reducing her offensive or defensive powers by only an increase in size of 1700 tons and cost of from 12 to 15 per cent then it must be admitted the advantage lies on the side of the Battleship as against the largest size of armoured cruisers . . ."[46] But Fisher was highly skeptical of the American claims that major improvements in battleship design could be achieved without commensurate increases in displacement, and believed in any case that both the main battery gun caliber and armour protection should be reduced in order to gain a further increase in speed.[47]

In November 1901, Fisher was promoted to the rank of Admiral and in February 1902 left the Mediterranean Fleet to assume the post of Second Naval Lord, followed in 1903 by his becoming Commander-in-Chief at

Portsmouth. There he continued to manifest a strong interest in armoured cruisers of the largest size. "Some silly idiots in the past," he told visitors to the naval base on 12 September 1903, "used to write letters to the newspapers with the heading 'Monstrous Cruisers'! It's the 'Monster' that will gobble up all the small fry when the day of battle comes!"[48]

Professional naval architects at home and abroad, in the meanwhile, had explored alternative solutions to the problem of capital ship design for the Royal Navy. In 1902, Chief Constructor Henry Deadman of the Royal Corps of Naval Constructors, acting as deputy for Sir William White, who was then ill and on the eve of retirement, broadly suggested, without giving details, that Britain should build battleships of such a size and cost that other powers would be unable to match them, an idea that was dismissed by Rear-Admiral W. H. May, the Controller. In 1903, both Philip Watts, White's successor as Director of Naval Construction, and J. H. Narbeth, the Assistant Director of Naval Construction, outlined schemes for battleships that would be armed with a uniform-caliber armament of 12-inch guns in place of the mixture of big-guns and heavy-caliber quick-firers of existing vessels, which, however, were not adopted.[49]

The ideas of the Italian naval architect Colonel Vittorio Cuniberti on capital ship design, which were published in the 1903 edition of *Fighting Ships* in an article entitled "An Ideal Battleship for the British Fleet," were similar to those that had been discussed within the Department of Naval Construction.[50] Cuniberti was skeptical of the effectiveness of long-range shooting with quick-firers. "What results can reasonably be expected from the discharge of the smaller guns at such great distances," he maintained, "is hard to say; nor can the slender expectation of, let us say, chancing to hit the captain of the opposing ship in the eye with a lucky shot, at all justify such a waste of ammunition."[51] The destruction of enemy battleships could be better effected, Cuniberti argued, through a close range action using big-guns. His ideal battleship was thus to have such a superiority in speed that it would be able to close the range rapidly to the point where its heavy-caliber armament could make hits, which in effect would have made it as fast as any armoured cruiser. Cuniberti's hypothetical warship, in addition, would be protected by heavy armour that would give it the capacity to withstand hits from medium-caliber quick-firers without suffering damage. The most distinctive feature of the proposed vessel, however, was the elimination of the secondary battery and the mounting in its place of additional heavy-caliber guns to produce an all-big-gun armament of twelve 12-inch guns. The increased number of big-guns, Cuniberti believed, would permit "at least one fatal shot on the enemy's belt at the water-line before she has a chance of getting a similar fortunate stroke at us from one of the four large pieces now usually carried as the main armament."[52] "Secure in her exuberant protection," Cuniberti's ideal battleship, which he called "our 'invincible'," was to be able to

swiftly descend on her adversary and pour in a terrible converging fire at the belt.

45

Having once disposed of her first antagonist, she would at once proceed to attack another, and, almost untouched, to despatch yet another, not throwing away a single round of her ammunition, but utilizing all for sure and deadly shots.[53]

Cuniberti's "invincible" was, however, highly impracticable for several reasons. In the first place, a close range action exposed a battleship to serious damage, or even destruction, by torpedoes, a problem for which Cuniberti provided no solution. Secondly, Cuniberti's scheme of employing big-guns did not eliminate the element of chance that had been the basis of his criticism of long-range shooting with quick-firers because the relative superiority in the number of big-guns enjoyed by Cuniberti's all-big-gun vessel over a conventional battleship was not so great as to preclude the possibility of the latter being able to inflict fatal damage on the former. And finally, the combination of heavy armament, thick armour and high speed called for by Cuniberti would have resulted in prohibitive increases in battleship size and cost—a factor which appears to have been the grounds for the rejection of the proposals of Deadman, Watts and Narbeth.[54] But within little more than a year of the publication of Cuniberti's article of 1903, Sir John Fisher would be convinced that technical changes and new methods of gun-laying and aiming had made the big-gun a more effective weapon at long range than the quick-firer, which led him to advocate the construction of high-speed, all-big-gun armed capital ships that he believed would cost little more than existing battleships but would be far more effective.

3 Development of Big-Gun Technology and Technique

The technical shift in favor of the big-gun began with an improvement in the chemistry of propellants. In the late 1880s, a special committee of chemists appointed by the British War Office had developed "cordite," a mixture of nitrocellulose, nitroglycerine and petroleum jelly. Cordite was more than twice as powerful as the black or brown powder then in service, and more even, consistent, and slower in combustion, which meant that a projectile could be fired more accurately and at higher muzzle velocities. Cordite replaced black and brown powder in the Royal Navy during the early 1890s, and was accompanied by the adoption of longer gun barrels and the wire-winding method of gun construction, which were both required to exploit the greater capabilities of the new explosive. The first of the new model big-guns, the 12-inch Mark VIII, which was first mounted in the battleships of the *Majestic* class, was smaller than the 13.5-inch guns of earlier battleships, but was more effective because of its higher performance.[55]

Over the course of the 1890s, the rate of fire of the 12-inch gun was significantly improved by changes in the systems of ammunition supply and loading. By the end of the decade, the 12-inch guns mounted in the latest battleships were capable of firing at an average rate of nearly once a minute, which was double that of the 13.5-inch guns of the Naval Defence Act battleships.[56] Faster rates were impracticable for technical reasons, and for a time the big-gun thus remained a less effective weapon than the quick-firer at longer ranges, where limitations in gunlaying and aiming methods still meant that a significant number of hits could only be obtained by firing a large number of shots in rapid succession. But changes in those methods of gunlaying and aiming, when combined with the improvements that had been made in big-gun ballistics and rate of fire during the 1890s, were to give the big-gun a marked advantage over the quick-firing gun when ranges were long.

At sea, the problem of gunlaying is complicated by the roll, pitch and yaw of a moving ship. Roll causes the elevation of guns that are trained to fire across the broadside to alter substantially and continuously, except at the instant when the rolling motion of the ship in one direction has slowed to a stop before starting its return. From the age of sail until the late 1890s, shipboard guns in the Royal Navy were laid so that they would come on to the target at the end of a roll, at which time they were fired. The correct setting of gun elevation for horizontal fire[57] depended upon an assessment of the amplitude of the roll, which was not always easy to make with precision. In addition, the gunner had to anticipate the appearance of the target in his sight to allow for the time delay between the visual act of sighting and the physical act of pulling the trigger or lanyard to discharge the gun that was inherent in the slowness of human reflexes. Aiming was also made more difficult by changes in elevation caused by pitch, and deviations in training caused by yaw, which became significant as range increased or in an immoderate sea. Aim was thus approximate rather than exact and, as a result, hits could only be made at short ranges where the target was so large that the inevitable small errors in the elevation and training of the gun with respect to the target at the instant of firing did not matter. And furthermore, the restriction of firing only on the roll reduced the effective rate of fire of quick-firing guns.[58]

In 1898, however, Captain Percy Scott, a particularly inventive British naval officer with a strong interest in gunnery, devised an alternative method of gunlaying. Scott began by replacing the open sights of a 4.7-inch quick-firing gun with a telescopic sight, which significantly reduced angular error in aiming,[59] and mounted it in such a manner that it followed the vertical and horizontal training of the barrel but was unaffected by recoil. In addition, Scott altered the gear ratio of the elevating mechanism of the gun in order to facilitate rapid movement. He then developed methods of training his gunners to keep their aim through the telescope continuously on the target through their ship's rolling and pitching by quickly elevating and depressing the barrel, and through their ship's yawing by swinging the barrel from side to side. Scott's system of "continuous aim" gunlaying neutralized the effect that a ship's motion had previously exerted on the gun in relation to its target. As a consequence, the percentage of hits was greatly increased at the then standard practice ranges of 1,600 yards or less.

On 26 May 1899 Scott demonstrated the effectiveness of his methods when the 4.7-inch guns of his protected cruiser *Scylla* made 56 hits out of 70 shots during the Annual Prize Firing, which was six times better than *Scylla* had done the previous year without continuous-aim, and more than twice as good as the fleet average. After developing additional training techniques, Scott repeated his success with 6-inch guns in the large protected cruiser *Terrible* in 1901. Although quick-firing guns were light enough to be rapidly elevated and depressed, and trained back and forth, by manpower, 12-inch guns were too heavy to be laid manually, while the hydraulic elevating and training controls of even the latest model big-gun mountings could not be made to act quickly enough to enable gunners to follow their targets with continuous-aim.[60] The Admiralty was nevertheless convinced of the effectiveness of Scott's approach, and in April 1903 he was appointed Captain of *Excellent*, the Royal Navy's gunnery school at Portsmouth, with a mandate to train a new generation of efficient naval gunners.[61]

At ranges that were much greater than the 1,400 to 1,600 yards of the Annual Prize Firings, the holes made in a target by the largest projectiles were too small to be seen even with the assistance of a telescopic sight, and while the splash of a projectile was still easily visible, its proximity to the target was much more difficult to ascertain than was the case when ranges were lower. Individual gunners could not, therefore, assess the effect of their shots, and thus were unable to make the necessary adjustments in the setting of their sights when misses occurred. But in firing experiments that were carried out at ranges of from 5,000 to 6,000 yards in 1899 and 1900, gunnery officers of the Mediterranean Fleet found that the accuracy of naval artillery fire could be determined by discharging several guns together in a "salvo", whose projectiles fell at about the same time and within a relatively small area. A salvo whose splashes were all either short or over the target indicated that the gunsights were incorrectly set for elevation. A salvo that resulted in splashes that fell both short and over, on the other hand, indicated that there were projectiles in between that might be hitting, which meant that the sights were correctly set.[62]

The tasks of coordinating the firing of several guns, spotting the splashes of several projectiles of the salvo and correcting the sights of several guns, had to be "controlled" by a centralized system of command, a process that gave rise to the term "fire control." In 1901, Captain Edward W. Harding of the Royal Marine Artillery, who had served in the Mediterranean Fleet during the critical years of 1899 and 1900,[63] wrote a series of articles on fire control in the *United Services Magazine*. In 1902, he produced a second series of articles that were entitled "The Tactical Employment of Naval Artillery," which appeared under the pseudonym 'Rapidan' in the "Traction and Transmission" monthly supplement to the journal *Engineering*. In April 1903, these articles were collected and published with the same title and under the same pseudonym to become the first book on fire control.[64] In December 1904, Percy Scott advocated the use of fire control in a lecture, "Remarks on Long Range Hitting," which he gave at *Excellent*.[65] And in late 1903 and early 1904, two Admiralty appointed committees—one in the battleship *Victorious* and the other in the battleship *Venerable*—conducted a series of fire control experiments in which Harding's book was used as a rough guide.[66] The reports from the two ships were evaluated by Harding, who in December 1903 had been assigned to the Ordnance Department, and who presented the findings of the fire control committees in the Admiralty secret printed report *Fire Control: A Summary of the Present Position of the Subject*, which was issued in October 1904.[67]

During the experiments of the fire control committees, the 12-inch guns of the *Victorious* and *Venerable* must have been fired on the roll because, as has been explained, big-guns were then incapable of being laid for continuous-aim.[68] But the imprecision in aim that was the result of firing on the roll appear to have been mitigated significantly by the approximate nature of the salvo system, in which projectiles fell on an area rather than on a point as would have been the case with a projectile that had been fired from a single gun, and as a consequence the experiments revealed that 12-inch guns could score a significant number of hits at long range for the first time. A 6-inch gun could still fire more rapidly than a 12-inch gun, although the extent of this superiority was no longer as great as it had once been because of the increases in the rate of fire of the 12-inch gun that had been achieved during the 1890s. The many splashes made by a large number of rapid-firing 6-inch guns, moreover, tended to obscure the target, which made it more difficult to evaluate the accuracy of firing than was the case with the fewer splashes made by a smaller number of slower firing 12-inch guns. In addition, the 6-inch projectiles were less accurate than 12-inch projectiles when ranges were long because they were much smaller and were fired at a comparable muzzle velocity. And finally, 6-inch projectiles had much less effect on impact because their explosive capacity was far smaller than that of a 12-inch projectile.

Harding's preference for the 12-inch big-gun over the 6-inch quick-firer was unequivocal. "12-inch guns are controlled and rendered effective with comparative ease," he concluded in the printed Admiralty report,

> whereas the more numerous 6-inch guns were extremely difficult to make effective. As regards effect, the 6-inch guns are vastly inferior, and, although a greater rate of hitting per gun may be expected at moderate ranges, about 4,000 yards, the value of the hits is insignificant having regard to rapidity of fire compared with that of the 12-inch. In comparing the value of hits by mere weight of metal alone, the value of the 12-inch is four to five times that of the 6-inch. . . . the heavier gun with its flatter trajectory can be brought on to the target more quickly and easily than the smaller, and therefore the hitting will commence earlier.[69]

12-inch guns that could be laid by continuous-aim could be expected to demonstrate an even greater superiority over the 6-inch gun than had been found by the fire control committees, and by mid-1904, there was probably good reason to believe that such a capability would be provided by the new rapid-action elevating and training controls of the Vickers BVIII mounting that was being developed for the battleships of the 1904–05 program.[70] The implications were plain. With the advent of fire control and the prospect that big-guns could be laid by continuous-aim, and given the necessity of fighting at long range to avoid the threat of torpedoes, there were strong reasons to substitute vessels that were armed with big-guns only for battleships armed with both big-guns and medium-caliber quick-firers.

Fisher had played an important, if not a direct, role in the development of fire control. In 1899 and 1900 while Commander-in-Chief in the Mediterranean, he had continued the long-range firing experiments—begun in 1898 by his predecessor, Admiral Sir John Hopkins—which led to the practice of firing salvoes described earlier.[71] The lessons of the Mediterranean long-range experiments may have caused Fisher to consider the desirability of uniform-caliber armaments. In his Mediterranean papers, he mocked the practice of equipping ships with quick-firing batteries that included guns of three different sizes by suggesting that it was the result of no more than a wish to have "representatives of all calibers" as if "you were peopling the Ark."[72] In his comments to the Admiralty of June 1901 on the fast battleship question, Fisher called for a simpler mixed-caliber system that would consist of a "uniform armament of 7 1/2 inch guns" in association with a battery of 10-inch guns,[73] and in his memoirs he claimed to have discussed the uniform-caliber armament issue with William Henry Gard, the Chief Constructor of the Malta Dockyard, as early as in 1900.[74] In February and March 1902, Fisher prescribed a mixed-caliber armament for his ideal armoured cruiser,[75] but in July 1904, he called for uniform-caliber armaments for both battleships and armoured cruisers in a paper that outlined the reforms that he planned to introduce on his assumption of office as First Sea Lord in the coming October.[76]

In his paper of July 1904, Fisher called for a uniform-caliber armament of new model 10-inch guns rather than 12-inch guns for future battleships.[77] The smaller gun, which had been much improved over the 10-inch guns of *Renown*, was lighter and thus could be mounted in larger numbers, possessed a higher rate of fire, and fired a projectile of considerable power.[78] Harding's summary of the findings of the fire control committees, however, which was issued in October just before Fisher became service chief, made it clear that there was nothing to be gained and much to be lost by sacrificing hitting power for a larger number of faster firing guns.[79] Fisher had prior knowledge of the work of the fire control committees,[80] and undoubtedly either read the report, or was informed of its contents by Captain R. H. S. Bacon, his naval assistant.[81] "Now the result of all long-range shooting," he argued in papers given to Lord Selborne on the day that he took office,[82]

has gone to prove that if we wish to make good shooting at 6,000 yards and above, the guns must be fired slowly and deliberately, and the shots marked, preferably one gun at a time. Hence the use of a large number of guns disappears, and the advantage of a few well-aimed guns with large bursting charges is over-whelming. . . . The fast ship with the heavier guns and deliberate fire *should* absolutely "knock out" a vessel of equal speed and many lighter guns, the very number of which militate against accurate spotting and deliberate hitting.

The speed of firing at long ranges is no longer limited by the loading of the gun, but by the limitations imposed to obtain accuracy of fire. Suppose a 12-inch gun to fire one aimed round each minute. Six guns would allow a deliberately aimed shell with a huge bursting charge every ten seconds. Fifty per cent of these should be hits at 6,000 yards. Three 12-inch shells bursting on board every minute would be hell![83]

Fisher's description of the shots being marked "preferably one gun at a time" indicated perhaps an imperfect understanding of the principles of the salvo system,[84] but whatever the case he was convinced that advances in fire control had swung the balance in favor of the 12-inch gun by the time he became First Sea Lord on 20 October 1904.

4   The All-Big-Gun Armoured Cruiser

Fisher's conversion to the concept of a uniform caliber armament of 12-inch guns did not necessarily mean that he was committed to the construction of battleships. By 1904, he had come to the conclusion that torpedoes launched by submarines or fast surface craft had made such vessels practically obsolete. Fisher was particularly concerned by the development of the submarine, whose potential he had recognized as early as 1902 while in command of the Mediterranean Fleet.[85] In that year, Britain built her first submarines, and in 1903 trials were carried out with these vessels from Portsmouth while Fisher was in command of the naval base.[86] He was impressed by the performance of the submarines at this time[87] and by the views of the officer supervising them, Inspecting-Captain of Submarine Boats R. H. S. Bacon.[88] Fisher, in addition, may have known of the outcome of the torpedo experiments carried out on the armour-plated ram *Belleisle* in September 1903, which revealed that coal bunkers afforded little protection against torpedoes and thus indicated that battleships were more vulnerable to underwater attack than had previously been thought to be the case.[89] In any event, Fisher wrote a paper in December 1903 for the Committee of Imperial Defence, in which he argued that the submarine's ability to sink transports and even large warships would make the invasion of Great Britain or the naval bombardment of foreign shores impossible,[90] and in early 1904 he informed Rear-Admiral Prince Louis of Battenberg, the Director of Naval Intelligence, that:

(a)   The Submarine is coming into play in Ocean Warfare almost immediately.
(b)   Associated with a Whitehead Torpedo 18 ft. in length it will displace the gun and absolutely revolutionize Naval Tactics.
(c)   No single Submarine ever built or to be built will be ever obsolete.
. . . I stake my reputation on the absolute reliability of these three statements. The deduction is—"Drop a Battleship out of the programme" (if it be necessary on account of financial necessities) but at any cost double the output of submarines.[91]

By the summer of 1904, Fisher was willing to suggest that the construction of battleships be stopped altogether. In the paper written in July 1904, in which he described his intended reforms, he maintained that

Formerly, transports or military operations could be covered by a fleet of battleships with the *certainty* that nothing could attack them without first being crushed by the covering fleet! NOW, ALL THIS HAS BEEN ABSOLUTELY ALTERED!

A battle fleet is no protection to anything, or any operation, during dark hours, and in certain waters *is no protection in daytime* because of the submarine.

Hence what is the use of battleships as we have hitherto known them? NONE! Their one and only function—that of ultimate security of defence—is gone—lost![92]

These views were amplified in the papers submitted to Lord Selborne upon Fisher's taking office as First Sea Lord on 20 October 1904. Fisher then argued that

> There is good ground for enquiry whether the naval supremacy of a country can any longer be assessed by its battleships. To build battleships merely to fight an enemy's battleships, so long as cheaper craft can destroy them, and prevent them of themselves protecting sea operations, is merely to breed Kilkenny cats unable to catch rats or mice. For fighting purposes they would be excellent, but for gaining practical results they would be useless.[93]

But although destroyers and submarines arguably were capable of replacing the battleship in the role of coast defence, neither type possessed the range or sea-keeping qualities that would have enabled them to operate effectively along Britain's far-flung lines of maritime supply, which thus meant that armoured cruisers were still required for commerce protection. Fisher was convinced, therefore, that a country's naval strength had to be measured in terms of armoured cruisers, destroyers and submarines, rather than in terms of battleships. He put the case plainly to Selborne on 20 October 1904:

> Of what use is a battle fleet to a country called (A) at war with a country called (B) possessing no battleships, but having fast armoured cruisers and clouds of fast torpedo craft? What damage would (A's) battleships do to (B)? Would (B) wish for a few battleships or for more armoured cruisers? Would not (A) willingly exchange a few battleships for more fast armoured cruisers? In such a case, neither side wanting battleships is presumptive evidence that they are not of much value.[94]

But Selborne rejected Fisher's suggestion that battleships were no longer necessary and that Britain's naval supremacy could be maintained with armoured cruisers and torpedo craft only. "I quite agree that the battleship type and armoured cruiser type are merging into each other," the First Lord noted in the margin of one of the papers submitted to him by Fisher on 20 October 1904, "but I am quite sure that if two Powers were equally provided with submarines, destroyers, and armoured cruisers, and one Power had in addition a squadron of ships in which extreme speed had been sacrificed to a more powerful armament = battleships, and the other Power had no such ships, then the Power which had the battleships must win."[95] "The battleship is essential," Selborne insisted in a note in the margin at a later point in the same paper, "just as much as 100 years ago."[96]

Fisher, from past experience, must have known that his views were likely to provoke strong disagreement,[97] and he had anticipated the objections of his patron and others by conceding from the start that his radical proposals were not to be considered as immediately practical. "All are agreed," he wrote in his paper of July 1904, "that battleships must for the present be continued . . ."[98] In the papers given to Selborne on 20 October 1904, Fisher stated that "at the present moment, *naval experience is not sufficiently ripe to abolish totally the building of battleships* so long as other countries do not do so."[99] In his July paper, however, Fisher noted, as he had in the Mediterranean, that "no one can draw the line where the armoured cruiser becomes a battleship any more than when a kitten becomes a cat!"[100] and in fact his disclaimers were undermined by his proposals for a fast battleship and a heavily armed armoured cruiser that could hardly be distinguished from one another. "Fundamentally the battleship," he maintained to Selborne in October, "sacrifices speed for a superior armament and protective armour," adding that "it is this superiority of speed that enables an enemy's ships to be overhauled or evaded, that constitutes the real difference between the two."[101] But Fisher's proposed 21-knot fast battleship was 3 knots faster than the *Lord Nelson* class battleships authorized under the 1904–05 estimates and just as fast as the *Cressy* class armoured cruisers that had entered service only two years before.[102] The new model battleship, he thus admitted ingenuously in his July paper, was to be nothing else than "*a glorified armoured cruiser.*"[103]

The distinction between the battleship and the armoured cruiser was further obscured by Fisher's call for armaments for the two types that were practically equivalent. The battleships of the *Lord Nelson* class, authorized under the 1904–05 estimates, were to have a mixed-caliber armament of four 12-inch guns and ten 9.2-inch guns, while the *Minotaur* class armoured cruisers of the same program year were to have a mixed-caliber armament of four 9.2-inch guns and ten 7.5-inch guns, which gave the battleships a more than two-to-one advantage over the armoured cruisers in the weight of large—that is, 9.2-inches and over—caliber projectiles that could be fired in a given period.[104] In his July paper, Fisher advocated uniform-caliber armaments of sixteen 10-inch guns for his proposed battleship, and sixteen 9.2-inch guns for his proposed armoured cruiser,[105] which because of the much higher rate of fire of the smaller gun would have given the armoured cruiser a more than 50 per cent advantage over the battleship in the weight of large caliber projectiles that could be fired in a given period, although this great difference would have been reduced to near parity by the limitations in rapid-firing imposed by fire control.[106] The equivalence in fire power was disrupted briefly in the papers submitted to Lord Selborne in October, in which Fisher abandoned the 10-inch gun for the 12-inch gun in the battleship while leaving the armament of the proposed armoured cruiser unchanged.[107] But comparability in fire power was restored shortly after Fisher became First Sea Lord when an informal committee of his seven close advisors[108] agreed that 12-inch

53

guns were appropriate for armoured cruisers "on the unanswerable plea," in the words of R. H. S. Bacon, a participant in the discussions, "that ships, of the size and tonnage necessary . . ., should have an additional use in being able to form a fast light squadron to supplement the battleships in action, and worry the ships in the van or rear of the enemy's line."[109]

In November 1904, Fisher collected a number of his papers, including portions of his July print and the material that had been submitted to Selborne in October, which included the First Lord's marginal comments, printed them under the title of *Naval Necessities*, and sent copies to his colleagues on the Board of Admiralty and a select group of senior naval officers.[110] In his comments on the papers, Vice-Admiral Lord Charles Beresford, then Commander-in-Chief of the Channel Fleet, on 19 December 1904 insisted that "a Battleship will beat an Armoured Cruiser now," that "speed is possible with Armoured Cruisers, which is not possible with Battleships owing to the fact that they have different duties to perform, both the strategy and tactics being of a different character" and that therefore he could "not agree in saying that the day of the Battleship is past."[111] To counter the arguments and influence of such critics, Fisher had persuaded Selborne in August 1904 to appoint a special committee of experts to consider the question of the design of warships to be built under the estimates of 1905-06. Fisher explained to Viscount Esher on 21 August 1904 that he had already "got the designs out of what had to be" but that it would be "a politic thing to have a committee of good names" so that opponents "will fire away at them and leave me alone!"[112]

Fisher's "Committee on Designs" was appointed in an Admiralty letter of 22 December 1904.[113] Seven of the fourteen members were naval officers, including the Director of Naval Intelligence, the Engineer-in-Chief of the Fleet, the Rear-Admiral in command of the Torpedo and Submarine Flotillas, and the officers about to become the Controller and the Director of Naval Ordnance.[114] The seven civilian members included the Director of Naval Construction, the Superintendent of the Admiralty Experimental Works, and the Chief Constructor of the Portsmouth Dockyard.[115] Six out of seven of Fisher's informal committee of close advisors were members of the Committee on Designs, with the seventh man given the position of secretary.[116] Fisher, while not a member of the the committee, was designated its chairman in the appointing letter.[117] The instructions issued to the members of the committee stipulated that it consider, in addition to the designs of three types of surface fast torpedo craft, the designs of a fast battleship of 21 knots and an armoured cruiser of 25 knots, which were both to be provided with uniform-caliber armaments of 12-inch guns.[118] Before the committee could meet, however, decisions were made by the Admiralty in response to an unanticipated deterioration in the financial situation, which in effect predetermined a building policy that heavily favored the construction of armoured cruisers as opposed to battleships.

Selborne had been allowed a large increase in the size of the 1904-05 estimates by promising the Cabinet in May 1904 that substantial reductions would be made the next year,[119] but by the fall of 1904, the financial picture for the government was far worse than had been predicted the previous spring. "I am sorry to tell you," Selborne informed Fisher on 17 October 1904, "that the Revenue is dropping so fast that it looks like a deficit on the estimated revenue of the current year of £2,000,000 and on that of next year of ! ! !"[120] Matters had not improved by December, and Fisher was then asked to reduce the next year's building program. On 30 December, E. G. Pretyman, the Admiralty's Parliamentary and Financial Secretary, reported to Selborne that Fisher was "prepared to accept reductions in light of Russian losses[121] and because rapid progress in existing large ship construction 'warrant a corresponding delay in laying down other large ships especially if such rapid building is possible.'"[122] Under the Selborne plan adopted in 1902, three battleships and four armoured cruisers were to have been laid down annually.[123] The 1905–06 program, however, had been prejudiced the previous year by the need to purchase two small Chilean battleships on top of that year's quota of three battleships in order to prevent their acquisition by the Russians for use against Japan, a British ally, which reduced the schedule by one battleship.[124] The need to make economies, moreover, resulted in a further reduction of one battleship and one armoured cruiser. The original planned battleship–armoured cruiser annual construction ratio of three-to-four was thus transformed by the course of events into a ratio of one-to-three, an outcome that favored Fisher's preference for the armoured cruiser.

Fisher was not, however, satisfied with the priority given to the armoured cruiser over the battleship by circumstances alone, and in the Committee on Designs he attempted to establish the position in principle. The printed proceedings of the Committee on Designs, which met in ten sessions in January and February 1905, shed little direct light on the line of argument that Fisher then took,[125] but there can be little doubt that he called for the cancellation of the battleship and the construction of only the armoured cruisers. Fisher insisted that he had done so in correspondence with various individuals from 1908 to 1912, and in a letter he wrote to *The Times* in 1919.[126] In three instances he mentioned that Lord Kelvin, the distinguished practical physicist and a member of the committee, had supported him,[127] and Kelvin's biographer, on the basis of information supplied by Fisher,[128] wrote in 1910 that the famous scientist had been "disposed on the whole towards favoring the swift armoured cruiser" over the battleship during the meetings of the Committee.[129] Selborne, moreover, was convinced that Fisher had by this time concluded that the battleship was obsolete. "Fisher believed that the torpedo as used by torpedo boat destroyers & submarines," Selborne wrote to A. J. Balfour, the Prime Minister, on 23 August 1905 describing the First Sea Lord's views of the previous March, "was going to make narrow seas (*very widely interpreted*) impossible for battleships . . . ."[130]

Fisher also argued in the Committee on Designs that an armoured cruiser was little more vulnerable than a battleship to big-gun fire. Much improved high–explosive armour-piercing shells had been introduced in 1903, and the Royal Navy was on the verge of adopting its first "capped" projectiles, which greatly increased penetration.[131] An armour-piercing projectile of the latest model 12-inch gun would thus be capable of piercing the 11 inches of armour proposed for the protection of the waterline and main armament of the new battleship at anticipated battle ranges.[132] Both the new model battleship and armoured cruisers would in any case be vulnerable to big-gun high-explosive shells given the impossibility of protecting large areas outside of the belt and armament with medium armour because of the increase in weight that this would have entailed.[133] There were thus grounds to believe that heavy armour was useless, and that the best that could be done was to provide protection over vital parts that would be just sufficient to resist big-gun high-explosive shells. For such a purpose, the six to eight inches proposed for the belt and armament of the new armoured cruisers would be adequate. Fisher's 1905 views on the question were revealed several years later in an exchange of letters with Winston Churchill, who was then First Lord. On 12 April 1912, Churchill, after being informed of further advances in big-gun armour-piercing projectiles that seemed to have rendered heavy armour ineffective, suggested to Fisher that it might thus be dispensed with.[134] On 22 April, Fisher replied that "it is just astounding how all the arguments you use are precisely identical with those employed by me with the support of Lord Kelvin in the verbal & informal discussions that took place on the ever memorable meetings with that great man in regard to the [Committee on Designs]."[135]

In papers submitted to the Committee on Designs, Fisher presented the case for both the battleship and the armoured cruiser. "*The Battleship,*" he then maintained, "*is the embodiment of concentration of gun-power,*" while "*the Armoured Cruiser is the embodiment of Armed Speed.*"[136] But if he did not attack the battleship in principle, he did argue that its essential characteristics would be embodied in the proposed all-big-gun armoured cruiser, and thus implied that the proposed all-big-gun battleship might be superfluous. The all-big-gun armoured cruiser, Fisher noted, would be fast and powerful enough to "annihilate everything that floats except the proposed battleship . . ."[137] He then cited the Japanese contention that such vessels "will be able if needs be to lie in the line of battle" because of their "uniform armament of 12-inch guns, which is the armament of the battleship."[138] "Indeed," he continued, "these armoured cruisers are battleships in disguise."[139] Fisher concluded with a veiled appeal for the armoured cruiser on the grounds of economy. The Japanese, he observed, were about to combine the battleship and the armoured cruiser to produce a "glorified armoured cruiser" because "they cannot at present afford to have both, nor can they afford to go to our displacements."[140] But all of Fisher's tactical, technical and financial arguments were to no avail, and Kelvin remained the only voting member of the Committee on Designs willing to give up the battleship.[141] There was nothing to be gained, however, by disrupting the consensus that had been established within the committee for the proposed battleship and armoured cruisers and in the end both Fisher and Kelvin supported the recommendations of the majority.

In February 1905, the "First Progress Report" of the Committee on Designs outlined the particulars of a 21-knot battleship armed with ten 12-inch guns and a 25-knot armoured cruiser armed with eight

12-inch guns.[142] The report recommended that turbine engines, whose practicability had been demonstrated recently in a number of small commercial and naval vessels,[143] be used in both types in place of the less efficient reciprocating engines that had equipped all major steam-powered warships in the past, in order to obtain the high speeds and reliability required on the lowest possible displacement.[144] The report also made recommendations in regard to the arrangement of the armament. The 12-inch guns of the battleship were to be disposed in such a way that eight guns could fire on each broadside and six guns could fire directly ahead or astern, which would give it a two-to-one superiority in big-guns over a conventional battleship with a mixed-caliber armament in a broadside to broadside engagement, and a three-to-one superiority in big-guns during a chase.[145] The 12-inch guns of the armoured cruisers were to be arranged in a different pattern that allowed six guns to be fired on the broadside or directly ahead or astern, which would enable them to out-big-gun a conventional battleship with a mixed-caliber armament by three-to-two in a broadside to broadside encounter, and by three-to-one, as was the case with the new model battleship, in a chase.[146] "The armoured cruisers," an addendum to the "First Progress Report" thus noted, "are not comparable with anything existing; they are, in reality, fast battleships."[147]

In 1904, Fisher had advanced economic arguments in favor of the uniform-caliber armament. "If all guns are of the same calibre," he had maintained, "the total amount of ammunition can be very largely reduced—there is also an immense advantage in only having to provide spare articles and fittings for one type of gun instead of two or three—observe the immense advantage of interchangeability of parts."[148] The uniform-caliber armaments of the battleship and armoured cruisers proposed by the Committee on Designs were more expensive than the mixed-caliber armaments of the battleships and armoured cruisers of the past,[149] which contributed to increases of 10 per cent in the over-all cost of the battleship and of no less than 28 per cent in the overall cost of the armoured cruisers as compared with the costs of their immediate predecessors.[150] But the Committee on Designs made it clear in an addendum to their "First Progress Report" that they believed that the introduction of uniform-caliber 12-inch gun armaments for both the battleship and the armoured cruisers would result in large savings. They were convinced that future engagements would be fought at long ranges where only guns of the largest caliber could be counted as effective. Under such circumstances, the four new model vessels would out-big-gun six conventional battleships in a broadside to broadside action, and equal the big-gun fire power of no fewer than twelve conventional battleships in a chase. The proposed battleship and armoured cruisers could thus be justified on the grounds of economy because the increases in fighting power were great enough to reduce the number of ships that would have to be built to counter foreign conventional battleships, which would result in savings that outweighed the increases in the cost per unit. The committee noted, therefore, that besides the "fighting arguments in favour of the new design, the purely financial side of the question is the most important."[151]

The general design of the battleship and armoured cruisers recommended by the Committee on Designs were approved by the Board of Admiralty on 17 March 1905.[152] The detailed design of the battleship was approved by the board on 15 May,[153] and that of the armoured cruisers on 7 July.[154] As early as in May 1905, the London technical journal *Engineering* published a roughly accurate description of the proposed new battleship.[155] The particulars of the armoured cruisers, in marked contrast, were kept strictly secret. In a meeting of the board on 17 July 1905, Fisher explained "the extreme importance of keeping 'Secret' the designs of the new cruisers,"[156] and, on 12 August, the board decided that all negotiations with the building firms would have "to be carried out so far as practicable by personal discussion, and as little writing as possible to pass."[157] In the absence of official information, the 1906 edition of *Fighting Ships* thus reported rumors of a uniform-caliber armament of eight or ten 9.2-inch guns for the proposed new armoured cruisers.[158] The new battleship, which was named *Dreadnought*, was laid down at Portsmouth on 2 October 1905. The Admiralty intended to finish her in a year, instead of the normal period of two-and-a-half years, in order to gain experience with the new systems of propulsion and armament as quickly as was possible.[159] To expedite the building process, the 12-inch guns and mountings allocated to the previous year's two battleships of the *Lord Nelson* class were diverted to *Dreadnought*; the additional mountings for the armoured cruisers, however, would require several years to manufacture, and these vessels were thus not laid down until the spring of 1906, and were not expected to complete until mid-1908.[160] The armoured cruisers were known as the *Invincible* class after the name of the leading ship,[161] which may well have been inspired by Cuniberti's "invincible" of 1903.

In the meanwhile, Fisher continued his campaign for a policy of building only armoured cruisers, but under the guise of combining the battleship and the armoured cruiser into a single type. At the end of February 1905 Fisher wrote to Balfour:

Pith of Cruiser—

She is a battleship in disguise! ! !

She is the coming Battleship.

Why? Because of speed!

That's why *really* only *one* Battleship.

Now elaborating a new design.—Get rid of distinction of Battleships and Armoured Cruisers.

Simply *Armoured* Ships![162]

"There is no hyperbole in the statement," Fisher later argued in the report of the Navy Estimates Committee of 16 November 1905, "that the gun-power and armour protection embodied in the new armoured cruiser design" meant "that no existing battleship could safely encounter her at the long ranges at which her superior speed would enable her to impose an action."[163] "How far will it be practicable in future [*sic*]," Fisher then asked, "to build all our armoured vessels to a single design, combining the speed of the armoured cruiser with the offensive and defensive strength of the battleship?"[164] He concluded that

> it is, indeed, so clear that if the armoured cruiser and the battleship could be combined in a single type, a tremendous advantage would be placed in the hands of our Admirals that the matter demands most serious consideration . . . Battle squadrons so composed would possess a flexibility hitherto unattainable, and a power hitherto undreamt of. That such a combination can scarcely be discarded as a purely visionary and preposterous compromise is shown by the Italian designs of Cuniberti . . .[165]

Two weeks later, on 2 December 1905, Fisher convened a special meeting of the four Sea Lords; the Directors of Naval Intelligence, Ordnance, and Construction; and various captain assistants, commanders and civilian secretaries.[166] On this occasion, Fisher ordered the formation of what amounted to a second Committee on Designs that was to consist of the Directors of Naval Intelligence and Ordnance, the captain assistants of the First Sea Lord and Controller, two captain assistants of the Director of Naval Intelligence, and two commanders, with Captain C. L. Ottley, the Director of Naval Intelligence, to act as chairman, and W. Graham Greene, a civilian and head of the Naval Branch, to serve as secretary.[167] Fisher stated that the committee would consider, among other things, "the fusion of the battleship and the armoured cruiser."[168] He informed the meeting that in a parliamentary paper about to be issued,[169]

> the terms "Battleship" and "Cruiser" had been discarded, and the term "Armoured Vessels" was substituted in the place of both. The aim was to have only one type. The Armoured Cruiser design of this year had rather less armour and armament but greater speed than the Battleship design, but practically the new Armoured Cruiser was a Battleship. It was desired to bring about a fusion of the two designs by the next year; it seemed possible for this to be done, and it would be a great assistance if the Committee would look into the matter.[170]

But the need to develop an economical means of containing the dual threat posed by French and Russian battleships and armoured cruisers had ceased to exist following the heavy Russian naval losses suffered in defeats inflicted by the Japanese in 1905 and the ruin of Russian finance because of the war, which made a rapid naval recovery highly unlikely. The hostility of France's relations with Germany—the only other European naval power of major consequence—ruled out the possibility of a naval alliance between these two nations, French naval power alone could offer no real threat to Britain's naval security, and in any case the signing of the *Entente Cordiale* in April 1904 had laid the diplomatic basis for friendly Anglo-French relations. This left the rapidly expanding German fleet by itself as the only serious potential danger. The German navy, however, while strong in battleships, had few armoured cruisers, and little in the way of overseas bases to supply them even if she had; the British Isles, moreover, blocked easy access from German ports to the high seas, which compromised a German cruiser strategy from the start.[171] In short, by the end of 1905 it was clear that whatever armoured cruiser peril still remained could be met by existing vessels, and that further British big-ship construction should be devoted to battleships. Britain's position was so improved that Lord Cawdor, who had succeeded Selborne as First Lord in March 1905, stated in December 1905 in the parliamentary paper referred to by Fisher in the meeting on 2 December, that no more than four "large armoured ships" would have to be laid down annually,[172] which was three ships less per year than had been called for by Selborne in 1902.

The recommendations of the "Fusion Design" committee, whose report was ready in January 1906, reflected an appreciation of the change that had taken place in Britain's strategic position. Fisher's combination battleship–armoured cruiser was to have had the armament and armour of *Dreadnought*, but the speed of an *Invincible*. The committee argued, however, that the cost of such a vessel as compared with a *Dreadnought*-type battleship would force a reduction in the number of ships that could be built, with no gain in fire-power to make up the difference, which would mean that in 1909 Britain would "only have a bare numerical superiority over Germany in new Armoured Vessels."[173] "Moreover," the committee report observed, "if we commence to build the 'Fusion' class, Germany's answer should be, and probably would be, ships of equal tonnage but carrying a greater number of guns pro rata to the tonnage and sacrificing something in point of speed or coal endurance. In that case our ships would be decidedly inferior to theirs in gun-fire."[174] Though the committee report admitted that a division of "Fusion" class vessels would be of great value "as a fast 'Flanking' Division," they insisted that Britain had first to establish a clear numerical superiority in all-big-gun battleships before such a unit could be provided for.[175] The committee believed that the three "Invincibles" satisfied Britain's requirements for new armoured cruisers, and their report thus concluded that the four vessels scheduled to be laid down in 1906 "should be Battleships of a speed similar to the 'Dreadnought,' . . ."[176] By way of a postscript, the committee report did suggest that the question of the "Fusion" class might be reopened after 1906, and that the 12-inch guns originally specified for the design might be replaced by new model 13.5-inch guns.[177]

There is no record of Fisher's reaction to the report of the "Fusion Design" committee. He was in no position, however, to overturn the conclusions reached by a committee of his own making, which had been composed of many of his strongest supporters, given the heavy opposition to his policies that had developed outside of the Admiralty during 1905.[178] The fall of the Conservatives in December 1905 and the election in January 1906 of a strong Liberal government that was committed to a policy of stringent economy, moreover, had practically ruled out any possibility of combining high speed, heavy armament, and thick armor in a single vessel by increasing the cost per unit. As it was, the Liberal Cabinet insisted that the new First Lord, Lord Tweedmouth, reduce naval expenditure, and on 26 May 1906 the four Sea Lords agreed to limit the 1906–07 program to three ships instead of the four called for by Lord Cawdor the previous December.[179] In accordance with the recommendations of the "Fusion Design" committee report, all three vessels were to be battleships.[180] The reduction in numbers posed a serious problem for a Royal Navy that in the not too distant future would have to have "dreadnoughts" in large quantity to match the all-big-gun battleship fleets that were certain to be built by foreign powers. In September 1906, however, Fisher's hopes for a cheaper naval strategy based on armoured cruisers rather than battleships were rekindled when he learned of Arthur Hungerford Pollen's proposals for a highly advanced system of fire control, which the inventor promised would give the Royal Navy a lasting monopoly of long-range hitting.

Notes to Chapter 2

1 Elie Halevy, *A History of the English People in the Nineteenth Century*, Vol. 6: *The Rule of Democracy, 1905-1914*, translated by E. I. Watkin (New York: Barnes and Noble, 1961; first published, 1932), pp. 214–9; E. L. Woodward, *Great Britain and the German Navy* (Oxford: Oxford University Press, 1935), pp. 100–20; R. C. K. Ensor, *England, 1870-1914* (Oxford: Clarendon Press, 1936), pp. 363–5; and Arthur J. Marder, *The Anatomy of British Sea Power: A History of British Naval Policy in the Pre-Dreadnought Era, 1880-1905* (New York: Alfred A. Knopf, 1940), pp. 515–45, and *FDSF*, Vol. 1, pp. 43–5. The meticulous Ruddock F. Mackay, however, appears to have been somewhat uneasy about such an interpretation, for which see his *Fisher of Kilverstone* (Oxford: Clarendon, 1973), p. 325.
2 On a displacement of 11,880 tons (full load), the *Inflexible* carried a main armament of four 16-inch guns and could steam 14.75 knots; the *Dandolo*, on a displacement of 12,071 tons (full load), carried a main armament of four 17.7-inch guns and could steam 15.6 knots, *CFS*, pp. 26, 340.
3 *FGDN*, Vol. 1, pp. 110–1.
4 Ibid. Fisher's "Mrs. Somebody" was Hannah Glasse, the author of the celebrated 18th century cookbook *The Art of Cookery made Plain and Easy*. The proverb "First catch your hare" does not appear in Glasse's book, but it may have been suggested by her phrase "Take your hare when it is cased." See *DNB*, s.v. "Glasse, Hannah," by Ronald Bayne. In later years, Fisher would again decorate arguments for high speed in warships with the proverb, but make the attribution to Glasse. See "Notes on the Imperative Necessity of Possessing Powerful Fast Armoured Cruisers and their Qualifications" (n.d. [February 1902]), F. P. 4198, FISR 5/9, C.C. [henceforward cited as "Fast Armoured Cruisers"] and Fisher to Churchill, 14 January, 1912, quoted in part in Winston Churchill, *The World Crisis* (New York: Charles Scribner's Sons, 1923), Vol. 1, p. 147.
5 A more complete description of the gunlaying problem is provided later in this chapter in the discussion of the gunnery reforms of the late 1890s.
6 Peter Padfield, *Guns at Sea* (London: Hugh Evelyn, 1973), pp. 205–6. For Fisher's apparent awareness at this time that long-range naval gunnery did leave much to be desired, see Fisher to Admiral Sir Geoffrey T.

Phipps Hornby, 24 October 1882, quoted in Mackay, *Fisher of Kilverstone*, p. 160.

7 The four muzzle-loading guns of *Inflexible* each weighed 80 tons, compared with the 45 tons each of the four breech-loading guns of *Collingwood*. On trials, *Inflexible* steamed 14.75 knots on 8,407 I.H.P., in comparison with the 16.6 knots on 8,369 I.H.P. of *Collingwood* on her trials. See Oscar Parkes, *British Battleships: A History of Design, Construction and Armament*, new revised edition (Hamden, Conn.: Archon Books, 1972), pp. 256, 303.

8 Reminiscence of Nathanial Barnaby, in Barnaby to Fisher, 15 January 1910, F.P. 2025, FISR 3/3, C.C., and also in Lord Fisher, *Memories* (New York: George H. Doran, 1920), pp. 249-50.

9 Fisher to Barnaby, 25 January 1883, in F.P. 2025, FISR 3/3, C.C., and also in *FGDN*, Vol. 1, p. 114. In *Memories*, Fisher produced a corrupt text of this letter by capitalizing every letter in one sentence for effect, and adding a phrase at the end. See Fisher, *Memories*, p. 250, and compare with the text given in the Fisher Papers or Marder.

10 Fisher to Barnaby, 23 January 1883, quoted in part in Fisher to Barnaby, 25 January 1883, in F.P. 2025, FISR 3/3, C.C., and Fisher, *Memories*, p. 249.

11 See Chapter 1.

12 For the speeds of British battleships laid down between 1883 and 1896, see *CFS*, pp. 29-35.

13 For the history of the development of the quick-firing gun, see *NA, 1894*, p. 394; *NA, 1896*, pp. 330-382; *NA, 1905*, pp. 396, 405; and Captain H. Garbett, *Naval Gunnery: A Description and History of the Fighting Equipment of a Man-of-War* (London: George Bell, 1897), pp. 177-87. For the use of the terms "quick-fire" for 4.7-inch guns and "rapid-fire" for 6-inch guns, a distinction not observed in the present work, see Officers of the United States Navy, *Naval Ordnance: A Text-Book prepared for the use of the Midshipmen of the United States Naval Academy*, rev. edn (Annapolis, Maryland: United States Naval Institute, 1917), p. 65.

14 Parkes, *British Battleships*, pp. 354-55; Mackay, *Fisher of Kilverstone*, pp. 192-3.

15 The 13.5-inch gun weighed 67 tons, compared with the 7 tons of a 6-inch, a quick-firing gun. See *NA, 1896*, pp. 380, 382.

16 Parkes, *British Battleships*, pp. 370-1.

17 Ibid., pp. 392-3, and Mackay, *Fisher of Kilverstone*, pp. 204-8.

18 *Renown* enjoyed a clear superiority in speed over the *Majestic* class vessels of the Spencer program, and was perhaps somewhat faster than the *Canopus* class. For the *Majestic* and *Canopus* class battleships in the Mediterranean while Fisher was in command, see Parkes, *British Battleships*, pp. 388-9, 398-9.

19 *FGDN*, Vol. 1, p. 174.

20 Ibid., p. 177.

21 *Extracts from Confidential Papers: Mediterranean Fleet, 1899-1902* [henceforward cited as *Extracts*](15 October 1902), p. 3, F.P. 4702, FISR 8/1, C.C.

22 Ibid., p. 10.

23 Ibid., p. 26. For the range of the Annual Prize Firings, see *NA, 1913*, p. 312.

24 *Extracts*, p. 31.

25 Ibid., pp. 10-11.

26 *FGDN*, Vol. 1, p. 208.

27 See Chapter 1, section 5.

28 Both types were capable of exceeding their designed maximum speeds—*Renown* on trials made 19.75 knots, and while *Cressy* did not quite make her

designed speed of 21 knots, her sister *Hogue* achieved 22.06 knots. *CFS*, pp. 34, 68.

29 For the characteristics of the *Cressy* and *Drake* class armoured cruisers, see *CFS*, pp. 68-9.

30 *Extracts*, p. 89.

31 Ibid.

32 Ibid., p. 75.

33 For the characteristics of the smaller *Monmouth* and *Devonshire* class armoured cruisers, see *CFS*, pp. 70-1.

34 See Fisher to Admiral Sir Wilmot Fawkes, 12 December 1900, F.P. 54, FISR 1/2, C.C.[in *FGDN*, Vol. 1, but incomplete], and Fisher to Vice-Admiral Sir Arthur Knyvet Wilson, 12 February 1902, FGDN, Vol. 1, p. 227.

35 "Fast Armoured Cruisers."

36 *FGDN*, Vol. 1, p. 235.

37 Ibid., p. 231.

38 See Chapter 1.

39 William Laird Clowes, "The Best Types of Battleships. Symposium," in Fred T. Jane (ed.), *Fighting Ships*, (London: Sampson Low Marston, 1901), p. 344.

40 Ibid.

41 For "Guerre de course," the strategy of commerce raiding, see Marder, *Anatomy*, pp. 84-104.

42 Fred T. Jane, "Are 12-inch Guns in Battle-Ships the Best Value for the Weight Entailed: A Plea for Ships Designed to Suit Our Strategical Needs," *Journal of the Royal United Services Institution*, Vol. 47 (January-June 1903), p. 174.

43 Ibid., p. 175.

44 Ibid.

45 *Extracts*, p. 123.

46 Fisher to the Admiralty Permanent Secretary, 25 June 1901, in "Lecture and Discussion at United States Institute [*sic*] on Battleships and Armoured Cruisers," Adm. 1/7521, P.R.O. [henceforward cited as "Lecture and Discussion"] Adm. 1/7521, P.R.O.

47 Ibid.

48 "A Visit to Portsmouth and Osborne on 12 September 1903. (Being a Leaflet to illustrate the Chief Points of Interest.)" (1903), F.P. 4928, FISR 8/37, C.C.

49 R. A. Burt, *British Battleships of World War One* (Annapolis: Naval Institute Press, 1986), pp. 19-20.

50 Cuniberti, however, had once been in agreement with those who preferred the armoured cruiser over the battleship. See his proposals for an 8,000 ton vessel armed with a uniform-caliber main armament of 8-inch (203 mm) guns in Great Britain, Admiralty, Naval Intelligence Department, "The New Type of Armoured Ship," No. 589 [draft print of article by Cuniberti translated from the *Marine Rundschau* of May and June 1900 that was subsequently cancelled following the Italian decision not to build vessels described] (1900), Adm. 1/7464A, P.R.O.

51 Colonel Vittorio E. Cuniberti, "An Ideal Battleship for the British Fleet," in Fred T. Jane (ed.), *Fighting Ships*, (London: Sampson Low Marston, 1903), p. 407.

52 Ibid., p. 408.

53 Ibid.

54 Burt, *British Battleships of World War One*, pp. 19-20.

55 For brown powder and cordite in the Royal Navy, see Garbett, *Naval Gunnery*, pp. 215-28; Vivian B. Lewes and J. S. S. Brame, *Service Chemistry: Being a Short Manual of Chemistry and Metallurgy and their Application in the Naval and Military Services*, 5th edn (London: Edward Arnold, 1922); Tenney L. Davis, *The Chemistry of Powder and Explosives*, 2 Vols (New York: John Wiley, 1943), Vol. 2, pp. 287-330; Frank Douglas Miles, *Cellulose Nitrate: The Physical Chemistry of Nitrocellulose, its Formation and Use* (New York: Interscience Publishers, 1955); and John Campbell, "Cordite," in *Warship*, Vol. 2 (1978), pp. 138-40. For big-gun design and performance, see Peter Hodges, *The Big Gun: Battleship Main Armament 1860-1945* (Annapolis, Md.: Naval Institute Press, 1981), p. 37.

56 For the development of British naval big-guns and their mountings, see Hodges, *The Big Gun*. For comparisons of average rates of fire, see Fred T. Jane (ed.), *Fighting Ships* (London: Sampson Low Marston, 1905), p. 34. For comparisons of maximum possible rates of fire, see Parkes, *British Battleships*, pp. 345, 384, 396.

57 For horizontal fire, see the beginning of Chapter 3.

58 For the problem of firing on the roll, see Captain C. Hughes-Onslow, "Section IV: Modern Naval Gun Practice," in *Fire Control* (Royal Naval War College, Portsmouth, 1909), P.P.

59 Philip R. Alger, *The Groundwork of Practical Naval Gunnery: A Study of the Principles and Practice of Exterior Ballistics, as Applied to Naval Gunnery and of the Computation and Use of Ballistic and Range Tables*, 2nd edn (Annapolis, Md.: United States Naval Institute, 1917), p. 251.

60 For the question of elevating and training controls, see 1980 memorandum by N. J. M. Campbell to author via Captain S. W. Roskill, and Hodges, *The Big Gun*, p. 51.

61 For the development of continuous-aim gun-laying, see Admiral Sir Percy Scott, *Fifty Years in the Royal Navy* (New York: George H. Doran, 1919), pp. 92-9, 143-63; Peter Padfield, *Aim Straight: A Biography of Admiral Percy Scott* (London: Hodder and Stoughton, 1966), pp. 78-9, 114-27; and Elting E. Morison, *Men, Machines, and Modern Times,* (Cambridge, Mass.: M.I.T. Press, 1966), pp. 17-24

62 For long range firing in the Mediterranean and the discovery of the salvo method, see Admiral Sir Frederick Dreyer, "A Brief History of the Development of Fire Control in the Royal Navy," undated typescript mimeograph copy, P.P., and Admiral Sir R. H. Bacon, *The Life of Lord Fisher of Kilverstone*, 2 Vols (London: Hodder and Stoughton, 1929), Vol. 1, pp. 251-2.

63 For Edward W. Harding and the development of fire control, see "Proof of Evidence of Colonel E. W. Harding" (January 1920), P.P.; an untitled memorandum that appears to be a draft of the preceding, P.P.; the testimony of Harding in RCAI, *Minutes*, Vol. 9 (1 August 1925), p. 5, P.P. and *NA, 1913*, p. 322.

64 "Rapidan," *The Tactical Employment of Naval Artillery* (London: Offices of Engineering, 1903), N.L.M.D. and P.P. [Churchill College].

65 Percy Scott, "Gunnery," a reprint of lectures, 1902-05, in the Arnold White Papers, WH 1/65, N.M.M.

66 Untitled Harding memorandum [cited above in note 63], P.P.

67 Great Britain, Admiralty, Gunnery Branch [Edward W. Harding], *Fire Control: A Summary of the Present Position of the Subject* (October, 1904), N.L.M.D. [hereafter cited as Gunnery Branch, *Fire Control*]. For Harding's authorship, see RCAI, *Minutes*, Vol. 9 (1 August 1925), p. 5, P.P.

68 For the inability of big-guns to be laid by continuous-aim, see Director of Naval Ordnance (Rear-Admiral Sir John Jellicoe) Memoranda and Minute: "Director for Turret Firing" (12 December 1907), Adm. 1/7955, P.R.O.

69 Gunnery Branch, *Fire Control*, p. 5. For the original reports of the fire control committees, see "Reports of Committees on Control of Fire" (2 July 1904), Adm. 1/7758, P.R.O. and Marder, *Anatomy*, pp. 522-3. See also "Remarks on Report of Joint Committee on Fire Control in Action" (29 May 1904), Adm. 1/7757, P.R.O.

70 For question of elevating and training controls and the Vickers BVIII mounting, see 1980 memorandum by N. J. M. Campbell to author via Captain S. W. Roskill, and Hodges, *The Big Gun*, p. 51.

71 Fisher's "Notes for Successor" (n.d., but probably 1902), p. 5, F.P. 4196, FISR 5/8, C.C., and Bacon, *Life of Lord Fisher*, Vol. 1, p. 251.

72 *Extracts*, p. 10.

73 "Lecture and Discussion," Adm. 1/7521, P.R.O.

74 Fisher, *Memories*, pp. 127-8. In his memoirs Fisher claimed that he discussed the idea of the all-big-gun battleship *Dreadnought*. Because he then favored quick-firers over big-guns, it would seem that he meant the principle of uniform-caliber armaments rather than all-big-gun armaments in particular.

75 See "Fast Armoured Cruisers," and Fisher to Selborne, 26 March 1902, in *FGDN*, Vol. 1, p. 235.

76 Print on "Admiralty House, Portsmouth," stationery (undated, but see Mackay, *Fisher of Kilverstone*, pp. 310-1), F.P. 4932, FISR 8/38, C.C..

77 Ibid. For the influence of Sir Andrew Noble, the chairman of the Elswick Ordnance Company, on Fisher with regard to the new model 10-inch gun, see Parkes, *British Battleships*, p. 468, and Noble to Fisher, 21 August 1904, in *FP*, Vol. 1, pp. 31-2. For the possible influence of Philip Watts, the Director of Naval Construction, who also favored smaller caliber big-guns, see Burt, *British Battleships of World War One*, p. 39.

78 For the characteristics of the various marks of 10-inch gun, see Parkes, *British Battleships*, p. 437, and N. J. M. Campbell, "British Naval Guns 1880-1945, No. 5," in *Warship*, Vol. 6 (1982), pp. 43-5.

79 To a lesser degree, the new model 10-inch gun suffered from the same disadvantages as the 6-inch gun when it came to fire control. In editions of *Fighting Ships* published before 1906, the new model 10-inch guns were given an average rate of fire that was more than 50 per cent higher than that of a 12-inch gun—that is, a rate of fire of 1.5 rounds per minute, as opposed to less than one round per minute. From 1906, the tables of average rates of fire in *Fighting Ships* were adjusted to account for the effect of fire control, which reduced the average rate of fire credited to the newer 10-inch guns to the same level as that of the 12-inch gun.

80 Admiral of the Fleet Sir Hedworth Meux to Fisher from H.M.S. *Victorious*, 25 May [1904], F.P. 126, FISR 1/4, C.C..

81 For Bacon's influence on Fisher over the question of the new model 10-inch gun versus the 12-inch gun, see Parkes, *British Battleships*, p. 468.

82 *FP*, Vol. 1, p. xxiv. For the misdating of certain documents in *FP*, Vol. 1, see Mackay, *Fisher of Kilverstone*, p. 311.

83 In *Naval Necessities*, Vol. 1, N.L.M.D., for the most part included in, and henceforward cited from, *FP*, Vol. 1, p. 74.

84 D. K. Brown, "The Design and Construction of the Battleship Dreadnought," in *Warship*, Vol. 4 (1980), p. 44. Scott, however, did call for single ranging shots with 12-inch guns. See Scott, "Gunnery," p. 34, and also Arthur

Hungerford Pollen's discussion of the limitations of relying on ranging shots without accurate knowledge of the change of range in "A.C.: A Postscript" (mid-1905), in *PP*, pp. 61–4. For Fisher's knowledge of Scott's work by this time, see Fisher to A. K. Wilson, 16 March 1902, F.P. 95, FISR 1/3, C.C.

85 *Extracts*, p. 73. See also Fisher's speech at the Royal Academy Banquet, *Times* [London], 4 May 1903.

86 For the first British submarines, see Michael Wilson, "The First Submarines for the Royal Navy," in *Warship*, Vol. 6 (1982), pp. 266–70.

87 "Invasion and Submarines," F.P. 4940, FISR 8/39, C.C.

88 Mackay, *Fisher of Kilverstone*, pp. 297, 302.

89 Parkes, *British Battleships*, pp. 271, 413–414.

90 "Invasion and Submarines," F.P. 4940. See Mackay, *Fisher of Kilverstone*, pp. 299–302.

91 Fisher to Battenberg (January 1904?), F.P. 112, FISR 1/3, C.C.

92 "Admiralty House, Portsmouth," portions of which are included in, and henceforward cited from, *FP*, Vol. 1, pp. 30–31.

93 *FP*, Vol. 1, p. 41.

94 Ibid.

95 Selborne printed marginal note (omitted in FP, Vol. 1, p. 31), *Naval Necessities*, Vol. 1, p. 40, N.L.M.D.

96 *FP*, Vol. 1, p. 41.

97 For prior opposition to Fisher's views on capital ship design, see the letters of Admiral Walter Talbot Kerr, Vice-Admiral A. K. Wilson, Rear-Admiral Reginald Custance and Rear-Admiral W. H. May of June and July 1901, in "Lecture and Discussion," Adm. 1/7521, P.R.O.; views of Captain H. J. May in Great Britain, Admiralty, Intelligence Department, "Exercises carried out at the Royal Naval College Greenwich. . .," No. 653 (May 1902), Adm. 1/7597, P.R.O.; and views of Vice-Admiral A. K. Wilson and Admiral Sir Cyprian Bridge, "Tactical Value of Speed as Compared with Extra Armour and Guns. Discussion on Captain May's Paper," No. 653A (November 1902), Adm. 1/7601, P.R.O.

98 *FP*, Vol. 1, p. 28.

99 Ibid., p. 41.

100 Ibid., p. 28.

101 Ibid., p. 41.

102 *CFS*, pp. 40, 68.

103 *FP*, Vol. 1, p. 31.

104 The four 12-inch guns and ten 9.2-inch guns of the *Lord Nelson* could fire 11,400 pounds of projectiles in a minute, as compared with the 4,560 pounds that could be fired by the four 9.2-inch guns of the *Minotaur* during the same period. See *Fighting Ships* (1905), p. 34.

105 "Admiralty House, Portsmouth," but not included in *FP*, Vol. 1.

106 The sixteen 10-inch guns of Fisher's proposed battleship could fire 12,000 pounds of projectiles in a minute, as compared with the 18,240 pounds that could be fired by his proposed armoured cruiser during the same time period; on the assumption that the employment of fire control would reduce the rate of fire of both the 10-inch gun and the 9.2-inch gun to roughly one round per gun per minute, the battleship would enjoy an advantage of a little less than four-to-three over the armoured cruiser in the weight of projectiles that could be fired within the same time period. See *Fighting Ships* (1905), p. 34 and Fred T. Jane (ed.), *Fighting Ships* (London: Sampson Low Marston, 1906), p. 41.

107 *FP*, Vol. 1, p. 45.

108 Fisher's informal committee of seven close advisors were Captains Henry B. Jackson, John R. Jellicoe, R. H. S. Bacon and Charles Madden; Commander Wilfrid Henderson; W. H. Gard, then Chief Constructor of the Portsmouth Dockyard, and Alexander Gracie, the managing director of the Fairfield Shipbuilding Company. See Fisher to Selborne, 19 October 1904, in *FGDN*, Vol. 1, pp. 330-1.

109 Bacon, *Life of Lord Fisher*, Vol. 1, p. 256.

110 *FP*, Vol. 1, pp. 2,4.

111 "Ship Design," comments by Beresford (19 December 1904), F.P. 4218, FISR 5/11, C.C.

112 *FGDN*, Vol. 1, p. 325.

113 See *Report of the Committee on Designs* (1905), N.L.M.D., given in, and herein cited from, *FP*, Vol. 1, pp. 199-200.

114 The seven naval officer members of the Committee on Designs were: Rear-Admiral Prince Louis of Battenberg, the Director of Naval Intelligence (replaced during the deliberations of the Committee by Captain C. L. Ottley, who succeeded Battenberg as D.N.I. in early 1905); Engineer Rear-Admiral Sir John Durston, Engineer-in-Chief of the Fleet; Rear-Admiral Alfred L. Winsloe, Commanding Torpedo and Submarine Flotillas; Captain Henry B. Jackson, who was about to become Controller of the Navy; Captain John R. Jellicoe, who was about to become the Director of Naval Ordnance; Captain Reginald H. S. Bacon, Naval Assistant to the First Sea Lord; and Captain Charles E. Madden, who was about to become a Naval Assistant to the Controller. See ibid., p. 199.

115 The seven civilian members of the Committee on Designs were: Philip Watts, the Director of Naval Construction; Lord Kelvin, the renowned physicist; J. H. Biles, Professor of Law at Glasgow University and a member of the Institution of Naval Architects; Sir John Thornycroft, a prominent marine engineer; Alexander Gracie, the managing director of the Fairfield Shipbuilding Company; R. E. Froude, the Superintendent of Admiralty Experimental Works; and W. H. Gard, the Chief Constructor of the Portsmouth Dockyard. See ibid., pp. 199-200.

116 This was Commander Wilfrid Henderson; in addition, E. H. Mitchell, an Assistant Constructor, was appointed Assistant Secretary. See ibid., p. 200.

117 Ibid., p. 199.

118 Ibid., pp. 200-1.

119 See Chapter 1.

120 Selborne Papers, Mss. Selborne 42, Bodleian Library.

121 By the end of 1904, Russia had lost one battleship and one armoured cruiser in the war with Japan.

122 Selborne papers, Mss. Selborne 42, Bodleian Library.

123 See Chapter 1.

124 Parkes, *British Battleships*, p. 452.

125 *FP*, Vol. 1, pp. 224-53.

126 Fisher to Arnold White, 15 August 1908, *FGDN*, Vol. 2, p. 189; Fisher to Viscount Esher, 13 September 1909, *FGDN*, Vol. 2, p. 266; Fisher to Cecil V. Fisher, 4 April 1912, *FGDN*, Vol. 2, p. 445; and *The Times* [London], 9 September 1919.

127 Fisher to Viscount Esher, Fisher to Cecil V. Fisher, and *The Times* [London], see ibid.

128 Silvanus P. Thompson to Fisher, 12 October 1909, F.P. 1960, FISR 3/3, C.C.

129 Silvanus P. Thompson, *The Life of William Thomson, Baron Kelvin of Largs*, 2 Vols (London: Macmillan, 1910), Vol. 2, pp. 734-5. See also Kelvin to Fisher, 3 January 1905, F.P. 144; in this letter, Kelvin wrote: "Many thanks for the papers which I received from you this morning. I have read them through with much interest. The paramount importance of high speed, not only for scouts but for fighting ships other than submarines is made very clear . . ."

130 Balfour Papers, Add. Mss. 49708, ff 88-91, British Library.

131 Ian Hogg and John Batchelor, *Naval Gun* (Poole, Dorset: Blandford, 1978), p. 104.

132 For the battle ranges of 4,000 to 8,000 yards expected in 1905, see Gunnery Branch, *Fire Control*, p. 5. Under testing-ground—i.e., ideal—conditions, the armour-piercing projectile of a 12-inch Mark X gun (adopted for the *Lord Nelson* class) was capable of penetrating more than 17 inches of the toughest armour plate at 5,000 yards; under battle conditions, where the impact of the projectiles tended to be oblique rather than normal, penetrating effect was substantially reduced, but even 11-inches of armour was probably not proof against a 12-inch Mark X armour-piercing projectile at 7,000 yards; see *Fighting Ships* (1906), p. 41 (the data for the 12-inch Mark XI gun listed actually applies to the Mark X model); and FP, Vol. 2, p. 273.

133 For the vulnerability of most battleships to 12-inch high-explosive projectiles, see *FP*, Vol. 2, p. 275.

134 Churchill to Fisher, 12 April 1912, F.P. 568, FISR1/11, C.C.

135 Fisher to Churchill, 22 April 1912, F.P. 570, FISR 1/11, C.C.

136 Great Britain, Admiralty, *Report of the Committee on Designs* (1905), N.L.M.D., FP, Vol. 1, pp. 217, 220.

137 Ibid., p. 221.

138 Ibid.

139 Ibid.

140 Ibid.

141 See note 127.

142 *FP*, Vol. 1, pp. 202-9. For the important role that J. H. Narbeth, the Deputy Director of Naval Construction, may have played in the recommendations of the committee in favor of the uniform-armament of 12-inch guns, see Burt, *British Battleships of World War One*, pp. 39-40.

143 For the development of the turbine engine, see Alexander Richardson, *The Evolution of the Parsons Steam Turbine* (London: Offices of Engineering, 1911).

144 *FP*, Vol. 1, p. 205.

145 Ibid., pp. 210-11, 284. In the tables giving the number of guns that could be fired at various bearings, only four guns were listed as being able to fire directly ahead or astern in the battleship and armoured cruiser designs selected by the Committee on Designs. The report noted, however, that "although the two designs adopted have only been credited with right ahead and right astern fire of four 12-in. guns, it is hoped that the blast screens to be fitted, and the distance of the broadside guns from the foremost and after turrets, may enable a chase fire of six 12-in. guns to be obtained." Ibid., p. 211.

146 Ibid., pp. 211, 290.

147 Ibid., p. 212.

148 Ibid., p. 33.

149 The cost of the uniform-caliber armament of the battleship was £113,200, as compared with £110,400 for the mixed-caliber armament of each of the *Lord Nelson* class; the cost of the uniform-caliber armament of the armoured cruisers

was £90,000, as compared with the £70,150 for the mixed-caliber armament of each of the vessels of the *Minotaur* class. See Great Britain, Parliament, House of Commons Papers, *Appropriation Accounts*, 1906–07 (1908), and 1907–08 (1909).

150 The cost of the proposed battleship (including guns) was £1,813,100, as compared with the roughly £1,653,000 for a *Lord Nelson*; the cost of the proposed armoured cruisers was roughly £1,753,000, as compared with the roughly £1,400,000 for a *Minotaur*. See ibid.

151 *FP*, Vol. 1, p. 214.

152 *Board Minutes* [Admiralty] 1905, Adm. 167/39, P.R.O.

153 Ibid.

154 Ibid.

155 "Speed of Warships," *Engineering* (26 May 1905), p. 675.

156 Discussion by Members of the Board at Portsmouth 17 July 1905 . . .," Adm. 1/7812, P.R.O.

157 Board Meeting 12 August 1905 . . .," Adm. 1/7812, P.R.O. For Fisher's concern for strict secrecy in the case of the particulars of the armoured cruisers, see also Fisher to Tweedmouth, 13 October 1906, in "Naval Policy, Strategy, Tactics, etc.," Adm. 116/942, P.R.O.

158 *Fighting Ships* (1906), p. 57.

159 Bacon, *Lord Fisher*, Vol.1, p. 261.

160 Ibid.

161 See the sketch of the proposed armoured cruiser with the name "Invincible" in Great Britain, Admiralty, *Report of the Committee on Designs* (1905), N.L.M.D. In the Ship's Cover papers of 1905 [N.M.M.], the names *Immortalite* and *Raleigh* were given to the other two vessels, these names only later being changed to *Indomitable* and *Inflexible* to match, apparently, that of the namesake of the class, for which see John A. Roberts, *Warship Monographs: Invincible Class* (London: Conway Maritime Press, 1972), p. 5. For Fisher's attraction to Cuniberti's ideas, see Fisher's reference to the Italian in the Navy Estimates Committee report in the text below. Fisher and Cuniberti were also both early proponents of oil fuel. See Fisher to Selborne, 24 December 1901, in *FGDN*, Vol. 1, p. 220, and "Liquid Fuel for Boilers in H.M. Ships. Cuniberti System of Fuel burning in Italian Navy" (16 January 1902), Adm. 1/7594C, P.R.O.

162 Balfour Papers, Add. Mss. 49710, ff 180-5, British Library.

163 Great Britain, Admiralty, *Report of Navy Estimates Committee* (16 November 1905), p. 14, N.L.M.D.

164 Ibid.

165 Ibid., pp. 14-15.

166 This was not a meeting of the Board of Admiralty; see *Board Minutes* [Admiralty] 1905, Adm. 167/39, P.R.O.

167 The names of the members of the committee were: Captain C. L. Ottley, the Director of Naval Intelligence; Captain J. R. Jellicoe, the Director of Naval Ordnance; Captain R. H. S. Bacon, the Assistant to the First Sea Lord; Captain Charles Madden, the assistant to the Controller; Captains Stuart Nicholson and Harry Jones, the two assistants to the Director of Naval Intelligence; and Commanders H. Orpen and T. E. Crease. See Minutes entitled "Saturday, 2nd December 1905," in *Naval Necessities, IV, 1905-07*, N.L.M.D. [not included in *FP*].

168 Ibid.

169 "A Statement of Admiralty Policy," in Great Britain, Parliament, *Parliamentary Papers* (Commons), 1906, Vol. 70 (Accounts and Papers, Vol. 6) Cmnd. 2791 [Lords, 1906, Vol. 14].

170 Minutes, *Naval Necessities, IV*, N.L.M.D.
171 See memorandum by the Director of Naval Intelligence [Ottley] "The Protection of Ocean Trade in War Time" (April 1905), p. 51, Adm. 116/866B, P.R.O.
172 "A Statement of Admiralty Policy"; both Oscar Parkes and Arthur J. Marder have interpreted this document, which was known as the "Cawdor Memorandum," as having stated a minimum program. [See Parkes, British *Battleships*, p. 497, and *FDSF*, Vol. 1, p. 126]. The wording of the paper, however, suggests rather that it was a maximum program, and this was the construction that Fisher put on it in 1906. See Lord Fisher, *Records* (New York: George H. Doran, 1920), p. 111.
173 "Report of Committee appointed to consider the Questions of the Provisions of a Parent Vessel for Coastal Destroyers, the Utilization of Mercantile Cruisers, and the Fusion Design of Armoured Vessel," in *Navy Estimates Committee 1906-7* (10 January 1906), pp. 20-1, F.P. 4711, FISR 8/6, C.C.
174 Ibid.
175 Ibid.
176 Ibid.
177 Ibid.
178 In particular, see Anonymous [Rear-Admiral Sir Reginald Custance], "A Retrograde Admiralty," *Blackwood's Edinburgh Magazine*, Vol. 177 (May 1905), and Admiral Sir Cyprian Bridge, "Naval Strategy and Tactics at the Time of Trafalgar," *Transactions of the Institution of Naval Architects*, Vol. 47 (1905). See also, Bacon to Fisher, 15 April 1906, in *FGDN*, Vol. 2, p. 76.
179 "Memorandum of a Meeting of the Sea Lords at the Admiralty on Saturday, 26th May, 1906, to consider future SHIPBUILDING ARRANGEMENTS, &c.—held in accordance with the wishes of the FIRST LORD, to consider and advise him as to possible reductions," in *Naval Necessities, IV*, N.L.M.D. The Cabinet accepted the reduction of one ship as adequate on 12 July 1906; see Cab. 37/83, 65, P.R.O.
180 *FP*, Vol. 2, pp. 259-60 (n.d., but see *Naval Necessities, III*, N.L.M.D., for original document and the date of 2 July 1906).

[3]

The Conception and Initial Development of the Pollen Fire Control System, 1900-1906

1 Introduction

(a) RANGE-FINDING IN THE ROYAL NAVY BEFORE 1906

The significance of Pollen's proposals of 1906 cannot be appreciated fully without first understanding the history of the Royal Navy's previous efforts to find a solution to the problem of naval range-finding.

In the last years of the age of sail, gunlaying and aiming techniques were such that the effective range of even the largest naval guns was at best no more than 700 yards.[1] Within this distance, projectile trajectories were practically flat and the time of flight of the projectile a matter of only a few seconds.[2] By the end of the Napoleonic Wars, gunnery experts in the Royal Navy had concluded that, under such conditions, the best hitting results could be obtained by laying guns to fire their projectiles parallel to the surface of the sea—that is, to apply no elevation to the guns beyond that which was necessary to compensate for the effect of firing on the roll—a practice that was known as "horizontal fire."[3] From the mid 19th century, the adoption of steam propulsion enabled warships to achieve higher speeds and the ability to move independently of wind and wave, but at the cost of increased yaw, pitch and roll, which exacerbated the gunlaying and aiming problem.[4] Thus in spite of minor improvements in gunlaying and aiming equipment, and very great increases in the size of projectiles and muzzle-velocity, the effective range of naval ordnance through the late 1880s was still so short—less than 2,000 yards under even ideal conditions[5]—that projectile trajectories remained practically flat and projectile times of flight nearly instantaneous. British naval guns as a consequence continued to be laid and aimed in order to achieve horizontal

71

fire,[6] which meant that there was no need for accurate range-finding to set the sights.

In the mid-19th century, Sir Howard Douglas, the preeminent British authority on naval gunnery, had maintained that "in all cases of gunnery an accurate knowledge of the distance is of the first importance,"[7] but his suggested methods of determining ranges at sea were mechanically too crude to achieve satisfactory results under anything except ideal conditions. The lack of an effective naval range-finder was in any case a matter of small significance so long as naval guns were laid and aimed for horizontal fire, and probably for this reason the Royal Navy made little effort to solve the problem for many years. Interest in naval range-finding may have been stimulated, however, by the advent of quick-firing guns in the 1880s, whose high rate of shooting enabled them to make hits at greater than point-blank ranges.[8] In June 1889, the question of naval range-finding instruments was referred to the Director of Naval Ordnance, Captain John Fisher, by the Ordnance Committee after it had learned of the experiments of Lieutenant Bradley Fiske of the United States Navy. Although Fisher was advised by the captain of *Excellent* that ranges could best be obtained by trial shots from quick-firing guns, he informed the Director of Artillery on 29 June 1889 that a "simple and easily manipulated range-finder suitable for use on board ship" would be "a great advantage."[9]

After two years of further discussion of naval requirements for a range-finder,[10] the War Office, on behalf of the Admiralty, issued an advertisement for a range-finder for the navy "capable of measuring ranges up to at least 3,000 yards with a maximum error of 3 per cent."[11] A "Committee on Naval Range Finders" was appointed by the Admiralty in March 1892 to evaluate the four instruments that were submitted in response to the War Office notice.[12] Following competitive trials in the second-class protected cruiser *Arethusa* in April 1892, the committee selected the instrument manufactured by the Glasgow firm of Barr & Stroud, which had been designed in 1888,[13] for further tests.[14]

This oblong instrument, which was operated by a single observer, was pivot mounted on a pedestal. When trained on the target so that the line of sight from one end formed a right angle with respect to its longitudinal axis, the oblique angle formed by the line of sight to the target at the opposing end of the instrument was then measured by an arrangement of mirrors, lenses and the adjustment of a moving prism to obtain what was known as "coincidence," which through a trigonometric calculation gave the range to the target. The adjustment of the prism was carried out through the movement of a roller in an action that was known as making a "cut." After further trials at *Excellent* and on board several naval vessels in regular service, the Director of Naval Ordnance reported in November 1893 that the Barr & Stroud range-finder was accurate to 1 per cent at 3,000 yards, easy to manipulate, workable at night, and insensitive to changes in temperature.[15] It was, as a consequence, adopted for service and appears to have entered into general use in 1899.[16]

The first Barr & Stroud naval range finder did not, however, provide either a final or complete solution to the sight-setting problem. In the first place, the effective range of the instrument was limited by factors that were inherent to its optical design. The base of the production Barr & Stroud range-finder—that is, the distance between the ends of the instrument from which the lines of sight were established—was four and a half feet, which allowed accurate range taking at up to approximately 4,000 yards.[17] An extension of the effective range could only have been achieved by lengthening the base, but it was impracticable to build a framework capable of supporting such a longer device with the necessary rigidity.[18] Yet advances in gunlaying and aiming described in the previous chapter prompted the Admiralty as early as in 1901 to order firing practice with heavy-caliber guns at ranges that were as high as 6,000 yards, the results of which were highly unsatisfactory.[19]

The operator of the Barr & Stroud range-finder, moreover, was confronted with a number of not insignificant difficulties. If the target was to be kept in view, the range-finder had to be elevated and depressed, and trained back and forth, in order to compensate for yaw, pitch and roll, and furthermore trained to take account of any change in position of the target relative to that of the firing ship. Making the cut involved an awkward adjustment of a roller, the task of reading the range off the scale was both difficult and prone to error, and the interruption of making cuts by the need to read the scale reduced the number of ranges that could be observed in a given time. And finally, the range-finder operator, who was standing, had to keep his balance while carrying out all these operations, which was not an easy thing to accomplish when the ship had much motion.[20]

Under the most favorable conditions, therefore, the operator of a range-finder still required several seconds to adjust his instrument to take each range, and then had to read his finding and transmit it to the guns, which took additional time. Under unfavorable conditions that might occur in battle, range taking was likely to be slower still and prone to error. Thus if the courses and speeds of the opposing warships were such as to produce rapid changes in range, data could not be obtained by range-finder observation with sufficient speed or consistency to allow continuous sight-setting. In addition, the observation of the target in a battle was likely to be interrupted by mist, gunsmoke or shell splashes, which would from time to time prevent any ranges from being taken. And finally, the extension of firing ranges resulted in commensurate increases in the time of flight of the projectile,[21] which meant that the range and bearing of the target could change significantly during the interval between the instant of firing and the moment of impact.

Accurate sight setting when ranges were long under conditions that were likely to occur in action thus required a range-finding instrument that was capable of precise measurement at greater distances, a means of using occasional range-finder observations to generate a rapid flow of range data that was independent of continuous observation of the target, and the correction of generated ranges for any change in range—and observed bearings for any change in bearing—that might be produced by the relative motion of the firing ship and target during the time of flight of the projectile.

By 1906, piecemeal and uncoordinated efforts had resulted in a measure of progress. In 1902, Lieutenant John Dumaresq of the Royal Navy invented a trigonometric slide rule calculator, which was known as a dumaresq after its inventor. The dumaresq, when set with the courses and speeds of the firing ship and target and the target bearing, indicated both the change of range rate and the deflection. In 1904, the Admiralty began experiments with a mechanical device that generated ranges independently of observations of the target. The machine, which had been developed by Vickers, the large armaments firm, consisted of a clockwork motor—that is, a spring–drive mechanism—that drove a pointer around a circular dial that was marked with a sequence of ranges. After the pointer had been set to a starting range and the motor set to run at a speed that corresponded to a change of range rate, the Vickers range indicator or, as it was known, the "clock", then indicated ranges in terms of that change of range rate. The initial setting of the pointer on the dial was provided by a single range observation from the range-finder. The change of range rate was determined in either one of two ways. It could be calculated on paper by simply dividing the difference between two ranges obtained from the range-finder by the time between the observations, which could be measured with a stop-watch. Alternatively, the change of range rate could be calculated on the dumaresq.[22]

An important advance was also made in range-finding. The report on the long-range firing experiments of late 1903 and early 1904, which concluded that big-guns could be fired with effect at ranges that were as high as 8,000 yards, induced the Admiralty in 1904 to issue a requirement for a range-finder that was "capable of measuring ranges up to at least 7,000 yards with a maximum error of 1 per cent, and beyond up to 10,000 yards with proportionate error."[23] The advertisement led to the development of a 9-foot base single–observer instrument by Barr & Stroud, and a 10-foot base single–observer instrument by the firm of Thomas Cooke & Sons of York, which were offered to the Admiralty in 1906. In both cases, the extension of base length that was necessary for accuracy at greater ranges was made possible because the polished metal plates that had been used in range-finders of the single–observer type as reflectors beforehand, were replaced by pentagonal prisms whose two surfaces of reflection cancelled minor shifts of alignment, which meant that a framework that was capable of keeping the range-finder perfectly rigid along its longitudinal axis was not required. After trials that were concluded by mid-1906, the Admiralty adopted the new model Barr & Stroud range-finder.[24]

Major difficulties, none the less, remained. The effectiveness of the dumaresq was seriously compromised by the absence of any means of measuring the target course and speed, the settings of which, as a consequence, had to be guessed. In addition, both the stop-watch/Vickers Clock and dumaresq/Vickers Clock combinations were incapable of accounting adequately for changes in the change of range rate. Given firing ship and target courses and speeds that were constant, the range could not only remain unchanged or change at a constant rate, but could also change at a rate that was itself changing at a constant rate. The change of range rate computed by the stop-watch method could thus result in a highly inaccurate setting of the Vickers Clock, because the change of range rate could alter considerably during the time interval between the two range observations that were used to compute a single change of range rate. A dumaresq, on the other hand, could be made to indicate the continuous variation in the change of range rate through the continuous adjustment of its setting for target bearing, because the target bearing varied in proportion to changes in the change of range rate. The continuous variation in the change of range rate indicated by the dumaresq could not, however, be represented by the Vickers Clock, whose motor could not be made to vary in speed continuously. The result was that as the speed of the Vickers Clock was altered in steps in the attempt to repeat the continuous alteration in the change of range rate indicated by the dumaresq, the range indicated by the clock would become increasingly inaccurate.

In the absence of effective instruments, the not inconsiderable gunnery progress of the Royal Navy during the first few years of the new century was the result of changes in practice procedures and methods of evaluation. Between 1884 and 1904, the gunnery of the fleet had been tested by the Annual Prize Firing, in which a ship steamed at low speed on a set course and fired at a stationary target at ranges of from 1,400 to 1,600 yards. The fleet average percentage of hits to shots fired during these events was always well below 50 per cent because of the inadequacy of improvised targets, the haphazard evaluation of results, and the absence of incentives for good shooting. Under the direction of Percy Scott, who became the first Inspector of Target Practice in February 1905, the Annual Prize Firings were replaced in 1905 by the Gunlayer's Test and Battle Practice. In the Gunlayer's Test, gunners fired from a stationary ship at a stationary target at a range of 2,000 yards, while in Battle Practice, gunners were required to shoot at a stationary target from a ship steaming at low speed on a set course at ranges of from 5,000 to 7,000 yards. The new system introduced a well-designed standard target, annual listings of warships ranked by their shooting scores, promotions for officers whose ships performed well, and courts of inquiry for ships with low scores. As a result of Scott's efforts, the average fleet percentage of hits to rounds fired in the Gunlayer's Test increased from 56 per cent in 1905 to 79 per cent in 1907, while the average fleet Battle Practice score, which was calculated on a points system rather than in percentages of hits to shots fired, more than doubled during the same period.[25]

In the Gunlayer's Test the range did not change, while in Battle Practice range-finding was simplified by the fact that the target course and speed settings required for the dumaresq were known from the start—being constant factors—while the very low change in the change of range rate that was the result of the slow speed of the firing ship and stationary position of the target meant that discontinuous settings of the Vickers Clock with rates from the dumaresq probably did not result in great errors in the generation of the range. In war, however, enemy fleets were unlikely to remain stationary or steam on courses and at speeds that would oblige the limitations of British gunnery equipment. Thus in spite of the great improvements in gunnery achieved under the direction of Scott, the development of new fire control instruments was essential if long-range firing under the conditions that were likely to be encountered in battle was to become practicable.

Pollen's proposed fire control system of 1906 depended upon the new model Barr & Stroud range-finder to provide ranges, but in addition consisted of mechanisms of his own design that were intended (1) to improve the accuracy of range and bearing observation, (2) to use the observed ranges and bearings to measure the speed and course of the target with precision, (3) to generate ranges—and bearings as well—from the integration of target and own ship course and speed data in a manner that took exact account of any continuous alteration in the change of range rate, (4) to correct generated ranges and bearings for time of flight and other ballistical factors and (5) to transmit rapidly the corrected ranges and bearings to the gunsights. Within seven years, Pollen was able to translate his ideas into a practicable system, which not only constituted a major advance in the technique of naval surface gunnery, but also marked a milestone in the development of the modern computer.

(b)   ARTHUR HUNGERFORD POLLEN

There appears to have been nothing in the family background, upbringing, education, early employment or political disposition of Arthur Joseph Hungerford Pollen that would have predisposed him to pursue a career as an inventor of sophisticated devices that served the needs of naval gunnery. His father was John Hungerford Pollen, a prominent Tractarian who had followed Newman into the Catholic church and who was a noted artist and author.[26] Much of his boyhood and adolescence were spent in the company of the artistic associates of his parents, which included such Bohemians as the adventurer-poet Wilfrid Scawen Blunt.[27] At the Oratory School in Birmingham, Arthur Pollen proved himself to be a gifted student, musician and athlete. He matriculated at Trinity College, Oxford, studied history, and graduated with honors. In 1893, he entered Lincoln's Inn to begin a career in law, and while a legal novice supplemented his income by writing as a critic of art, literature, drama and music for the highly respected *Westminster Gazette*, a position he obtained through J. A. Spender, the prominent journalist and a friend.[28] In politics he was a Liberal and in 1895, he unsuccessfully contested a parliamentary seat at Walthamstow, Essex.

Pollen possessed certain talents, on the other hand, that would play an important part in his success in the field of naval gunnery. He was an experienced shot, who, in the words of his son, was familiar with the problem of "the judgement of speed and distance required to bring down driven grouse in full flight."[29] Pollen was, in addition, an accomplished debater, who had made his mark as an undergraduate at the Oxford Union, the famous forensic society, as an advocate of unfashionable causes such as Irish Home Rule. In later years his ability to present his case persuasively would often, though not always, win the support of naval skeptics. And in 1898, he became the managing director of Linotype

& Machinery, Ltd. (henceforward the Linotype Company), England's leading manufacturer of newspaper equipment, following his marriage to the daughter of the firm's chairman. As the director of a company that was engaged in the production of precision machinery of highly complex design,[30] Pollen proved himself to be a skilled businessman and technical innovator,[31] attributes which were to be of great value when he turned his attention to the development of instruments for naval service. For all this, Pollen might well have confined his work to the world of private industry in the ordinary course of events. But in 1900, a mere chance happening that took place while he was on vacation prompted him to investigate the problem of setting the sights of naval ordnance with accurate data.[32]

2 Pollen and Fire Control, 1900-1906

In February 1900, Pollen travelled to Malta to visit an uncle, Sir Clement La Primaudaye, R.N., the Superintendent of Police. While there he by coincidence met a cousin, William Goodenough, a lieutenant in the Royal Navy who would later win distinction at the Battle of Jutland. Goodenough invited his relation to witness a seagoing practice shoot, and Pollen thus sailed on board H.M.S. *Dido*, a second-class protected cruiser armed with 6-inch and 4.7-inch guns, in the company of the battleship *Empress of India*, whose armament was composed of 13.5-inch and 6-inch guns. During the gunnery exercise, the two ships took turns firing and towing the target, and because their courses were parallel and speeds equal, the range of approximately 1,500 yards did not change. That very morning Pollen had read in a copy of *The Times*, which had been posted from London, that naval 4.7-inch guns used on land against the Boers in the war in South Africa had been effective at five miles (8,800 yards). He thus asked his service companions why practice took place at ranges that were much less than those to which the guns of the cruiser—and the even more powerful guns of the battleship—were evidently capable of firing accurately. Pollen was then told that the range limitation was imposed largely by the lack of an efficient range-finder.[33]

Intrigued by the problem posed by aiming big-guns at distant and moving targets from a moving ship, Pollen began to consider methods of measuring the greater distances to which naval artillery could fire accurately, but which could not be measured with precision by the existing single-observer Barr & Stroud range-finder. Shortly after returning from the Mediterranean, Pollen conceived of a range-finding system that did not resort to reflecting surfaces, and thus by-passed the mirror alignment factor that restricted the base length of the existing service instrument. Two observers who were to be separated by the length of a ship's superstructure were to ascertain the target's bearings simultaneously, which were then to be transmitted by electrical signals from the observation positions to a pantographic calculator that instantaneously combined the observed data with the known distance between the observers to produce an indication of the target range.

By July 1900, Pollen, and an associate who appears to have been Mark Barr, an independent scientist and inventor, had designed a ranges-from-bearings pantographic calculator.[34] Pollen also exploited the technical resources of the Linotype Company by having its engineers consider the hypothetical case of two armoured cruisers, initially 10,000 yards apart, approaching each other at full speed on parallel courses that were separated by a distance of 1,500 yards. Their analysis of these circumstances, which had been chosen to pose the problem of rapidly changing range, disclosed the fact that the range would change by nearly 900 yards during the 30 second interval that it took a 6-inch projectile, aimed to hit its target at the starting range, to travel 10,000 yards, and that the range would not only change, but would change at a rate that was itself changing at a constant rate. Further study revealed that the change of range rate would alter in such a manner in most realistic cases of convergence or divergence.[35] The target bearing, on the other hand, changed only when the change of range rate was changing, and at a much slower rate than the change of range. Changes in target bearing were, in addition, much easier to perceive than changes in target range. Thus in comparison with the change in range, the change in bearing posed a smaller, if not entirely negligible, problem.

As a result of the studies of his engineers, Pollen concluded that the gun sights would have to be set with observed ranges that had been given a correction for the change in range during the time of flight of the projectile. He recognized, moreover, that the correction would have to take into account the continuous variation in the change of range rate. The rate at which the change of range rate changed was determined by the courses and speeds of the firing ship and target. Because the course and speed of the firing ship would of course be known, the data problem was reduced to the question of finding the target's course and speed. Pollen decided that this could best be accomplished by plotting simultaneously observed ranges and bearings in sequence on a chart to produce a scale picture of the target's movement, from which its course and speed could be measured. The determination of the required range corrections from the integration of this discovered with known data, he assumed, would then be a "mere matter of calculation."[36]

A method of measuring the target bearing was essential for both the two–observer range–finding system and the plot. The latter, in particular, required bearings that were precisely accurate with respect to the course of the ship. A ship under way, however, does not move along a perfectly straight path, but is constantly weaving back and forth as helm is applied to compensate for the deflecting force of wave motion, a phenomenon known as yaw. Pollen at first hoped that the effects of yaw could be neutralized with an observing instrument that corrected observed bearings through the action of a magnetic compass. This scheme, however, was rejected on the advice of Lord Kelvin, England's preeminent practical physicist and a director on the board of the Linotype Company, who pointed out that the electrical mechanisms of Pollen's proposed device and the blast of the ship's guns would disrupt the magnetic field of the compass and prevent its accurate operation.[37] As an alternative, Pollen settled in December 1900 on the correction of azimuth observations with a gyroscope.[38]

On 26 January 1901, Pollen, with nothing more concrete in hand than drawings of his pantographic calculator, wrote to Lord Walter Kerr, the First Sea Lord and a family friend, describing his two–observer range-finding system and offering it to the Admiralty to develop.[39] Kerr referred Pollen to Selborne, the First Lord, to whom he restated his case in a letter dated 4 February.[40] On Selborne's advice, Pollen submitted his proposal formally via the Admiralty Permanent Secretary on 25 February in a printed statement entitled *The Pollen System of Telemetry*.[41] In this pamphlet, Pollen estimated that observation with his gyroscopically corrected two–observer scheme would be possible, given a base of 150 feet, at 10,000 yards with an error of just over 1 per cent, and at 20,000 yards with an error of just over 3 per cent. Ranges of less than 5,000 yards could not be measured conveniently, and were to be left to the existing Barr & Stroud instrument to determine. Pollen maintained that the employment of his instruments would "double the effective range of every gun from 6" to 12" calibre in the fleet," which would "enable fire to be opened on the enemy at distances at which he could not possibly reply, and would enable a ship equipped with it to keep out of the enemy's range until he was destroyed or put out of action—a revolution in naval battle tactics."[42]

The Admiralty, however, informed Pollen on 7 February 1901 that the offer of his system had been declined on the grounds that it "does not seem to the Admiralty to offer them advantages sufficiently good to warrant their buying the secret."[43] Pollen's appeals later that month for further consideration were refused.[44] An animus against the two–observer approach must have played a major role in the decision: the use of widely separated observers posed the problem of insuring the simultaneity of bearing observations that was essential for accuracy, exposed a great deal of electrical circuitry to enemy shell fire, and required the use of three sets of instruments and observers to command an all round view. These considerations, in any case, had led to the rejection of the two–observer systems that had been submitted for trial in the Royal Navy's range-finder competition of 1892.[45] And in addition, the Admiralty appears to have not seen the need for a more efficient range-finder in spite of their orders of February 1901 for gunnery practice at distances that exceeded the maximum effective range of the Barr & Stroud instrument.[46]

Pollen's prospectus did impress Rear-Admiral Lord Charles Beresford, then Second-in-Command of the Mediterranean Fleet, who wrote on 17 March 1901 that the "advantages claimed for your system, provided they can be realized, are undoubtedly of the greatest value . . ."[47] But although Beresford believed that Pollen had made out a good case for a trial of his range-finding system, the Admiralty remained disinterested. Pollen's advances to the Elswick Works of W. G. Armstrong, Whitworth & Company were no more successful—the offer of his system to the large armaments firm for consideration was summarily refused in August 1902.[48] Pollen nevertheless continued, in the meanwhile, to develop his ideas,[49] and with the assistance of William Henry Lock, the manager and secretary of the Linotype Company, and Mark Barr, designed an improved ranges-from-bearings calculator. The patent for this device had been applied for in March 1902, and a complete specification was submitted in December of that year.[50] In 1903, Pollen was strongly urged during a second trip to Malta to develop his ideas by naval officers whose interest in the possibilities of long-range firing had probably been stimulated by the recent advances that had taken place in gunlaying and aiming.[51] Pollen also learned at this time that the service knew of no method of calculating ranges from the integration of target and firing ship courses and speeds as he had assumed it had.[52] In May 1904, Pollen and Lock applied for additional patents for mechanisms that were part of the two-observer range-finding system. And during the spring of 1904, Pollen turned again to Lord Kelvin for advice, laying before him the entire question of providing accurate data for long-range firing at sea. Kelvin, Pollen later recalled, was "much interested" and "extremely sympathetic," but also warned that "it is a very big project. You have ten years' hard work before you."[53]

Encouraged by his informal naval contacts, better equipped with draft plans of his proposed instruments and fortified by the counsel of Lord Kelvin, Pollen approached the Admiralty once more to propose that funds, which he estimated would amount to less than £1,000, be made available to develop his system.[54] Pollen's efforts were backed by the political influence of his father-in-law, Sir Joseph Lawrence, who in 1901 had been elected to represent Monmouth boroughs as a Conservative, and who had received his knighthood in 1902. Lawrence wrote to Selborne on 24 May 1904 in support of his son-in-law's project, and again on 27 May after it had been rejected.[55] When consulted a second time, presumably as a result of Lawrence's pressure, the Director of Naval Ordnance, Captain Henry D. Barry, maintained on 31 May that Pollen's instruments were "in no sense a range finder," and he furthermore complained that he had found the Pollen family to be, from personal experience, "pushing & persistent."[56]

Pollen's proposals were again rejected on 8 June, but he had an interview with the First Sea Lord, Lord Walter Kerr, and the Controller, Rear-Admiral W. H. May, on 9 or 10 June,[57] during which he "gave an explanation of the system, and informed them that, while the observing instruments and other mechanisms necessary for the system had not been completely designed, their general design had been determined."[58] On 2 July, Pollen was then informed that no further action could be taken until he provided the Admiralty with prototypes of his bearing observation instruments and a written description of a complete system of obtaining the data required to set the gun sights. He thus turned to the task of completing detailed plans of his instruments.[59]

At this time Pollen also consulted a number of senior naval officer gunnery experts, and at Torbay met with a committee of gunnery lieutenants chosen from the ships of the Channel Fleet who had been unofficially authorized to advise him by Vice-Admiral Lord Charles Beresford, the Commander-in-Chief of the Channel Fleet, who it will be recalled had previously been receptive to Pollen's proposals.[60] In July

Pollen was thus able to write a *Memorandum on a Proposed System for Finding Ranges at Sea and Ascertaining the Speed and Course of Any Vessel in Sight,* in which he described his two-observer range-finding scheme and a system of plotting observed ranges and bearings. The plot was to be made by orienting a long paper in a direction corresponding to the direction of the firing ship's course, and moving it by rollers at a rate corresponding to the firing ship's speed, while a fixed pencil drew a line on the paper that would thus represent the movement of the firing ship. Simultaneously observed ranges and bearings from the two-observer range-finding system would then be marked on the plot to form a sequence of points that, when meaned with a straight line, produced a scale record of the movement of the target relative to that of the firing ship.[61]

This "true-course" plot was to be used in one of two ways. The target's course and speed could be measured from the plot with a ruler and protractor. With this information the course and speed of the firing ship could be matched with that of the target, and the range thus kept long and constant. A single range from the range-finder would then be sufficient to enable the firing ship to destroy the target which, presumably because it had no effective range-finder of its own, would be unable to reply. Alternatively, the plot could be extrapolated. The target's range could then be measured off the plot at a point far enough into the future to account for the change in range during both the time it took to measure the range and transmit it to the gunsights, and the time of flight of the projectile. By such means, the plot itself would be used to integrate the courses and speeds of the firing ship and target, and in the process produce corrected ranges with respect to any variation in the change of range rate. The averaging of the observed ranges and bearings on the plot, moreover, would eliminate the errors of individual observations, thus increasing the accuracy of the data measured off the plot.[62]

Pollen circulated his print in the fall of 1904, after which he requested interviews with Selborne and Sir John Fisher, the new First Sea Lord, in November.[63] Selborne's response is not known and Fisher denied Pollen an audience,[64] but the Admiralty did appoint a special committee, which examined his patent materials on 16 December 1904.[65] By this time Lock had completed the design work on both a bearings recording and transmission mechanism—that together with the observing instruments and the calculator comprised the two-observer range-finding system—and a plotter.[66] All these instruments were described to the committee, along with a device called a "crab machine," which was meant to provide a convenient method of extrapolating the relative movement of the firing ship and target into the future. The new instrument was to be set with the known course and speed of the firing ship, an initial range and bearing from observation or off the plot, and the target's course and speed as measured from the plot. By a mechanical trigonometric calculation, this data was to be combined and made to control the compass and length of a pivoting, extending arm—hence the sobriquet. The movement of the arm determined the position of a token that represented the target, the position of the firing ship at all times being held as stationary. This "virtual course"[67] plan could be arranged to represent the relative positions of the two ships at a given future time. A glass pane covering the mechanical scale diagram supported a ruler and protractor, which could then easily be manipulated to measure the required future range and bearing.[68]

Pollen estimated that the cost of trials instruments, including compensation for his past expenses and a margin of profit, would be £2,500. The committee, however, had misgivings about the bearing observation mechanism, considered the expense of Pollen's proposals to be excessive, and as a consequence did not recommend a trial. Pollen thus turned to the task of redesigning his gear to meet the criticisms of the committee,[69] and on 21 December 1904 asked the Admiralty to name such financial terms that would enable them to agree to a trial so that he could decide whether or not he could "arrange for the deficiency to be borne in some other quarter."[70] Pollen, moreover, had in the meanwhile recognized that his system was unsatisfactory in at least one other important respect, and also that the naval authorities had yet to understand the nature of the sight-setting problem and thus could not appreciate the significance of his proposed solution.

The several manual operations required by the "crab machine" to obtain future range and bearing would prevent data from being obtained quickly enough when the range was changing rapidly, and Pollen, therefore, with the assistance of Harold Isherwood, a Linotype Company engineer, conceived of an instrument that would work automatically. His mechanical range generator of late 1904 was very different in principle and effect from the dumaresq/Vickers Clock combination, of whose existence he was in any case apparently ignorant until a meeting with Percy Scott in May 1905.[71] Pollen's proposed device solved the problem posed by the non-existence of any motor whose speed could be varied continuously with precision by combining the processes of calculation and indication in such a way that a constant speed drive produced a variable speed result. This was to be accomplished by having a clockwork motor that ran at a constant speed actuate a mechanism that, after having been set with the courses and speeds of the firing ship and target, and a range and a bearing, continuously reproduced the virtual course movement of the two ships. This mechanical action would, in turn—through a simple mechanical linkage—be used to control a pointer on a dial, whose indication of the range would reflect any continuous variation in the change of range rate because such variation was inherent to the replicated relative motion of the two ships.[72]

In order to educate Admiralty skeptics, Pollen restated his ideas at some length in a pamphlet entitled *Fire Control and Long Range Firing*, which was written in December 1904.[73] In this print he pointed out that naval artillery could fire more rapidly than ranges could be observed, which meant that the sights could not be set accurately with observed ranges for every shot when the range was changing; that under battle conditions, the view of the target was likely to be obscured by shell splashes or smoke, preventing range-finding by observation altogether; and, that when the range was long and changing rapidly, the sights would have to be set with ranges that had been corrected for the time of flight of the projectile and other ballistical factors. Pollen maintained that mechanically generated ranges, on the other hand, could provide data as fast as the guns could be fired, could be based upon a record of past observations which would mean that accurate data could be supplied to the guns even when the view of the target was obscured, and could automatically factor in the required corrections. He insisted, however, that single–observer range-finders and spotting could not determine the required initial range data with sufficient accuracy, and that account would have to be taken of the fact that the change of range rate would most likely be changing continuously. Accurate long-range gunnery, Pollen thus concluded, would require a two–observer range-finding system to obtain the initial range and bearing data, a true–course plotter to determine the target's course and speed, a "change of range machine" that would calculate the range and bearing not by "a fixed amount per minute but the actual amount of change," and a mechanism that computed and added in the various correction factors.

Pollen also criticized the existing service practice of placing the range-finder, dumaresq, and Vickers Clock together in a mast-top position. While the situation of the observing and calculating instruments and their operators together with the spotter enabled the entire fire control team to communicate easily in face to face conversation, Pollen pointed out that such an exposed and unarmoured arrangement was highly vulnerable to enemy fire. He thus suggested that the observation instruments be placed on the main deck or superstructure, where they could be protected by armour shields, and that the plotting and calculating instruments be housed behind the armoured belt and beneath the armoured deck, an arrangement that was to be made possible by the extensive use of electrical communications. The accuracy of the proposed system was presumably to be such that a spotting position in the mast-top would be, if not unnecessary, at least of greatly reduced importance.[74]

In January 1905, Pollen circulated his print, and approached the Admiralty with an offer to supply his instruments for trial if paid just for his material costs, estimated to be less than £1,000,[75] a figure that might have been suggested by the Admiralty in response to Pollen's letter of the previous month. In any case, Pollen's proposal was considered in February by Captain John Jellicoe, who in that month replaced Captain Barry as Director of Naval Ordnance. At this time, a combination of circumstances favored Pollen. In the first place, Jellicoe's appointment was attributable, in part, to his favorable attitude towards gunnery innovation.[76] In the second place, Jellicoe was then involved in the discussions concerning the impact of fire control on capital ship characteristics in the Committee on Designs, which were centered on the issue of long-range firing.[77] And finally, Jellicoe was advised on matters of range-finding by Captain Edward W. Harding, Royal Marine Artillery, a recognized authority on fire control and a member of the late special committee that had interviewed Pollen in December 1904, who was convinced both of the soundness of Pollen's understanding of the fire control problem as a whole and of the practicability of Pollen's proposed solution.[78]

In February 1905, the naval members of the late special committee reversed the negative conclusions of their earlier report after inspecting a prototype bearing observation unit that had been built by Linotype Company engineers, who had taken account of criticisms that had been made by the committee in December. Meetings between Jellicoe and Pollen then led to preliminary experiments with the inventor's bearing observation instruments in the old armoured cruiser *Narcissus* on 20 March 1905 at the inventor's expense. The trials were supervised by Harding,[79] who wrote a highly favorable report on 3 April 1905,[80] after which serious negotiations ensued.[81]

By this time Harold Isherwood had produced preliminary sketches of the change of range machine.[82] He had not, however, been able to develop a practicable design of the continuously running gyroscope required to correct bearing observations against yaw.[83] Pollen's proposal of terms thus included a request for funds to perfect the gyroscope. But the Ordnance Department insisted that yaw would not be a significant factor, and categorically refused to provide support for the project. Pollen nevertheless decided to proceed to a trial without the gyroscope, in the hope that even a partially successful demonstration would lead to an Admiralty commitment to develop his system completely.[84] On 17 April 1905, he thus offered to supply prototypes of the observing and plotting instruments, and the change of range machine, in return for payments of £1,500 for manufacturing costs, £2,000 for the expenses that he had incurred in the preceding four years developing the designs of those elements of his system that were to be tried, and £1,000 for his services up to and including the trial period.[85] On 3 May 1905, Pollen was informed that his terms would be granted.[86]

Pollen remained highly skeptical of the practicability of true–course plotting without bearings that were corrected by gyroscope against yaw, and in May 1905 consulted Percy Scott on the matter when he attended the fleet gun calibration trials off the south coast of Ireland in Bantry Bay. Scott had preferred ranging on the fall of shot over ranging from computations of the change of range[87] but that March had been persuaded by Jellicoe to support the idea of giving Pollen's system a trial.[88] He could suggest nothing helpful, however, in regard to bearings, though his conversations with Pollen appear to have been cordial.[89] On his return from Bantry Bay, Pollen resubmitted the problem of determining a target's position relative to that of the firing ship to his engineers at the Linotype Company in the hope that a method that did not require bearings could be formulated. The mathematical analysis of his employees conclusively demonstrated, however, that bearings in conjunction with ranges were a prerequisite to any calculation of the target's speed and course.[90] It was perhaps after this point in 1905, that Pollen commissioned Mark Barr to develop an electrically driven gyroscope, an undertaking that was not to be abandoned in the absence of success until 1911.[91]

At some point after the agreement with the Admiralty in May, but before the start of the trials in September, Pollen wrote a pamphlet entitled *A.C.: A Postscript*, the initials standing for "aim correction," the term preferred by the author to "fire control," while the sub-title referred to his previous print, *Fire Control and Long Range Firing*. In this work, Pollen modified his earlier views by expanding his list of ballistical correction factors that would have to be applied to calculated ranges and bearings. In answer to those such as Percy Scott who had believed that spotting would be an adequate method of range-finding, Pollen pointed out that account had to be taken not only of the distance by which the last salvo missed, but also of the change in range that would occur during the time interval between the last salvo and the next, a task of such complexity that hitting by means of spotting would be reduced to the level of mere chance. And in reply to Jellicoe's criticism of 14 April 1905 that a two-observer system positioned on the longitudinal axis of the ship could not be trained on targets directly ahead,[92] Pollen questioned the tactical validity of the "end-on" approach.[93] He concluded by recommending the replacement of the 12-inch by the 13.5-inch gun in the interests of achieving greater accuracy at long range and greater penetrating power, and the increase of deck armour at the expense of vertical armour in order to resist the effects of plunging fire that would occur when ranges were long and shell trajectories were, as a consequence, curved.[94]

By September 1905, the observing and plotting instruments were ready for trial. The telescope units were manufactured by the firm of Thomas Cooke & Sons of York, while the remaining range-finder mechanisms and the plotter were built by the Linotype Company.[95] Isherwood, however, had not been able to translate his preliminary sketches of the change of range machine into a fully practicable working design,[96] and Pollen's costs on the observing and plotting instruments were far higher than he had expected. The agreement with the Admiralty had made provision for a delay in the delivery of the change of range machine, and its manufacture was, therefore, suspended, pending the outcome of the trials of the observing and plotting instruments.[97]

The range-finding system consisted of two telescope units that were to be separated by the approximately 150-foot length of a battleship's superstructure, an electrical bearing transmission mechanism and a range-from-bearings calculator. When the telescope units were each trained on the target, their angles of bearing were to be electrically recorded as rapidly as possible; the transmitting mechanism was designed to send to the calculator only those bearings from the two units that had been observed simultaneously; the calculator would then automatically compute the range. The plotter consisted of a table with rollers that moved a long sheet of paper over the table surface, above which was positioned a swinging arm with an adjustable length, at whose base was fixed a pencil that was permanently depressed to mark the paper, and at whose end was fixed a pencil that marked the paper only when depressed by hand. The plot was produced by moving the paper at a speed corresponding to that of the firing ship, setting by hand the angle of the arm with the target bearing and its length with the simultaneously observed range and depressing the pencil at the end of the arm to mark the paper once for each setting of the arm. A straight line drawn through a succession of such marks would average the data and depict the movement of the target, while the pencil at the base of the arm drew a line that depicted the movement of the firing ship; the resulting scale picture could then be measured with special rulers and a protractor to determine the target's course and speed, and range from the firing ship.[98]

On 25 September 1905 the Admiralty appointed a committee under the presidency of Vice-Admiral Alfred A. Chase-Parr to carry out the trials.[99] The committee was instructed to evaluate the accuracy of range-taking with the two-observer range-finder, the accuracy of range-taking off the plot, the capacity of the range-finder to measure the distance to the fall of shot, the accuracy of course and speed data produced by the plot, the rapidity with which the system of range-finding and plotting could be made to function, and the extent to which the instruments were affected by gun blast and exposure to sea-going conditions.[100] Pollen's instruments were installed at Portsmouth in the battleship *Jupiter* in September and October. Many changes had to be made in the experimental gear before a satisfactory set-up was achieved,[101] and thus preliminary experiments with a small boat were carried out in port from 25 September through 17 November. The sea-going trials began in *Jupiter* on 18 November and continued until 19 January 1906.[102] In December, Pollen's commitment to supervise the trials in person required his continued presence on board *Jupiter*, and as a consequence he at this time resigned his executive position of Managing Director of the Linotype Company, although he remained connected to the firm as a director,[103] while Isherwood left the Linotype Company to devote all of his attention to the fire control problem as an employee of Pollen.[104]

The trials revealed four major technical problems. In the first place, the faulty design of the bearings transmission mechanism resulted in the frequent sending of non-simultaneous bearings to the calculator, which thus computed ranges that were inaccurate.[105] Secondly, the manual manipulation of the plotting arm and pencil proved to be too slow, and too liable to human error.[106] Thirdly, when the ship yawed a great deal due to heavy winter seas, there were many instances when the two telescopes could not be trained through a wide enough arc to keep the target continuously in sight, which greatly reduced the number of bearing observations that could be made in a given time.[107] But the most serious problem was posed, as Pollen had feared, by the effect of yaw on the bearing observations required for the plot. While valid ranges could be calculated from yaw-affected bearings—so long as they were taken simultaneously—a satisfactory plot could not be obtained without bearings that were nearly perfectly accurate with respect to the mean course-line travel of the ship—that is to say, without bearings that were yaw-free.

After discovering that bearings taken with a magnetic compass were also critically affected by yaw, and thus were useless even for the sake of experiment,[108] Pollen improvised a system of gyroscopic correction. A Whitehead gyroscope of the type used in torpedoes was made to work a dial that would indicate the extent of deviations from mean course. As bearings were received, they were corrected by the amount indicated on the dial before being plotted with the simultaneously observed range. The spring-wound drive of the Whitehead device limited plotting runs to only four minutes, but this was long enough to demonstrate that plotting was feasible if gyroscopically corrected bearings could be provided.[109] And while the trials in *Jupiter* were still in progress, Pollen was informed that both Barr & Stroud, and Thomas Cooke & Sons, had developed the more efficient single-observer range-finders described earlier in this chapter, and that Isherwood, who probably had left the Linotype Company in December with Pollen to devote his full attention to naval gunnery, had come up with a method of providing continuous gyroscopic correction.[110]

At the end of January, Pollen thus cancelled further trials in *Jupiter* and began to rework his system in light of the latest technical developments.[111] On 2 February 1906, he wrote to Chase-Parr and recommended that the two-observer range-finding system should be replaced by one of the new model single-observer instruments that would soon be available, at least until the problems with the train of the bearing telescopes and the faulty transmitting mechanism could be overcome, which he warned "must take some little time." Although a 9-foot or 10-foot base single-observer instrument would not be as accurate as a perfected 150-foot base two-observer system, Pollen noted that the few successful plotting runs in *Jupiter* had indicated that a certain amount of range error, so long as it was constant, and given accurate bearings, would not affect the integrity of the course and speed measurements from the plot. He also informed Chase-Parr that he had devised a mechanism that would record the bearing of the range-finder line of sight relative to the keel line of the ship, and transmit that bearing simultaneously with each range observation.[112]

At this time Pollen was approached by representatives of the navies of France and the United States, who were interested in learning more about his work.[113] The inventor was determined, however, to have his system developed for the exclusive use of the Royal Navy, and thus refused the offers made to him. On 13 February, Pollen wrote to Jellicoe to describe the new combination range-finder and bearing-indicator.[114] A copy of this letter was sent to Lord Tweedmouth, the new First Lord, on 14 February, along with a covering letter in which Pollen suggested that a British monopoly of his perfected system would result in great savings in naval expenditure. "Supposing we are the first power to develop long range hitting at a moving target," he argued,

> We can then gradually reconstitute our Fleet, in view of the knowledge we should have. We might well keep the secret for 5 or 6 years. In that time we should have constructed probably twenty armoured ships in the light of the tactical requirements of our new accomplishment. The revolution in naval fighting would then have cost us nothing. But if we are to suppose that other powers are to acquire the art of long range hitting, either before us or concurrently with us, then the requirements of naval supremacy will make it necessary for us to build with far greater rapidity and in much greater numbers.[115]

The report of Chase-Parr's committee, which was considered by the Board of Admiralty in March 1906,[116] was unfavorable, the committee attributing the failure of Pollen's system to the training difficulties with the telescopes, electrical difficulties and the lack of a continuous-running gyroscope. The committee report also noted that attempts to range the fall of shot were unsuccessful.[117] The Admiralty thus informed Pollen on 22 March that they were "not prepared to incur any further expenditure in the development of the two observer Range-finding System," but encouraged the inventor to submit his proposals for a method of "ascertaining with accuracy the rate of change of range of a moving object in connection with a single observer range-finder."[118] In his response of 27 March 1906, Pollen maintained that the technical shortcomings revealed by the trials could be easily overcome, described his gyroscope proposals in detail, explained the circumstances which had defeated efforts to determine the fall of shot while arguing that failure in this matter was of little significance, and noted that his financial losses stemming from the experiments thus far amounted to over £1,300.[119]

Pollen provided Jellicoe with sketches of his "one-observer system of Aim Correction" in a meeting on 4 April.[120] Over the course of the next two and a half months, Pollen and Isherwood worked out detailed designs, drafts of which were explained to Jellicoe in personal interviews as they were completed.[121] Continuous gyroscopic action was to be achieved through the use of two gyroscopes, which were to work in alternation. A blast of compressed air would activate one of the gyroscopes, which would then be engaged to provide bearing correction. Before it lost sufficient speed to compromise the correction process, the second gyroscope would be set into motion by a blast of compressed air and instantaneously engaged while the first gyroscope was disengaged. The disengaged gyroscope would then be reactivated by a blast of compressed air and reengaged when the engaged gyroscope had run its turn, the process repeating itself continuously.[122]

Two methods of gyroscopically correcting bearings were developed. In the first, the gyroscope mechanism was to be incorporated into the plotter, where the bearings would be corrected after they had been observed by, recorded at and transmitted from, the observing instrument. In the second, the gyroscope mechanism controlled a motor that stabilized the range-finder and bearing indicator mounting against yaw by altering its train, an action that would both correct the bearings as they were being observed and relieve the range-taker of the task of constantly re-laying his instrument. The range-taker's difficulties were to be further reduced by improvements to the connection between the roller and the moving prism, which would make it easier to obtain a satisfactory "cut," and the replacement of the range-finder range scale that had to be read with an electrical mechanism, which enabled the range-taker to transmit the range indicated by a "cut," and the bearing of the moment as well, to the plotter by simply pressing a button. The plotter was improved—in light of the difficulties experienced with manual operations during the *Jupiter* trials— by the design of powered devices that automatically translated the electric range and bearing signals from the observing instrument into settings on the moving arm, and depressed the marker.[123] The design of the change of range machine was essentially the same as that of the device that was delivered to the Director of Naval Ordnance on 14 May in fulfillment of obligations contracted the year before,[124] but was provided with a mechanical scheme of correcting the computed ranges and bearings for ballistical factors, and the change of range and bearing during the time of flight of the projectile.[125]

In May 1906, while his system was being redesigned, Pollen collected portions of the texts of six letters which he had written between December 1905 and May 1906—four of which were addressed to an anonymous admiral, one to an unnamed captain, and one to Vice-Admiral Chase-Parr—and had them printed in a pamphlet entitled *Extracts from Letters Addressed to Various Correspondents in the Royal Navy principally from H.M.S. "Jupiter"*. In this work, Pollen criticized the existing state of gunnery in the Royal Navy, summarized the experience of the trials in *Jupiter*, advanced the technical arguments in favor of his mechanized approach to fire control and discussed the advantages of possessing a monopoly of long-range hitting.

The ideas about capital ship design, tactics and strategy, and their interrelationship, that Pollen put forward in the *Jupiter Letters* were strikingly similar to those of Fisher. He maintained that a British monopoly of long-range hitting would mean that a "numerical superiority in ships will be of very secondary importance" because "no enemy could approach his hitting range without passing through a fire zone of ours which should be impassable."[126] Immunity from hits, in turn, suggested changes in capital ship design. Pollen contended that if the *Dreadnought* strategy had been "to build a ship that no foreign ship could destroy at some critical range, and to arm her so that at and beyond that range her armament would pierce any foreign ship afloat, and engine her so that she could keep that range," then the development of a viable system of fire control must open the way to further changes in capital ship design that would enable Britain to "out-'Dreadnought' the 'Dreadnought'."[127] The new designs, he suggested, should be armed with 13.5-inch rather than 12-inch guns, and have "armour less vertical, more horizontal."[128] "But beyond everything," Pollen insisted, "you must have speed—for this is the determining factor both in choosing an initial range, and maintaining it with the minimum of change. Tactically, it is second in importance only to technical perfection in the use of guns. Protection—i.e., armour—is a bad third."[129]

Pollen argued that a British monopoly of long-range fire control—by vastly improving the capabilities of existing ships, and by allowing the design of a new generation of capital ships superior to those of any foreign fleet—would, in turn, both secure naval supremacy and lead to a reduction in naval expenditure. "It would pay a hundred times over," Pollen thus concluded,

> to cut the new building programme in half, and devote a couple of millions a year to nothing but practice, experiments, instruments—anything to raise the average hitting capacity of the 200 big guns we have already, rather than swell the list of guns that cannot hit at all.

Suppose you spend seven or eight millions a year to get five more "Dread-nought's." Well, you have 40 more 12in. [*sic*] guns available for your next battle. But if you spend a fifth of this and can treble the efficiency of all the guns you have, you gain the equivalent of 600 new guns.

That will be a piece of new construction worth having; a secret worth working for, and finding; and once found, better worth guarding than any secrets of design that the womb of the pregnant future may conceal. [130]

Pollen sent copies of his print to a number of naval officers, including Fisher. [131] On 8 June, Pollen submitted drawings of the Isherwood gyro-scope mechanism, along with extracts from a report that endorsed the design, which Pollen had commissioned from Charles Vernon Boys, one of England's leading applied physicists and an expert on gyroscopes. [132] On 18 June, Pollen sent the Admiralty a final collection of general arrangement drawings of his system. In his covering letter, he noted that the detailed design of the mechanisms for gyroscope correction at either the range-finder or the plot had yet to be worked out, but that the drawings and descriptions as they stood were "sufficient for a judgement to be formed as to the probability of this system giving useful results, and should enable a decision to be come to as to the advisability of any further trial being made, and consequently secrecy being maintained." [133] Pollen then expressed his intention to develop his system with private capital for sale abroad in the event that the Admiralty declined to develop it in secret, and thus asked that a decision be reached quickly in order to allow him, in the case of a refusal, to file for foreign patents at the earliest possible date. [134]

A three man committee headed by Jellicoe evaluated the submissions [135] and, in addition, Jellicoe sought the advice of the Inspector of Target Practice (Percy Scott) and his staff, the captain and staff of H.M.S. *Excellent*, the Whale Island Experimental Staff, the Director of Naval Intelligence, and the captain and staff of the War College. [136] In late June a conference of the committee and at least some of the naval gunnery experts that had been consulted concluded that a trial of Pollen's revised system was justified. "I was delighted," wrote Harding to Pollen on 29 June 1906,

when the conference on Tuesday decided strongly in favour of a trial of the new A.C.: much writing and talking has had its effect at last: Crooke [*sic*] is quite a tower of strength as although he is never a wild enthusiast, he always sees a point and his opinion is that "plotting" is the only scientific way of finding speed and course. He was rather against secrecy, as his opinion [is] that nothing can be kept secret: however he was overruled in that: as I said that even if we couldn't always keep it secret, the system embodied a fundamental principle rather than a matter of detail and was bound to lead to tremendous and radical developments in our ideas of gunnery and naval tactics, so that even a period of secrecy meant a very great start: that view was accepted, [sic] Percy Scott turned round and said to me "that is exactly the point I was going to make." [137]

Backed by the leading gunnery experts of the navy, Jellicoe advised Rear-Admiral Sir Henry B. Jackson, the Controller and his immediate superior, that it would be worth acquiring the secrecy rights to the system and funding the costs of prototypes for trial. But Jackson, who had been involved with the development of gyroscopes for torpedoes, where difficulties had been overcome only after great effort, was highly skeptical of the claim that the Pollen-Isherwood gyroscope mechanism—upon which the success of the entire Pollen fire control system depended—could be made to work without prolonged and prohibitively expensive development. He refused, therefore, to agree to the proposal. Jellicoe thus asked Pollen whether or not the feasibility of plotting could be proved using a single-observer range-finder, a magnetic compass, and a manual plotting table, in the hope that a success with cheap extemporized equipment would persuade Jackson to support a more ambitious experiment.[138] But Pollen rejected such a plan, citing the lessons of the *Jupiter* trials, which had clearly shown that no successful demonstration could be made without the proper instruments.[139]

Jellicoe concurred,[140] and turned to the alternative of lowering initial costs by reducing the system to a bare minimum. Because the change of range machine would be of little use without a practicable means of obtaining accurate data to set it, the decision was again made to put off its development until after the trials of the observing and plotting instruments were successful. For the sake of experiment, Pollen suggested that the place of the change of range machine could be taken by a dumaresq whose target bearing setting was stabilized against yaw by a gyroscope. Pollen and Harding discussed the possibility of further reducing expenses by replacing the true-course with a virtual-course plot. This solution was rejected as offering almost nothing in the way of economy. The two then considered the alternative of plotting separate range and bearing rates, presumably for conversion into course and speed readings via a dumaresq "cross-cut."[141] This approach was also dismissed on the grounds that savings would be small—not more than a few hundred pounds (£s)—while the disadvantages in practice would be considerable. These were, that when the change of range rate was altering rapidly, coincidence range-finders could not be made to take ranges quickly enough to provide the near continuous stream of data that was required, and that frequent interruptions in the observations of ranges and bearings by smoke, haze, mist or shell splashes would lead to critical errors in the rate plots.[142]

But projected costs were sufficiently reduced by the limitation of the trials to a test of the plotting and observing instruments, that Harding was able to persuade Jackson to lay aside his misgivings for the moment,[143] and on 7 August 1906 the Board of Admiralty, minus Fisher and Vice-Admiral Sir Charles C. Drury, the Second Sea Lord, decided to open negotiations with Pollen for the rights to his system.[144] Thus on 8 August 1906 Pollen was invited to attend a conference the next day at the Admiralty building to discuss terms.[145] On 9 August, as requested, Pollen met with Jackson, Jellicoe, Harding, two members of the Contract Department and the Controller's private secretary, who kept detailed minutes.

The Admiralty officials first asked Pollen to name an amount that he would accept in return for the supply of his observing and plotting instruments for trial, and a secrecy agreement that would hold until the outcome of the trial was decided. Pollen stated a figure of £8,000—£3,400 for costs, £1,000 for profit and £3,600 for losses incurred during the period 1902-1906 on gyroscope development[146] and the *Jupiter* trials.[147] Pollen then asked that, in the event of a successful trial and a decision in favor of acquiring the system for the exclusive use of the Royal Navy, he be guaranteed a minimum order to equip 12 ships a year for five years and that he be paid a royalty on each set of instruments supplied plus a royalty for every year that his equipment was in service—terms that were roughly calculated to amount to at least £300,000 spread over a 15 year interval. He insisted, moreover, that his rights over his system should extend beyond the technical provisions of his patents, which would require the Admiralty to pay infringement penalties if any devices working on the same principles, though not technically identical, were put into service.[148]

Pollen was told that the Admiralty should not have to pay for his earlier losses, particularly because the *Jupiter* trials had been unsuccessful, and was offered £4,500 for new instruments and his services only. No formal position was taken on the monopoly price question, "though half Mr. Pollen's figures was casually mentioned as more nearly approaching reasonableness." In the course of discussion, the Admiralty officials pointed out that "inventors usually have to perfect their inventions at their own expense, or else grant very favorable terms to others who will find the money for them"; that the navy already had a good system of fire control that was in the process of improvement, "and that his system was not therefore of such value to use in H.M. Navy as it might conceivably be to other Navies not so well equipped at present"; that it was "doubtful" that the extension of Pollen's rights beyond his patents could be admitted and that in view of the financial and technical assistance that he had received from the navy in the past and would have to receive in the future "he ought to be prepared to offer terms, both for trial and acquisition, which the Admiralty would accept."[149]

In reply, Pollen argued that his terms had been formulated with the unperfected state of his system taken into account; that if the Admiralty would not accept his terms there were others that would; that he considered "that the value of a ship as a fighting unit was about doubled by having this apparatus, hence his large ideas of its worth"; and that the price that he asked was only just "in consideration of his giving up all his foreign markets, from which he thinks he could obtain much more if he be left free to do so." Pollen thus refused the Admiralty's counter-proposals, and the meeting ended in deadlock.[150]

After a meeting with Lord Tweedmouth, the First Lord, the next day, on 10 August Pollen wrote to the Admiralty and offered to supply trial observing and plotting instruments for an immediate payment of £6,500. The £1,500 reduction from the original estimate was apparently made acceptable by a separate agreement that allowed Pollen £800 for his earlier losses that were due to modifications in the equipment for the *Jupiter* trials that had been requested by the Admiralty,[151] and by a reduction of Pollen's profit margin to £300, a sum which the inventor warned left "practically no cover for the risk of the expenses exceeding the estimate." Pollen continued to insist that his monopoly terms were justified, but offered to submit the question to arbitration, subject to the restrictions that he be allowed to resume the foreign rights to his system if the awarded sum was less than half, and the British rights also if the award was less than a quarter, of the terms that he had first asked. And he again requested that any agreement would require the Admiralty not to employ another system of taking ranges and bearings simultaneously for use in conjunction with a gyroscopically corrected plot "whether in detail exactly as I have claimed in my patents or not, except subject to agreement with me, as if the method actually used were a method validly protected by my patents." Such a clause, Pollen explained, was necessary since modifications in the course of his system's development might mean that "in years to come the fact that the invention is mine may not seem so obvious."[152]

The Admiralty, in its reply to Pollen's letter on 21 August, agreed to the immediate payment of £6,500 for the observing and plotting instruments; further negotiations of the monopoly payment question subject to arbitration as suggested by Pollen, but with a maximum limit of £90,000; and the recognition of his claim to be the sole inventor of a system of using simultaneously observed ranges and bearings in conjunction with a gyroscopically corrected plot. The Admiralty refused, however, to bind themselves not to "employ any such system except subject to agreement with you."[153]

In his response to the Admiralty of 22 August, Pollen refused to agree to the arbitration limit of £90,000 and refuted charges made at the conference that his association with the navy had enabled and would enable him to gain knowledge of service fire control methods that could be sold to foreign navies. With regard to the question of what he had learned from the existing service system of fire control, he observed that its "real and incommunicable value" did "not lie in its somewhat threadbare secrets, but in the amazing skill, experience, and resourcefulness of the officers engaged in it, which enables them to triumph over inferior material." In answer to the suggestion made at the conference that he required immediate Admiralty financial backing to proceed with the development of his system, Pollen noted that he had

arranged for a revolving and rocking turntable to be made for testing my system on shore before its installation on shipboard. There is no difficulty whatever in setting up both range finder and charting table on a yawing platform—varying the extent and speed of movement—trying the instruments at all bearings and combinations of pitch and roll—keeping an exact measure of all the regular movements, and testing the efficiency of the correcting mechanism, and thus being able to demonstrate conclusively what their performance at sea will be. Whether the Admiralty see fit to give an order now or not, I intend that these shore trials shall be exhaustively made before the instruments are sent to sea. They will be ready in December—and these tests will be carried on through January and February until every imperfection is removed, and the performances of the system are not only satisfactory but constant.[154]

In a letter of 23 August 1906 Pollen presented the Admiralty with an estimate of the price that he would charge for production models of his observing and plotting instruments, and suggested that the purchase of a certain number of units per annum at an agreed price, which would spread payments over a number of years, might be preferable to the lump sum purchase of his rights over his system.[155] On 24 August, he wrote to the Admiralty to insist that in so far as any agreement that involved the sale of his rights over his system was concerned, the terms would have to provide for a royalty of £120,000, half of which was to be paid upon the decision to adopt his system and the balance in two installments of £30,000 each within two years, and a manufacturing agreement that allowed him a fair commercial profit.[156] And on 27 August, he wrote to Tweedmouth to explain his position. In his 13 page double-spaced typed letter, Pollen justified his monopoly price not only in terms of the decisive influence his system was likely to have in any war, "but because the development it will make inevitable in material and methods must be so radical that it will be of prime financial importance that their control shall remain with this country, and the ruinous expenditure avoided that must follow from the competitive pressure the possession of the system by rival powers would entail." "What I have to sell is not instruments," he then argued in defence of his stipulation that the Admiralty recognize that his rights as an inventor extended beyond his patents,

> but a system, the embodiment of certain laws of gunnery which I have been the first to codify. My instruments as at present designed will no doubt soon be superseded by others that embody the essential features of my system more completely. The monopoly of instruments is only incidental. It is the knowledge of the system which they make workable, and the exclusive knowledge of it, to which high, possibly supreme, value attaches.[157]

In his acknowledgement of 29 August, which Tweedmouth apparently wrote before reading Pollen's very long letter, the First Lord warned the inventor that "to me you seem altogether [to] overrate the present value of the ideas[,] good [,] but incomplete which you are offering to the Admiralty."[158] Tweedmouth, however, reconsidered his views within a few days and on 3 September, wrote to Pollen to say that

> I am most interested in your range and course finding experiments,[159] thoroughly appreciate how invaluable a successful result from them would prove, most anxious they should succeed, and that our Navy should reap the full advantage; . . . But potential values are hard things to assess, and so I and my advisers have to be cautious, though it does seem to me our offer was a liberal one.

"My doubt about your present line is," Tweedmouth then wrote in reference to Pollen's letter of 22 August, in which he had informed the Admiralty of his intention to test his equipment on land by means of a moving platform, "not conducting the experiments on a ship at sea where the practice has at last to take place."[160]

In Pollen's reply of 7 September, the inventor maintained that objections on the grounds of the difficulties of assessment were met by his willingness to submit the question of the value of his system to arbitration after trials had proved its practicability, and that the factory tests of his equipment on land were only meant as a preliminary to full-scale trials at sea. Pollen concluded by observing that

> the real difficulty of the position is that everybody at the Admiralty is so much overworked that no one of authority can give connected attention to the *whole* negotiation; and, following logically from this, everyone dreads having to make out a case to the Treasury for a very unusual transaction, when the reasons for the transaction being unusual are only incompletely grasped.
>
> I never have had, and have not now, the slightest doubt but that ultimately the business arrangements that I have proposed will be understood to be just as moderate and reasonable as the technical proposals I have made are at last admitted to be both logical and important. [161]

Harding, in the meanwhile, had written a "Memorandum upon the Professional and Financial Value of the A.C. System," in which he established the military requirements for, and technical arguments in favor of, the Pollen system, and answered the business objections that had been raised by the scheme's opponents. In his covering letter to Jellicoe of 4 September 1906, Harding wrote that his intention was to present "a record of the considerations affecting the Admiralty point of view, and to define clearly and beyond future criticism the basis upon which the Admiralty offer [to the inventor for monopoly] is calculated." "It is assumed throughout the inquiry," he added, "that a trial has been recommended, because there appears a reasonable probability of success . . ."[162] "I have got out," Harding wrote less formally to Pollen on the same day, "a regular snorter for the D.N.O., if [*sic*] it doesn't convince him nothing will!"[163]

Harding began his report by stating the Admiralty's requirements for a system of long-range fire control. The chief tactical requirements were "first that the individual ship should be able to envelope any required target in a heavy and continuous stream of hits up to extreme ranges, and secondly that a group of ships should be able to envelope simultaneously a given target with such a stream of hits, without material diminution of accuracy of the fire of the individual ship." The technical requirement determined by the above tactical requirements was "primarily accurate and continuous knowledge of the Gun Range of any and all possible targets," the "Gun Range" being here defined as the sum of the actual, or "Geometric," range at the moment of firing plus the change of range that occurred during the time of flight of the projectile.

Harding pointed out that because optical instruments could not give the geometric range with sufficient accuracy and because the determination of the change of range could be based upon nothing more than a guessed estimate of the target's course and speed, the existing system of finding the gun range depended mainly upon the observation of the fall of shot. But it was practically impossible, he noted, to range on the fall of shot when more than one ship was firing on the target because the gunners of one vessel could not distinguish their shell splashes from those caused by the firing of the other engaged ships, preventing the effective employment of concentration of fire tactics. Harding thus insisted upon reducing the reliance on ranging on the fall of shot to "the lowest possible limits" through the development of a system of precisely measuring the factors that determined the gun range. Observed data, he contended, would have to be plotted in some form, and then averaged to neutralize the errors of individual readings. Harding then considered methods of plotting data. He again rejected the separate range and bearing rate plots approach as "obviously unsatisfactory," choosing instead the "more correct method" of a plot of simultaneously observed ranges and bearings from which the target's course and speed could be measured, his reasons being essentially those discussed earlier with Pollen.

Harding was convinced that Pollen's observing and plotting instruments would be capable of providing the precisely accurate target course and speed data that he believed would be required by any practicable system of long-range fire control. Pollen's approach, he maintained, marked a "great advance in principle" because it recognized the "necessity for accurate data and substituted a system of exact observation for one of merely personal estimation." "The very simplicity of the solution," Harding argued,

> showing as it does the essential complexity of the problem, tends to strengthen the conviction that in principle it is the final solution. In the present state of our knowledge it is impossible to affirm that there is any simpler or more practical solution of the Rangefinding problem and therefore it must be regarded as the only solution. Obviously if the development of the requisite mechanism is hampered by the necessity of avoiding infringement of the original patents, a method of obtaining the same results will be extremely difficult.

The "national and professional importance" of the Pollen system, Harding then explained,

> lies in the fact that it is the only method by which a factor essential to the further development of Naval Artillery technique can be supplied. Its value is further enhanced when is considered the effect of its reaction upon Tactical thought and upon the efficiency of guns and gun appliances.
>
> (The effect of the introduction of recent Fire Control methods is a measure of the technical developments which may be expected.)
>
> Moreover by its reaction on Tactical thought, to the extent that it induces the formation of a definite Tactical system based on sound principles and on a definite standard of technical efficiency, it immensely simplifies the problems of Construction and ultimately reacts on Strategical possibilities and methods.
>
> Thus its national value cannot be regarded only from the point of view of ingenious instruments for obtaining even a great advance in Artillery technique but must be looked upon as an essential link in a far reaching chain of development. It is from this point of view that the inventor regards the system and this now explains much of his apparently exaggerated talk as to its value.

But in spite of the uniqueness of the solution required by the range-finding problem and the enormous value of such a solution if found,

Harding argued that the Pollen system was not likely to be discovered by others. "Undoubtedly the idea of plotting the course can occur and has occurred to many," he observed, "but ignorance as to its importance, the obvious difficulties in the way of its successful application and its apparent complexity have deterred would-be inventors from following up the idea." "The problem of making the Range Finder automatically record ranges," Harding noted by way of illustration, "is one that Messrs. Barr and Stroud have hitherto not looked at, nor has the idea been suggested by the great warship building firms." The "necessity for some form of gyroscopic control," he added, "is probably totally unrecognized." All foreign admiralties but the German, Harding believed, had yet to turn their attention to the range-finding problem. In the case of the Germans, who were thought to be "probably the most advanced" of all other naval powers in regard to gunnery, he explained "that a certain effectiveness of technique has been taken for granted, improvements have taken place along obvious lines only and that the tendency has been to devote attention to tactics divorced to a certain extent from technique." Harding thus contended that "the probability of independent anticipation in the ideas and instruments of the A.C. system is exceedingly small, in fact negligible." He was convinced, moreover, that the perfected system's essentials could be kept secret "long enough to enable the reactions of the system upon Artillery Technique and Tactics to take full effect."

Harding then turned to the question of whether or not Pollen's rights over his system should remain uncompromised in the event of post-trial improvements contributed by others. He argued that Pollen's insistence upon the unqualified recognition of his interests in spite of any such post-trial alterations was justified, pointing out that "the improvements in details of the mechanism which might be possible are comparatively immaterial" because the success of the trials had to be "practically absolute" to justify the purchase of monopoly in the first place. In any case, Harding maintained, Pollen was the party best suited by talent and temperament to develop the system beyond the successful prototype stage. "Throughout the negotiations," he observed, Pollen had

> laid more stress on the principles involved and their effect on the science of Gunnery, on the *idea* that is to say, than on the details of the mechanism; hence as this is his dominant mental attitude he will naturally use every endeavour to provide the mechanism to work the idea and also to develop in practical form the corollaries of the system. When this attitude of mind is contrasted with that of the majority of firms supplying mechanisms to the Government, the probability of material improvements seems small. The driving force supplied by the endeavour to develop a dominant idea is infinitely greater than mere pride in any mechanism even when spurred by competition. It may be said, then, that no decided advantage is likely to be gained by an attempt to deprive the original inventor of his interest in the matter, and that, if anything, it would be the reverse.

Harding concluded his report with an evaluation of Pollen's monopoly terms. He first explained that the inventor's stipulation that there be

97

a royalty in addition to commercial profit was a practice that was "universally the case" in such matters. Harding secondly defended Pollen's high percentage of profit on each unit to be manufactured, arguing that the large capitalization costs combined with the relatively small numbers of units that were to be produced meant that a substantial unit profit was necessary to ensure that Pollen received a reasonable net profit. And thirdly, Harding refuted the claim that the Admiralty deserved a reduction in the monopoly price in return for having funded the development and trials of the system, contending that the Admiralty's payment of costs was not an action required by the inventor to alleviate the risk of financial loss in the event of failure, "but because the probable success of the invention and its value if successful has justified the attempt to obtain a monopoly and therefore the sum thus spent must be looked upon as an insurance against the possible acquisition of the invention by other powers or as money spent in research . . ."

On the matter of specific financial terms Harding argued that the purchase of Pollen's rights over his system would in the long run cost far less than an agreement to buy instruments. That "developments," he maintained,

> and important developments will follow is morally certain so that it is a question whether it would not be wise policy to pay an apparently inflated value for the system as it is at present, with the certainty that all developments initiated by the inventor would not increase the Royalty cost of the Gunnery system as a whole. In a sense, of course, this procedure would be paying for a problematic increase in the value of the original invention, but it has the advantage that should the increase occur, and it is almost certain to do so, in possibly an inherently expensive form, no additional Royalties are involved and furthermore the principle of paying large lump sums at a time is avoided.

In any case, as Harding had stated previously, the Pollen system would be "of immense national value as a monopoly, and the instruments offered, when their constituents are analyzed, make a large group of patents, so that when the intrinsic value of the System and its probable effect on Naval development are considered together with the value and number of the instruments offered, an apparently large price for the acquisition of the monopoly appears justified."[164]

Harding's paper played a major role in the breaking of the stalemate in the negotiations between Pollen and the Admiralty. Vice-Admiral Sir Charles Drury, the Second Sea Lord, perhaps at the prompting of Tweedmouth, raised the matter with Fisher, who was then on vacation in Carlsbad, Germany, and his communication appears to have contained either the Harding report or a precis of its contents rendered by Jellicoe. "*Pollen's invention is simply priceless,*" Fisher thus informed Tweedmouth on 10 September 1906 from Carlsbad, "and I do hope we may hesitate at nothing to get ITS SOLE USE. We shall NEVER be forgiven hereafter if we do not! Jellicoe's arguments are so cogent and convincing that it's useless my enlarging on them!"[165] Unlike the Admiralty officials who had on 9 August informed Pollen that his inventions were not regarded as being comparable to a weapon of "first class importance" such as the Whitehead torpedo,[166] Fisher had the highest estimation of what was being offered. "The case," he observed on 14 September to Tweedmouth, again from Carlsbad, "is marvelously like the introduction of the Whitehead torpedo. We could have had the absolute monopoly of that wonderful weapon (and Mr. Whitehead body and soul into the bargain!), but the Admiralty of that day haggled over £80,000. But thanks to you, I hope we shan't make such an idiotic mistake over Pollen!"[167]

On 12 September, Pollen had sent a memorandum to the Admiralty that put forward proposals regarding the form of a possible agreement,[168] and on 18 September 1906, the Board of Admiralty agreed to meet Pollen's terms.[169] The official offer, which embodied understandings that had been reached later that same day in a meeting between the inventor and Jellicoe and Edmund Robertson, the Admiralty Parliamentary and Financial Secretary,[170] was made in an Admiralty letter to Pollen dated 21 September 1906. According to this document, Pollen was to receive an immediate payment of £6,500 for trial observation and plotting instruments. To satisfy the Admiralty conditions for complete success, Pollen's equipment would have to "be worked at sea in a ship of war under moderately bad conditions of weather, the ship having a fair motion of pitch, roll and yaw," "to give the change of range of one moving ship observed from another with such degree of accuracy that with an initial range of 8,000 yards, the error does not exceed 80 yards in 3 minutes," all "within two minutes from the commencement of observations, both ships steering a steady course (excluding ordinary yaw), speed not to exceed 16 knots." In the event of a successful trial and an Admiralty decision to adopt the instruments for service, Pollen was to be paid a sum of £100,000 for the rights over his system and for royalties covering the installation of the system in 40 ships and a royalty of £1,000 for each additional ship above the first 40 ships up to a second 40 ships. No royalty payments were to be charged for ships fitted with the system after 80 had been so equipped. And Pollen's right to supply the system to the Admiralty was restricted by a limit on profits of 25 per cent over the cost of manufacture.

Pollen was enjoined to preserve the secrecy of his system, to assign all patents to the government, to refrain from applying for foreign patents, to communicate to the Admiralty any improvements that he might devise in his system and to accept "such further provisions for ensuring the secrecy of the system and the monopoly of the Admiralty as Their Lordships may consider necessary." The Admiralty refused to include the clause that would have prevented the Royal Navy from employing any system of plotting based upon gyroscopically corrected range and bearing data without Pollen's agreement. The inventor's long term rights over his system regardless of alterations were adequately protected, however, by the clause that bound him to give to the Admiralty any improvements that he might devise.[171] This condition had appeared in the agreement of 3 May 1905, and had again been suggested by Pollen after he had been advised by legal counsel that such a provision would set up a collaborative relationship between him and the Admiralty that would, in

99

the language of a later legal analysis of the clause, obligate both parties to act as "a trustee of the interests of the other," the actions of each party being ultimately subject to "the principles governing all fiduciary relations."[172]

There can be little doubt that in September 1906, Fisher acted on Pollen's behalf in the belief that a British monopoly of long-range hitting would enable his lightly protected all-big-gun armoured cruisers to engage even foreign dreadnought battleships with impunity. Fisher may have considered the Pollen factor as early as in January 1905, when he could have been informed of Pollen's work by Lord Kelvin, who was then advising the Committee on Designs on, among other things, fire control instruments.[173] Fisher was given a copy of the *Jupiter Letters* in May 1906; he could hardly have missed Pollen's contention that the adoption of his system would enable British capital ships to hit their targets at ranges at which an opponent could not reply effectively, and that such a capability suggested the construction of vessels of higher speed, heavier fire power and less armour, which would be much superior to the not yet completed *Dreadnought*. In any case, in the fall of 1906, shortly after the question of the development and trial of Pollen's instruments had been settled, Fisher once again declared his preference for the new model armoured cruisers over the new model battleship. "3 'Invincibles' building," he wrote to Tweedmouth on 26 September 1906, "*which vessels (in my opinion) superior to Dreadnoughts.*"[174]

Notes to Chapter 3

1 Peter Padfield, *Guns at Sea* (London: Hugh Evelyn, 1973), p. 160.
2 For the approximate time of flight of projectiles [derived from figures on the muzzle-velocity of projectiles] fired from muzzle-loading guns in the late sailing era, see General Sir Howard Douglas, *A Treatise on Naval Gunnery 1855*, reprint (London: Conway Maritime Press, 1982; 1st edn, 1820; 4th edn, 1855), p. 27.
3 For "horizontal fire," see Padfield, *Guns at Sea*, pp. 121, 132, 138–46.
4 Douglas, *Naval Gunnery*, pp. 410–11.
5 Padfield, *Guns at Sea*, p. 204–6. Although British naval big-gun open sights of the 1880s and 1890s were graduated to over 5,000 and 6,000 yards respectively, their effectiveness at such ranges would have been practically nil because of large angular errors inherent in the open sight system, and the lack of sight calibration, which did not become standard practice in the Royal Navy until 1905. For open sights and angular error, see Philip R. Alger, *The Groundwork of Practical Naval Gunnery: A Study of the Principles of Exterior Ballistics, as Applied to Naval Gunnery and of the Computation and Use of Ballistic and Range Tables*, 2nd edn. (Annapolis, Md.: United States Naval Institute, 1917), p. 251. For calibration, see *PP*, p. 376.
6 Padfield, *Guns at Sea*, p. 211.
7 Douglas, *Naval Gunnery, 1855*, p. 377.
8 See Chapter 2.
9 "Range-finders for Naval Service," in Admiralty, Gunnery Branch, *MRPQ/DNO* (July to December 1889), p. 9, N.L.M.D.

10 "Rangefinder [*sic*] for the Navy—Conditions it should fulfil," in *MRPQ/DNO* (January to June 1891), pp. 255-6, N.L.M.D.
11 "Rangefinder for the Navy," ibid, pp. 158-60.
12 "Naval Range Finders [*sic*].—Appointment of Committee to carry out Trials," in idem., *MRPQ/DNO* (January to June 1892), pp. 75-7.
13 Barr & Stroud, Ltd., *The Principles of Rangefinding together with Descriptive Notes on the Barr & Stroud Rangefinders and their Principal Features*, pamphlet no. 42 (Glasgow and London: by the author, n.d.), p. 41.
14 Great Britain, Admiralty, Gunnery Branch [Commanders Frederic C. Dreyer and C. V. Usborne], *Pollen Aim Corrector System, Part I: Technical History and Technical Comparison with Commander F. C. Dreyer's Fire Control System* (1913) [henceforward cited as Dreyer and Usborne, *Technical History*], pp. 4, 13-7, N.L.M.D.
15 "Barr and Stroud Range Finder.—Particulars of," in idem, *MRPQ/DNO* (January to December 1893), p. 293. For a full discussion of range-finder optics and mechanisms, see Alexander Gleichen, *The Theory of Modern Optical Instruments*, trans. by H. H. Emsley and W. Swaine, 1st edn, (London: HMSO, 1918).
16 For the year of entry into general service of the Barr & Stroud range-finder, see financial accounts in *Controller of Navy's Portion of the Vote*, Vols 1899-1900, N.L.M.D.
17 For the accuracy of the first production Barr & Stroud naval range-finders, see Great Britain, Admiralty, Gunnery Branch, *Handbook for Naval Range-Finders and Mountings: Book I*, (November 1921), Appendix I, "Tables of Approximate Uncertainty of Observation with Range-finders of various Base Lengths and Magnifications, under Favourable Conditions of Observation," pp. 153-6, N.L.M.D.
18 Ibid., p. 16.
19 "Long Range Firing with heavy Guns—Instructions for," in Admiralty, Gunnery Branch, *MRPQ/DNO* (July to December 1903), pp. 145-6, N.L.M.D., and Percy Scott, *Fifty Years in the Royal Navy* (New York: George H. Doran, 1919), pp. 163-5.
20 "A. H. P. Statement to 1911," n.d. but probably 1912, P.P. [henceforward cited as "A. H. P. Statement," P.P.].
21 For times of flight of the projectile of British naval ordnance at various ranges, see Admiralty, Gunnery Branch, *Range Tables for His Majesty's Fleet. 1910* (1911) N.L.M.D.
22 For the dumaresq and Vickers Clock, see Great Britain, Admiralty, *Half-Yearly Summary of Progress in Gunnery*, No. 7 (July 1906), pp. 22-3, N.L.M.D, and *PP*, pp. 371-3.
23 Dreyer and Usborne, *Technical History*, p. 4.
24 Ibid.; Wilfrid Arthur Greene, legal brief: "The Claim of the Argo Company and Mr. Pollen before the Royal Commission" [henceforward cited as Greene, brief], part 2, p. 17; "Notes of a Meeting held at the Admiralty in the Board Room on 9th August 1906," *CCB*, P.P.; "Summary," statement of the Dreyer case for the Royal Commission on Awards to Inventors, p. 5, courtesy of Sir Desmond Dreyer to the author, 1979; and Great Britain, Admiralty, *Half-Yearly Summary of Progress in Gunnery*, No. 7 (July 1906), pp. 15-17, N.L.M.D.
25 For the Annual Prize Firings, the Gunlayer's Test, and Battle Practice, see *NA, 1913*, pp. 311-14, and Scott, *Fifty Years in the Royal Navy*, pp. 189-92.
26 For the elder Pollen, see Anne Pollen, *John Hungerford Pollen 1820-1902* (London: John Murray, 1912).

27 For Arthur Hungerford Pollen's close relations with Blunt and his family, see Elizabeth Longford, *A Pilgrimage of Passion: The Life of Wilfrid Scawen Blunt* (New York: Alfred A. Knopf, 1980).

28 For Spender's references to his friendship with Pollen, see John Alfred Spender, *Life, Journalism and Politics*, 2 Vols (London: Cassell, 1927), Vol. 2, p. 24. For Pollen's correspondence with Spender, see Chapter 6, and Epilogue.

29 Anthony Pollen, *The Great Gunnery Scandal: The Mystery of Jutland* (London: Collins, 1980), p. 20.

30 For a description of the machines manufactured by the Linotype Company, which was the British subsidiary of the Mergenthaler Company, an American firm, see George Iles, *Leading American Inventors* (New York: Henry Holt, 1912), s.v. "Ottmar Mergenthaler," pp. 393–432.

31 In the index of patents at the Patent Office, Pollen's name is associated with no fewer than 29 patents related to printing machines during the period 1903 to 1910.

32 For Arthur Joseph Hungerford Pollen (1866–1937), see obituary in *The Times* (London, 29 January 1937); *Who Was Who, 1929-1940*, s.v. "Pollen, Arthur Joseph Hungerford"; and Anthony Pollen, *Great Gunnery Scandal*.

33 Pollen was to write several accounts of the events of February 1900. The most complete source, however, is to be found in the brief submitted by Wilfrid Arthur Greene, Pollen's attorney to the Royal Commission on Awards to Inventors hearings of 1925. Greene's narrative was, of course, based upon information supplied by Pollen. See Greene, brief, part 2, pp. 1-2, P.P., and also Anthony Pollen, *Great Gunnery Scandal*, p. 20.

34 The British Patent Office index of inventors and their patents lists Archibald Barr of the instrument firm of Barr & Stroud as the co-inventor with Pollen of a range-finding calculator, a patent specification for which was submitted on 18 July 1900 (British Patent 12,952/1900), but which was later withdrawn. The association of Archibald Barr and Pollen was probably an error, the intended reference being Mark Barr.

35 Greene, brief, part 2, pp. 2-3, P.P.

36 Arthur Hungerford Pollen, *The Gun in Battle* (by the author, n.d. [1913]), p. 20, P.P. [*PP*, p. 309].

37 Pollen, *The Gun in Battle*, p. 6.

38 Ibid., and Arthur Hungerford Pollen, *Notes, Etc., on the Ariadne Trials* [not to be confused with a pamphlet of a similar title printed in 1908] (by the author, April 1909), p. 24, P.P. [*PP*, p. 213].

39 Pollen to Kerr, 26 January 1901, P.P. For Kerr's relations with the Pollen family, see Anthony Pollen, *Great Gunnery Scandal*, p. 22.

40 Pollen to Selborne, 4 February 1901, *CCB*, P.P.

41 Pollen to the Admiralty Permanent Secretary, 25 February 1901 [print], and Arthur Hungerford Pollen, *The Pollen System of Telemetry* (by the author, 1901), both in P.P. [*PP*, pp. 8-13, *PST* only].

42 Pollen, *PST*, p. 1 [*PP*, p. 9].

43 W. B. Fawkes to Pollen, 7 February 1901, P.P.

44 Pollen to W. B. Fawkes, 12 February 1901; Fawkes to Pollen, 19 February 1901; Pollen to Fawkes, 20 February 1901, P.P.

45 "Report of Committee on Naval Range Finders" (1892), reprinted in full in Dreyer and Usborne, *Technical History*, pp. 13-17.

46 Untitled, undated printed history probably prepared for the Royal Commission on Awards to Inventors hearings by either Pollen or Greene [henceforward cited as 'Untitled printed history, RCAI'], paragraph 6, P.P.

47 Beresford to Pollen, 17 March 1901, P.P.
48 W. G. Armstrong, Whitworth, & Company, Ltd. to Messrs. The Linotype Company, Ltd., 27 August 1902, P.P.
49 F. E. D. Acland [a consulting engineer] to Pollen, 1, 3, and 15 September 1902, P.P.
50 British patent 6838/1902 (20 March 1902), P.O.L.
51 Untitled printed history, RCAI, paragraph 6, P.P.
52 Greene, brief, part 2, p. 8, P.P.
53 Pollen, *Gun in Battle*, p. 22, P.P. [*PP*, p. 310].
54 Pollen memorandum on two–observer range–finding, 9 May 1904, in Adm. 1/7733, P.R.O., and Great Britain, Admiralty, *Pollen Aim Correction System: General Grounds of Admiralty Policy and Historical Record of Business Negotiations* (February 1913), [henceforward cited as *Record of Business Negotiations*], p. 21, N.L.M.D.
55 Lawrence to Selborne, 24 May, and Lawrence to Selborne, 27 May 1904, in Adm. 1/7733, P.R.O.
56 Barry minute, 31 May 1904, in Adm. 1/7733, P.R.O.
57 List of papers not in Pollen business files, P.P., gives the date 10 June, Pollen to the Admiralty Permanent Secretary, 21 December 1904, P.P. gives the date as 9 June.
58 Pollen to the Admiralty Permanent Secretary, 21 December 1904, P.P.
59 Pollen to Vincent Wilberforce Baddeley, secretary to the First Lord, 5 July 1904, in Adm. 1/7733, P.R.O., and Pollen to the Admiralty Permanent Secretary, 21 December 1904, P.P.
60 Pollen to Selborne, 14 November 1904, in Adm. 1/7733, P.R.O.
61 Arthur Hungerford Pollen, *Memorandum on a Proposed System for Finding Ranges at Sea and Ascertaining the Speed and Course of Any Vessel in Sight* (by the author, n.d. [August or September, 1904]), p. 4, P.P. [*PP*, pp. 17–18].
62 Ibid., pp. 6, 8.
63 Pollen to Baddeley, 24 November 1904, in Adm. 1/7733, P.R.O.
64 W. F. Nicholson to Pollen, 19 November 1904, P.P.
65 The committee members were: Captain Henry F. Oliver and Lieutenant Thomas B. Crease, Royal Navy; Captain Edward W. Harding, Royal Marine Artillery and Captain B. J. W. Locke from the War Office. See typescript "Proof of Evidence of Colonel E. W. Harding, R.M.A.," dated January 1920, paragraph 6, P.P. For the date of the hearing, see Pollen to the Admiralty Permanent Secretary, 21 December 1904, P.P.
66 British patent 23,872/1904 (4 November 1904), P.O.L.
67 *PP*, p. 370.
68 Colonel Edward W. Harding, R.M.A., testimony, in Great Britain, Royal Commission on Awards to Inventors, *Minutes of Proceedings* [henceforward cited as RCAI, *Minutes*], Vol. 9 (1 August 1925), p. 6, P.P.; and British patent 14,305/1906 (22 June 1906), P.O.L. For the delays in submitting patent applications, see Wilfrid Arthur Greene, in RCAI, *Minutes*, Vol. 2 (29 June 1925), p. 22, P.P.
69 For the views of the committee and Pollen's response, see Captain Edward W. Harding, R.M.A. to the Director of Naval Ordnance, "Report on Pollen System of Range Finder" (3 April 1905), P.P.
70 Pollen to the Admiralty Permanent Secretary, 21 December 1904, P.P. For the negotiations of November, 1904, see ibid., and "Proof of Evidence of Colonel E. W. Harding, R.M.A.," paragraph 5, P.P., and *Record of Business Negotiations*, p. 21.

71 Greene, brief, part 2, p. 14, P.P.
72 The Pollen mechanical range generator of 1904 was covered by British patent 595/1906 (9 January 1906), which is not available from the P.O.L.; for references to the patent and descriptions of the device, see Wilfrid Arthur Greene in RCAI, *Minutes*, Vol. 2 (29 June 1925), pp. 21–2, testimony of Arthur Hungerford Pollen in RCAI, *Minutes*, Vol. 9 (1 August 1925), p. 43; and testimony of Harold Isherwood in RCAI, *Minutes*, Vol. 10 (3 August 1925), pp. 104–5, P.P.
73 For Mark Barr's advice on technical matters discussed in this print, see Barr to Pollen, 6 and 15 October 1904, P.P.
74 Arthur Hungerford Pollen, *Fire Control and Long Range Firing: An Essay to define certain principia of Gunnery, and to suggest means for their application* (by the author, n.d. [author's manuscript note: "written in December 1904, 25 copies to various officers in January 1905]), P.P. [*PP*, pp. 23–54].
75 *Record of Business Negotiations*, p. 21.
76 See Admiral Sir John Fisher to Selborne, 29 October 1904, *FGDN*, Vol. 2, pp. 46–7.
77 See Chapter 2.
78 "Proof of Evidence of Colonel E. W. Harding" (January 1920), pp. 3–4, P.P.
79 For a detailed description of the experiments, see Harding to Pollen, 21 March 1905, P.P.
80 Captain Edward W. Harding, R.M.A., to the Director of Naval Ordnance, "Report on Pollen System of Range Finder" (3 April 1905), in P.P.
81 *Record of Business Negotiations*, p. 6.
82 Wilfrid Arthur Greene in RCAI, *Minutes*, Vol. 2 (29 June 1925), pp. 21–2; testimony of Arthur Hungerford Pollen in RCAI, *Minutes*, Vol. 9 (1 August 1925), p. 43; and testimony of Harold Isherwood in RCAI, *Minutes*, Vol. 10 (3 August 1925), pp. 104–5, P.P.
83 For one of Isherwood's experimental designs, see British patent 23,846/1906 (26 October 1906), P.O.L.
84 Greene, brief, part 2, pp. 13–14, P.P.
85 *Record of Business Negotiations*, p. 21. For the exact date of Pollen's offer, see C. I. Thomas (for the Admiralty Permanent Secretary) to Pollen, 3 May 1905, *CCB*, P.P.
86 Ibid. For Pollen's acknowledgement of the Admiralty agreement and the formal contract, see Pollen to the Admiralty Permanent Secretary, 4 May 1906 and draft "Memorandum of Agreement . . ." (n.d.), in P.P.
87 For Scott's views on the dumaresq, see Percy Scott, "Remarks on Long Range Hitting," Lecture (15 December 1903), in "*Gunnery*', a reprint of four lectures of 1902–5, in WH1/65, Arnold White Papers, N.M.M..
88 Harding to Pollen, 21 March 1905, P.P.
89 Greene, brief, part 2, p. 14, P.P.
90 Greene, brief, part 2, pp. 14–15, P.P. For the mathematical analysis, see Harold Isherwood, "On the Relationship of 'Change of Range' to 'Time'," pp. 21–7, in Arthur Hungerford Pollen and Harold Isherwood, *Reflections on an Error of the Day* (by the authors, September 1908), P.P. [not included in *PP*].
91 Greene, brief, part 2, p. 34A, P.P.
92 Jellicoe to Pollen, 14 April 1905, P.P.
93 Pollen observed that "range errors will always greatly exceed deflection errors, and that consequently at any great range the probability of hitting a battleship will always be three times as great if she is end on to the guns than if she is broadside on." At long range, moreover, the shell trajectories would

be curved, exposing the relatively lightly armoured deck along its length. And finally, an end-on, as opposed to an oblique approach that allowed broadside fire, would reduce the number of guns that could be brought to bear on the enemy. See *A.C.*, paragraph 23, P.P. [*PP*, pp. 64–5].

94 Arthur Hungerford Pollen, *A.C.: A Postscript* (by the author, n.d. [1905]), P.P. [*PP*, pp. 55–69].

95 Thomas to Pollen, 3 May 1905, *CCB*, P.P.

96 Wilfrid Arthur Greene in RCAI, *Minutes*, Vol. 2 (29 June 1925), p. 37, and testimony of Harold Isherwood in RCAI, *Minutes*, Vol. 10 (3 August 1925), pp. 104–5, P.P.

97 Thomas to Pollen, 3 May 1905, *CCB*, and Pollen to Tweedmouth, 14 February 1906, P.P.; Pollen, *Gun in Battle*, p. 21, P.P. [*PP*, p. 310] and *Record of Business Negotiations*, pp. 6, 21.

98 See British patent 23,872/1904 (4 November 1904), P.O.L.

99 The members of the "Finding and keeping Ranges at Sea" committee were Vice-Admiral Alfred A. Chase-Parr, Captain Frederick Tower Hamilton (H.M.S. *Excellent*), Captain Herbert A. Warren, Captain Bernard Currey, Lieutenant Ralph Eliot and Commander Francis H. Mitchell, who acted as secretary. See "List of Committees, 1906," Admiralty print (31 December 1906), in Adm. 1/7882, P.R.O.

100 Typescript memorandum: "Instructions for the Committee Appointed to Carry out Trials of 'Aim Corrector' System of Range Finding &c. in H.M.S. 'Jupiter'" (25 September 1905), DRYR 2/1, Dreyer Papers, C.C.

101 Pollen to the Admiralty Permanent Secretary, 27 March 1906, P.P.

102 Log book of H.M.S. *Jupiter* (15 August 1905–20 September 1906), Adm. 53/22479, P.R.O.

103 Pollen to the Admiralty Permanent Secretary, 14 May 1906, P.P., and Anthony Pollen, *Great Gunnery Scandal*, p. 248.

104 Anthony Pollen, *Great Gunnery Scandal*, p. 68

105 Pollen to Chase-Parr, 2 February 1906, in Arthur Hungerford Pollen, *Extracts from Letters addressed to various Correspondents in the Royal Navy principally from H.M.S. "Jupiter"* (henceforward cited as the *Jupiter Letters*) (by the author, [May] 1906), p. 37, P.P.

106 Greene, brief, part 2, pp. 18–19, P.P.

107 Pollen to Beresford, 21 June 1906, p. 5, P.P.

108 Greene, brief, part 2, p. 16, and Wilfrid Arthur Greene in RCAI, *Minutes*, Vol. 1 (22 June 1925), p. 43, P.P.

109 Pollen testimony in RCAI, *Minutes*, Vol. 9 (1 August 1925), p. 45, P.P.

110 Greene, brief, part 2, p. 19, P.P. For Isherwood's system of using two gyroscopes in alternation, see below.

111 Ibid.

112 Pollen to Chase-Parr, 2 February 1906, in *Jupiter Letters*, P.P. [*PP*, pp. 87–92].

113 Pollen to Admiral Sir Arthur Knyvet Wilson, 18 December 1907, P.P.

114 Pollen to Jellicoe extract, 13 February 1906, in RCAI, *Minutes*, Vol. 9 (1 August 1925), pp. 12–13, P.P.

115 Pollen to Tweedmouth, 14 February 1906, P.P.

116 For the month in which the report was considered by the Board of Admiralty, see Admiralty Permanent Secretary to Pollen, 22 March 1906, P.P. The only meeting of the Board in March 1906 took place on the 13th, for which see *Board Minutes* [Admiralty] 1906, Adm. 167/40, P.R.O.

117 "Pollen Aim-Correction System: Extracts from report of Committee" (March 1906), P.P.

118 Admiralty Permanent Secretary to Pollen, 22 March 1906, P.P.
119 Pollen to the Admiralty Permanent Secretary, 27 March 1906, P.P.
120 Pollen to the Admiralty Permanent Secretary, 3 April 1906, P.P.
121 Greene, brief, part 2, p. 19, P.P.
122 Pollen to the Admiralty Permanent Secretary, 27 March 1906, P.P., and British Patent 23,846/1906 (26 October 1906), P.O.L.
123 Pollen to the Admiralty Permanent Secretary, 18 June 1906, *CCB*, P.P.
124 Pollen to the Admiralty Permanent Secretary, 14 May 1906, P.P.
125 Greene, brief, part 2, pp. 20-1, P.P.
126 Letter II (January 1906), in *Jupiter Letters*, p. 26, P.P. [*PP*, p. 81].
127 Letter V (February 1906), in *Jupiter Letters*, p. 45, P.P. [*PP*, p. 94].
128 Ibid., p. 44, and Letter VI (May 1906), in *Jupiter Letters*, p. 54, P.P. [*PP*, pp. 93-4, 99].
129 Letter VI (May 1906), p. 54 [*PP*, p. 99].
130 Ibid., p. 55 [*PP*, p. 100].
131 See Captain Charles E. Madden, the Naval Assistant to the Controller, to Pollen, 25 May 1906, P.P., which informed the inventor that he was about to "hand Sir John Fisher your very interesting book on Range Finding & Keeping." For a list of the many others that received a copy of this print, see *PP*, p. 379.
132 Reference to this communication is to be found in Pollen to the Admiralty Permanent Secretary, 18 June 1906, *CCB*, P.P. No copy of the Boys report of 1906 [not to be confused with the Boys report of 1912, which has survived in the Pollen Papers] has been found.
133 Ibid.
134 Ibid.
135 The record of Harding's testimony before the Royal Commission on Awards to Inventors gives the names of Jellicoe, a Captain Percy Smith, and a Commander Crook, as the members of the committee. See RCAI, *Minutes*, Vol. 9 (1 August 1925), p. 14, P.P. Commander Henry Ralph Crooke was then assigned to the Ordnance Department. The Captain Percy Smith mentioned was probably meant to be Commander Bertram H. Smith, a participant in the *Jupiter* trials. See list of officers associated with the recommendations to the Board of Admiralty in regard to the Pollen system from 1905 to 1907, made up by Pollen in 1908, an untitled and undated typescript (henceforward cited as "list of officers 1905-1907"), P.P.
136 Greene, brief, part 2, p. 22, and "list of officers 1905-1907," P.P.
137 Harding to Pollen, 29 June 1906, incomplete, P.P.
138 Greene, brief, part 2, pp. 24-5, P.P.
139 Arthur Hungerford Pollen, *Note on the Possibility of Demonstrating the Principle of Aim Correction without the use of Instruments designed for the Purpose (Sent to the Director of Naval Ordnance, July 1906)* (by the author, presumably July 1906), P.P. [*PP*, pp. 101-4].
140 Jellicoe to Pollen, 31 July 1906, *CCB*, P.P.
141 *PP*, p. 373.
142 Greene, brief, part 2, pp. 25-30, and "Proof of Evidence of Colonel E. W. Harding," pp. 7-8, P.P.
143 "Proof of Evidence of Colonel E. W. Harding," p. 7, and testimony of Harding in RCAI, *Minutes*, Vol. 9 (1 August 1925), pp. 15-16, P.P. See also Harding to Pollen, 22 July 1906, and Harding to Pollen, 2 August 1906, P.P.
144 *Board Minutes* [Admiralty] 1906, Adm. 167/40, P.R.O. The board members present on 7 August were: Tweedmouth; Jackson; Captain Frederick S.

Inglefield, the Fourth Sea Lord; Edmund Robertson, the Parliamentary and Financial Secretary, and C. Inigo Thomas, acting for MacGregor.

145 C. Inigo Thomas (for the Admiralty Permanent Secretary) to Pollen, 8 August 1906, *CCB*, P.P.
146 Much of it attributable probably to Barr's work on the electrically driven gyroscope. See Greene, brief, part 2, p. 34A.
147 For Pollen's detailed recounting of his losses stemming from the *Jupiter* trials, see Pollen to the Admiralty Permanent Secretary, 14 May 1906, P.P.
148 "Notes of a Meeting held at the Admiralty in the Board Room on 9th August 1906," *CCB*, P.P.
149 Ibid.
150 Ibid.
151 *Record of Business Negotiations*, pp. 7, 21.
152 Pollen to the Admiralty Permanent Secretary, 10 August 1906, *CCB*, P.P.
153 C. Inigo Thomas (for the Admiralty Permanent Secretary) to Pollen, 21 August 1906, P.P.
154 Pollen to the Admiralty Permanent Secretary, 22 August 1906, P.P.
155 Pollen to the Admiralty Permanent Secretary, 23 August 1906, P.P.
156 Pollen to the Admiralty Permanent Secretary, 24 August 1906, P.P.
157 Pollen to Tweedmouth, 27 August 1906, P.P., and in Arthur Hungerford Pollen, *Notes, Etc., on the Ariadne Trials* (April 1909), pp. 28-9, P.P. [*PP*, 216–22].
158 Tweedmouth to Pollen, 29 August 1906, P.P.
159 For Tweedmouth's interest in scientific shooting with small-arms, which may have attracted him to Pollen's approach to naval gunnery, see Ishbel Maria Gordon, Countess of Aberdeen, *Edward Marjoribanks Lord Tweedmouth, K.T. 1849-1909: Notes and Recollections* (London: Constable, 1909), p. 24.
160 Tweedmouth to Pollen, 3 September 1906, P.P., and in *Notes, Etc., on the Ariadne Trials*.
161 Pollen to Tweedmouth, 7 September 1906, P.P.
162 Harding to Jellicoe, 4 September 1906, P.P.
163 Harding to Pollen, 4 September 1906, P.P.
164 Captain Edward W. Harding, Royal Marine Artillery, "Memorandum upon the professional and financial value of the A.C. system" [henceforward cited as the "Harding Report"], *CCB*, P.P.
165 Fisher to Tweedmouth, 10 September 1906, *FGDN*, Vol. 2, p. 87.
166 "Notes of a Meeting held at the Admiralty in the Board Room on 9th August 1906," CCB, P.P.
167 Fisher to Tweedmouth, 14 September 1906, *FGDN*, Vol. 2, p. 88.
168 "Memo. to C. I. Thomas Esq." [dated in pencil, 12 September 1906], P.P.
169 *Board Minutes* [Admiralty] 1906, Adm. 167/40, P.R.O. The Board members present at the meeting of 18 September 1906 were: Tweedmouth; Drury; George Lambert, the Civil Lord; Robertson, the Parliamentary and Financial Secretary; and MacGregor.
170 Reference to the meeting of 18 September 1906 in Admiralty Permanent Secretary to Pollen, 21 September 1906, *CCB*, P.P.
171 Ibid.
172 Greene, brief, part 2, p. 39, P.P.
173 Silvanus P. Thompson, *The Life of William Thomson, Baron Kelvin of Largs*, 2 Vols (London: Macmillan, 1910), Vol. 2, pp. 734-5.
174 Fisher to Tweedmouth, 26 September 1906, *FGDN*, Vol. 2, p. 91.

Part II
1906-1914

"Live forces break through forms, and shape results to suit requirements".

Sir Lewis Namier, *England in the Age of the American Revolution*

[4]

Conflict: The Fisher Strategy Disrupted, 1906-1908

1 The Effect of the Dreadnought on British Naval Finance

The all-big-gun battleship H.M.S. *Dreadnought* was laid down on 21 October 1905 and commissioned for trials with a nucleus crew on 1 September 1906. Her completion after only a year of construction, which was a third of the normal time required by a battleship, was made possible by the simplicity of the hull design, the advance purchase of material, special labor arrangements and the use of big-gun mountings that had originally been allocated to the two battleships of the 1904–05 program, whose completions were as a consequence delayed.[1] *Dreadnought* ran her Official Steam and Gun Trials during October, which demonstrated that she could make her designed speed, that her artillery was in good working order and that her hull could withstand the effect of firing full broadsides.[2] The success of these preliminary tests, which removed a measure of uncertainty as to the practicability of the radical changes in armament and propulsion,[3] and an experimental battle practice in December 1906 that demonstrated that 12-inch guns were more accurate than smaller caliber guns,[4] was followed in late 1906 and early 1907 by the laying down of a class of three nearly identical vessels.

Other naval powers were slow to respond with equivalent vessels of their own for technical and financial reasons.[5] Japan had laid down two turbine-engined battleships in the spring of 1905, but had given them mixed-caliber armaments. The United States had laid down two uniform-caliber armament battleships in December 1906, but had not equipped them with turbines. France did not lay down any battleships in 1904, 1905 or 1906, and while the class of five battleships begun in 1907 and 1908 were provided with turbines, they retained a mixed-caliber armament. Russia did not lay down any new battleships between 1905 and 1909. The United States would not begin the construction of vessels that were equipped with both an all-big-gun armament and turbines until November 1907, Japan and Russia not until 1909 and France not until 1910.

The threat that had been posed by the combined naval might of France and Russia since the 1880s, was substantially diminished by the heavy Russian naval losses in the Far East in 1904 and 1905, which left Germany as Britain's principal naval rival. The German battleship program, however, was completely disrupted by the advent of the *Dreadnought*. In 1904, the German navy had drawn up the plans of a mixed-caliber armament battleship, of which two were to have been laid down in 1906. The German Admiralty learned of the *Dreadnought*'s basic characteristics in 1905,[6] but concern over political difficulties in the Reichstag that would have attended increases in naval expenditure resulted in a reluctance to increase the size and thus the cost of battleships;[7] German designers thus improvised an all-big-gun arrangement on the hull of the 1904 design by replacing the secondary battery with big-guns. The resulting eight big-gun armament, however, did not compare favorably with the ten big-gun battery of the British design, and the project was therefore cancelled. It subsequently took more than a year to prepare the plans of a larger and more heavily armed battleship class, which postponed the laying down of the first two German all-big-gun vessels until June 1907. As it was, these battleships, and the six that followed them, had to be given reciprocating engines because the output of Germany's limited capacity to produce turbine machinery was required for the all-big-gun armoured cruiser program. Germany's first turbine propelled all-big-gun battleships were therefore not laid down until 1910.[8]

Fisher was elated by the delays in foreign battleship programs in general, and the disruption of the German battleship program in particular. "We have stopped," he boasted to an unknown correspondent on 3 January 1907, "all foreign ship-building for 16 months."[9] "Everyone is in a fog," he again crowed to Arnold White, the arch-imperialist journalist and a close friend, five days later on 8 January,

> and a good thing too! The truth is we don't want anyone to know the truth. It keeps the foreigners mystified. We shall have four Dreadnoughts ready to fight before a single foreign Dreadnought is launched.[10]

"In March of this year *it is an absolute fact* that Germany had not laid down a single Dreadnought," Fisher wrote to King Edward VII on 4 October 1907,

> nor had she commenced building a single big ship for 18 months (*Germany has been paralyzed by the Dreadnought!*). The more the German Admiralty looked into her qualities, the more convinced they became that they must follow suit, and the more convinced they were that the whole of their existing Battle Fleet was utterly useless *because* utterly wanting in gun power![11]

"The German Admiralty has wrestled for one and a half years with the Dreadnought problem," Fisher reported to the Prince of Wales on 16

October 1907, "trying to evade it by smaller ships and mixed armament, and, having been paralyzed for 18 months, they have swallowed her whole!"[12]

The delays in foreign battleship construction were far greater than the Admiralty had anticipated. In October 1906, Captain Sir Charles Ottley, the Director of Naval Intelligence, informed the Cabinet that

> although even at the time when the late Board of Admiralty[13] reached the momentous decision to build the "Dreadnought," a strong belief prevailed at Whitehall that the leap forward would prove of great value to this country, by bewildering foreign ship-builders and thereby delaying the construction of warships abroad, yet it was impossible at that early date to foresee how completely the appearance of the new model would bring naval design work in foreign Admiralties to a standstill . . . In deciding to construct the "Dreadnought" it seems then that the British nation "builded better than they knew." The breathing space the nation has consequently enjoyed has been measured not by a few weeks but by months, if not by a year.[14]

The delays in foreign battleship building programs, which came on top of the heavy Russian losses in the Far East, enabled Britain to lay down fewer all-big-gun battleships and armoured cruisers than the four per year specified by the "Cawdor Memorandum" of 1905.[15] Three slightly improved *Dreadnoughts*—mentioned previously—were laid down under the 1906–07 estimates, three more essentially similar vessels were ordered under the 1907–08 estimates and only one somewhat improved battleship and one slightly improved armoured cruiser were laid down under the 1908–09 estimates.[16] As a consequence, the £8.4 million spent on battleship and armoured cruiser construction in fiscal year 1905–06 fell to £7.9 million in 1906–07, to £6.5 million in 1907–08 and to no more than £5.5 million in 1908–09.[17] As a result of these reductions and those achieved through Fisher's administrative reforms,[18] and in spite of rising costs in other areas, the net naval estimates of 1906–07, 1907–08 and 1908–09 were kept between £31 and £32 million, which was £5 million less per year than the peak of £36.9 million that had been reached in fiscal year 1904–05.[19]

The upsetting of foreign battleship programs did not, however, provide a lasting solution to the problem posed by the limited financial resources available for British capital ship construction. In his memorandum of October 1906, Ottley had warned the Cabinet that "up to the year 1909 our position will be satisfactory in regard to battleships, but from that time onwards, unless the building programme is well sustained, we shall be drifting year by year into a more and more precarious position; because our potential enemies will thenceforward be adding larger numbers of 'Dreadnoughts' to their fleets than we shall . . ."[20] In other words, within a matter of only a few years, Britain would have to match the all-big-gun construction of the next two leading naval powers with comparable vessels that were more expensive than the smaller battleships that had been laid down before 1905 if she were to maintain the two-power standard, which would necessarily lead to great increases in naval expenditure.

The introduction of a more powerful and faster battleship that might again overturn the building programs of foreign navies did not seem practicable. In the 1906 edition of *Fighting Ships* in an article entitled "A New 'Ideal' Ship," Cuniberti returned to the subject of a "supreme" warship suited to "Britain the Wealthy." As a result of his study of the Russo-Japanese War, Cuniberti had concluded that the 12-inch gun was not as effective against armoured targets as he had imagined in 1903. He thus urged that a new "Ideal" British battleship be armed with eight 16-inch guns, which at 10,000 yards would penetrate "the thickest plates of the enemy and maintaining at that distance an energy . . . sufficient to damage a vessel so thoroughly that one blow would be sufficient to render it unserviceable." Cuniberti ended, however, on a temporizing note, writing that

> the displacement that such a vessel would require, constructed as we have described with the internal arrangements for safety against underwater explosions of whatever nature, with efficient external defence against projectiles, and finally with such great powers of attack, being armed with eight guns of 16 inches, would be so great that we should be absolutely forced to forego the very high speed necessary for future actions in which submarines would take part, or else we should have to adopt engines of such enormous power, as would be incompatible with the structure of the vessel and with the spaces required on board for other purposes.
>
> At the present moment, therefore, it does not appear practicable to pass with one step only to an increase of 4 inches in the calibre of the guns we propose to adopt . . . and in that case we must content ourselves for the moment with an increase of something less than this.[21]

Fisher, on the other hand, believed that big-gun armoured cruisers of even greater speed and fire power than those under way, which would be far less expensive to build than battleships of comparable performance, could upset the building programs of foreign powers in the manner of the *Dreadnought*.[22] Fisher's colleagues at the Admiralty were opposed, however, to the further construction of vessels of the *Invincible* type. In early 1907, an improved *Invincible* that had been projected in December 1906 for the 1907–08 program was cancelled.[23] Although documentary evidence explaining the decision is lacking, the board probably acted in the belief that large outlays on big-gun armoured cruisers were not required for the reasons given by the special committee of December 1905.[24] And in June 1907, Rear-Admiral John Jellicoe, the Director of Naval Ordnance, urged that the armoured cruisers scheduled to be laid down under the 1908–09 estimates be given 9.2-inch instead of 12-inch guns in order to reduce their size and cost,[25] a proposal that the full Board of Admiralty unanimously approved on 12 June 1907.[26]

There were compelling reasons for Fisher to vote with the majority on the board against the big-gun armoured cruiser, in spite of his own views on the subject. From the spring of 1907, Admiral Lord Charles Beresford—then the Commander-in-Chief of the Channel Fleet and an officer of great popularity and influence who had opposed Fisher's proposals to replace the battleship with the armoured cruiser in 1904—had openly challenged Fisher's leadership of the navy, and by so doing had added considerable weight to an already vigorous public campaign that had been waged by critics of the First Sea Lord's policies since 1905. In the face of so serious an external threat, Fisher could not have risked dividing the board over such a major issue as capital ship design. There was, moreover, clearly much to be said for waiting on events. With foreign all-big-gun battleship programs still lagging, a second design trump was not urgently required. In addition, the successful trials of the yet to be completed *Invincible* class and the Pollen fire control system were bound to strengthen the case for the armoured cruiser. The development of the Pollen system, however, was to be disrupted by changes at the Admiralty that nullified the agreement that had been reached in September 1906.

2 The Vicissitudes of the Pollen System, 1906-1908

(a) FORMAL CONTRACT NEGOTIATIONS

The Admiralty letter of 21 September 1906 embodied a commitment in principle to support the development of the Pollen system in order to obtain exclusive rights to its use if perfected. Further negotiations were required, however, before agreement could be reached on the wording of a preliminary draft formal contract. Difficulties began with Pollen's letter of 25 September, a response to the Admiralty offer, in which he suggested that he be paid the full sum of £100,000 in the event that the Admiralty decided to equip more than 4 ships with his system even though the trials were not completely successful; that he be paid £50,000 to keep his system secret even though the trials were not successful and the system was not adopted for service, and that he be paid £5,000 a year to improve his system if trials should reveal that further development was required to enable it to be successful.[27] The Admiralty reply of 15 October, categorically rejected the first proposal, maintained that provisions for arbitration covered the second providing that "the award of the Arbitrators shall be absolutely binding on both parties without any limitations," and suggested the postponement of discussions on the third until circumstances raised the question.[28]

Pollen's letter to the Admiralty of 17 October stated that the Admiralty's agreement to binding arbitration without limitation made his suggestions unnecessary, proposed a minor change in language with regard to the setting of his profit margin on manufactured instruments, and pointed out that the language of the complete success conditions was such that minor shortcomings in the performance of his system could lead to an unfavorable judgement that was substantially unwarranted.[29] In a letter of 25 October, the Admiralty accepted Pollen's proposals regarding his profit margins and suggested that the conditions of success be modified by an explanatory clause that would meet Pollen's concerns.[30] Agreement on the provisional language of the formal contract was reached in a meeting at the Admiralty on 29 October, and embodied in an Admiralty letter of that date to which Pollen replied on the same day giving his assent.[31] The conclusion of these

115

preliminary negotiations cleared the way for the payment to Pollen of the agreed advance payment of £6,500 on 8 November,[32] the delay of which had caused the inventor some distress.[33]

The tentative agreement was meant to apply only to the gyroscopically stabilized range and bearing instruments, the data transmission system, and the plotter. On 2 November 1906, Pollen thus had offered to assign to the Admiralty for their consideration, as a matter of course, the patents of other fire control devices that he might invent—such as a change of range clock—that could be used in conjunction with the instruments covered by the tentative agreement.[34] The Admiralty accepted Pollen's offer in a letter of 7 November, but at this time warned him that, if the design of the new instruments embodied features that would reveal the principles upon which the instruments covered by the draft formal contract worked, they could not be offered to foreign navies in the event that the Admiralty did not adopt them for service because the sale of such instruments to third parties would violate the secrecy provisions of the main agreement then in preparation. Pollen would not, therefore, be allowed royalties—that is, payments in compensation for lost foreign sales—in the event that such instruments were adopted for service, because the secrecy provisions of the main contract had precluded the possibility of foreign sales in the first place.[35]

While the negotiations just described were nearing their conclusion in early November, Pollen printed a pamphlet, *Some Aspects of the Tactical Value of Speed in Capital Ships*, for private circulation. His defence of high speed in large armoured warships, which was directed against articles that had been published that October in *Blackwood's Edinburgh Magazine* and the *United Service Magazine*[36] that had been critical of the *Dreadnought*, put forward arguments that suggest that he was aware that the armoured cruisers of the *Invincible* class were armed with big-guns, which was then a closely held secret.[37] A small, fast squadron acting independently of a slower main force of battleships, Pollen maintained, could be deployed against an engaged section of the enemy line of battle in order to achieve a decisive local superiority of force that "would give, under modern conditions, the effect that Nelson got at Trafalgar." The fast squadron, furthermore, would be able to complete the victory by pursuing and engaging "a few very slightly damaged battleships, which might have survived the first brunt of the action and be retreating." While even the latest armoured cruisers lacked the fire power to perform these tasks successfully, Pollen observed that "fast ships, armed with 12in. [*sic*] guns, with an extra knot or two of speed, would prove absolutely invaluable . . ." He then mentioned not only the *Dreadnought*, but "the new 25 knot capital ships"—that is, the all-big-gun armoured cruisers.[38]

Pollen left England for the United States on 10 November for six weeks to do business in connection with the Linotype Company.[39] Official correspondence with the Admiralty did not resume until 11 March 1907, at which time the Admiralty forwarded a draft formal contract to Pollen for his inspection.[40] On 15 March, Pollen wrote to the Admiralty to take strong exception to provisions in the document that he believed were prejudicial to his interests and that had not been discussed previously. These were, first, that Pollen's right of exclusive manufacture of the instruments of his system would last for only so long as his patents were recognized as valid, second, that the inventor would be required at all times to maintain a skilled staff of assistants to improve his system, and, third, that in the event that arbitration was necessary to determine the value of instruments which were not completely successful in trials, the judgement be based upon trials results only without consideration for "any points in which the invention, though apparently promising, may require further development before actually achieving the results looked for, it being agreed that the terms for any such developments, if desired by the Commissioners are matters for subsequent arrangement between them and the Inventor."[41]

Pollen reiterated and amplified his objections in a letter to the Admiralty of 5 April,[42] and on 16 April sent a memorandum to the Admiralty in which he dealt with the issue of possible patent infringements.[43] He then consulted his attorney, Ernest B. Hawksley, in the course of preparing emendations to the draft formal contract.[44] The Admiralty, for its part, replied to Pollen's letter of 15 March in April with a vigorous defence of the provisions of the draft formal contract in question, which closed with the observation "that their Lordships do not concur that the matters referred to have been dealt with in the draft agreement in a manner contrary to the manner in which they are dealt with in the correspondence."[45] Following an unofficial conversation with a member of the Contracts Department on 17 April, Pollen surmised that the aim of that department was to overturn the perpetual royalty agreement[46] and that he was suspected of behavior "verging on sharp practice."[47]

The draft formal contract with changes that reflected the views expressed in Pollen's letter of 15 March was dispatched to the Admiralty on 21 May.[48] The Admiralty required two months to prepare their reply, which was sent to Pollen's attorneys on 19 July. In this document the Admiralty refused to agree to the arrangement to purchase instruments from Pollen at a royalty of 25 per cent in perpetuity and to obligate themselves to pay Pollen the full award of £100,000 in the event of complete success being achieved at any time after the first trial, stipulated that Pollen provide specific guarantees that his instruments did not infringe previous patents, and proposed a number of minor changes.[49] In his reply to the Director of Navy Contracts of 22 July, Pollen insisted upon his royalty rights and maintained that his provision of a guarantee on the matter of previous patents was "at great variance with the whole purport of the agreement, which is that the Inventor is submitting a system and not patented devices," but agreed to set a time limit on the Admiralty obligation to pay him the full award in the event that his system achieved complete success in trials.[50]

Agreement on the minor changes proposed in the Admiralty letter of 19 July was reached in a meeting in the office of the Director of Navy Ordnance on 23 July,[51] and the questions of royalty arrangements and the time limit on trials appear to have been settled not long thereafter in meetings and through correspondence.[52] The issue of Pollen's indemnifying the

Admiralty in the event of patent infringement, however, remained out-standing. The Admiralty position was derived from the standard practice of the Contract Department of requiring the manufacturers of naval equipment such as guns or engines to provide an indemnity in case of patent infringement.[53] Pollen's position was expressed in legal terms by Russell Clarke, a patent expert whom he had retained in addition to Hawksley, in an opinion that was sent to the Director of Navy Contracts on 30 July.[54] Clarke observed that the indemnity clause desired by the Admiralty

> would be a proper one, if the transaction contemplated were that Mr. Pollen should sell to the Admiralty certain patented instruments manufactured by him, under patents of which he himself retained the control. If the article sold is an infringement of a third party's patent the manufacturer is the proper person to be sued, and if the Plaintiff elects to sue the user, it is natural that the user should require an indemnity from the manufacturer. If I sell a man a manufactured article, it may well be that there ought to be a covenant for quiet enjoyment, either expressed or implied.
>
> This however does not appear to be the contemplated arrangement. Although in many cases apparatus is to be obtained through Mr. Pollen, the primary effect of the arrangement is to transfer the Pollen patents and secrets to the Admiralty, and in this case the covenant is quite out of place. . .
>
> A patent therefore does not purport to confer any right to make or use, and therefore an indemnity such as suggested is quite unsuitable.[55]

A conversation with "a member of the Gunnery Branch" on 30 July left Pollen with the feeling that his position was not yet understood,[56] and he thus presented his position in his own words at some length in a private letter to F. W. Black, the Director of Navy Contracts, on 31 July 1907.

In his letter, Pollen observed that the year before he had offered to sell his instruments exclusively to the Admiralty at a price that was subject to arbitration in the event of disagreement, in which case he would "have been in the position of a person commercially exploiting patented goods, and each sale to the Admiralty would naturally have carried with it an implicit indemnity against claims for infringement . . ." Pollen reminded Black that it was the Admiralty who had "preferred to buy out my commercial position outright" and "as they have bought my profits outright so they have bought my liabilities and my risks." "It is not," Pollen argued, "reasonable to ask to have it both ways" and went on to write that he could not "help thinking that there has been a good deal of confusion of thought about this for the reason that the person or persons who drafted the agreement have not clearly understood what the essential nature of the transaction is." Pollen then concluded

> that even if we were absolutely certain that no infringement had taken place or could take place, we are no nearer being certain that nobody can make any claim or bring any suit for infringement. The possibility of such claims is one of the ordinary risks of commerce: and I repeat that had I been left in a commercial position vis a vis to the Admiralty, it is a risk that I would have cheerfully taken; but as the whole purpose and object of the Admiralty has been to take over the commercial position themselves, and to leave us in the position of an

expropriated patentee, it is of course as I think quite demonstrably inconsistent to leave me with what may possibly be the most onerous of all the commercial liabilities without any elasticity of profit which the possibilities of commercial development might have enabled me to make to counterweight the risk.[57]

But the Admiralty appears not to have been persuaded by Pollen's arguments, and did not respond to the revised draft formal contract that Pollen had submitted on 25 July with a revised draft of their own until 26 November.[58] A meeting between Admiralty officials and Pollen took place that same day, but an agreement on the indemnity clause was not reached, which may have prompted the Admiralty to inform the Treasury that the payment of £50,000 to Pollen "in connection with his aim-correcting apparatus, which, though provided for, cannot be made this year."[59] Pollen suggested in a letter to the Admiralty of 19 December, however, that he could agree to "not without the written assent of the Commissioners knowingly make use of . . . any British Patent for the time being in force of which he may not then be the owner or licensee and he shall at all times use reasonable diligence to prevent such use."[60] The Admiralty accepted the proposed clause as a substitute for the one that they had previously insisted upon on 21 December,[61] and after further correspondence to resolve questions of detail,[62] the formal contract was signed on 18 February 1908.

The formal contract differed from the Admiralty offer of 21 September 1906 in a number of respects. The conditions of success were modified by changes in language that specified that Pollen's system perform "with reasonable regularity to the satisfaction of the Commissioners," which precluded a judgement of failure for exceptional shortcomings in performance, and the addition of a stipulation that Pollen's system would not be held accountable for errors in the indicated rates that were shown to have been the result of incorrect settings of the dumaresq for the speed of the test warship. Arbitration procedures were specified, which were to come into effect in the event of disputes arising over the interpretation of any part of the contract. The Admiralty, moreover, was bound to do their best to maintain the secrecy of Pollen's system, to provide him with facilities to test his instruments under sea-going conditions, to supply him with whatever non-confidential information that was required to enable him to improve and develop his system, and not to use any portions of Pollen's system for purposes other than fire control without his consent.

New provisions regarding Pollen's obligations made his rights of manufacture contingent upon his continued direction of a skilled staff that would be charged with the task of improving and developing his instruments; required him to obtain the written consent of the Admiralty before making use of patents other than his own; prevented him from transferring his interest—as a whole or in part—in the arrangement between him and the Admiralty, as given in the contract, to another party without the Admiralty's consent; limited the wages of those hired to manufacture the components of the system to levels that were comparable to the wages paid for similar work by other companies; gave the Admiralty the right to approve the choice of sub-contractors; stated the terms upon which the completed instruments would be delivered and received, or rejected in the case of substandard material, workmanship, or inoperation; and empowered the Admiralty to determine the terms of liquidation in the event of Pollen's bankruptcy.[63]

The final agreement had been achieved in the face of financial difficulties that had arisen suddenly in November 1907, when the Admiralty discovered that rising costs and unanticipated expenses would produce an increase in the 1908-09 estimates that was twice what had been expected. The Cabinet categorically refused to accept the Admiralty's position that the additional spending was essential, and in February 1908 the navy was left with an increase that was even less than the amount proposed before the previous November.[64] There can be little doubt that the climate of severe financial restriction magnified the distaste of the Department of Navy Contracts, and others as well, for the terms demanded by Pollen—which in effect committed the Admiralty both to bear the full cost of experiments and to reward the inventor handsomely in the case of success—an unprecedented arrangement that to those who did not appreciate the military importance of what was being offered appeared to be unjustified. The grudging acquiescence of the Admiralty's business office to the formal contract of 1908, indeed, may only have been given in the hope if not the knowledge that changes in the Naval Ordnance Department had probably made it certain that the Pollen system would be rejected regardless of the outcome of the trials.

(b) THE NAVAL ORDNANCE DEPARTMENT IN OPPOSITION

The payment of £6,500 to Pollen in November 1906, mentioned previously, had enabled him to proceed with the development of his instruments for trial in the absence of a definitive agreement with the Admiralty. While work was in progress in the spring, he printed *Notes on a Proposed Method of Studying Naval Tactics*, a pamphlet for private circulation in which he argued the case for his "tactical machine," a derivative of the "crab machine" of 1904. This device, when set with course and speed data, would display the relative positions of the firing ship and target, or of two opposing fleets, which could then be manipulated to indicate how that relative position might appear at selected moments in the future. Pollen maintained that his tactical machine would in peacetime enable naval officers to practice conveniently "how to approach, when to increase and when to decrease speed, how to seek and ensure superiority of position, the right counterstroke to each possible attack the enemy may develop," and in actual battle would assist in the determination of the most effective deployment.[65] The tactical machine was the subject of Pollen's one meeting at the Admiralty with Sir John Fisher, an interview that lasted only five minutes, which probably took place in the spring of 1907. Pollen later recalled that at this time the First Sea Lord "instantly appreciated the value of the Tactical Machine."[66]

Work on the gunnery instruments, in the meanwhile, had advanced rapidly, and on 11 June 1907 prototypes were inspected at the Linotype

Company's works at Broadheath, which was near Manchester, by a party of naval officers that included Rear-Admiral Sir Henry Jackson, the Controller; by now Rear-Admiral John Jellicoe, the Director of Naval Ordnance; and Jellicoe's assistant, Captain (R.M.A.) Edward W. Harding. Pollen was then able to demonstrate the method by which the automatic arm and marker of the plotter would be activated by the electrical signals of the data transmission system. The capability of the gyroscopically stabilized range-finder and bearing-indicator mounting was demonstrated by its ability to keep the range-finder trained steadily on a point marked on an opposing wall while the platform upon which the mounting and range-finder were placed was swung from left to right in a manner that simulated the effect of a yawing ship. And, in addition, the visitors were shown drawings of the projected change of range machine, and assemblies of certain of its principal mechanisms.[67]

The members of the visiting party were much impressed by what they had seen,[68] and Pollen had every reason to believe that he had greatly increased the Admiralty's confidence in the prospects of a completely successful trial. But in August 1907 Jellicoe, with whom Pollen had developed a cordial personal relationship,[69] left the Ordnance Department to become Second-in-Command of the Atlantic Fleet, and was replaced by Captain R. H. S. Bacon. Bacon was a confidant of Fisher, who had served as the First Sea Lord's assistant and as the first commanding officer of the *Dreadnought*. In 1903 Fisher had noted that he was "acknowledged as the cleverest officer in the Navy,"[70] and there can be little doubt that he was an officer of considerable ability. Bacon's technical specialization, however, had been in torpedoes rather than gunnery, which together with what appears to have been a propensity to overvalue the benefits of drill and discipline,[71] may have led him to underestimate the necessity of developing mechanical methods of sight-setting. He was, in addition, opposed to the employment of complicated machinery for fire control purposes, which he believed would be less reliable in service than a mechanically simpler system that was based on manual operations. There is good reason to believe, therefore, that Bacon was determined from the start to prevent the adoption of Pollen's mechanized system of fire control.[72]

Bacon's objectives were undoubtedly also those of Lieutenant Frederic C. Dreyer, a young naval officer who had by this time established a considerable reputation as a gunnery specialist. Dreyer had passed the advanced course in gunnery at H.M.S. *Excellent* with honors in 1899. In 1903, he became gunnery officer of the newly commissioned battleship *Exmouth*, which in 1904 became the flagship of Vice-Admiral Sir Arthur Knyvet Wilson, the Commander-in-Chief of the Channel Fleet. Dreyer's great ability as a trainer of gunlayers expert in the methods of Percy Scott was demonstrated when *Exmouth* took first place in the Channel Fleet in Battle Practice, the Heavy Gunlayer's Test, and the Light Gunlayer's Test for three years in succession from 1904 to 1906. Wilson made Dreyer his Gunnery Staff Officer, in which capacity he served as the admiral's chief advisor on all gunnery matters.[73] It was while serving under Wilson that Dreyer's rivalry with Pollen as an inventor of fire control instruments had begun.

In May 1905, Dreyer had left *Exmouth* temporarily to serve on Percy Scott's Gunnery Calibration Committee. It was at this time that he first met Pollen, who had been allowed to witness the calibration trials in the battleship *Commonwealth* in Bantry Bay off the southern coast of Ireland as a part of the preparation for the forthcoming trials of his instruments in the battleship *Jupiter*. Pollen thoroughly explained his ideas in a long conversation with Dreyer, who in addition received a copy of *Fire Control and Long Range Firing*. The two established friendly relations, and in the spring of 1906 Dreyer was present at a dinner that Pollen gave at the Queen's Hotel in Swansea to a group of naval officers, who afterwards were given an explanation, illustrated by plans, of the automatic plotter, the gyroscope mounting and the clock. Dreyer then showed a great interest in Pollen's work, and later questioned the inventor closely while giving him a tour of the *Exmouth*.[74]

On 31 October 1906 Pollen sent Dreyer a copy of the *Jupiter Letters* and asked for "any reflections you may have to make after you have struggled to the end of all of them."[75] Dreyer did not reply until 15 December, and then refused to offer an opinion on the grounds that "I have never seen your gear & do not know how you actually overcome the many great mechanical difficulties which must exist & what degree of accuracy you obtain . . ."[76] He had, however, a reason for evasion other than intellectual reticence, for only five days earlier, on 10 December, he had submitted the design of a change of range rate calculator to Wilson, who forwarded it to the Admiralty for consideration.[77]

Dreyer's "rate of change" calculator consisted of a long strip of paper moved at a constant speed by a clockwork motor, an ink pad that marked the paper when depressed, a rule calibrated in yards that moved along a slide that ran parallel to the travel of the paper, and a fixed scale calibrated in knots. The operator was supposed to calculate the change of range by marking the moving strip with the ink pad at the moment that the range–finder operator called out a range, following the movement of the mark with the rule calibrated in yards by moving the rule down the slide, and stopping the movement of the rule when a second range was called out, at which point the second range as read on the sliding rule would be opposite a number on the fixed scale that would indicate the change of range in knots, which could then be set on the Vickers Clock.[78] In principle, the Dreyer calculator did nothing more than divide the difference between two ranges by the time interval between the moments at which the two range observations were made, and while perhaps an improvement over the existing system of determining the time interval with a stop-watch and writing out the calculations, the device took no account of the problems posed by the continuous change in the change of range rate or of error in the range observations and involved a number of time–consuming manual operations that were, in addition, subject to human error. There can be little doubt, in spite of the absence of documentary evidence, that the Ordnance Department dismissed Dreyer's design as unworthy of serious consideration.

Dreyer's success as a fleet gunnery officer, however, had impressed Fisher, who specially assigned him to the *Dreadnought* from January to April 1907 in order to advise Bacon on gunnery.[79] Dreyer's official connection with the development of the Pollen system began in April 1907 with his appointment to the Naval Ordnance Department. In June 1907, Dreyer was among those officers who witnessed the demonstration of Pollen's partially completed instruments at Broadheath, and Pollen later recalled that Dreyer had been "very cordial in his congratulations."[80] At the same time, however, Dreyer and his older brother, Captain John Tuthill Dreyer of the Royal Artillery, were designing an improved change of range calculator, which they called a "Position Finder for Determining Rate of Change of Range," a description and the plans of which were submitted to the Admiralty on 2 July 1907. In the covering letter that accompanied the submission, Frederic Dreyer noted "that the rate of change of range is a variable *which alters from instant to instant.*"[81] The new device thus offered an improved method of setting the ranges and reading off the change of range rate. But while the new arrangement made it easier to obtain a succession of change of range rate readings, the result was still a discontinuous set of individual change of range rates that had each been calculated by the division of the differences between two range observations by the time interval between the moments of their being made, and that thus imperfectly represented the continuous change in the change of range rate.

Harding, who had been responsible for fire control projects at the Naval Ordnance Department while Jellicoe was its head, would most likely have rejected Dreyer's new proposals as inadequate. But when Bacon became the Director of Naval Ordnance in August 1907, he transferred Harding to other duties, and replaced him with Dreyer, who was thereby placed in a position to advance the cause of his own inventions. Dreyer's calculator was probably for this reason given a trial by the staff of the *Excellent* in the battleship *Revenge* during the fall of 1907[82] which was, however, not successful.[83] In September 1907, Dreyer met Pollen by chance while the inventor was on his way to Portsmouth to choose a position for his instruments on the protected cruiser *Ariadne*, which had been assigned to him as a trials ship, and Pollen later recalled that Dreyer on this occasion "told me he hoped it would be his duty to crab me when the time came."[84]

The selection of Admiral of the Fleet Sir Arthur Knyvet Wilson to umpire the official trials insured that Dreyer's desire to play a major role in the blocking of Pollen would be fulfilled. When Pollen informed the Admiralty in November 1907 that his instruments were ready for trial, Wilson, who had retired in the spring of 1907, was asked by the Admiralty to inspect the experimental gear and develop a program of experiments. Wilson accepted the offer, and at this time or not long afterwards Bacon assigned Dreyer to be his assistant. Wilson's nomination undoubtedly originated with Bacon, who must have been aware of his dependence upon Dreyer for advice on all gunnery matters. Wilson possessed other qualifications which suited the determination of the Director of Naval Ordnance to secure the rejection of the Pollen system. Wilson, it was generally known, had resented the detachment of the *Jupiter* for experiments with Pollen's equipment.[85] And though not possessed of expertise in naval gunnery, the admiral was universally regarded as an officer of unrivalled seamanship, tactical brilliance and unqualified devotion to the interests of the Royal Navy, whose judgement on practically any matter related to the service was bound to be accorded the utmost respect.

Wilson's inspection of Pollen's equipment in the *Ariadne* and an evening dinner with the inventor took place on 20 November 1907. Pollen later recalled that his relations with Wilson were at this time cordial.[86] Wilson's report of his discussions indicated that Pollen and the Admiralty were in disagreement over the time that the Admiralty would be allowed to come to a decision following the conclusion of the trials, a matter that was settled in the course of the negotiations over the formal contract,[87] but otherwise Pollen had little cause for concern when Wilson informed him on 4 December that he had agreed to an Admiralty request that he serve as the judge of the official trials, and enclosed a program of experiments.[88]

The inventor may, however, have had at least a suspicion that difficulties were in the offing with the receipt of Wilson's letter of 8 December, which asked him to send "a written statement showing exactly what are the advantages you claim for your system as fitted in the Ariadne and for which the Admiralty are asked to pay £100,000 . . ."[89] Pollen thus provided Wilson, and Bacon and Dreyer as well, with a copy of a print entitled *An Apology for the A.C. Battle System*, which he had originally prepared a few months before as a lecture for the War Course program at Portsmouth that had been postponed at Bacon's request pending the outcome of the trials.[90] In this work, Pollen addressed the opponents of his system, who, he argued, believed that the fire control problem could be solved by little more than an extension of the methods of intensive drill and new practice procedures that they had championed over the past few years in the name of up-to-date naval gunnery. But such opposition to the mechanization of fire control, Pollen warned, was that of progressives whose policies had been overtaken by new developments. There was not, he observed with perhaps excessive candor,

> a more pathetic spectacle than the warnings of the adventurous against any adventure but their own. Hence there is no conservatism like that of the progressive. It was not the duffers, but the greatest astronomers in the world, who found Galileo's discovery hard to swallow.[91]

To illustrate the operation of his proposed fire control system, Pollen described a situation in which an armoured cruiser of the *Invincible* class steaming at its top speed of 25 knots would begin firing at ranges of at least 7,000 to 8,000 yards at an enemy vessel steaming at an equal speed and on a steeply converging course. Although such circumstances posed the problem of change of range rates that would approach 1,500 yards a minute and would be continuously varying, Pollen predicted that two hits out of every three shots fired would be possible through the employment of a fully mechanized system of fire control that was to consist of the gyroscopically stabilized range-finder, the automatic true-course plotter, a calculator to compute ranges, a separate calculator to compute bearings and a system of automatic sight-setting. In addition, the fire control system was to be augmented by the "tactical machine."[92]

The explanations given by Pollen in his print did not satisfy Wilson, who on 11 December wrote

> I have read your lecture but it does not quite answer my question which was, exactly the advantages you claim for your system as fitted in the Ariadne and for which the Admiralty are asked to pay £100,000. As far as I can see the only paragraphs in the lecture which refer to the apparatus which is fitted in the Ariadne are 17 and 18 and possibly part of 23. The rest I understand has not even been designed and in any case is not included in the portion of the system for which the Admiralty would obtain their £100,000.
>
> I understand that you claim to have improved the accuracy of the Range finder by your method of mounting. That we can test during the experiments. Also that your method of charting gives the data for keeping the sights adjusted better than any other means. That is mainly a function of the accuracy of the data and the time required to make it available for use. That also we can test.
>
> Am I right in the above and is there anything further that you claim. If so what is it?[93]

Any doubts that Pollen may have had as to Wilson's hostility, were erased shortly thereafter at the house of the Commander-in-Chief of the Portsmouth naval base following a second inspection of the inventor's instruments that took place in mid December.[94] Pollen later recalled that Wilson at the moment of parting

> turned upon me and in a peremptory and angry voice and with a very stern expression of countenance, told me he had been horrified at finding no means of getting the data obtained by my plotting table to the guns, and said, "You will have to explain to me some time or other why on earth the Admiralty should pay you £100,000 more than to Barr and Stroud or any other maker of Fire Control instruments that have got to be used for your system." I was completely taken aback by his mentioning, before a number of officers who were strangers to me, and the Admiral's domestics, the purchase price, which had hitherto been regarded as strictly confidential. . . . recovering myself with great difficulty, I replied that I would send him such explanations as I could in writing.[95]

On 17 December, Pollen attempted to explain his position to Wilson in a long letter. Pollen maintained that his instruments would determine the course and speed of an enemy ship, that present methods of obtaining such data were inadequate, and that the accurate knowledge of the target course and speed would greatly increase the effectiveness of the dumaresq and Vickers Clock. He observed that

> if, then the A.C. system gets the right data for hits at longer distances than they can now be got, and if it enables the present Fire Control System to get

these data to the guns, it must add an efficiency to these ships that they do not now possess. If that efficiency means that more hits are made in a given time at a given range, it increases the value of such ships in proportion. If it enables sustained hitting to be maintained at a range now impossible, it increases the value incalculably.

A mechanized system of fire control, Pollen concluded, would be easier to protect with armour than the manual system then in use and less prone to human error.[96] In reply to Pollen's letter of the day before, Wilson wrote on 18 December that "I think you have made your claims quite clear. I hope the experiments will be able to prove how far they are justified."[97]

Pollen again wrote to Wilson on 18 December to justify his financial terms. He explained that he had originally asked for payment of his instruments on a ship by ship basis but that it was the Admiralty who had insisted upon the high fixed award that would cover an indeterminate large number of instruments. "In my private opinion," Pollen admitted,

> the arrangement I proposed would have been a more businesslike one for the Admiralty to have made. However I had the choice of closing with their terms or being practically compelled to choose between throwing the whole thing over or making it common property.[98]

On 19 December, Pollen wrote to Wilson to make suggestions about the coming trials, including a request that tests be made at ranges of 10,000 and 12,000 yards, which was considerably above the 8,000 yards specified by Wilson in the plan of experiments that had been sent to the inventor on 4 December. Pollen's letter was accompanied by a volume that consisted of the *Jupiter Letters* and the *Notes on a Proposed Method of Studying Naval Tactics*.[99] Wilson's reply of 20 December did not respond to Pollen's request regarding tests at longer ranges, and noted that he already possessed copies of the two prints.[100]

Preliminary trials in the second week of December, which will be described in the next section, had by this time exceeded even Pollen's expectations of success, but he could have been under no illusions as to the seriousness of his political predicament. In January, just before the official trials, Rear-Admiral Sir Henry Jackson, the Third Sea Lord and Controller, warned Pollen that "If your gear can be broken down, Wilson will break it—so look out . . ."[101]

(c) THE *ARIADNE* TRIALS

Preliminary trials of Pollen's gyroscopically stabilized range-finder and bearing-indicator, the electrical data transmission system and the automatic plotter began on 7 December 1907.[102] In these tests, the range-finder was operated by Lieutenant Gore Langton; the table by either Lieutenant George Gipps or Isherwood; and D. H. Landstad, who was one of Pollen's draughtsman, looked after the gyroscopes and recorded the extent of yaw for the purposes of analysis afterwards.[103] The armoured cruiser *Shannon* was tracked by the instruments in the *Ariadne* while both ships steamed at speeds and on courses that were such as to pose the problem of moderately high and continuously changing change of range rates. The first trial runs were undertaken in relatively calm weather, but on 9 December a heavy storm struck, resulting in very rough seas during trial runs that were made the next day. The gyroscopically stabilized range–finder and bearing–indicator, however, proved to be capable of compensating for the very considerable yaw of the *Ariadne* caused by the extreme conditions, which enabled the range–taker to make numerous and accurate range and bearing observations, which were transmitted without mishap to the automatic plotter, which in its turn produced a clear chart of the *Shannon*'s movements relative to that of the *Ariadne*. Accurate measurements of the *Shannon*'s course and speed were thus made by Pollen's system although the courses and speeds of both test ships were such that the change of range rates were as high as over 500 yards a minute and varying continuously, and the ranges were as great as 12,000 yards.[104]

The preliminary trials, which demonstrated that Pollen's instruments were easily capable of satisfying the requirements for complete success embodied in the formal contract then under negotiation, impressed a number of prominent gunnery officers. "Hamilton, Captain at Whale Island, and Chatfield, his commander, came out to Spithead the other day," wrote Pollen to his wife in late December 1907 or early January 1908,

> to look at our instruments and inspect some of the tests we have made with them. Both appeared to be surprised and pleased by the results, which indeed have surpassed all expectations. . . . After Hamilton and Chatfield's visit, Gipps asked them for a passage back to the beach, and when he came on board again next morning, he told me that as they pushed off Hamilton asked his commander what he thought of it. To which Chatfield replied, "What am I to think about a fellow who discovers a problem that we did not know existed, and then proceeds to solve it completely?"[105]

On 26 December 1907, Jellicoe had written to Pollen congratulating him on the success of the preliminary trials in the *Ariadne*.[106] In a second letter that was probably written a few days later in acknowledgement of his receipt of a copy of *An Apology for the A.C. Battle System*, Jellicoe, who must have been aware of Pollen's difficulties with Wilson and the Naval Ordnance Department, wrote that

> the great necessity is to convince those who have the decision of the value or rather the need of a method of obtaining correct rate of change and your notes for the lecture are very convincing to those who know the difficulties now. To those who do not appreciate these difficulties, it will not be so easy to demonstrate it.[107]

In the meanwhile, Dreyer, who had been assigned to advise Wilson during the trials, had worked together with the admiral to concoct a complete manual scheme of obtaining sight-setting data. Their approach was based upon a virtual course and speed plot that was to be produced from ranges obtained from a 9-foot base Barr & Stroud range-finder on a standard mounting, and bearings from an improvised telescope-torpedo director observing instrument that made no correction for yaw.[108] The Wilson-Dreyer system required five men to make the range and bearing observations and to transmit the findings, five men to plot the observations and to measure off the virtual speed and course or range rate and deflection rate, five men to set the clock and calculate corrected ranges and bearings, and one man to transmit the corrected ranges and bearings to the gun positions, a total of sixteen men.[109] Pollen's mechanized system of observation, transmission of data and plotting, and proposed mechanized system of computing, transmission of results and sight setting, on the other hand, could be operated by only two men—one man to make the observations, and the other to measure the target's true course and speed off the plot and to set this data on the clock. Although Pollen's mechanized system risked the possibility of mechanical failure where the Wilson-Dreyer manual approach to all intents and purposes did not, the *Jupiter* trials had already demonstrated that manual methods were too slow when the change of range rates were high and changing, and, moreover, were unreliable because of the likelihood of human error.

In the official trials that took place in January 1908, Pollen's equipment in *Ariadne* recorded the movement of a second test vessel, the pre-dreadnought battleship *Vengeance*, while unbeknownst to Pollen, the Wilson-Dreyer system was tested simultaneously in *Vengeance* by having it track the movements of the *Ariadne*. Although the trials were concerned with the accuracy of the observing and plotting methods only, the performances of the competing mechanized and manual approaches were evaluated on the basis of the accuracy of ranges produced by the dumaresq-Vickers Clock combination after being set with data taken from the plots. The Wilson-Dreyer gear was worked by a team of naval personnel under the direction of Dreyer. In *Ariadne*, Langton and Landstad served as before, Isherwood manned the table, Gipps operated the dumaresq and the Fleet Paymaster manipulated the clock.[110] During the trials of January, Gipps later recalled, "the presence of the Admiral [that is, Wilson] rattled Isherwood a bit and being rather a nervous man he made one or two slips," which "in no way should have affected the judgement of the gear"[111] but which, Pollen remembered, Wilson observed "with great amusement."[112]

The *Ariadne* departed from Portsmouth on 8 January for Torbay, where the first series of official trials were to take place. According to the program formulated by Wilson in December, the test area was to consist of a rectangle that was approximately 8,000 yards long and 2,500 yards wide, whose corners were marked by four moored destroyers. Pollen recalled that

> two days were spent in trying to fix the position of these four destroyers so as to plot their position on the chart. A party of officers had been sent by the Hydrographers Department, and these, with the help of the Navigating officers, proceeded to take bearings and cuts with a view to fixing the positions. The

result of each observation was sent up as fast as it was made to the "Ariadne," but no two observations agreed, with the result that by the afternoon of the second day, we were no nearer getting to an agreed position of the destroyers. It so happened that at this moment, "Ariadne" had veered round into a position in which the range could be taken of each destroyer in succession, and the A.C. instruments were used to construct a plot. In comparing this with the tentative chart already made, we found that it agreed with it as to the positions of two of the destroyers, and supplied two new positions for the others, and that all these four positions, as found by us, resulted in more observations agreeing than by any other arrangement.

Admiral Wilson accepted this position, and the official trials began.[113]

In each of the tests that were carried out on 11 and 13 January 1908, the two trials vessels entered the opposite ends of the rectangle on prearranged courses and speeds that were unknown to each other, but which did not pose change of range rates that were greater than 500 yards per minute. At the point at which the trials vessels were estimated to be 8,000 yards apart, a gun was fired from the *Ariadne* and a flag hauled down simultaneously to mark the beginning of the test period, which was five minutes in duration. Both trials vessels dropped buoys at the beginning, at two minutes after the beginning and at the end of the test period, the positions of which were determined by observations from the moored destroyers and a record of the movement of the trials vessels thus charted. The accuracy of the ranges generated from the plotted data in both ships were checked against the record produced from the location of the buoys, and both methods of plotting were found to have produced valid plots. The success of the Wilson-Dreyer system, however, had been possible only because yaw had been minimized by the calm waters of Torbay in good weather, visibility had been excellent, the maximum range had been relatively low, and courses and speeds had been such as to produce only moderate change of range rates.

The trials did not pass without incident between Wilson and Pollen. "One of the runs was abortive," Pollen recalled,

because the Admiral's orders for the gun to be fired were not carried out, and the observers were, consequently, not ready. The Admiral was very much put out by this, and, before all of my employees in the plotting station and with several officers of the ship present, he again opened up on the question of the £100,000, as he had at the Admiral's House. I had to tell him that I could not discuss the matter in the presence of strangers, but would see him in the cabin afterwards.[114]

The second series of tests were to take place on the open sea, where conditions for plotting were less favorable than the enclosed waters of Torbay. Destroyers could not be moored to mark the testing zone and thus the speeds, courses and ranges produced by plotting and the dumaresq-Vickers Clock combination were to be checked against readings from speed logs, compasses and range finders. The course and speed of each test ship was determined by a lottery in which courses varying by half a degree and speeds from eight to fourteen knots were written on slips of paper, placed in a cap and then drawn. The outcome of the drawing was such that the course and speed of the *Ariadne* was practically identical to that of the *Vengeance*. Under such conditions the change of range would be almost non-existent, and the virtual plot of the Wilson-Dreyer system would thus be useless because the small change in the relative position of the two vessels would mean that the simultaneously observed ranges and bearings would simply be superimposed over one another. Dreyer suggested, therefore, that the virtual plot be replaced during the trial by a manual plot of ranges against time—sometimes referred to as a "time curve"—from which a single change of range rate could be measured. This expedient suited the particular conditions of the trial as determined by the lottery, because the alteration in the change of range rate would be negligible. Dreyer's method, moreover, did not require bearings, which conveniently eliminated difficulties that would otherwise have been caused by yaw produced by the wave action of the open sea.

In the single test run carried out on the open sea on 15 January 1908, the *Ariadne* gear was operated as before, but in the *Vengeance*, the virtual plot was replaced by an improvised time-and-range plot operated by Dreyer and an assistant. This consisted of nothing more than a table on which was placed a chart showing a time-and-range graph. On this graph, ranges were marked in pencil and the sequence of ranges meaned with a ruled pencil line, after which the slope of the line was measured with a protractor to obtain a change of range rate. Wilson again umpired from the *Ariadne*. The two trials vessels steamed on roughly the same course and at the same speed—as had been determined by the lottery—in clear weather, in a moderate sea and separated by a distance of 8,000 yards. Fifty minutes after the trial had begun, Wilson received a flag signal from the *Vengeance* that informed him of the success of the time-and-range plot. He then called a halt to all further testing, and told Pollen that his system had been superseded by one that was "vastly superior."[115]

Wilson provided Pollen with several reasons for his decision. In the first place, he maintained that whatever success Pollen's instruments had achieved was due to the excellence of the Barr & Stroud range-finder. Secondly, Wilson expressed his objection to the mechanical complexity of Pollen's approach by quoting Voltaire's maxim: "The best is the enemy of the good." When Pollen requested a trial in which the sea conditions were less moderate, the range was longer, the maximum change of range rate was much higher and the change of range rate was itself changing rapidly, Wilson refused, arguing that the parallel course and equal speed conditions of the just completed sea-going trial had best approximated the conditions that would occur when hostile fleets actually approached each other, and that even a high change of range rate or rough weather did not affect the difficulty of plotting.[116] After dismissing Pollen with these remarks, Wilson went on board the *Vengeance*, which left the company of the *Ariadne* to carry out further trials with the manual virtual course, and time-and-range plotting systems. These tests, which were limited to tracking the movements of passing steamers, were quickly concluded.[117]

Wilson had given Pollen permission to submit any comments that he might have in writing, and Pollen availed himself of the offer in a printed letter with enclosures of 24 January 1908. Pollen at this time cautiously questioned the capacity of the manual alternative, whose exact nature had not been revealed to him, to perform adequately under less than ideal conditions of courses and speeds, rough weather, or in battle where the personnel would be likely to suffer casualties or make errors under the stress of action. In addition, he pointed out the inconsistency of the trials proceedings and judgement with the previous attitude of the Admiralty, which had emphasized the importance of the capacity of a fire control system to function under difficult circumstances. And finally, Pollen asked whether or not his automatic system of observation and plotting, while less than a complete system of getting the data required to set the gunsights, might be considered as a complement to the manual methods of calculating such data rather than simply being rejected out of hand. Pollen's letter was accompanied by a full technical description of his instruments, and copies of the charts made in the preliminary trials of December with explanatory notes.[118]

Wilson was not to be moved. In his report to Bacon of 31 January 1908, he claimed that the gyroscope arrangement was unworkable and that the instruments in general were mechanically unreliable, and thus recommended that the Pollen system be rejected.[119] In late February or early March, Wilson then submitted a report to Bacon in which he provided a description of the manual fire control system that had been tried in the *Vengeance*, which had been slightly modified as a result of experience gained in the trials and post-trial experiments. A Chetwynd liquid compass, which was then just entering service with the fleet, replaced the improvised telescope-torpedo director arrangement that had previously served as a source of bearings,[120] and the Dreyer time-and-range plot was added to the virtual-course plot scheme for employment when the conditions of courses and speeds were such that there was little change in the relative position of the firing ship and target. While admitting a number of difficulties, Wilson maintained that the navy's fire control requirements had been essentially satisfied by the complete system of observation, plotting, calculation, data transmission and sight-setting that he described in detail in his report. "The methods by which hits can be obtained at long ranges in practice firing," he observed, "are now generally well understood, so that, now this primary difficulty having been more or less solved, greater attention can be directed to the problem of how the materiel and personnel employed to ensure good long-range shooting can be best protected during an action . . ."[121]

Wilson's charge that Pollen's instruments were mechanically unreliable were categorically repudiated by Gipps. "The gear from a mechanical point of view," he wrote to Captain Constantine Hughes-Onslow on 12 December 1908, "behaved splendidly, the results obtained were accurate and instantaneous and came well within the acceptance conditions laid down by the admiralty." "The gyroscopes used in the Ariadne," he stated later, "ran practically continuously for some 5 hours per day during the whole of the trials without any attention[;] they have since run in this ship for two months and given most satisfactory results." Gipps noted that the performance of the gyro-stabilized mounting was such that accurate readings were obtained "in weather in which the guns could not have been laid with sufficient accuracy to fire." The Pollen gear, he believed, was "far ahead of anything that we have got or are likely to get unless we adopt automatic methods."[122]

Wilson's unfavorable report of 31 January 1908 on Pollen's instruments, and later favorable report on his own manual alternative, were read by Harding shortly after they had been submitted to the Naval Ordnance Department. Harding, whose official connection with fire control matters had been severed by Bacon, but who had understandably remained deeply interested in the fate of the Pollen system, later recalled that Wilson's recommendations were

> so wholly inconsistent with the plain evidence of the results obtained in the test runs that I was wholly unable to understand how anyone, even rudimentarily familiar with the problem, could have come to such a conclusion. It seemed to me it was not a case of the "ARIADNE" results being merely better than the "VENGEANCE" results, for it was not a matter of degree at all, but of kind.[123]

In Battle Practices and further experiments carried out in 1908 and 1909, the Wilson-Dreyer system was later found to be completely unworkable.[124] Wilson's recommendations, nevertheless, were to become the basis for the rejection of the Pollen system.

(d) THE REJECTION OF THE POLLEN SYSTEM

Pollen was not without influence at the Admiralty. On 17 January 1908, which was two days after the sea-going tests had concluded, he wrote to Captain E. J. W. Slade, the Director of Naval Intelligence and a good friend. Although plainly exhausted and dispirited, Pollen gave a long account of the *Ariadne* trials, and suggested that Slade consult C. Inigo Thomas, who had succeeded Sir Evan MacGregor as Admiralty Permanent Secretary and who was another supporter. Pollen was also in communication with Commander Thomas E. Crease, a confidant of Fisher and a long-time sympathizer.[125] In response to a letter from Crease, Pollen wrote on 12 February 1908 that "I quite agree with you that the situation is a difficult one, and that the principal hope of a right decision being come to will not rest upon the gunnery verdict (which is a foregone conclusion) but upon the political aspect."[126] Pollen thus once again produced a print for private circulation, in the hope that a clear statement of the nature of the conflict between manual and mechanized methods of fire control would enhance his political position.

The pretext for such a printed address was provided by the Director of Naval Ordnance. "How far mechanisms should supersede the human brain," Bacon wrote privately to Pollen on 26 February 1908, "involved serious practical considerations."[127] Pollen's lengthy reply of the next day, copies of which were printed and probably circulated at the Admiralty,[128] confronted the issue of mechanized versus manual methods of fire control squarely. "The real issue, then, as to the Admiralty taking or rejecting the A.C. system," he observed, "turns on confidence and no confidence in machinery." "Now which," Pollen then asked,

> is the best to have—a lot of complicated people with a lot of complicated heads, or one complicated machine? The errors of a machine can be ascertained by experiment, and they repeat themselves exactly, and therefore can be allowed for in the results. As far, therefore, as instrumental errors are concerned, they can be said not to exist, because they can be ascertained and counteracted. But human errors are in their nature incalculable.

"The issue between A.C. and no A.C. is, I think," Pollen concluded several paragraphs later

> exactly as you state in your letter, and I cannot help thinking that in a matter of such crucial importance as getting hits in battle, it is quite inevitable that, as in every other sphere of human activity, the future must be with the machine. The history of progress is epitomized in the phrase "scientific method."[129]

Bacon was not to be convinced. "The flexibility of the powers of a man either cerebral or mechanical," he wrote to Pollen on 2 March 1908,

> has to be balanced against the rapidity of operation of a machine. The liability to error of both from different causes is a variation of the problem and the available spare men must be balanced against the available spare machines. It is as I have previously pointed out the knowledge of the adaptability of men & matter at sea which draws the only distinctive line between sea & land experience.[130]

Pollen's surrejoinder of 6 March closed the correspondence. After reiterating his arguments in favor of mechanized means of gunnery, Pollen countered Bacon's claim to special insight as a seaman with observations characteristic of his own professional training and religious practice. "In any matter of importance," he maintained,

> the motto of Vincent of Lerins "securus judicat orbis terrarum"[131] is to be remembered. This is acted on in English law by leaving matters of fact to the jury and only law to the judge. Even the Pope, to be accepted as infallible by the faithful, has to speak in the name of, and after consultation with, the *whole* Church. He cannot be rushed into "ex cathedra" pronouncements by "ex parte" and unexamined statements.[132]

Pollen at this time also sought redress through appeals to higher authority. By the terms of the formal contract which had not been signed until a month after the trials, the Admiralty was bound to accept or to reject the Pollen system within one calendar month of the last day of trials—that is, by 14 February—a deadline that was extended to 14 March, as a result, apparently, of the late signing of the agreement.[133] Pollen had not been informed of any decision by the end of February, and thus on 1 March 1908 called upon Tweedmouth, who agreed to show him "the substance of Admiral Wilson's report" and "to consider the question of further trials."[134] The next day, on 2 March, Pollen wrote to Tweedmouth to confirm his request for information and further trials in writing.[135] Tweedmouth appears to have been convinced that Pollen's instruments had not been evaluated fairly, and insisted that further tests be made. Thus C. I. Thomas informed Pollen on 6 March that the Admiralty had decided "to carry out further trials with your Aim Correction Apparatus, in accordance with the provisions of the agreement dated 18th February, 1908, before arriving at a decision as to its adoption or non-adoption in the Service."[136]

Pollen did not receive the Admiralty letter of 6 March until 9 March, at which time he wrote in reply to accept the Admiralty's proposal of further trials. In his letter, he offered to send Isherwood "at a moment's notice" to prepare his instruments, which had been exposed to the elements without attention on the *Ariadne* for seven weeks, for the new trials, but noted that other work would prevent him from being present at all times during the trials. "I shall of course be much interested," he wrote, "in any trials that their Lordships may carry out, but I regret that my business engagements put it out of the question of my being able to attend continuously." "No doubt," Pollen added, "before the question of my attending actually arises, I shall be informed more fully what trials are proposed, and how it is suggested they should be conducted."[137] On the evening of 9 March, Pollen met with Tweedmouth briefly, who invited him to "call again the next day with any suggestions he wished to make with regard to trials."[138]

Tweedmouth, however, was unable to keep the promised appointment on 10 March, and Pollen instead on that day communicated his suggestions for trials conditions in writing. In his "Memorandum" of 10 March 1908, Pollen maintained that the *Ariadne* trials should have taken the form of "a judicial proceeding, or scientific investigation," which, he observed, implied

(1) An impartial head.
(2) Competent expert technical, tactical, and mechanical assessors.
(3) Thorough comprehension of the intention and object of the gear, and the policy of the Board of Admiralty.
(4) Exhaustive experiments to verify or disprove the claims made for the system.
(5) A thorough consideration of the tactical and other developments that must follow upon success.
(6) An equally thorough consideration of such improvements as obviously would improve the results or facilitate their use.

Pollen, in addition, insisted that "the person whose gear was on trial should have been heard with regard to each experiment, and any experiments he asked for should have been made," and that "the report of the Commission trying his system should have been submitted to the Admiralty, together with the inventor's comments on all finding of [sic] and inferences from matters of fact." These conditions, he concluded, had been the case with the *Jupiter* trials.[139]

Pollen's "Memorandum" of 10 March 1908 was accompanied by a letter in which the inventor thanked the First Lord for his intervention, to which he attributed the Admiralty's decision to hold new trials.[140] But on the very day that Pollen wrote his letter and "Memorandum," Thomas in his capacity as the Admiralty Permanent Secretary replied officially to Pollen's letter of 9 March, in which the inventor had accepted the Admiralty offer of further trials, to inform him of the Admiralty's decision not to conduct further trials on the grounds that Pollen had refused their offer! The "further trials proposed in the Admiralty letter of the 6th March . . .," Thomas explained,

> were suggested out of consideration for yourself. By your letter of the 9th March, you do not appear to wish these further trials to take place. In the absence of such further trials, the Agreement between yourself and the Admiralty will expire on the 14th instant.

The Admiralty, Thomas continued, had "accordingly determined to decide the question on the basis of the trials that have already taken place," and after having made "a full and careful consideration," had rejected the instruments.[141]

The Admiralty's decision to hold additional trials of 6 March and the reversal of that position on 10 March, which the pretext given in the Admiralty letter of 10 March could not disguise, were not established by votes of the board, which did not meet between 24 February and 31 March 1908.[142] The decision of 6 March in favor of Pollen was presumably made informally by Jackson, Fisher and Tweedmouth. Tweedmouth was undoubtedly convinced that Pollen had not received fair treatment, but his capacity to support the inventor—which was probably not strong to begin with[143]—was almost certainly damaged on 9 March when he failed in a speech in the House of Lords to provide a satisfactory explanation of his correspondence in February with the German emperor over the British navy estimates.[144] Fisher, on the other hand, and probably Jackson as well, appear to have been persuaded by Dreyer that the service had produced a cheap and effective alternative to the Pollen system. Dreyer, wrote Fisher to Julian Corbett, the naval writer, on 10 March, has "the brain of a Newton!," although the First Sea Lord admitted that "only 1 in a 100 could understand him."[145]

By this time, the technical issues may have been further obfuscated by Wilson's report on his manual system of fire control, which was submitted in early or mid March. In an accompanying memorandum, Bacon observed that

> the actual obtaining of change of range, which was the sole object of the "Ariadne" and "Vengeance" trials, forms but a small feature of this report, and is a comparatively simple matter, but the interpretation of the results obtained; the estimation of deflection; the calculation of the rate of change, both by the time curve and plotting methods; the application of the ballistic corrections,

and the corrections due to wind, course and speed of the enemy, and hence obtaining the accurate gun range, is a piece of splendid work, and cannot fail to mark a very great advance in accurate practical gunnery.

Bacon thus recommended that Wilson's report be printed for restricted circulation, that time and range plotting equipment be fitted in all warships that were equipped with range-finders "as quickly as possible," and that the complete Wilson fire control system be fitted in four battleships and two armoured cruisers of the latest design for further trials.[146]

Wilson's report, Hughes-Onslow was later to note in his War Course paper of 1909, was "generally recognized to be most difficult to follow."[147] Fisher and Jackson had little technical understanding of the latest advances in gunnery, which meant that they were incapable of exposing subtle prevarication when it came to the arcana of fire control. Of Fisher's trusted advisors on gunnery, Jellicoe and Scott had been transferred to sea duty and were as a consequence not immediately available, while Lord Kelvin—who had understood Fisher's concept of the all-big-gun armoured cruiser, the nature of the fire control problem in general and the character of the Pollen fire control system in particular—had died in December 1907. Jackson thus expressed his agreement with Bacon's remarks and recommendation in a note on the bottom margin of the Bacon memorandum. "Concur with Controller," Fisher wrote under Jackson's note on 21 March 1908, while Tweedmouth simply initialled the paper beneath Fisher's concurrence a week later on 27 March.[148]

Pollen, in the meanwhile, was understandably infuriated by the Admiralty letter of 10 March, in which he had been informed of the decisions not to hold the trials promised in the Admiralty letter of 6 March and not to adopt his instruments. At this date, he later recalled to Lieutenant George Gipps, "my temper had been rather worked up, and, distrusting my mental condition, I took a few days before I replied."[149] "Yours of March 6th, saying the Lords had ordered further trials," Pollen maintained in his delayed response of 25 March 1908, "did not inform me that they were ordered out of consideration for me; nor did mine of March 9th say, nor can be supposed to mean, that I did not desire them." "My whole contention, since protesting in January, against the character of the Torbay tests," he continued, "has been that there have so far been no trials at all." "That I have refused further trials," Pollen then insisted, "is utterly unfounded." He concluded with a recounting of the history of the development of his system and his relations with the Admiralty and a refutation of charges which appear to have been made in the Wilson report of 31 January 1908 that his system was mechanically unreliable.[150]

A copy of Pollen's letter to the Admiralty Permanent Secretary was also sent to each member of the Board of Admiralty on 25 March. In a covering letter, Pollen argued that the Admiralty had rejected his instruments through "a complete, though undoubtedly sincere, misrepresentation of the details and purpose of my system; and that this misrepresentation itself has been due to the underlying principle of my gear neither having been understood, nor consequently tested." After stating his conviction that "the final rejection of my system on demonstrably mistaken grounds" would "be made impossible" once the facts had been recognized by the board, Pollen offered to resubmit the question of financial terms to impartial arbitration and to improve his instruments on the basis of the experience of the *Ariadne* trials, reasoning that

> if I am willing to have the question of terms impartially decided, and able to submit material improvements, it is possible for the Board to re-investigate the question, without necessarily animadverting on the character or adequacy of the recent trials, or even reconsidering their decision, which was limited to not purchasing for £100,000.

Pollen concluded with assurances that his representations were in no way directed against the character of Wilson. "That he was not informed of the principles I was working on," Pollen noted,

> and consequently mistook the purpose of my invention, is undoubtedly to be regretted—but to point this out does not involve any arrogation of the right to criticize him, in a matter in which he could have had no motive but to act for the best interests of the Service, of which he is perhaps the greatest living ornament. [151]

On 25 March, Pollen also discussed the possibility of obtaining new trials with Slade, who had already proposed to Thomas that Pollen "should be absorbed into the Service & given a salary to develop the whole question of range getting & aim correction." [152] Fisher may by this time have suspected that all was not well. "In reply to your letter just received," the First Sea Lord wrote to the inventor on 26 March 1908, "as you will remember you much interested me in Sir C. Ottley's room long ago but I don't presume to put my judgement in opposition to that of far finer brains than I possess yet you may be sure so far as my personal influence has play every care will be given to your representation." [153]

On 31 March, the full Board of Admiralty met to discuss, among other things, the Pollen system. [154] The next day, on 1 April, Pollen met at the Admiralty with Thomas, who told him that the Board had refused to reconsider the decision of 10 March, but that they would be willing to compensate Pollen for his losses to date and award him a fee in recognition of his contribution to the development of fire control theory. [155] In response to the Admiralty's request for his estimate of his losses and an appropriate fee, Pollen, in a letter written to the Admiralty Permanent Secretary on 1 April, accounted his losses as having amounted to £4,700 and suggested a recognition fee of £10,000. "If an agreement can be arrived at on this basis," he stated in his letter, "I should feel that my long association with the Navy, and with the Admiralty, which has been a matter of the greatest pride and satisfaction to me, had been severed in a fashion which deprived me of any ground whatever for personal complaint . . ." [156] In a letter of 23 April 1908, the Admiralty offered to pay Pollen £11,500 and give back the instruments tried in the *Ariadne*, including the range-finder, while he in return was to agree not to divulge the secret of his system to any foreign power for two years, during which time the patents of his instruments would remain in the possession of the British government.[157]

On 27 April 1908 Pollen replied to the Admiralty, stating that he would accept the offer on the condition that the two year term was lowered to one year.[158] His cooperative attitude may have been based upon inside knowledge of the board's deliberations, provided perhaps by Thomas, Slade, or Crease. "The Ariadne thing," he explained to George Gipps on 30 April,

> as it stands, is, of course, while perfectly successful, exceedingly incomplete as a fire control system, it being, indeed, only the beginning of one; and I reckon it will take me a full year to get all the other instruments designed, built, and running to my satisfaction. In binding myself, therefore, not to approach any foreign power for a year, I am not in the slightest degree hurting the commercial development of the thing, and, by accepting the money, I am getting the working capital necessary for me to carry on with it without the necessity of making it public. This is virtually understood, I think, at the Admiralty; and, although the transaction takes the form of a final closing up of the thing, I think it is thoroughly understood by Jackie & Co. that the thing will be re-opened.[159]

In a letter of 4 May, the Admiralty informed Pollen that the board was "prepared to meet you half way and substitute 18 months for 2 years as the period during which the patents are to remain sealed,"[160] an arrangement to which Pollen agreed.[161] After further correspondence to arrange details,[162] Pollen was informed on 18 June 1908 that Treasury approval for the transaction had been obtained, and the question of his relations with the Admiralty was thus settled for the time being.[163]

Notes to Chapter 4

1 D. K. Brown, *A Century of Naval Construction: The History of the Royal Corps of Naval Constructors, 1883-1983* (London: Conway Maritime Press, 1983), pp. 90-1.

2 For the results of steaming trials and tests of *Dreadnought*, see John Wingate, *H.M.S. Dreadnought*, in John Wingate (ed.), *Warships in Profile*, 3 Vols. (New York: Doubleday, 1971-4), Vol. 1, pp. 10-14.

3 Oscar Parkes, *British Battleships: A History of Design, Construction and Armament*, new and revised edition, (Hamden, Conn.: Archon, 1972), p. 479.

4 "Experimental Battle Practice carried out by H.M.S. 'Britannia'", *MRPQ/DNO*, 1906, pp. 36-9, N.L.M.D.

5 Siegfried Breyer, *Battleships and Battle Cruisers, 1905-1970*, trans. by Alfred Kurti (New York: Doubleday, 1973; f. p. in German, 1970), pp. 196, 331, 392, 418-19.

6 In a public address at Barrow in November 1904, Albert Vickers had called for the construction of an all-big-gun battleship, which may have caused the German naval attache in London to report the next month that Vickers had produced plans for such a vessel. See J. D. Scott, *Vickers: A History* (London: Weidenfeld & Nicolson, 1962), pp. 54-5. The basic characteristics of the

Dreadnought were not settled until early 1905, however, and the German Admiralty may not have learned of these until the *Engineering* article of May 1905, for which see Chapter 2.

7 V. R. Berghahn, *Germany and the Approach of War in 1914* (New York: St. Martin's Press, 1974), pp. 61-4.

8 Ibid., pp. 263-4, and Peter Padfield, *The Battleship Era* (London: Pan Books, 1975; f.p. 1972), p. 195.

9 Fisher to an unknown correspondent, 3 January 1907, *FGDN*, Vol. 2, p. 112.

10 Fisher to Arnold White, 8 January 1907, ibid., p. 113.

11 Fisher to King Edward VII, 4 October 1907, ibid., pp. 139-40.

12 Fisher to the Prince of Wales, 16 October 1907, ibid., p.148.

13 By the term "the late Board of Admiralty," Ottley meant the change in First Lords, the service members of the board having remained the same.

14 "Comparative Battleship Strength and Recent Admiralty Policy, October 1906" (15 October 1906), a memorandum by Captain Charles Ottley, in "Admiralty policy: Replies to criticism" [henceforward cited as "Comparative Battleship Strength"], Cab. 37/84, 80, *Cabinet Papers*, P.R.O.

15 See Chapter 2.

16 For the reductions in the building programs of fiscal years 1906-07, 1907-08, and 1908-09, see "Memorandum of a Meeting of the Sea Lords at the Admiralty on Saturday, 26th May, 1906, to consider future SHIPBUILDING ARRANGEMENTS, & c.—held in accordance with the wishes of the FIRST LORD, to consider and advise him as to possible reductions," in *Naval Necessities*, IV, 1905-7, N.L.M.D.; "Memorandum relative to Meeting, under Presidency of the Prime Minister, on Thursday, July 12, at 10, Downing Street" (17 July 1906) by Lord Tweedmouth, in Cab. 37/83, 65, P.R.O.; and *Board Minutes* [Admiralty] (12 June 1907), Adm. 167/41, P.R.O.

17 See Appendix, Tables 8 and 9.

18 For the nature and effect of Fisher's administrative reforms, see Admiral Sir R. H. Bacon, *The Life of Lord Fisher of Kilverstone: Admiral of the Fleet*, 2 Vols (London: Hodder and Stoughton, 1929), Vol. 2, pp.1-28.

19 See Appendix, Table 3. For Fisher's claim that his economies so exceeded the expectations of both Selborne and Cawdor, the Conservative First Lords, that they were reluctant to accept the reductions offered by their service advisors, see Fisher to Tweedmouth, 5 October 1906, *FGDN*, Vol. 2, p. 96. See also Fisher to Selborne, 2 August 1904, *FGDN*, Vol. 1, pp. 321-2. For a fuller discussion of naval finance under the Liberal government from 1906, see Chapter 6, section 1.

20 "Comparative Battleship Strength."

21 Vittorio Cuniberti, "A New 'Ideal' Ship," in Fred T. Jane (ed.), *Fighting Ships, 1906-7* (London: Sampson Low Marston, 1906), pp. 456-9. When an armament of eight 16-inch guns was mounted in a battleship for the first time (the Japanese *Nagato* class of 1916), the hull displaced 34,000 tons—or nearly twice that of the *Dreadnought*'s 18,000 tons.

22 See Chapters 2, 5, and 6.

23 "Board Meeting to Consider the Details of the Armament and Construction of the two Vessels intended for the 1907-8 programme" (11 December 1906), in Adm. 167/40, P.R.O.

24 See Chapter 3.

25 "Armament of Cruisers: Statement by Rear-Admiral Sir John Jellicoe, when Director of Naval Ordnance, on the Subject of the Armament of the Cruisers for the 1908-9 Programme" (June 1907), in Great Britain, Admiralty, Navy

Estimates Committee, *Report upon Navy Estimates for 1908-9* (November 1907), F.P. 4724, FISR 8/11, C.C.

26 *Board Minutes* [Admiralty], 12 June 1906, Adm. 167/41, P.R.O. For the reversal of this decision, see Chapter 5.

27 No copy of this letter appears to have survived, but its contents are summarized in Admiralty Permanent Secretary to Pollen, 15 October 1906, P.P.

28 Ibid.

29 Pollen to the Admiralty Permanent Secretary, 17 October 1906, P.P.

30 Admiralty Permanent Secretary to Pollen, 25 October 1906, P.P.

31 Admiralty Permanent Secretary (MacGregor) to Pollen, 29 October 1906, and Pollen to the Admiralty Permanent Secretary, 29 October 1906, both in P.P.

32 Pollen to the Accountant General to the Navy, 8 November 1906, P.P.

33 Pollen to Tweedmouth, 12 October 1906; Tweedmouth to Pollen, 13 October 1906; Pollen to Tweedmouth, 31 October 1906; Tweedmouth to Pollen, 2 November 1906; Pollen to the Admiralty Permanent Secretary, 2 November 1906; and Admiralty Permanent Secretary (MacGregor) to Pollen, 3 November 1906, all in P.P.

34 Pollen to the Admiralty Permanent Secretary, 2 November 1906, P.P.

35 Admiralty Permanent Secretary (MacGregor) to Pollen, 7 November 1906, P.P.

36 "Maga" [Vice-Admiral Sir Reginald Custance], "The Speed of the Capital Ship," *Blackwood's Magazine*, Vol. 180 (October 1906), p. 435-51, and "Black Joke," "Tactical Speed," *The United Service Magazine*, Vol. 155 (October 1906), pp. 1-15.

37 See Chapter 2.

38 Arthur Hungerford Pollen, *Some Aspects of the Tactical Value of Speed in Capital Ships* (by the author, November 1906), *PP*, pp. 106-13.

39 Pollen to the Admiralty Permanent Secretary, 2 November 1906; Pollen's business secretary [probably Godfrey Hedges] to the Admiralty Permanent Secretary, 15 November 1906; and Greene, brief, part 2, p. 40, all in P.P. Greene gives a return date of March 1907 but no date of departure. The Pollen correspondence of the time clearly states a departure date of 10 November and arrangements for a trip of six weeks duration, while a letter from Jellicoe of 1 January 1907 indicates that Pollen was present in London on that date. The Greene statement was thus probably in error, and appears to have been based upon a 1912 memorandum by Pollen, which gave an approximate time of return of late February or early March (see "A. H. P. Statement to 1911," n.d. but probably 1912, P.P. [henceforward cited as "A. H. P. Statement," P.P.]). Pollen's error perhaps stemmed from the fact that official contract correspondence between the Admiralty and Pollen did not resume until March 1907.

40 Admiralty Permanent Secretary (MacGregor) to Pollen, 11 March 1907, P.P.

41 Pollen to the Admiralty Permanent Secretary, 15 March 1907, P.P.

42 Pollen to the Admiralty Permanent Secretary, 5 April 1907, P.P.

43 "Mr. A. H. Pollen's Memorandum on Patent Position re Barr and Stroud," 16 April 1907, P.P.

44 Godfrey Hedges to Ernest B. Hawksley, 18 April 1907, and Pollen to Hawksley, 13 May 1907, P.P.

45 Admiralty Permanent Secretary (C. I. Thomas) to Pollen, April [no day] 1907, P.P.

46 Hedges to Hawksley, 18 April 1907, P.P.

47 Pollen to a Mr. Minter, 18 April 1907, P.P.
48 Director of Navy Contracts (F. W. Black) to Hollams, Sons, Coward & Hawksley, 23 May 1907, P.P.
49 Director of Navy Contracts (F. W. Black) to Pollen, 19 July 1907, and the Admiralty Permanent Secretary to Hollams, Sons, Coward & Hawksley, 19 July 1907, P.P.
50 Pollen to the Director of Navy Contracts, 22 July 1907, P.P.
51 Pollen to the Director of Navy Contracts, 24 July 1907, P.P.
52 Ibid., and [Hedges?] to Russell Clarke, 25 July 1907; Memo. from Mr. Pollen to Mr. Russell Clarke, 26 July 1907; and Pollen to the Director of Navy Contracts, 26 July 1907, P.P.
53 "Memo. from Mr. Pollen to Mr. Russell Clarke," 26 July 1907, P.P.
54 Pollen to the Director of Navy Contracts, 30 July 1907, P.P.
55 Russell Clarke, "Admiralty Commissioners and A. H. Pollen, Esq. Opinion," 29 July 1907, P.P.
56 Pollen to F. W. Black, 31 July 1907, P.P.
57 Ibid.
58 Admiralty Permanent Secretary (Thomas) to Pollen, 26 November 1907, P.P.
59 Admiralty to the Treasury, 26 November 1907, in Great Britain, Parliament, *Appropriation Account, Navy* (1907-8), p. 121. For Pollen's suspicions regarding this letter, which were perhaps unwarranted, see Arthur Hungerford Pollen, *Notes, Etc., on the Ariadne Trials* (London: Argo Company, April 1909) [*PP*, p. 223].
60 Pollen to the Admiralty Permanent Secretary, 19 December 1907, P.P.
61 Admiralty Permanent Secretary (W. Graham Greene) to Pollen, 21 December 1907, P.P.
62 [Godfrey Hedges?] to the Admiralty Permanent Secretary, 23 December 1907, P.P.
63 Formal Contract, dated 18 February 1908, *CCB*, P.P.
64 Ruddock Mackay, *Fisher of Kilverstone* (Oxford: Clarendon Press, 1974), pp. 387-92.
65 Arthur Hungerford Pollen, *Notes on a Proposed Method of Studying Naval Tactics* (by the author: spring, 1907), *PP*, pp. 114-30.
66 Untitled, undated, typescript memorandum written in 1909, apparently by Pollen, in P.P. For the subsequent history of Pollen's tactical machine, see *PP*, p. 237.
67 For the date of the inspection, see the Admiralty Permanent Secretary (Thomas) to Pollen, 21 May 1907, P.P. For what took place at the inspection, see "Proof of Evidence of Colonel E. W. Harding" (January 1920), p. 12, and testimony of Arthur Hungerford Pollen, in RCAI, *Minutes*, Vol. 9 (1 August 1925), pp. 82-3, P.P.
68 Ibid.
69 See Jellicoe to Pollen, 10 August 1907, and Jellicoe to Pollen, 25 August 1907, P.P.
70 Quoted in Ruddock F. Mackay, *Fisher of Kilverstone* (Oxford: Clarendon, 1973), p. 297.
71 Admiral Sir Reginald Bacon, *A Naval Scrap-Book; First Part: 1877-1900* (London: Hutchinson, n.d. [1925]), pp. 33-4.
72 For Bacon's views on gunnery, see Pollen to Bacon, 27 February 1908; Bacon to Pollen, 2 March 1908; Pollen to Bacon, 6 March 1908; Pollen to Bacon, 16 December 1908; and Bacon to Pollen, 16 July [1909]; P.P.

73 For Dreyer's early career, see Admiral Sir Frederic Dreyer, *The Sea Heritage: a Study of Maritime Warfare* (London: Museum Press, 1955). For Wilson's reliance on Dreyer's advice on matters pertaining to gunnery, see Admiral Sir Edward E. Bradford, *Life of Admiral of the Fleet Sir Arthur Knyvet Wilson* (New York: E. P. Dutton, 1923), p. 22.

74 Testimony of Arthur Hungerford Pollen in RCAI, *Minutes*, Vol. 9 (1 August 1925), p. 80, P.P. See also Dreyer to Pollen, 22 March 1906, P.P.

75 Pollen to Dreyer, 31 October 1906, P.P.

76 Dreyer to Pollen, 15 December 1906, P.P.

77 Description of the Dreyer calculator, dated 10 December 1906, DRYR 2/1, Dreyer Papers, C.C., and Dreyer, *Sea Heritage*, p. 55.

78 Ibid.

79 Jellicoe to Dreyer, 11 December 1906, DRYR 3/2, Dreyer Papers, C.C.; Captain R. H. S. Bacon, "Report on Experimental Cruise" (16 March 1907), Adm.116/1059, P.R.O.; and Bacon, *The Life of Lord Fisher*, Vol. 1, p. 267.

80 Testimony of Arthur Hungerford Pollen, in RCAI, *Minutes*, Vol. 9 (1 August 1925), p. 83, P.P.

81 Frederic C. Dreyer to [the Admiralty Permanent Secretary?], 2 July 1907, DRYR 2/1, Dreyer Papers, C.C.

82 Testimony of Frederic C. Dreyer, in RCAI, *Minutes*, Vol. 11 (4 August 1925), p. 18, P.P.

83 Letter to an unknown correspondent, 2 November 1910, in Arthur Hungerford Pollen, *The Quest of a Rate Finder* (by the author, November 1910), P.P [*PP*, p. 264].

84 Testimony of Arthur Hungerford Pollen, in RCAI, *Minutes*, Vol. 9 (1 August 1925), p. 84, P.P. See also Pollen to Dreyer, 18 December 1907, P.P. In his memorandum of 1912 ("A. H. P. Statement," P.P.), Pollen gave the date of his meeting with Dreyer as 25 October 1907, but the date of his letter to Dreyer is given incorrectly. All things considered, the date given in his later testimony seems to be the better choice.

85 Pollen to Wilson, 28 May 1906, P.P.

86 Anthony Pollen, *The Great Gunnery Scandal: The Mystery of Jutland* (London: Collins, 1980), p. 56.

87 Admiralty Permanent Secretary to Pollen, 23 November 1907; "Notes of principal points discussed at meeting at D.N.O.'s room on November 26th 1907"; and Formal Contract, dated 18 February 1908, P.P.

88 Wilson to Pollen, 4 December 1907, and also the Admiralty Permanent Secretary (Thomas) to Pollen, 5 December 1907, P.P.

89 Wilson to Pollen, 8 December 1907, P.P.

90 For the background and text of this print, see *PP*, pp. 131-55.

91 Ibid., p. 135.

92 Ibid., pp. 144-51.

93 Wilson to Pollen, 11 December 1907, P.P.

94 Ibid., and Pollen to Wilson, 18 December 1907, P.P.

95 "A. H. P. Statement," P.P. See also Lieutenant George Gipps to Captain Constantine Hughes-Onslow, 12 December 1908, P.P.

96 Pollen to Wilson, 17 December 1907, in Arthur Hungerford Pollen, *Notes, Correspondence, etc., on the Pollen A.C. System, installed and tried in HMS Ariadne* (by the author, 1908), in *PP*, pp. 167-71.

97 Pollen to Wilson, 18 December 1907 [noted by Wilson in his reply to have been a letter of 17 December], and Wilson to Pollen, 18 December 1907, P.P.

98 Pollen to Wilson, 18 December 1907, P.P.

99 Pollen to Wilson, 19 December 1907, P.P.
100 Wilson to Pollen, 20 December 1907, P.P.
101 Pollen to George Gipps, 26 August 1911, P.P.
102 Pollen to the Admiralty Permanent Secretary, 9 December 1907, P.P.
103 Gipps to Captain Constantine Hughes-Onslow, 12 December 1908, P.P.
104 Ibid.; Captain A. S. Lafone to Pollen, 16 January 1908; and Arthur Hungerford Pollen, *Notes, Correspondence, etc., on the Pollen A.C. System, installed and tried in H.M.S. Ariadne, December, 1907-January, 1908* (by the author, 1908); P.P.
105 Pollen to his wife, no date, but clearly written in either late December 1907 or early January 1908, P.P. For the subsequent friendship between Chatfield and Pollen, see Hobart Chatfield-Taylor to Chatfield, 22 January 1943, in CHT/8/1, Chatfield Papers, N.M.M.
106 Jellicoe to Pollen, 26 December 1907, P.P.
107 Jellicoe to Pollen, no date, but probably late December 1907, P.P.
108 The telescope was mounted on a torpedo director, which consisted of a flat plate with a circular bearing scale engraved on its face. The bearing observation was made by training the telescope on the target, and reading off the bearing from the scale as indicated by the train of the telescope in relation to the scale. Such an arrangement, however, made no allowance for the effect of yaw because the bearings were taken with respect to the keel-line, rather than the course-line movement, of the ship from which the observations were made.
109 For the Wilson-Dreyer system, see "Report of Admiral of the Fleet Sir A. K. Wilson on Rate of Change Experiments," in Great Britain, Admiralty, Gunnery Branch, *Fire Control* (1908), bound together with other reports in *Miscellaneous Gunnery Experiments, 1901-1913*, N.L.M.D. [henceforward cited as Gunnery Branch, *Fire Control* [1908], N.L.M.D.]; "Battle Practice" and "Plotting" in Captain C. Hughes-Onslow, *Fire Control* (Royal Naval War College, Portsmouth, 1909), P.P.; and the testimony of Frederic C. Dreyer, in RCAI, *Minutes*, Vol. 11 (4 August 1925), p. 18, P.P.
110 Gipps to Captain Constantine Hughes-Onslow, 12 December 1908, P.P. Pollen's description of the arrangements, which was given many years after the event, is somewhat different and perhaps not altogether accurate. In any case, see testimony of Arthur Hungerford Pollen, in RCAI, *Minutes*, Vol. 9 (1 August 1925), p. 51, P.P.
111 Gipps to Hughes-Onslow, 12 December 1908, P.P.
112 Testimony of Arthur Hungerford Pollen, in RCAI, *Minutes*, Vol. 9 (1 August 1925) p. 51, P.P.
113 "A. H. P. Statement," P.P.
114 "A.H.P. Statement," P.P.
115 Untitled, undated printed history, probably prepared for the Royal Commission on Awards to Inventors hearings by either Pollen or Greene, paragraph 34, P.P. For the competitive trials of 11, 13 and 15 January, see the log of H.M.S. *Ariadne*, Adm. 53/17318, P.R.O.; Pollen, *Notes, Correspondence, etc.*, P.P. [PP, pp. 159-71].; Pollen, "A. H. P. Statement"; Wilfrid Greene, in RCAI, *Minutes*, Vol. 3 (6 July 1925), pp. 3-12; and testimony of Frederic C. Dreyer, in RCAI, *Minutes*, Vol. 11 (4 August 1925), pp. 18, 22-4 and Vol. 12 (5 August 1925), pp. 5-6, P.P.
116 Pollen to Captain E. J. W. Slade, 17 January 1908; Pollen to Wilson, 24 January 1908, in *Notes, Correspondence, etc.* and Pollen to George Gipps, 26 August 1911, P.P.

117 Gunnery Branch, *Fire Control* (1908), N.L.M.D.
118 Pollen, *Notes, Correspondence, etc.* For the circumstances surrounding the production of this print, see Pollen to Wilson, 18 January 1908; Pollen to Wilson, 21 January 1908; Wilson to Pollen, 23 January 1908; [Hedges?] to Wilson, 24 January 1908; Wilson to Pollen, 26 January 1908; and Pollen to Wilson, 27 January 1908; P.P.
119 No copy of Wilson's report of 31 January 1908 has yet been discovered, but see Pollen's summary of Wilson's criticisms in Pollen to the Admiralty Permanent Secretary, 25 March 1908, in Arthur Hungerford Pollen, *Notes, etc., on the Ariadne Trials* (by the author, April 1909; not to be mistaken with the printed work of a similar title of 1908), P.P. [*PP*, pp. 195-236]; and Pollen's detailed discussion of the minor technical shortcomings of the *Ariadne* gear in his memorandum to George Gipps of 29 January 1908, P.P. In his report, Wilson may also have reiterated his contention that the Pollen gear was unnecessary because of the excellence of the Barr & Stroud range-finder, for which see Great Britain, Admiralty, *Pollen Aim Correction System: General Grounds of Admiralty Policy and Historical Record of Business Negotiations* (February 1913), p. 8, N.L.M.D.
120 Bearings obtained from a Kelvin compass were critically affected by yaw because of the rapid response of its pin-pivoted indicator. Yaw had less effect on bearing readings obtained from a liquid compass because the movement of its floating indicator was much slower.
121 "Report" in Gunnery Branch, *Fire Control* (1908), N.L.M.D.
122 Gipps to Hughes-Onslow, 12 December 1908, P.P.
123 "Proof of Evidence of Colonel E. W. Harding" (January 1920), p. 13, P.P.
124 See Chapter 5.
125 See Crease to Pollen, 5 November 1904, 11 November 1904, 13 March 1905, 28 March 1905 and 5 April 1905, P.P.
126 Pollen to Crease, 12 February 1908, incomplete draft letter. No copy of Crease's letter to Pollen has been found.
127 Bacon to Pollen, 26 February 1908, P.P.
128 Pollen to C. I. Thomas, 28 February 1908, P.P.
129 Pollen to Bacon, 27 February 1908, P.P.; abridged printed version in *PP*, pp. 172-7.
130 Bacon to Pollen, 2 March 1908, P.P.
131 "The verdict of the world is conclusive." For more on the use of this quotation, see *PP*, p. 388.
132 Pollen to Bacon, 6 March 1908, P.P.
133 Admiralty Permanent Secretary (Thomas) to Pollen, 10 March 1908, in Pollen, *Notes, etc.*, p. 34, P.P. [*PP*, p. 230].
134 Ibid., p. 34 [*PP*, p. 223].
135 Pollen to Tweedmouth, 2 March 1908, ibid., p. 36 [*PP*, pp. 225-6].
136 Admiralty Permanent Secretary (Thomas) to Pollen, 6 March 1908, ibid., p. 38 [*PP*, p. 227].
137 Pollen to the Admiralty Permanent Secretary, 9 March 1908, ibid., pp. 38-9 [*PP*, pp. 227-8].
138 Pollen ibid., p. 34 [*PP*, p. 223].
139 "Memorandum" ibid., p. 40 [*PP*, p. 229].
140 Pollen to Tweedmouth, 10 March 1908, ibid., pp. 39-40 [*PP*, pp. 228-9].
141 Admiralty Permanent Secretary (Thomas) to Pollen, 10 March 1908, ibid., p. 41 [*PP*, p. 230].
142 *Board Minutes* [Admiralty] 1908, Adm. 167/42, P.R.O.

143 For the rejection of Tweedmouth's proposals to build battleships with mixed-caliber armaments for the 1908–09 program, see Tweedmouth to Sir George Clarke, 25 April 1908, in *The Effectiveness of Naval Fire. Memorandum by Sir George S. Clarke, and Remarks thereon*, Admiralty confidential print, F.P. 4982, FISR 8/45, C.C.

144 For the Tweedmouth affair, see *FDSF*, Vol. 1, pp. 140-2.

145 Fisher to Julian Corbett, 10 March 1908, FISR 1/6, F.P. 296, C.C. See also Fisher's Secretary (Walker?) to Corbett, 9 March 1908, and Dreyer to Julian Corbett, 10 March 1908, both in RIC/9/1, Richmond Papers, N.M.M.

146 Bacon Memorandum and Minute, March 1908, in Adm. 1/8010, P.R.O.

147 Hughes-Onslow, *Fire Control*, "Section III: Plotting," p. 4, P.P.

148 Bacon Memorandum and Minute, March 1908, Adm. 1/8010, P.R.O.

149 Pollen to Gipps, 30 April 1908, P.P.

150 Pollen to the Admiralty Permanent Secretary, 25 March 1908, in Pollen, *Notes, etc.*, pp. 43, 46–7 [*PP*, pp. 232-6].

151 Pollen to each member of the Board of Admiralty, 25 March 1908, ibid., p. 42 [*PP*, pp. 231-2].

152 Slade Diary, 1908, entry for 25 March, MRF/39/3, N.M.M.

153 Fisher to Pollen, 26 March 1908, P.P.

154 *Board Minutes* [Admiralty] 1908, Adm. 167/42, P.R.O.

155 Pollen to the Admiralty Permanent Secretary, 1 April 1908, *CCB*, P.P.

156 Ibid.

157 Admiralty Permanent Secretary (Thomas) to Pollen, 23 April 1908, *CCB*, P.P.

158 Pollen to the Admiralty Permanent Secretary, 27 April 1908, P.P.

159 Pollen to Gipps, 30 April 1908, P.P.

160 Admiralty Permanent Secretary (Thomas) to Pollen, 4 May 1908, P.P.

161 An allusion to this agreement is to be found in Pollen to the Admiralty Permanent Secretary, 11 May 1908, P.P.

162 Admiralty Permanent Secretary (Thomas) to Pollen, 9 May 1908,; Pollen to the Admiralty Permanent Secretary, 11 May 1908; and Pollen to the Admiralty Permanent Secretary, 28 May 1908; P.P.

163 Admiralty Permanent Secretary (Thomas) to Pollen, 18 June 1908, P.P.

[5]

Confusion:
Fire Control and Capital Ship
Design,
1908-1909

1 *The Gunnery Muddle, 1908-1909*

At the Lord Mayor's banquet at the Guildhall on 9 November 1907, Sir John Fisher had boasted that as a result of the recent efforts of the Admiralty, the strength of the Royal Navy was such that he could say to his countrymen "sleep quiet in your beds." The First Sea Lord was particularly extravagant in his report on the progress of naval gunnery. "The gunnery efficiency of the Fleet," he maintained

> has surpassed all records—it is unparalleled—and I am lost in wonder and admiration at the splendid unity of spirit and determination that must have been shown by everybody from top to bottom to obtain these results.[1] I am sure that your praise and your appreciation will go forth to them, because, remember, the best ships, the biggest Navy . . . is no use unless you can hit. You must hit first, you must hit hard, and you must keep on hitting. If these are the fruits I don't think there is much wrong with the government of the Navy. . . . our object has been the fighting efficiency of the Fleet and its instant readiness for war; and we have got it. And I say it because no one can have a fuller knowledge than myself about it, and I speak with the fullest sense of responsibility.[2]

Fisher's remarks provoked a highly critical three-part series of articles entitled "Fool Gunnery in the Navy" in the February, March and April 1908 numbers of *Blackwood's Magazine*, written by an anonymous naval officer under the pseudonym of "St Barbara," the patron saint of artillerymen. In the first article, the writer addressed matters raised by the promulgation by the Admiralty in November 1907 of new Battle Practice rules. Although he was gratified by the fact that the stationary targets that had been standard in Battle Practice since 1905 were to be replaced by towed targets, the author noted that the action "was an innovation which all thinking men have been urging for some two or three years past," and that "it is extremely doubtful whether sufficient can be built in time to be used for the firing of all fleets in 1908." St Barbara also greeted the news that hits with 12-inch guns would in the future count more than hits with 6-inch guns, with the observation that "seeing that the former does six times the damage of the latter, one can only wonder why it is that they [the Admiralty] did not come to such an obvious conclusion five years ago."

St Barbara insisted, furthermore, that additional changes were necessary. He maintained that, in so far as battle practice rules were concerned, the time period of firing—eight minutes—was too short; that more than a single battle practice per year was required to keep fleet gunnery efficient; that hits made at the beginning of a battle practice run should count more than those made towards the end in order to encourage early hitting; and that all ships should carry out battle practice under comparable and not necessarily favorable conditions of wind, wave and visibility. Secondly, St Barbara argued that those gunnery personnel who were charged with the task of controlling fire were inadequately trained and were so few in number that ships lacked an effective reserve in the likely event of casualties occurring in battle. He thus called for major changes in the frequency and character of battle practice, and the setting up of new gunnery schools devoted solely to the production of officers trained in practical fire control technique.[3]

In his second article, St Barbara denounced the Gunlayer's Test on technical, financial and pedagogical grounds; advocated its abolition; and described an alternative system of training gunlayers. He criticized Battle Practice, on the other hand, because it only tested the gunnery prowess of individual ships, which he believed promoted a spirit of competition that led to "illicit effort, instead of the study of war," and thus insisted that provision had to be made for gunnery exercises that involved the simultaneous firing of groups of ships in preparation for the fleet action that was certain to be fought in the event of hostilities with a major naval power. St Barbara then outlined proposals for a sweeping reorganization of the Naval Ordnance Department, the gunnery schools and the training procedures of the fleet, whose result, it was hoped, would be gunnery training in the schools and battle training in the fleet instead of the combination of both in the latter, which was then said to be the case. In the conclusion to this piece, he alluded to the recent trials in the *Vengeance* and *Ariadne*, but otherwise declined comment because of their confidential character.[4] In his third article, St Barbara dealt with questions related to the use of light guns against torpedo craft and in particular to the problem of night-fighting.[5]

In all three articles, the writer condemned the leadership of the Admiralty in no uncertain terms. "In the work of destruction of an enemy by guns," he wrote in the first of the series, "the fleet are not properly led or assisted by the Admiralty Board," and later that "the Admiralty have no gunnery policy whatsoever beyond advertisement."[6] "Naval gunnery,"

St Barbara claimed in his second, "is only efficient up to Admiralty standards." "The writer," he continued, "considers he has shown those standards to be poverty-stricken, viewed from a fighting standpoint."[7] And in the third, St Barbara stated that

> although the Administration have, in the case of heavy guns, made some sort of attempt to attain daylight efficiency, they have most signally failed and neglected during the past five years to give a proper lead to the sea-going fleets in developing the art which is to save the ship from an intelligent enemy after the sun has set. To have failed in a matter of such imperative urgency lays them open to a much more wholesale condemnation than any neglect of daylight fighting.[8]

The charges made in the first two articles were dismissed rather than answered in an Admiralty confidential print of March 1908, which may have been written by R. H. S. Bacon, the Director of Naval Ordnance. The author largely avoided the issues raised by St Barbara by arguing that Admiralty policy had been governed by the need to educate the navy into accepting the practicability of long-range firing. "The Navy had to be taught," he wrote,

> that hitting at such ranges was possible, and that it would become in time a mere commonplace. Now that this has been done, further progress can be and is being made apart from mere hitting and the firing generally can be made to approximate annually more closely to battle conditions. To have confused this instruction by attempting too much while the possibility of hitting at such ranges was scoffed at generally in the Navy would have been absurd and suicidal to progress. . . . The Navy must be taught by practical experience as well as by direct instruction; for this time is required. No doubt we may confidently expect annually the question of the ingenuous critic as to why the improvements decided on for the next year's instruction were not tried the year before. The question is so simple and the answer so obvious.[9]

The Admiralty's position was not without merit. Attempts to fire at extended ranges before 1905 in the absence of proper instruments or a program of training had resulted in failure and discouragement. The introduction of the Gunlayer's Test and Battle Practice in 1905 had provided a uniform system of testing and evaluating fleet gunnery performance where none had previously existed. The changes in Battle Practice rules of 1907 were significant improvements. And the training proposals called for by St Barbara would have required great expenditure on up-to-date equipment for non-combatant establishments that was already in short supply in the fleet, at a time when financial constraints had forced the Admiralty to reduce the level of spending on ammunition by a quarter.[10] St Barbara, nevertheless, probably represented a large constituency within the service, who believed that their careers were threatened by the actions of what they viewed as a capricious and artificial system of gunnery evaluation, a fear that was not completely unjustified. And their anxieties were only further exacerbated by the commitment of the Naval Ordnance Department to impractical methods of fire control.

The Wilson-Dreyer system, it will be recalled, consisted of both manual virtual-course and time-and-range plotting. Bacon, the Director of Naval Ordnance, however, appears to have preferred the latter over the former on the grounds of its greater simplicity, and thus pressed for its adoption without its erstwhile partner. In March 1908, he reported that the "general results" of the experiments in the *Vengeance* "have been communicated verbally to the different fleets so that in a very short time the time curve method will be in general use and good practical results in firing at moving objects should be obtained."[11] Dreyer, on the other hand, argued the case for the use of both manual virtual-course and time-and-range methods of plotting in a lecture given in the spring of 1908 to the officers in training from the Channel Fleet at H.M.S. *Excellent*. "The 'one & only' Dreyer," wrote a witness to the affair–known only by his nickname, which was "Hooligan"—to George Gipps, "came down from the Admiralty today at great expense & personal inconvenience to endeavor, in language suited to our indifferent mental capacities, to explain to us benighted 'back enders' the epoch making 'Vengeance' method of fire control." After describing the Wilson-Dreyer approach, which was characterized as an "entirely unpracticable method of hitting the enemy," the writer noted that "in the heckling which followed [Dreyer's presentation] he refused to discuss Pollen's A.C."[12]

A lack of confidence in the advice on fire control offered by the Naval Ordnance Department drove many officers to seek the assistance of Pollen. Not long after the *Ariadne* trials, Pollen had manufactured a manual version of his true-course plotting instrument and supplied them at cost to 15 or 20 gunnery lieutenants who were personal friends, and these were in turn more or less copied by other naval officers who were concerned by the difficulties that would be posed by that year's Battle Practice, which would be the first to involve shooting at a moving target. The result was that, of the 54 warships that participated in the 1908 Battle Practice carried out during the summer and fall, 8 used manual virtual-course plotting, 13 used manual time-and-range gear and 33—the overwhelming majority—used manual true-course plotting, including all the ships of the Home Fleet and nearly all those of the Atlantic Fleet.[13]

Although the performance of the true-course plotting board suffered from the inherent limitations of manual operation and yaw-affected bearings, the results were better than those achieved with the manual virtual-course or time-and-range plotting that had been recommended by the Admiralty. In his 1909 report for the Naval War College,[14] Captain Constantine Hughes-Onslow noted that the Wilson-Dreyer system had "not been found satisfactory by those who have tried it," and that "no instance has come to light of any Ship making successful use of the Virtual Plot combined with a Time and Range diagram."[15] He observed, on the other hand, that "several ships" that used Pollen's manual gear achieved "great success"[16] and that true-course plotting "appears to have met with general acceptation as being the best method to employ."[17] Pollen was informed in late 1908 by many naval officers, including members of the Board of Admiralty, that in Battle Practice both manual virtual–course and time–and–range plotting "had been complete failures."[18] The Admiralty's own review of the 1908 Battle Practice reported that the success rate of true–course plotting was 55 per cent, virtual–course plotting was 50 per cent and time–and–range plotting was 31 per cent.[19]

Many officers in the fleet were impressed by the successes achieved with Pollen's manual plotter. On 11 October 1908, Lieutenant Roger Backhouse wrote to Pollen to ask him for

> a plotting table with the next batch you make. There is no immediate hurry for it but I should like it if possible in a month or 6 weeks. My own amateurish Table did good work but now I think I would like to have the more exact instrument.[20]

Admiral Lord Charles Beresford, the Commander–in–Chief of the Channel Fleet, reported Lieutenant Ernest K. Arbuthnot to Pollen on 17 October 1908, was "so much impressed" with the Pollen true–course plotting instrument "that the remaining 5 ships that have to do their B.P. are all to use it." "I propose to lend the board to someone for their B.P. if possible," Arbuthnot added later in his letter, "as the more widely it is used the better."[21] Lieutenant K. G. B. Dewar and 12 others[22] purchased a slightly improved version of Pollen's manual table that was produced in 1909,[23] while the Ordnance Department was forced by service demand to issue a near–exact copy of Pollen's manual true–course plotting table in 1909.[24]

Pollen had a low opinion, however, of manual plotting of any sort, including his own. The manual true–course plotting table, he informed Captain Herbert Richmond on 17 June 1909,

> was built with a full knowledge that it would be utterly impracticable for anything except the very easy conditions of modern Battle practice [*sic*], and was only lent or sold to the officers who have it for the reason that, in the absence of anything better, it might be found to be better than nothing. I think experience shows that, in the generality of ships, it is so little better than no system at all, that in all probability gunnery efficiency would be increased if greater reliance were placed on guesswork and spotters trained for that.[25]

Pollen's objections to manual plotting in any form, and time–and–range plotting especially, were put into the form of a pamphlet that was printed in September 1908 under the title *Reflections on an Error of the Day*.[26] Pollen's general critique of time–and–range plotting was backed by a detailed analysis of the mathematical issues written by Harold Isherwood, Pollen's design engineer, in a separate section entitled "On the Relationship of 'Change of Range' to 'Time.'" In addition to the specific question of plotting techniques, Pollen's main text discussed the *Ariadne* trials, the problems of Battle Practice, and the necessity of mechanized fire control. "Proposals that have any prospect of success," he insisted with regard to last point, cannot . . . be dismissed with such threadbare arguments of prejudice as, for instance, that automatic gear is too complicated or too costly. The reason it is complicated is that the operation is so; the test of gear being too complicated is not its complexity, but its being reliable; and, to prove whether gear is reliable or not, trials must be made extending over sufficient time, and over a sufficient number of conditions as to weather, distance, rapidity and variation in change of range, the detection of change of course, etc., to enable the true facts to be known, and prevent condemnation being come to on baseless assumptions.[27]

Pollen's print, which was widely circulated in the service, outraged Dreyer.[28] On 18 October 1908, he wrote a long letter to Captain Constantine Hughes-Onslow, who had asked him to provide a description of his plotting system.[29] Dreyer admitted at the outset that he had "spent a lot of time . . . trying to develop Range plotting *without* bearings" but that he had "happily dropped it before B.P." and that true-course plotting "still holds the day . . ." The latter method, he maintained, had been invented years before by Colonel Henry Watkin for the coast artillery, and attributed its successful application in the navy solely to the advent of the 9-foot Barr & Stroud range-finder. Pollen, he charged, had "stirred up some agitators to believe that his auto-system is the best, but a searching analysis I think reveals the fact that the simple kitchen table methods [a reference to the kitchen table upon which his time-and-range chart had been placed] are better than the complicated machinery game and produce the same result as the latter only does when in adjustment."

Dreyer's opposition to mechanical complexity was whole-hearted and unequivocal. "The simpler we keep our ships," he insisted,

> the better. A Chetwynd compass in the transmitting station and a pointer that is worked by the R.F. training, a deal kitchen table and a range bar that is all we want.
>
> We are quite sure that we know how to adjust a simple compass, but of the gyro gear we are *by no means sure*.

Dreyer believed that the automatic transmission of range data was inherently unreliable. "A few people even now hanker for the auto-plot," he argued,

> not realizing that even with the auto-plot they must provide a man with brains to extract the *rate of change* from it.
>
> A lot of rubbish re auto-transmission to the sights is *loosely* talked of, but the cold fact remains that you must have the man of brains to decide when to throw out and when to include the R.F. readings as sent down.

"In action," he rationalized, "it is very likely that one range every 5 mins. will be all one will get, so that will not want to be automatically plotted . . ."[30]

Bacon personally explained his views on mechanized fire control in an informal meeting with Pollen that took place on 15 December 1908. Bacon then argued that sophisticated fire control methods were unnecessary because poor visibility in the North Sea, where he anticipated that the next naval war would be fought, would restrict battle ranges. "Our guns," he maintained, "are enormously over-ranged already." He insisted, moreover, that a fire control system that was capable of dealing with high and changing change of range rates was not required because either side in a fleet action was capable of steaming at speeds that would prevent such conditions from occurring. In addition, Bacon feared that the adoption of a practicable mechanized system of fire control would lead to the abandonment of practice in manual methods of gunnery, which would result in a reliance on machinery that he apparently found unacceptable. And finally, Bacon believed that mechanized fire control would not work at long ranges as Pollen had claimed because existing range-finders were ineffective at such great distances.[31]

In 1909, the Ordnance Department issued a report on the last year's Battle Practice, which stated that "considering how recent the general use of Plotting is, the results obtained were on the whole satisfactory . . ." It then went on to dismiss the value of plotting, warning that

> too much reliance must . . . not be placed on Range Plottings, as it is very doubtful to what extent ranges can be obtained of an efficient enemy once the latter has opened fire, and if the Plotting does lose its effectiveness as soon as fire is opened then it should be borne in mind that *the successful use of Plotting before fire is opened to set the Dumaresq correctly can be greatly discounted by the enemy's Admiral altering the course of his ships "together," say, one point or so at the moment that either side opens fire. . . . It therefore becomes imperative to ensure that the Plotting system does not become so incorporated in the Fire-Control system as to cause the latter to fail when the Plotting does.*[32]

Such a counsel of despair, however, could not conceal the failure of manual methods of fire control.

The drawbacks of manual gunnery and the necessity of adopting an automatic approach were evident to a number of Pollen's service correspondents. Pollen forwarded excerpts from the letters of two such officers to Jellicoe on 18 January 1909. "The Oxford crew," observed the first writer,

> could not row a race against Cambridge at a day's notice, and the "Dreadnought" could not go out and do a good Battle Practice without weeks of practice. If, within six weeks of any given Battle Practice, the Admiralty sent telegraphic orders to do another, it is a moral certainty that practically no, or very few, hits would be made. . . . The worst of the existing organization is that it can neither be extemporized nor kept at Concert pitch. . . . Until you can reduce the personnel of Fire Control to five or six skilled people, whose skill does not depend upon drill but upon their general intelligence, you cannot count upon fighting efficiency as a *constant*.

The second officer observed, in a lighter style, that

> it is a distinct argument in favour of automatic machinery that it does not share the inheritance of ills to which flesh is heir. Your Change of Range Machine is very unlikely to get appendicitis at the critical moment. I suggest to you for a

motto "No matter if the Commander gets the Quinzy, the Pay Master the pip, the Midshipman the mumps, the Chaplain the chilblains, or a Lieutenant the leprosy, as long as someone touches the button, *we do the rest.*"[33]

Bacon's opposition to mechanized methods of gunnery included mechanized gunlaying as well as sight-setting. The Petravic system of automatically discharging guns at a predetermined point during a ship's roll with the aid of gyroscopes was tried in September 1908 but rejected as "being not suitable for adoption under sea going conditions," a decision that appears to have been prompted by the same distrust of gyroscopes that had operated in the case of the *Ariadne* trials.[34] The Naval Ordnance Department even declined to support the work of Percy Scott, who like Petravic also sought to improve the laying and firing of big-guns in a seaway but whose approach was fundamentally different. It will be remembered that big-guns could not be laid by continuous-aim because of the shortcomings of existing elevating and training controls, and thus had to be laid instead at fixed angles of elevation and train. Firing took place at the top or bottom of the roll after the signal of a bell, the goal being a simultaneous discharge of several guns that would produce a closely bunched group of projectiles upon which the effectiveness of the salvo system depended. But because the judgement of the roll varied from gunner to gunner, the firing of several guns after the bell signal did not occur exactly at the same instant, with the result that the roll produced by even a moderate seaway was enough to cause the projectiles of a salvo to scatter over a wide area, which greatly reduced the chances of making hits. The smoke from adjacent guns or seaspray thrown up by a ship steaming at high speed, moreover, could momentarily obscure a gunner's view of the target through his sight and prevent him from firing on the top or bottom of the roll after the bell signal, which by reducing the number of projectiles in a salvo also decreased the probability of making hits.

In August 1905, Scott had submitted a paper to the Ordnance Department in which he described a new method of sighting and firing big-guns that were laid at a fixed elevation and train. Scott proposed that the elevation and train, and the moment of firing, of all the big-guns of a ship be determined by a device called a "director," which was to be located high on a mast and operated by a single observer. The director was to consist of a master sight whose setting for the target's range and bearing would be translated into appropriate instructions for the elevation and train of each big-gun by an instrument called a "converger," and of some means of firing the guns simultaneously on the top or bottom of the roll by either an electrical signal triggered by the director observer, or by an order of the director observer that would be transmitted to the various gun stations and immediately carried out. The employment of such a system of "director firing," Scott maintained, would both place the sighting process above any interference from seaspray or gunsmoke and ensure that firing was simultaneous, or very nearly so. Accurate hitting would then be possible, according to Scott, at very long ranges, which were held to be 7,000 to 8,000 yards.[35]

Scott's proposals were evaluated favorably by Jellicoe, who was then Director of Naval Ordnance. The use of the director system to achieve simultaneous firing would, he argued, produce accurate results even if continuous-aim gunlaying for big-guns could not be perfected. The alternative of continuing to fire salvoes after a bell signal, Jellicoe maintained on the other hand, would be practicable only if continuous-aim with big-guns were to become possible, and even then only one out of four guns would have their sights on the target while the remainder would not fire, or fire and miss. The adoption of the director system, he observed, would also place the real sight and layer above smoke and bursting shell, away from the blast of neighboring guns, and in closer proximity to the range-finder. Jellicoe thus recommended that trials be undertaken to test the feasibility of that portion of Scott's scheme that was related to gun elevation, it being "more important, and also easier carried out, than the proposals regarding training."[36]

An elementary prototype of Scott's director, which was capable of coordinating gun elevation only, was tested in the battleship *Africa* in early 1907 with unsatisfactory results because no allowance in the functioning of the mechanism was made for the effects on gun elevation caused by the tilt of the turret roller paths[37] and because the swaying of the pole mast upon which the director was mounted produced severe distortion.[38] The replacement of Jellicoe by Bacon later that year then appears to have ended Ordnance Department support for director firing, presumably on the grounds of the mechanical complexity of the instruments required to make it work. In 1908, the Admiralty refused to provide Scott with the funds to build a director system for trials in his armoured cruiser *Good Hope*, and he was thus "forced to beg, borrow, or steal all the necessary material"[39] for an improvised director that was designed and constructed by his torpedo officer, Lieutenant Charles Rice.[40] In the first trial, which took place on 10 February 1909, the performance of guns laid by the director was inferior to that of those that were independently laid,[41] but nevertheless was apparently good enough to convince Scott of the superiority in principle of director over independent gunlaying.[42] In trials carried out in May, by which time Scott had left the *Good Hope*, the results with director firing were more favorable, although to what degree is not clear.[43] Official support for the development of director firing was in any case not forthcoming.[44]

Scott and Pollen thus found themselves sharing the status of gunnery outcasts. In a letter to Scott of 26 March 1909, Pollen put forward arguments in favor of mechanized gunnery and complained of the continuing refusal of the Admiralty to recognize the necessity of developing more effective methods of fire control, closing with the phrase "as a rule you know two of a trade don't agree."[45] Scott replied that Pollen's arguments were "unanswerable to anyone who understands what you are talking about, in this case two of a trade agree."[46] Rear-Admiral Richard Henry Peirse, a close associate of Scott who became Inspector of Target Practice in March 1909, quickly became a strong supporter of Pollen's ideas.[47] By the late spring, the entire Inspectorate had been transformed into a bastion of opposition to the policy of the Ordnance Department,[48] an attitude that was clearly reflected in their reports on the Battle Practice of 1909.

The reports of the Inspectorate on the attempts by the big-gun armoured cruiser *Inflexible* in March and the Atlantic Fleet in August to fire in rough weather, were particularly revealing. During the *Inflexible* shoot, gunlaying was so adversely affected that the report stated that "some form of director may prove the best remedy under conditions other than those of smooth water . . ." The statement on the performance of the Atlantic Fleet noted that the effect of less than calm weather in one case "caused the plotting to break down entirely," that for all ships it was impossible to obtain "accurate readings of the range finder as at present fitted under the conditions which existed," and that "some form of gyro controlled range-finder such as [the] Pollen instrument is an absolute necessity if plotting is to be undertaken in a seaway with any hope of success." Automatic sight-setting was found to be essential as well. "With a rapid rate," the report conjectured, "say two fleets or ships approaching one another at 15 knots, sightsetting would defeat most men, and if the changes were made for every 25 yards the sight would have to be moved 40 times a minute, an obvious impossibility."

In his general remarks on plotting, the I.T.P. noted that "all except one ship plotted the true course and speed of the enemy." He then maintained that "one of the principle [sic] sources of error appeared to be inaccuracy of the bearings" and that "mistakes and delays in the actual plotting and communications were also very common, but are characteristic of any manual system." For these and other reasons, the I.T.P. concluded that

(1) Plotting is not yet sufficiently developed to be of practical use under general service conditions. The time available for plotting and the steady course of the target were favourable to accurate results [but] these were not generally obtained.
(2) The future of plotting depends upon the development of the range-finder mounting, a more accurate method of obtaining bearings and measuring the observing ship's speed, and the accuracy and rapidity with which the observations are converted into rate. . . .[49]

Opposition to the Ordnance Department also surfaced at the Royal Naval War College at Portsmouth. In the fall of 1908, the War College had assigned Captain Constantine Hughes-Onslow the task of investigating the fire control problem. Hughes-Onslow had proceeded in the hope of doing "absolutely impartial justice to every system, *apart* from any official views that may be *held*."[50] He began his work ignorant of the Dreyer-Pollen controversy, but found Dreyer's response to his query for information, described earlier, so offensive that he sought Pollen's counsel, and quickly became an enthusiastic supporter.[51] Hughes-Onslow's comprehensive and detailed study of fire control was completed in August 1909,[52] and constituted a damning indictment of the Ordnance Department's insistence on manual methods of fire control. "In Battleships," he pointed out, the personnel of the Fire Control amounts to forty or fifty Officers and men, according to class of Ship, and it is very keenly realized that by some means a reduction of this huge number must be effected, as it is impossible to divert so many individuals from their other duties without considerable dislocation. *The momentous fact is revealed that these operators are taken very largely from the torpedo personnel so that it would be impossible to use these essential weapons, which now have an effective Range of 7,000 yards, simultaneously with the Guns. Hardly anything could be more serious than this aspect of the case.*

"*In recent trials,*" Hughes-Onslow went on to say, "*it has been found that even with a trained personnel gross errors have been made* such as applying the Rate of Change the wrong way, and several ruined their Battle Practice this year owing to this very mistake being made.*"

Hughes-Onslow dismissed objections to automatic methods of fire control on the grounds of mechanical complexity. "The opinion has been advanced," he wrote,

that we require to keep our Ships simple and that rough and ready methods are preferable to a highly developed Automatic System. This opinion can hardly be considered sound as it appears possible that an Automatic System might be produced which would be exceedingly reliable and thus eliminate the human errors just alluded to. Furthermore it is impossible to keep our Ships simple, but we can insist that they be efficient, and it appears more likely that we shall realize this desideratum with Automatic Gear than with any rough and ready or Manual System involving the human errors which are quite certain to be realized by the employment of a large personnel.

Our Ships are not simple at present and it is impossible to keep them so. Would a resuscitated Officer of a hundred years ago think them simple? Is an Electric Compass, the mechanism of a Whitehead Torpedo, or the inside of a Submarine particularly simple? The question only needs to be put to be immediately answered in the negative, but in connection with Plotting it will certainly be eventually found that the most efficient System is also the simplest because it is when things go wrong that complications arise.

In regard to Automatic Sight Setting it should be noticed that in the latest Service Sight there are 5 Corrections to be applied in addition to the ordinary setting for Range and Deflection and that 3 of these Corrections are constantly altering during the course of the Battle, so this gives the Sight Setter no less than 5 changing settings to his Sight! Now it is a matter of common knowledge that the Sight Setter, although assiduously exercised, may, in the excitement of Battle Practice, frequently set his Sight wrong; so we need not be surprised that Officers of great experience and judgement say they would not allow the Corrections to be touched in case the last state of affairs should be worse than the first.

Hughes-Onslow then addressed the issues of visibility conditions in the North Sea and the vulnerability of fire control teams that consisted of many men to disruption.

It is also stated that as the visibility of the North Sea is frequently limited to 8,000 yards, or even less, that it is not necessary to employ a System of Plotting which is designed for Long Range but it appears evident that every ship in the British Navy should be prepared to fight under all circumstances and in any condition, *as one cannot predict the day or the weather for the decisive action on which the fate of the Empire may depend.*

A most serious consideration is that with any form of Manual Plotting prolonged training is absolutely necessary for the more important operators, a senior Officer who is a great authority and who has been associated with this kind of work throughout his career, stating that in his opinion it would take several months to obtain the requisite proficiency, especially as the personnel have to be trained together and in co-operation. Yet we know that at any moment one of the most essential operators may be removed owing to a variety of causes, such as sickness, with the result that the efficiency of the whole System is lost for a considerable time till some one else can be trained.

Advances in fire control, Hughes–Onslow maintained, were necessary for tactical, strategic and financial reasons. "With the advent of the hot-air Torpedo," he argued, "the Range of this weapon has been so enormously increased that every possible step must be taken without delay to ensure the utmost extension of effective Gun Range." Hughes–Onslow was also convinced that a monopoly of long-range hitting would confer significant advantages for a worthwhile period of time. "The specious argument has been advanced," he wrote,

that the expense of an Automatic System is hardly justified by the advantages gained therefrom, as no doubt Foreign Countries would soon follow suit. This argument is not justified because it would apply in all directions in regard to preparation for War, and the best we can hope to do is to keep ahead for the time being, besides which directly some Foreign Power had acquired it the need for our following suit would be imperative. Steps would then have to be taken in a great hurry to obviate our backwardness, involving extra expense while risking efficiency. *The Navy that has a perfected Fire Control first can with safety effect large economies in construction, etc., as it would be at such an enormous advantage for the time being.*

This argument only holds good for the Navy whose Fire Control, under any conditions of Day or Night action, is substantially superior to that of any possible adversary. It appears that the British Navy may be put in this position of superiority which might hold good for several years, if steps were taken to maintain secrecy, and which can be done as we know next to nothing of German preparations.

In an appendix, Hughes–Onslow described Pollen's instruments at length, included illustrations that had been provided by the inventor, and in his main text informed the reader that Pollen's gyroscopically stabilized observing instruments were reputedly capable of "taking Bearings accurately to within 1/4 of a degree, even when there is considerable yaw, roll and pitch," and of "enabling the Ranges also to be observed accurately even when the Ship has considerable motion, and in conditions when the ordinary Range Finder would be quite unreliable," advantages which were said to be "*of enormous importance if they can be substantiated.*" On the other hand, he repeatedly condemned the Wilson-Dreyer system[53] and called for competitive trials that would subject both the Pollen and Wilson-Dreyer systems to poor visibility, rough weather and high and changing change of range rates.[54]

Hughes–Onslow was also inclined to favor director firing. His discussion of the subject was prefaced by a detailed analysis of ship movement, which included the phenomenon of net vertical motion—later known as heave—as well as roll, pitch and yaw. The effects of these four factors on gunlaying, he argued, was critical to the point that big-guns could not be laid and fired by existing continuous-aim or fixed elevation methods in even moderately rough seas. Hughes–Onslow acknowledged that there were serious difficulties with director firing, that the latest big-gun mountings were more easily laid by continuous-aim than previous models, and that more information from trials was required before a definitive answer to the gunlaying problem could be reached. His preference in principle for director firing over alternative forms of gunlaying was nevertheless evident. "In fact it appears that any system of individual firing," he wrote,

> employing controlled elevation with continuous aim, is a very dangerous playmate as it involves many operators each with his own and perhaps varying Personal Error, besides which, except with the most recent power worked guns, the elevating gear is not capable of dealing with anything like rapid motion of the ship.
>
> On the other hand firing at a Fixed elevation, rolling the sights on, is bound to realize the error due to roll; but if the firing is made simultaneous by means of a Director, and controlled by one specialized and highly educated Officer, it is thought that these errors may be dealt with by means of a Spotting Correction, or even . . . by making an allowance on the target if the Ship is rolling regularly.[55]

Hughes–Onslow's findings would have a great effect on the policy of the Ordnance Department.[56] Fisher, however, remained unaware of the fact that long-range fire with big-guns under anything but ideal conditions of wind and sea was as yet impossible, and thus in the meanwhile had pressed forward with his campaign to replace the battleship with the armoured cruiser.

2   Fisher and the Battle Cruiser, 1908-1909

The three all-big-gun armoured cruisers of the *Invincible* class were laid down in the spring of 1906, launched a year later, and completed between the spring and fall of 1908. In armament they were more powerful than any battleship except the *Dreadnought*, to which they were not far inferior, while they were faster than any armoured cruiser. In August 1908, H.M.S. *Indomitable*, the first of the *Invincible* class to be completed, maintained a record average speed of over 25 knots for three days with remarkably low coal consumption when returning from Canada.[57] "The *Indomitable* really did what was claimed for her, 25.13 knots," Fisher boasted to Arnold White, a journalist friend and confidant, on 15 August 1908,

> as I went to Chatham and overhauled her logs and registers, but I don't propose to give any official statements, as they would be of use to the Germans. I've no doubt your clear mind sees what the *Indomitable* means. I should have none else

myself! and said so when she was designed, the same time as *Dreadnought*, but I was in a minority of one! *You had to have Moses before Paul! You couldn't have had the New Testament without the Old first!* The *Dreadnought* paved the way to the *Indomitable*. It's no use one or two knots superiority of speed—a dirty bottom brings that down! It's a d—d big six or seven knots surplus that does the trick! THEN you can fight HOW you like, WHEN you like, and WHERE you like! But what babes one has to deal with![58]

The German reaction to the *Invincible* class, in the meanwhile, had forced the Admiralty to reconsider its plans to build smaller armoured cruisers. In 1907, the German navy had laid down an armoured cruiser, the *Blücher*, which was armed with 8.2-inch guns on the apparent presumption that the British armoured cruisers of the 1905–06 program would be armed with 9.2-inch guns as attributed to them in the 1906–07 edition of *Fighting Ships*.[59] The *Blücher* was heavily outclassed by the British units, which were in fact armed with 12-inch guns, and not much superior to the smaller uniform–caliber 9.2-inch gun armed British armoured cruisers projected for the 1908–09 program in June 1907.[60] When, however, the German navy in 1908 made public their intention to build all-big-gun armoured cruisers under the 1907–08 and 1908–09 programs that surpassed the *Invincible* class in cost and in all likelihood in size and fighting power, the Admiralty cancelled the 9.2-inch gun armoured cruisers scheduled for the 1908-9 program and instead approved plans on 31 March 1908 for an improved *Invincible*, which later was named the *Indefatigable*.[61]

On 8 September 1908, Fisher informed Viscount Esher that he had got Sir Philip Watts, the Director of Naval Construction, "into a new *Indomitable* that will make your mouth water when you see it! (and the Germans gnash their teeth!)"[62] On 17 September, in a letter to Watts, Fisher for the first time on record used the term "battle cruiser" when referring to what had formerly been known as the all-big-gun armoured cruiser. And Fisher's letter to Watts made it clear that he believed that the new generic name described a warship type that would be far superior to the dreadnought battleship while costing little more to build. What was to become the *Indefatigable* was at this time referred to as the "Sanspareil," and Fisher explained that

> If we go to work the same way as we did with *Dreadnought* we shall succeed, because [it is] so obviously silly to refuse an increase of 25 per cent of power in the "Sanspareil", with only an increase of 4 per cent in cost and 5 per cent in displacement. . . . If you remember, the opposition succumbed at once against *Dreadnought* when it was seen that such an increase of power resulted from so small an increase in expense and displacement.

"The best is the cheapest," Fisher then maintained, "The British Navy only travels First Class. It ain't numbers, it's quality."[63]

Fisher's hopes for an improved *Indomitable* by no means diminished his enthusiasm for the bird in hand. The 25 knots and 12-inch guns of the *Invincible* class gave them a five knot superiority in speed and a larger caliber main armament than the first two German dreadnought battleships, which in September 1908 were still more than a year away from being completed.[64] "It's quite impossible to refute the arguments for the 'Indomitable' class," Fisher insisted in his letter to Watts of 17 September, "because their speed—their big fat margin of 5 or 6 knots of speed—permits them to do just what they damn please and fight *any one* and not care whether their bottoms are dirty or whether they have an extra 1,000 tons of coal on board: the whacking big excess of speed makes them absolutely independent."[65] In what may have been a reference to the complaints of Brassey and others,[66] Fisher then complained that "any silly fool in the street can see this, but naval experts with enormous brains can't."[67]

Fisher appears to have had some knowledge of the difficulties that were experienced in Battle Practice during the summer of 1908, but was assured by Vice-Admiral Sir William May, the Second Sea Lord, on 23 September 1908, that performances had much improved.[68] Any remaining doubts as to the long-range gunnery efficiency of the fleet that he may have harbored were probably dispelled by the results of the first Battle Practice of the *Indomitable*, which took place on 16 January 1909. "18 hits out of 31 rounds," wrote Rear-Admiral Sir Frederick Inglefield, the Commander-in-Chief of the Fourth Cruiser Squadron,[69] two days later. He went on to say that

> of the 15 rounds fired on the first run of 4 minutes, 13 were direct hits on the target. I believe this to be a "record" under present Battle Practice conditions (with speed of target 8 knots, course and speed unknown to firing ship, "Indomitable" steaming 15 knots and distance of target 8,300 to 8,600 yards). In the second run of 4 minutes after turning 18 points, 5 hits were scored out of 16 rounds. This less good result was due to a small error in spotting: the shooting was very good and very true for direction. The accuracy and reliability of guns and instruments was most satisfactory, as was also the good organization and careful training of both Officers and men.

Inglefield considered the *Indomitable* "a splendid type of fighting vessel" and noted that "a squadron of Armoured Cruisers with such high speed, heavy armament and so handy to manoeuvre, will be dangerous for the enemy to tackle."[70]

"The *Indomitable*," Fisher thus wrote on 10 February 1909 to Reginald McKenna, who had replaced Tweedmouth as First Lord the previous April, ". . . in her first 15 rounds hit the target 13 times at a range of over 4 miles, the target 1/14th her own size."[71] The warships of the British fleet in home waters, Fisher informed Arnold White on 21 March 1909,

> could each and all hit the target. Not one good and one bad! Look at the battle-practice report. See the *Indomitable* hitting a target 14 times smaller than herself 13 times out of 15! At what distance? 5 miles![72]

The Battle Practice performance of the *Indomitable*'s sister ship *Invincible* in 1909 further reinforced Fisher's confidence in British naval gunnery. On 28 August 1909, he wrote to Viscount Esher of "the unexampled advance in gunnery (the *Invincible* with her 12-inch guns hitting the target

1/14th her own size 15 *times out of 18 at 5 miles,* she herself going 20 knots and the target also moving at an unknown speed and unknown course) . . ."[73]

Fisher's conviction that all was well was further reinforced in the fall of 1909 by other misleading reports of Battle Practice success. On 29 October 1909, Fisher confided to Archibald Hurd, the naval journalist, that

> Madden[74] gave me a wonderful and spontaneous account of the increasing gunnery efficiency of the fleet. Fancy making certain practice at 15,000 yards!! Just under 9 shore miles!!! *but don't mention this.*

In what could only have been a reference to the Wilson-Dreyer system, Fisher then observed that "the new system of Fire Control is quite excellent and knocks Pollen into smithereens . . ."[75]

By this time, the development of a new model 13.5-inch gun had led Fisher to press for the construction of battle cruisers that were far more powerful than the *Invincible* class, the *Indefatigable* or even the *Dreadnought* and her sisters. Fisher had considered the prospect as early as January 1908. On 22 January 1908, Captain Edmond J. W. Slade, who had replaced Ottley as the Director of Naval Intelligence in December 1907, wrote in his diary that "Sir J. has now got the 13.5 [-inch] gun on the brain—Bacon is at the bottom of it . . ." Fisher's plan, Slade explained, was to "spring" the 13.5-inch gun armed vessels on Germany as had been done with the *Dreadnought* "so that she shall be obliged again to spend money outside the ordinary Naval Estimate."[76] On 3 February, Slade noted that he had

> discussed the 13.5 gun [*sic*] ship with Bacon & Sir P. Watts. She is to be 500 tons more than the St. Vincent, will cost £2,000,000 and will have 8 guns all firing on one broadside.[77]

A secret memorandum of 18 March 1908 that may have been written by Bacon or Dreyer as part of a campaign to distract Fisher's attention away from the issues raised by the Pollen controversy, noted that

> the substitution of 13.5-inch for 12-inch will involve an extra displacement of no more than 2,000 tons. It is considered safe to estimate that a 13.5-inch "Dreadnought" type of ship will throw into an enemy 50 per cent. more weight of shell in a given time, on any bearing, than the "Dreadnought." Thus, by a 10 per cent. increase of displacement, we secure a 50 per cent. increase of weight of shell thrown in . . .
>
> Generally, it may be said that the advantages of long range, ease of fire control, and the rest of the arguments advanced in favour of a single type armament nearly all apply with equal force to making the type of gun the heaviest possible within the practical limits of tonnage of a battleship.[78]

Slade, however, was opposed to the development of the new gun "until we can collect information & data from what the Dreadnought & her sisters can do,"[79] and perhaps for this reason the order to begin the design of the 13.5-inch gun was not given by the First Lord until 21 October 1908.[80]

161

On 20 November 1908, the Board of Admiralty approved the design of a battle cruiser of the *Indefatigable* type for the 1909–10 program, acting on information supplied by the Intelligence Department that projected German battle cruisers would be no larger.[81] Rear-Admiral Sir John Jellicoe, who had become Third Sea Lord and Controller that October, subsequently learned through a confidential private source that the new German vessels would be substantially greater in size than had been reported, and was convinced that the just-approved British battle cruiser would have to be cancelled and replaced by a much more capable design.[82] In addition, Bacon by this time had probably concluded that the battleship should be replaced by a more powerful type of battle cruiser, a view that he was to express publicly only a few months later in the spring of 1910.[83] The Board of Admiralty on 18 August thus approved the design of a battle cruiser of unprecedented speed and gun power to be built instead of the *Indefatigable* that had been planned previously.[84]

The name *Lion* for the new battle cruiser was approved by the board on 27 October 1909.[85] An expansion of the 1909–10 program resulted in an order for a second vessel of the same type named *Princess Royal*.[86] Both warships were armed with 13.5-inch guns in place of the 12-inch pieces that had previously been standard, which practically doubled the weight of projectiles that could be fired in a single broadside, and were, moreover, equipped with engines of almost twice the power of earlier battle cruisers, which increased their speed from 25 to 27 knots. They were in fact the largest, most costly and fastest capital ships yet attempted, and whereas the displacement of the *Invincible* class had been less than the *Dreadnought* and her sisters, and that of the *Indefatigable* less than the battleship built under the same estimate, the *Lion* class displaced nearly 4,000 tons—or 18 per cent—more than their 13.5-inch armed battleship counterparts of the 1909–10 program.[87] "*Do you know,*" crowed Fisher to Arnold White on 13 November 1909,

> that the ships we have just laid down are as far beyond the Dreadnought as the Dreadnought was beyond all before her! And they will say again, "D—n that blackguard! Again a new era of Dreadnoughts!" But imagine the German "wake-up" when these new ships by and by burst on them! *70,000 horsepower!!! and guns that will gut them!!!*[88]

By the fall of 1909, Fisher believed that the stage had been set for the replacement of the battleship by the battle cruiser. "The very wonderful thing is," he had written to Viscount Esher on 13 September 1909,

> that dear old Kelvin and the First Sea Lord wanted 'Indomitables' alone and *not Dreadnoughts*; but we had a compromise as you know, and got 3 'Indomitables' with the Dreadnoughts; and all the world now, headed by A. K. Wilson, have got 'Indomitables' on the brain! Hip! Hip! Hurrah![89]

Fisher's enthusiasm was not entirely misplaced, for by this time the Admiralty had reversed its position on gunnery once again, and had ordered new trials of the Pollen system and of Percy Scott's director.

3 *Gunnery Progress and Disaster, 1908-1909*

(a) OFFICIAL NEGOTIATIONS

By the end of 1908, Pollen had good reason to believe that the Admiralty would look upon new proposals to develop his system with favor. Battle Practice had exposed the shortcomings of the manual methods that had been recommended by the Ordnance Department. Jellicoe had become Third Sea Lord and Controller in October, which made him Bacon's immediate superior, and although he had warned Pollen in August that he would be "bound by the actions already taken to a very large extent,"[90] Pollen could not help but be encouraged by the return to the Admiralty of one of his strongest supporters. Isherwood had not only improved the range-finder mounting and plotting table, but completed the designs of a change of range machine, automatic sights and spotting correction mechanisms, which together with the observing, plotting and transmitting devices made up a complete system of fire control. And finally, Pollen had taken steps to increase the private financial resources that were available to support his work by forming the Argo Company.

In a printed letter of 5 January 1909, Pollen informed the Admiralty in his capacity as Governing Director of the Argo Company of the existence of the new firm, of the fact that the drawings of the instruments that constituted a complete system of fire control had been completed, and of the ability of his company "to supply any instrument in quantities, or singly for experiment," with payment not to be made "before the gear is accepted as satisfactory." Pollen then pointed out that the analysis upon which his system was based had "stood the test of the ablest expert scrutiny," that the gear now offered was no longer purely experimental as had been the case with that tried in the *Ariadne* but was "in all respects fitted to its purpose as integral parts of a fighting ship's equipment," that the system had "excited a great deal of interest" among many naval officers and that "an apparently important body of opinion exists to the effect that it should, if successful, add very notably to the fighting efficiency of ships and fleets." Pollen thus suggested that his system should be subjected to comprehensive trials and a decision with regard to its adoption by the service made before the expiration of the secrecy agreement in the fall of that year. Pollen's letter was accompanied by a prospectus which included descriptions of the new gunnery instruments, and also of a new model mechanical compass.[91]

Pollen's hopes for a quick decision in his favor were not realized. In January and early February, the First Lord, First Sea Lord and Controller were preoccupied with the question of the 1909-10 estimates, which had provoked a furious debate within the government,[92] and the board was unable to discuss Pollen's proposals until 12 February. At this time, the board directed Bacon, who was present, to prepare a statement for the next meeting that was to take place in a week later, which would describe "the trials which he considered it desirable should be made with parts of the mechanism."[93] Bacon thus arranged a meeting with Pollen,[94] which took place on 15 February. Pollen was then asked to provide cost estimates for the range-finder mounting and electrical transmission gear only, and informed that "it had been decided not to reconsider the question of monopoly or a possible extension of the period of secrecy."[95] Bacon reported to the board on 18 February, the matter was further discussed and the Admiralty Permanent Secretary was instructed to obtain an assurance from Pollen that terms of the formal contract with regard to the conditional payment of £100,000 in the event of success was no longer in effect.[96]

Pollen replied to the verbal query of the Admiralty Permanent Secretary for his views on the subject of payment in the event of success on 22 February to the effect that he was willing to submit all questions of financial remuneration to arbitration.[97] On 4 March, the board again met to discuss Pollen's proposals, and the matter was left in the hands of Fisher. According to this arrangement, the First Sea Lord was to meet with Bacon, who had not been present, and formulate an agreement with regard to a service trial of Pollen's complete system of fire control instruments, which would then be submitted to the inventor.[98] Growing impatient in the absence of any official word, Pollen wrote on 10 March to the Admiralty Permanent Secretary to ask for a formal decision. He heard nothing until 24 March, at which time Jellicoe informed him unofficially in a brief conversation that trials of his system would take place in the pre-dreadnought battleship H.M.S. *London*.[99] The Argo Company, however, was not formally requested to submit a tender for the supply of a complete system of fire control suitable to control the entire main armament of the test ship until 2 April.[100]

Pollen's reply, which was sent the same day as the Admiralty letter, pointed out that the Admiralty's delay in coming to a decision and the need to design and manufacture additional equipment for the firing trials that were proposed—which were more extensive than Pollen had anticipated—meant that he could not deliver a complete system of instruments for trial until well after the existing secrecy agreement expired in November. There was, in addition, a problem of costs being substantially greater than he had beforehand supposed. Pollen noted that he had earlier estimated that trial instruments would cost approximately £6,800. To this figure he added £4,150 for the additional gear, and £6,540 for the extension of the secrecy agreement for the year requested by the Admiralty, a total of £17,490, or well over twice what had been previously quoted. Pollen noted that the instruments would be manufactured by the Linotype Company, and concluded with a request for the ballistical data of the 12-inch guns mounted in the *London*, which were required to design the sights.[101]

The Admiralty was unwilling to put up anywhere near the sum given by Pollen, and on 7 April requested that tenders be submitted for a set of observing, plotting, calculating and spotting correcting instruments with and without automatic sights, which would be sufficient for a less ambitious program of tests.[102] Pollen's reply of 14 April informed the Admiralty that a minimal system without automatic sights and the spotting correcting devices would cost £6,400, while their inclusion would push the price to £8,500. Pollen promised that if a decision was reached immediately, he could deliver the observing and plotting instruments by

June, the change of range machine in July and the automatic sights by November. He also pointed out that if the trials were to involve turning by the firing ship, a mechanical compass would be a necessity, for which he would ask £650.[103]

On 21 April, the Admiralty informed the Argo Company that they were ready to accept the tender to supply the less expensive set of instruments, made no mention of the mechanical compass, noted that they expected that there would be sufficient time for trials before the expiration of the secrecy agreement, insisted that the late delivery of instruments would require Pollen to extend the period of secrecy by an equivalent amount of time at no cost to the Admiralty, and asked for tenders for range and deflection indicators that were to be used in lieu of automatic sights.[104] After an exchange of correspondence,[105] Pollen agreed on 1 May 1909 not to charge the Admiralty for extensions of secrecy that were made necessary by delays in the delivery of instruments for which the Argo Company was responsible, and in addition that so long as the Admiralty was honestly engaged in the process of trying the instruments, the Argo Company was bound to "raise no difficulties, nor make any charge, in respect of any reasonable extension of the period of secrecy that may be thought desirable before a final decision is come to."[106]

After further correspondence,[107] the Admiralty on 8 June 1909 formally ordered a set of instruments from the Argo Company for trial according to the terms that had been negotiated through previous correspondence.[108] According to this agreement, the gyro-stabilized range-finder mounting and automatic plotting table were to be delivered by 15 July 1909, and the change of range machine by 15 August 1909. No delivery date was specified for the observer's correcting mechanisms, and payment was to be made for each group of instruments upon delivery. On 21 June, the Admiralty accepted the tender of the Argo company for range and deflection indicators, and for the 600 feet of electrical cable that would be required to connect the instruments. The Admiralty communication also asked the firm to tender for receivers that would indicate the range and bearing sent by the observing instruments to the plotter, to quote prices and delivery dates for an order for at least 30 gyroscopically stabilized range-finder mountings in combination with either indicators or an automatic plotting table, and to give alternative figures for an agreement that embodied secrecy and monopoly and one that was calculated on a commercial basis only.[109] Pollen provided the Admiralty with his terms for a production order for instruments on 23 June 1909.[110]

In spite of these agreements and negotiations, Pollen nevertheless had a number of reasons to be dissatisfied with his relations with the Admiralty. In March 1909, Pollen had learned that the Ordnance Department would soon issue a manual true-course plotting table that he believed infringed his patents, but his attempts to obtain an explanation of what he regarded as a flagrant violation of the secrecy agreement between him and the Admiralty that was still in effect were unsuccessful.[111] On 11 May, he had asked for a clarification of the Admiralty position on arbitration with respect to the settlement of a monopoly agreement in the event of either a successful or partially successful trial in response to his letter of 22 February.[112] On 20 May, the Admiralty informed the Argo Company that the matter would not be considered until after the conclusion of the trials.[113] On 14 May, the Admiralty had suggested that the range-finder be placed in the spotting top.[114] On 17 May, Pollen pointed out that to do so was unnecessary and undesirable and its proposal by the Admiralty was "doubtless due to there having as yet been no opportunity for pointing out the nature and purposes of the A.C. system to their Lordships' advisers."[115]

Much worse was to follow. On 4 June, Pollen protested to the Admiralty that it had been intimated to him that the trials would again take the form of a competition with service equipment, that he and his employees would be excluded from the ship during trials and that he would not be allowed to test his gear at sea or train officers in their use before the trials. Pollen thus asked that steps be taken to ensure an impartial evaluation, that he and his engineers not be excluded from the test ship, that he be given the opportunity before the final trials to test his instruments thoroughly to ensure that they were "seaworthy and not likely to break down under service conditions" and that he be allowed to provide instruction to those officers who would be manning his instruments.[116] Although the Admiralty agreed in a letter of 21 June 1909, to allow Pollen to train officers thoroughly as he had requested,[117] it appeared that the Ordnance Department retained both the means and the will to prevent a fair trial, the concluded negotiations for the purchase of instruments notwithstanding.

(b) PRIVATE COMMUNICATIONS

During the first six months of 1909, Bacon's obstruction had forced Pollen to appeal privately to the senior members of the Board of Admiralty for equitable treatment. Reginald McKenna, the First Lord, had not been unwilling to consider Pollen's case. In December 1908, he responded to Pollen's request for an interview with a note in which he wrote that it would give him "much pleasure" to discuss the the gunnery question after his return to London in late January.[118] An apparently brief conversation took place on 18 February 1909, at which time McKenna expressed his intention to come to an understanding of what the gunnery debate was about, although he informed Pollen that he had been advised that "we have means of doing all that you say the A.C. Battle system does; and this is shown by the fact that the 'Indomitable' has in Battle Practice got 13 hits out of 15 shots."[119]

Later that day Pollen responded with a long letter in which he first criticized the character of proceedings that had surrounded the *Ariadne* trials, warned that the same mistakes were about to be repeated, and asked for an impartial investigation that would at least establish matters of fact. He then demonstrated that the *Indomitable*'s performance in Battle Practice misrepresented the true state of British naval gunnery by calling attention to the following issues:

(1) First, what was the change of range? Supposing that the speeds and courses of ship and target were similar to other practices this year—for half the

time there would have been a comparatively small change of range and for the other half a maximum of about 200 yds. a minute.

This is no guide to what could be done at 1,000 yds. per minute.

(2)   Next, what were the weather conditions, i.e. what was the extent and the speed in degrees per second, of the yaw, the roll, and the pitch during this practice? . . . .

(3)   Again, what was the rate of fire maintained? If the "Indomitable" was given eight minutes to fire 32 rounds the conditions were not very exacting in this respect.

(4)   Did the target ship keep a steady course during the practice, and for how long before the shooting was the "Indomitable" plotting?

With two "Indomitables" firing at each other the change of range might conceivably be 1,600 yds. a minute, and this might be under very severe weather conditions with very quick and considerable pitch and roll; and if the target ship changed course it would be a vital matter for gunnery efficiency to find out how soon after the target had changed course, the new data for securing hits could be got on to the sights. . . .

The point surely is not that under a given set of conditions the "Indomitable" got 80.6 per cent of hits, but that, had she been up against another "Indomitable" fitted with an automatic system, would she have got any hits at all? because if the other "Indomitable" had an automatic system she might have opened fire sooner and fired quicker, and got in with her 13 hits out of 15 shots before the "Indomitable" had been able to fire a round. . . .

(5)   Finally, the case given you says "13 out of 15". This sounds like one run at the target before the turn. What did she do on the other run? Was it on the minimum change of range run, or the maximum change run that this record was made? Was the target and the rate picked up immediately after the turn was over? These are the crucial points.[120]

In closing, Pollen maintained

(1)   That the A.C. system is the right system of gunnery and inevitable.

(2)   That monopoly can be kept long enough to be of supreme national value, and consequently

(3)   That no reasonable trouble or expense should be spared to ascertain whether these two propositions are based on right reason and a right appreciation of the truly ascertained facts.

(4)   That the "a priori" opinions of those who have not investigated either the facts of gunnery to-day or the nature of my solution, cannot be of such value as to be a sufficient guide in deciding these questions.

(5)   Finally that to wound the susceptibilities of those who have pre-judged the question without evidence is not such a serious matter as to risk the loss of any advantage to the national safety.[121]

The failure of the Admiralty to come to a decision with regard to trials of his system prompted Pollen to write to McKenna once again on 22 March to ask for an interview. Pollen expressed the fear

that those who succeeded in turning the Ariadne trials into mockery last year may do their best to prevent my getting a prompt and fair trial now.

My first reason for wishing to see you therefore is that, as you have said you take personal responsibility for all that the Admiralty does, it is right you should know what has been done in this matter, so that you should be precisely aware of what it is you are taking responsibility for.

Pollen then informed the First Lord of communications that he had had with men who hoped to use the gunnery issue to attack the government in the press and in Parliament.[122] Pollen explained that

> to supply powder and shot for a Unionist attack upon a Liberal Government can never be part of my programme; and in this matter the efficiency of the Fleet and national safety are more important than anything else. I have accordingly told these gentlemen, who, I hope, are as good patriots as they are partisans, that if their object is the efficiency of the Fleet, they will be defeating their object by drawing the attention of foreign powers to a secret system of enormous fighting value, nor would their doing so accelerate the introduction of this system into the English Navy. I hope, therefore, that I have prevented this matter being publicly discussed. But naturally I should like to hear from you whether this assurance I have given has any foundation.

In a postscript, Pollen reviewed the history of his relations with the Admiralty, and pointed out that he had learned that the Ordnance Department had issued a copy of his manual plotting board in violation of agreements between him and the Admiralty that were still in force.[123]

In a letter of 23 March McKenna informed Pollen that a trial of his complete system had been approved, and a meeting between the two men took place on 26 March.[124] After further delays in reaching a final agreement, Pollen wrote yet again to the First Lord on 20 April. He reported that he had, in a recent trip to Germany, "by a curious accident"—which he did not describe—discovered that the German navy in the fall of 1908 had "adopted exactly the same hand worked imitation of the A.C. system as you have been led to adopt after the utter failure of the Dreyer system." After briefly stating the case for his conception of gunnery, and bitterly accusing Bacon of ignorance and prejudice, he questioned the capacity of the Admiralty to come to a decision in the face of the predisposition of the Ordnance Department to oppose his scheme. Pollen ended his letter with a plea for an impartial inquiry by service gunnery experts, and a request for an interview.[125] McKenna wrote on 22 April simply that he had read Pollen's letter "with great interest" but noted that Pollen had undoubtedly received the official letter of 21 April, in which the Admiralty had accepted the Argo Company's tender of 14 April for trials instruments.[126]

Pollen's private communications with the First Lord appear to have worked in his favor, although the lack of McKenna correspondence makes any precise assessment impossible. There can, however, be no doubt of Pollen's failure to influence Fisher, whose earlier support had by 1909 turned to hostility.

Fisher could not have been ignorant of or pleased by Pollen's cordial relations with Admirals Lord Charles Beresford and Sir Reginald Custance, who were two of his harshest critics.[127] It will be remembered that Beresford had been a supporter of Pollen's ideas as early as in 1901, while Pollen and Custance had begun to correspond no later than 1905.[128]

In the spring of 1908, Pollen almost certainly communicated with both officers on the subject of the *Ariadne* trials.[129] That summer, Pollen corresponded with Beresford and Custance, and dined with the latter.[130] In August, Beresford asked the Admiralty to allow Pollen to witness a Battle Practice, a request that was refused.[131] In September, Beresford's report to the Admiralty on the Battle Practice firings of the Channel Fleet noted that it was the unanimous opinion of the gunnery officers under his command that Pollen's manual true-course plotting scheme was superior to the methods recommended by the Ordnance Department.[132] Pollen, for his part, by his criticisms of the policy of the Ordnance Department, provided both men with at least indirect support for their campaign against the leadership of the Admiralty, and one of his letters in particular contained language of a personal character with regard to Fisher that was by no means friendly.[133]

In a letter of late 1908, Pollen asked Fisher for an interview. Pollen began by thanking the First Sea Lord for his support in the past, and then went on to say that

> in backing me as you have done you have been right from the first and will be easily proved right in the end. But there has been a whole mountain of misunderstandings. Those who have been the innocent victims of these have misrepresented my conduct and my system until both are unrecognizable. I am confident that in 10 minutes the whole fabric can be destroyed. Will you give me the chance?[134]

Fisher refused to comply with Pollen's request, and the inventor could do little more than simply send the First Sea Lord a copy of the letter and prospectus of 5 January 1909, in which he described his proposals, accompanied by a brief note that excused the recipient of any obligation to reply.[135] Fisher deeply distrusted written argument,[136] however, and Pollen's communication probably had little, if any, positive effect. Fisher explained his position with regard to Pollen not long afterwards. "I had been told," he wrote to Arnold White on 4 April 1909, "that Pollen's ramifications were extraordinary and his newspaper influence very considerable, and his being a Roman Catholic of immense support to him. I have consistently refused to have anything to do with him or see him."[137] The next day he informed McKenna that he had been advised that Pollen "ought to be denied access to the Admiralty" because the inventor had allegedly begun to play a behind-the-scenes role in the latest public attacks on the navy's leadership.[138]

Pollen also experienced some difficulties with Jellicoe. Although the Third Sea Lord and Controller continued to sympathize with Pollen's cause, he had begun by the spring of 1909 to find the inventor's claims upon his time vexing[139] and his financial terms unreasonable.[140] In April 1909, moreover, Pollen printed *Notes, Etc., on the Ariadne Trials*, an account of the *Ariadne* trials and aftermath in which he vented all the bitterness and frustration that had built up over the preceding year by accusing Bacon, Wilson and Dreyer of ignorance, stupidity and dishonesty.[141] Pollen appears to have believed that this document would serve his cause by forcing a showdown with Bacon. "What I want to do," he wrote on 17 May 1909 to Gipps,

> is to precipitate—or rather have Bacon to precipitate—a row with me, on which I can produce a précis that I have drawn up of the Ariadne fiasco. He must either take this lying down, or face the music of the whole thing.[142]

One of Pollen's most important service supporters assured him that his statement was not inappropriate in form or content. "The precis [*sic*] of the whole question," wrote Rear-Admiral Richard Peirse, the Inspector of Target Practice, on 16 May 1909, "is most interesting reading, admirably lucid & in my opinion most moderate in tone considering the circumstances."[143] Jellicoe, who had strong personal ties to Wilson,[144] does not appear to have concurred in this judgement, and his angry reaction prompted Pollen to apologize. "Your rebuke is quite deserved," Pollen wrote to Jellicoe on 1 June 1909,

> and I am sorry I was violent. If I did not get a fair trial in the Ariadne, it was not because Sir Arthur Wilson, Captain Bacon, and Commander Dreyer were dishonourable men, but because the trials took the form of a competition, and these Officers were the inventors and advocates of the competing system. Partisans, as has already been said, cannot be impartial; prejudice makes even the justest unconsciously unjust.[145]

Some damage appears to have been done in spite of Pollen's expressions of regret, and for a time in subsequent correspondence the two men addressed each other more formally.

In a remarkable manner, however, the cooling of Pollen's friendship with Jellicoe was counteracted by a dramatic improvement in his relations with his leading opponent. In mid July 1909, the circulation of preliminary copies of Hughes-Onslow's survey of fire control[146] induced Bacon to reconsider his view of gunnery. "Yes, your Essay has been downed," wrote Captain Robert F. Scott (soon to find fame as a polar explorer), who was then assigned to the Ordnance Department,[147] to Hughes-Onslow on 17 July 1909,

> but not without having created the desired effect. There has been a great change in the whole policy which you would be very interested to hear. I will only say that Mr. Pollen is in high spirits.

In a postscript, Scott noted that "the D.N.O. went arm in arm with Pollen to Manchester[148] and came back much impressed. He is now sincerely anxious for the experiments to succeed."[149] Pollen's letter of congratulations to Bacon upon his promotion to Rear-Admiral resulted in a revealing as well as friendly reply. "If I differ from you as I have done," Bacon wrote on 16 July 1909,

> it is because I am convinced I am right!!!-but I am always willing to be convinced I am wrong[;] as you say-we are all working for the good of the

country & really the more diverse our views the greater the ultimate gain, the more severe the criticism & selection the better the product. I sincerely wish you every success with your apparatus & that it will help us in our work. My definition of success may be too flavoured with a hatred of complications but this will do no harm as an antidote. [150]

The change in Bacon's attitude appears to have resulted in an informal agreement that allowed Pollen and his engineers to remain on board the trials ship throughout the trial period. And although the civilians were not to be permitted to witness the operation of the instruments while they were being tested, the improved relations with the Ordnance Department gave Pollen at least the hope of a fair trial.

(c) TRIALS AND TRIBULATIONS

On 21 April 1909, the Admiralty had informed the Argo Company that the projected trials would not take place in the pre-dreadnought battleship *London* as had been originally planned. [151] On 14 May, the Admiralty provided the Argo Company with ballistical data and other information on the 9.2-inch gun for the purposes of designing the change of range machine, which suggested that an armoured cruiser might be chosen as the test ship, but no vessel was named. [152] By August, however, the Admiralty had selected the armoured cruiser *Natal*, which was part of the Home Fleet, to carry out the trials of the Argo gear and, on 13 August, Pollen and Isherwood attended a conference on board that ship. [153] Design and manufacturing difficulties appear to have been the cause of some delay in the completion of the test instruments, and as a consequence the gyroscopically stabilized range-finding apparatus, electrical transmitting gear, indicators and plotting table were not delivered until 25 September 1909, and the delivery of the change of range machine postponed indefinitely. [154] Pollen got his way with regard to the placement of the range-finder, it being mounted on the bridge platform, while the plotting table was installed in the lower conning tower. [155]

The gear fitted in the *Natal* in September differed from that tried in the *Ariadne* two years before in a number of ways. The range-finder mounting was improved through the replacement of the double gyroscope mechanism by a single gyroscope that was kept continuously in motion by a jet of compressed air, which resulted in a mechanically less complex and more compact arrangement. [156] The new plotting table had been designed to allow plotting to take place while the ship in which it was fitted was turning. This was to have been achieved in the following manner. Instead of moving the paper while the marking arms were fixed in position, the marking arms were to be moved on a framework to correspond with the speeds of the firing ship and target while the paper chart was pinned in place on a flat surface that could be pivoted around an adjustable center to represent the turning motion of the ship. The Ordnance Department, however, apparently did not believe that the capacity to plot while turning justified the increase in mechanical complexity, [157] and thus the plotting table as supplied did not incorporate the pivoting feature although other changes were made that allowed the operator to measure the target course and speed much more rapidly.[158]

The *Natal* was commanded by Captain Frederick C. Ogilvy, one of the most distinguished gunnery officers in the fleet.[159] One of his officers later recalled that he

> was a man of dynamic personality. He had been Torpedo Officer of the *Terrible* when Percy Scott was in command and had been infected with his Captain's enthusiasm. He was a small man with a comic face, always wore an eyeglass, and was like an animated bottle of champagne.[160]

Ogilvy had previously been in charge of experiments with manual plotting in the pre-dreadnought battleship *Revenge*, and had been convinced by the experience that manual methods of fire control were impracticable.[161] In large part as a result of his efforts, the *Natal* in 1909 set a fleet record in the Gunlayer's Test, an achievement that was acclaimed in the press as well as the service.[162] Ogilvy was also an enthusiastic proponent of director firing. During the late summer or early fall of 1909, he had on his own initiative seen to the construction of a prototype director, which was tested in the *Natal* in October, apparently at the same time as the evaluation of Pollen's equipment.[163]

There are no records of the trials of the incomplete Argo system that were carried out in October 1909 other than the brief mention of plotting exercises in the *Natal*'s log.[164] Pollen was not allowed to witness the operation of his gear at sea,[165] but he appears to have been informed that plotting was carried out successfully.[166] Although there may have been a few minor mechanical difficulties,[167] the instruments greatly impressed Ogilvy. He also agreed that the ability to plot while turning was essential, and urged Pollen and Isherwood to improvise means by which this could be accomplished with the existing machine.

"I scarcely dare believe," Pollen wrote to Hughes-Onslow on 1 November 1909 from the *Natal*,

> in my good fortune. Ogilvy is not one in a thousand, but just one only. His grasp both of principle and detail is, in my experience, unique. We have had great talks. I have not presented him with advocacy. He has studied the pamphlets –and descriptions closely; he knows the gear intimately; his eye for a drawing is infallible, it is like a great conductor's for a score—he does not have to hear the music—he can read it. F.O. can see a machine in a drawing and he is even more anti-polyanthropist than I am. It is a new one on me to find a sea captain insisting on making the gear more complete both as a scientific solution of the problem and as eliminating still more mental and manual operations. But then –he is both the best mechanic and the hardest thinker on war that I encountered. He is ruthless in telling me our shortcomings and defects—all of his suggestions are invaluable. To him the employment of the gun in action-as contrasted with battle practice—is everything.
>
> You cannot realize what it means to me. The great change in our plotting system which we have funked all these years on the grounds that it was an extra complication he, with his eye for sea fighting, insists on as a primary necessity; it is, of course, making the table plot irrespective of helm—i.e., our

course is no longer a straight line, only true when we are on a straight line, but is itself accurately plotted. This makes Captain and Admiral free to manoeuvre as they please, knowing the guns will be ready to open [fire] the moment they [are] steady, and they can choose the course to steady on *without notice* to the plotting station. No more bother about turns etc. It is a great improvement, but one we should not have dared to make unless we had his authority behind us.

Ogilvy had withheld his general opinions of Pollen's work until after he had observed the gear in operation, which for a time had caused the inventor some worry. "It was only yesterday [31 October]," Pollen explained to Hughes-Onslow,

that he really spoke out about his belief in the whole show. I was for some time rather nervous. I wondered if he was not rather carried away by his interest in the machinery and not interested in the purpose and object of it all, but I was quite mistaken. From what he said yesterday, I gather that like me, he takes the machinery for granted. It is either right, or can be made right. The purpose is everything; the means nothing. He said "You have done a much bigger thing in analyzing the problem and showing what must be done, than in producing means for doing it. You will have a tougher job making people understand all it means, than in making the gear succeed."

Ogilvy believed, however, that Pollen would win in the end. "He is quietly indignant," Pollen confided to Hughes-Onslow, "over the way that Reginald Bacon has treated me, and what is worse the Service, but thinks the thing is safe now." "He showed me a letter," Pollen wrote later in his very long communication,

he had written yesterday: "Pollen is either right or has got to be made right: the necessity for his system is overwhelming: and it is the only possible one."
So you see that I am getting educated and have found the friend and protector that I and the system needed. It is a wonderful stroke of luck the best of all the good offices Jellicoe has done me. F.O.'s selection was entirely his I believe. Anyway it is going to do the trick.[168]

Ogilvy's good opinion of Pollen's work was shared by Rear-Admiral Prince Louis of Battenberg, the Commander-in-Chief of the Atlantic Fleet, whose vessels joined the ships of the Home Fleet in late October. He had become a strong supporter of Pollen after reading the *Jupiter Letters* in the summer of 1906, and in January 1909 had expressed views on gunnery that differed sharply from those of Wilson, Bacon, and Dreyer.[169] On 30 October, Pollen was the guest of honor at a dinner on board Battenberg's flagship, the pre-dreadnought battleship *Prince of Wales*. "We had," Pollen reported to Hughes-Onslow,

great doings Saturday. Atlantic Fleet here en masse, dinner on flagship in my honour in the evening: P.L. vocal in my praises, "the most important project now proceeding anywhere in the world: the future of naval fighting depends on your success", and so forth. Very gratifying.[170]

173

A week and a half later, however, Pollen and Isherwood were ordered off the *Natal* by Admiral Sir William May, the Commander-in-Chief of the Home Fleet, who believed that their presence on board during forthcoming gunnery exercises would be inconsistent with an Admiralty circular letter of the previous spring, which had warned officers that relations with Pollen were to be governed by the strict enforcement of regulations regarding the secrecy of service fire control equipment.[171] As a result of an oversight, Pollen and Isherwood received no warning of the order of departure and, as a consequence, were unceremoniously hustled over the side on the evening of 10 November.[172] Angered by such treatment, Pollen met with Bacon on 13 November, to discuss the possibility of establishing a framework of mutual trust that would not only preclude such actions in the future, but allow naval officers to assist freely in the process of perfecting his instruments for service use. Bacon apparently sympathized with Pollen's predicament and responded by suggesting that the two parties come to a comprehensive agreement with regard to secrecy and the purchase of Pollen's system. Pollen thus wrote to the Admiralty Permanent Secretary on 16 November, outlining his terms and proposing a conference to settle the matter.[173]

Pollen was gratified by Bacon's response,[174] but troubled by a premonition of disaster. "The fact is," he confided to Ogilvy on 16 November 1909,

> I am really worried. To tell the truth I left Weymouth–after watching the good ship [the *Natal*] steam out—with a very heavy heart. Somehow we seem on the eve of serious trouble. Your parting words that the success of the gear is assured were comforting. I know that the Lords [of Admiralty] at least do trust you.

Pollen was particularly concerned by the fact that Fisher had decided to retire at the beginning of the new year, in the wake of the equivocal judgement of his leadership of the Admiralty that had been rendered by a sub-committee of the Committee of Imperial Defence.[175] Pollen was by this time fairly certain "that Wilson is to succeed Fisher early in the year," and he confessed that "in the back of my mind I have an instinct that if we cannot secure monopoly and co-operation before this last event—the gear will be lost to the Navy . . ."[176]

Even the resignation of Bacon from the navy to take up the managing directorship of the Coventry Ordnance Works, a decision which may have been attributable at least in part to his by now manifest failure as Director of Naval Ordnance, was the cause of some regret to Pollen, who wished him well in a friendly letter of 23 November, which was answered with an equally cordial letter the next day.[177] Bacon's departure must have been responsible in part for the delay in the setting up of the conference over terms that Pollen had formally requested on 16 November, and which the Admiralty had acknowledged on 18 November. Further correspondence between Pollen and the Admiralty had ensued,[178] but no date had been set by early December, which prompted Pollen to write privately on 2

December to the Acting Director of Naval Ordnance, Captain Arthur W. Craig, to ask whether the Admiralty still wanted to reach a comprehensive agreement, and to urge that if so, it be settled before Fisher's departure, "for obvious reasons, if an agreement is not signed by that date, all chances of monopoly will be gone forever."[179]

In the meanwhile, Ogilvy had informed Pollen that further tests of his instruments had been carried out with success, but in the absence of the Argo Company's engineers, the gear was apparently mishandled, which resulted in its breakdown sometime between 16 and 18 November. Pollen thus dispatched one of his employees to the *Natal* to make repairs and to supervise subsequent operations,[180] but complained in his letter to Craig of 2 December of the restrictions on himself and his engineers that had led to the mechanical difficulties in the first place.[181]

On 4 December, Craig assured Pollen that a conference was in the offing and that he believed that an agreement with regard to the gyro-stabilized gear was a certainty. He encouraged Pollen, moreover, to complete the modifications to the plotting table that had been suggested by Ogilvy as quickly as possible and to delay work on the change of range machine if necessary.[182] Also on 4 December, F. W. Black, the Director of Navy Contracts, asked Pollen by telephone to submit a statement of terms for a production order for the components of his system, which Pollen provided in a letter written that day.[183] Pollen wrote a second letter to Black on 7 December to add a statement with regard to royalties.[184] A conference between Pollen, Craig, Black and Charles Minter (an associate of Black from the Contracts Department) took place on 10 December, at which time several alternative sets of terms were discussed, and a verbal commitment made by the Admiralty representatives to buy 75 gyro-stabilized range-finder mountings and 50 plotting tables, an order worth some £187,000.[185] On 23 December, Pollen met with Bacon's successor as Director of Naval Ordnance, Captain Archibald Gordon Henry Wilson Moore, to settle questions about payment for secrecy and the financing of the plant required to manufacture instruments for a production order.[186] By this time, however, Pollen's prospects for a satisfactory agreement with the Admiralty had been irreparably damaged.

In November, Pollen had provided the officers of the *Natal* with a gift of oysters, one or two of which proved to be contaminated with typhoid germs.[187] In a letter to Pollen of 18 November, Ogilvy complained that he "had a bad attack of liver and am rather cheap."[188] On 2 December, Pollen wrote to Craig that "Captain Ogilvy is so horribly sick as to be incapable of doing anything."[189] On 4 December, Craig informed Pollen that Ogilvy had been relieved of his command of the *Natal*.[190] Ogilvy died on 18 December of heart failure.[191]

Ogilvy had been one of Pollen's strongest and most intelligent supporters and next to Scott the leading proponent of director firing. In November, moreover, Fisher had selected him to assume command of the *Excellent*,[192] a position that would have greatly enhanced his authority in gunnery matters, which might well have led to the rapid adoption of both the Pollen system and director firing. His death, therefore, was nothing less than a disaster for the cause of mechanized gunnery in the Royal Navy. In his absence, both the Argo gear and director control were to suffer major setbacks in 1910, with the result that the gunnery efficiency of the fleet under the less than ideal conditions that were likely to occur in battle remained a matter of serious doubt. This parlous state of affairs was largely overshadowed, however, by a very great improvement in the financial circumstances of the government, which from 1909 enabled Britain to increase dramatically the amount spent on the navy.

Notes to Chapter 5

1 For the improvement in fleet gunnery practice between 1905 and 1907, see Chapter 3, section 1.
2 Admiralty print, "The Guildhall Banquet" (November 1907), F.P. 4852, FISR 8/27, C.C.
3 St Barbara, "Fool Gunnery in the Navy—I," *Blackwood's Magazine*, Vol. 183 (February 1908), pp. 308-16.
4 St Barbara, "Fool Gunnery in the Navy—II," *Blackwood's Magazine*, Vol. 183 (March 1908), pp. 442-60. For St Barbara's response to Pollen's query, see St Barbara to Pollen via Blackwood, 6 March 1908, P.P.
5 St Barbara, "Fool Gunnery in the Navy—III," *Blackwood's Magazine*, Vol. 183 (April 1908), pp. 598-610.
6 "Fool Gunnery—I," pp. 309, 314.
7 "Fool Gunnery—II," p. 452.
8 "Fool Gunnery—III," p. 598.
9 Admiralty print, "Improvement in Naval Gunnery" (March 1908), F.P. 4868, FISR 8/29, C.C. For a view of the Admiralty's reaction to the St Barbara articles, see K. G. B. Dewar, *The Navy From Within* (London: Victor Gollancz, 1939), pp. 112-3.
10 See Appendix, Table 11.
11 Bacon Memorandum and Minute, March 1908, in Adm. 1/8010, P.R.O.
12 Hooligan [a nickname—an officer of that name is not to be found in the Navy List] to George Gipps, n.d., P.P.
13 Admiralty, Gunnery Branch, "Information Regarding Fire Control, Range-Finding, and Plotting"(1909), pp. 2, 30, N.L.M.D. [henceforward cited as "Information Regarding Fire Control"]; and Backhouse to Pollen, 11 October 1908; Captain C. Hughes-Onslow, *Fire Control* (Royal Naval War College, Portsmouth, 1909) [henceforward cited as Hughes-Onslow, *Fire Control*], "Section III.: Plotting," pp. 9-11; and "A. H. P. Statement," P.P.
14 For which see this section, below.
15 Hughes-Onslow, *Fire Control*, "General Remarks and Conclusion on Plotting," p. 2, P.P.
16 Ibid., "Section III.: Plotting," p. 9, P.P.
17 Ibid., "General Remarks and Conclusion on Plotting," p. 2, P.P.
18 "A. H. P. Statement," P.P. For the figures that indicate that much higher percentages of hits to rounds fired were achieved by ships that used true-course plotting as compared with those which used time-and-range plotting, see Pollen to the Admiralty Permament Secretary, 22 February 1909, P.P.
19 "Information Regarding Fire Control," p. 30.

20 Backhouse to Pollen, 11 October 1908, P.P.

21 Lieutenant Ernest K. Arbuthnot to Pollen, 17 October 1908, P.P. For Beresford's admiration of the Pollen manual plotter, see also Captain Sir Douglas E. R. Brownrigg, 2 October 1908, P.P. For more on Beresford's support of Pollen, see this chapter, section 3(b).

22 Dewar, *The Navy From Within*, p. 104; Pollen to Captain Herbert Richmond, 17 June 1909, P.P.

23 Arthur Hungerford Pollen and Harold Isherwood, *The Pollen Manual Charting Table as privately supplied to and used in certain H.M. Ships* (London: The Argo Company, 1909), P.P.

24 "Information Regarding Fire Control," pp. 10-12. In 1912, Pollen recalled that following the Admiralty issue of a manual true-course plotter in 1909, he "returned to each of the officers who had bought a plotting-table from me a cheque for the amount he had paid for it." "A. H. P. Statement," P.P.

25 Pollen to Richmond, 17 June 1909, P.P.

26 For Pollen's explanation of his motives in writing this print, see text of print and "A. H. P. Statement," P.P.

27 Ibid., pp. 16-17 [*PP*, pp. 190-1].

28 *PP*, pp. 386-7.

29 Pollen to Wilfrid Greene, 28 July 1925, P.P.

30 Dreyer to Hughes-Onslow, 18 October 1908, P.P. For the effect of the letter on Hughes-Onslow, see this section, below.

31 Pollen draft letter to Bacon dated 16 December 1908, that was apparently not sent, being replaced by a somewhat different letter dated 18 December 1908, P.P.

32 "Information Regarding Fire Control," p. 2.

33 Unnamed officers quoted by Pollen in Pollen to Jellicoe, 18 January 1909, P.P.

34 "Obry (Petravic) Gun Firing Apparatus, Trial of & report on," D.N.O. (17 September 1908), Adm. 1/8011, P.R.O., and Admiral Sir Frederic C. Dreyer, *The Sea Heritage: A Study of Maritime Warfare* (London: Museum Press, 1955), p. 85. The Petravic gunlaying gear was adopted by the German navy, but does not appear to have been used until after the battle of Jutland, for which see N. J. M. Campbell, *Battlecruisers: the design and development of British and German battlecruisers of the First World War era* (London: Conway Maritime Press, 1978), pp. 49, 57. For the possibility that the Petravic system was ineffective, see "General Information collected by Mr. J. W. French, Technical Expert, N.I.A.C.C., from various sources, and more particularly from the German Liaison Officer, Lieut.-Commander Renken," in Great Britain, Admiralty, Naval Staff, Intelligence Division, *Reports on Interned German Vessels: Part V.—Gunnery Material* (October 1920), p. 6, Adm. 186/243, P.R.O.

35 Percy Scott, "Proposed Method of fighting the guns of the most powerful ship in the world, namely H.M.S. 'Dreadnought,'" (1905) in "Director for Turret Firing," Adm. 1/7955, P.R.O.

36 Jellicoe Memoranda and Minute, 17 August 1905, Adm. 1/7955, P.R.O.

37 For the problem of tilt, see E. Altham, "Notes on Director Firing" (19 June 1913), Adm. 1/8330, P.R.O.

38 Percy Scott, "Proposed Method of fighting the guns"; and Great Britain, Admiralty, Technical History Section, *Fire Control in H.M. Ships*. Series: *The Technical History and Index: A Serial History of Technical Problems Dealt with by Admiralty Departments*, part 23 (December, 1919), p. 4, N.L.M.D.

39 Admiral Sir Percy Scott, *Fifty Years in the Royal Navy* (New York: George H. Doran, 1919), p. 201.
40 Ibid. For a discussion of the *Good Hope* director, see Hughes-Onslow, *Fire Control*, "Section IV-Modern Naval Gun Practice," pp. 14–18.
41 Ibid., p. 17.
42 Scott, *Fifty Years*, p. 232.
43 Hughes-Onslow, *Fire Control*, "Section IV—Modern Naval Gun Practice," p. 17.
44 Scott, *Fifty Years*, p. 209, and Peter Padfield, *Aim Straight: A Biography of Admiral Sir Percy Scott* (London: Hodder & Stoughton, 1966), p. 190.
45 Pollen to Scott, 26 March 1909, P.P.
46 Scott to Pollen, n.d., P.P.
47 For the early development of the important relationship between Pollen and Peirse, see Pollen to Peirse, 30 March 1909; Peirse to Pollen, 1 May 1909; and Peirse to Pollen, 16 May 1909, P.P.
48 Pollen to Gipps, 17 May 1909, P.P.
49 Staff of the Inspector of Target Practice, "Battle Practice, 1909," typescript memorandum, P.P.
50 Hughes-Onslow to Gipps, 11 December 1908, P.P.
51 Hughes-Onslow, Pollen wrote many years later, was

immensely surprised that Dreyer, a total stranger, writing to him in response to a service inquiry, should go out of his way to make a personal attack upon me. This seemed to him a wholly un-english thing to do, and he therefore made it his business to make my acquaintance, and . . . formed the opinion that I had been very unjustly treated; believed that there was a great deal of personal animus behind the opposition to me, and therefore gave me Dreyer's letter although it was marked confidential, as he thought it only just to me that I should know the kind of opposition that I was up against.

Pollen to Wilfrid Greene, 28 July 1925, P.P. See also Gipps to Hughes-Onslow, 19 December 1908, P.P.
52 Although the last section of this work is dated 1 August 1909 ["Section IV—Modern Naval Gun Practice," p. 25], preliminary drafts were circulated as early as in July, for which see Captain Robert F. Scott to Hughes-Onslow, 17 July 1909, P.P.
53 Described above in this section.
54 Hughes-Onslow, *Fire Control*, "General Remarks and Conclusion on Plotting."
55 Ibid., "Section IV-Modern Naval Gun Practice."
56 See this chapter, section 3(b).
57 John Roberts, *The Invincible Class* (London: Conway Maritime Press, 1972), p. 11.
58 Fisher to White, 15 August 1908, in *FGDN*, Vol. 2, p. 189. For the effect of a "dirty bottom"—that is to say, fouling-on a ship's speed, see note by Richard M. Anderson, *Warship International*, Vol. 23 (No. 4, 1986), p. 416.
59 Fred T. Jane (ed.), *Fighting Ships, 1906-7* (London: Sampson Low Marston, 1906), p. 57.
60 See Chapter 4 above and Admiralty confidential print, "Statement by Rear-Admiral Sir John Jellicoe, when Director of Naval Ordnance, on the Subject of the Armament of the Cruisers for the 1908-09 Programme" (November 1907), p. 3, F.P. 4850, FISR 8/27, C.C.

61 *Board Minutes* [Admiralty], 31 March 1908, Adm. 167/42, P.R.O.
62 Fisher to Esher, 8 September 1908, in *FGDN*, Vol. 2, p. 195.
63 Fisher to Watts, 17 September 1908, ibid.
64 The particulars of the first German dreadnought battleships were correctly described for the first time in the 1908 edition of the *Naval Annual*. The first two vessels of the class of four were not completed until October and November 1909.
65 Fisher to Watts, 17 September 1908, in *FGDN*, Vol. 2, pp. 195-6.
66 *NA, 1908*, pp. 83-91.
67 Fisher to Watts, 17 September 1908, in *FGDN*, Vol. 2, pp. 195-6.
68 Fisher to May, 28 September 1908, ibid., p. 196.
69 The *Indomitable* was not under Inglefield's command, being assigned at this date to the Nore Division of the Home Fleet, but he had been a member of the Board of Admiralty at the time of the Committee on Designs in 1905 as Fourth Sea Lord, and doubtless knew of Fisher's special interest in the new warship.
70 Inglefield to Fisher, 18 January 1909, F.P. 345, FISR 1/7, C.C.
71 Fisher to McKenna, 10 February 1909, *FGDN*, Vol. 2, p. 221.
72 Fisher to White, 21 March 1909, ibid., p. 234.
73 Fisher to Esher, 28 August 1909, ibid., p. 261. For the misleading character of the *Indomitable* and *Invincible* Battle Practice performances, see this chapter, sections 1 and 3(b).
74 Captain Charles Madden, then naval secretary to the First Lord.
75 Fisher to Hurd, 29 October 1909, HURD 1/4, Hurd Papers, C.C.
76 Entry of 22 January 1908, in the Slade diary, MRF/39/3, N.M.M.
77 Entry of 3 February 1908, in the Slade diary.
78 "A discussion of the Relative Merits of the 13.5-inch and the 12-inch gun as the Armament for Battleships," pencil dated 18 March 1908, DRYR 2/1, Dreyer Papers, C.C. For Dreyer's role in the development of the 13.5-inch gun, see Dreyer, *The Sea Heritage*, pp. 59-60.
79 Slade Diary, 1908, entry of 3 January, MRF/39/3, N.M.M.
80 "New Design 13.5 inch B.L. gun: Tender for supply of one to V.S.M. design 19788 G." (1909), Adm. 1/8064, P.R.O.
81 *Board Minutes* [Admiralty], 20 November 1908, Adm. 167/42, P.R.O., and Admiral Sir R. H. Bacon, *The Life of John Rushworth Jellicoe* (London: Cassell, 1936), pp. 161-2.
82 Bacon, *The Life of John Rushworth Jellicoe*, pp. 161-2.
83 Rear-Admiral R. H. S. Bacon, "The Battleship of the Future," *Transactions of the Institution of Naval Architects*, Vol. 57 (1910), pp. 1-21. For a discussion of this work, see Chapter 6, section 3.
84 *Board Minutes* [Admiralty], 18 August 1909, Adm. 167/43, P.R.O.
85 Ibid., 27 October 1909, Adm. 167/43, P.R.O.
86 See Chapter 6, section 1.
87 Oscar Parkes, *British Battleships: A History of Design, Construction and Armament*, new and revised edn. (London: Seeley Service, 1957), p. 531.
88 Fisher to White, 13 November 1909, *FGDN*, Vol. 2, p. 277. When speaking of ships just laid down, Fisher was, of course speaking loosely—the *Lion* was not begun until later that month, and the *Princess Royal* not until the spring of the next year.
89 Fisher to Esher, 13 September 1909, *FGDN*, Vol. 2, p. 266.
90 Jellicoe to Pollen, 18 August 1908, P.P.
91 Pollen to the Admiralty Permanent Secretary, 5 January 1909, P.P.

92 For the preoccupation of the Admiralty with the estimates, see *FDSF*, Vol. 1, p. 159. For Jellicoe's busy schedule, see Jellicoe to Pollen, 6 January 1909, P.P.

93 *Board Minutes* [Admiralty], 1909 (12 February 1909), Adm. 167/43, P.R.O.

94 Bacon to Pollen, 13 February 1909, P.P.

95 Pollen to the Admiralty Permanent Secretary, 15 February 1909, P.P.

96 *Board Minutes* [Admiralty], 1909 (18 February 1909), Adm. 167/43

97 Argo to the Admiralty Permanent Secretary, 22 February 1909, P.P.

98 *Board Minutes* [Admiralty] 1909, (4 March 1909), Adm. 167/43, P.R.O.

99 Draft of a letter that was not sent to McKenna, dated 24 March 1909, and Pollen to Jellicoe, 26 March 1909, P.P.

100 Admiralty Permanent Secretary to the Argo Company, 2 April 1909, P.P.

101 Argo Company (Pollen) to the Admiralty Permanent Secretary, 2 April 1909, P.P.

102 Admiralty Permanent Secretary to the Argo Company, 7 April 1909, P.P.

103 Argo to the Admiralty Permanent Secretary, 14 April 1909, P.P.

104 Admiralty Permanent Secretary (Thomas) to the Argo Company, 21 April 1909, P.P.

105 Argo Company (Pollen) to the Admiralty Permament Secretary, 22 April 1909, and reference to an Admiralty letter of 30 April 1909, in Argo Company (Pollen) to the Admiralty Permanent Secretary, 1 May 1909, P.P.

106 Argo Company (Pollen) to the Admiralty Permanent Secretary, 1 May 1909, P.P.

107 Admiralty Permanent Secretary to the Argo Company, first week of May, 1909; Admiralty Permanent Secretary to the Argo Company, 7 May 1909; Argo Company to the Admiralty Permanent Secretary, 11 May 1909; Admiralty Permanent Secretary to the Argo Company, 14 May 1909; Admiralty Permanent Secretary to the Argo Company, 14 May 1909; Argo Company to the Admiralty Permanent Secretary, 17 May 1909; Admiralty Permanent Secretary to the Argo Company, 20 May 1909; Argo Company to the Admiralty Permanent Secretary, 25 May 1909; Argo Company to the Admiralty Permanent Secretary, 4 June 1909; and Argo Company to the Admiralty Permanent Secretary, 7 June 1909, P.P.

108 Director of Navy Contracts (Black) to the Argo Company, 8 June 1909, with covering letter, P.P.

109 Admiralty Permanent Secretary to the Argo Company, 21 June 1909, P.P.

110 The Argo Company to the Admiralty Permanent Secretary, 23 June 1909, P.P.

111 For Pollen's queries, see Bacon to Pollen, 19 March 1909; Pollen to Bacon, 22 March 1909; Argo Company to the Admiralty Permanent Secretary, 28 April 1909; draft letter from the Argo Company to the Admiralty Permanent Secretary, 28 April 1909, that was apparently not sent; Admiralty Permanent Secretary to Pollen, 7 May 1909; Pollen to the Admiralty Permanent Secretary, 11 June 1909; Pollen to Russell Clarke, 20 July 1909; Pollen to the Admiralty Permanent Secretary, 21 July 1909; Opinion of Russell Clarke dated 27 July 1909; Pollen Secretary to the Admiralty Permanent Secretary, 30 July 1909; and Admiralty Permanent Secretary to Pollen, 30 July 1909, P.P. For the settlement of this question, see Chapter 6, section 2.

112 Argo Company (Pollen) to the Admiralty Permanent Secretary, 11 May 1909, P.P.

113 Admiralty Permanent Secretary to the Argo Company, 20 May 1909, P.P.

114 Admiralty Permanent Secretary to the Argo Company, 14 May 1909, P.P.

115 Argo Company (Pollen) to the Admiralty Permanent Secretary, 17 May 1909, P.P. For Pollen's views on the placement of fire control instruments, see Chapter 3, section 2.
116 Pollen to the Admiralty Permanent Secretary, 4 June 1909, P.P.
117 Admiralty Permanent Secretary to the Argo Company, 21 June 1909, P.P.
118 McKenna to Pollen, 31 December 1908, P.P.
119 Quoted by Pollen in Pollen to McKenna, 18 February 1909, P.P.
120 Pollen to McKenna, 18 February 1909, P.P. For the circumstances of the *Indomitable* shoot, see this chapter, section 2.
121 Pollen to McKenna, 18 February 1909, P.P.
122 For the possible identity of these men, see discussion of Pollen's relations with Admirals Beresford and Custance, in this section.
123 Pollen to McKenna, 22 March 1909, P.P.
124 For a reference to McKenna's letter of 23 March 1909, a text of which does not seem to have survived, see Pollen to McKenna, 20 April 1909, P.P. For the meeting between Pollen and McKenna of 26 March 1909, see Pollen to Percy Scott, 26 March 1909, P.P.
125 Pollen to McKenna, 20 April 1909, P.P.
126 McKenna to Pollen, 22 April 1909, P.P.
127 "In Fisher's time," recalled Admiral Sir Henry Oliver, "one was on thin ice; it did not do to hob-nob with old friends in the United Services Club who were in the opposition camp." For Oliver's reminiscence, see Admiral Sir William James, *A Great Seaman: The Life of Admiral of the Fleet Sir Henry F. Oliver* (London: H. F. & G. Witherby, 1956), p. 117.
128 Custance to Pollen, 8 May 1905, P.P.
129 Pollen to Gipps, 30 April 1908, and Pollen to Custance, 10 July 1908, P.P.
130 See Beresford to Pollen, 10 July 1908; Beresford to Pollen, 26 August 1908; Pollen to Custance, 3 June 1908; Pollen to Custance, 10 July 1908; Custance to Pollen, 11 July 1908; Pollen to Custance, 11 August 1908; and Custance to Pollen, 15 August 1908; all in P.P.
131 Beresford to Pollen, 26 August 1908, P.P.
132 Beresford to Pollen, 27 September 1908, P.P.
133 "Of course," Pollen wrote to Beresford on 7 September 1908, "those who knew you and the facts knew that there was only one condition on which the hatchet could be buried, and that is that our Oriental friend had surrendered to you and not you to him. It is of course obvious to everybody who know the elements of the facts that the white flag can never go up on the King Edward."
134 Undated draft letter, probably December 1908, P.P.
135 Pollen to Fisher, 5 January 1909, P.P.
136 "Set a man before a sheet of paper," Fisher said, "and he has time to tell lies." Quoted by A. G. Gardiner in Admiral Sir R. H. Bacon, *The Life of Lord Fisher of Kilverstone, Admiral of the Fleet*, 2 Vols (London: Hodder and Stoughton, 1929), Vol. 1, p. 241.
137 Fisher to White, 4 April 1909, in *FGDN*, Vol. 2, p. 241.
138 Fisher to McKenna, 5 April 1909, F.P. 376, FISR 1/8, C.C. Fisher believed that Pollen was "taking a hand" in the controversy caused by the public revelation that Bacon had in 1906 made unfavorable reports to Fisher about Beresford, for which see *FGDN*, Vol. 2, pp. 211-12. See also Fisher to Arnold White, 4 April 1909, and Fisher to George Lambert, 5 April 1909, in *FGDN*, Vol. 2, p. 241, 241n.
139 Jellicoe to Pollen, 6 January 1909; Pollen to Jellicoe, 10 March 1909; Jellicoe to Pollen, 11 March 1909, and Jellicoe to Pollen, 1 April 1909; P.P.

140 Pollen to Jellicoe, 15 April 1909, and Jellicoe to Pollen, 15 April 1909, P.P.
141 Arthur Hungerford Pollen, *Notes, Etc., on the Ariadne Trials* (London: Argo Company, April 1909) [*PP*, pp. 194-236].
142 Pollen to Gipps, 17 May 1909, P.P.
143 Peirse to Pollen, 16 May 1909, P.P.
144 Jellicoe's past associations with Wilson may have made him particularly sensitive to Pollen's criticisms of the admiral. In 1891, Wilson had chosen Jellicoe to be his commander in the battleship *Sans Pareil*, a position he fulfilled with great success until he was invited to become flag commander to Admiral Sir George Tryon in April 1893. In June 1893, after Tryon's flagship had sunk after a collision, Wilson invited Jellicoe on board his ship and treated him with special consideration. For Jellicoe's past relationship with Wilson, see Bacon, *Jellicoe*, p. 65, and John Winton, *Jellicoe* (London: Michael Joseph, 1981), pp. 40-4.
145 Pollen to Jellicoe, 1 June 1909, P.P.
146 See this chapter, section 1.
147 For Scott's support of Pollen's ideas, see Scott to Pollen, 15 June 1909, P.P.
148 Bacon's trip to the Linotype works near Manchester appears to have taken place on 8 July 1909, for which see Bacon to Pollen, 1 July 1909, P.P.
149 Scott to Hughes-Onslow, 17 July 1909, P.P.
150 Bacon to Pollen, 16 July 1909, P.P.
151 Admiralty Permanent Secretary to the Argo Company, 21 April 1909, P.P. The Admiralty provided no explanation, but *London* may have been unavailable because of changes in her refitting schedule, for which see Parkes, *British Battleships*, p. 410.
152 Admiralty Permanent Secretary to the Argo Company, 14 May 1909, P.P.
153 Argo Company Secretary to the Admiralty Permanent Secretary, 11 August 1909, P.P.
154 Argo Company to the Director of Navy Contracts, 6 September 1909, and the Admiralty Permanent Secretary (Thomas) to the Argo Company, 29 October 1909, P.P.
155 For the placement of the range-finder, see photograph of the arrangement, to the author courtesy of Anthony Pollen. For the placement of the plotting table, see Arthur Hungerford Pollen, *To Rear-Admiral the Hon. Stanley C. J. Colville, CVO, CB* (by the author, July 1910) [*PP*, pp. 246-7].
156 British Patent 11,795/1909 (19 May 1909); Argo Company Prospectus, "The Pollen A.C. Battle System" (5 January 1909), p. 9, P.P.; Great Britain, Admiralty, *Handbook for Argo A.C. Range-Finder Mounting* (1912), PLLN 1/3, Pollen Papers, C.C.
157 Pollen to Hughes-Onslow, 1 November 1909, and Arthur Hungerford Pollen, *The Quest of a Rate Finder* (by the author, November 1910) [*PP*, p. 265].
158 Argo Company Prospectus, "The Pollen A.C. Battle System" (January 5, 1905), p. 9, P.P., and British Patent 5031/1909 (2 March 1909).
159 For Ogilvy's high reputation in the service, see *NA, 1913*, p. 322.
160 Admiral Sir William James, *The Sky was Always Blue* (London: Methuen, 1951), p. 65. For Ogilvy's relations with Scott, see Padfield, *Aim Straight*, p. 190.
161 Pollen, *Quest of a Rate Finder* [*PP*, p. 264].
162 James, *The Sky was Always Blue*, pp. 65-7.
163 The log of the *Natal* noted that director firing exercises were carried out on 13 and 25 October 1909, Adm. 53/23981, P.R.O. For a description of the *Natal* director, see Peter Padfield, *Aim Straight*, p. 190

164 Log of H.M.S. *Natal*, 7 April 1909–14 April 1910, Adm. 53/23981, P.R.O. Plotting exercises are noted on 12 and 14 October only.

165 Pollen to the Admiralty Permanent Secretary, 13 April 1910, P.P.

166 See typescript copies of what appear to have been hand-written letters from Pollen to his wife, dated 26 and 27 October, and 1 November. In the last letter Pollen wrote "we have done a little—but very little plotting—the gear works well—and with any luck we should get some fine plots to show before we get to Portland, where I understand we are to plot against the fleet."

167 For example, see Ogilvy to Pollen, 18 November 1909, P.P.

168 Pollen to Hughes-Onslow, 1 November 1909, typescript copy made by Anthony Pollen from draft handwritten letter, P.P.

169 Battenberg to Pollen, 15 August 1906, and 29 January 1909, P.P.

170 Pollen to Hughes-Onslow, 1 November 1909, typescript copy made by Anthony Pollen from draft handwritten letter, P.P.

171 Pollen to Harding, 19 November 1909, P.P. For the Admiralty circular letter, see Great Britain, Admiralty, *Pollen Aim Correction System: General Grounds of Admiralty Policy and Historical Record of Business Negotiations* (February 1913), p. 9, N.L.M.D.

172 Pollen to Harding, 19 November 1909, P.P.

173 Pollen's terms of 16 November were that the Argo Company be paid £1,112 to cover the cost of each set of instruments, £2,224 royalty for each ship fitted, with the royalty to amount to a minimum of £9,000 per year for so long as use continued. Pollen to the Admiralty Permanent Secretary, 16 November 1909, P.P. (See "Points for Discussion" [for conference at the Admiralty, 10 December 1909] for terms, which are missing in the copy of the letter of 16 November).

174 Ibid.

175 Mackay, *Fisher of Kilverstone*, p. 417.

176 Pollen to Ogilvy, 16 November 1909, P.P.

177 Pollen to Bacon, 23 November 1909, and Bacon to Pollen, November 24, 1909; P.P.

178 Pollen to the Admiralty Permanent Secretary, 22 November 1909; Pollen to the Admiralty Permanent Secretary, 25 November 1909; Admiralty Permanent Secretary to the Argo Company, 29 November 1909; F. W. Black to Pollen, 29 November 1909; and F. W. Black to Pollen, 2 December 1909; P.P.

179 Pollen to Craig , 2 December 1909, P.P.

180 Pollen to Gipps, 18 November 1909, P.P.

181 Pollen to Craig, 2 December 1909, P.P.

182 Craig to Pollen, 4 December 1909, P.P.

183 In his letter, Pollen gave prices for each instrument calculated on the basis of their being ordered in lots of 25 or more; proposed that secrecy be maintained by the Argo Company without charge until March 1914 so long as orders equalled or exceeded £30,000 per annum and suggested that after five years if goods to the value of £250,000 or more had been ordered, the Admiralty would have the right to submit the manufacturing contract to arbitration if a satisfactory agreement could not be reached through negotiations with the Argo Company. Pollen to Black, 4 December 1909, P.P.

184 Pollen wrote to Black to add that a royalty of £250 per annum per ship for as long as the Admiralty wished to preserve secrecy would also be charged. Pollen to Black, 7 December 1909, P.P.

185 "Points for Discussion" [for a conference at the Admiralty], 10 December 1909, and "A. H. P. Statement to 1911," (1911), p. 66, P.P.; and "Proof of

Evidence of Vice-Admiral Arthur Craig-Waller, C.B.," n.d., Craig Waller Papers, N.L.M.D.

186 Pollen to Moore, 23 December 1909, P.P.

187 Vice-Admiral Sir Francis Pridham, who was a lieutenant on the *Natal* at the time, to Anthony Pollen, 14 May 1973, courtesy of Anthony Pollen.

188 Ogilvy to Pollen, 18 November 1909, P.P.

189 Pollen to Craig, 2 December 1909, P.P.

190 Craig to Pollen, 4 December 1909, P.P.

191 Obituary, *The Times* [London] (20 December 1909).

192 Fisher to Ogilvy, 9 November 1909, courtesy of Ogilvy's daughter via Anthony Pollen.

[6]

Compromise: Financial Revolution and Technological Reaction, 1909-1914

1   Radical Finance and Dominion Aid

Between 1900 and 1903, the Conservative–Unionist government had increased taxes to the limit acceptable to the electorate in order to meet expenses arising from the Boer War. In spite of this effort, less than a third of the expenditure on the fighting was defrayed out of current income, while non-war related expenditure continued to rise, which led to heavy borrowing. In 1903, Joseph Chamberlain, the Colonial Secretary, proposed the alternative of replacing free trade with a system of imperial preference that would, he argued, both protect British agriculture and industry and generate revenue that could be spent on the defence of the empire. Chamberlain's call for tariffs bitterly divided the government and was highly unpopular with an electorate that favored cheap food more than it feared import-induced unemployment. The government fell in December 1905, and in the general election of January 1906, which was fought over the issues of the late government's policy on education, financial practices and its equivocal position on free trade, the Conservative-Unionist party suffered a crushing defeat.[1]

The Liberal government did not have time to prepare a budget of its own before the start of the new fiscal year, and thus adopted the draft navy estimate for 1906–07 that had been prepared under the old regime. The navy estimate was nevertheless substantially lower than that of the previous year because of Fisher's administrative reforms and reductions in new construction, which had become possible because of heavy Russian naval losses in the Far East and delays in German capital ship construction that were caused by the introduction of the all–big–gun battleship *Dreadnought*.[2]

185

A Liberal policy of economy in its own right was not established until the discussions of the estimates for 1907-8, which took place in the summer of 1906. At this time, H. H. Asquith, the Chancellor of the Exchequer, obtained reductions in the size of the 1906-7 building program, the personnel of the fleet, the number of ships in commission and the scale of maneuvers; the deferment of certain new works construction; and a promise to reduce the battleship building program for 1907-8 by one vessel if forthcoming armament negotiations at The Hague were successful. With the failure of The Hague talks, however, the contingent battleship was ordered.[3]

The negotiations between the Admiralty and the Cabinet over the 1908-9 estimates were protracted and bitter. In November 1907, the government refused flatly to accept the Admiralty's proposals for an increase in the estimates of £2 million, which was double the figure that had been put forward previously. In December, the service members of the Board of Admiralty countered with a memorandum in which they insisted that any reduction in their financial recommendations would jeopardize national security. After more than a month of negotiations, a compromise was reached in February 1908 that gave the Admiralty somewhat less than half of the increase that they desired, which was enough to preserve the building program substantially intact but at the cost of further significant reductions in spending on practice ammunition and major repairs to ships.[4]

Very substantial savings in naval spending were achieved during the first three years of Liberal rule. It will be recalled that expenditure on the navy had risen significantly in practically every year between 1889 and 1904. For three fiscal years from 1906-7 to 1908-9, however, the navy estimates were held at a level that was on average some 15 per cent below the high point that had been reached in 1904-5. The temptation to pass additional Naval Works Acts was, moreover, resisted successfully,[5] and although funds authorized by previous legislation were utilized, the amount borrowed annually for naval works between fiscal years 1906-7 and 1908-9 fell to less than a third of the figure of 1905-6. The reductions in overall naval spending are even more impressive when it is remembered that from 1905-06, £1.3 million were required out of the Works Vote of each year's navy estimates to pay for the annuities arising out of earlier spending under the Naval Works Acts.

The savings achieved from fiscal years 1906-7 to 1908-9, were in large part attributable to decreases in the construction of battleships and first-class cruisers. The Selborne program of 1902, which had called for the ordering of seven battleships and first-class cruisers per year from 1903-4 through 1906-7, was reduced by the Conservative-Unionist government to four units in 1905-6. Under the Liberals, the building programs of 1906-7 and 1907-8 fell to three battleships, and the program of 1908-9 provided for only one battleship and a single battle cruiser. Expenditures on the construction of battleships and first-class cruisers thus declined substantially, falling from £8.4 million in 1905-6, to £7.9 million in 1906-7, to £6.4 million in 1907-8 and finally to £5.5 million in 1908-9.[6] Through 1907, the protests of extreme navalists and the opposition in Parliament over the inadequacy of British capital ship construction carried relatively little force in light of the improved relations with France, the financial and naval prostration of Russia, and the delays in the German all-big-gun capital ship building programs. But by the end of 1908, Germany had laid down no fewer than 9 dreadnought battleships or battle cruisers to Great Britain's 10, and although none were yet in service while 4 British units had joined the fleet, there appeared to be prospects of Germany achieving parity if not superiority in new model capital ships within a few years unless the building program for 1909–10 was greatly increased.

In January 1909, the Sea Lords as a body advised Reginald McKenna, who had replaced Lord Tweedmouth as First Lord in 1908, that eight battleships and battle cruisers would have to be ordered under the 1909–10 estimates to meet the German threat. Within the Cabinet, McKenna pressed for a minimum of six vessels, while his Radical colleagues insisted upon no more than four. After bitter debate, the Cabinet agreed to a compromise in February, which provided for the laying down of four capital ships within the coming financial year and four additional vessels if circumstances required it. The refusal of the government to agree unequivocally to an eight ship program provoked a storm of criticism in the Unionist press, and culminated in an opposition call for a vote of censure in the House. Although the Conservative–Unionist motion was defeated overwhelmingly, in July, the government announced that the contingent four ships would be ordered that financial year without prejudice to the next year's program, in response to the decisions by Austria and Italy to begin the construction of all-big-gun battleships, which threatened Britain's position in the Mediterranean.[7]

From 1906 through 1908, while Asquith had been Chancellor of the Exchequer, the financial policy of the Liberal government had been to apply savings in military and naval expenditure, and surplus tax revenue, to liquidate debts in order to free funds for spending on social reform that would otherwise have been spent on debt servicing.[8] Income from taxation, however, had fallen sharply in 1908 as a result of an economic downturn that had begun at the end of 1907, and as late as the spring of 1909 there was no indication of a recovery in sight. In addition, spending under the Old Age Pensions Act passed in 1908 was scheduled to come into full effect in fiscal year 1909–10, a situation that was aggravated by the fact that enrollments, and thus the prospective costs, were much higher than had been anticipated. In fiscal year 1909–10, moreover, savings from the consumption of surplus naval stores without replacement, which had on average reduced spending by over £1 million per annum between 1905–6 and 1907–8, and by over half that amount in 1908–9, would because of the depletion of stores fall to little more than £150,000,[9] and there would also for the first time be no left-over borrowed funds from Naval Works Acts to offset the payment of Naval Works Acts annuities out of the navy estimates. The government's agreement to a building program that was four times the size of that of the previous fiscal year, therefore, complicated what was already an extremely difficult financial situation.

David Lloyd George, a leading Radical who had succeeded Asquith as Chancellor of the Exchequer in the spring of 1908, had vigorously objected to the building proposals of the Admiralty during the late winter and spring of 1909. While fearful that unrestrained naval spending would consume revenue from planned tax increases that he hoped to apply to social problems, he was by no means oblivious to the dangers posed by German capital ship construction to Britain's naval supremacy, which he was determined to uphold. As early as in July 1908, he had informed the German ambassador "that if he had to borrow 100 millions for the Fleet, he would do so, in order to maintain our relative strength *vis-à-vis* to Germany."[10] And in November 1908, even before the onset of the naval scare, Lloyd George was, according to a Treasury colleague, apparently encouraging "ministers to spend, so that he may have justification for the extra millions he proposes to ask for next year."[11]

Following the first Cabinet alarm in December 1908 over the German naval threat, Lloyd George responded in February 1909 to the demand for an immediate large increase in dreadnought construction in 1909-10 with an alternative proposal that was intended to provide enough capital ships to overmatch German building over a five year period. The Admiralty was to be allowed to accelerate construction in the first years of the program if necessary by borrowing against funds approved for later years in an arrangement reminiscent of the Naval Defence Act of 1889 and, in addition, the government was to take steps to ensure that the building capacity existed to provide enough big-guns and mountings to outfit twelve dreadnoughts a year. But the Chancellor of the Exchequer's plan was rejected after it was opposed both by the First Lord as inadequate and by other ministers on the grounds that the approval of spending beyond a single fiscal year compromised Parliament's control of finance.

Lloyd George had by this time come to terms with at least the possibility that six dreadnoughts would have to be laid down in the coming fiscal year, but the rejection of his proposals, which he believed were far sounder than those of the Admiralty, may have provoked his use of abusive language in Cabinet that, according to Asquith, alienated most of his colleagues. Lloyd George's ostentatious resistance to large naval increases, on the other hand, was perhaps motivated by the need to placate back-bench Radicals with a strong show of opposition. And in addition, there is evidence that suggests that Lloyd George and Churchill contrived the Cabinet controversy over the navy estimates in order to discredit McKenna, who was strongly opposed to the land taxes planned by the Chancellor of the Exchequer.[12]

Lloyd George's budget, which was considered by the government in March and April, resorted to sharp increases in income tax, death duties, and stamp duties on all sales and stock transactions; increased taxes on the consumption of liquor, tobacco and the use of automobiles; and a tax on real estate capital gains. In spite of the severe criticism of its provisions by a significant minority of the Cabinet, the draft survived substantially intact and was presented to the Commons at the end of April. After furious resistance by the Conservative-Unionist party, the budget passed its third reading on 4 November 1909 by 379 votes to 149. On 30 November, the Lords rejected the measure on the grounds that its extraordinary character required a favorable "judgement of the country"—that is, a general election won by the Liberal party and its allies—before they would be willing to give their consent. This action of the Lords provoked a constitutional crisis that would not be resolved until their power was sharply curtailed by the passage of the Parliament Act in August 1911, but the victory of the Liberal party and its supporters in the general election held in January 1910 was followed by the final passage of the budget in April.[13]

The executive collection of most taxes with the voluntary cooperation of the taxpayers covered the bulk of the government's expenditures in fiscal year 1909–10, but the non-application of taxes affected by Lloyd George's controversial changes caused substantial deficits that had to be covered by borrowing. The reduced income of 1909–10 was subsequently counterbalanced in 1910–11 by the retroactive collection of taxes due the previous fiscal year. The yield of taxes was also substantially increased by an improvement in economic conditions, which was manifest by the second half of 1909. In April 1910, Asquith estimated that the disruption caused by the budget controversy had resulted in direct costs of £1.3 million and "indirectly a vast deal more."[14] The new taxes nevertheless greatly improved the government's financial position. The average of the sums collected during 1909–10 and 1910–11 was £167.8 million, an increase of £16.2 million, or roughly 10 per cent, over that collected in 1908–9. The continued dynamic performance of the economy resulted in further increases in tax yields. Although no new taxes were levied, income in fiscal year 1911–12 was £185.1 million, that of 1912–13 £188.8 million and that of 1913–14 £198.2 million—the last figure representing an increase over the income of 1908–9 of over 30 per cent.[15]

Spending on social welfare out of tax revenue went from £2.1 million in fiscal year 1908–9, to £19.7 million in 1913–14,[16] by which time the National Insurance Act was providing a measure of protection for the general population against sickness and unemployment.[17] The increase of £17.6 million in per annum spending on social welfare during this period, however, was very nearly matched by the annual increase in naval spending. Expenditure on the navy out of tax revenue rose from £32.2 million in 1908–9 to £48.7 million in 1913–14, an increase of £16.6 million. In the spring of 1909, moreover, New Zealand and Australia each offered to pay the costs of building one dreadnought. After consultation with the Admiralty, it was decided that the two Dominion units should be battle cruisers, and in addition that the Australian contribution would provide for the construction of a balanced fleet unit that would include cruisers and destroyers. In effect, the assistance of the Dominions increased British naval spending by some £2 million per annum from 1910–11 through 1913–14.[18]

A comparison of spending on capital ship construction and capital ship authorizations during the first four years of Liberal rule from 1905–6 to 1908–9, and during the second four years from 1909–10 to 1912–13, reveal the extent to which the Lloyd George budgets and Dominion aid improved

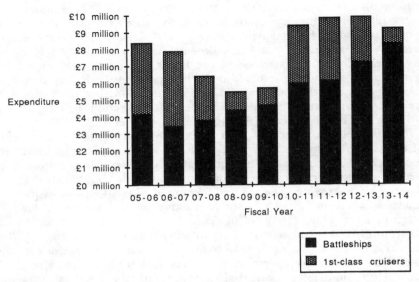

Figure 3: *Expenditure on battleships and first-class cruisers, 1905-1913*

Britain's naval position. Effective expenditure on battleships and battle cruisers—that is, including the colonial contributions—increased from £28.1 million during the period from 1905–6 to 1908-9, to £34.7 million during the period from 1909-10 to 1912-13, a rise of 23 per cent (see Figure 3). Including the two ships contributed by the Dominions, the 1909-10 program amounted to no fewer than 10 units of capital rank. Four battleships and one battle cruiser were ordered under the 1910-11 estimates, an identical program in fiscal year 1911-12 and four battleships in 1912-13. The number of capital ships ordered during the four years from 1909-10 to 1912-13, as a consequence, was double that of the four years from 1905-6 to 1908-9, rising from 12 to no less than 24 units.[19] This was accomplished at the same time that spending on fuel, ammunition, and the construction of the second-class cruisers and destroyers that were required to support the capital units in a fleet action, was also increased substantially.[20]

On 12 November 1908, Asquith had stated to the Commons that the Liberal government would uphold the two-power standard, which was then defined as a numerical superiority of 10 per cent over the combined capital ship forces of the next two largest navies. Asquith's phrasing was equivalent to that used by Selborne in 1901,[21] but by 1908, both France and Russia, who had been formally allied, had been displaced as the second and third strongest naval powers by Germany and the United States, who were regarded as most unlikely diplomatic or naval partners.[22] Apart from the diplomatic drawbacks of including a friendly power—that is, the United States–in calculations of British naval requirements, there was the distinct possibility that Germany's dreadnought program would so exceed even that of the United States that a two-power standard plus 10 per cent

190

would not result in the construction of enough British dreadnoughts to provide a safe margin of superiority over the German navy. "It is quite conceivable," Asquith was advised in May 1909,

> that in the future we may be confronted with a situation in which there would be only one great fleet in Europe besides our own. In such a case the margin of strength which we should have by building up to a standard of equality with any physically possible combination of two Powers might not be adequate against the single European Power. It may become necessary to have, apart from the two-Power standard, an independent standard of strength measured by a given percentage of superiority over any individual European Power. . .
>
> The probability that our whole fleet would have to be divided, and that each part would have to be superior to the foreign squadron against which it was sent, entails upon us the need for considerable superiority over any one Power. We must therefore have such a margin of superiority over one Power as might conceivably render the two-Power standard insufficient provision.[23]

A one-power standard calculated as being a force equal to that of Germany plus a margin of 60 per cent, first appeared officially in April 1909 in a report of the Admiralty's Committee on Manning Requirements.[24] In October 1909, Rear-Admiral Alexander Bethell, the Director of Naval Intelligence, prepared a diagram illustrating the numbers of ships that would have to be laid down through April 1914 in order to maintain a 60 per cent superiority over the German navy, an exercise that was repeated in December 1911 for Winston Churchill, who had taken over the Admiralty from McKenna that October.[25] On 29 December 1911 Churchill proposed that the 60 per cent standard be formally adopted,[26] and on 18 March 1912 he proclaimed the new standard to the Commons.[27]

In fiscal year 1913-14, a two-power standard plus a margin of 10 per cent in cumulative dreadnought starts would have required the laying down of 3.4 more dreadnoughts than called for under the one-power plus 60 per cent standard, but in all other fiscal years between 1909-10 and 1913-14, the difference was smaller. The equivalence of the two standards was closer when considering cumulative dreadnought launches, and closer still when considering cumulative dreadnought completions. In calendar year 1909, a one-power standard in cumulative completions would have been one vessel higher than a two-power standard, and in calendar year 1913, the one-power standard in cumulative launches and completions was practically identical to that of a two-power standard. It would not be unreasonable to conclude, therefore, that as it turned out the replacement of the two-power standard by the one-power standard did not result in a significant change in the accepted measure of British naval security.[28]

Calculations of the Royal Navy's first-line strength in capital ships between 1909 and 1914 were complicated by the questions of whether the two pre-dreadnought battleships of the *Lord Nelson* class—whose heavy-caliber secondary battery made them nearly as powerful as the early all-big-gun units—and the two battle cruisers contributed by the Dominions in 1909 could be taken into account. According to a memorandum written by the Director of Naval Intelligence in 1913 neither the

Lord Nelson class nor the Dominion vessels were counted up to December 1911; in December 1911 it was decided to count the two vessels of the *Lord Nelson* class as dreadnoughts but only until April 1917 while the Dominion vessels were not included; and after December 1911 the *Lord Nelson* class was counted as decided in December as well as one of the two Dominion vessels.[29]

In both fiscal and calendar years from 1909 to 1912, by the criterion given by the D.N.I. in 1913, neither the one-power nor two-power standard was achieved in cumulative dreadnought starts, but both standards were closely approximated and even exceeded in terms of cumulative dreadnought launches and completions.[30] The occasional shortfalls in completed dreadnoughts amounted at most to a single unit plus a fraction, which in light of the Royal Navy's enormous quantitative and significant qualitative superiority in pre-dreadnoughts should not have been cause for serious anxiety insofar as the maintenance of the power standards was concerned. After 1909, however, the integrity of both standards was called into question by changing international circumstances.

The fact that Britain could no longer count upon her pre-dreadnoughts as an adequate safe-guard in the Mediterranean in the face of the dreadnought programs of the Italian and Austro-Hungarian navies, prompted navalists in 1910 to reiterate their earlier demands for a "two-keels-to-one" standard in capital ships over Germany.[31] In response to changes in the German navy law and the deteriorating Mediterranean situation, Churchill declared in his speech to the Commons of 18 March 1912 that German capital ship construction above current levels would be met on a "two-keels-to-one" basis, and that the maintenance of Britain's position in the Mediterranean would require that "as the vessels of the pre-Dreadnought type declined in relative fighting value, our ratio of new construction will have to rise above the 60 per cent. standard."[32] On 10 July 1912 Churchill informed the Committee of Imperial Defence that the Admiralty planned by 1915 to have a force of eight dreadnoughts in the Mediterranean while maintaining a 50 per cent superiority in dreadnoughts in home waters, a scheme that was announced to the Commons in March 1913.[33]

The carrying out of the new arrangement depended upon further colonial contributions and the continued construction of dreadnoughts by Britain in large numbers. In December 1912, the Federated States of Malaya offered to pay for a battleship and in February 1913, the Canadian House of Commons passed legislation that would have provided for the building of three dreadnoughts. The Malayan offer resulted in the addition of a fifth unit to the class of battleships ordered under the 1912-13 estimates, but in May 1913, the Canadian Senate rejected the bill passed by the lower house and the matter was never revived.[34] The failure of the Canadian project deprived the Royal Navy of units that were to have been deployed in the Mediterranean by 1915, and changes in capital ship design had made it practically impossible for Britain to make up for the shortfall on her own by ordering more than four capital ships per annum.

The adoption of the 13.5-inch gun for four of the ten vessels ordered in 1909-10 had raised the price of a battleship by some 14 per cent, and that of a battle cruiser by no less than 36 per cent, over the 12-inch gun armed vessels of the same program. Increases in the cost of battleships were relatively modest in 1910-11 and 1911-12, and although major increases in speed and protection for the single battle cruiser of the 1911-12 program made it some 24 per cent more costly than the vessels of 1909-10 and 1910-11, no further warships of this type were ordered until after the outbreak of war. Beginning with the 1912-13 program, however, and continuing through 1913-14 and 1914-15, the 13.5-inch gun was superseded by the 15-inch gun, which resulted in the construction of battleships that were more than 30 per cent more expensive than their immediate predecessors, and some 60 per cent more than the 12-inch gun battleships of the 1909-10 program.[35]

In 1909 and 1912, the Admiralty had entertained hopes that the adoption of more powerful guns would disrupt German capital ship construction in the manner of the *Dreadnought*, which would have allowed a corresponding reduction in the size of British building programs.[36] In 1909, however, the Germans had not matched the new model British warships with comparably armed units, which enabled them to maintain their building pace, while in 1912, the Germans adopted the 15-inch gun for battleships if not for battle cruisers, and modified the navy laws to allow for the construction of three more capital ships, although in the event only two additional units were ordered.[37] The Admiralty, for its part, felt obliged to uphold Britain's numerical lead in dreadnoughts, the Royal Navy's apparently increased qualitative advantage in capital ship armament notwithstanding. British expenditure on battleship and battle cruiser construction from fiscal year 1910-11 on thus remained well above the amount spent in 1908-9.

Although the large annual increases in the navy estimates described earlier, which were in large part the consequence of the increases in spending on capital ships, resulted each year in serious disagreements between navalists and economists within the Cabinet, and protests from Radical back-benchers in the Commons,[38] conflicts within the Liberal party in fiscal years 1910-11, 1911-12, 1912-13 and 1913-14 were mitigated by the fact that the tax increases introduced in 1909-10 produced sufficient additional revenue to support both rising expenditure on the navy and social reform. The combination of the second-year peak costs of the 15-inch gun battleships of the 1913-14 program and the still heavy third-year costs of the 1912-13 program, however, made a substantial increase in the 1914-15 navy estimates practically inevitable, which together with higher spending on social welfare and education raised the prospect of state expenditure exceeding the level of income.

In public speeches in October and November 1913, Churchill had warned that much higher navy estimates were to be expected, and indeed his draft estimates for 1914-15, which were presented to the Cabinet in December, showed an increase of some £3 million over that of the previous year. The First Lord's proposals bitterly divided the Cabinet, a situation that was exacerbated by his upward revision of his figures in January 1914, which reversed a tentative agreement that had provided for a reduction. Attention was again focused on the question of the size of the battleship building program, with the Admiralty insisting upon four ships while the economists within the Cabinet demanded a reduction to two.

Lloyd George's categorical refusal to accept the Admiralty's position, provocative statements to the press, threat of resignation, and support of a back-bench Radical revolt, appeared to bring the government to the brink of destruction. His actions, however, may have been calculated to placate both his Radical following in the House and economist subordinates at the Treasury while preparing the way for further substantial increases in taxation that would not only provide for the capital ships required by the navy but increased spending in other areas as well. In February 1914, he agreed to an increase in the navy estimates of somewhat less than the £3 million requested in December, which allowed a program of four battleships, in return for a pledge from Churchill of substantial reductions in the navy estimates of 1915-16.[39]

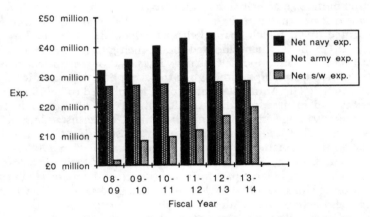

Figure 4   *Net expenditure on defence and social welfare, 1908–13*

Lloyd George's budget for 1914-15 was adopted by the Cabinet in late April, and presented to the Commons in May. In spite of strenuous objections from a faction of Liberal back-benchers, who with the support of the opposition forced the government to modify or abandon certain provisions that would have resulted in heavier taxes for the wealthy, the budget nevertheless passed in July, and through increases in the income tax rate, the extension of the principle of graduation to the supertax introduced in 1909-10, the steeper graduation of death duties and reductions in payments to the sinking fund, provided for an increase in revenue of over £11 million above that of the previous fiscal year.[40] In fiscal year 1914-15, the spending increase on social welfare amounted to £1.1 million, while the navy estimate was higher by £2.7 million.[41]

Between fiscal years 1908-9 and 1914-15, Britain's annual net expenditure (that is, expenditure chargeable against current revenue) increased for social welfare by 900 per cent, for the navy by 60 per cent and for the army by 8 per cent (see Figure 4). In actual amounts, however, the increase in net spending on the navy and army during this period exceeded that on social welfare. The total of increases in net expenditure on social welfare above the 1908 level from 1909-10 through 1914-15 came to £74.8 million. The total of increases in British net expenditure on the navy above the 1908 level during the same period equalled £70.7 million, while that for the army amounted to £6.9 million, the combined figure coming to £77.6 million.[42] It would appear, therefore, that the bounty produced by Lloyd George's Radical budgets purchased guns and butter in practically equal measure.

The fiscal policy of the Liberal government from 1909 to 1914, unlike that of its Conservative-Unionist predecessor between 1900 and 1905,[43] was politically viable not only because social legislation benefited the working masses, but because the middle class gained significant tax reductions. The burden of the new taxes imposed by the 1909-10 and 1914-15 budgets fell on the wealthy to such an extent that the great majority of income tax payers found themselves paying less than they had when the Liberals had come to power in 1905.[44] The social legislation of 1908 and 1911, moreover, made the national government responsible for the care of many who would otherwise have been supported by the poor law, which worked to the advantage of ratepayers, most of whom were middle class.[45]

Although in 1909 Admiral Sir John Fisher had opposed Lloyd George over naval increases and in general distrusted him,[46] by 1914 he had come to an understanding of the Chancellor of the Exchequer's approach to finance and politics, and, in light of what it had accomplished for the navy, seems to have approved of it. Fisher was apparently convinced, indeed, that even more could be done in the way of reducing taxes on workers and raising taxes for the wealthy. "I do wish Lloyd George," he wrote to McKenna's wife on 10 April,

> would take the duty off tea, sugar, and tobacco (not cigars). He would sweep up the whole agricultural vote, as the farm labourers now drink nothing but sweetened tea and their tobacco is their one and only luxury! He could recoup himself by increasing the death duties, by making transfer of property before death equally taxable, and by increasing the income tax of those above £10,000 a year pro rata up to £100,000 a year.[47]

But in the 1910 general elections, there had been substantial losses of middle-class voters to the Conservative-Unionists. The successful revolt of Liberal MPs who represented wealthy interests against the 1914-15 budget, moreover, was a strong sign that the tax revenue of the state could no longer be increased substantially at the expense of the rich and to the advantage of others.[48] The financing after 1914 of large increases in spending on either the navy or social welfare without recourse to borrowing might, therefore, have posed difficulties that even so devious and imaginative a politician as Lloyd George would have been unable to overcome.[49]

The financial situation of the German government as compared with that of Britain, on the other hand, was far worse. The imperial government did not have the authority to levy income taxes, a power that was reserved to the states, and could not substantially increase taxes on consumption, which had reached prohibitively high levels, without risking serious political consequences. Much of its spending on the navy, as a result, had to be financed through loans. Borrowing equal to roughly a quarter of annual expenditure on the navy took place from fiscal year 1908 through 1911-12, and even after the rate of new capital ship construction was reduced, amounted to 17 per cent in 1912-13, and 11 per cent in 1913-14. In effect, therefore, the construction costs of more than half the German all-big-gun capital ships completed before the outbreak of war were covered by loans. From 1912, moreover, increased spending on the army meant that there was little prospect of the imperial government gaining financial support from the states for the navy. Britain's naval position *vis-à-vis* Germany after 1909 was thus probably far stronger than a simple comparison of capital ship numbers and gun caliber, which already showed to her considerable advantage, would indicate.[50]

The fiscal prodigies of the Liberal government, with the assistance of the Dominions, were, as it turned out, sufficient to assure Britain's naval supremacy in the critical North Sea, while France, with whom Britain was practically allied, possesed a navy that was capable of defending essential British interests in the Mediterranean.[51] The situation in 1914 with regard to the gunnery efficiency of the Royal Navy's battleships and battle cruisers, however, was by no means so satisfactory.

2   The Vagaries of Fire Control

(a)   NEGOTIATIONS, A NEW AGREEMENT AND *NATAL* TRIALS (II) [1910]

It will be recalled that on 10 December 1909, representatives of the Admiralty had agreed to place a large order for gyro-stabilized range-finder mountings and plotting tables, which was to be confirmed at the beginning of the new year. The Admiralty's position at this time was a reflection of the confidence of both Captains Ogilvy and Craig in the ultimate mechanical practicability and high military value of the Argo system.[52] The situation was changed completely over the course of December, however, by the death of Ogilvy and the replacement of Craig by Captain Moore as Director of Naval Ordnance. Moore was critical of the mechanical reliability of the gyro-stabilized range-finder mounting, believed that further development with the advice of naval experts would be required before it could be made ready for service use, and doubtful that plotting was of any value. The Contracts Department, for its part, believed that Pollen's profit margins were excessive.[53] These unfavorable assessments were consistent with, if not in part prompted by, the views of Admiral Wilson, the new First Sea Lord, who was adamantly opposed to any monopoly agreement.[54]

On 18 January 1910, the Admiralty asked the Argo Company to state its terms for a production order for the gyro-stabilized range-finder mounting, transmitting gear, receivers and the plotting table, in various combinations, and with and without secrecy conditions. The firm was also informed that no definite order would be forthcoming until further trials of its instruments were carried out, and that in any case a decision would not be reached until after 31 March.[55] In a second letter to the Argo Company of the same date, the Admiralty—in response to a request made by Pollen in December for modifications of the terms covering secrecy payments beyond the time allowed for trials after the delivery of instruments agreed to the previous May—offered to begin payments before the time stipulated earlier, conceding that delays in the delivery of instruments had been caused in part by changes requested by the Admiralty.[56] Pollen's dissatisfaction with the offer with regard to secrecy payments led to further correspondence, which soon resulted in a compromise that appears to have favored the Argo Company.[57] The protracted negotiations over the far more important question of the Admiralty order for instruments, however, were to have a different outcome.

Pollen was given an explanation of the Admiralty's change in position on the purchase of his instruments in an interview with Moore that took place sometime between 18 and 20 January.[58] In a letter to the Admiralty of 22 January, Pollen provided the price estimates requested on 18 January, reminded the Admiralty that the Argo Company required £30,000 to acquire the additional manufacturing capacity needed to fulfill a large order for instruments, again observed that the raising of capital from private sources might compromise secrecy, suggested that a pre-payment of £30,000 might be made in return for a net reduction of £9,000 in the total price of his instruments, and assured the Admiralty that while design difficulties had been very considerable, no problems were anticipated with respect to manufacture.[59] Pollen wrote privately to F. W. Black, the Director of Navy Contracts, on 11 and 16 February to argue the case for his pre-payment proposals.[60] Black informed Pollen on 22 February, however, that the question of pre-payment would not be considered until a definite decision had been reached with regard to the purchase of instruments.[61]

Pollen had viewed the Admiralty commitment of the previous December to place a large order for gyro-stabilized range-finder mountings and improved plotters, as the basis for the cooperative relationship between the Argo Company and the Admiralty that he believed was essential if his system was to be perfected in secret.[62] The Admiralty's indecisiveness not only threatened the principle of cooperation, but jeopardized the arrangements that Pollen had made in December to acquire the additional manufacturing capability that was required for production in quantity.[63] In addition, Pollen seems to have suspected that the delays were prompted by the hostility of the First Sea Lord, which raised the question of whether or not the Admiralty was acting in good faith. In a brief conversation with an important Admiralty official—probably Jellicoe—on 1 March, Pollen appears to have been told that Wilson's opinions were not the obstacle that he supposed.[64] Thus reassured, though still doubtful, Pollen wrote privately that same day to C. I. Thomas to explain that he was willing to accept terms for the gyro-stabilized mounting that allowed him no profit but only on the understanding that losses would eventually be made good by orders for the complete system in the event that it was successful in trials, and "if the fraudulent contractor theory is dropped and I am put into the position of untrammeled and real cooperation with the Service."[65]

In the meanwhile, further trials of the Argo gyro-stabilized range-finder mounting had been carried out in the *Natal* on 17 February with an Argo Company electrician in attendance,[66] and were completely successful, Captain Reginald Hall, the commanding officer, reporting that "the Pollen gear was well worth more than three times as much as the Service range-finder and mountings."[67] The Admiralty, however, required additional trials, which took place on 8 March, and another month of deliberation before it was able to come to a decision.[68]

On 11 April 1910, the Admiralty informed the Argo Company that it was willing to order 15 mountings and sets of range and bearing receivers at a cost of £1,000 per unit, to be delivered by 15 March 1911; that secrecy rights would not be required; that in the absence of secrecy restrictions Pollen would be free to sell his gear on the open market, which meant that no advance payment would be offered to enable him to set up production; and that no arrangement to order additional mountings could be made and that any such order would only be forthcoming if prices were substantially reduced. The Admiralty letter also stated that trials of the change of range machine, which had been delivered to the *Natal* in late February,[69] and the modified plotter, would be "carried out as opportunities offer," and that while the decision as to their adoption would be left open, secrecy rights, as in the case of the mounting order, would not be purchased.[70]

In light of the fact that the service gear cost approximately £400, Hall's assessment would have justified a price for the Argo mounting of at least £1,200, if not the £1,750 quoted by Pollen in January. The Directors of Naval Ordnance and Navy Contracts believed, however, that the costs of manufacturing the mounting and receivers amounted to less than £800,[71] and that while the Argo mounting was worth having, little would be gained by purchasing secrecy rights because it was "recognized that as gyroscopic working was being so universally considered in many directions, it was only a question of time before it was generally tried for range-finders."[72] The Admiralty reasoned, moreover, that the abandonment of secrecy would enable the Argo Company to profit from foreign orders, which in turn would allow it to lower its charges to the Admiralty.[73] There may, in addition, have been a political factor, because Wilson remained adamantly opposed to any purchase that involved secrecy terms.[74]

Pollen replied to the Admiralty offer on behalf of the Argo Company–in temperate language on the advice of Jellicoe[75]—on 13 April 1910. In his letter, he maintained that the costs of manufacturing exceeded the £1,000 per set of instruments offered, that "unless extraordinary and costly measures were adopted, it would be impossible to deliver by 15th

March 1911," and that, therefore, it was "a commercial and industrial impossibility for us to accept the order at the price mentioned." Pollen then explained that although profits from foreign trade would enable the Argo Company to reduce charges to the Admiralty on repeat orders, the amount of the reduction could not be estimated in advance in the absence of knowledge of how large the volume of foreign purchases was likely to be, and that the Argo Company would be unable to persuade foreign navies to order unless the Admiralty lifted certain restrictions on the publication of his patents and provided an official letter "expressing the Admiralty's satisfaction with the result of both series of trials, and its consequent desire forthwith to begin the installation of our gear in H.M. fleet." Pollen concluded with a promise that prices would be reduced in repeat sales to the Royal Navy, profits from foreign trade permitting, in consideration of the contributions made by the service to the development of his instruments.[76]

On the same day of his official reply to the Admiralty offer, Pollen in a private communication with Reginald McKenna, the First Lord, proposed an alternative. "We are quite content," he wrote,

> to continue working without profit (should this be the Board's wish) if only secrecy can be maintained until the system has been thoroughly tried. We have no misgivings as to the result when it is tried. We ask no compensation for risking the loss of patents abroad, and we shall always be content with a fair commercial profit. All we ask is that we may be enabled for the present to carry on without loss. We could do this if you would order 45 sets, instead of 75, for delivery between Aug. 1911 and Sept. 1913—and advance £25,000 of the price—£78,750. An order in these terms would leave no divisible profit at all.

Pollen then insisted that his arrangements to acquire the necessary production facilities required the advance, and that without delay; advised that even large foreign sales were not likely to result in significant reductions in the price of his instruments; argued that his original monopoly terms had been reasonable; and observed that the acceptance of his current proposal involved risks of overspending that were small in comparison with the benefits that many service gunnery experts believed were obtainable.[77]

Pollen sent a copy of his letter to McKenna to Jellicoe on 13 April[78] along with a more detailed financial critique of the Admiralty's proposals. "The real difficulty about a small order," he wrote,

> is that we cannot complete in less than 18 months—that means £9,000 Argo charges; and all the preliminary expenses £4,000 may have to be written off against that order, if no more of the type made are ordered later: a net charge of £13,000 against 15 sets! The cheapest thing would be to order 100 sets for delivery in 36 months—our head charges would then be £220 per set, against £460 per set for 75 in 60 months, or £860 for 15 in 18 months.[79]

In a second letter to Jellicoe of the same date, Pollen explained that he would not ask for compensation for the loss of foreign business but only a "fair commercial profit." "What a fair profit is," he argued, should not be difficult to settle. Appoint an Admiralty representative to watch the Argo Company. Appoint your own firm of auditors. Take the accounts as from say July 1st present debts being paid first. You shall be satisfied what the profits are, and that the expenditure is not excessive. If profits are too good, prices should be reduced. We shall not quarrel. At present we are to take all the risks. We *must* make prices that are safe. But I am quite willing to repay if the event shows we have asked too much. Can anything be fairer? Or we can arbitrate . . .[80]

Pollen revealed his bitter frustration with the Admiralty in a letter to A. J. Spender, which was also written on the day of his letters to the Admiralty, McKenna and Jellicoe. The Admiralty, Pollen informed his friend,

have written to me offering me a price 60% below what I quoted, and saying that future orders are to be cheaper still, because now that I am free to go abroad I shall be able to develop so enormous a business that production will be cheapened and I can charge them less. Note the argument. A method of Fire Control is developed in the British fleet by public money, and when only a fraction of it is tested, the best judges in the world at once see that it will supersede everything that foreign navies now have. But this does not occur to them as a reason for monopolizing it, but is hailed as a godsend because with this vast demand, the cost per unit to the British navy can go down. . . . I enclose you a copy of my official letter to the Admiralty, in which I take their argument as seriously as it can be taken, and a personal letter to Mr. McKenna in which I try feebly to protest without letting myself go on the absurdities of the situation.[81]

Pollen's representations were not without their effect on Jellicoe, who asked both the Directors of Naval Ordnance and Navy Contracts to submit written estimates of what in their personal opinion would constitute a fair manufacturing price per unit for an order of 15 sets of the Argo gyroscopically-stabilized range-finder mounting, and associated range and bearing indicators. Their reports of 18 April gave figures which closely approximated the quotation given by Pollen to Jellicoe on 13 April of per unit cost on an order for 100 sets of instruments. Black, in addition, maintained that his estimate made ample allowance for contingencies, while Pollen had called for an additional 20 per cent charge as a hedge against unforeseen difficulties. On the other hand, Black conceded that Pollen's pioneering work "may deserve liberal remuneration," that "there is much to be said for an increase of the number of sets and to be spread over a longer time and for some increase of price if the offer is much below 75 sets," that a price of £1,200 per set on an order of 30 sets—which was £160 per set more than Moore's estimate for 15 sets—would not be unreasonable, and that there was "no objection in principle—subject to Treasury sanction" to the Admiralty paying Pollen the advance that he had requested.[82]

Jellicoe also sought the advice of Rear-Admiral Peirse, the Inspector of Target Practice, who spoke and wrote strongly in favor of maintaining secrecy.[83] McKenna read the reports of Moore and Black, and was probably informed by Jellicoe of the views of Peirse. On 19 April, Pollen wrote privately to the First Lord, with whom he had just had a short and apparently difficult meeting. In his communication, Pollen asked for a fee of £540 per month to cover the administrative expenses of the Argo Company, an order for 45 mountings and receiver sets at £1,750 per set, and an agreed rate of profit of 60 per cent above cost for repeat orders, in return for the maintenance of secrecy, periodic independent audits of the Argo Company's accounts, and the settlement of all disputes by arbitration upon the request of either party. [84] After what must have been hard bargaining, Pollen submitted a much reduced set of terms in an official letter to the Admiralty on 22 April, [85] which were then discussed by the full board in a meeting on 27 April. Following contentious debate, [86] the board gave general approval for an agreement along the lines of Pollen's letter and directed Jellicoe to arrange the details. [87]

On 29 April 1910, the Admiralty informed the Argo Company that it was willing to purchase 45 mountings with indicators on a monopoly basis at a price of £1,350 per set, which included payment for the overhead charges of the Argo Company and compensation for secrecy over a three year period. The Admiralty letter also offered to provide an advance of £15,000, and to pay £270 upon the acceptance of the offer and an additional £270 to extend secrecy on the plotting unit to 15 July 1910. Pollen for his part was bound to commit himself and Isherwood to continue working for the Argo Company during the three years covered by the secrecy agreement; to disavow the contract signed on 18 February 1908, which freed the Admiralty from any obligation to pay Pollen the £100,000 award in the event that his instruments were completely successful in trials; to withdraw claims against the Admiralty for patent infringements with regard to manual plotting tables; [88] to agree that the Admiralty would be charged a "fair commercial rate of profit only" on orders for any additional equipment that was considered to be part of the Aim Correction system; and to submit to a number of lesser requirements. [89] The Argo Company accepted the conditions "without qualification" on the day that they were offered, [90] although Pollen appears to have verbally reserved the right to raise the issue of restoring the price cut agreed to in the event that the order proved to be unprofitable. [91]

The Admiralty's volte-face was in part prompted by the protests of influential naval officers who were strong supporters of Pollen and his ideas. [92] In addition, McKenna at least may have been aware of Pollen's communications with E. G. Pretyman, a prominent Conservative politician who had been Financial Secretary to the Admiralty at the time of the *Jupiter* trials in 1905, [93] and feared that the failure to reach an agreement with the Argo Company would lead to dangerous parliamentary complications. On the other hand, Pollen's acceptance of the Admiralty's unfavorable terms of purchase for only a portion of his fire control system, which provided a margin of profit that was too small to enable the Argo Company to carry on experimental work on the remaining instruments, was made possible by the assurances given to him by a number of his naval supporters that they, in the event of necessity, would provide endorsements that would enable the Argo Company to raise funds privately and in such a way as to avoid giving explanations that might compromise secrecy.[94]

Arrangements for the trial of Pollen's plotter, receivers and clock were completed by the end of April, the plotter delivered to the *Natal* by early May,[95] and a pre-trial program of experiments carried out between 24 May and 9 June.[96] These preliminary tests revealed that the modifications to the plotting table to allow plotting while the firing ship was turning were faulty in design; that difficulties caused by the design shortcomings were exacerbated by damage to the wooden parts of the prototype table that was the result of the very high temperature of the lower conning tower—caused by heat from an adjacent boiler room—where the table was situated; that the placement of the clock in a separate compartment made it impossible to supply it with data from the table with sufficient rapidity; that the range and bearing receivers suffered from a number of serious design defects and had to be redesigned and rebuilt; and that the electrical system was unreliable. Pollen believed, however, that his instruments could be made fully practicable with additional design work in a short time and that results that were good enough to demonstrate the military value of his system were obtainable if his engineers were allowed to keep the gear in operation during the official trials.[97]

On 15 June, however, the employees of the Argo Company were removed from the *Natal* without notice on the instruction of the Director of Naval Ordnance, and in spite of Pollen's strong protests on 16, 17 and 18 June, the order barring them from the ship was allowed to stand.[98] The absence of expert technical supervision was worsened by the fact that the *Natal* had that spring just recommissioned with a fresh crew, which meant that her fire control team had had no previous experience with each other or with Argo equipment.[99] Lieutenant Wilfrid G. H. Cree, who had been trained during the preliminary trials to operate the plotter was, moreover, taken ill in mid June, which meant that an even less well-prepared replacement worked the gear during the official trials.[100] These took place between 16 and 29 June,[101] in the form of a competition with manual true-course and manual virtual-course plotting systems, supervised by a committee headed by Rear-Admiral S. C. G. Colville, which had been appointed by Admiral Sir William H. May, the Commander-in-Chief of the Home Fleet.[102]

The Argo instruments suffered from numerous mechanical and electrical failures during the official trials, which prompted Pollen to send a long printed letter of explanation to Colville on 1 July 1910.[103] Pollen's anticipation of an unfavorable evaluation, however, was not fulfilled. Lieutenant Reginald Plunkett, the torpedo officer of the *Natal*, reported on 28 June 1910 to Commander W. W. Fisher, a member of Colville's committee, that

> the electrical gear can be made just as reliable as any other fire control system that we now possess. The mechanical gear, barring breakdowns, is already good and can be further improved. All those who know the gear thoroughly will

202

support me in this statement. If such results are practically within our grasp, it seems desirable that we should make a whole hearted attempt to materialize them for the good of the Service.[104]

Plunkett's views were also those of Captain Reginald Hall, the commander of the *Natal*.[105] Colville's committee concluded that the automatic system of plotting fitted in the *Natal* was "far superior to any manual method"; that the range–finder mounting, redesigned range–receiver, and clock should be adopted for service; and that the plotter should be fitted in four ships whose officers were to cooperate with the Argo Company in order to perfect it for service "as quickly as possible."[106]

Pollen at this time continued to receive encouragement from Prince Louis of Battenberg. In April 1910, the royal admiral had been among those who promised a letter of endorsement, and in May, he had even offered to nominate Pollen for a peerage, a suggestion that Pollen had discouraged on the grounds that such recognition would jeopardize his efforts to develop an advanced system of gunnery in secret. In July, after receiving a printed copy of Pollen's letter to Colville, Battenberg expressed concern over the inventor's difficulties with the Admiralty, and offered to speak to the new king, George V, about the situation. Pollen politely declined the proposal by replying that "the subject is perhaps still too controversial for such august intervention."[107] But in spite of such support, Pollen was again to be disappointed by the decisions of the naval authorities.

The Admiralty did not follow the recommendations of the Colville committee. On 19 August 1910, the Argo Company was informed that the plotting table would not be adopted, that the clock had been found to be defective in certain respects, that an improved clock design was required before the Admiralty could consider further trials, and that shortcomings in the range and bearing receivers currently on order would have to be rectified.[108] Pollen, in the meanwhile, had decided to redesign the plotter and clock from start to finish in order to produce instruments that could not be faulted on technical grounds.[109] In his reply to the Admiralty of 25 August, he stated, among other things, his intention to redesign the table without financial assistance from the service, to redesign the clock and incorporate modifications that would meet the Admiralty's criticisms of the instrument tested in the *Natal*, and to correct the shortcomings of the receivers.[110] In a meeting with the Director of Naval Ordnance the next day, Pollen was informed that the Admiralty had decided that plotting in all forms was impracticable.[111]

The Admiralty's rejection of plotting was probably at least in part based upon a report of 25 April 1910 by Admiral W. H. May, who observed that recent tactical exercises of the Home Fleet

carried out under conditions representing thick weather (i.e. a visibility of 5,000 to 8,000 yards) do not furnish one single instance where a plot could have been obtained, which either would not have delayed the opening of fire or which could have remained correct for a period long enough to render it of service.

203

In clear weather May maintained that plotting was still "extremely difficult" and

> even if it is in certain cases carried out successfully, the facts adduced are those which no longer apply when fire has to be opened, for it is the enemy's course and speed when in battle formation, assumed either just before or in answer to our move that is required, and to obtain this by plotting entails either a delay in answering his final move or a delay in opening fire when we have formed and he is in process of forming. In either case this delay is undesirable.

May then noted that from "extensive trials" it had been learned that estimates of the target course by eye after "a little experience" resulted in "rather less" average error than was the case in plotting in Battle Practice "though on the latter the course was known to within two points either way and the range not exceeding 9,000 yards, whilst in these tests at sea there have been no limits to the course or the range, observations being recorded up to 36,000 yards."[112]

May's report, based as it was on experiments with manual plotting and an otherwise as yet unperfected system of centralized fire control, amounted to a devastating critique of the fire control methods recommended by Wilson, Bacon and Dreyer, but was largely inapplicable to the automatic system advocated by Pollen. Thus Rear-Admiral Peirse, the Inspector of Target Practice, in his commentary to Moore on May's report, pointed out that in clear weather

> by the aid of a good range finder and a really perfect automatic plot capable of giving quick and reliable results independently of any alterations of course and speed of one's own ship, a correct initial range and, what is even more important, a correct rate could be predicted as the Fleet were turning up into line to open fire.

Peirse also observed that

> the main reason now why there may be delay in *opening* fire when controlled from the principal position is the difficulty experienced in transmitting quickly the bearing of the target to the guns. As soon as this difficulty is overcome there should be no delay whatever . . .[113]

Moore, however, was inclined to apply May's criticisms of manual plotting to automatic plotting, and to believe that estimates by eye or by spotting the fall of shot made plotting in any form unnecessary. In his response to the remarks of the I.T.P. of 24 May 1910, he wrote that

> the more accurate ballistics and higher powers of our later guns have so extended the battle range, that fire must be opened before hand plotting can produce sufficiently accurate results to be of any practical value. The guns under these circumstances become the quickest and most accurate range finder and good rates can be obtained by estimate and spotting the range.
> It is interesting to note how small was the error in estimating enemy's course by eye as shown in [May's report]. It is remarkable also that the error was

1 Nine-foot base Barr & Stroud rangefinder on prototype gyro-mounting as set up on HMS *Natal*, 1909

2. Ten-foot base Barr and Stroud rangefinder on production Argo gyromounting, c. 1913.

3   A.C. Course and Speed Plotter, Mark IV (helm-free plotter) c. 1913

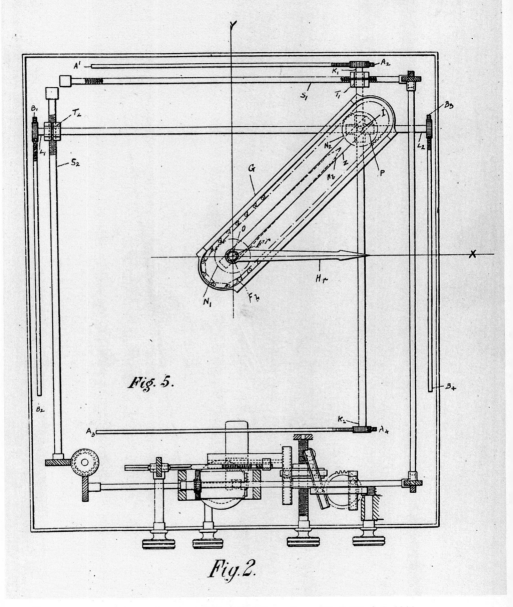

4 Patent diagram, main mechanism, Argo Clock Mark I, 1911

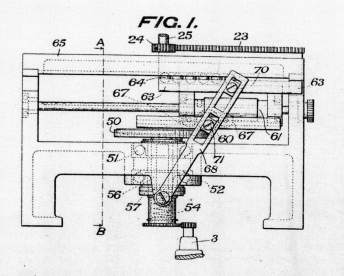

FIG. 1.

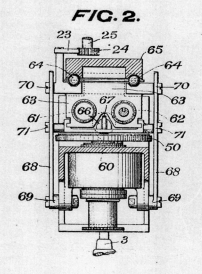

FIG. 2.

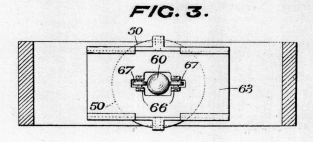

FIG. 3.

5   Patent diagram, ball and disc variable speed drive,
Argo Clocks, Marks II–IV, 1912

6   Argo Clock Mark V, c. 1913

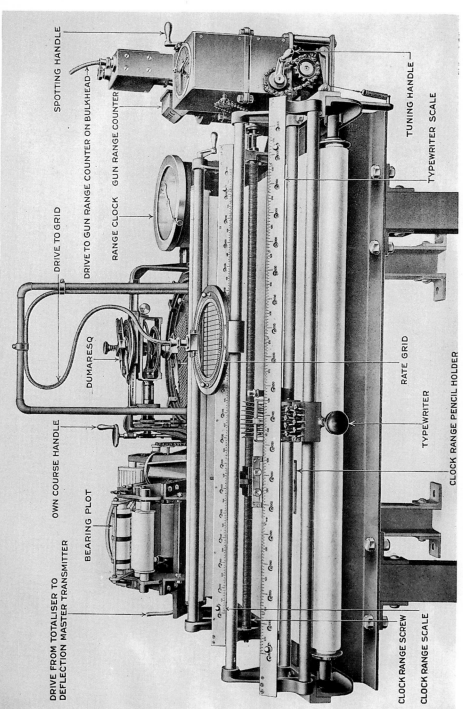

SPOTTING HANDLE

DRIVE TO GRID

DRIVE TO GUN RANGE COUNTER ON BULKHEAD

RANGE CLOCK   GUN RANGE COUNTER

TUNING HANDLE

TYPEWRITER SCALE

OWN COURSE HANDLE

DUMARESQ

RATE GRID

TYPEWRITER

CLOCK RANGE PENCIL HOLDER

DRIVE FROM TOTALISER TO
DEFLECTION MASTER TRANSMITTER

BEARING PLOT

CLOCK RANGE SCREW

CLOCK RANGE SCALE

7   Dreyer Table, Mark I

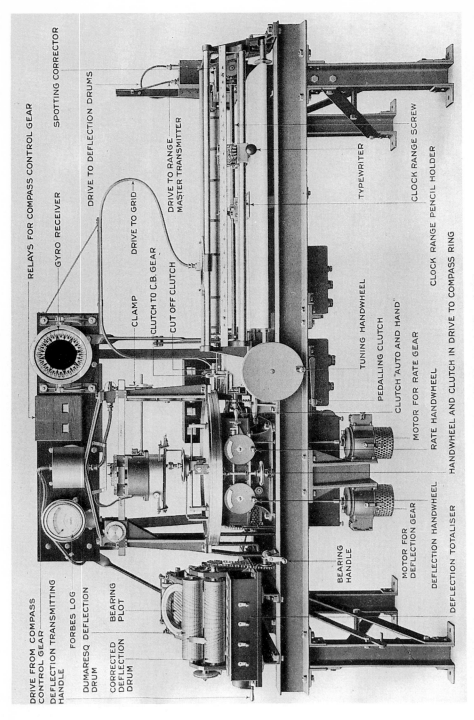

DRIVE FROM COMPASS
CONTROL GEAR

DEFLECTION TRANSMITTING
HANDLE

FORBES LOG

DUMARESQ DEFLECTION
DRUM

CORRECTED
DEFLECTION
DRUM

BEARING
PLOT

RELAYS FOR COMPASS CONTROL GEAR

GYRO RECEIVER

SPOTTING CORRECTOR

DRIVE TO DEFLECTION DRUMS

CLAMP   DRIVE TO GRID

CLUTCH TO C.B. GEAR

CUT OFF CLUTCH

DRIVE TO RANGE
MASTER TRANSMITTER

TYPEWRITER

CLOCK RANGE SCREW

CLOCK RANGE PENCIL HOLDER

CLOCK RANGE
PENCIL HOLDER

TUNING HANDWHEEL

PEDALLING CLUTCH

CLUTCH "AUTO AND HAND"

MOTOR FOR RATE GEAR

RATE HANDWHEEL

HANDWHEEL AND CLUTCH IN DRIVE TO COMPASS RING

BEARING
HANDLE

MOTOR FOR
DEFLECTION GEAR

DEFLECTION HANDWHEEL

DEFLECTION TOTALISER

8   Dreyer Table, Mark IV and IV★

generally smallest between 8,000 and 10,000 yards, the accepted battle range of to-day, and one at which officers unconsciously chiefly practise their eyes.

It is possible that automatic plotting or even modified hand plotting by means of the Gyro controlled Range Finder with automatic transmission of bearings and ranges may in very clear weather enable a correct rate to be predicted shortly before battle range is reached.

The "NATAL" trials should throw much light on this question. Still as the C-in-C points out it will usually be found that when opening fire becomes practicable the Fleets will turn at once into battle formation and the rate will alter immediately, in most cases from a very large to a very small one, and the gun cannot wait on a plot for a new rate. Early hitting above all things is necessary.

It is hoped with the new Gyro Control to get accurate R.F. readings up to 12,000 or 13,000 yards, but it is doubtful if we shall progress much further than this for some time although the matter is receiving earnest consideration. For the time being the effective gun range is outdistancing the R.F. and plotting in any form is receding in comparative value.[114]

Moore's rejection of the Argo plotter may in addition have been motivated by his preference for an alternative plotting system that had just been brought to his attention, and about which more will be said later. His dissatisfaction with the Argo clock, on the other hand, appears to have been based upon a less than careful analysis of its features. In the Admiralty's letter of 19 August, the Argo Company had been informed that it was "essential" that any improved clock be capable of being set with a range rate alone in the manner of the Vickers Clock in addition to the provision for setting with course and speed data. In his reply of 25 August, Pollen pointed out that the instructions for setting the existing instrument with the range rate only were "engraved on the dial provided for the purpose." Rear-Admiral Peirse, who had examined the clock on board the *Natal* the previous week, found the Admiralty's slip "amazing" and could "see no excuse for such a material point having been overlooked."[115]

By the fall of 1910, a majority of the service had come to share Moore's low opinion of plotting in any form, word of which was communicated to Pollen by a number of his service correspondents, "Plotting," wrote one officer in October,

> so long the centre of our hopes, has collapsed. For three years we have been doing our best with it. We have tried it with your gear, with Admiralty gear, and with no gear at all. We have tried virtual plotting and rate curve making. But all have been equally disappointing, and for the moment we are in a state of chaos.

". . . In last year's Battle Practices," wrote another,

> the plotted course of the 6 to 8 knot target was something like 14 deg. out on average. The target's speed was so low that it is difficult to say what the average speed error would be in action; judging from P.Z.[116] and manoeuvre results, the errors would be considerable, and if the speed were higher we might be less likely to get as near as 14 deg. to the course.

Naturally, the common verdict is that plotting is dead.

In November 1910, Pollen printed portions of these two letters as well as an extract from one other, together with "an omnibus reply, made up and amplified from the original answers to them" in which he gave an account of the development of his system through the *Natal* trials and argued the case for automatic true-course plotting. This work was entitled *The Quest of a Rate Finder*.[117]

By the end of November, Pollen had completed a formal essay on the relationship of fire control and naval tactics. In this piece, he was critical of the tactics of long range fighting upon which the policy of building "the bigger and faster ship, and the bigger gun" was based. The practice of manoeuvering to keep the range long, Pollen observed, presupposed "a very defensive sort of fighting," which he believed was unlikely to be productive of decisive results even when practiced in conjunction with a perfect system of fire control. As an alternative, Pollen maintained that British ships should close as rapidly as possible to medium ranges where a large percentage of hits to rounds fired could be made. This movement would result, at least initially, in very high and changing change of range rates, which would mean that an advanced system of fire control would be required in order to achieve hits during the approach. Such a system of change of range proof fire control would, moreover, enable an Admiral to maneuver freely in the knowledge that his guns were unaffected.

On a higher plane, Pollen warned that until mastery of weapons was gained, "neither the tactics of battle, nor the strategy of peace preparation for it, can be founded on anything but sand." That mastery, Pollen then stated, depended first and foremost upon the rapid securing of information that was essential for the accurate aiming of artillery. "Just as quickness of brain in the leader is more than quickness of foot in the men," he wrote,

> so superior speed in getting and using accurate knowledge of the enemy's movements is, tactically, of infinitely greater value than superior engine speed.
> And high engine speed can be made of tactical value only if you have means of getting the knowledge necessary for using it.
> Thus action speed is not engine speed, but Admiral speed. It cannot be measured by the volume of steam that causes the revolutions of the screws; but it can be measured by the swiftness of the knowledge that feeds the convolutions of the directing brain.

Pollen's essay, which was entitled *Of War and the Rate of Change*, was circulated, together with *The Quest of a Rate Finder*, from January 1911, and appears to have had many readers.[118]

(b) FINANCIAL DIFFICULTY, TECHNICAL IMPROVEMENT AND COMPETITION [1911]

The Pollen system was probably not the only victim of Wilson and Moore's predilection to oppose new technical developments in gunnery. In trials carried out in 1909 and 1910 against the old battleship *Edinburgh*, the Naval Ordnance Department discovered that when trajectories were curved—and the impact of the shell against a vertical plate therefore oblique rather than perpendicular—which would occur when ranges were long, the existing heavy-caliber armour-piercing projectile was incapable of penetrating.[119] On 18 October 1910, Jellicoe, acting in his capacity as Controller, asked the Ordnance Board to design a new armour-piercing shell.[120] By November 1911, however, the First Sea Lord and his Director of Naval Ordnance, had concluded that firing at long range should be carried out with high-explosive shells that would, among other things, wreck an opponent's fire control and consequently reduce the effectiveness of his fire at an early stage in the action; armour-piercing projectiles were to be reserved for close-range work, where trajectories were flat and the impact of projectiles thus normal rather than oblique, which may have justified the decision not to develop a new model armour-piercing projectile.[121]

The fortunes of Percy Scott's director firing fared no better than those of the Pollen system or Jellicoe's request for more efficient ammunition. In March 1910, extensive trials were carried out in the dreadnought battleship *Bellerophon* with a crude prototype director, which controlled elevation but not training as had been the case in the earlier trials in the *Africa*, and was without an adequate system of communication between the director and guns. Director firing in these tests, as a consequence, was found to be both slower and less accurate than independent gunlaying. The report on the experiments by Captain Hugh Evans-Thomas, the commander of the *Bellerophon*, was highly critical of the director both in practice and in principle, and although strongly challenged by the I.T.P., undoubtedly contributed a good deal to service prejudice against its adoption. A much more sophisticated director, which was designed to control both elevation and training, was fitted in the dreadnought battleship *Neptune* in 1910, and tested thoroughly in March 1911. These trials were successful enough to convince Jellicoe to advise its adoption, but his recommendations were not followed, which may have been the result of the opposition of Moore. The *Neptune* director subsequently broke down in battle practice after suffering a combination of mechanical and electrical failures.[122]

Scott continued to develop the director, and having won the confidence of Trevor Dawson, an executive of Vickers, was supported by the resources of Britain's largest armaments manufacturer.[123] Pollen's efforts to perfect his system, on the other hand, were handicapped by a serious shortage of working capital. Most of the £15,000 advance from the Admiralty that had been paid by June 1910 on the order for mountings and indicators,[124] was spent immediately to acquire production facilities for the 45 mountings and indicators through the purchase of shares in Thomas Cooke & Sons of York.[125] The Argo Company then suffered losses on the order when the Admiralty refused to accept suggestions for improvements in the design of the mounting, which forced the firm to produce another set of drawings, causing a great delay and additional expense.[126] The Argo Company, moreover, had to support the development of the new plotting table and clock out of its own resources, which by early 1911 had been practically exhausted.

At this point, Pollen approached a number of wealthy men with a request for financial assistance, backed by letters signed by Vice-Admiral Prince Louis of Battenberg, Admiral Lord Charles Beresford, Rear-Admiral E. J. W. Slade, Rear-Admiral Richard Peirse and Captain Osmond de Beauvoir Brock, to the effect that "as there was no other solution of the Fire Control problem in sight, nor indeed conceivable, it was a practical certainty that the system would before very long, be adopted" and that the investment "would not only serve a patriotic purpose, but should be remunerative as well."[127] The letter from the five prominent naval officers, who had promised Pollen such support the previous spring upon hearing of the unfavorable terms of the Admiralty order for the mountings and indicators,[128] was sufficient to raise over £19,000 by February 1911 through the sale of Cumulative Preference and Participating shares in the Argo Company.[129] This was enough to enable Pollen and his associates to proceed with the development of the plotter and the clock, and most likely because the Admiralty had expressed interest in the latter and disinterest in the former, work on the clock received priority.

The fundamental problem of clock design was to produce an instrument that was capable of indicating the range even when it was changing at a rate that was itself changing, which required that a pointer be driven across a dial at a speed that changed continuously. The motors of Pollen's day, however, could not be made to vary in speed continuously with the degree of accuracy that was required for the purposes of fire control. In the clock tested in the *Natal*, which was to become known as the Argo Clock Mark I, this difficulty had been overcome by an arrangement in which a motor that ran at a constant speed produced a continuously variable speed result. This was achieved through a mechanism that was driven by an electric motor that ran at a constant speed, which after having been set with the courses and speeds of the firing ship and target, and a range and a bearing, continuously reproduced the virtual course movement of the two ships—that is, the motion of the target relative to the firing ship, the latter being held to be stationary. This action was in turn—through mechanical linkages—used to control the movement of a pointer on a dial marked with ranges, and a pointer on a dial marked with bearings, whose indications of the range and bearing would reflect any continuous variation in the change of range and change of bearing rates, because such variation was inherent to the replicated motion of the two ships. Alternatively, the Argo Clock Mark I could be set with a range rate and a range in the manner of the Vickers Clock and would then simply indicate the range as produced by an unchanging change of range rate (see Diagram 1).[130]

The Argo Clock Mark I could not, however, compute ranges and bearings accurately while the firing ship was turning, because its mechanism was incapable of integrating the turning motion of the firing ship with the straight motion of the target to produce the virtual replication of relative movement that was required. The desirability of being able to calculate as well as plot while the firing ship was turning was evident to Pollen even before his discussions in the fall of 1909 with Ogilvy, and early in that year Isherwood had investigated the possibility of designing

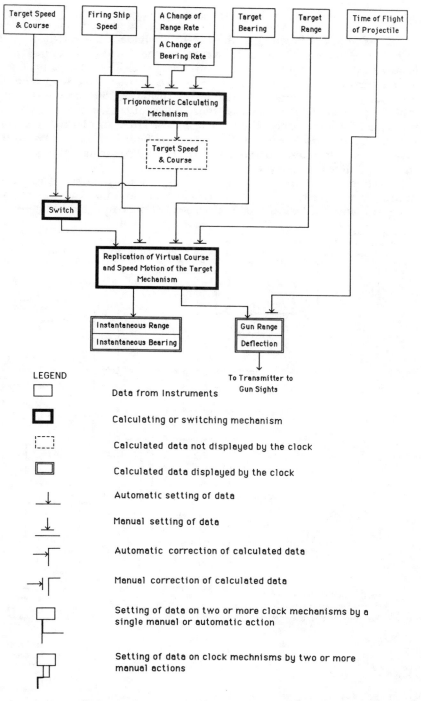

Target Speed & Course	Firing Ship Speed	A Change of Range Rate / A Change of Bearing Rate	Target Bearing	Target Range	Time of Flight of Projectile

Trigonometric Calculating Mechanism

Target Speed & Course

Switch

Replication of Virtual Course and Speed Motion of the Target Mechanism

| Instantaneous Range / Instantaneous Bearing | | Gun Range / Deflection |

To Transmitter to Gun Sights

LEGEND

Data from Instruments

Calculating or switching mechanism

Calculated data not displayed by the clock

Calculated data displayed by the clock

Automatic setting of data

Manual setting of data

Automatic correction of calculated data

Manual correction of calculated data

Setting of data on two or more clock mechanisms by a single manual or automatic action

Setting of data on clock mechnisms by two or more manual actions

Argo Clock, Mark I, 1912, Legend for Schematic Diagrams

a "helm-free" clock based upon the disc–ball–cylinder differential analysers that had been devised by Lord Kelvin in the 1870s, which had been inspired by ideas formulated by his brother, James Thomson, a professor of engineering at Glasgow University.[131] Kelvin may have suggested the disc–ball–cylinder scheme to Pollen in the spring of 1904, at which time, it will be recalled, the two had thoroughly discussed the fire control problem.[132] Alternatively, Pollen may have learned of the method from Charles Vernon Boys who, it will also be remembered, had advised the inventor on gyroscopes in 1906, and who had a particular interest in the study of differential analyzers.[133]

In Kelvin's instruments, a disc revolving at a constant speed imparted motion to a ball resting on its surface, which in turn caused a long cylinder in contact with the ball to rotate. The speed of the ball could be altered by

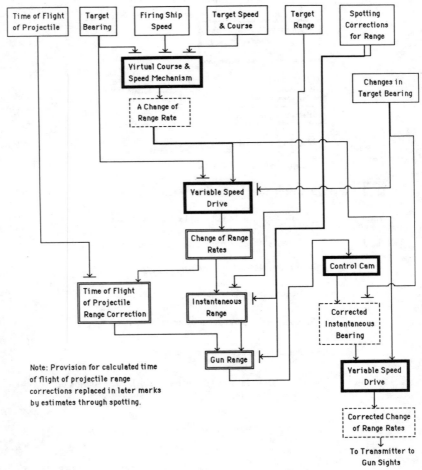

Note: Provision for calculated time of flight of projectile range corrections replaced in later marks by estimates through spotting.

Argo Clock, Mark II, 1911

210

moving it along the diameter of the disc: movement from the edge of the disc to its center would reduce the speed of the ball from its maximum to nil, while further movement from the center to the opposite edge would increase the speed of the ball from nil to its maximum in the opposing direction; the changing motion of the ball was imparted to the cylinder. Isherwood's initial attempts to apply this mechanism to the calculation of change of range rates failed because of the occurrence of slippages between the disc and ball that were caused by excessive friction between the ball and the cylinder as the ball was shifted along the diameter of the disc. This problem was not overcome until 1911, when the cylinder was replaced by two parallel rollers that were mounted in a frame that moved along a slide, an arrangement that allowed the rollers to travel with the ball as the ball was moved along the diameter of the disc, eliminating friction that would have caused slippage. The discovery of this solution led to the design of the Argo Clock Mark II (see Diagram 2).[134]

The calculating mechanism of the Argo Clock Mark II consisted of a disc, a ball and two closely spaced parallel rollers that were mounted on a slide. The ball was positioned between the disc and the two rollers, and firm contact between the three units was maintained by a spring that pushed the disc towards the rollers. An electric motor controlled by a governor rotated the disc at a constant speed, the rotation of the disc caused the ball to spin, and the spin of the ball in turn caused the rollers to rotate. The initial distance of the ball from the center of the disc was determined by the setting of a change of range rate on a dial. The movement of the ball along the diameter of the disc depended upon changes, if any, in the target bearing.

If the courses and speeds of the firing ship and target were such that the range was constant, or changing at a constant rate, there would be no change in the target bearing. In the former case (constant range), the ball would be placed at the center of the disc and would not, therefore, spin. In the latter case (change of range at a constant rate) the ball would be displaced from the center of the disc, but its position would not alter, and the ball would thus spin at a constant speed. If, on the other hand, the courses and speeds of the firing ship and target were such that the change of range rate was itself changing—which could occur when both courses were straight or when the firing ship was turning—the target bearing would change. By moving the ball along the diameter of the disc at a speed that corresponded with the change in target bearing, the speed at which the ball was spun would vary in accordance with the change in the change of range rate.

The change of range rate that was required to set the initial position of the ball along the diameter of the disc could be obtained from a time-and-range plot. Alternatively, the Argo Clock Mark II was equipped with a virtual-course-and-speed calculating mechanism–in essence a dumaresq—that converted target speed, course and bearing, and firing ship speed, settings into a change of range rate setting, e.g. which then determined the position of the ball. The bearings that determined the subsequent movement of the ball along the diameter of the disc were obtained by observation. The calculation of the target range was accomplished by the geared connection of one of the rollers of the disc-ball-roller mechanism—hereafter referred to as a variable speed drive—to a pointer that rotated around a dial marked with a succession of ranges. After being set to an initial position that was determined by a range observation, the pointer rotated around the dial at a speed determined by the actions of the variable speed drive. The pointer thus indicated the ranges as marked on the dial face in accordance with the change of range rate, whether it was nil, constant or varying. A second variable speed drive, which was set with bearings generated from ranges calculated by the first variable speed drive that were corrected for the time of flight of the projectile, generated predicted rather than instantaneous ranges that were transmitted by a step-by-step system to follow-the-pointer sights.[135]

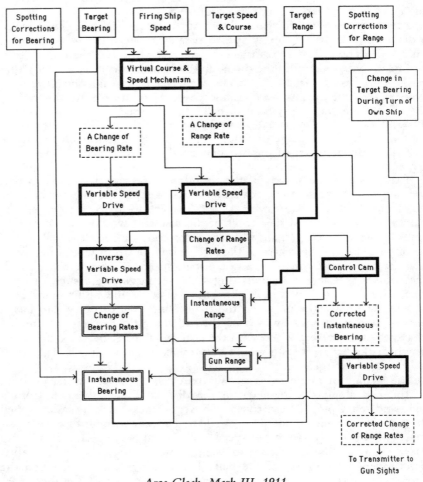

Argo Clock, Mark III, 1911

A written description and the blueprints of the Argo Clock Mark II were sent to the Admiralty on 15 May 1911.[136] In a meeting with Pollen on 22 May, Commander Joseph C. W. Henley, an assistant to Moore—who had been promoted to the rank of Rear-Admiral in March—suggested that the new clock should have the capability of generating bearings—as did the Argo Clock Mark I—and provision to be set with either speed and course or change of range and bearing rates.[137] To meet these requirements, Isherwood designed an arrangement of two additional variable speed drives, which when set with the target bearing, a change of bearing rate and a continuous supply of changing ranges from the range-calculating disc-ball-roller, not only indicated the instantaneous bearing, but supplied the range-calculating variable speed drive with a continuous supply of changing bearings. When set with a range and a bearing, and either courses and speeds or change of range and bearing rates, and so long as the firing ship and target steamed on straight courses at constant speeds, the clock would thus generate ranges and bearings without the need for further bearing correction. If the firing ship turned the automatic setting of calculated bearings was superseded by hand set bearings obtained by observation (see Diagram 3).[138]

This modified design, which was known as the Argo Clock Mark III,[139] was then further improved by the addition of mechanisms that adjusted the setting of the virtual course and speed mechanism that converted known data into the change of range and bearing rates that were set on the variable speed drives, in accordance with any changes that might be made in the settings of the dials that indicated the computed ranges and bearings. Corrections in the settings of the range and bearing dials could be made whenever the computed data differed from observed ranges and bearings that were presumed accurate. Occasional individual range and bearing observations could, in this manner, be used not only to check the accuracy of the computed data, but to increase the accuracy of subsequent calculations as well.[140] The drawings of this further developed design, which was known as the Argo Clock Mark IV, were for the most part completed by the end of November 1911 (see Diagram 4).[141]

While the clock had been under development, Pollen and the Argo Company had carried on with other work. In 1910, Pollen had suggested to Thomas Cooke & Sons that the capacity of range-finders to operate when light was dim—which would occur at dusk or when vision was partially obscured by mist, haze or gunsmoke—could be improved by replacing prism reflectors with mirrors and adopting a novel system of optics.[142] By March 1911, a prototype had been built and tested with success. It was subsequently loaned to H.M.S. *Excellent*, and although design defects revealed in the course of lengthy trials were remedied, the instrument was nevertheless rejected, probably on the grounds that it was too expensive.[143] In the late spring or early summer of 1911, Admiralty trials of the Anschütz gyro-compass revealed that its gyroscope was superior to the Argo device, and capable of controlling both the compass and the mounting. In July 1911, the Admiralty thus asked the Argo Company to modify the mounting to allow the substitution

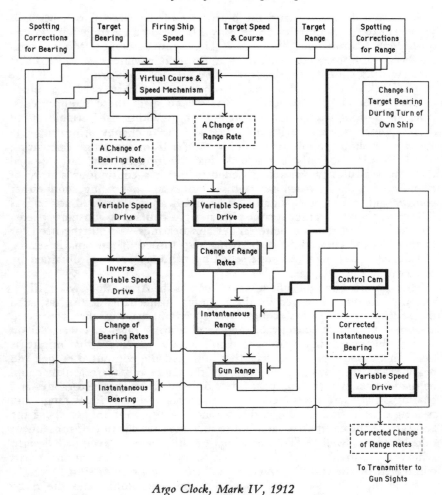

Argo Clock, Mark IV, 1912

of the Anschütz for the Argo gyroscope, to which the Argo Company agreed in February 1912, the arrangement applying to 20 units only, because by this time 15 sets had been delivered and 10 others were then under construction.[144]

The Argo Company also explored an alternative to true–course plotting. On the suggestion of Captain Reginald Hall, the firm designed a simple attachment to the plotting table in the *Natal* that would enable it to plot change of range and bearing rates simultaneously, and on 12 November 1910 the modification was offered formally to the Admiralty. Although rate plotting was incapable of producing useful results while the firing ship was turning, Pollen believed that its mechanical simplicity and cheapness would make it suitable as a back-up to a true–course plotting system. Trials were approved on 4 January 1911,[145] and while no records of the experiments in the *Natal* have survived, the Argo offer of a new model rate plotting device, which was ordered by the Admiralty in August for installation in the dreadnought battleship *Orion*, suggests that they were carried out successfully.[146]

The preoccupation of the Argo Company with the production of the mounting, and the development of the clock and rate plotter, delayed design work on the improved helm-free/true-course plotter, which probably did not begin in earnest until late 1911 or early 1912. The improvised helm-free/true-course plotter tested in the *Natal* had suffered from a number of minor and easily rectifiable mechanical and electrical shortcomings. There was, however, in addition a serious flaw in design. The capacity to replicate the turning motion of the firing ship had been achieved by fixing the paper chart on a board that was placed on top of a set of spiked wheels whose motion was controlled by differential gears. A board of considerable weight was used in order to set up enough friction with the spiked wheels to avoid slippage, but the trials at sea in the summer of 1910 had revealed that the pitch and roll of the *Natal* caused the heavy board to develop enough momentum to shift position, and by so doing spoil the plotting.[147]

This fundamental design defect was eliminated by replacing the paper and heavy board arrangement with a stiff paper chart—whose small mass prevented the ship's motion from generating a significant amount of momentum—that was moved from below by a pair of rubber rollers controlled by differential gears, and which had a pair of rubber roller idlers pressing down from directly above the drive rollers to hold the paper in place. The moving marking arm of the earlier plotting tables was abandoned, and in its stead a fixed arm was positioned over the center of the smooth horizontal surface upon which the stiff paper was placed. An unmoving pencil at the end of the arm marked the position of the target, while a second pencil that marked the position of the firing ship was mounted to slide along the arm, with the roller mechanism described above moving directly under the second pencil along a slot in the horizontal surface (see Figure 5).

Changes in range and bearing that occurred when the course of the firing ship was constant were reproduced by the motion of the controlling rollers and the movements of the roller mechanism along the slot and pencil along the fixed arm, while the turning motion of the firing ship was replicated by the rotation of a platform upon which the controlling rubber roller mechanism was mounted, the axis of movement corresponding to the vertical second pencil. Working drawings of this instrument, which was known as the "A. C. Course and Speed Plotter, Mark IV," were completed by the fall of 1912.[148]

In order to develop the clock and plotters, Pollen had increased the staff of the Argo Company, by hiring additional draughtsmen (probably in 1910). In addition, two naval officers, Lieutenant George Gipps, who had operated Pollen's gear in the *Ariadne* trials, and Lieutenant Gerard Riley, who had served in the *Natal* under Ogilvy (probably in early 1911) were permitted by Vice-Admiral Sir Francis Bridgeman, the Second Sea

215

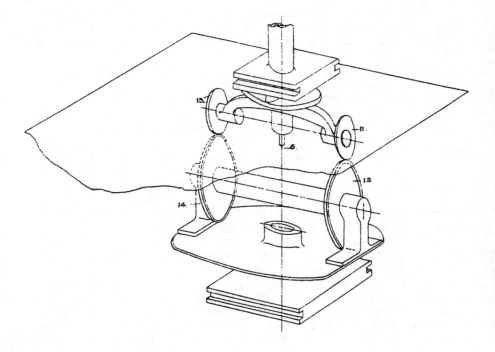

Figure 5 *Moving pencil and roller mechanism, A. C. Course and Speed Plotter*
Mark IV
Source: *Technical History*

Lord, to be employed by the Argo Company as technical advisors.[149] In
1911 and 1912, the salaries paid to Pollen and his staff amounted to some
£8,000, while expenditure on overhead incidentals came to about £3,000,
per annum expenditure in the years named thus totalling approximately
£11,000. This greatly exceeded the £6,000 per year allowed for in the order
for the mountings and indicators. The separate costs of developing the
instruments, moreover, were very considerable, expenditure on the clock
alone amounting to an estimated £13,700. By the end of 1911, therefore,
the Argo Company again found itself short of cash—the capital raised
earlier in the year through the sale of preference shares notwithstanding—a
situation that was rectified only through the agreement of the Admiralty
to pay what amounted to another advance on the mountings order.[150]

The Admiralty was less cooperative when it came to the provision
of information required by the Argo Company to design a local system
of fire control that was intended as a back-up to the centralized main
system. The Argo turret control was to consist of the new Pollen-Cooke
range-finder, a mounting that incorporated a solving mechanism that could
calculate a change of range rate from two range observations and a change
of bearing rate from two bearing observations, and a clock that could be

set by the rates calculated at the mounting. In July 1911, Gipps sent 72 serving officers a memorandum describing the arrangement and asking for opinions. 25 replies were received by September, including a long and favorable letter from Captain A. E. M. Chatfield, an officer of great ability who later became First Sea Lord. Commander Roger Backhouse, on the other hand, though a Pollen supporter, thought it improper for a serving officer to supply information to a private firm, a view shared by the Admiralty, which reprimanded the Argo Company, and informed the fleet that private communications between naval officers and the firm violated regulations.[151]

As a result of the Admiralty injunction, a number of correspondents informed Gipps that they could not repond to his memorandum. "I am prevented from saying anything about your interesting scheme," wrote one officer from the *Orion*, "by an order which has just come out that no reply is to be given." The writer then added that "an enemy hath done this!"[152] This was, indeed, the case. A copy of the Gipps memorandum had been sent to Commander Frederic Dreyer, who in July had complained to Henley, a good friend. Henley, after raising the issue with Moore, drafted the Admiralty injunction against the Argo Company.[153] Dreyer had good reason to deny Pollen the benefit of service advice, for at this time he was himself at work on a mechanized system of fire control that he intended to put up as an alternative to the Argo gear.

While serving in the *Vengeance* in January 1908 during the *Ariadne* trials, Dreyer had explored the possibilities of rate plotting. At this time, separate change of range and bearing rates were plotted manually, and the results set on a dumaresq, which having been set with the known course and speed of the firing ship and the target bearing, indicated the target's course. The dumaresq was then reset with the just determined target course together with the course and speed of the firing ship and the target bearing, so that it indicated a change of range rate (i.e, making a cross–cut). Changes in the change of range rate were taken into account by adjusting the setting for changes in target bearing. Range rates indicated by the dumaresq could then be used to set a Vickers Clock, which generated ranges.[154]

Under Battle Practice conditions, when rates were low and the change in the rate relatively small, the use of rate plots to set a dumaresq produced a reasonably accurate estimate of the target course and speed, while the inherent limitations of the dumaresq-Vickers Clock combination were also less evident.

Dreyer's method would not have produced satisfactory results, however, if forced to contend with the high and changing change of range and bearing rates, and interruptions in visibility that Pollen and others believed were likely to occur in battle. Under such conditions, the inability of the time–and–range and time–and–bearing plots to contend with the changing rates would mean that the dumaresq would give an inaccurate indication of the target speed, the occasional obscuring of the target would cut off the supply of bearings required to reset the dumaresq, while continuous changes in the range rate could not be represented accurately by the Vickers Clock, whose drive speeds, it will be recalled, could only be altered in discrete steps. Although he was advised of at least some of these drawbacks by Pollen while visiting the Argo works in York in early 1910 with Captain Craig,[155] Dreyer nevertheless continued to apply himself to the formulation of a system of fire control based upon rate plotting and the mechanical principles embodied in the dumaresq and Vickers Clock.

In November 1909, Dreyer had left the Ordnance Department to become Commander of the dreadnought battleship *Vanguard*, which was then just completing. While serving in this ship, he improvised a mechanized system of plotting ranges and bearings against time, which was tried with success in Battle Practice. In July 1910, Dreyer submitted a description of his instrument to the Admiralty, in which he argued that inaccuracies caused by measuring change of range and bearing rates from time–and–range and time–and–bearing plots while the rates were changing were inconsequential, and were far outweighed by the advantage of being able to set the Vickers Clock with a mean of several ranges—what was called "the mean Rangefinder Range of the moment"—taken from the time–and–range plot.[156] Dreyer's proposal was backed by recommendations in favor of its adoption from Captain J. B. Eustace of the *Vanguard* and Admiral May, the Commander-in-Chief of the Home Fleet.

Moore and others at the Ordnance Department opposed the automatic plotting of ranges and bearings, apparently preferring manual methods.[157] On 13 August 1910, Moore, however, approved May's recommendations and ordered the adoption of Dreyer's scheme "in order to protect the Admiralty from any developments of Mr. Pollen or others."[158] A secret patent covering the automatic plotting of ranges and bearings separately to obtain change of range and change of bearing rates that were to be used in conjunction with a dumaresq and Vickers Clock as previously described was thus drawn up, and assigned to Dreyer on 23 September 1910.[159] Then in October, Moore became worried that the automatic method of plotting ranges and bearings, which necessarily involved the automatic transmission of ranges and bearings, would constitute an infringement of Argo patents.[160] This matter, it would seem, caused Dreyer to substitute a manual method of plotting ranges for the automatic means described in his secret patent, which was to become a standard feature of the production variants of his system.

The manual range plotting mechanism consisted of a typewriter with 10 lettered keys that was mounted on a saddle that moved along two parallel supporting bars. The bars were mounted over a moving paper roll, the axis of the bars being perpendicular to the direction of the paper path. The position of the saddle was determined by moving it until a pointer that travelled with it indicated the range that was to be plotted on a graduated range scale that was situated under one of the bars. One of the keys of the typewriter was then depressed, which marked the moving paper. The availability of ten keys meant that each of the several range-finders of a ship could be coded with a letter, and the plot thus marked in such a way as to indicate not only the range but the instrument that had observed it. For all the ingenuity of this arrangement, it must have been slower and more prone to error than Pollen's system of automatic plotting, if not as ineffective, perhaps, as the manual plotting methods that had failed previously. Automatic plotting of bearings, on the other hand, seems to have been retained, perhaps in the belief that the change to manual plotting of ranges was sufficient to circumvent Pollen's claims.[161]

In December 1910, Dreyer became Flag Commander to Jellicoe, who had succeeded Battenberg as Commander-in-Chief of the Atlantic Fleet. In early 1911, the firm of Elliot Brothers manufactured an instrument that combined Dreyer's rate plotting elements with a dumaresq and Vicker's Clock, which was first tested in the *Prince of Wales*, Jellicoe's flagship.[162] While Dreyer was at sea, Keith Elphinstone, an engineer at Elliot Brothers, with the support of the Ordnance Department, began design work on an improved clock. While this was in progress in May, at which time Henley was in daily consultation with Elphinstone, the Ordnance Department received the description and plans of the Argo Clock Mark II. Moore's assistant had previously kept Dreyer fully informed of confidential matters relating to the Argo Company,[163] and by July at the latest, both Elphinstone and Dreyer were familiar with the mechanical details of the Argo Clock. Elphinstone, in addition, was a frequent visitor to the Cooke's works at York, and in October 1911 with Henley examined both the clock, which was then under construction, and all the drawings.[164]

The new model Dreyer-Elphinstone Clock was at best an imperfect development of the dumaresq-Vickers Clock combination. A separate dumaresq was used to calculate the target course and speed from settings of the target bearing, and change of range and bearing rates from the plots. This data was then set on the dumaresq that was part of the Dreyer gear, and through the cross-cut method integrated with the firing ship course and speed and target bearings to calculate change of range of bearing rates that were then transmitted automatically via a mechanical linkage to the clock. The basic mechanism of the clock consisted of two disc-roller units, one of which generated ranges and the other bearings. Each disc rotated at a constant speed, which imparted motion to a roller, the speed and direction of motion being determined by the position of the roller on the disc, which was controlled by the settings of the dumaresq. The generated bearings, on the other hand, controlled the bearing setting of the dumaresq, which in addition could be altered by the action of a gyro compass whenever the firing ship made a turn.[165]

The clock mechanism bore an unmistakable resemblance to the disc-ball-roller arrangement of the Argo Clock, which in light of the proceedings described above, was probably not coincidental—this, in any case, was the judgement of a government tribunal that met in 1925.[166] The plagiarism of the Argo instrument, if such it was, however, was incomplete and in operation thus far less efficient. In the first place, the absence of adequate provision to reduce friction during the translation of the roller along the diameter of the disc probably resulted in slippage that introduced errors in the generation of ranges and bearings. Secondly, the cast iron discs of the Dreyer-Elphinstone Clock were undoubtedly more susceptible to wear than the hardened steel discs of the Argo device, which over time was bound to reduce accuracy further. And thirdly, when observed bearings could not be obtained because the target was obscured and the change of bearing changed at a rate that was itself changing, the control of the bearing setting of the dumaresq by the bearings produced by the setting of an unchanging change of bearing rate on the clock would constitute an additional source of inaccuracy.

As in the case of the resort to manual range plotting, the adoption of an inferior variable speed drive mechanism may have been attributable to concern over the problem of patent infringement. In any event, to compensate for inaccuracies in the speed and course settings of the dumaresq that were the result of the limitations of rate plotting—if not for the inherent defective operation of the clock mechanism, which may not have been fully appreciated—the Dreyer-Elphinstone Clock was made to drive a marking pencil that plotted generated ranges alongside the plot of observed ranges. By this means, ranges generated by the clock could be quickly compared with observed ranges and the clock settings adjusted whenever the plots diverged.[167] This ingenious method of "feed-back" correction did much to enable the various production marks of the Dreyer Table, as it was known, to produce acceptable results under the unrealistic and easy conditions of Battle Practice, and this was to be a major factor in the rejection of the far superior Argo system.

(c)   MONOPOLY CRISIS AND THE *ORION* TRIALS [1912]

The obstruction of Admiral A. K. Wilson had played an important role in the disruption of the development of the Pollen system, new model armour-piercing projectiles and probably director firing as well. He also had stood squarely in the way of the adoption of a naval staff system. But Wilson's stubborn opposition to technical and organizational change discredited his leadership, and, following the replacement of McKenna by Churchill as First Lord, he was forced to resign and was succeeded by Admiral Sir Francis Bridgeman in November 1911.[168] Moore, on the other hand, kept his place as Director of Naval Ordnance, and although his private relations with Pollen were friendly,[169] he remained nevertheless a determined opponent of true-course plotting and secrecy agreements with the Argo Company. And Henley, a strong supporter of Dreyer's cause, continued to serve as Moore's assistant. Pollen's political standing was even more seriously threatened, however, by the growth of a close professional relationship between Jellicoe and Dreyer.

In his memoirs, Dreyer recalled that his first meeting with Jellicoe had taken place in March 1895 when the two had tied for first place in a naval rifle match at Malta.[170] By 1906, Jellicoe had been impressed by Dreyer's gunnery success under Wilson in the Channel Fleet.[171] Jellicoe undoubtedly disagreed with Dreyer's preference for manual over automatic methods of fire control,[172] but this does not appear to have diminished his respect for Dreyer's overall professional capacity, and Pollen's one known direct attack in print on Dreyer's gunnery knowledge and integrity appears to have earned the inventor a sharp rebuke.[173] In November 1910, Jellicoe, on being appointed to take command of the Atlantic Fleet, asked Dreyer to become his flag commander, an offer which was accepted. When

Jellicoe moved on to take command of the Second Division of the Home Fleet in December 1911, Dreyer accompanied him.[174] While serving under Jellicoe, Dreyer had ample opportunity to display his considerable talent for command and to demonstrate the operation of the prototype of his fire control table that had been built by Elliot Brothers, which was fitted in both of Jellicoe's flagships.

The strengthening of the Dreyer-Jellicoe connection coincided with the final stages in the development of the Pollen system. In March and April 1912, a prototype Argo Clock Mark IV was exhibited in the London offices of the Argo Company, and its operation observed by "the First Lord of the Admiralty, by three of the four Sea Lords, by the Directors of Ordnance and Contracts and their principal advisers and assistants, by the Inspector of Target Practice and his staff, by the Captain and officers of H.M.S. 'Excellent', by the officer commanding the War College, by the representatives of the various intelligence branches and many other expert officers."[175] Rear-Admiral Charles Briggs, the Third Sea Lord and Controller, was subsequently advised by all the gunnery authorities named that the acquisition of the clock on a monopoly basis was a matter of "vital importance."[176] On 18 March, Pollen offered to lend the clock to the Admiralty for sea trials, asking only that the Argo Company be reimbursed for expenses.[177] On 10 April 1912, Moore in an interview and a letter informed Pollen that he would recommend the adoption of the clock for the five battleships of the *King George V* class pending the outcome of sea trials and an agreement over prices.[178]

In his interview with Moore of 10 April, Pollen maintained that he could not quote prices and delivery dates for the five clocks without knowledge of Admiralty plans for future orders. "I am reluctant to quote," Pollen explained in a letter to Moore on 11 April,

> because it is impossible to make so small a number at commercial prices, and I would not like to have the first impression of price be one that would not be defensible if clocks were supplied in quantities. The cost will be high for two reasons. First, the actual manufacturer's cost will be much higher, because it would not be worth while making jigs, templates, etc. or purchasing the special grinding and other machinery necessary. The absence of jigs and such machines necessitates the employment of a higher grade of labour, and much higher wages of supervision, while the time that the clock would take means a general increase in all standing charges. In addition to this it would be necessary for me to contribute a great deal of supervision from our own staff, whom I can ill spare for this work, and for whose services I pay at a scale that such services would not justify. Even at this increased cost it would still be a difficulty to shove them through without a considerable amount of extra plant for purchase of which we should have to find capital, and this capital is difficult for us to find so long as we are tied to secrecy.

Pollen thus suggested three alternative courses of action:

> The first is for the Admiralty to acquire the monopoly of our system, the second is to tell us at once that we are free to supply our devices elsewhere, and the

third to give us a sufficiently large order for plotting tables, rangefinders and new mountings to enable us to raise the capital requisite for manufacturing the clocks on a commercial basis.[179]

On 17 April, Pollen again wrote to Moore to inform him that the addition of a spotting pointer to the clock, which would indicate ranges that incorporated spotting corrections, would cause a four- to six-week delay in the availability of the clock for sea trials. Pollen then noted that he would be unable to supply the five clocks to the *King George V* class on schedule unless he had a definite order and thus suggested that, in light of the highly favorable response of those who had examined the clock, an order might be made in advance of the sea trials. Pollen concluded his letter by urging Moore to consider also an immediate order of either his true-course or rate plotter, a prototype of the latter unit, by this time, having already been delivered to the dreadnought battleship *Orion*.[180] On 20 April, Moore informed Pollen that he would press for an order for five clocks "without waiting for results of the trial one."[181] In his reply of 22 April, Pollen suggested that if the Admiralty went on to order enough clocks for both the central and local control of all dreadnought battleships and battle cruisers built and building—which would come to between 170 and 180 instruments—that he could supply them at the rate of two per week beginning six months from the receipt of the order at a price that would be less than half of that for a limited order for five.[182]

It will be remembered that in the spring of 1910, Pollen had reserved the right to request a renegotiation of the mountings order, and pressing financial need[183]—which, however, turned out to be only temporary[184]—prompted Pollen on behalf of the Argo Company to ask the Admiralty on 13 May 1912 for an additional payment on the mounting order that would restore the £18,000 cut from the original quotation of 1910 and provide another £8,000 to cover the unanticipated costs of necessary improvements in the mountings. As an alternative to the payment of £26,000, Pollen asked that "an immediate relief from all secrecy obligations under the contract may be extended to us," which would enable the Argo Company to raise capital on the strength of prospective sales of the system on the open market.[185] On 20 May, Pollen wrote again to the Admiralty to suggest that the Argo Company would be willing to equip a ship with a complete fire control system for trial in return for payments that would relieve "our imminent financial embarrassments" and a separate financial arrangement for extensions of secrecy beyond December of the current year.[186]

These matters were still under consideration when on 7 June 1912 the Admiralty informed the Argo Company that "without waiting for the preliminary trial in H.M.S. 'Orion' already arranged for, it is desired to have a quotation from you for supply of sufficient apparatus for a more extended trial, should such be desired, and also for supply in quantities in the event of the trials resulting in the adoption of the Clock." To this end, the Argo Company was asked to quote prices and delivery dates for an order for five clocks and a separate order for five rate plotters, and also separate alternative prices for orders for 14 clocks and 14 plotters, and 96 clocks and 96 plotters, under monopoly and also non-monopoly terms.[187] The Argo reply to the Admiralty of 10 June 1912 gave price and delivery date estimates as requested.[188] The company refused, on the other hand, to suggest a price for maintaining secrecy of the clock and plotter only, observing that

> our system must be regarded as an entirety, and to be of commercial value must be put on the market as a whole. We have no wish to keep it secret unless it is felt that some national object is served by so doing; and in this event we prefer that the Admiralty should suggest the consideration, and failing agreement we are willing that the matter should be referred to the independent arbitration of two persons selected one by each side, who should coopt a third: the unanimous decision of two to be binding on both sides.
>
> We are not disposed to discuss the further maintenance of secrecy for a limited period. We have already done this for some years without consideration, and have thereby jeopardised Patent protection in foreign countries, and cannot continue this risk beyond the 31st of December next . . . .[189]

In June, the prospects of a favorable reply to his request for a resettlement of the mountings order, an immediate large order for clocks, and a decision in favor of monopoly, were clouded, however, by Admiralty umbrage over imputations that had been made against Dreyer by Pollen. In his letter to Moore of 11 April 1912, Pollen had noted that

> his attention has been drawn to the fact that Commander Dreyer has brought out an automatic clock which is in some sense a competitor to ours. Bearing in mind that Commander Dreyer was taken to see the "Ariadne" gear in the course of construction, and promptly produced the "Vengeance" imitation, that he saw our first automatic clock and has now produced an imitation, I think it not unreasonable to stipulate that until the monopoly question is settled no competing inventor should be allowed access to our machine.[190]

Moore gave no sign of having taken offence at these remarks in subsequent correspondence.[191] Pollen was thus stunned to receive a letter from the Admiralty on 20 June 1912 that informed him that his private letter of April had been treated as an official communication from the Argo Company, for which he was officially censured.[192]

Moore maintained that the difficulty had occurred because the envelope which contained Pollen's letter had not been marked "private," but there is good reason to believe that the supposed mishap was no accident. In the first place Moore was determined to block the advance of the Argo Company. In mid May, he had replaced Briggs as Third Sea Lord and Controller. Moore made sure, however, that his elevation to the board in no way diminished his involvement with the Pollen question by removing this issue from the jurisdiction of his successor at the Ordnance Department and assuming direct responsibility for the matter from his position of higher authority.[193] Secondly, Moore believed that the refusal of the Argo Company to consider monopoly on an *à la carte* basis was an unfair means of forcing the Admiralty to order his entire system[194]—which in his mind might have justified underhanded action on his part. Thirdly, Moore probably had good reason to fear that Pollen's good relations with important board members such as Battenberg, a long time supporter, and Churchill, with whom Pollen had been communicating since April 1912, would lead to a decision in his favor.[195]

And finally Moore's behavior, if not suspicious, was certainly curious. Pollen, writing to J. A. Spender several months later, asked

> If this letter was one that even as between two friends ought not to have passed from me to Moore, why did Moore reply in a purely friendly and chaffing way without the slightest comment on the character of my letter? Why did he reopen further private and chaffing correspondence with me later? Why did he not at once bring the matter forward for official censure? Why wait nearly four months [actually two months] to bring it to the notice of those who were no longer his superiors but his colleagues? I think the reason is obvious.[196]

Although Pollen was able to have his letter expunged from the official file and the Admiralty letter of reproof withdrawn,[197] he was certain that Moore had succeeded in damaging his standing with Battenberg, Churchill and perhaps Bridgeman as well.[198]

Whatever the case, the affair was followed by a succession of unfavorable notices from the Admiralty. On 22 June 1912, the Argo Company was informed that its request for either a financial resettlement of the mountings order or an immediate release from secrecy restrictions was denied, on the grounds that the original contract had allowed a fair margin of profit and that the firm's financial difficulties were of its own making.[199] On 12 August 1912, the Argo Company learned that the promise made in April to allow representatives of the firm to attend the trials of the clock in the *Orion* had been withdrawn.[200] On 20 August 1912, the Director of Navy Contracts notified the Argo Company that no rate plotters would be required, that only five clocks would be ordered at a price that would have to be "greatly below the £2,400 originally quoted," and that advance payment would not be possible.[201] And on the same day, the Admiralty Permanent Secretary, in a separate letter, advised the Argo Company that the monopoly agreement covering the firm's entire system would be allowed to lapse at the end of the year.[202]

The Department of Navy Contracts was almost certainly opposed in no uncertain terms to additional payments for the mountings or an early release from secrecy obligations, and its opinion would have been an important—perhaps even critical—factor in the Admiralty's verdict, regardless of the actions of Moore.[203] The Admiralty's breach of promise with regard to the presence of representatives of the Argo Company on board the *Orion* during trials, which Pollen regarded as a strong sign that Moore had succeeded in turning the board against him on personal grounds, was in fact probably attributable to the assignment of that ship to forthcoming trials with Scott's director. The rejection of the Argo rate-plotter was most likely due to the fact that it was nearly four times the cost of the Dreyer rate plotting gear and not appreciably superior in performance.[204] The decision to abandon monopoly over the Argo system even before the sea trials of the clock had taken place, however, may well have been affected by the development of a personal animus against Pollen on the board.

Moore, in any case, had advised the First Lord and other Sea Lords on 13 August 1912 that the Argo Company

> possesses no knowlege that the Service is lacking, indeed the whole of the knowledge it has of the Fire Control necessities has been derived from the exceptionally privileged position in which Mr. Pollen has been placed by the Admiralty; everything that the Argo Company professes to achieve with its instruments, can be equally well performed with the Dreyer instruments; except that the Argo Company still advocates "True Course and Speed plotting" as an essential, whereas the Service and Dreyer prefer the "Time and Range" and "Time and Bearing" curve systems. (The True Course and Speed system has been tried over and over again and always fails). His clock may or may not prove better than Dreyer's, under monopoly terms it will certainly be more expensive. I do not see any reason for continuing the privileged position of this inventor, he has been handsomely and generously paid for his work in the past, and in my opinion it is full time that he was placed in the same position as all other inventors. . . .[205]

Moore's counsel, according to Battenberg, convinced his colleagues that the renewal of the monopoly agreement with the Argo Company was unnecessary, if not undesirable.[206]

By early July 1912, Pollen had concluded that the political tide was not in his favor at the Admiralty, and turned to Rear-Admiral Peirse for assistance. Peirse was at this time probably one of the service's most respected senior gunnery officers, having served as the Inspector of Target Practice from February 1909 to January 1911, commanded the First Battle Squadron of the Home Fleet from February 1911 to January 1912, after which he had been assigned to assist Percy Scott in preparing trials of a new model director. Pollen informed Peirse in early July 1912 that there were indications that monopoly would not be renewed and, after alternative methods of influencing Admiralty policy were discussed in subsequent correspondence, the two agreed that Peirse should approach various members of the board and others on Pollen's behalf.[207] In the third week of July, the Admiral, who had not been able to view the clock in London earlier in the year, paid a visit to the Argo Company works in York in order to see a demonstration before it was installed in the *Orion*.[208] In late July, Peirse was provided with the drawings of both the clock and the new model true-course plotter, the latter being still under design. After spending "an instructive hour" of study, Peirse was able to tell Isherwood on 29 July that he had "mastered all the essential details," adding that "the simplicity & ingenuity of the Clock mechanism is delightful."[209]

On 25 August, Peirse reported to Pollen that he had sent Churchill a memorandum after speaking with him briefly, and had had many talks with Scott while on board H.M.S. *Thunderer*, the trials ship for the director. "I have succeeded in getting Percy Scott entirely on the right side," Peirse wrote in his letter, "& he is now also preparing a paper on the subject of the deplorable state of our Gunnery in which incidentally he is making a strong point of our total lack of Rate Finding & Rate Keeping instruments, which he will address to the First Lord." Peirse, having been informed by Pollen of the abandonment of monopoly by the Admiralty, regretted that his appeal to Churchill had been to no avail, but he assured Pollen that he had not yet lost hope.[210] On 7 September, Peirse wrote to Battenberg to express his views on the question of maintaining secrecy in no uncertain terms. "To throw over Mr. Pollen now," he argued

> and allow him to give the fruits of his ten years experience (all gained at our expense) to some Foreign Power would in my opinion be nothing short of a National disaster.
>
> The Director from what I have seen of it here, undoubtedly promises to give us the *best system of firing* & one might add the *only system* when the ship is rolling.
>
> What we still require is the means of placing these concentrated broadsides on the Enemy and keeping them there.
>
> Pollen's apparatus is without any doubt whatever, the one best calculated to give us this.[211]

Peirse's letter was accompanied by a copy of the same memorandum that he had submitted to Churchill, and also to Bridgeman and Jellicoe.[212] Peirse began his paper by asserting that in the Battle Practices of the preceding three years "our failure to obtain a large percentage of hits on the target has been chiefly due to the employment of an *incorrect Rate* of change of Range." Peirse then insisted that true-course plotting was essential, that present methods of determining the rate amounted to nothing better than guesswork, that the "the only instruments . . . which hold out any hopes of success . . . are those devised by Mr. Pollen," that the Argo gear tested in the *Natal* had been "undoubtedly sound" and should have been developed, and that monopoly should not be abandoned until the complete Argo system had been thoroughly tested. Peirse warned that

> we are now only teaching our Officers and Men to fire at a target moving at 8 knots! with a "Rate of change" limited to 350 yards a minute.
>
> Judging by the small and disappointing percentage of hits obtained under these elementary conditions what chance have we with our present crude methods of making any hits at all when the Enemy may be steaming at any speed between 15 and 30 knots with a "Rate" of anything up to 1600 yards a minute?
>
> This is rather a pitiful admission and all very well with an unlimited ammunition supply and at moderate range, but the time when hits will tell is at the commencement of an action when
>
> (a)   The range is a maximum and consequently when the rate of fire must be deliberate.

(b) When the danger space is a minimum.

(c) When the "Rate of change" of range is large and rapidly varying due to a steep approach.

These are the difficult conditions when hits will be of supreme value as largely influencing the result of the Battle.[213]

On 16 September, Pollen wrote at length to Peirse, giving a history of his difficult relations with Moore that included a full account of the private letter affair; refuting the argument that his knowledge of service methods of fire control compromised national security; and offering his favorable view of director gunnery.[214] On 18 September, Pollen discussed his case with Battenberg.[215] Peirse met with Battenberg on 19 September, and subsequently reported to Pollen that he had received "a sympathetic hearing" and been assured that a further inquiry would be made into the matter.[216] Battenberg was true to his word, and on the same day met with Moore, asking for his comments on Peirse's letter and memorandum of 7 September, and Pollen's letter to Peirse of 16 September, which Peirse had left him. In his letter to Battenberg of 19 September, Moore simply refused to give his views on Pollen's letter on the grounds that it was a "personal" communication, and limited his remarks to the subjects raised in the Peirse letter and memorandum.

Moore maintained that payments for monopoly to the Argo Company amounted to blackmail, and that Dreyer offered a system of comparable performance at a lower price. "It is perfectly true," he wrote,

> that by placing Mr. Pollen in the position of a favoured inventor, we have put him in possession of the most confidential items of our Fire Control system, and we are being constantly pressed by Mr. Pollen to pay him large sums of money to keep that information for our exclusive use (His way of putting it is in the form of saying we pay him consideration for the restriction of his profits by limiting his market). Each time we pay him thus (monopoly rights) he gains more Confidential knowledge and thus his most valuable marketable article rises in proportion, so that monopoly prices rise, it is a chain round our necks being forged more and more relentlessly. If there was no other system achieving equal results with Pollen's then there would be no choice (or very little) for us; but there is another system; it is almost identical, it is Dreyer's; the mechanical details are different but with one exception [rate as opposed to true-course plotting] the principles are the same . . . . Mr. Pollen has always made a great parade of his patriotic feelings preventing him from seeking other markets, but if we propose to accept that kind offer of patriotism without paying him for it, he threatens to go abroad and *trade upon the Confidential knowledge he has acquired by reason of his specially favoured treatment.* I believe that both Dreyer's & Pollen's systems will produce about equal results. Dreyer's is the more developed at present, but Pollen's workmanship is probably better & less liable to get out of order. If Pollen's table proves better than rate plotting, then it is a question of how much better compared to price, but meanwhile everything with Pollen hangs up, because of the demand for Monopoly money (it might almost be called Hush money).
>
> . . . . I think the time has long since arrived when we should shake ourselves free, and let Mr. Pollen prove the truth of his contention that he has a waiting market elsewhere.[217]

Battenberg does not appear to have been completely satisfied by Moore's response, because on 20 September Pollen was able to report to Peirse that he had been verbally advised by someone at the Admiralty that representatives of the Argo Company would be allowed on board the *Orion* for four days of pre-trial experiments, a promise that was confirmed in writing on 24 September.[218] Pollen also informed Peirse that he had just been to the *Orion* and had pointed out to her officers that the ship "must do something quite extraordinary with the gear if there is to be any hope whatever of saving it, and I need not tell you, who know the kind of men that are in the 'Orion', that they are in a state of friendly determination to save it at all costs from the Wilhelmstrasse."[219] The first set of pre-trial experiments took place during 23-5 September, and the second from 30 September through 2 October.[220] In October, Pollen, writing to an unknown correspondent, was able to report complete success. "We were given the range of a fixed mark," he wrote,

> whose distance from the ships had been exactly ascertained. Our Clock was set to its bearing and range and to our own course and speed. Our ship, the *Orion* then described a quadrilateral figure, whose sides measured between eight and nine miles, and the three turns executed in describing it were made under full helm, and aggregated more than three full right angles. And, in the course of these nine miles, speed was worked up from cruising speed to the highest speed possible in the time. As the experiment was carried out at the entrance to Bantry Bay, it was easy to complete it by steering the ship to the exact point at which it commenced; and this was a point which, in the circumstances, could be, and was, exactly fixed by the navigators; thus verifying, beyond cavil, the margins within which we could do what we had set out to do. The task was to keep the range of the fixed mark and its line of aim throughout the run, without having transmitted to us any range or bearing corrections of any kind whatever. At the end of the run, it was found that we had the range within twenty-five yards, and the bearing within half a degree. And, as we had been without further data about the target, we had, in fact, proved that we could have kept an invisible target under accurate indirect fire just as easily as a visible target under direct fire throughout the run.[221]

While Peirse corresponded with both Captain Montague Browning, the Inspector of Target Practice, and Jellicoe on the fire control question,[222] Pollen attempted to influence Churchill. In his private letter to the First Lord of 21 October, Pollen supposed that the objections to extending the secrecy agreement due to expire were the cost of monopoly, the lack of success of the Argo gear in the past and the doubtfulness of success in the future, and the "thought that there is no necessity for so complete and elaborate system as ours, but that a less complete and cheaper solution will be adequate." With regard to the third point, Pollen observed that

> range, speed and course finding must first be available however high the relative speed, so as to enable a "Lion" at top speed to fight another "Lion" at top speed if she wished. And next, that to be ready for war, the "Lion" must be able to get the data for doing this whether she is on a steady course or under helm.

228

The proposed Service methods of getting speed and course cannot do either ot these things, because they are not designed to attempt to do them.

. . . . It is a simple fact that all proposed Service solutions of this [that is, the fire control] problem are not only posterior to mine in time, but inferior, first, in accuracy, second in the swiftness of the necessary operations[,] thirdly in being designed to cope with a very greatly restricted set of conditions.

Pollen then argued that the Admiralty would be forced by the adoption of his system by foreign navies to purchase his gear in any case. "If, then, my system is right," he wrote, "and I do not think that without a thorough investigation you can be sure that it is not, may you not be driven to adopt it to regain mere equality, when perhaps at no greater cost you might now be able to keep it, at any rate for some years, and with it gain a vast, if only temporary, superiority." Pollen then warned that

the day my system becomes public property you have no secret of any kind left in your naval gunnery. In as far as you have adopted a restricted and mutilated form of my system you have obviously no secret of any value. Outside of this system, or of what you have adopted of it, you have not today on board ship, a single Fire Control instrument or process that is not supplied in the open market to any foreigner who wishes to ask for it.

Pollen concluded his letter to Churchill with an offer to "accept any financial arrangement that you personally might decide on," on condition that "a small impartial committee of experts" be appointed "who would hear the case both for my system and for every actual or projected Service substitute and not only report to you on the facts, but recommend whether monopoly should be preserved or not."[223]

On 26 October 1912, Churchill's secretary informed Pollen that the First Lord had read his letter and was "making further inquiry."[224] On the same day, the Director of Navy Contracts notified the Argo Company that their revised tender of 27 September 1912 for five additional clocks at a price of £2,133 each had been accepted.[225] Churchill's deliberations would require more than a month and in the meanwhile Pollen drew much satisfaction, and perhaps encouragement as well, from the outcome of the trials of director firing. On 15 October, Peirse had reported that a preliminary shoot with the director in H.M.S. *Thunderer* had been highly successful.[226] Better news followed. On 13 November, in trials held in rough weather off Berehaven, Ireland, the *Thunderer*, using the director, made more than six times as many hits as the *Orion*, which was not fitted with a director, conditions being equal for both ships.[227] "I gather from the papers," Pollen wrote to Scott on 19 November,

that your courageous work of the last eight years is really crowned with success at last. I assure you this is as gratifying to those who have watched and admired your efforts as it can be to you. For my own part, I rejoice especially for two purely selfish reasons: firstly, that your success is a severe kick in the stomach to a crowd of wiseacres who were just as much my opponents as yours, and I take an unchristian delight in seeing my enemies discomfited. Secondly, it seems to me that the wider the scope of conditions in which effective aiming and firing can take place, the greater the need of accurateness in means of finding out what the range and the rate is, so that the best results may be got from your firing system.

The real truth about the cursedly inept gunnery policy that has prevailed since 1907 is that neither Bacon nor Moore were either of them in the minutest degree Artillerists: by this I mean that there was not a single branch of practical naval artillery technique in which—I won't say they were experts—in which they were even competent to understand the leading points. They neither understood the scientific principles or the essence of gunlaying—a field that you have made so particularly your own; nor yet the requirements of Fire Control—the field to which my humble efforts have been confined. The consequence is they have been bang off the track, and absolutely wrong on every point in connection with both of them.

It certainly gives me a most venemous delight to see you "down" those b——dy know-alls, who for years have had the whole Aegis of official infallibility to conceal the imbecile folly of their childish heresies. A bas Bacon, Conspuez Dreyer, Moore a la lanterne; for the rest, full steam ahead.[228]

The next day, Pollen was able to tell Peirse that

> I saw P. Scott this morning, and had the greatest difficulty in holding him down on the floor. I gather from what he tells me that the success of the thing is undoubted. I am really exceedingly glad.[229]

At about this time Pollen had good news from another, and more directly related quarter. On 27 September 1912, Pollen had asked Professor Charles Vernon Boys to evaluate an Argo range-finder that had been redesigned to rectify shortcomings revealed by the informal service trials, the new model helm-free/true-course plotter and clock. Boys, who was one of England's leading practical physicists, and who it will be recalled had been consulted in 1906 on the question of gyroscopes, accepted the commission, and after careful study of the plans and descriptions of the gear, which included a visit to the Argo works at York, sent Pollen his report in the second week of November.[230] In his report, Boys noted that the Argo range-finder's higher efficiency in dim light "should not only lengthen the hours in which action can take place, and give ranges of greater individual accuracy, but should also make the quicker reading of ranges possible . . ." Boys was convinced, furthermore, that the mechanism of the plotting table was "perfectly adapted to do the work required of it, and, seeing how difficult and complicated the problem is, it is comparatively simple."

Boys reserved his highest praise, however, for the clock, which he described as being "as near perfection as any mechanism which I have ever examined critically." "I have followed the development of the integrating machine," Boys then wrote,

> in its various forms for over 30 years, including the ball, disc and cylinder integrator used by Lord Kelvin in his harmonic analyser. I have no hesitation in saying that the integrating mechanism used in the "Clock" is the most perfect of all that has been done in this direction. It has the advantage also that the working surfaces may be made of hardened steel, with an accuracy exceeding 1/10,000 inch by well recognised and standard workshop methods, that the

motions in all cases are pure rolling without sliding, and appreciable wear should be unknown. Perfect as the integrators are as an element in the design of the "Clock" the manner in which they are cross connected so as to provide a constant mechanical solution of the ever varying triangle of velocity is equally so, and the conception and execution of the "Clock" as a whole represents in my opinion the high water mark of invention in this field.

"I should like to add," he concluded,

> that it is surprising that you should have reached so perfect a conclusion in the short time of six years since you first consulted me. The problem is one of such difficulty that it must have required immense perseverance to have kept in mind the main desideratum, and to have persuaded Mr Isherwood to find the mechanical solutions of a series of problems of great technical difficulty. Thanks to his genius, to the excellent use you have made of your practical experiments at sea, and to the constructive skill that has been available you now have a perfected whole which could not have been produced without such a fortunate combination of minds and circumstances.[231]

Pollen sent copies of the Boys report to Churchill, Jellicoe and Peirse in the third week of November.[232] Although the reactions of the First Lord are not known, Jellicoe read the paper with "a great deal" of interest,[233] while Peirse believed that it was "admirable & ought to carry great weight . . ."[234]

Even better tidings were in store. On 19 and 20 November, the official trials of the Argo Clock were carried out in the *Orion*.[235] The 20 minute test run with the guns firing full charges involved ranges that varied from 12,400 yards at the start to 8,750 yards at the end, the *Orion* steaming at 15 knots while the target was towed at 8 knots. Inaccurate ranges and bearings, which were set directly on the clock,[236] at first resulted in an incorrect rate being generated by the clock, but by the time the guns opened fire 9 minutes into the run the clock had been provided with accurate data. Craig reported that

> at 11 minutes the helm was put over for a turn of 67 degrees, but this alteration of course in no way affected the firing, which continued throughout the turn, 3 hits being made in that time. When the ship was steadied the rate on the clock although not absolutely correct was sufficiently accurate to enable hits to be obtained with no difficulty continuously throughout the remainder of the run . . . .
> During the firing time 40 rounds were fired, 14 hits are calculated to have been made. The target was so damaged that hits could not have been counted.
> The large alteration of course at 11 minutes did not interfere with the rapidity or accuracy of the firing, nor did it in any way complicate the working or reduce the accuracy of the clock which transmitted the range correctly & kept the rate during the turn.[237]

The tests in which the guns were fired using 3/4 charges were somewhat less successful, due solely to the inaccuracy of ranges and bearings taken during a very large turn, but the results were nevertheless impressive.[238]

Pollen was not informed of the detailed outcome of the official trials and, in particular, would not learn of the difficulties caused by the inaccuracy of the data until mid December, but had reason to believe that they were generally quite successful. "I heard a very satisfactory account," Peirse wrote to Pollen on November 28, 1912, "of the recent firing trials in 'Orion.' Craig speaks enthusiastically," Peirse went on, "& considers it far ahead of any other instruments for keeping the range."[239]

In the meanwhile, a Dreyer table that incorporated the clock designed in 1911 had been tried in 1912 in the dreadnought battlehip *Monarch*, which was part of the Second Division of the Home Fleet commanded by Jellicoe, who undoubtedly observed the proceedings with interest.[240] The 1912 experiments with the Dreyer table, however, appear not to have been extensive, involving neither use in conjunction with guns firing nor rigorous tests of instrumental accuracy.[241] Pollen knew that Dreyer's instrument existed, and his speculations to Peirse in November 1912 as to its character were essentially accurate. But in the absence of exact knowledge, he was unable to do more than produce general critiques of rate–plotting and the dumaresq–Vickers Clock combination.[242] Dreyer, on the other hand, was able to respond in late 1912 with a typescript technical memorandum that contained detailed technical comparisons of his own gear and the Argo Clock, which to the technically innocent could have carried considerable force.

"The Argo Clock as a piece of ingenious mechanism is no doubt very attractive," Dreyer began, "but it is not a practical instrument." He went on to criticize the Argo device for lacking an alternative hand drive, a dumaresq that gave a "Bird's Eye View" [that is, a schematic picture] of the relationship of the firing ship and target, a connection between with a gyro–compass that would automatically correct for changes in the firing ship course, and a system of tuning the clock for the "Mean Rangefinder Range of the moment" by inspection [that is, the feedback system described earlier], all of which, he pointed out, were included in his "Monarch Table." Dreyer also maintained that his instrument was capable of keeping the rate even when the target was obscured simply by setting a constant bearing rate on the bearing clock whose generated bearings could then be set on the dumaresq.[243] In an historical set of remarks which may have accompanied the technical memorandum, Dreyer characterized Pollen's instruments as plagiarizations of the work of Watkins and his own manual methods of 1908 as a success.[244]

Dreyer's technical memorandum was misleading from a number of standpoints. In the first place, his method of using generated bearings from a bearing clock set with a constant bearing rate to set the dumaresq would not produce usable results if the bearing rate was changing rapidly, which meant that his table would not work accurately as he claimed if the bearing rate was changing rapidly and bearing observation was impossible because the target was obscured. Secondly, while the features of his instrument that he correctly explained possessed a number of advantages, these were not enough to compensate for the serious limitations inherent to his approach, which have already been described. Thirdly, Dreyer's comparison of his complete system with only a single component of Pollen's was unfair. And in so far as Dreyer's historical remarks are concerned, it should be clear from what has been related in earlier chapters that his charges and claims were far-fetched.

Dreyer's technical and historical observations nevertheless appear to have influenced the judgement of the Admiralty in his favor, although even his supporters would have admitted that he had overstated his case with regard to the Argo Clock. On 6 December 1912 Colonel Stephen Hungerford Pollen, Arthur Hungerford Pollen's brother and a retired army officer, was granted an interview with Churchill and Moore. In his notes of the meeting, Stephen Pollen recollected that

> (a) I understood Admiral Moore to say that in his opinion the Argo Clock was mechanically superior to the Service Clock, but that its superiority was not sufficient to warrant a large price being paid for it or for monopoly.
> (b) Admiral Moore also stated that "the price asked for monopoly was excessive."
> (c) The First Lord of the Admiralty told me that guided by his technical advisers he was prepared to say that he had no objection to our selling the Clock in the open market after the 1st of January.

Churchill at this time refused to accept the proposals that Arthur Hungerford Pollen had put forward in his letter of 21 October—namely that the decision as to price be left in his hands on condition of the formation of an impartial committee of experts to review the matter in its entirety—but was impressed by Stephen Pollen's argument that "the real point at issue would not be whether our navy had a Clock slightly inferior only to the Argo, but it would be that foreign powers who now had no similar Clock, would have one admittedly superior to that used by the British Navy." Churchill thus asked Pollen "to quote for a large number of Clocks, the price to be calculated on the basis that the Admiralty should be our only customer."[245]

In early December, Bridgeman had resigned at Churchill's request and been replaced by Battenberg, who had been Second Sea Lord. Battenberg's former position on the board was filled by Jellicoe. For Pollen, however, these appointments of his long time friends and patrons proved to be a great disappointment. As early as October 1912, Battenberg had made it clear to Pollen that he intended to stand by the board's decision to allow the monopoly agreement to expire.[246] On 17 December, Battenberg told Pollen—perhaps by telephone—that the performance of the Argo Clock and the Dreyer gear were equivalent. In his written reply of that day, Pollen argued that the Argo and Dreyer systems were "quite different in aim and have quite different practical results," and complained that this was not clear because the official trials of his clock had been compromised by the setting of the clock with inaccurate data, which he had not known until he received an account from a private source on 11 December [for which see below]. After pleading for additional trials Pollen asserted that

> my clock has not been fairly tried against its competitor. My plotting is rejected

untried and unexamined. The Board is again told that the cheap imitation is as good as the costly original, and once more judgement is given against me without my being allowed to advocate my own cause or to produce evidence or my witnesses, or knowing anything of the case I have to answer.

His letter was accompanied by a copy of the letter which was his source of information on the *Orion* trials, a memorandum that compared the Argo and Dreyer systems, and a memorandum that discussed the difference between rate-finding and rate-keeping. Pollen closed with a request for a personal interview.[247]

The letter of Pollen's naval officer informant, who had been given first-hand accounts of the *Orion* trials by two of the participants, was revealing. "We all agree," Pollen's correspondent wrote,

> that you and Dreyer have totally different aims, but that it would be difficult to prove this unless you can get a fair trial of your Clock as a Clock against the corresponding part of his system.
>
> Everyone here is very strongly of opinion [*sic*] that the recent trials have not been fair to you. The Dreyer gear has not been put through the same tests as yours, and your Clock has throughout been tried as if it were a complete Fire Control system, i.e. the "Orion" had to get the data to put on it as well as keep them right when they got them. They did not always succeed in getting the right ranges and some of the runs appear to have been pretty bad, and these have been counted against you, as if it were a fault in your Clock to give bad results when wrong data are put upon it.[248]

Battenberg telephoned the next day to reply to Pollen's letter and enclosures. He then maintained that the "question had been thoroughly thrashed out"; that the Admiralty's decision "was made in the light of all the facts"; that trials of the Argo Clock that had taken place under Jellicoe's direction had convinced both Jellicoe and the board that "the Dreyer gear was for practical purposes as good and as accurate" as the Argo Clock; that while "it was admitted" that the Argo Clock "was more accurate and could be used in more difficult conditions than the Dreyer Clock" that "nobody wanted a Fire Control system that could be used when there was a change of range of 2,000 yards a minute, which was not a practical possibility; and that the Dreyer Clock was sufficiently accurate for all conditions which would arise in war."[249]

In an interview at the Admiralty between the Pollen brothers and Moore that had taken place on 11 December 1912, the Argo Company had, in response to Churchill's request of 6 December, quoted a price of £1,600 per clock on an order for 150 units, with a stipulation for an advance payment of £50,000.[250] The Dreyer-Elphinstone Clock, however, had cost about £500,[251] and Battenberg thus informed Pollen that there was "no possibility of coming to an agreement" on a large clock order because the cost of the Argo instrument "was so much higher than the cost of the Dreyer Clock" that the Admiralty had concluded that they could make no offer which the Argo Company could accept.[252] Battenberg's verbal notice of the Admiralty's decision not to place a large order for Argo Clocks was confirmed by an official letter that was written the next day.[253] On 30 December, the Admiralty informed the Argo Company that it would purchase the Argo Clock installed in the *Orion* in addition to the five clocks on order for the *King George V* class as per terms that had been quoted in November.[254] On 31 December 1912 the special relationship between the Admiralty and the Argo Company that for seven years had kept his inventions off the open market ended.

(d) THE LAST CAMPAIGN AND AFTERMATH [1913-1914]

On being informed that monopoly would not be renewed, the Argo Company had asked the Admiralty on 22 August 1912 that arrangements necessary to enable the firm to file foreign patents immediately in the new year be made.[255] The Admiralty assented to this request on 26 September 1912.[256] The Admiralty then agreed on 21 November to extend secrecy for technical reasons to 31 January 1913, and this was later extended to 31 March .[257] In November and December, the representatives of the Argo Company and the Admiralty met and corresponded to discuss the question of whether or not the Argo rate plotter infringed service secret patents, but the issue remained unresolved.[258] On 6 December, Churchill and Moore had assured Stephen Pollen that the Admiralty would have no objection to the foreign sale of the Argo Clock.[259] But on 17 January, Pollen was informed by Captain F. C. T. Tudor, the Director of Naval Ordnance, that the Admiralty was considering a prohibition on the foreign sale of the Argo Clock on the grounds that it incorporated features that would reveal service secrets. Pollen immediately had an interview with Moore, who then told him that he had no knowledge of any such deliberations, after which Pollen wrote to the Director of Navy Contracts on 18 January for a clarification of the matter.[260]

Pollen would receive no answer to his query for a month, and in the meanwhile, his efforts to secure a reconsideration of his system by the Admiralty resulted in a serious increase in bad feelings. Pollen had advised his service friends that the Admiralty had abandoned monopoly and that his system would soon be placed on the open market. A considerable number of officers, including no fewer than eleven admirals,[261] responded with letters or in person. On 20 January 1913, extracts from several of these letters, whose authors were not identified, were sent by Stephen Pollen to Churchill, along with a covering letter that asked that his brother be granted an interview. On 21 January, Arthur Pollen discovered that one of his extracts contained observations that were critical of both Jellicoe and Moore by name, which had been unintentionally included. He thus asked Churchill's secretary that day to withdraw the first set of extracts and to replace it with a substitute, which he stated would be sent as soon as it had been made.[262]

No copy of the original set of extracts that were sent to Churchill seems to have survived, but three other collections exist that contain passages that mention officers by name and that may have been part of the original set.[263] In one of these, an unknown officer wrote that "Dreyer and Jellicoe have been together and effectually blocked anything like clear thinking on the matter."[264] The original set of extracts probably also contained those sections of letters that were included in the revised set of extracts which, while not mentioning names, denounced the Admiralty in no uncertain terms. One officer, for example, wrote that he was "absolutely disgusted with the behavior of the Board on the whole question." Another wrote that he was "deeply grieved and disappointed to hear that the Admiralty are giving up exclusive rights," that he could not "imagine on what grounds the decision was arrived at," and that "there is nothing in the Service in the same street with the Argo Clock." And a third exclaimed that the "news not only disgusted me, but also made me wonder who is responsible for what in my humble opinion is crass stupidity."[265]

This attempt of the Pollens to influence Churchill badly misfired. On 22 January 1913 James Masterton-Smith, the First Lord's private secretary, stated in reply that Churchill "desires me to observe that the step you appear to have taken of obtaining from a number of officers afloat opinions reflecting upon Admiralty decisions is irregular . . ." He in addition noted that the offending extract was "grossly improper and offensive in its character" and that it had been shown to the two officers involved. And finally, Masterton-Smith wrote words to the effect that the First Lord was unable to reopen the question of monopoly or the clock.[266] On 23 January, Pollen wrote an apology to Moore, who on 25 January responded with a letter that expressed his outrage at considerable length.[267] Jellicoe accepted Pollen's regrets in a letter that was also written on 23 January, with understanding, although he closed his short note with the admonition that "your correspondence with officers afloat has led, and must necessarily have led, to some of the younger officers expressing views which are—to put it mildly—not in the best interests of discipline."[268]

Pollen, in his letter of apology to Jellicoe, had admitted that he had "made a serious error in tactics in urging monopoly so strongly upon you and your colleagues,"[269] and on 4 February advised the board of the Argo Company that "the wisest course is to recognise that monopoly is definitely given up, and that to attempt any further action by the Company would only lead to exasperating the Admiralty, which may be detrimental to our commercial interests."[270]

But on the very day of his statement to the Argo Company board, Pollen informed E. G. Pretyman, the former Conservative Financial Secretary to the Admiralty, of his state of affairs and appealed for assistance. In his letter of 4 February, which was accompanied by a set of extracts, Pollen suggested that "I do not think it would be any use a single member of Parliament moving in this matter, but that if it is worth doing anything, it is worth making a front bench question of it, and approaching the Prime Minister privately before raising it in the House."[271] In his reply of 5 February, Pretyman observed that "the question of which system is finally adopted appears to me to be quite separate from that of preserving the monopoly & secrecy of both systems, & this latter is the only question which could be effectively raised in Parliament, as the other must solely be one for the judgement of experts." Pretyman added that he planned to consult Jellicoe, whom he knew and regarded highly, before bringing the Argo question to the attention of the Conservative leadership.[272] On 13 February, Pretyman, after making his inquiries, advised Pollen that he had been told that "the A.C. depends upon other secret patents which are govt. property & which cannot be communicated elswhere." He had thus concluded that the Admiralty were "quite alive to the necessity for secrecy & the responsibility must rest with them."[273]

On 20 January 1913, Black, the Director of Navy Contracts, had suggested that "it might be advisable to pay Mr. Pollen and the Argo Co., a certain sum for services rendered." This proposal was strongly opposed, however, by Captain Tudor, the Director of Naval Ordnance. It will be recalled that responsibility for matters relating to the Argo Company had been assumed by the Controller in the spring of 1912. Tudor, however, appears to have demonstrated a hostility to the Argo Company that was at least as great as that of Moore—it was Tudor, after all, and not Moore who seems to have originated the idea of trying to prohibit the publication of certain patents related to the Argo Clock—and perhaps for this reason had by January 1913 been given charge of the case. On 18 February, in reply to the proposal of Black, Tudor maintained that the Argo Company had already been fully remunerated, had benefited greatly from the assistance of naval officers, that it was "impracticable" to pay the Argo Company

> a sum sufficient to tempt them to forego their plan of offering their inventions to Foreign Governments; and that a reversal of the decision made in 1912, not to continue to pay for the secrecy and monopoly of these patents would be the signal for Mr. Pollen to demand a continually higher price for this secrecy and monopoly as he had already done on two previous occasions, in 1906 and 1909.

Tudor also argued that "the Pollen system was not at that time of the first importance to the Navy, in view of the alternative apparatus available."[274]

Tudor's views carried the day, and his scheme of obstructing the foreign sale of the Argo Clock officially adopted. On 21 February 1913, the Admiralty informed the Argo Company that the dials that were used to set the range and bearing rates on its clock would indicate to a foreign purchaser of the instrument that the service system was based on rate plotting, that the mechanism controlled by the dials that translated the settings into estimates of the target course and speed revealed "the same Service secret," that therefore no clocks incorporating these features could be sold to foreign navies, and that any breach of this stipulation "would constitute an infringement of the Official Secrets Act."[275] Pollen thus consulted his patent attorney, Russell Clarke,[276] whose advice was communicated to the Admiralty via Coward, & Hawksley, Sons & Chance, the firm that represented the Argo Company. On 15 March 1913, they stated to the Admiralty that "our clients are advised that the Admiralty are bound to re-assign the patents and that the only alternative to publication is for them to be kept secret by agreement," that "failing any such agreement our clients will proceed at once to apply for foreign Patents . . .," and that "prosecution under an Act of Parliament" had "no possible application in their case."[277]

Pollen had, in the meanwhile, opened another political front in February with the private publication of a lengthy essay, which was entitled *The Gun in Battle*. As in previous prints, Pollen explained the general nature of his instruments, the history of their development, and the technical and therefore tactical limitations of the existing service system of gunnery. With his perfected system nearly complete, Pollen could now claim that the employment of his fire control apparatus would enable naval artillery "to keep an enemy under practically continuous fire, so long as the target is within the zone in which the gun can be trusted to shoot in the terms of the sight, irrespective of the relative velocities set up by the courses and speeds adopted, and unhampered by voluntary or involuntary changes of own course." Such capability would mean that a warship would be "free to race and free to turn, and free to hit while doing either," which had not previously been the case. This, he argued, made "a complete revolution in all preconceived notions of Naval Tactics" a certainty.[278]

The considerable force of Pollen's writing had in the past won him widespread support that had influenced the actions of the Admiralty. Recognition that this had been so appears to have prompted the Admiralty to produce a long three part commentary on the Pollen case for restricted circulation. Part one, a technical history and technical comparison, was written by Dreyer and Commander C. V. Usborne of the Ordnance Department. Part two, a report on the patent aspects of the case, was written by James Swinburne, a patent attorney retained by the Admiralty. Part three, an explanation of the general grounds of the Admiralty's policy and a historical record of the business discussions and transactions, was probably written by the Director of Navy Contracts or a member of his staff.

The technical history and comparison was the longest of the three papers, amounting to over 60 pages of text supported by many drawings and diagrams. As in Dreyer's historical memorandum of late 1912, Pollen's plotting system was dismissed as a mere plagiarization of the Watkins system. In the account of the 1910 trials, in which it will be recalled the Argo system in the *Natal* had been tried against manual rate and virtual-course methods of plotting, the reader was informed that "none of the three systems could be said to be satisfactory, but the 'Virtual' system in 'Africa' was the best of the three,"[279] a statement flatly contradicted by the findings of the Colville committee, which had been in charge of the tests.[280] And in spite of the fact that Colville and his associates had repudiated the manual methods tested in no uncertain terms, and strongly urged the Admiralty to acquire additional sets of Argo instruments for further testing and development, Dreyer and Usborne, in their conclusions, observed that

the Committee who carried out the "Natal" trials commenced their report to the Admiralty as follows:—

If it is necessary, in order to hit an enemy, that her track should first be drawn on a chart, the automatic method of doing so, as arranged for in "Natal," is far superior to any manual method.

They could not recommend that such a track was necessary.

After naming the members of the Colville committee, the authors maintained that "there is no doubt that these officers considered the question thoroughly and purely from a war point of view, and had they seen any real advantage to be gained by such a track, they would have recommended it to the Admiralty."[281]

The section which listed and discussed the "assumptions as to the conditions under which actions will be fought" was, if not deliberately misleading, practically self-destructive in argument. Dreyer and Usborne maintained that an admiral might try to open fire "under difficult conditions in the hope that the enemy will be unable to cope with them," after which they noted that an admiral "may engage at a high range, or with a high rate of change of range, so as to turn his gunnery to the best account." The two officers had previously stated, however, that "an Admiral will always be fully cognisant of the capabilities and limitations of the guns and fire control fittings and arrangements of his fleet, he will guide his tactics accordingly, endeavouring so to control the tactical situation that the task of the guns will always be one to which they are fully equal." After warning that alterations in course were seriously detrimental to the accuracy and rapidity of firing and thus should not be resorted to, the authors admitted that both changes in course and speed after firing had opened would be unavoidable.[282]

After being described in great detail, the Dreyer and Argo systems were evaluated with respect to a list of "the requirements of an ideal fire control system." The Argo system was faulted mainly for not having a method of determining the average of several plotted ranges (in other words, the "mean range finder range of the moment") for direct setting or correction of the clock; the use of true course plotting, which was dismissed on the basis of the results of the defective runs carried out by the *Natal* in the summer of 1910; and the absence of an alternative hand drive for the clock. The description of the Dreyer Table, on the other hand, which was written by Dreyer, not surprisingly failed to mention any of the defects that have been discussed previously, and Usborne's critique maintained that the instrument was considered to have embodied all the features of the "ideal fire control system." In the summary of the report the two authors concluded that the Dreyer Table was

in every way a practical instrument designed to meet the real requirements of Naval action, in so far as we can foresee them, and no one but a Naval Officer, working with ample personal experience of fire control behind him, could have produced it.

Similarly, the A.C. system is the embodiment, perhaps the most perfect embodiment, of a system conceived by a civilian. The system is an attractive one, and may have real advantages, but it is not based on a full apprehension of the real conditions of action, and cannot be compared in value with the Dreyer.[283]

James Swinburne, in his nine-page report on the patent aspects of the Pollen case, began by stating that he did "not differ as to anything" in what appears to have been the historical narrative produced by Dreyer and Usborne,[284] but warned later on that he had "no knowledge of [the] history, except as gathered from the patent specifications." Swinburne advised that the patents protecting the Dreyer and Argo systems were not in conflict, and also noted that the Dreyer Clock's capacity to indicate ranges graphically next to the range plot was a valuable feature which the Argo Clock did not possess. But there could be no doubt as to his preference for the Argo instrument. "Pollen's arrangement as a machine," he observed, "is much more complete than Dreyer's, and given accurate data it will do much more." With the addition of certain features of the Dreyer table, such as the generation of a range graph by the clock, Swinburne maintained that the Argo Clock "would be, as far as I understand the matter, really ahead of the present system, though it is behind it taken just as it stands." There was no question that "to allow the Pollen clock to be sold to other Powers would be giving them all the knowledge that is embodied in the Dreyer."[285]

The report of the Contracts Department on the Admiralty's business relations with Pollen and the Argo Company, which was over thirty pages long, portrayed Pollen as an inventor who had been generously treated by the Admiralty, who in return had sought unreasonably high profits in his negotiations, and whose threats to sell his system abroad amounted to blackmail. The decision to abandon monopoly was defended on the grounds that

> the Pollen system is not of first importance to the Navy in view of the alternative Service apparatus available. . . ., that any features of the Pollen system which it may be thought desirable to instal can now be obtained on ordinary commercial terms . . ., that secrecy and monopoly in such apparatus cannot be preserved for any very long time . . ., that if secrecy had been continued the Argo Company would have obtained more and more insight into Service conditions, &c., and could have thus taken away more and more valuable information when the inevitable moment of release from secrecy eventually arrived. . . ., that the Aim Corrector or Pollen system considered as a whole will not, in the opinion of technical experts, be of great advantage to any foreign nation adopting it, owing to certain inherent defects of the system. . . ., [and] that trials will be the necessary consequence, should any foreign nation consider the system favourably, and that should they, after such trials, decide to incorporate a part of the Pollen system into their own systems, as H.M. Navy did in 1910, it can confidently be anticipated that by the time their decision has taken effect the British Navy will have approached much nearer perfection in respect of such part, and will have nothing to fear from such a course.[286]

A draft of the historical section of the Dreyer-Usborne report, which was finished by late February or early March, and the Contracts Department report, which was printed in March, probably had a great influence on Churchill. In February, the First Lord—in response to the representations of John Walter, the owner of *The Times* and a large shareholder in the Argo Company, who had urged that steps be taken in the national interest to prevent public disclosure of the Argo patents—apparently agreed to make an offer for monopoly.[287] On 24 March, however, Churchill wrote in reply to a subsequent communication with Walter that "you may entirely dismiss from your mind the idea that the point at issue involves a risk of national disaster such as you appear to imagine."[288] In March and April, Usborne drafted the section of the *Technical History and Technical Comparison* that dealt with the Argo system with the assistance of Pollen, who in April was able to report that a prototype of his new true course plotting table had been completed.[289] In May, the complete Dreyer-Usborne report was printed for restricted circulation, which was just before Churchill was confronted by inquiries in the press and in Parliament about the fire control question. But although the Swinburne report, whose contents raised serious doubts as to the wisdom of Admiralty policy, was completed in early March, it was not printed until August—that is, not until after the furor in the press and in Parliament had subsided and negotiations between the Admiralty and the Argo Company had finally broken down.[290]

The Admiralty did not reply to the letter from the legal representatives of the Argo Company of 15 March until 30 April, at which time they took strong exception to the accusation that the rights of the inventor and his firm had been disregarded, and restated and explained their position at considerable length.[291] While the Admiralty and the Argo Company's lawyers were engaged in further legal correspondence,[292] Pollen took a number of steps that he hoped would lay the groundwork for an amicable settlement. In May, he retained Robert Bannatyne Finlay, a distinguished lawyer who had served as Attorney-General, to give his view of the question of the Argo Company's right to publish their complete patents, in the hope that such an authoritative opinion, which Pollen's attorneys had assured him must favor the Argo Company, would carry some weight with the Admiralty.[293] On 10 June, the board of directors of the Argo Company decided to accommodate the Admiralty to the extent of having the foreign patent for the clock drawn in a way that omitted the rate dials but allowed for their addition at a later date pending the completion of Finlay's opinion,[294] although this was not communicated to the Admiralty until 30 June in a meeting, about which more later.

On 2 June, Stephen Pollen had once again sought an interview with Churchill and when this was refused, on 13 June asked that the question of the rate dials and mechanism of the clock be submitted to the judgement of an independent legal authority, a request that was also turned down.[295] Churchill's refusal to deal with the Pollens may have had something to do with resentment of the fact that by mid June the Argo Clock had become a matter of public controversy. As early as in May, John Walter had anticipated that the abandonment of secrecy issue would become the subject of a press debate in which "it might be necessary for *The Times* to take a part," and had both resigned his position on the board of the Argo Company and disposed of his shares in order to avoid charges of conflict of interest.[296] And in mid June 1913, Pollen informed the editors of the leading newspapers that the Admiralty had abandoned secrecy and that the embargo against published references to his system, which he had requested them to enforce in the national interest in the spring of 1910, had ended.[297]

The fact that this was the case had been virtually announced by the publication of an account of the Argo system in an article on gunnery by Commander C. N. Robinson in the 1913 issue of the *Naval Annual*, which had appeared in late May or early June. After giving a history and general description of Pollen's system, Robinson noted that Pollen had "apparently succeeded in perfecting instruments of incalculable value for finding and keeping the rate at long range."[298] On 19 June 1913, the *Western Daily Mercury* published a favorable account of the development of the Pollen system based upon the article in the *Naval Annual*. This piece, however, mistakenly reported that the Admiralty had adopted the Argo system which, the author believed, illustrated "the willingness of the Naval authorities to deal with private inventors when they really have anything to offer worth acceptance—thereby disproving the traditional belief that Whitehall is hopelessly unapproachable in this respect."[299]

Newspaper reports of the great success of the *Orion* in Battle Practice presented a very different view of the relations between the Argo Company and the Admiralty. In mid June, the excellence of the shooting of the *Orion* in Battle Practice was such as to prompt Percy Scott to exclaim upon being told of the results that it was "either a lie or a miracle."[300] The connection between the Argo Clock and the *Orion*'s success was first reported in an article in *The Times* on 21 June. The *Orion*, *The Times* stated, had "broken all 'records',", and that "unless the firing of other ships is very exceptional, her performance cannot be eclipsed." The paper then noted that these results, as well as those obtained in the experimental firings of the previous November under much more difficult conditions, had been obtained through the use of the Argo Clock. On 23 June, the *Daily Chronicle* reported that the Admiralty had rejected the Pollen system, but the next day noted that Pollen had informed the paper that negotiations were still in progress so that "the announcement that the foreign patents had already been taken out, and secrecy consequently already lost, is premature."[301]

On 27 June, *The Times* provided additional information on the *Orion*'s Battle Practice, noting that "she is credited with between 40 and 45 per cent. of [hits] to rounds fired" and that "her number of hits would have been 50 per cent. higher but for certain deflection errors that crept in." *The Times* correspondent then stated that the *Orion* "is the only ship so far fitted with the Pollen Clock" and that "there seems to be a widespread feeling here that as soon as these appliances are in more general use the conditions of battle practice should be made more exacting, so as to ascertain exactly what extension of gunnery possibilities the Pollen system throws open." On 28 June, the *Daily Chronicle* revealed that Robert Harcourt, a Liberal MP, intended to ask the First Lord to provide the House of Commons with answers to the following questions:

Whether an automatic fire-control system invented by a Mr. Pollen was in whole or part used by H.M.S. Orion at her recent battle practice.

Whether the good firing results obtained by that ship are attributable to the use of this system.

Whether it is intended to adopt the Pollen system or any other fire-control system in the British Navy.

Whether the Admiralty has co-operated with Mr. Pollen in the development of his system; and

Whether it is proposed to take any steps to prevent it being acquired by other nations.[302]

Harcourt's questions were formally addressed to Churchill in Parliament on 30 June. "I am informed," the First Lord stated in reply,

that some portions of Mr. Pollen's apparatus were used, but they were not used in accordance with the Pollen system. The good shooting was not attributable either to the Pollen apparatus or to any employment of the Pollen system. It is not intended to adopt the Pollen system, but to rely on a more satisfactory one which has been developed by service experts. In reply to the last part of the question, the Admiralty has given Mr. Pollen considerable assistance, in the hope of obtaining a valuable system of fire-control in the Navy. The results obtained with his system, and the principles underlying it, are such that it is not proposed to take any steps to prevent him making public use of all its essential features. This he can do without divulging official secrets connected with the service system, and he will, of course, be precluded from disclosing service secrets, of which his connection with the Admiralty has given him knowledge, or from any infringement of the Official Secrets Act, which, I have every confidence, will be respected.

Churchill closed by observing that the discussion of fire control questions in the newspapers "could not lead to any intelligible conclusion, or be attended by any public advantage" and that in so far as the technical aspects of the particular case at hand were concerned, that he had "been guided by the representations of my naval colleagues and the advice of the experts, on whom the Admiralty must rely."[303]

Churchill's contention that the Argo Clock had not been used in accordance with the Pollen system was presumably based upon the fact that it was set with data from the Argo rate plotter, a "system" that Dreyer claimed had originated with him.[304] Pollen's response to the First Lord's remarks, were limited to a brief statement printed in *The Times* on 1 July that noted that competitive trials had not taken place.

This was followed the next day, however, by a letter to the editor of *The Times* written over the pseudonym "Emeritus." The writer was actually none other than Sir Charles Inigo Thomas, the late Admiralty Permanent Secretary who had been privy to the negotiations between Pollen and the Admiralty in that capacity from 1907 through 1911. Thomas criticized the failure of the board to base its decision on competitive trials, pointed out that it was Pollen who had "led naval thought" in the direction of systematically taking account of relative motion as the prerequisite to effective naval gunnery, maintained that the service had put forward an inferior variant of Pollen's work in 1908 as a superior alternative, suggested that further trials with the existing service alternative might demonstrate that history had been repeated, and observed that Churchill's predecessors had not simply relied on the advice of experts, but insisted upon conclusive trials. Thomas's concluding paragraphs were particularly strong. "For 14 years Mr. Pollen has worked at his invention," he wrote,

> and successfully kept it secret in the interests of the country, but to his own commercial detriment. In these circumstances it seems less than just, and much less than generous, that the First Lord should in his speech have included a covert threat of using the Official Secrets Act against him.
>
> That there is a strong feeling in the Navy in favour of the A.C. system is undeniable. With the experts divided, and no definite authoritative results by which the controversy can finally be settled, it is surely premature to part with a secret of which so high an opinion is held, for the believers in the Pollen system are quite as eminent in professional attainments as the official experts who are once more in opposition to it.
>
> Lastly, the wisdom of giving up a fire control system acknowledged to be the foundation of our own, developed entirely within the Navy and largely at public expense, must be very questionable, especially in the absence of any evidence that foreigners possess any system as scientifically thought out or as thoroughly developed.[305]

Although the absence of evidence makes it impossible to establish the exact extent of his involvement with the press and with Harcourt's queries, Pollen appears to have at least entertained some hope that the Admiralty would be made to soften its position, if not reconsider it altogether, as a result of public pressure.[306] But in a meeting on 30 June, at which time Hawksley advised representatives of the Admiralty that the Argo Company was willing to omit, for the time being, reference to the rate dials and associated mechanism of the Argo Clock,[307] he was informed verbally by Black, the Director of Navy Contracts, that in addition to these, the Admiralty would now insist upon the excision of additional features, a position that was confirmed in writing on 3 July.[308] In a second meeting at the Admiralty on 4 July, between Russell Clarke on the one hand, and Black, Minter and Usborne on the other, Pollen's patent counsel pressed for the withdrawal of the proscription of one of the additional mechanisms on the grounds that it had already been published in a patent taken out by Barr & Stroud, a request that was subsequently turned down by Usborne in a telephone conversation with Clarke.[309]

After Pollen had met with the Argo board, the Argo Company's attorneys and Russell Clarke, the Argo Company informed the Admiralty on 8 July that the new restrictions and the fact that the Admiralty had, according to Hawksley, refused to have the matter submitted to arbitration, showed that "the views of the Company and of the Admiralty are irreconcilable, and leaves the Company no alternative but to have its rights to the two patents determined by the Courts."[310] In a second letter to the Admiralty of the same date the Argo Company stated that we shall apply for foreign patents on the inventions in dispute, and shall show our apparatus to the representatives of foreign powers in its present complete form on the 20th day of July, unless in the meantime Their Lordships offer to consent to an arbitration as to who is entitled to the invention, or move to restrain us by injunction from taking this course, or commence a prosecution under the Official Secrets Act.[311]

In its reply of 12 July, the Admiralty expressed surprise at the "entirely different attitude" taken by the firm in their letters of 8 July, noted that the question of the omission of the additional mechanisms was considered to be still negotiable, and offered to reopen discussions.[312] Two days later the Argo Company categorically refused the Admiralty's offer. "From previous correspondence," Pollen explained in a letter of 14 July,

we had understood that the Admiralty's demands were based upon the assertions (1) that the disputed linkages were Service inventions, and (2) that they were communicated to us in the course of confidential relations with the Navy. We are advised that were they truly Service inventions, and communicated to us, the Admiralty would have legal grounds for demanding their suppression; but if they were our own unaided inventions, and not communicated to us by the Service, then the Admiralty could have no legal grounds for such a demand, whatever the consequences of publication.

Up to July 3rd, therefore, the issue seemed to be one of ownership only. We then realised that our conception of the Admiralty position was at fault. On that day as set out in your letter, a proposed method of setting our Clock, which is already accessible to the public, was objected to on the ground that it "would risk the disclosure of the Service secret system." We are advised that such a risk does not of itself afford any legal ground for objecting to our patent, and consequently that the Admiralty is taking ground outside the law. In other words, while we are founding our case on what is purely a matter of fact, namely, whose is the invention? the Admiralty are founding theirs on an administrative necessity, namely, to prevent a device being put upon the market which could endanger the secrecy of the Service system.

At the time of the interviews, our willingness to take out a partial patent was due to the fact that we hoped the question of ownership was one on which we could convince Their Lordships' advisers; but if the Admiralty's position is based not on ownership but on policy, any such attempt must be a mere waste of time.[313]

"I have been besieged by journalists and politicians," Pollen had confided to Spender on 11 July 1913, "who want me to help them attack the Admiralty for adopting an inferior form of Fire Control."[314] But the inventor had good reason to believe that further public debate over the question of monopoly would only have increased the intransigence of the Admiralty and compromised secrecy as well, while additional delays in the application for foreign patents would have jeopardized the financial interests of the Argo Company.

By the summer of 1913, moreover, Pollen's strongest sources of service support had been dispersed or otherwise rendered ineffective. In December 1912, Peirse had been appointed to command British naval forces in the East Indies. Percy Scott, who had been the target of a vituperative personal attack in the press and inquiries in Parliament beginning in early 1913, had announced that he would retire from the service in March.[315] The Inspectorate of Target Practice had supported Pollen strongly against the Ordnance Department since 1908. But Peirse's successor as Inspector of Target Practice, Captain Montague Browning, who took office in 1911, while a believer in the Argo system, was also a Beresfordite and thus a bitter foe of Percy Scott and director firing.[316] There can be little doubt that the Admiralty came to the opinion that such conflict between the Ordnance Department and the Inspectorate over gunnery fundamentals could no longer be tolerated, and in August 1913 the latter was abolished.[317] Pollen's confidence in the strength of his legal position, on the other hand, was bolstered by Finlay's opinion on the Argo case, which was given on 23 July 1913 and confirmed that given earlier by Clarke.[318]

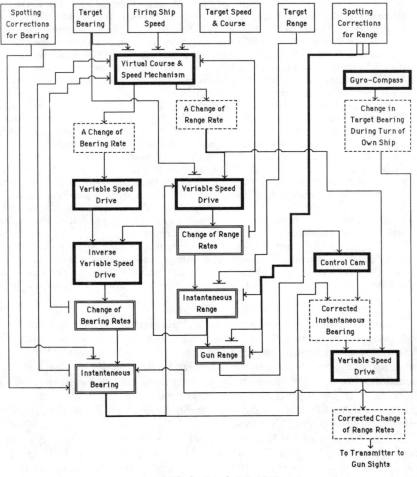

Argo Clock, Mark V, 1913

246

Further correspondence between the Argo Company and the Admiralty over the patent question in July and August was unproductive, and the negotiations came to an end.[319] On 10 September 1913 the Argo Company advised the Admiralty that the Mark IV Clock had been improved by the addition of a gyroscope that corrected the bearing setting of the clock when the firing ship was turning, and offered to demonstrate a prototype of the new instrument, which was known as the Argo Clock Mark V, in five weeks (see Diagram 5).[320] This offer was declined on 8 October.[321] In early September, the Argo Company, in accordance with advice contained in Finlay's opinion, informed the Admiralty that they would file for foreign patents within the next several weeks "unless in the meantime their Lordships apply for an injunction restraining the Company from taking such Action."[322]

In September 1912, Pollen had opened negotiations through Sir Charles Ottley, who had been Director of Naval Intelligence from 1905 to 1907 and appears to have been a Pollen supporter,[323] with the Armstrong Whitworth Board in the hopes of securing a satisfactory manufacturing agreement that would enable the Argo Company quickly to produce its instruments in quantity. The discussions had broken down in 1913, however, when the large armaments firm was informed by the Admiralty that the Official Secrets Act would bar the sale of certain parts of the Argo system.[324] The Argo Company's lack of capital, which hampered its preparations to sell abroad, appear to have been to some extent remedied in mid 1913 by a new share issue amounting to £25,000, of which a certain proportion was accepted by Cooke & Sons in partial payment for goods manufactured.[325] In September 1913, the Argo Company published *The Necessity of Fire Control*, a brief and lucid explanation of the principles upon which its instruments were founded, which was meant to acquaint potential foreign buyers with Pollen's basic ideas on gunnery.[326]

The Argo Company began its sales campaign in September, probably having in stock at this time 3 Argo Clock Mark IVs, 3 Pollen-Cooke Range-finders with improved mountings, and one helm-free/true-course plotting table (A.C. Course and Speed Plotter, Mark IV), all of which had been ordered from Cooke & Sons in late 1912 in addition to the five Argo Clocks (the sixth was in the *Orion*) that were to go to the Royal Navy.[327] By the summer of 1914, the Argo Company had reached agreements with Russia and Austria-Hungary,[328] negotiations with Brazil and Chile were practically concluded,[329] and discussions with favorable prospects were underway with the United States.[330] Interest had been expressed, in addition, by Turkey, Greece, Italy and France.[331] It would appear that the major problem for Pollen was not lack of orders, but rather the difficulty of expanding the manufacturing capacity of Cooke & Sons to meet foreign demand.[332]

The Argo Company, perhaps partly in deference to the Admiralty's wishes but probably mainly in the belief that rate-plotting was useless, did not at first market or even mention the existence of an Argo rate-plotter, although one, it will be remembered, had been built for the *Orion*.[333] In the course of discussing fire control requirements with foreign buying commissions, however, Pollen learned that the plotting of ranges and bearings to obtain separate range and bearing rates was employed by practically all other navies. "Almost every Commission," Pollen wrote to Craig after his sales campaign had begun,

> has asked us whether we can adopt our plotting system to rate plotting, if we have tried rate plotting and what our opinion of it is. So far I have not found one case where they wish to persist with it after they have heard the argument pro true course plotting and contra rate plotting. . . . [334]

But a French report on the Argo system indicates that the French navy, at least, remained convinced in the efficacy of rate plotting,[335] and foreign interest in this method seems to have been such that the Argo Company asked the Admiralty for permission to market a rate plotter, a request that was apparently granted on the condition that it did not incorporate a means of "graphically indicating in the plotting chart the gun range in use on the clock."[336]

The reasons that the Russian naval command decided in favor of the Argo system were explained to Pollen after the sale by what may have been the Russian Naval attaché in London. "I do not think that our ordnance advisers," wrote the Russian officer in a revealing letter,

> would have recommended such elaborate instruments, only as a substitute for present organisation, although their value in diminishing errors is not disputed. They said that even this advantage might not justify devices that require special functionaries to keep them in order. It was the consideration of the tactical question by the General Staff that overcame all objections. The possibility that its success will enable long range fire to be effective, while the firing ship is manoeuvering, would be an advance in the art of naval warfare which, we frankly admit, cannot be too dearly purchased.
>
> I must tell you, that the refusal of the British Admiralty to try your system, after keeping it a secret for so long, did for some time appear a serious objection to our minister. It was your analysis of the action conditions, and your explanation of your instrumental synthesis of the operations which these conditions made necessary, that carried the decision in your favour.[337]

The breakdown of discussions with the Argo Company in late July prompted the Admiralty to issue an order to all major naval commands that communication with Pollen or representatives of the Argo Company on any matter pertaining to gunnery was strictly prohibited.[338] Although the Admiralty did not immediately reply to the notice and actions of the Argo Company in September 1913 with regard to the complete disclosure of their patents, the question of taking the issue to the courts was at least considered. In February 1914, however, Tudor advised against taking civil action against the Argo Company, on the grounds that

> if this matter be brought into the Law Courts, there is always the possibility of our fire control system becoming known.
>
> It is also considered that it would be bad policy to do this, for the advantages to be gained are small, and it is probable that the Admiralty's reasons for prosecuting the Argo Co. would be misunderstood.[339]

No mention was made of the legal weakness of the Admiralty case. In April 1914, the Director of Naval Ordnance was reduced to counselling that "it is considered most undesirable" that an Admiralty letter to the Argo Company that contained stipulations against the disclosure of service secrets

> should take the form of a warning. Up to the present such letters seem to have had the opposite effect to that desired, and it is suggested that the communication should take the form of a request: should this be refused, it will leave the Admiralty in a far more dignified position than if a warning had been issued.[340]

(e) TECHNOLOGY, TACTICS, FINANCE AND POLITICS

The Admiralty's abandonment of the monopoly of the Argo system, refusal to place more than a limited order for the Argo Clock and relative indifference to the sale of the Argo system abroad after its legal bluff to restrict foreign sales had been called, can be explained to a great extent by the effect that certain technical, tactical, financial and political considerations had on the views of the Sea Lords on the naval gunnery question between 1912 and 1914.

Deliveries of both the Argo range-finder mounting and production Dreyer tables were well under way in 1912, and the new gear probably had been supplied to most if not all of Britain's dreadnoughts by late 1913. The operator of a range-finder on an Argo mounting could record and transmit more than twice as many ranges as an observer using a range-finder on a conventional mounting. In the firing trials carried out against the old battleship *Empress of India* in November 1913,[341] for example, Captain C. S. Hickey of the dreadnought battleship *Vanguard* reported that in seven minutes, 4 observations had been made with the range-finder in the main top and 10 with the range-finder in "A" turret, but that no less than 23 were obtained with the range-finder on the Argo mounting.[342] The combination of a more effective mounting for one instrument and the use of additional instruments greatly increased the number of range observations, and thus the potential accuracy of the range plot. The Dreyer tables, for all their shortcomings, nevertheless constituted a marked improvement over previous service fire control gear. These changes would have been enough to result in a substantial improvement in the gunnery performance of the Royal Navy under the prevailing conditions of Battle Practice.

It will be recalled that in September 1912, Vice-Admiral Peirse had maintained that the change of range rate in Battle Practice was 350 yards per minute. But in the *Orion*'s Battle Practice of 1912—which was probably typical—this rate was in effect for only the ten minutes before firing began, after which a change in course was made to reduce the change of range rate to 100 yards per minute, with firing taking place for ten minutes at ranges of between 8,000 and 7,000 yards.[343] If the experience of the *Vanguard* can be taken as a guide, a Dreyer rate plotter that was equipped to receive ranges from several range-finders—including one on an Argo mounting—would have been capable of being supplied with no fewer than five ranges a minute.[344] It would not, therefore, have been difficult to extract at least one "mean range-finder range of the moment" per minute from the time-and-range plot that approximated the instantaneous range, which given the low change of range rate, and very considerable margin for error for range that was allowed by both the relatively large "danger space" at ranges of less than 10,000 yards[345] and the fact that the projectiles of a big-gun salvo spread along a line 200 yards wide,[346] would have been frequent and accurate enough to correct the rate setting on the Vickers or Dreyer-Elphinstone Clock so that hits could be made.

This meant that the service system of gunnery came in effect to depend less upon the correct estimation of the target's course and speed as derived from a setting on the dumaresq of the change of range and bearing rates, and much more on the continuous correction of the clock by the output of "mean range-finder ranges of the moment" from the time-and-range plot. On 22 April 1914 the Director of Naval Ordnance thus wrote with regard to the indication of the "mean range-finder range of the moment" by the time-and-range plot, that

> it is the opinion of Gunnery Officers that it is the chief advantage of the present Dreyer's Fire Control Table, and has become the foundation of that system of fire control known as rangefinder control, which has produced such excellent results, and which will increase in importance as rangefinders increase in numbers and accuracy.[347]

Prior to the adoption of the Argo mounting and the Dreyer rate-plotter, service gunners had made do with various crude methods of manual plotting using observations from a single range-finder,[348] which must have meant that plotted ranges were too few in number to obtain either an accurate estimate of the rate or a close approximate of the instantaneous range. In 1911, as a consequence, a change in Battle Practice rules that made the conditions somewhat more difficult resulted in a sharp decline in performance that gave the Admiralty serious cause for concern. The fleet's performance in Battle Practice in 1912 and 1913—following the introduction of the new equipment—appears to have improved substantially.[349]

In November 1912, moreover, the dreadnought battleship *Colossus*, which was equipped with a rate plotter, dumaresq, Vickers Clock and the standard outfit of 9-foot base range finders, had achieved good results in experiments that involved firing at 14,000 yards, and although other conditions must have been extraordinarily favorable, Jellicoe and the Admiralty had been impressed.[350] In his memoirs, Dreyer maintained that the *Colossus* trials "demonstrated the sound lines on which naval gunnery was developing,"[351] and there can be little doubt that their apparent success had something to do with the Admiralty's decision of December not to maintain the secrecy of the Argo Clock.[352]

By 1912, it is probable that the first 15 dreadnought battleships and battle cruisers had been equipped with dumaresqs and Vickers Clocks. The Admiralty may have believed, moreover, that these 12-inch gun units had been superseded by the 13.5-inch gun capital ships of the 1909 program and their successors, and were thus unworthy of expensive upgrading. In any case, these units, with one exception, were the recipients of the Dreyer Table Mark I, which amounted to little more than a combination of a rate-plotter, dumaresq and Vickers Clock.[353] Outfits of dumaresqs and Vickers Clocks were most likely never ordered for the later 13.5-inch gun capital ships, which left the way open to their equipment with up-to-date instruments. Their newer design, in addition, made them more attractive candidates for costly improvement with brand new fire control gear.

Four of the 13.5-inch battleships and one battle cruiser were equipped with a Dreyer rate plotter that had been modified for use with the five Argo Clock Mark IVs, a combination that became known as the Dreyer Table Mark II. The *Orion* appears to have retained her Argo rate plotter and Argo Clock Mark IV. Four other battleships and two battle cruisers were equipped with the Dreyer rate plotter and the Dreyer-Elphinstone Clock, a combination that was known as the Dreyer Table Mark III. One battleship was equipped with an improved version of the Dreyer Table Mark III, which was known as the Dreyer Table Mark IV. For reasons that are not clear, one 12-inch gun battleship, the *Hercules*, was given a Mark III table, while one 13.5-inch gun battleship, the *Marlborough*, was fitted with a Mark I table.[354] Thus of the 28 British all-big-gun battleships and battle cruisers in service in July 1914, no fewer than 15, or more than half, were making do with second-class fire control gear, a state of affairs that was a measure, perhaps, of the strength of the Admiralty's faith in range-finder control.[355]

The belief that meaned ranges were sufficiently accurate for gunnery purposes, and over-confidence in the capability of the existing 9-foot base Barr & Stroud range-finder,[356] may also explain why none of the completed dreadnoughts were equipped with 15-foot base instruments, although these had been tested as early as 1909 and were under order in quantity by July 1914 for the battleships of the 1913-14 and 1914-15 programs.[357] The absence of urgency that characterized the Admiralty's attitude towards longer-base range-finders seems to have extended, moreover, to gunlaying instruments. By the summer of 1914, only a third of the dreadnoughts—which included none of the battle cruisers—had been fitted with directors.[358] And of these, not all used their instruments in Battle Practice, which were carried out under such ideal conditions of wind, wave and weather that higher scores could be achieved with independent laying.[359]

Range-finder control and independent gunlaying were, however, incapable of producing satisfactory results when firing conditions were more difficult than those of Battle Practice. In the spring of 1913, Rear-Admiral Beatty, the Commander-in-Chief of the Battle Cruiser Squadron, at the suggestion of Captain A. E. M. Chatfield, a Pollen supporter, had asked Admiral Sir George Callaghan, the Commander-in-Chief of the Home Fleet, for permission to carry out firing practice at near full speed, with a number of turns, and at ranges of 12,000 yards, in order "to find out defects in our material."[360] Callaghan was at first opposed, but Chatfield secured the backing of Callaghan's flag captain, Roger Backhouse, who was another Pollen sympathizer, and the exercise was approved. None of Beatty's battle cruisers were at this time equipped with either Argo Clocks or directors, and Chatfield later recalled that the exercise, which was carried out on 5 June 1913 revealed "weaknesses . . . from which we learnt valuable lessons."[361]

There can be little doubt that the experiment exposed the inadequacy of the service system of fire control and gunlaying under those conditions that involved shooting while maneuvering and steaming at high speed, which may have given rise to the rumor—reported in *The Times* on 27 June 1913—that all battle cruisers were to be equipped with both the Argo Clock and the Scott director.[362] The Admiralty, however, reproved Callaghan for having authorized such trials without their approval,[363] all battle cruisers were still without directors more than a year later, and only the battle cruiser *Queen Mary*, which was commissioned in the fall of 1913, received an Argo Clock Mark IV. The Admiralty's opposition to the trials and subsequent failure to take action may be explained in part by doubt that any system of fire control or gunlaying was capable of enabling battle cruisers to fire effectively at distant targets when steaming and changing course at full speed,[364] and concern that attempts to achieve what was considered to be impracticable would only assist Pollen's efforts to gain a rehearing of his case. A preoccupation with the fire control needs of a battleship as opposed to those of a battle cruiser action may also have been a factor.

Much of the Admiralty's satisfaction with the existing service system of fire control can, in addition, be explained by their assessments of the gunnery capabilities of the German navy. The Admiralty was probably aware that the German navy did not have a system of graphically meaning ranges and that sight-setting depended upon either rangefinder observations or ranges generated by a device that was comparable to the Vickers Clock that had been set with guess-estimates of the rate.[365] Reports on this clock prompted Captain Morgan Singer, the Director of Naval Ordnance, to observe in 1914 that the German system of fire control "could not compete with a high and varying change of range."[366]

There were, in addition, other strong indications that the Germans intended to fight a short range action. All German dreadnoughts, unlike practically all British dreadnoughts except those that entered service from 1914 onwards, possessed heavy secondary batteries. The Admiralty was aware that in the German equivalent of Battle Practice the main and secondary batteries were fired together at ranges that were as low as 2,200 yards, and that in maneuvers German torpedo craft worked in close conjunction with the battle line. In 1912, a special committee of the Department of Naval Ordnance had concluded, therefore, that the Germans intended to seek a short-range engagement in order to use fire from their secondary batteries to destroy the weakly protected secondary batteries of the British battleships, which would enable their torpedo craft to deliver an effective attack.[367] German capital ships also lacked the mast-head spotting positions that the British believed were essential for effective spotting when ranges were long.

In 1914, Pollen's Russian naval correspondent wrote that the lack of high observation positions and the German allocation of only one or two unarmoured range-finders per ship had indicated to the Russian naval command

> that point blank ranges will be sought, when the speed of the change of range and accuracy of range knowledge are both immaterial. Point blank ranges, it is believed [by the German Navy], can be sought successfully and at little risk, by making a defensive use of the change of range, which arises from closing at high speed, for this, ex hypothesi, must be fatal to the hitting power of the enemy's artillery.

The Russian officer then informed Pollen

> that our people think, that the British Admiralty are quite aware of German views as to naval gunnery; indeed, it is thought that German military principles and doctrines have become more acceptable and carry greater authority with your Board, than used to be the case. Many things combine to show, that the present Board of Admiralty are no longer relying on the hope, that future battles will be fought at very long ranges, and that their policy of adopting more powerful guns has, as its primary motive, the capacity to destroy an enemy by a single blow. That the heavier shell may give an advantage at long ranges in favourable conditions, appears to be only a secondary consideration.[368]

The Admiralty, in short, appears to have believed that the German navy would seek a short-range engagement (that is, one that was probably fought at much less than 10,000 yards) by closing rapidly and that while neither side would be able to hit consistently during the approach phase, once the two battle lines had turned on to roughly parallel courses the advantages of range-finder control based upon time-and-range plotting, and heavier caliber main armaments, would give the British battle fleet a decisive fire power superiority.

The Admiralty view of the fire control question must also have been affected by financial considerations. The cost of an Argo Clock Mark IV, even assuming an order in quantity, would have been £1,350, while that of a helm-free/true-course plotter could not have come to much less than £1,000.[369] The cost, therefore, of outfitting a single capital ship with the Argo system—not including the Argo mounting, which had already been purchased—would have amounted to at least £2,350. The cost of the Dreyer rate plotter was £138, while that of the Dreyer-Elphinstone Clock was £500.[370] The total amount required to outfit a single battleship with even the Dreyer Table Mark III or IV could not have exceeded £700, which was less than one third that of the sum that would have been spent on the Argo equivalent. And it should be remembered that 15 dreadnoughts received only the Dreyer Table Mark I—which meant merely adding a rate plotter to the dumaresq and Vickers Clock already in service—which for all 15 ships could have cost no more than £2,070, or less than what would have been spent on a single unit with Argo gear.

As it was, the equipping of 6 dreadnoughts with the Dreyer Table Mark II or Argo plotter and an Argo Clock Mark IV (at the limited production price of £2,133 each) must have involved charges of some £13,300, as compared with the £6,970 spent on providing the other 22 capital ships with all-service instruments. The supply of the entire dreadnought battle fleet with Argo plotters and clocks, at semi-limited production prices—that is, in quantities greater than 5 but fewer than 96—would probably have amounted to well over £70,000, or three times what was actually spent on the mix of Argo and service gear.[371] Economies in naval spending demanded by the Liberal government in the face of sharply rising expenditure on capital ship construction had forced a considerable reduction in even so basic a gunnery commodity as practice ammunition,[372] and given the conviction that German tactical intentions were such as to make it unnecessary to possess a fire control system that was capable of dealing with high and changing change of range rates when ranges were long, there can be little doubt that the "cost-effectiveness" issue weighed heavily in the Admiralty's deliberations.

There was, finally, a political factor. In December 1912, the apostasy of Battenberg and Jellicoe, who had been long-time supporters of Pollen, ensured that the monopoly of the Argo Clock, as well as of the entire Argo system, would not be secured for the Royal Navy. Although Jellicoe was probably convinced of the technical superiority of the Dreyer Table,[373] Battenberg appears to have acted as he did in order to avoid dividing the Sea Lords, whose authority was then being threatened by the First Lord. By October 1912, Churchill's habit of taking actions without consulting the service members of the board had resulted in serious discord,[374] and in November 1912, Churchill had all but forced Bridgeman, who as First Sea Lord had staunchly opposed the First Lord's assumption of prerogatives normally exercised by the Sea Lords, into retirement.[375]

Jellicoe, who had rejoined the Admiralty as Second Sea Lord as a replacement for Battenberg, who had risen to take the place of Bridgeman as First Sea Lord, later recalled "it did not take me long to find out that Mr. Churchill, the First Lord, was very apt to express strong opinions upon purely technical matters; moreover, not being satisfied with expressing opinions, he tried to force his views upon the Board." Jellicoe went on to observe that Churchill's "wonderful argumentative powers" enabled him to "make a weak case appear exceedingly strong," which became

> a positive danger when the First Lord started to exercise his powers of argument on his colleagues on the Board. Naval officers are not brought up to argue a case, and but few of them can make a good show in this direction. Moreover, if one is apt to be over-ridden in argument, as was certainly the case with one of the Sea Lords on the Board at that time, it made the position very difficult for the remainder of the Board.[376]

On those several occasions when, as has already been related, Churchill raised the Pollen question, Battenberg, who was probably the weak member of the board referred to by Jellicoe,[377] may have found it expedient, regardless of any misgivings, to support both Jellicoe and Moore in the interest of maintaining the collective service front upon which he depended in the absence of the will or ability to stand up to Churchill on his own. Pollen later recalled that in December 1912, he had begged his friend

> to put his foot down and insist upon a competitive trial between the two systems—the trial that Churchill had promised me verbally in the summer. But it was all to no purpose. I got the impression that he was so intent on being First Sea Lord that he wouldn't risk any hostile opinions amongst his colleagues. He seemed to be not sure of his hold over Churchill. There was too much at stake. He came very near admitting as much to me when after the war I met him for the first time since 1912 and for the last time altogether. It was a tragic story.[378]

And once the Sea Lords had placed themselves in opposition to the adoption of the Pollen system, they could not allow either the deliberation of an impartial committee of experts or the carrying out of a competitive trial, whose outcomes might have raised questions of their capacity to advise the First Lord on technical matters, which in turn would almost certainly have encouraged Churchill's propensity to interfere. For Pollen then, the problem with Churchill may not have been that he was an unwilling or incapable advocate, but rather that he was so much the reverse that his support of the Argo cause raised larger issues of civil versus naval—to say nothing of amateur versus professional—control of policy. But in any case, the combination of the united front put up by the Sea Lords and the technical complexity of the issues, which undoubtedly prevented Churchill from feeling entirely confident of his ground, put the First Lord off the hunt.

Service confidence in the Admiralty's gunnery policy was by no means complete. In an addendum to the gunnery orders issued to the Home Fleet on 5 November 1913, Admiral G. A. Callaghan warned his command that it was not to be supposed

> that reliance should be placed unhesitatingly on plotted results; on the contrary, until it is reported that the plot is a good one, and the concurrence of the spotter is obtained to "R.F. control" being adopted, the range should be maintained in the usual manner by means of the Dumaresq and range clock. The degree to which the range plots can be trusted will depend on the spread of the R.F.s, [sic] as well as on the experience of the officer in charge of the table.

Callaghan later observed that range-finder control was likely to be compromised by "lapses from accuracy to which R.F. operators are liable"; "unfavourable light, smoke, or other interference with R.F. observers" and "the range being too great for the accuracy of the R.F.s." He thus suggested that gunnery officers would have to be prepared, in the event of these conditions arising, "to revert to the alternative system, *i.e., maintaining the Range by means of the Rate*, for which purpose a Dumaresq is essential, and should always be ready."[379]

The service alternative to the Pollen system may have satisfied the requirements of a battleship action under favorable conditions, but without fire control instruments that could deal with high and changing change of range rates, and the disruptions of visibility that were bound to occur in battle, battle cruisers manifestly lacked the capability to hit at long range while maneuvering and steaming at high speed. In spite of this fact, Fisher persisted in his belief that British capital ships possessed the ability to hit before they could be struck in return, that heavy armour was thus unnecessary and that, therefore, the battleship should be replaced by the battle cruiser.

3 "The Romance of Design": Fisher and the Battle Cruiser, 1910-1914[380]

Although Fisher retired from the service in February 1910, he subsequently attempted to influence, if not control, the direction of Britain's naval affairs through the communication of his ideas to friends in the press, industry and government. By the spring of 1910, the implementation of the Lloyd George budget was assured by the Liberal victory in the general election, and Fisher must have recognized that great increases in spending on the navy were now possible. In April 1910, he thus greeted W. T. Stead's call in *The Standard* for a "2 keels to 1" capital ship program measured against that of Germany with enthusiasm, on the grounds that such a policy would produce a navy that was strong enough to dominate the Pacific as well as the Atlantic.[381] The creation of an effective two–ocean navy was not, however, to be based simply upon increased numbers, but would require changes in capital ship design as well. "The keel is laid (though no one knows it)," he confided to Gerard Fiennes, a journalist and friend, on 14 April 1910,

> of that great Pacific Fleet, which is to be in the Pacific what our Home Fleet is in the Atlantic and North Sea—the *Mistress of that Ocean as our Home Fleet is of the Atlantic.* So don't go blazing away at a want of something which is truly coming, but you can "cocker it up" [that is, gloss it over] by judicious phrasing to keep our Pacific children [the Dominions] to their task. The 3 'New Testament' ships, with their attendant satellites, will be in the Pacific in 1913. That marks the first step.[382]

The "New Testament" ships meant battle cruisers, while "attendant satellites" referred to destroyers, and the significance of such a combination had been revealed a month before.

On 16 March 1910, Rear-Admiral Reginald Bacon presented a paper at the spring meeting of the Institution of Naval Architects entitled "The Battleship of the Future." Bacon at this time maintained that the invention and improvement of the torpedo had exposed the battleship to effective attack by smaller vessels, that the deployment of battleships in close-order linear formations increased the likelihood that torpedoes would hit, that larger hulls were less susceptible to critical damage from torpedoes than smaller hulls, that within anticipated battle ranges—which Bacon estimated to be 6,000 yards—armour-piercing projectiles "could penetrate any thickness of armour that could be practically mounted in a ship," and that high speed was of great strategical and tactical value. He thus concluded that

> the functions of the large cruiser will, therefore, be assumed by the battleship, high speed will become more and more necessary, and armour protection will be less accentuated than at present. The link between the ocean-going destroyer and the battleship will become closer, and we may reasonably expect that the huge monsters of the future will always be accompanied by torpedo craft of high seagoing speed as defensive and offensive satellites.
>
> The battleship as now known will probably develop from a single ship into a battle-unit consisting of a large armoured cruiser with attendant torpedo craft. Line of battle, as we now know it, will be radically modified, and the fleet action of the future will, in course of time, develop into an aggregation of duels between opposing battle units.[383]

Bacon's ideas may have been an important factor in the design of the *Lion* class battle cruisers, to which he had probably been an important contributor as Director of Naval Ordnance. Fisher, in any case, was convinced that the advent of the *Lion*, which was to be armed with the new 13.5-inch gun, was comparable in significance to that of the *Dreadnought*. "Observe the Lion," he wrote to J. A. Spender on 8 August 1910,

> launched yesterday. None of your shore-going people can in the least realize her unparalleled power! The *Dreadnought is a flea-bite to her!* The 13-inch gun and 70,000 horsepower give fighting results . . . [384]

"The Lion," he insisted to Reginald McKenna, the First Lord, on 22 August 1910, "[is] as superior to the *Dreadnought* as the *Dreadnought* to all before her . . ."[385] And on 15 October 1910, Fisher advised Arthur J. Balfour, the leader of the Conservative-Unionist opposition, that

> our magnificent new 13 1/2-inch gun being put in our ships now building before they, the Germans, had any inkling of it has knocked them into a cocked hat! It is as superior to the 12-inch as the 12-inch to a pea-shooter! [386]

Bacon's concept of a super battle cruiser must have closely approximated Fisher's own views on capital ship design.[387] On 19 July 1910, Fisher had advised Fiennes that Bacon's paper was "worth your study."[388] The next year Fiennes wrote *The Ocean Empire: Its Dangers and Defence*, in which he maintained that the *Lion* class would "be capable of taking their own part in a fleet-action, equally with the newest and best battle-ships" and that the effective defence of the empire depended upon the ability of the battle cruiser to steam long distances at high speed.[389] Fisher may also have discussed the battle cruiser question with Julian Corbett, an historian and friend.[390] In Corbett's *Some Principles of Maritime Strategy*, which was published in 1911, the writer wondered whether the existing distinctions between battleships, cruisers and flotilla vessels were justifiable, and suggested in particular that the battleship and cruiser might be combined. "What Nelson felt for," Corbett noted, "was a battleship of cruiser speed."[391]

In the fall of 1911, the Admiralty was considering the design of the capital ships of the 1912-13 program, and in particular whether or not to replace the 13.5-inch gun with an even larger piece, and whether or not to change fuel from coal to oil. Winston Churchill, the new First Lord, asked Fisher for his views on the subject, which were given in secret meetings at the Admiralty in late October and repeated during a meeting on the Admiralty yacht in mid November. Fisher, in addition, wrote a series of letters to Churchill in which he presented a clear and comprehensive statement of his radical conception of the battle cruiser.

From the beginning, Fisher expressed his strong opposition to proposals to build fast battleships rather than battle cruisers and the retention of the 6-inch gun secondary battery that had been introduced with the ships of the 1911-12 program. On 9 November 1911, Fisher insisted to Churchill that a new model battle cruiser named *Non-Pareil* would

> work out half a million sterling cheaper and 50 per cent more powerful than the d—d hybrid you mentioned to me.
> . . . . For God's sake don't have either armour or the 6 inch gun for the Anti-Torpedo armament. *It's silly utter rot! Speed—Big Gun* and *Cheapness* those are the 3 Fundamentals—& you can have them.[392]

Like Bacon, Fisher was convinced that heavy armour was useless and that the torpedo threat could be neutralized by increasing the size of the hull, which was to be minutely subdivided to contain flooding in the event of a hit. On 10 November, he urged Churchill to "*reduce armour and increase subdivision.*"[393] On 13 November, Fisher again wrote to Churchill to explain that

> You only want enough thickness of armour to make the shell burst outside, and in most places where armour is put you don't want it at all. And as for the Torpedo Bogey '*Size & Subdivision*' is the War Cry![394]

Fisher was convinced that the fire control problem had been solved by the adoption of uniform-caliber armaments and that as a consequence the possession of a larger big-gun would enable British capital ships not only to hit harder, but to hit before they could be hit in return. Fisher thus differed from Bacon in believing that actions would take place at long ranges. "The 15 inch gun with big case shot," he maintained to Churchill on November 10, "will sweep everything into perdition up to the horizon!"[395] In his letter to the First Lord of 13 November, Fisher argued that German capital ships would be ground

> into tooth powder! when they can't reach the *Non-Pareil*!
> For superiority of speed—preponderance of gun calibre—and unity of armament (which means Fire Control in excelsis) enables you to
>
> I   Hit *First*   I   *When* you *Like*
> II   Hit *Hard* and to fight II   *How* you *Like*
> III Keep on Hitting   III *Where* you *Like*[396]

Churchill must have been convinced by Fisher at first, because on 10 November he informed Battenberg that he intended to press for the construction of 4 battle cruisers.[397] But by the end of the month

Churchill seems to have been persuaded by the Controller, Rear-Admiral Sir Charles Briggs, and Director of Naval Ordnance, Captain A. G. H. W. Moore, that the construction of battleships was still essential, and that the 1912-13 program should include both types.[398] Fisher was outraged. On 3 December, his letter to Churchill referred to "those two Slugs you have now got as Controller and Director of Naval Ordnance who want you to perpetuate Battleships of the *Tortoise* type all armour and no speed and inadequate armament and d—d costly as compared with a *far cheaper, far faster* and *63 per cent more powerful ship*!!"[399] "I absolutely disagree," Fisher wrote again to Churchill three days later,

> with your two effete experts. They woke me at 4 am with a start! A nightmare! The British Fleet were Spithead Forts, splendid armour but they couldn't move! The first desideratum of all is Speed! Your fools don't see it—They are always running about to see where they can put on a little more armour! to make it safer! *You don't go into Battle to be safe!* No, you go into Battle *to hit the other fellow in the eye first* so that he can't see you! Yes! you hit him first, you hit him hard and you keep on hitting. *That's your safety!* You don't get hit back! Well! that's the improved 13 1/2 inch gun! but dissociated from *dominating speed*—Big Speed—30 knots—you don't care a d—n then whether your bottoms dirty or a compartment bashed in with a torpedo making you draw water because you have a big margin of speed over your Noah's Ark Dreadnoughts of 21 knots![400]

Fisher was certain that the introduction of a new model capital ship of greatly superior design would upset German building plans as had been the case with the *Dreadnought*. "THE GREAT SECRET," he explained to the First Lord on 13 February 1912,

> IS TO PUT OFF TO THE VERY LAST HOUR THE SHIP (big or little) *that you mean to build* (or PERHAPS NOT BUILD HER AT ALL!). You see all your rival's plans fully developed, their vessels started beyond recall, and then in each individual answer to each such rival vessel you plunge with a design 50 per cent. better! knowing that your rapid shipbuilding and command of money will enable you to have your vessel fit to fight as soon if not sooner than the rival vessel. Sometimes, as in one famous year, you can drop an armoured ship and put the money into acceleration of those building because you have a new design coming along, so don't be a d—d ass and deliberately lay down a ship which you know is obsolete by some sudden vast step in old Watts' brain! "*Sufficient for the year is the programme thereof.*"[401]

On several occasions, Fisher had stated that his proposed battle cruiser should be armed with eight or ten 15-inch guns, steam 30 knots, and cost less than £2 million.[402] On 22 April, Fisher once again pleaded the case for such vessels, asserting that "There MUST be the 15 inch gun . . . . There MUST be sacrifice of armour . . . . There must be further VERY GREAT INCREASE OF SPEED . . . . your speed must vastly exceed your possible enemy!"[403] In May 1912, however, the Admiralty settled on a compromise, which provided for the construction of a single group of vessels that to a great extent combined the attributes of the battleship and battle cruiser. The final fast battleship design approved by the Admiralty in July 1912, which was to become the *Queen Elizabeth* class, incorporated the 15-inch gun and oil fuel propulsion that Fisher had demanded, and was given heavy armour protection and a secondary battery of 6-inch guns, which limited speed to 24 knots—still 3 knots greater than the *Dreadnought*—and raised costs to £2.6 million.[404]

Fisher's immediate reaction to the new type does not seem to have been recorded, but by the fall of 1912 he was calling for the introduction of an even more radical variant of the battle cruiser. As early as in August 1910, Fisher had predicted to McKenna that a "coming 'Motor Battleship'" would be "as superior to the *Lion* as the *Lion* to the *Dreadnought!*"[405] In the fall of 1912, Fisher, not long after his assumption of the chairmanship of the Royal Commission on Fuel and Engines, a body that was charged with the task of providing information on oil as fuel for major warships,[406] began to insist upon the adoption of diesel engines for capital ships. On 14 September 1912, he provided Viscount Esher with a brief description of his proposals for a 25-knot diesel battleship that was to be named H.M.S. *Incomparable.*[407] In the early morning of 17 September 1912, Fisher produced a sketch of his imaginary vessel, which was to be armed with eight or ten 16-inch guns and a secondary battery of 6-inch guns. A central citadel that contained the armament and propulsion machinery was to be protected by a 16-inch thick belt and heavy armoured deck, with little or no armour on the ends. Fisher at first specified a speed of "26 knots at least," but then noted "Reduce the thickness of the armour and the number of 6-inch guns as necessary to get the *minimum of 30 knots speed.*"[408]

In his letter of 14 September, Fisher had informed Esher that he had approached Churchill with an offer to supervise the construction of an *Incomparable* in Canada as part of the anticipated Canadian dreadnought program. Following the rejection of this scheme, Fisher advised Esher on 20 September that he was planning to build his vessel with private funding. "The one all-pervading, all absorbing thought," he argued,

> is to get in first with motor ships before the Germans! Owing to our apathy during the last two years, they are ahead [with internal combustion engines]! *They have killed 15 men in experiments* [with oil engines] *and we have not killed one!* And a d—d fool of an English politician told me the other day that he thinks this creditable to us!

Fisher then gave Esher a vivid portrait of his conception. "Imagine a silhouette," he wrote,

> presenting a target 33 per cent less than any living or projected battleship! No funnels—no masts—no smoke—she carries over 5,000 tons of oil, enough to take her round the world without refuelling! *Imagine what that means!* Ten motor boats carried on board in an armoured pit in the middle of her, where [the] funnels and the boilers used to be. Two of these motor boats are over 60 feet long and go 45 knots! and carry 21-inch torpedoes that go 5 miles! *Imagine these let loose in a sea fight!* Imagine projectiles over a ton weight! going a mile or more further than even the 13 1/2-inch gun (which gun has rightly staggered humanity!).[409]

Fisher was certain that the elimination of funnels would make warships more difficult to identify and fleets less likely to betray their presence. "The one sole vital point for the Navy about the internal combustion engine," he maintained to Sir Charles Parsons, the manufacturer of marine turbine machinery,

> is that you get rid of a mass of funnels. I've seen a fleet 20 miles off and each ship spelling her name to me by her funnels! And a single jet of black smoke has in my experience disclosed a fleet 40 miles off![410]

Fisher's ideas apparently impressed designers at Vickers, who drew up detailed plans and an artistic illustration of a 25-knot diesel engine battleship that resembled the admiral's sketches.[411] On 14 October 1912, Fisher informed Parsons that "Vickers are absolutely confident they can produce a 25-knot Dreadnought equal to any building or projected ship and capable of going round the earth without refueling."[412] "I wish you could see your way," Fisher wrote again to Parsons on 3 November, "to the continuance of the turbine in connection with the internal combustion principle. . . ."[413]

But Parsons pointed out that the power-to-weight ratio of high-power diesel engines was not yet great enough to allow their use in large warships, an opinion that Fisher accepted, if reluctantly. "It's quite wonderful," he replied to Parsons in December 1912, "your getting such results with steam and as you truly say it makes the diesel with all its complications retire into the background, but remember there are always those funnels."[414] Fisher put the case for diesel engines in capital ships to Churchill as late as in March 1913,[415] but does not appear to have raised the subject thereafter.

In the spring of 1912, Fisher's flight of fancy with regard to the battle cruiser may have been temporarily disturbed by unsatisfactory reports of the results of the 1911 Battle Practices, which raised serious questions about the state of gunnery in the Royal Navy. On 5 March 1912, Fisher advised Churchill that the matter of deficiencies in naval gunnery was "far more important than the German Menace or the Coal Strike or Plural Voting! If you don't give your personal attention to it, we shall find ourselves in the background when Armageddon comes along." But as in 1908, he lacked any understanding of the technical issues, and as a consequence reduced the gunnery question to a matter of changing personnel. Fisher urged Churchill to seek the counsel of Jellicoe and called for the replacement of Briggs by Richard Peirse as Controller, Moore by Frederick Tudor as Director of Naval Ordnance and Montague Browning as Inspector of Target Practice by either Edward Phillpotts or Mark Kerr. Churchill promised on 9 March to give the gunnery problem "my closest personal attention as soon as the Estimates are disposed of,"[416] but while he replaced Moore by Tudor as Fisher had suggested, he passed over Peirse, for whom he seems to have had a personal distaste, and substituted Moore for Briggs while keeping Browning.[417]

Fisher's intervention was thus not without effect, but in light of the account given earlier of the Argo story in 1912 perhaps inadvertently disastrous for British naval gunnery. The appointment of Peirse to the Controllership would have practically guaranteed a fair hearing for the Argo Clock and plotter, if not the adoption of the Argo system. But the removal of Briggs, who by the spring of 1912 was prepared to adopt the Argo Clock, and the succession of Moore, who was an inveterate opponent of Pollen's approach to fire control, paved the way for the abandonment of monopoly and ultimately the rejection of the Pollen system. Fisher was given a chance to retrieve the situation when Pollen, at the suggestion of J. A. Spender, a mutual friend, wrote to him on 25 June 1912 to ask for a meeting at which he could explain his views. On 27 June, however, Fisher informed Pollen by telegram that "I am unable to see you as circumstances make it impossible that I can intervene."[418]

Any fears that Fisher may have had with regard to the gunnery efficiency of the fleet were dispelled by assurances that the adoption of Dreyer's instruments would meet the fire control needs of the Royal Navy. On 20 October 1913, Fisher thus informed Rear-Admiral Sydney Eardley-Wilmot that "the long range firing now is quite wonderful with the latest arrangement of a whole lot of big range finders and they have made wonderful practice at *15,000* yards!!!"[419] But in the absence of fire control instruments that could produce accurate results both when ranges were long and the change of range rates were high and changing, British battle cruisers lacked the means of hitting their all-big-gun opponents before they could be hit in return. The use of superior speed to keep the enemy at a distance thus offered no protective benefit, and under these circumstances, the sacrifice of armour protection became practically impossible to justify.

Jellicoe as well as Fisher had preferred the continued development of battle cruisers over the introduction of the more heavily protected but slower fast battleship, but the two in 1912 had been unable to get their way.[420] By 1913, Admiralty opinion had turned even further in the direction of giving British capital ships better protection. On 23 October 1913, Eustace Tennyson D'Eyncourt, who had succeeded Sir Philip Watts as Director of Naval Construction in the previous year, wrote that

it is held by some authorities that much less armour should be carried on our ships and the weight so saved should be used for increasing the number of guns, the argument being that the best protection is to overwhelm and silence the enemy's guns by one's own fire; but it must not be forgotten that immediately this principle is adopted and the defensive armour reduced, the enemy is in a position to increase the number of guns of somewhat smaller calibre which are able to pierce the thinner sides of the ships opposed to them, and can accordingly bring a much greater number of guns to bear, so that the argument to abolish or reduce armour quickly recoils upon those who actually adopt it in principle. Under present conditions, probably with 8 or 10 heavy guns, as now adopted in our battleships, together with a powerful A.T. armament, there are as many guns assembled in one ship as can be well trained and fought to the best possible advantage, so that if a considerable amount of armour can be carried as well, it is all clear gain; and in view of the fact that good gunnery is of the very first importance, and taking into consideration the devastating effect of modern high explosive shells, it appears absolutely necessary to protect not only the stability, the vitals, and the armament of the ship, but also the crews, to enable them to work the guns with a sense of reasonable security to themselves from the enemy's fire, as without this feeling it is almost certain that the crew will not be capable of obtaining the best results.[421]

Moore, the Third Sea Lord and Controller, was not in complete agreement with D'Eyncourt. In a minute written on 6 January 1914, he maintained that the suppression of enemy fire by one's own was preferable to depending upon armour for protection. But Moore was convinced that the sacrifice of both armour and fire power for high speed in the latest battle cruisers had been taken to extremes. "It is very difficult," he observed,

> to defend battle cruisers of the "Lion" type, which are very large and very expensive, where offence has been considerably and defence very greatly sacrificed so that they cannot be expected to engage with success the more powerful battleships that their superior speed enables them to overhaul; unless the tactical advantages are supposed to outweigh their otherwise inferior military capacities, by enabling a number of them to outflank a battleship line, and crush by the accumulated superiority of gun-fire the leading ship or ships, a rôle they may seldom have an opportunity of playing.[422]

The views of D'Eyncourt and Moore probably account for the fact that the *Royal Sovereign* class battleships of the 1913–14 and 1914–15 programs were more heavily armoured and much slower than the *Queen Elizabeth* class of 1912–13, and that no battle cruisers were authorized under these estimates.[423]

The sketch design of the *Royal Sovereign* class was approved by the Admiralty in May 1913.[424] The absence of any reference to the reversion to the construction of slow battleships with thick armour in Fisher's correspondence of this period[425] may be explained in large part by the fact that his imagination by this date had been captured by the submarine. "*Submarines,*" he insisted to Arnold White on 13 March 1913, "*are the coming Dreadnoughts . . .*"[426] In June, he associated the submarine and diesel propulsion. "For many, many years," he wrote to Sir Francis Hopwood, the Civil Lord of Admiralty, on 6 June 1913,

> I have been unceasingly and assiduously devoting both my waking and even my sleeping thoughts to submarines, and *oil and the oil engine* is the germ of their vitality. . . . . *The oil engine will govern all sea-fighting, and all sea-fighting is going to be governed by submarines . . .*[427]

By the fall of 1913, Fisher had concluded that in addition to diesel powered submarines for coast defence and distant operations off foreign shores, steam-propelled submarines would have an important role to play in a battle fleet action. "If the submarine," he explained to Arthur J. Balfour on 4 September 1913,

> (as some urgently and with great force and reason advocate) is to be a partial

substitute for battleship strength or battleship preponderance and not simply a
substitute for destroyers, then the root of the matter is "surface speed", and
the submarine must possess a strategic speed which will enable it effectively to
overhaul or circumvent a Battle Fleet, so that it can come into action without
fail and be counted on as a decisive weapon. This speed can be attained at the
present time and in the immediate future by no other path except by those of
size and steam. . . . Without any doubt whatever a fast Battle Fleet which can
be accompanied always by submarines under all circumstances would possess
an overwhelming fighting advantage.[428]

On 29 November 1913, Fisher informed Julian Corbett that "we
have *3,000* trained submarine officers and men, and are 2 keels to 1
against Germany and MORE SO."[429] A week later, however, he warned
Churchill that the German construction of submarines for foreign nations
would give them the capacity to out-build Britain in war.[430] In February
1914, Fisher complained to Jellicoe that Germany enjoyed a large numerical
superiority in submarines suited for overseas work.[431] In May, Fisher again
wrote to Jellicoe, urging that "for God's sake, do get on SOMEHOW with
building more submarines at once, *no matter what drawbacks.*"[432] And in
June, Fisher welcomed the prospect of the hostile naval powers building
dreadnoughts that he expected would be useless in war in the face of the
submarine. "Austria and Italy," he explained to Corbett on 22 June 1914,
"will continue to dig out vigorously to build Dreadnoughts against each
other, and the Grand-Admiral Köster, the head of the German Navy
League, will carry his point for 2 extra Dreadnoughts, so the Triple
Alliance will lavish their money on vessels that will be securely blockaded
by our submarines, as the Mediterranean and North Sea will be securely
locked up."[433]

Fisher's apparent indifference from 1913 to the course of surface capital
ship design may also have been attributable to his confidence in the
extent of the Royal Navy's quantitative and qualitative superiority in
dreadnoughts over Germany. Britain at all times had maintained the 60
per cent numerical standard in completed dreadnoughts, and from 1912
laid down at least twice as many dreadnoughts per annum as did Germany.
Of the 29 British and Dominion dreadnoughts that had entered service
by July 1914, 13 were armed with 13.5-inch guns, 3 additional similarly
armed vessels were nearing completion, and 10 units armed with 15-inch
guns were building. All of the 18 German dreadnoughts commissioned
by the same date were armed with nothing larger than 12-inch guns, and
of the 10 units under construction, 6 were armed with 12-inch guns and
only 4 with 15-inch guns.[434]

It was by no means certain, however, that the Royal Navy's capital ships
were technically superior to those of Germany. The gun-caliber advantage
of British dreadnoughts had been secured by sacrifices in armour that left
them inferior to their German counterparts in protection against artillery
projectiles. The narrowness of British docks, in addition, had restricted
the beam of British battleships, which adversely affected their capacity to
resist hits by torpedoes. Such weaknesses troubled Jellicoe, who by 1914
had begun to harbor serious doubts about the capital ship design policy

that had been pursued since 1905 and to which he had been a major contributor. On 14 July 1914, he advised Churchill that

> besides having a considerably thicker armour over their main belt and for the protection of their guns, the Germans carry thick belt protection to the ends of the ships to a far greater extent than we do and their armour is carried up much higher on the side than is ours in ships of the same date of construction. . . . The inferiority of the protection of the British ships against guns and torpedoes is very striking.

After comparing British and German battleships class for class, Jellicoe concluded that "it will be seen therefore that far from the British ships showing a superiority [in displacement] the exact opposite is usually the case and assuming equality in design it is highly dangerous to consider that our ships as a whole are superior or even equal fighting machines."[435]

Scarcely two weeks after Jellicoe had offered his views, hostilities with Germany commenced. British expenditures in the ensuing war dwarfed previous peacetime outlays on defence, which made earlier concerns about excessive spending on national security seem exaggerated. The loss of three battle cruisers at the battle of Jutland in 1916, on the other hand, raised fundamental questions about the soundness of prewar British naval technology, particularly with regard to capital ship design and fire control.

Notes to Chapter 6

1 Bernard Mallet, *British Budgets, 1887-88 to 1912-13* (London: Macmillan, 1913), pp. 148-254; Richard A. Rempel, *Unionists Divided: Arthur Balfour, Joseph Chamberlain and the Unionist Free Traders* (Newton Abbot: David & Charles, 1972); Alan Sykes, *Tariff Reform in British Politics, 1903-1913* (Oxford: Clarendon, 1979); and A. K. A. Russell, *Liberal Landslide: The General Election of 1906* (Newton Abbot: David & Charles, 1973).

2 Mallet, *British Budgets*, p. 254.

3 H. H. Asquith, "Naval Expenditure" (8 July 1906), Cab. 37/83, 63, and Lord Tweedmouth, "Memorandum relative to Meeting under Presidency of the Prime Minister, on Thursday, July 12, at 10, Downing Street" (17 July 1906), Cab. 37/83, 65, both in *Cabinet Papers*, P.R.O.

4 G. H. Murray, "Naval and Military Expenditure" (18 November 1907), Cab. 37/90, 98; Lord Tweedmouth, "Future Battleship Building" (21 November 1907), Cab. 37/90, 101; Lord Tweedmouth, "Navy Estimates 1908-09" (18 December 1907), Cab. 37/90, 112; all in *Cabinet Papers*, P.R.O.; and *Board Minutes* [Admiralty], 1908, Adm. 167/42, P.R.O.; and Ruddock F. Mackay, *Fisher of Kilverstone* (Oxford: Clarendon, 1973), pp. 387-92.

5 Lord Tweedmouth, "Memorandum relative to Meeting, under Presidency of the Prime Minister, on Thursday, July 12, at 10, Downing Street," Cab. 37/83, 65, and H. H. Asquith, "Naval Expenditure" (8 July 1906), Cab. 37/83, 63, both in *Cabinet Papers*, P.R.O.

6 See Appendix, Tables 8 and 9.

7 *FDSF*, Vol. 1, pp. 151-71. See also Paul G. Halpern, *The Mediterranean Naval Situation 1908-1914* (Cambridge, Mass.: Harvard University Press, 1971).

8 Bruce K. Murray, *The People's Budget 1909/10: Lloyd George and Liberal Politics* (Oxford: Clarendon Press, 1980), pp. 93–108.

9 Great Britain, Parliament, House of Commons, *Parliamentary Papers, 1914*, Vol. 53 (*Accounts and Papers*, Vol. 4), "Navy Estimates for the Year 1914-15 with Explanations of Differences," p. 4. It should be noted that in comparison with increased spending made necessary by the depletion of stores, the matter of reductions in proceeds from the sale of obsolete warships—another of Fisher's administrative measures of economy—in 1908-9 was insignificant, amounting to not much more than £100,000 relative to the peak years of 1905-6 and 1906-7; the 1908-9 figure, indeed, was over £10,000 higher than that of the previous year. For the proceeds from the sales of warships, see Great Britain, Parliament, *Parliamentary Papers*, 1905-6 to 1913-14, "Appropriation Accounts (Navy)."

10 Esher journal entry, 23 July 1908, Maurice V. Brett and Oliver, Viscount Esher, ed., *Journals and Letters of Reginald Viscount Esher*, 4 Vols (London: Ivor Nicholson & Watson, 1934-38), Vol. 2, pp. 329-30.

11 Edward David (ed.), *Inside Asquith's Cabinet: From the Diaries of Charles Hobhouse* (London: John Murray, 1977), pp. 73-4.

12 Michael G. Fry, *Lloyd George and Foreign Policy*, 2 Vols (Montreal: McGill-Queen's University Press, 1977), Vol. 1, pp. 105-29, and Murray, *The People's Budget*, pp. 127-30. For highly suggestive evidence not cited by either Fry or Murray in support of the possibility that Churchill was playing a double game, see Fisher to Churchill, 4 March 1909, in *FGDN*, Vol. 2, pp. 226-7.

13 For detailed accounts of the budget of 1909-10, see Mallet, *British Budgets*, pp. 298-313, and Murray, *The People's Budget*.

14 Quoted by Mallet in *British Budgets*, p. 312.

15 See Appendix, Table 1. For the growth in British GNP between 1909 and 1914, see B. R. Mitchell, *European Historical Statistics, 1750-1920*, abridged edition (New York: Columbia University Press, 1978), p. 416.

16 Great Britain, Parliament, Board of Trade, *Parliamentary Papers*, 1919, Vol. 52 (*Accounts and Papers*, Vol. 21), Cmd. 491, "Statistical Abstract for the United Kingdom in Each of the Last Fifteen Years from 1903 to 1917," pp. 6-7.

17 For the National Insurance Act, see Bentley B. Gilbert, *The Evolution of National Insurance in Great Britain: The Origins of the Welfare State* (London: Michael Joseph, 1966).

18 See Appendix, Tables 3, 4 and 5. For the complicated background to the Dominion contributions to British naval power, see Donald C. Gordon, *The Dominion Partnership in Imperial Defense, 1870-1914* (Baltimore: Johns Hopkins University Press, 1965).

19 Ibid.

20 Appendix, Tables 9, 10 and 11.

21 See Chapter 1, section 5.

22 Although Fisher considered the question of a naval war against such a combination to the point of drafting rough plans, they were not taken seriously. "Sir J. has now evolved an idea of distributing the Fleet with the object of facing a combination of the U.S. & Germany," wrote Rear-Admiral Edmond Slade, then Director of Naval Intelligence, in his diary on 22 July 1908, "which is the most hopelessly puerile thing that he could possibly bring out." Slade Diary, 1908, MRF/39/3, N.M.M., and see also *FDSF*, Vol. 1, pp. 183-4.

23 Unknown writer, memorandum entitled "Two-Power Standard," dated May 1909, Ms. Asquith 21, Bodleian Library, Oxford.

24 Captain Thomas Jackson (the Director of Naval Intelligence), "The Genesis of the Sixty per cent. Standard" (March 1913) [henceforward cited as "Genesis"], in Cab. 37/118, 6, *Cabinet Papers*, P.R.O. This may be the memorandum referred to in *FDSF*, Vol. 1, pp. 183–4.

25 "Genesis."

26 Winston Churchill, printed memorandum dated 29 December 1911, in "Estimates and Finance, 1912," Adm. 116/1294B, P.R.O.

27 *FDSF*, Vol. 1, p. 183.

28 For the comparison of standard, see Appendix, Tables 18, 19, 20 and 21.

29 "Genesis."

30 See Appendix, Tables 19, 20 and 21.

31 *FDSF*, Vol. 1, p. 216.

32 Quoted in Halpern, *Mediterranean Naval Situation*, pp. 16–17.

33 *FDSF*, Vol. 1, pp. 297, 313; Halpern, *Mediterranean Naval Situation*, pp. 40–2.

34 Gordon, *The Dominion Partnership in Imperial Defense*, pp. 248–67, and Richard A. Preston, *Canada and "Imperial Defense": A study of the origins of the British Commonwealth's defense organization, 1867–1919* (Durham, N.C.: Duke University Press, 1967), pp. 387–461.

35 See Appendix, Tables 16 and 17.

36 See Chapter 5, section 2, and Chapter 6, section 3.

37 For the German response to the British changes in capital ship armament, see Siegfried Breyer, *Battleships and Battle Cruisers, 1905–1970*, trans. by Alfred Kurti (Garden City, New York: Doubleday, 1973), p. 280; *FDSF*, Vol. 1, p. 284; and Holger H. Herwig, *"Luxury" Fleet: The Imperial German Navy 1888–1918* (London: George Allen & Unwin, 1980), pp. 81–2.

38 *FDSF*, Vol. 1, pp. 214–21, 311–16.

39 Ibid., pp. 314–27; F. W. Wiemann, "Lloyd George and the Struggle for the Navy Estimates of 1914," in A. J. P. Taylor, ed., *Lloyd George: Twelve Essays* (New York: Atheneum, 1971), pp. 71–91; Morris, *Radicalism Against War*, pp. 341–7; and Fry, *Lloyd George and Foreign Policy*, pp. 169–81. For Lloyd George's predilection to follow Churchill's lead, see in addition David (ed.), *Inside Asquith's Cabinet*, pp. 155–60. Note in particular Hobhouse's entry of 27 January, which suggests that Lloyd George's letter to Churchill of that date, quoted in *FDSF*, Vol. 1, pp. 323–4 and elsewhere, may have been intended as much or even more to placate his economist subordinates at the Treasury than to admonish the First Lord. For Lloyd George's frivolous pretext for his capitulation to Churchill's program of four battleships, see Randolph S. Churchill, *Winston S. Churchill*, 2 Vols (Boston: Houghton Mifflin, 1967), Vol. 2, pp. 661–2.

40 Peter Rowland, *The Last Liberal Governments*, 2 Vols (New York: St. Martin's, 1971), Vol. 1, pp. 325–7, and Murray, *The People's Budget*, pp. 303–10.

41 See Board of Trade, *Statistical Abstract*, pp. 6–7, and Appendix, Table 3.

42 See Board of Trade, *Statistical Abstract*, pp. 6–7, and Appendix, Tables 3–5.

43 For an analysis of fiscal policy and party politics, see H. V. Emy, "The Impact of Financial Policy on English Party Politics before 1914," *Historical Journal*, Vol. 15 (1972), pp. 103–31.

44 Murray, *The People's Budget*, pp. 310–14.

45 Great Britain, Parliament, House of Commons, *Parliamentary Papers*, 1914, Vol. 40 (*Reports*, Vol. 30), Cmd. 7315, "Final Report of the Department Committee on Local Taxation: England and Wales," pp. 7–9; and George L. Bernstein, *Liberalism and Liberal Politics in Edwardian England* (London: Allen & Unwin, 1986), pp. 146–7. For poor law expenditure between 1890 and

1914, see B. R. Mitchell, *Abstract of British Historical Statistics* (Cambridge: Cambridge University Press, 1962), pp. 416, 418, 424.

46 Fisher to McKenna, c. 8 April 1909, in *FGDN*, Vol. 2, p. 242.

47 Fisher to Pamela McKenna, 10 April 1914, in *FGDN*, Vol. 2, p. 503.

48 Murray, *The People's Budget*, pp. 302, 312.

49 For the opposition within the Cabinet to Lloyd George's tactics, see Walter Runciman to Robert Chalmers, 24 June 1914, in Avner Offer, *Property and Politics, 1870-1914: Landownership, Law, Ideology and Urban Development in England* (Cambridge: Cambridge University Press, 1981), p. 396. For Lloyd George's willingness to consider unorthodox, not to say far-fetched, political expedients in his search for the means to meet both Britain's social welfare and defence requirements, see Bernard Semmel, *Imperialism and Social Reform: English Social-Imperial Thought, 1895-1914* (Cambridge, Mass.: Harvard University Press, 1960), pp. 240-6 and, most recently, Bentley B. Gilbert, *David Lloyd George, a political life*, Vol. 1 *The Architect of Change, 1863-1912* (London: B. T. Batsford, 1987), pp. 413-26.

50 For the finances of the German imperial government, see Paul M. Kennedy, *The Rise of the Anglo-German Antagonism 1860-1914* (London: George Allen & Unwin, 1980), pp. 356-60, and Carolyn Webber and Aaron Wildavsky, *A History of Taxation and Expenditure in the Western World* (New York: Simon & Schuster, 1986), p. 353. For German borrowing on the navy, see Board of Trade, "Financial Position of the German Empire" (1 October 1909), pp. 19-25, Cab. 37/101, 133, *Cabinet Papers*, P.R.O.; Winston Churchill, [German naval expansion: financial difficulties] (3 November 1909), pp. 1-2, *Cabinet Papers*, Cab. 37/101, 147, P.R.O.; and Archibald Hurd and Henry Castle, *German Sea-Power: Its Rise, Progress, and Economic Basis* (London: John Murray, 1914; f.p. 1913), pp. 252-5, 377. For German naval finance and politics, see V. R. Berghahn, *Germany and the Approach of War in 1914* (New York: St. Martin's, 1973), pp. 104-24, 145-64, and Herwig, *Luxury Fleet*, pp. 89-92.

51 Halpern, *Mediterranean Naval Situation*, pp. 47-149.

52 See Chapter 5.

53 Pollen to Slade, 24 January 1910, P.P., and Great Britain, Admiralty, *Pollen Aim Correction System: General Grounds of Admiralty Policy and Historical Record of Business Negotiations* (February 1913) [henceforward cited as *Record of Business Negotiations*], p. 11, N.L.M.D.

54 Draft letter, Pollen to J. A. Spender, 17 September 1912, not sent, and Pollen to Rear-Admiral E. J. W. Slade, 6 January 1911, P.P.

55 Admiralty to Argo, 18 January 1910, P.P.

56 Admiralty to Argo, 18 January 1910 (ii), P.P.

57 Argo to the Admiralty, 22 January 1910; Argo to the Admiralty, 25 January 1910; Admiralty to Argo, 2 February 1910; Admiralty to Argo, 16 February 1910; Admiralty to Argo, 19 February 1910; and Argo to the Admiralty, 23 February 1910; P.P.

58 C. I. Thomas to Pollen, 21 January 1910, P.P.

59 A copy of this letter is not to be found in the Pollen Papers. For draft letters from Argo to the Admiralty in reply to the letter from the Admiralty to Argo of 18 January 1910, that were apparently not sent, see Argo to the Admiralty, 21 January 1910 [one page missing] and 22 January 1910, P.P. For reference to the fact that a letter from the Argo Company in reply to the Admiralty letter of 18 January 1910 was sent on 22 January, see Pollen to Black, 16 February 1910, P.P. For a summary of the contents of this letter, see *Record of Business Negotiations*, p. 12.

60 Pollen to Black, 11 and 16 February 1910, P.P.
61 Black to Pollen, 22 February 1910, P.P.
62 Draft letter that was not sent, Argo to the Admiralty, 21 January 1910 [one page missing], P.P.
63 Draft letter from Argo to the Admiralty, 22 January 1910, apparently not sent.
64 Identical letters from to Pollen to C. I. Thomas and Rear-Admiral Sir Richard Henry Peirse, 1 March 1910, and P.P.
65 Ibid.
66 Admiralty to Argo, 4 February 1910, P.P.; log of Natal from 7 April 1909-14 April 1910, Adm. 53/23981, P.R.O.
67 *Record of Business Negotiations*, p. 12.
68 Ibid. and *Natal* log.
69 Argo to the Admiralty, 23 February 1910, P.P.
70 Admiralty to Argo, 11 April 1910, P.P.
71 *Record of Business Negotiations*, p. 12, and "D.N.O.'s Estimate," dated 18 April 1910, MCKN 3/14, and Director of Navy Contracts Memoranda, dated 18 April 1910, MCKN 3/15, McKenna Papers, C.C.
72 *Record of Business Negotiations*, p. 12.
73 See Pollen's analysis, Argo to the Admiralty, 13 April 1910, P.P.
74 Draft letter, Pollen to Spender, 17 September 1912, not sent, P.P.
75 Pollen to Jellicoe, 13 April 1910, P.P.
76 Argo to the Admiralty, 13 April 1910, P.P.
77 Pollen to McKenna, 13 April 1910, P.P.
78 Another copy was sent to Prince Louis of Battenberg, for which see Battenberg to Pollen, 15 April 1910, P.P.
79 Pollen to Jellicoe, typescript, 13 April 1910, P.P.
80 Pollen to Jellicoe, manuscript, 13 April 1910, P.P.
81 Pollen to A. J. Spender, 13 April 1910, P.P.
82 "D.N.O.'s Estimate," dated 18 April 1910, MCKN 3/14, and Director of Navy Contracts Memoranda, dated 18 April 1910, MCKN 3/15, both in McKenna Papers, C.C
83 Peirse to Pollen, 21 April 1910, P.P.
84 Pollen to McKenna, 19 April 1910, P.P. Pollen's terms of address to McKenna were this time more formal than previously had been the case.
85 No copy of the letter from the Argo Company to the Admiralty of 22 April has survived, but see the reference to this letter in the Admiralty to Argo, 29 April 1910, P.P.
86 Draft letter from Pollen to Spender, 17 September 1912, that was apparently not sent, and Pollen to Slade, 6 January 1911, P.P. For Wilson's obstinacy, which had alienated McKenna by January 1910, see *FDSF*, Vol. 1, p. 213.
87 *Board Minutes* [Admiralty], 27 April 1910, Adm. 167/44, P.R.O.
88 See Chapter 5, section 3(a). For the correspondence over manual helm-free plotting tables, see Argo to the Admiralty, 28 April 1910, and the Admiralty to Argo, 9 May 1910, P.P.
89 Admiralty to Argo, 29 April 1910, with enclosure "X", P.P.
90 Argo to the Admiralty, 29 April 1910, P.P.
91 Pollen to Churchill, 24 June 1912, P.P.
92 Pollen to Rear-Admiral Arthur Limpus, 24 May 1910, and Captain Montague Browning to Pollen, 8 September 1911, PP.
93 Pollen to Pretyman, 4 February 1912, P.P.
94 Typescript fragment, apparently prepared for the use of Counsel, before the RCAI in 1924. See also Pollen to Beresford, manuscript draft letter, n.d. but

in April 1910; Beresford reply to the preceding, 16 April 1910; Beresford to Pollen, 24 April 1910; and Beresford to Pollen, 9 May 1910; P.P. For the names of the officers, who were to live up to their promise in 1911, see below, Chapter 6, section 2(b).

95 Pollen to Moore, 20 April 1910, and Admiralty to Argo, 28 April 1910, P.P.

96 Log book of H.M.S. *Natal* (10 May 1910–30 April 1911), Adm. 53/23982, P.R.O.

97 "Memorandum," undated but probably from Pollen to the Director of Naval Ordnance, 17 June 1910 [see reference to such a letter in Argo to the Admiralty, 21 June 1910, P.P.], P.P.; Pollen to Colville, 1 July 1910, in Arthur Hungerford Pollen, *To Rear-Admiral the Hon. Stanley C. J. Colville, CVO, CB* [July 1910], *PP*, pp. 245–52; and Arthur Hungerford Pollen, *The Quest of a Rate Finder* [November 1910], *PP*, pp. 264–7.

98 Pollen to Moore, 17 June 1910; Moore to Pollen, 17 June 1910; Argo to the Admiralty, 17 June 1910; Pollen to Moore, 18 June 1910; the Admiralty to Argo, 20 June 1910; and Argo to the Admiralty, 21 June 1910; P.P.

99 Lieutenant Reginald Plunkett, "Report by Torpedo Lieutenant of H.M.S. 'Natal'," 28 June 1910, P.P.

100 "Memorandum," undated but probably from Pollen to the Director of Naval Ordnance, 17 June 1910 [see reference to such a letter in Argo to the Admiralty, 21 June 1910, P.P.], P.P.

101 Log book of H.M.S. *Natal* (10 May 1910–30 April 1911), Adm. 53/23982, P.R.O.

102 Admiral William H. May, "Memorandum: Aim Corrector Trials," 31 May 1910, DRAX 3/3, Drax Papers, C.C. The other committee members were Captain A. P. Stoddart, Captain C. M. de Bartolomé and Commander W. W. Fisher.

103 Pollen, *To Rear-Admiral the Hon. Stanley C. J. Colville*, *PP*, pp. 245–54.

104 Lieutenant Reginald Plunkett, "Report by Torpedo Lieutenant of H.M.S. 'Natal'," 28 June 1910, P.P.

105 "Sir Reginald Hall's draft for a letter to Admiral Beatty, the First Lord, in support of A.H.P.'s plea for a private settlement of his case against the Admiralty," probably 1922, P.P. Pollen had by this time developed the highest respect for Hall's abilities. Hall, he informed Battenberg on 25 July 1910, "has a grip of the [gunnery] question not only in its immediate technical aspects but in its further tactical aspect, which is exceedingly strong. He is indeed a man of most powerful mind, and as he joins to this insatiable industry and thoroughness in all his ways, it would seem to be only necessary for his health to last for him to be of the supremest value to the Service." [Pollen to Battenberg, 25 July 1910, P.P.]

106 Colville Committee to Commander-in-Chief, Home Fleet, 1 July 1910, DRAX 3/3, Drax Papers, C.C.

107 Battenberg to Pollen, 15 April 1910; Pollen to Battenberg, 9 May 1910; Battenberg to Pollen, 11 May 1910; Pollen to Battenberg, 13 May 1910; Battenberg to Pollen, 20 July 1910; Pollen to Battenberg, 25 July 1910; and Pollen to Battenberg, 27 July 1910; P.P.

108 Admiralty to Argo, 19 August 1910, P.P.

109 Peirse to Pollen, 18 August 1910, P.P. "I quite agree with you," Peirse wrote in this letter, "that to avoid any risk of failure at the next demonstration, the provision of an entirely new table is much to be preferred, & especially if there is little to choose in the matter of time. Once get the gear working all right & to the satisfaction of the Ship's people, its success will soon make

itself known in the Fleet & then I think you may be pretty sure that the opposition will ultimately be broken down, in fact must be. But until then its opponents will always be able to shelter themselves behind the argument of unreliability & unseaworthiness."

110 Argo to the Admiralty, 25 August 1910, P.P.
111 Note at the end of the text of Argo to Admiralty, 25 August 1910, in the copy printed in the *CCB*, P.P.
112 Admiral W. H. May to the Admiralty Permanent Secretary, 25 April 1910, in "Gunnery: Effects on (a) plotting for range, (b) rate of change of bearing & range, (c) possibility of concentration of fire &c. of new developments in Fleet Tactics," Adm. 1/8051, P.R.O.
113 Peirse to Moore, 18 May 1910, ibid.
114 Moore, "Views on 'the possible effects on Gunnery Technique of new developments in Fleet Tactics'," 24 May 1910, ibid.
115 Admiralty to Argo, 18 August 1910; Argo to Admiralty, 25 August 1910; and Peirse to Pollen, 28 August [1910], P.P.
116 Tactical exercises were known as "P.Z. exercises" after the flag signal "P.Z.", which indicated that they were to be performed.
117 Arthur Hungerford Pollen, *The Quest of a Rate Finder* (by the author, November, 1910), in *PP*, pp. 260-2. For additional testimony that plotting was falling out of favor, see Battenberg to Pollen, 20 July 1910, P.P.
118 Arthur Hungerford Pollen, *Of War and the Rate of Change* (by the author, January, 1911), in *PP*, pp. 271-90.
119 For the *Edinburgh* firing trials of 1909-10, see D. K. Brown, "Attack and Defence, No. 5: Prior to World War I—Part Two," in Andrew Lambert, ed. *Warship Volume*, Vol. 9 (London: Conway Maritime Press, 1985), pp. 116–19.
120 Admiral Sir R. H. Bacon, *The Life of John Rushworth Earl Jellicoe* (London: Cassell, 1936), p. 162.
121 See D.N.O. memorandum, 3 November 1911; A. K. Wilson minute on same, 10 November 1911 [". . . it is considered that it would be generally inadvisable to change projectile after an action is commenced before definite results have been attained, and that in view of the wreckage produced on unarmoured portions, communications, and control stations &c., it would be generally advisable to begin with Lyddite at long range."]; and Admiralty to Commander-in-Chief Home Fleet and Vice-Admiral commanding the Second Division Home Fleet, 18 November 1911 and accompanying memorandum "Choice of Projectiles in Action"; all in IQ/DNO, Vol. 1 (1912), N.L.M.D. See also "Extracts from a Long-Course Lecture, by Lieutenant A. Domville, R.N., on the Latest Types of Projectiles, Their Uses in Action, and Effect," in Great Britain, Admiralty, Gunnery Branch, *Half-Yearly Summary of Progress in Gunnery* (January 1909), N.L.M.D.
122 For the vicissitudes of director firing in 1910 and 1911, see Director of Naval Ordnance, "Director Firing Gear: Transfer from 'Dreadnought' to 'Bellerophon.' Report of trials in 'Bellerophon'," Adm. 1/8145, P.R.O.; Great Britain, Admiralty, Technical History Section, *Fire Control in H.M. Ships. Series: The Technical History and Index: A Serial History of Technical Problems Dealt with by Admiralty Departments*, part 23 (December, 1919), p. 4, N.L.M.D.; Admiral Sir William James, *The Sky was Always Blue* (London: Methuen, 1951), p. 74; and Peter Padfield, *Aim Straight: a biography of Admiral Sir Percy Scott* (London: Hodder & Stoughton, 1966), p. 204. For Moore's opposition to director firing, see Pollen to Percy Scott, 19 November 1912, P.P.

123 Padfield, *Aim Straight*, p. 197.
124 Admiralty to Argo, 29 April 1910, Enclosure "X", paragraph 5, P.P.
125 Pollen to McKenna, 13 April 1910, P.P., and *Record of Business Negotiations*, pp. 15, 23. £13,600 worth of ordinary shares were bought at this time, followed by the purchase later that year of £3,000 of preference stock. See also 1913 memorandum "Issue of 6% Debentures," P.P.
126 Argo to the Admiralty, 14 July 1910; Admiralty to Argo, 3 August 1910; "Remarks on the R.F. Mounting," 31 August 1910; Argo to Admiralty, 13 May 1912, extracts; all in P.P.; and *Record of Business Negotiations*, p. 13. According to the Argo letter of 13 May 1912, the redesign work "involved four months work being done over again, necessitating a great deal of overtime work, additional draughtsmen, staff, etc. to make up for lost time."
127 Statement "to the Shareholders of the Argo Company Limited," 4 December 1923; typescript fragment, apparently prepared for the use of Counsel, before the RCAI in 1924; and Pollen to Peirse, 17 May 1925, P.P. According to Pollen's letter to Peirse, the endorsements were returned to their authors after they had accomplished their purpose.
128 See above.
129 The big investors included John Walter, the chairman of *The Times* [London], and Sir Julius Wernher, Otto Beit, Sir Kay Muir, Sir Joseph Lawrence, W. and G. Mosenthal, James Buchanon, F. Hamilton, Sir James Pender, S. H. Pollen, Alexander Isaac, Ernest Debenham and T. Cooke & Sons. For a complete list of Pollen's financial backers, see memorandum, "List of Subscribers," dated 9 February 1911. See also 1913 memorandum, "Issue of 6% Debentures"; and "Registrar of Members of the Argo Company Limited," dated 13 January 1913; P.P. By the end of 1911, the sale of Cumulative Preference and Participating Shares had raised £25,000.
130 For the Argo Clock Mark I, see British Patent 360/1911 (submitted 5 January 1911; accepted 1 August 1911).
131 James Thomson, "On an Integrating Machine Having a New Kinematic Principle," *Proceedings of the Royal Society*, Vol. 24 (1876), pp. 262-5; and William Thomson (Lord Kelvin from 1892), "On an Instrument for Calculating $[\int \phi(x)\psi(x)dx]$, the Integral of the Product of Two Given Functions," *Proceedings of the Royal Society*, Vol. 24 (1876), pp. 266-8.
132 See Chapter 3.
133 For the connection of Boys and Pollen in 1906, see Chapter 3. For the interest of Boys in differential analyzers, see his untitled report to the Argo Company of November 1912, in P.P.
134 Wilfrid Arthur Greene, brief: "The Claim of the Argo Company and Mr. Pollen before the Royal Commission" (1925), part 2, paragraph 41, P.P.
135 British Patent 19,627/1911, which describes the Argo Clock Mark II, is still restricted. For a complete technical description of the Argo Clock Mark II, however, see Argo Company memorandum, "The A.C. Range and Bearing Clock, Mark II" (8 May 1911), in P.P. For a detailed description of the disc-ball-roller mechanism, see British Patent 17,441/1912 (submitted 4 April 1912; accepted 24 October 1912). For the transmission of range and bearing via the Vickers step-by-step system to follow-the-pointer sights, and the fact that the original Argo transmitting system was synchronous, see Argo to Admiralty, 26 October 1910, and Director of Navy Contracts to Argo, 8 November 1910, P.P. For a clear description of the two systems of transmitting, see Alan Raven and John Roberts, *British Battleships of World War Two: The development and technical history of the Royal Navy's*

battleships and battlecruisers from 1911 to 1946 (London: Arms & Armour, 1976), p. 428.

136 Argo to the Admiralty, 15 May 1911, P.P.

137 Pollen to Isherwood, 22 May 1911, P.P.

138 For a precise mechanical description of automatic bearing generation in the Argo Clock Mark III, which presumably was the same as in the Argo Clock Mark IV, see Great Britain, Admiralty, Gunnery Branch, *The Argo Range and Bearing Clock, Mark IV* (10 January 1914), N.L.M.D.

139 Pollen to Peirse, 24 November 1912, P.P.

140 Argo Company, "Memorandum," 6 May 1913, P.P.

141 Argo to the Admiralty, 17 November 1911; F. W. Black to Argo, 20 November 1911; Argo to Henley, 28 November 1911; and Gipps to Pollen, 30 November 1911; P.P.

142 For the new optical design, see British Patent No. 3090/1912 (submitted 31 December 1912; accepted 31 December 1913). For the resort by Barr & Stroud to silvered mirrors for long-base naval range-finders in order "to give specially good illumination under high magnification," which appears to have taken place during the latter part of the First World War, see Barr & Stroud, Ltd., *The Principles of Rangefinding*, pamphlet no. 42 (Glasgow: by the author, n.d.), and Great Britain, Admiralty, Gunnery Branch, *Handbook for Naval Range-Finders and Mountings: Book I* (November 1921), N.L.M.D. For the post-war competitive trials at Fort Cumberland that revealed that the Cooke-Pollen range-finder was superior to Barr & Stroud instruments under low light conditions, see Great Britain, Admiralty, Gunnery Branch, *Progress in Gunnery Materiel, 1922-1923* (1923), p. 41, in Adm. 186/259, P.R.O. For the development and capabilities of the Anschütz gyro-compass, see Great Britain, Admiralty, Technical History Section, *The Development of the Gyro-Compass Prior to and During the War. Series: The Technical History and Index: A Serial History of Technical Problems dealt with by Admiralty Departments*, part 20 (October, 1919), N.L.M.D., and G. A. A. Grant and J. Klinkert, *The Ship's Compass*, rev. edn (London and Henley: Routledge and Kegan Paul, 1970; f. p. 1952), pp. 423-7.

143 Pollen to Jellicoe, 20 March 1911; Moore to Pollen 22 November 1912; Pollen to Moore, 26 November 1912; Charles Vernon Boys, untitled typescript report commissioned by the Argo Company [November,1912]; and Pollen to Balfour, 29 February 1916, P.P. In the absence of more complete documentation, it is impossible to give a detailed account of the events surrounding the development and trials of the Cooke-Pollen range-finder. It appears, however, that the service evaluation of this instrument was largely separate from that of the main part of the system.

144 Admiralty to Argo, 26 July 1911 [reference to which in Argo to Admiralty, 20 February 1912] and Argo to Admiralty, 20 February 1912, P.P.; and *Record of Business Negotiations*, p. 14. It should be noted that the Anschütz gyro-compass cost £2,300 per unit, or nearly £1,000 more than an Argo mounting and pair of indicators [*Record of Business Negotiations*, p. 14.]

145 Argo to the Admiralty, 12 November 1912; Admiralty to Argo, 29 November 1910; Argo to Admiralty, 29 November 1910; Pollen to Henley, 9 December 1910; Pollen to Black, 22 December 1910; Director of Navy Contracts to Argo, 4 January 1911; Argo to the Admiralty, 20 January 1911; Argo to the Director of Navy Contracts, 25 November 1912; and undated draft letter from Reginald Hall to Beatty [1922]; P.P. For Pollen's discussions of rate plotting with the officers of the *Natal*, see also Pollen to Plunkett, 26 September 1910;

Plunkett to Isherwood, 27 September 1910; Plunkett to Pollen, 27 September 1910; Plunkett to Pollen, 12 October 1910; Plunkett to Pollen, 24 January 1911; and Pollen to Plunkett, 31 January 1911; P.P.; and Plunkett, "Plotting systems" [1910], in Drax 3/3, Drax Papers, C.C.

146 Director of Navy Contracts to Argo, 2 May 1911, and Director of Navy Contracts, 11 August 1911, P.P.

147 *To Rear-Admiral The Hon. Stanley C. J. Colville*, in *PP*, pp. 246-9.

148 Charles Vernon Boys, untitled typescript report commissioned by the Argo Company [November 1912], P.P; and Great Britain, Admiralty, Gunnery Branch [Commanders Frederic C. Dreyer and C. V. Usborne], *Pollen Aim Corrector System Part I. Technical History and Technical Comparison with Commander F. C. Dreyer's Fire Control System* (May 1913) [henceforward cited as *Technical History*], pp. 28-30; N.L.M.D. Presumably, the Mark I plotter was the device mounted in the *Jupiter*, the Mark II that mounted in the *Ariadne*, and the Mark III that mounted in the *Natal*.

149 From the financial statements made in the Admiralty's *Record of Business Negotiations*, both Gipps and Riley appear to have been employed with the Argo Company from early 1911. Although the formal contract between Gipps and the firm for full time employment for four years is dated 19 September 1911, Gipps was clearly working for the firm in a major capacity at least as early as in July of that year. Riley, like Ogilvy, had partaken of the poisoned oysters in the *Natal* in 1909, and suffered some damage to his health. His employment with the Argo Company may have been attributable in part to Pollen's remorse. For Gipps, see "Memorandum of Agreement . . .," 19 September 1911, and Gipps to Pollen, 25 July 1911, P.P. For Riley, see Vice-Admiral Sir Francis Pridham to Anthony Pollen, 14 May 1973, quoted in part in Anthony Pollen, *The Great Gunnery Scandal: The Mystery of Jutland* (London: Collins, 1980), p. 261 [Riley's son later informed Anthony Pollen that Pridham was mistaken about the extent to which his father suffered from the oysters]. For the grant of permission to employ the two naval officers by the Admiralty, see Admiralty to Coward & Hawksley, Sons & Chance, 30 April 1913, P.P. For the attribution of the decision to allow Riley and Gipps to assist the Argo Company for 18 months to Vice-Admiral Sir Francis Bridgeman, the Second Sea Lord, in particular, see Anthony Pollen, *Great Gunnery Scandal*, p. 79.

150 *Record of Business Negotiations*, pp. 14-16. This account recorded that "in December 1911 Argo Company appealed to the Admiralty to pay for the first 15 sets in full, as delivered, instead of deducting from the price of each a proportion of the £15,000 advanced, and to defer the deduction of that sum until after 15 sets had been paid for in full. . . . The Admiralty, although realizing that the insecure financial position of Argo Company was due to causes for which the Company alone were responsible (and largely to their heavy expenditure on staff, &c.), agreed to make the slight concession asked by the Company, as it was recognized that they had put very high-class work into the apparatus, and had undoubtedly gone out of their way to try to give the Admiralty the monopoly." There is, unfortunately, no correspondence in the Pollen Papers on this matter.

151 "List of Officers to whom Argo Memo re Turret Control was sent—July 1911"; "Notes on points raised in the various replies received in answer to Memorandum re Turret Control," 2 August 1911; and Backhouse to Gipps, 22 July 1911, all in P.P.; and Gipps to Dreyer with memorandum, 18 July 1911, DRYR 2/1, C.C.; and *Record of Business Negotiations*, p. 15.

152 Gipps to Pollen, 8 August 1911, P.P. See also Backhouse to Gipps, 17 August 1911; Pollen to Gipps, 26 August 1911; Rear-Admiral Montague Browning to Pollen, 8 September 1911; and Rear-Admiral Arthur Limpus to Pollen, 29 September 1911, P.P.

153 Henley to Dreyer, 24 July 1911, DRYR 2/1, Dreyer Papers, C.C. Henley mentioned the fact to Dreyer that he had taken care not to mention Dreyer by name in connection with the Gipps memorandum issue, which may indicate that at this date he was not entirely sure of Moore's willingness to resort to any means of obstructing Pollen.

154 *Technical History*, p. 10.

155 Pollen to Peirse, 24 November 1912, P.P.

156 "Remarks by Commander F. C. Dreyer, R.N. on the question of how to best obtain and maintain the gun range in action," 22 July 1910, Adm. 1/8417, P.R.O. See also Dreyer, *The Sea Heritage*, p. 85.

157 Henley to Dreyer, 13 August 1910, DRYR 2/1, Dreyer Papers, C.C.

158 Moore memorandum and minute, 13 August 1910, in "Invention of Range-finding System," Adm. 1/8131, P.R.O.

159 Admiralty to Admiral W. H. May, 30 August 1910, and "Copy Final Specification of Commander Frederic Charles Dreyer's Invention . . .," 23 September 1910, DRYR 2/1, Dreyer Papers, C.C.

160 Dreyer to Captain J. B. Eustace, 22 October 1910, Adm. 1/8131, P.R.O.

161 Great Britain, Admiralty, *Handbook of Captain F. C. Dreyer's Fire Control Tables, 1918*, N.L.M.D.

162 *Technical History*, p. 12. For the development of this instrument, see Dreyer to Eustace with attached papers, 12 October 1910; and Dreyer to Eustace and attached papers and diagram, 22 October 1910; in DRYR 2/1, Dreyer Papers, C.C.

163 "Mr. Pollen appeared one day," Henley had written to Dreyer on 13 August 1910,

and informed me he was preparing a scheme for *Automatic Time and Ranges Plotting*. I said nothing about you having *already* got the Secret Patent for a Time and Range Board but I am pushing on the papers submitting that you should take out a Secret Patent for the whole system of T.&.R. and T.&.B. plotting whether done manually or automatically and also asking you for drawings of Auto T.&.R. and Auto T.&.B. board.

Mr. P. may have been on this T.&.R. scheme for some time but so far we have no information of any patent having been lodged. (Personally I expect he has heard of your scheme through somebody and that this has given him the idea). . . .

In view of Mr. P's sudden attack on T.&.R. I concur with you re secret patents and I hope you agree with me that the patent should cover the whole principle of T.&.R., and T.&.B. so as to keep him out of it.

Henley to Dreyer, 13 August 1910, DRYR 2/1, Dreyer Papers, C.C. See also Elphinstone to Dreyer, 10 July 1911; and Henley to Dreyer, 21 February 1911, DRYR 2/1, Dreyer Papers, C.C. For the frankness of Pollen's communications with Henley, see Pollen to Henley, 17 July 1911, P.P.

164 *The Great Gunnery Scandal*, pp. 136-7. See also Henley to Dreyer, 24 July 1911, DRYR 2/1, Dreyer Papers, C.C.; and RCAI, *Minutes*, Vol. 13 (6 August 1925), P.P.

165 *Technical History*, pp. 39-55, and *Handbook of Captain F. C. Dreyer's Fire Control Tables*.

166 For the complete text of the RCAI recommendation, see Anthony Pollen, *The Great Gunnery Scandal*, pp. 252-5.

167 *Handbook of Captain F. C. Dreyer's Fire Control Tables*, and *Technical History*, pp. 39-55.

168 For Wilson's failings as First Sea Lord and his removal, see *FDSF*, Vol. 1, pp. 213-14, 255-8.

169 See Moore to Pollen, 22 March 1911; Pollen to Moore, 14 November 1911; Moore to Pollen, 14 November 1911; Moore to Pollen, 15 May 1912; Pollen to Moore, 16 May 1912; and Moore to Pollen, 16 May 1912, P.P.

170 Dreyer, *Sea Heritage*, p. 27.

171 Jellicoe to Dreyer, 11 December 1906, DRYR 3/2, Dreyer Papers, C.C.

172 Jellicoe to Pollen, n.d. [December 1907], P.P.

173 See Chapter 5, section 3(a).

174 Dreyer, *Sea Heritage*, pp. 62-5.

175 Pollen, "Memorandum," 6 May 1912, P.P. See also Argo Secretary to Moore, 26 February 1912, and Pollen to Moore, 29 February 1912, P.P.

176 Sir Reginald Hall draft letter to Beatty, probably 1922, P.P. See also Pollen to Moore, 17 April 1912, P.P.

177 Argo to the Admiralty, 18 March 1912,, P.P.

178 No copy of Moore's letter has been found, but see the reference to this communication and the interview in Pollen to Moore, 11 April 1912, P.P.

179 Pollen to Moore, 11 April 1912, P.P.

180 Pollen to Moore, 17 April 1912, and Argo to the Admiralty, 20 February 1912, P.P. For the design of the Argo rate plotter, see British Patent 23,351/1912 (12 October 1912), P.O.L.

181 Moore to Pollen, 20 April 1912, P.P.

182 Pollen to Moore, 22 April 1912, P.P.

183 *Record of Business Negotiations*, pp. 17-18.

184 Pollen to Masterton-Smith, 23 July 1912, P.P. No details as to how the financial exigencies of the Argo Company were resolved are available.

185 Extracts from Argo to the Admiralty, 13 May 1912, P.P., and see also *Record of Business Negotiations*, p. 17.

186 Argo to the Admiralty, 20 May 1912, P.P.

187 Director of Navy Contracts to Argo, 7 June 1912, P.P.

188 Argo to the Director of Navy Contracts, 10 June 1912, P.P. For 5 clocks, the price per unit was £2,400; for 5 plotters, the price per unit was £500. For 14 clocks, the price was £1,850 each; for 14 plotters, £450 each. For 96 clocks, the price was £1,350 each; for 96 plotters, £400 each. In the case of 96 clocks, deliveries were promised at the rate of 2 per week within 8 months of getting the order.

189 Argo to the Director of Navy Contracts, 10 June 1912, P.P.

190 Pollen to Moore, 11 April 1912, P.P.

191 See Moore to Pollen, 13 April 1912, 20 April 1912, 15 May 1912 and 16 May 1912, P.P.

192 This letter was subsequently destroyed, but see reference to it in Pollen to Moore, 20 June 1912, P.P.

193 Draft letter that was not sent from Pollen to J. A. Spender, 17 September 1912, P.P.

194 See Moore to Prince Louis of Battenberg, 19 September 1912, in DS/MISC/20, #147, Battenberg Papers, I.W.M.

195 Pollen's relations with Battenberg have already been described. For his private communications with Churchill, which began after a lunch meeting in April

1912 arranged by J. A. Spender, see Pollen to Churchill, 14 May 1912 and 6 June 1912, P.P.

196 Draft letter that was not sent from Pollen to J. A. Spender, 17 September 1912, P.P.

197 Pollen to Moore, 20 June 1912 (i); Pollen to Moore, 20 June 1912 (ii); Pollen to Moore, 21 June 1912; Moore to Pollen, 21 June 1912; and Pollen to Moore, 22 June 1912, P.P.

198 Pollen to Peirse, 16 September 1912, P.P. Peirse passed Pollen's letter to Battenberg. The fact that Battenberg felt it necessary to confront Moore with the letter is suggestive. For Moore's evasive reply to Battenberg's query, see Moore to Battenberg, 19 September 1912, in DS/MISC/20, #147, Battenberg Papers, I.W.M.

199 Admiralty to Argo, 22 June 1912, P.P. See also *Record of Business Negotiations*, pp. 17-18.

200 Admiralty to Argo, 12 August 1912, P.P. The Admiralty letter of 25 April 1912 is known only through reference to it in the Admiralty letter of 12 August 1912.

201 Director of Navy Contracts to Argo, 20 August 1912, P.P.

202 Admiralty to Argo, 20 August 1912, P.P.

203 *Record of Business Negotiations*, p. 17-18.

204 Ibid., p. 15.

205 "Extract from 3rd Lord Minute" (13 August 1912), in DS/MISC/20, #174, Battenberg Papers, I.W.M.

206 The minutes of the meetings of the Board of Admiralty for 1912 do not record any discussions of the Argo case, but for the testimony of Battenberg, see Peirse to Pollen, 19 September 1912, P.P.

207 Peirse to Pollen, 8 July [1912]; Pollen to Peirse, 15 July 1912; Pollen to Peirse, 23 July 1912 (i); Pollen to Peirse, 23 July 1912 (ii); Peirse to Pollen, 24 July 1912; Peirse to Pollen, 27 July [1912]; and Pollen to Peirse, 29 July 1912; all in P.P.

208 Peirse to Pollen, 24 July 1912, P.P.

209 Peirse to Isherwood, 29 July 1912, P.P.

210 Peirse to Pollen, 25 August 1912, P.P.

211 Peirse to Battenberg, 7 September 1912, in DS/MISC/20, #147, Battenberg Papers, I.W.M.

212 Peirse to Pollen, 11 September 1912, P.P.

213 Rear-Admiral Richard Peirse, "Some Remarks on Mr Pollen's Plotting System" [August 1912], P.P.

214 Pollen to Peirse, 16 September 1912, P.P.

215 Pollen to Peirse, 18 September 1912, P.P. See also "Memorandum to H.S.H. Admiral Prince Louis of Battenberg," 18 September 1912, taken to the interview, and one copy of which was sent to Peirse, P.P.

216 Peirse to Pollen, 19 September 1912, P.P.

217 Moore to Battenberg, 19 September 1912, in DS/MISC/20, #147, Battenberg Papers, I.W.M.

218 Minter for the Director of Navy Contracts, to Argo, 24 September 1912, P.P.

219 Pollen to Peirse, 20 September 1912, P.P.

220 Log book of H.M.S. *Orion* (2 January 1912-23 April 1913), Adm. 53/24312, P.R.O.

221 Correspondent and exact date unknown, quoted by Anthony Pollen in *Great Gunnery Scandal*, p. 92.

222 Peirse to Pollen, 25 September 1912 and 27 September 1912, P.P.

223 Pollen to Churchill, 21 October 1912, P.P.
224 J. E. Masterton-Smith to Pollen, 26 October 1912, P.P.
225 Argo to the Director of Navy Contracts, 27 September 1912,, and Minter for the Director of Navy Contracts to Argo, 26 October 1912, P.P.
226 Peirse to Pollen, 15 October 1912, P.P.
227 For the director trials of 1912, see Captain Arthur W. Craig to Jellicoe, Vice-Admiral commanding Second Squadron, First Fleet, Home Fleet, 15 November 1912, in Craig-Waller Papers, N.L.M.D., and Peter Padfield, *Aim Straight*, pp. 209-10, and *Guns at Sea* (London: Hugh Evelyn, 1973), p. 248. For a detailed discussion of the characteristics of the director fitted in the *Thunderer*, see Lieutenant E. Altham, "Notes on Director Firing" (19 June 1913), Adm. 1/8330, P.R.O.
228 Pollen to Scott, 19 November 1912, P.P.
229 Pollen to Peirse, 21 November 1912, P.P.
230 Pollen to Boys, 27 September 1912; Boys to Pollen, 1 October 1912; Pollen to Boys, 7 October 1912; Pollen to Boys, 11 October 1912; Pollen to Boys, 19 October 1912; Boys to Pollen, 2 November 1912; Boys to Pollen, 10 November 1912; Pollen to Boys, 11 November 1912; Pollen to Boys, 13 November 1912; and Boys to Pollen, 15 November 1912; all in P.P.
231 Untitled and undated copy of report by Boys, P.P.
232 Pollen to Churchill, 18 November 1912, and Pollen to Peirse, 19 November 1912, P.P.
233 Jellicoe to Pollen, 22 November 1912, P.P.
234 Peirse to Pollen, 20 November 1912, P.P.
235 Log book of H.M.S. *Orion*, 2 January 1912-23 April 1913, Adm. 53/24312, P.R.O.
236 The clock must initially have been set with estimates of the target course and speed or of change of range and bearing rates from the Argo rate-plotter, after which occasional direct settings of ranges and bearings would have produced corrections in the generation of ranges and bearings.
237 Report of Captain Arthur W. Craig, "Full Charge Run," Craig Waller Papers, N.L.M.D.
238 Report of Captain Arthur W. Craig, "3/4 Charge Run," Craig Waller Papers, N.L.M.D.
239 Peirse to Pollen, 28 November 1912, P.P.
240 Dreyer and Usborne, *Technical History*, pp. 47, 55.
241 Pollen to Spender, 17 January 1913, P.P.
242 Pollen to Peirse, 24 and 29 November 1912, P.P.
243 [Commander Frederic Dreyer], "Some Comparisons between the Argo Clock and the Fire Control Table in 'Monarch,' " dated 1912, CCB.
244 Untitled set of remarks, written in late 1912, CCB.
245 Stephen Hungerford Pollen, "Memorandum," dated 6 December 1912, P.P.
246 Pollen to Battenberg, 24 October 1912, and summary of Battenberg to Pollen telegram, 25 October 1912, P.P.
247 Pollen to Battenberg, 17 December 1912, P.P.
248 Unnamed naval officer to Pollen, 11 December 1912, P.P.
249 Transcript from notes taken by Arthur Hungerford Pollen of a telephone conversation with Battenberg, dated 18 December 1912, P.P.
250 Statement dated 11 December 1912, P.P.
251 *Record of Business Negotiations*, p. 16.
252 Transcript from notes taken by Arthur Hungerford Pollen of a telephone conversation with Battenberg, dated 18 December 1912, P.P.

253 Admiralty to Argo, 19 December 1912, P.P.
254 Director of Navy Contracts to Argo, 30 December 1912, P.P. The Argo letter of 12 November 1912, which named the price for the Argo Clock installed in the *Orion*, is not to be found in the Pollen Papers. Information in the *Record of Business Negotiations*, p. 21, suggests that the price was the same as for the other clocks, that is, £2,133.
255 Argo to the Admiralty, 22 August 1912, P.P.
256 Admiralty to Argo, 26 September 1912, P.P.
257 Admiralty to Argo, 21 November 1912, and 20 January 1913, P.P. For the technical reasons which made the extensions of secrecy necessary to the Argo Company, see Argo to the Admiralty, 8 October 1912, P.P.
258 Argo to the Director of Navy Contracts, 25 November 1912, and 2 December 1912, P.P.
259 Stephen Hungerford Pollen, "Memorandum," dated 6 December 1912, P.P.
260 Argo to the Director of Navy Contracts, 18 January 1913, P.P.
261 Pollen to E. G. Pretyman, 4 February 1913, P.P. These included Beatty, Custance, Slade, Warrender and Wemyss for certain; probably Peirse, Beresford, Browning and Scott; and perhaps Bayly, Hamilton, Oliver or Poore. For the mention of the verbal messages of Beatty, Warrender and Wemyss, see Argo Company, "Governing Director's Report" (4 February 1913), P.P. For a list which may represent Pollen's naval correspondents in late 1912 or 1913, see untitled and undated list of officers found together with the extracts and Stephen Pollen letter, P.P.
262 Pollen to Masterton-Smith, 21 January 1913, P.P.
263 Pollen to Plunkett, 17 January 1913, with list of 20 extracts, in DRAX 3/4, Drax Papers, C.C.; undated set of 24 extracts, and set of 22 extracts, entitled "Revised extracts" and dated 4 February 1913 [sent to E. G. Pretyman], in P.P.
264 In Plunkett set of 20 extracts and undated set of 24 extracts, P.P.
265 Untitled and undated collection of extracts from letters to Pollen, P.P. The author of each extract was identified by a number code. This number was also marked on other letters received from the officer in question, and from an examination of these letters it has been possible to identify the first officer quoted as Slade, and second as Craig.
266 Masterton-Smith to Pollen, 22 January 1913, P.P.
267 Pollen to Moore, 23 January 1913 and Moore to Pollen, 25 January 1913, P.P. See also Pollen to Moore, 27 January 1913, P.P.
268 Pollen to Jellicoe, 23 January 1913 and Jellicoe to Pollen, 24 January 1913, P.P.
269 Pollen to Jellicoe, 23 January 1913, P.P.
270 The Argo Company Limited, "Governing Director's Report: February 4th 1913," P.P.
271 Pollen to Pretyman, 4 February 1913, P.P.
272 Pretyman to Pollen, 5 February 1913, P.P.
273 Pretyman to Pollen, 13 February 1913, P.P.
274 Typescript addenda to *Record of Business Negotiations*, pp. 1-2.
275 Admiralty to Argo, 21 February 1913 , P.P.
276 Opinion by Russell Clarke, 12 March 1913, P.P.
277 Coward & Hawksley Sons & Chance to the Admiralty, 15 March 1913, P.P.
278 Arthur Hungerford Pollen, *The Gun in Battle* (London: by the author, 1913), in *PP*.
279 *Technical History*, p. 7.
280 For the Colville report of July 1910, see this chapter, section 2(a).

281 *Technical History*, pp. 61-2. For the reservations of Captain W. W. Fisher, a member of the Colville Committee, with respect to rate-plotting, see Fisher to Plunkett, 19 October 1910, in DRAX 3/3, Drax Papers, C.C.
282 Ibid., pp. 18-19.
283 Ibid., p. 62.
284 According to the footnote on the first page of his commentary, Swinburne read only a portion of the Dreyer and Usborne report, which probably did not include the technical critique and conclusions, with which he would probably have been in at least some disagreement.
285 Great Britain, Admiralty, Contracts Department, *The Time and Range System: Report of J. Swinburne, F.R.S.*, dated 5 March 1913 [but from the printer's note at the bottom of the first page apparently not printed until August 1913], N.L.M.D.
286 *Record of Business Negotiations*, pp. 4-5.
287 Pollen to Spender, 24 March 1913, P.P.
288 Walter to Churchill, 17 March 1913, and Churchill to Walter, 24 March 1913, P.P.
289 See Pollen to Usborne, 18 March 1913; Pollen to Usborne, 21 April 1913; Pollen to Usborne, 29 April 1913, P.P.; and *Technical History*, p. 34n. See also Harding to Usborne, 12 January 1913, P.P.
290 The printing dates of the various reports are indicated by the printer's marks at the foot of the first page of each document.
291 Admiralty to Coward & Hawksley, Sons & Chance, 30 April 1913, P.P.
292 Hawksley to Pollen, 1 May 1913 (i); Hawksley to Pollen, 1 May 1913 (ii); C & H/S & C to the Admiralty, 1 May 1913; Pollen to Hawksley, 1 May 1913; C & H/S & C to Argo, 3 May 1913; C & H/S & C to the Admiralty, 5 May 1913; C & H/S & C to the Admiralty, 7 May 1913; Admiralty to C & H/S & C, 31 May 1913; C & H/S & C to the Admiralty, 2 June 1913; Admiralty to C & H/S & C, 6 June 1913; C & H/S & C to the Admiralty, 9 June 1913; Pollen to Hawksley, 10 June 1913; Admiralty to C & H/S & C, 16 June 1913; all in P.P.
293 Hawksley to Pollen, 26 May 1913; Argo Company, "Report of the Annual General Meeting . . ." (23 May 1913); and Hawksley to Pollen, 10 June 1913; P.P.
294 Pollen to Hawksley, 10 June 1913, P.P.
295 Stephen Pollen to Churchill, 2 June 1913; Churchill to Stephen Pollen, 4 June 1913; Masterton-Smith to Stephen Pollen, 11 June 1913; Stephen Pollen to Masterton-Smith, 13 June 1913; and Masterton-Smith to Stephen Pollen, 25 June 1913; P.P.
296 The Argo Company Limited, "Report of the Annual General Meeting . . ." (23 May 1913), P.P.
297 Pollen to Geoffrey Robinson, editor of *The Times*, 16 June 1913, P.P. For Pollen's efforts to keep his story out of the press in 1912, see Pollen to Percy Scott, 3 June 1912, P.P.
298 *NA*, 1913, pp. 319-20.
299 Clippings of the various newspaper accounts are to be found in PLLN 3/6, Pollen Papers, C.C.
300 Pollen to Beatty, 28 June 1920, P.P.
301 Clippings of the various newspaper accounts are to be found in PLLN 3/6, Pollen Papers, C.C.
302 Ibid.
303 Ibid.
304 For Dreyer's explicit use of this argument, see *Technical History*, p. 12.

305 *The Times*, 2 July 1913. For the complete text of the Emeritus letter, see the last print reproduced in *PP*. For the identity of Emeritus, see Pollen to Thomas, 22 October 1913, P.P. See also the response to the Emeritus letter in the *Naval and Military Record*, 9 July 1913.
306 "Secrecy can still be saved," Pollen wrote privately to Geoffrey Robinson, the editor of *The Times*, on 23 June 1913, "if the Admiralty desire it," in Pollen to Robinson, 23 June 1913, P.P.
307 Argo to the Admiralty, 30 June 1913, P.P.
308 Director of Navy Contracts to Argo, 3 July 1913, P.P.
309 Pollen draft letter to the Admiralty for the use of Hawksley, 5 July 1913, P.P.
310 Argo to the Admiralty, 8 July 1913, cover letter to Argo to the Admiralty, 8 July 1913, P.P.
311 Argo to the Admiralty, 8 July 1913, P.P.
312 Admiralty to Argo, 12 July 1913, P.P.
313 Argo to the Admiralty, 14 July 1913, P.P.
314 Pollen to Spender, 11 July 1913, P.P.
315 Padfield, *Aim Straight*, pp. 215-18.
316 Admiral Sir William James, *A Great Seaman: The Life of Admiral of the Fleet Sir Henry F. Oliver* (London: H. F. & G. Witherby, 1956), p. 119.
317 Ibid., p. 221.
318 Sir Robert Bannatyne Finlay, "Opinion" (23 July 1913), P.P.
319 Argo to the Admiralty, 22 July 1913, and Admiralty to Argo, 24 August 1913, P.P.
320 Argo to the Admiralty, 10 September 1913, P.P.
321 Admiralty to Argo, 8 October 1913, P.P.
322 Draft letter from Coward & Hawksley, Sons & Chance to the Admiralty, dated July 1913, but in light of the fact that the Admiralty letter of 24 August made no mention of such a communication from the Argo Company, probably not sent until early September.
323 See Fisher to Pollen, 26 March 1908, in Chapter 4, section 2(d).
324 Notes, which were generously supplied to the author by Hugh Lyon in 1979, taken from the "Board Minute Books, Schedule C 29, Book 3," and "Executive Committee Minute Book No. 1, Schedule C 33," in the Armstrong Whitworth Papers, Tyne and Wear County Record Office.
325 The Argo Company Limited, "Issue of 6% Debentures," no date, but about June or July 1913, P.P.
326 For the text of this print, see *PP*.
327 Undated Argo Memorandum, probably late 1912, P.P.
328 Pollen to [Mrs Pollen?], 5 November 1913, typescript excerpt; Riley to Pollen, 28 January 1914, typescript excerpt; Riley to Isherwood, n.d. but apparently January 1914; Riley to Pollen, 24 July 1914; and Pollen to Hawksley, 19 January 1915, P.P. The Russian order was for five complete sets of equipment, for which see "Memorandum on Fire Control," 1 August 1916, P.P. For the cancellation of the Austro-Hungarian order and the deliveries to the Russian navy, see the Epilogue.
329 Ibid., Riley to Pollen, 4 August 1914, P.P.
330 Riley to Pollen, 15 May 1914; Riley to Pollen, 18 May 1914; and Pollen [secretary?] to a Mr Dodge, 22 August 1914, P.P.
331 Pollen to [Mrs Pollen?], 16 September 1913; Argo to Rear-Admiral Mark Kerr, 17 January 1914; and Pollen to [Mrs Pollen?], typescript excerpt, 4 February 1914; P.P. For the breakdown of the Turkish discussions over cost, see Rear-Admiral Arthur Limpus to Pollen, 13 July 1914, and Pollen

to Limpus, 20 July 1914, P.P. For a translation of one report on the Argo system made to the French navy in 1913 or 1914, see undated report, "Pollen System" [henceforward cited as "Pollen System"] in the company records of Barr & Stroud, to the author courtesy of Mr Iain Russell. The report expressed a favorable view of the Cooke-Pollen range-finder, noted that Barr & Stroud believed that the Argo system as a whole was superior to that adopted by the Royal Navy, but was critical of the complexity of the plotting and calculating instruments, and concluded that existing French methods were superior.

332 Pollen to Hall, 15 January 1914, P.P. "I simply do not know how far the manufacturing capacity can be extended," Pollen confided to Hall, "as there is the very real difficulty of getting the right men as well as the right tools and space, and men cannot be extemporized."

333 Riley to Pollen, 13 November 1913, P.P.

334 Pollen to Craig, n.d., quoted by Anthony Pollen in *The Great Gunnery Scandal*, p. 114.

335 "Pollen System."

336 "Pollen Patents; Question of Civil Proceedings Against Argo Co.," dated February 1914, *IQ/DNO*, vol. 2 (1913), N.L.M.D.

337 Undated, untitled letter, P.P. For the conditions of the sea trials of the Argo system for what was probably the Russian navy, see Pollen to Rear-Admiral Arthur Leveson, 20 February 1914, P.P. For the complete success of these trials in June 1914, and the Russian desire to reequip immediately the entire battle fleet, see Pollen to Leveson, 19 June 1914, P.P.

338 Admiralty to various major commands, 29 July 1913, *IQ/DNO*, vol. 2 (1913), N.L.M.D.

339 "Pollen Patents; Question of Civil Proceedings Against Argo Co.," dated 2 February 1914,, *IQ/DNO*, Vol. 2 (1913), N.L.M.D.

340 "Pollen Patents: Re Civil Proceedings Against Argo Co.," incomplete, dated 22 April 1914, *IQ/DNO*, Vol. 2 (1913), N.L.M.D.

341 For a detailed description of these trials, see Great Britain, Admiralty, Gunnery Branch, *Report on Firings at H.M.S. "Empress of India," Carried out by First Fleet on the 4th November 1913* [henceforward cited as *Report on Firings at H.M.S. "Empress of India"*], N.L.M.D.

342 Captain C. S. Hickey to Admiral Callaghan, 5 November 1913, and also captain of the dreadnought battleship *King George V*, who reported comparable results with regard to range-finders on conventional mountings, in "Gunnery Practice at Sea: Sinking of 'HMS Empress of India'" (8 December 1913), in ibid. and Adm. 1/8346, P.R.O.

343 Battle Practice Chart, H.M.S. *Orion*, dated 1912, Craig-Waller Papers, N.L.M.D. The conditions under which the *Orion* shot were regarded by the Admiralty as "good," as opposed to the "very good" conditions that pertained for no fewer than 18 out of the 33 battleships tested. See Great Britain, Parliament, *Parliamentary Papers* (Commons), *1913*, Vol. 43 (*Accounts and Papers*, Vol. 3), Cmnd. 6765, "Result of Battle Practice in His Majesty's Fleet, 1912."

344 The *Vanguard* figures for range observation were, if anything, low. In a firing practice that took place on 20 December 1915, the Dreyer Table in the dreadnought battleship *Iron Duke* recorded 10 ranges a minute. The mean range was 7,000 yards, the sea was calm, and visibility was very good (13,000 yards), as would have been the case in a pre-war Battle Practice. See Great Britain, Admiralty, Naval Staff, Gunnery Division, *Extract of Gunnery Practices in Grand Fleet, 1914 to 1918: Battleships and Battle Cruisers* (March 1922), N.L.M.D.

345 *PP*, pp. 4, 360.
346 *NA, 1914*, p. 348.
347 "Pollen Patents: Re Civil Proceedings Against Argo Co.," incomplete, dated 22 April 1914, *IQ/DNO*, vol. 2 (1913), N.L.M.D. See also the report of the captain of H.M.S. *King George V, in Report on Firings at H.M.S. "Empress of India,"* p. 18, and Great Britain, Admiralty, Gunnery Branch, *Manual of Gunnery (Volume III) for His Majesty's Fleet, 1915* (1915), pp. 18–19, N.L.M.D.
348 *Technical History*, p. 24.
349 In 1911, only 4 out of the 12 dreadnoughts in service were to be found among the top 10 scoring capital ships, the superior gun-laying capability of the all-big-gun units notwithstanding—an indication that rate-finding and rate-keeping difficulties were posing serious problems. The Admiralty Permanent Secretary warned in the parliamentary report on the 1912 Battle Practice that "the conditions of the practice differed widely from those of previous years, and no comparison can be made." It can be noted, however, that in 1912, 8 of the 16 dreadnoughts in service were to be found among the top 10 scoring capital ships. In 1913, 9 dreadnoughts out of the 15 in service that year were among the top 10 highest scoring capital ships. 60 per cent of the dreadnoughts in service, in other words, were to be found in the top 10, and 90 per cent of the top 10 vessels were all-big-gun capital ships, as compared with the respective figures of 50 per cent and 80 per cent in 1912, and 33 per cent and 40 per cent in 1911. "Gunnery in the Royal Navy: Conference at Admiralty Dec. 1911/Jan. 1912; Report and action" (13 February 1913), in Adm. 1/8328, P.R.O.; Record of hits made by 22 battleships in the 1912 Battle Practice, Craig-Waller Papers, N.L.M.D.; Great Britain, Parliament, *Parliamentary Papers* (Commons), *1911*, Vol. 48 (*Accounts and Papers*, Vol. 4), Cmnd. 5957, "Result of Battle Practice in His Majesty's Fleet, 1911"; *idem, 1913*, "Result of Battle Practice in His Majesty's Fleet, 1912"; and *idem, 1914*, Vol. 54 (*Accounts and Papers*, Vol. 5), Cmnd. 7366, "Result of Battle Practice in his Majesty's Fleet, 1913."
350 For the range finder outfit of the *Colossus*, see "'Colossus' Report on Rangefinders," dated 20 May 1914, *IQ/DNO*, Vol. 3 (1914), N.L.M.D. For its fire control gear, see "Dreyer Rear-Admiral F. G. Fire Control Tables" (February 1916), submitted to the Royal Commission on Awards to Inventors, 1922, in T. 173/204, P.R.O. It should be noted that some of the information in this list was revised in light of material contained in "Dreyer's Fire Control Apparatus," dated 6 July 1914, *IQ/DNO*, vol. 3 (1914), N.L.M.D. For the 1912 long-range experiments and their effect on Jellicoe, see Bacon, *Jellicoe*, p. 180.
351 Dreyer, *Sea Heritage*, p. 86.
352 The captain of the *Colossus* at this time, ironically, was none other than William Goodenough, Pollen's cousin, whose invitation of 1900 to witness a firing practice at sea, it will be recalled, had prompted the inventor to begin his study of naval gunnery in the first place.
353 The dumaresq and Vickers Clock were connected by a mechanical linkage that automatically set the rate of the former to match the indications of the rate on the latter instrument. In addition, ranges indicated by the clock were marked on the plot, so that observed and calculated data could be compared, and corrections to the clock settings made if their paths differed.
354 The *Hercules* was Jellicoe's flagship from December 1911 to November 1912, and Dreyer was Jellicoe's flag commander. The Mark III Table may have been fitted in this vessel in 1912 in order to give Jellicoe the opportunity to

witness demonstrations of its capabilities. The Mark I Table that may have been displaced by this action would then have been available for installation in the yet to be completed 13.5-inch gun battleship *Marlborough*.

355 "Dreyer Rear-Admiral F.G. Fire Control Tables" (February 1916), submitted to the Royal Commission on Awards to Inventors, 1922, in T. 173/204, P.R.O.; "Dreyer's Fire Control Apparatus," dated 6 July 1914, *IQ/DNO*, Vol. 3 (1914), and *Handbook of Captain F.C. Dreyer's Fire Control Tables, 1918*, N.L.M.D. Apart from the differences noted in the text, the main distinctions between the various Dreyer table marks fitted to dreadnoughts were as follows. The Mark I table was completely manual in operation, with no motor-driven gear or any electrical connections. The Mark II table was similar to the Mark I except for the electrical connections to drive the Argo Clock Mark IV. The Mark III table had electric motors for the clock drives and paper rollers. The Mark IV table was similar to the Mark III, but substituted a new model "electrical dumaresq" for the previously standard mechanical instrument. The Mark IV★ table was fitted with a slightly modified range plotter, which was arranged to allow the plotting of somewhat longer ranges than was possible with the Mark IV. The Mark V table, which like the Mark IV★ was not introduced until after the outbreak of war, was essentially the same as the Mark IV★, differing only in the manner in which deflection was handled (for which see below). In the Dreyer Table Marks I, III-V, the dumaresq and clock were connected by a mechanical linkage that automatically set the rate of the former to match the indications of the rate on the latter instrument. In the Dreyer Table Marks I, III, IV, and IV★, the deflection was read off the dumaresq and manually set on a device, the Deflection Totaliser, which corrected this figure by taking account of ranges set manually from the clock and ballistical factors; the Totaliser then transmitted the corrected deflection to the gun stations. In the Dreyer Table Mark II, the Totaliser was probably set manually with ranges and bearings from the Argo Clock. In the Dreyer Table Mark V, the dumaresq and range clock were both mechanically connected to the Totaliser, and the dumaresq deflection and range thus set automatically. In all marks, the ranges indicated by the clock were marked on the plot, so that observed and calculated data could be compared, and corrections to the clock settings made if their paths differed; ballistical and spotting corrections were added automatically to the generated ranges, which were then transmitted from the clock automatically to the gun stations. In the Dreyer Table Mark V only, clock as well as observed bearings were plotted, and the two paths compared as in the case of calculated and observed ranges.

356 "'Colossus' Report on Rangefinders," dated 20 May 1914, *IQ/DNO*, Vol. 3 (1914), N.L.M.D.

357 "Invention of 15' Range Finder, Sea Going Trials of," dated December 1909, in Adm. 1/8051, P.R.O., and "Tender for Rangefinders &c.," 25 July 1914, and "Range-finder Mountings," 30 July 1914, *IQ/DNO*, Vol. 3 (1914), N.L.M.D.

358 "Practices of Ships Fitted with Director Firing," dated May 1914, *IQ/DNO*, Vol. 3 (1914), N.L.M.D. These were *Iron Duke, Marlborough, Neptune, King George V, Ajax, Audacious, Centurion, Monarch* and *Thunderer*.

359 Padfield, *Aim Straight*, pp. 211-12. For the reluctance of some officers to use the director, see ibid.

360 Lord Chatfield, *The Navy and Defence* (London: William Heinemann, 1942), p. 113. For the conditions and results of the high-speed trials, which actually took place in 1913 and not in 1914 as stated by Chatfield, see Rear-Admiral Sir David Beatty's Memorandum, .0142, 4 June 1913, and "Remarks on High

Speed Exercises, 5th June," .0142, 11 June 1913, both in the Drax Papers, DRAX 4/1, C.C.
361 Chatfield, *Navy and Defence*, p. 113.
362 "Naval and Military Intelligence: The Firing of the Orion," *The Times*, 27 June 1913.
363 Chatfield, *Navy and Defence*, p. 113.
364 Chatfield recorded that "opponents of [firing at] long ranges were . . . critical [of the trials] and considered the ammunition had been 'largely thrown away,'" ibid.
365 In 1914, Pollen's Russian correspondent advised him that the Russian navy did not think that the Germans had "in fact applied the automatic principle either to plotting the actual course, or to the French method of making curves of the velocity of the change in the distance and angle of bearing" [that is, rate plotting], for which see see undated, untitled letter from Russian naval officer to Pollen, P.P.
366 "Intelligence Information Obtained at Kiel," p. 155, in "Intelligence, 1914," Adm. 137/1013, P.R.O.
367 Ibid., and R. A. Burt, *British Battleships of World War One* (Annapolis: Naval Institute Press, 1986), pp. 212-3. See also Henry G. Thursfield, "Development of Tactics in the Grand Fleet: Three Lectures," delivered 2, 3 and 7 February 1922, in Thursfield Papers, THU 107, N.M.M. Thursfield maintained that before the First World War, "the heavy secondary armaments of the German ships, and the fact that they were known to practice attacks on an enemy engaged with the battlefleet by torpedo craft passing through the battle line, led to the firm conviction that the Germans would endeavour to fight a close range action." "So firm was this conviction," Thursfield added, "that our whole tactics were based upon it."
368 Ibid.
369 For the per-unit costs of a production Argo Clock Mark IV, see Argo to the Director of Navy Contracts, 10 June 1912, P.P. No tender for an Argo helm-free/true-course plotter trials prototype or production order was ever made. Pollen's quotations to the United States Navy for a plotting table was £2,062 and for a clock £2,312, so that a plotter price to the Royal Navy of about £1,000 does not seem unlikely, for which see Pollen to Commander Symmington, 29 April 1914, P.P. Consideration of the cost estimates made to the Greek government in 1914 for a complete system also supports an estimate of £1,000 for a production helm-free/true-course plotter, again allowing for the reduction in price that would have been made for a large order from the Royal Navy, for which see Argo to Rear-Admiral Mark Kerr, 17 January 1914, P.P.
370 *Technical History*, pp. 15, 16.
371 Argo to the Director of Navy Contracts, 10 June 1912, P.P.
372 Padfield, *Aim Straight*, p. 219.
373 Jellicoe to Dreyer, 10 June 1913, in DRYR 3/2, and Dreyer to Jellicoe, 14 June 1913, in DRYR 4/3, both in Dreyer Papers, C.C.; and Pollen to Hall, 15 January 1914, P.P.
374 J. S. Sandars to A. J. Balfour, 10 October 1912, Balfour Papers, quoted in Randolph S. Churchill, *Winston S. Churchill*, 2 Vols (Boston: Houghton Mifflin, 1967), Vol. 2, p. 610.
375 Ibid., pp. 611-12, and Bridgeman to Sir Francis Hopwood, 8 December 1912, quoted in *FDSF*, Vol. 1, p. 259.
376 Quoted in Bacon, *Jellicoe*, pp. 181-2.

377 Battenberg, Fisher wrote to Jellicoe on 20 December 1914, "was a cypher and Winston's facile dupe!", in *FGDN*, Vol. 3, p. 100. For Battenberg's nickname of "I concur," see Richard Hough, *The Great War at Sea, 1914-1918* (Oxford: Oxford University Press, 1983), p. 162.

378 Pollen to Custance, 23 October 1934, P.P.

379 Admiral G. A. Callaghan, "Home Fleets General Orders," "13. Fire Control Arrangements" and "14. Fire Control Organization" (25 October 1913); and "Enclosure No. I to Home Fleets General Order No. 14 of 5th November 1913," DRAX 1/9, Drax Papers, C.C.

380 Winston S. Churchill, *The World Crisis*, 6 Vols (New York: Charles Scribner's Sons, 1923), Vol. 1, title of Chapter 6.

381 Fisher to Esher, 8 April 1910, *FGDN*, vol. 2, p. 320. For Fisher's preference for the "2 keels to 1" over the "Two-power" standard on the grounds that the former did not involve building against the United States, see Fisher to J. A. Spender, 8 August 1910, ibid., p. 335.

382 Fisher to Gerard Fiennes, 14 April 1910, ibid., p. 321.

383 Rear-Admiral R. H. S. Bacon, "The Battleship of the Future," *Transactions of the Institution of Naval Architects*, Vol. 52 (1910), pp. 1-21.

384 Fisher to Spender, 8 August 1910, *FGDN*, Vol. 2, p. 335.

385 Fisher to McKenna, 22 August 1910, ibid., p. 337.

386 Fisher to Balfour, 15 October 1910, *FGDN*, Vol. 3, p. 31.

387 Pollen suspected this at once. On 18 March 1910, he wrote to the editor of the *Morning Post*, observing that

the public have the best of reasons for knowing that Admiral Bacon was the confidant of Lord Fisher. We have the First Lord's word for it that the lecturer of yesterday enjoyed the fullest confidence of the Board of Admiralty less than a year ago. The portentous question that faces us, therefore, is this:—Is this balderdash about non-combatant battleships just his own extemporized opinion or has he unconsciously revealed to friend and foe at last that imponderable and unknown quantity, the mind of the British Admiralty?

For Pollen's draft letter to the editor, *Morning Post*, 18 March 1910, see Pollen Papers, PLLN 3/6, C.C.

388 *FGDN*, Vol. 2, p. 332. See also Fisher to Fiennes, 14 April 1910, ibid., Vol. 2, p. 321.

389 Gerard Fiennes, *The Ocean Empire: Its Dangers and Defence* (London: A. Treherne, 1911), pp. 220-4.

390 For Fisher's relations with Corbett, see Donald M. Schurman, *Julian S. Corbett, 1854-1922: Historian of British Maritime Policy from Drake to Jellicoe* (London: Royal Historical Society, 1981).

391 Julian S. Corbett, *Some Principles of Maritime Strategy* (Annapolis: Naval Institute Press, 1972; f.p. 1911), pp. 105-27.

392 Randolph S. Churchill (ed.), *Winston S. Churchill: Companion Volume II, Part 2, 1907-1911* (Boston: Houghton Mifflin, 1969), p. 1325.

393 Ibid., p. 1329.

394 Ibid., p. 1332.

395 Ibid., p. 1329.

396 Ibid., p. 1332.

397 Churchill to Battenberg, 10 November 1911, DS/MISC/20, 46, Battenberg Papers, I.W.M.

398 For the Admiralty's commitment through April 1912 to build both battleships and battle cruisers, see Churchill to Fisher, 12 April 1912, F.P. 568, FISR 1/11, C.C.

399 Randolph Churchill, ed., *Companion Volume II, Part 2*, p. 1349.
400 Ibid.
401 Winston Churchill, *The World Crisis*, Vol. 1, pp. 106-7.
402 Fisher to Jellicoe, 13 December 1911, in *FGDN*, Vol. 2, p. 420; and Fisher to Churchill, 10 and 22 November, 3 and 30 December, 1911, in Randolph Churchill, *Companion Volume II, Part 2*, pp. 1329, 1341-2, 1349, 1365; and Fisher to Churchill, 16 January 1912, in Winston Churchill, *World Crisis*, Vol. 1, p. 146.
403 Fisher to Churchill, 22 April 1912, in Randolph Churchill, *Companion Volume II, Part 3*, p. 1546.
404 *Board Minutes* [Admiralty] (20 May, 19 June and 17 July, 1912) in Adm. 167/46, P.R.O. For the development of the *Queen Elizabeth* class, see R. A. Burt, *British Battleships of World War One* (Annapolis: Naval Institute Press, 1986), pp. 251-2.
405 Fisher to Reginald McKenna, 22 August 1910, *FGDN*, Vol. 2, p. 337. See also Fisher to J. A. Spender, 8 August 1910, ibid., p. 335. Fisher may have put forward his views to Lionel Yexley, with whom he sometimes corresponded on naval affairs. In 1911, Yexley wrote that a diesel propelled battleship would be under construction in 1912, for which see "The Battleship of the Future," in Lionel Yexley (ed.), *The Fleet Annual and Naval Year Book, 1911* (London: The Fleet, Ltd., 1911), pp. 39-44.
406 For Fisher and the Royal Commission, see Ruddock Mackay, *Fisher of Kilverstone* (Oxford: Clarendon Press, 1973), pp. 437-41.
407 Ibid., Vol. 2, p. 478.
408 Original sketch, entitled "H.M.S. 'Incomparable'," dated 17 September 1912, 2 pp., F.P. 4484, FISR 5/42; typescript of drawing notes, entitled "H.M.S. 'Incomparable'," 3 pp., F.P. 4283, FISR 5/17, C.C. Many of the characteristics of this design—apart from the proposal for diesel engines—originated with Churchill, for which see Churchill to Fisher, 12 April 1912, F.P. 568, FISR 1/11, C.C.
409 Fisher to Esher, 20 September 1912, *FGDN*, Vol. 2, pp. 478-9.
410 Fisher to Parsons, 6 October 1912, ibid., Vol. 2, p. 479.
411 For the set of plans of a 27,500 and 29,000 ton vessel and an illustration of the latter, see F.P. 5528, in FISR 12/5, C.C.
412 Fisher to Parsons, 14 October 1912, *FGDN*, Vol. 2, p. 481.
413 Fisher to Parsons, 3 November 1912, ibid., p. 482.
414 Fisher to Parsons quoted in A. C. Hardy, *History of Motorshipping: The story of Fifty Years of Progress which have had a Profound Influence upon the Development of Sea Transport during the Twentieth Century* (London: Whitehall Technical Press, 1955), p. 201. For more on the problem of applying diesel propulsion to high-speed large warships, and, in particular, the unlikelihood that it would work for battle cruisers, see Alexander Richardson, "Machinery Problems in High-Powered Warships," *NA,1912*, pp. 91-111.
415 Mackay, *Fisher of Kilverstone*, p. 441.
416 Churchill to Fisher, 9 March 1912, F.P. 559, FISR 1/11, C.C.
417 Fisher to Churchill, 5 March 1912, *FDGN*, Vol. 2, pp. 438-40. "You must make Admiral Peirse Controller," Fisher had written, "whether you like him or not."
418 Pollen to Fisher, 25 June 1912, and Fisher to Pollen, 27 June 1912, P.P.
419 Fisher to Eardley-Wilmot, 20 October 1913, F.P. 2255; see also Fisher to Yexley, 25 October 1913, F.P. 2257, both in FISR 3/6, C.C. Fisher, in addition, retained his confidence in Dreyer, for which see Dreyer to Fisher,

23 June 1914, F.P. 813, FISR 1/15, C.C.; and Fisher to Jellicoe, 23 April 1914 and 29 August 1914, in *FGDN*, Vol. 3, pp. 56, 202.

420 Jellicoe to Fisher, 29 December 1914, F.P. 890a, FISR 1/17, C.C.

421 "Minute by Director of Naval Construction" (23 October 1913), in "Armour Protection," Admiralty confidential print (March 1914), N.L.M.D.

422 "Minute by Third Sea Lord" (6 January 1914), in ibid.

423 For press comment on the decline of the battle cruiser, see Alan H. Burgoyne, "Recent Developments in Battleship Type" [12 March 1913] *Transactions of the Institution of Naval Architects*, Vol. 55, Part I (1913), p. 10; "New Battle Cruisers: The Trials of the Queen Mary," *The Times* [London] (22 May 1913), p. 5; and "Warship Design: III—The Dreadnought Policy," *The Times* [London] (15 October 1913), p. 12.

424 *Board Minutes* [Admiralty] 1913 (6 May 1913), Adm. 167/47, P.R.O.

425 Fisher does appear to have been concerned that D'Eyncourt would substitute coal for oil propulsion in the later vessels of the *Queen Elizabeth* class, for which see Watts to Fisher, 9 April 1913, F.P. 674, FISR 1/13, C.C. For Fisher's later claim that he opposed the construction of the *Royal Sovereign* class from the start, see Fisher to Asquith, 15 March 1916, *FGDN*, Vol. 3, p. 328.

426 Fisher to Arnold White, 13 March 1913, *FGDN*, Vol. 2, p. 484. See also Fisher to Balfour, May 1913?, *FGDN*, Vol. 3, pp. 33–4.

427 Fisher to Hopwood, 6 June 1913, *FGDN*, Vol. 2, p. 488.

428 Fisher to Balfour (?), 4 September 1913, ibid., Vol. 2, p. 491. Fisher may have initially opposed the use of steam in submarines on the advice of Rear-Admiral S. S. Hall, but was convinced of its utility for fleet submarines by Churchill, for which see Hall to Fisher, 4 July 1913, F.P. 708, and Churchill to Fisher, 30 August 1913, F.P. 720, both in FISR 1/13, C.C. For Fisher's belief that submarines had demonstrated their capacity to sink capital ships in recent maneuvers, see Fisher to Balfour, 8 September 1913, *FGDN*, Vol. 3, p. 34. For Balfour's belief that submarines had made the battleship obsolete, which seems to have been even greater than that of Fisher, see Balfour to Fisher, 25 October 1910, F.P. 499, FISR 1/10 and Balfour to Fisher, 2 November 1910, F.P. 500, FISR 1/10, C.C.

429 Fisher to Corbett, 29 November 1913, *FGDN*, Vol. 2, p. 494.

430 Fisher to Churchill, 6 December 1913, ibid., p. 496.

431 Fisher to Jellicoe, 3 February 1914, ibid., p. 498.

432 Fisher to Jellicoe, 25 May 1914, ibid., p. 507.

433 Fisher to Corbett, 22 June 1914, ibid., p. 508.

434 See Appendix, Tables 18 and 21.

435 Jellicoe to Churchill, 14 July 1914, A. Temple Patterson (ed.), *The Jellicoe Papers: Selections from the private and official correspondence of Admiral of the Fleet Earl Jellicoe of Scapa*, 2 Vols (London: Navy Records Society, 1966–69), Vol. 1, pp. 38-9.

Epilogue

1 Fisher and Pollen at War, August 1914-May 1916

(a) FISHER

Following the outbreak of war in 1914, Battenberg's position as First Sea Lord was made untenable by unwarranted public suspicion of his German origins and Churchill's dissatisfaction with his cautious direction of naval operations. He thus resigned and was replaced on 30 October 1914 by Fisher.[1] A few days after assuming office, the new First Sea Lord was alarmed by Percy Scott's report that only a third of the dreadnoughts had been equipped with directors and that, as a consequence, the gunnery efficiency of the British battle line was a matter of some doubt. In the first week of his administration, Fisher therefore appointed Scott "Adviser to their Lordships on matters connected with the gunnery efficiency of the Fleet," which gave him the authority to take whatever measures were necessary to fit the rest of the battleships and battle cruisers with directors in the shortest possible time.[2] Later in November, Fisher forcefully reminded Admiral Sir John Jellicoe, the Commander-in-Chief of the Grand Fleet, and Vice-Admiral Sir David Beatty, the Commander of the Battle Cruiser Force, that gunnery superiority over the German navy was essential.[3]

Jellicoe responded by convening a special conference of Grand Fleet gunnery officers that apparently expressed satisfaction with the existing arrangements for long-range firing, a judgement that must have been reported to Fisher.[4] In any case, Dreyer—who visited the Admiralty in April 1915 while his ship, the *Orion*, was refitting in Devonport—almost certainly assured the First Sea Lord that there was little to fear in so far as fire control was concerned. "I had a most interesting talk," Fisher wrote to Jellicoe on 23 April 1915, "with Dreyer. *I am devoted to him*. All is arranged as he wishes."[5] By May 1915, moreover, Scott had, by dint of prodigious effort, succeeded in extending director firing to the point that some two-thirds of the Grand Fleet's dreadnoughts were so equipped.[6] Fisher thus seems to have believed that the Royal Navy's long-range naval gunnery technique was equal to or better than that of the German fleet and that, as a consequence, a superiority in big-gun caliber would give British capital ships a decisive advantage in battle.

Fisher's faith in his ideas on gunnery and capital ship design was greatly strengthened by the outcome of an encounter between British and German naval units in the South Atlantic. On 8 December 1914, a German cruiser squadron under the command of Vice-Admiral Graf von Spee was intercepted by a British force led by Vice-Admiral Sir Doveton Sturdee off the Falkland Islands. In the ensuing action, two German armoured cruisers *Scharnhorst* and *Gneisenau*, which were much inferior in armament and speed to Sturdee's two battle cruisers, the *Invincible* and *Inflexible*, were overtaken and sunk in a long-range gunnery duel, the British vessels suffering only negligible damage. Fisher was exultant on hearing the news. "*Perhaps their guns never reached us!*" he speculated on 10 December after receiving preliminary reports of the engagement, adding "So it may have been like shooting pheasants: the pheasants not shooting back!"[7] Here, it seemed, was proof that a superiority in long-range hitting when combined with speed would produce decisive results, and Fisher thus began to press forthwith for the construction of battle cruisers of unprecedented size, speed and gun-power.

On 18 December, Fisher met with Eustace Tennyson D'Eyncourt, the Director of Naval Construction, to discuss the possibility of converting two recently laid down *Royal Sovereign* class battleships, upon which little work had been completed, into battle cruisers armed with four 15-inch guns. On 19 December, Fisher wrote to the D.N.C. and outlined his proposals for a new battle cruiser, which was to be called the "Rhadamanthus," at this time calling for a main battery of six 15-inch guns. On 21 December Fisher and D'Eyncourt came to an agreement on the dimensions, speed and armament of the new capital ship.[8] "I fear you have missed my point," Fisher argued to a skeptical Churchill that same day,

> about the 32-knot 'Rhadamanthus'! (*So quickly built and cheap!*) The only vessel that can '*catch*', not 'keep up with'—*she has to catch!!!!!!*—the German battle cruiser *Lützow*, of 28 knots, is the English *Tiger*, of 29 knots. (She can't be counted on for 30, I'm told!) *Anyhow, a few months out of dock* (even a few more tons of coal) *makes a superiority into an inferiority of speed in the list you gave me!* There's no '*commanding personality*' in that list! ONE 'Greyhound' amongst that lot of hares with the characteristics of the 'Rhadamanthus' would knock them all out! The big 5 knots of the 'Rhadamanthus' is wanted '*here and now*' (as the Salvation Army poster says!). *We have got to have 3 'Rhadamanthi'!*[9]

In the face of the opposition of the First Lord and others in the Cabinet and at the Admiralty to his proposals, Fisher turned to Jellicoe for support. "'*Battle cruisers and more battle cruisers*' is the watchword!" he wrote to the Commander-in-Chief of the Grand Fleet on 22 December, adding "Cumbersome battleships are rotten. Slow men and slow ships mean failure."[10] "*I am now alone here*," Fisher complained to Jellicoe the very next day,

> *fighting the battle for more battle cruisers!* I wish, when you have leisure, you would write me a casual sort of letter which I can show to the Cabinet (*not as if you were responding to my request; not an official memorandum*) that the supposed existing superiority in fast battleships that we now have is FALLACIOUS! . . . . *None of our existing ships have the necessary FUTURE speed!* We must have 32 knots speed to give us a margin of being long out of dock, and to give the necessary excess of speed to CATCH a 28-knot ship! *Millions* of SLOW *ships are no use!* SPEED IS EVERYTHING! . . . . it would save me an immensity of trouble if you would kindly send this letter on to Beatty, as being the Admiral commanding the Battle Cruiser Squadron, if he also could support me with a private letter *written in a casual way!* I have to resort to every stratagem to gain

my mind! If I don't get these 3 battle cruisers of 32 knots speed, I shall have to leave the Admiralty on January 25 next.[11]

On 29 December, Jellicoe responded belatedly to Fisher's call for support with a letter, in which he wrote that

> unless the policy of building much faster battle cruisers is reverted to, we shall find ourselves in a position of not having any sufficient number of vessels to catch and engage the increasing number of vessels of this type possessed by Germany.
>
> . . . . I am therefore most strongly of opinion that we should immediately, if we have not already done so, commence to lay down battle cruisers possessing a speed of at least 30 to 31 knots. If we can get higher speeds by the use of oil fuel, it is most eminently desirable to do so.
>
> . . . . The war, so far, has proved what you have yourself so often stated would be proved, first, the immense value of high speed, and secondly, the overwhelming value of the big gun. In every engagement that has taken place, this latter point has been most strongly emphasized, and for this reason, I am perfectly convinced that our new battle cruisers should carry 15″ guns.[12]

Fisher welcomed Jellicoe's missive, but by this date had "anticipated" it by having claimed the backing of the Commander-in-Chief of the Grand Fleet for his proposed battle cruisers in a letter to Churchill written on Christmas day![13] The First Lord appears to have set aside his objections by 27 December,[14] and two units, named *Renown* and *Repulse*, were ordered at the end of December.[15] These vessels were roughly comparable to the *Lion* class in displacement, but were significantly less well–protected, nearly 20 per cent faster and carried a main armament of six 15-inch rather than eight 13.5-inch guns. Both Churchill and Jellicoe believed that eight heavy caliber guns were necessary, the latter even suggesting in January that this should be secured by reverting to the 13.5-inch gun.[16] Fisher would have none of it. On 22 January 1915 he informed Jellicoe that the adoption of two additional 15-inch guns was "absolutely inadmissible, because of loss of speed from 33 knots which is almost certain, *great increase in draught of water, and displacement and cost.*" The 13.5-inch gun, he added in a postscript, was obsolete, and that "we shall go in for an 18-inch gun now."[17]

On 23 January, Fisher wrote again to Jellicoe and confided that "I'm getting out a new light cruiser, to be completed by Cammell Laird in 11 months: *33 knots* speed, *23 feet draught of water,* four *15*-inch guns!"[18] "Our North Sea experiences," Fisher explained to Churchill two days later,

> clearly indicate that a cruiser of 32 knots speed and 22 1/2 feet draught of water, carrying four 15-inch guns, associated with groups of 4-inch guns on turntables for dealing with destroyers, would as completely knock out all the German light cruisers as the *Invincible* knocked out the *Scharnhorst.* It would be a repetition of the old argument that the big gun and high speed, besides giving you certain victory, avoid having any killed or wounded. But chiefly is this type of vessel imperatively demanded for the Baltic, where she can go through the international highway of the Sound owing to her shallow draught.[19]

The big-gun broadside of the proposed warships was in fact substantially greater than that of an *Invincible*,[20] and the appellation of "light cruiser" for what were in fact battle cruisers was intended to deceive the Chancellor of the Exchequer, who had ruled that no sanction would be given for the construction of new warships that were larger than light cruisers.[21] The justification of building such vessels for use in the Baltic to cover a landing of troops on the Pomeranian coast was also a cover. "I had a fierce time," Fisher wrote to D'Eyncourt on 25 January, "with the First Lord—*Very Fierce!*—but we are to have two [large light cruisers] . . . if only we can make a good story for the Cabinet." "It's on the Baltic necessities," he noted later, "that we will carry these ships through the Cabinet."[22] Churchill had shown considerable interest in carrying out an offensive operation in the Baltic to relieve pressure on Russia,[23] but this was a program that Fisher did not seriously support.[24] Fisher's insistence on shallow draught, moreover, was probably motivated mainly by his belief that this characteristic enabled vessels to steam faster.[25]

On 25 January 1915, on the very day that Fisher raised the issue of the big-gun light cruisers with Churchill and D'Eyncourt, the case for building additional battle cruisers was strengthened by an unsatisfactory action that was fought between British and German battle cruisers off the Dogger Bank.[26] On 28 January, Fisher informed Asquith, the Prime Minister, that Jellicoe had advised him that "the battle cruiser action [Dogger Bank] showed most conclusively the absolute necessity of a BIG preponderance of these ships . . ."[27] Fisher then threatened to resign over the deployment of battle cruisers and fast battleships to the Dardanelles operation, which appears to have been averted only by the promise of approval for two big-gun light cruisers. "I had fierce rows with Winston and the Prime Minister," Fisher wrote to Jellicoe on 29 January, 1915

> and it was a near thing! I was six hours yesterday with them and War Council and sat till 8 p.m.! . . . . I got two more '*light cruisers*' carrying 15-inch guns yesterday, of 33 knots speed and 22 feet draught of water, and oil for 11,000 miles . . . so we are getting on![28]

On 8 February 1915, Fisher wrote to Jellicoe of having 14 battle cruisers in the North Sea within a year, a figure that included the *Renown, Repulse*, and the two big-gun light cruisers.[29] That same day the First Sea Lord advised Beatty that

> I don't believe the Battle Squadrons will be in this war. THE BATTLE CRUISERS will finish the job! IF ONLY THEIR GUNNERY IS PERFECTION! Imagine! the *Invincible*, which was the leading ship and did the whole fight and sunk the prize gunnery ships *Scharnhorst* and *Gneisenau*, had not a single person killed or wounded! The *Invincible* hit first, hit hard, and kept on hitting![30]

By the end of February, the designs of the big-gun light cruisers, which were named *Courageous* and *Glorious*, were completed by the Director of Naval Construction, and work on the two ships began in March and April.

On 5 March 1915, Fisher wrote a memorandum in which he called for the construction of four additional big-gun light cruisers,[31] but he was subsequently able to secure approval for only one additional unit, which was similar to the previous two vessels except for the adoption of two 18-inch in place of the four 15-inch guns and changes in the secondary armament. This vessel, which was named *Furious*, was laid down in June.[32]

In the late spring of 1915, Fisher conceived of a battle cruiser that was far larger, faster, and more heavily armed than any vessel then built or building. On 5 May, he asked D'Eyncourt "what is the longest ship and widest ship that Cammell Laird can build?" and about this same time he approached Major Albert George Hadcock, head of the Elswick Ordnance Manufacturing Department, to design a 20-inch gun. The new vessel, which was to be named the *Incomparable*, was to be 1,000 feet long, displace 40,000 tons, carry six 20-inch guns and steam 35 knots.[33] In January, it will be recalled, Fisher had got approval for additional battle cruiser construction over the strong objections of Churchill and Asquith by threatening to resign, and he may have hoped that similar tactics would enable him to get his way once more. In any case, in mid May Fisher tendered his resignation as First Sea Lord, again over the Dardanelles issue, after which he informed the Prime Minister that he would return if placed in "complete professional charge of the war at sea . . ." and if "the First Lord of the Admiralty should be absolutely restricted to policy and parliamentary procedure . . ."[34] The granting of Fisher's terms would have given him the power to proceed with the *Incomparable* on his own authority, but they were refused, and with his departure from the Admiralty, commitment to the development of a 20-inch gun battle cruiser evaporated.[35]

In June 1915, Fisher accepted the presidency of the Board of Invention and Research, a position of little power that had nothing to do with capital ship design.[36] On 22 January 1916, however, Asquith, the Prime Minister, sought the old admiral's advice with regard to reports that new German battleships would mount 17-inch guns.[37] On 24 January, in a brief and petulant reply, Fisher suggested that the Prime Minister seek responsible opinion—that is to say, that of Jellicoe[38]—but on 3 February, he wrote again to put the case for larger caliber big-guns and fast battle cruisers at great length. In his letter, Fisher argued that "the time has gone by for the 18-inch gun, and I have applied myself to a 20-inch gun and have a model of a battle cruiser that should immediately be proceeded with, to mount 6 such guns on a light draught of water . . ." Fisher justified the battle cruiser as follows:

> Even the Naval "bow-and-arrow" party now admit that the big gun and high speed decide the sea fight, and the twaddle talked about weather being mist and preventing advantage of superior range of fire is as ludicrous as was the opposition by the ancient Boards of Admiralty to the introduction of steam, the use of iron for shipbuilding instead of wood . . . Sir David Beatty sighted the German battle cruisers at 14 miles distance; at 10 miles he hit the German Blücher and practically killed her then! But with bigger guns than Beatty's 13 1/2-inch guns the battle will be concluded at far greater distances. . . . . War is audacity and imagination, big conceptions and quick decisions. Hit first, hit hard,

keep on hitting—that is the motto of the battle cruiser. No other type counts in the line of battle.[39]

Fisher's call for the construction of additional battle cruisers was strongly seconded by Beatty in a letter to Asquith of the same date.[40]

The correspondence of Fisher and Beatty with the Prime Minister coincided with deliberations at the Admiralty over capital ship design. In November 1915, the Treasury had granted the Admiralty permission to order an experimental battleship that would incorporate the lessons of war experience learned thus far. Sketch designs for a 30,000 ton, 25 knot fast battleship armed with eight 15-inch guns had been considered by the board in January 1916, but no agreement had been reached.[41] Jellicoe was then asked by the Board of Admiralty, perhaps at the prompting of Asquith, to offer his views. The Commander-in-Chief of the Grand Fleet, it will be recalled, had in 1912 wanted to build additional battle cruisers rather than the fast battleships that were actually approved, and in December 1914 had supported Fisher's battle cruiser program. In his letter to the board of 8 February 1915, he again made clear his preference for the construction of battle cruisers rather than battleships, arguing that several would be required to meet the threat of anticipated German construction, and in particular specifying 30 knots speed and guns larger than 15-inch.[42]

Following the receipt of Jellicoe's letter, the board instructed the Director of Naval Construction to prepare specifications for a battle cruiser armed with 15-inch or 18-inch guns and capable of at least 30 knots. In March, six sets of particulars[43] were presented to the board, which decided in favor of a 32 knot vessel armed with eight 15-inch guns. On 7 April 1916, the board approved the worked out design and on 13 April sanctioned orders for four units.[44] Fisher mistakenly believed that the projected vessels would be fast battleships rather than battle cruisers, and regretted that they would not be armed with 20-inch guns. "Replicas of the 'Furious' with 20-inch guns is the type, capable of being built in a year, if pushed . . .," he insisted to Commodore Charles de Bartolomé, the naval secretary to Arthur Balfour, the First Lord, on 18 April 1916,[45] and on 29 April, Fisher protested to Jellicoe that the projected battle cruisers were "of the 'Snail and Tortoise' type and have not the speed for the job,"[46] but he was mollified on learning that they were to be much faster than he had supposed. "Since I wrote to you about a fortnight ago," he wrote again to Jellicoe on 18 May 1916,

> and cursed the new design of battle cruiser of the "*Snail and Tortoise*" type, I find the speed has been increased from 25 to 32 knots! *So that's all right!*[47]

Fisher had good reason to be satisfied. Since the outbreak of the war he had been able, with the assistance of Jellicoe, to halt the construction of slow battleships and to arrange or instigate orders for no fewer than nine new battle cruisers, which together with the eleven prewar battle cruisers would have constituted a force that was practically equal in numbers and far superior in fire-power to the existing fleet of German all-big-gun capital ships. By May 1916, it could have appeared, to Fisher at least, that the battleship was on the verge of being replaced by the battle cruiser.

(b) POLLEN

The outbreak of the war in August placed the Argo Company in a precarious position with regard to its foreign sales. The fulfillment of the Austrian order had been made impossible by the state of hostilities between Britain and that power. The delivery of the Russian order was complicated by the closure of the Baltic to British shipping.[48] By the end of August, the discussions with the United States Navy for a trial of the Argo system had been suspended because certain American officers believed that the cost of the instruments was too high, that acceptable results could be achieved with simpler gear, and that plotting requirements might be met by an instrument then being developed by Elmer Sperry, a domestic inventor.[49] And by September, the takeover by the Admiralty of the Chilean battleship then nearing completion in Britain, and Brazil's cancellation for financial reasons of the battleship ordered from Vickers, ended any prospect of orders for fire control equipment from the navies of these countries.[50] The Argo Company's very capacity to fulfill any contracts that might be made was threatened, moreover, by the possibility that Thomas Cooke & Sons would close for want of large orders.[51]

Pollen, in desperation, turned to the Admiralty, where yet another change in command may have given him some hope of an opening. In September 1914, Rear-Admiral F. C. T. Tudor became Third Sea Lord and Controller, and was replaced as Director of Naval Ordnance by Captain Morgan Singer. Not long afterwards, Pollen contacted Singer, offering to supply any instruments that the Admiralty required, including gear that was then being completed for the Russian navy, at cost, a proposal that was apparently refused.[52] In mid October, Pollen wrote to Singer to inform him that the Argo Company could supply the navy with three new types of clocks. The Argo "automatic turret clock" was essentially an Argo Clock Mark IV that was much reduced in size for use in a turret for local control in the event of the failure of the main fire control system. The Argo "electrical rate clocks," numbers 1 and 2, which were simplified versions of the Argo Clock Mark II, were much cheaper than the other production Argo Clocks and differed from one another only in regards to their provisions for transmitting data. In spite of their low cost, Pollen argued that they would

> enable range to be kept during a turn, if the operator has a constant indication of bearing, and is assisted by an intelligent person using a Dumaresq. Their efficiency for this purpose would not equal the efficiency of the automatic Argo R. & B. Clock, but it would be very greatly ahead of anything else now in use.

Singer politely asked for price quotations, but did not place any orders.[53]

Given the Admiralty's refusal in September to take up Pollen's offer to supply instruments at cost, the Argo Company proceeded to complete the Russian order, which in the end consisted of three range-finders with indicators, two Argo Clock Mark Vs, and two gyroscopes (presumably for use with the clocks), but no plotting tables, which were cancelled. These instruments had left the factory by mid October, and were apparently shipped around Norway to Archangel.[54] The Russian payment for the order left the Argo Company solvent,[55] but without immediate prospect of further sales, and Pollen thus ceased operations and by the spring of 1915 had become a full-time war journalist.[56]

In early 1916, Pollen was informed that support for his instruments in the service had remained very strong. "I have heard a good deal lately from the Grand Fleet," a naval officer correspondent wrote,

> where, I understand, the disappointment at Argo Clock [*sic*] not being in all the new ships is very great. The ships that have them have always done extra-ordinarily well, and the Clocks have never given any trouble. Judging from the "Queen Mary's" battle practices, there is very little doubt that if the Clock ships were to compete with the non-Clock ships, in a searching test, the non-Clock ships would not only make no hits, but might not be able to fire at all. It would not be difficult to arrange battle conditions. They would have to include such elements as the ships firing during and immediately after turns, and cutting them off from all observations during the turn interval—just as Craig did in the "Orion" trials. This often happens in action through the target being obscured. In these conditions the Clock ships would have it all their own way.

On 1 February 1916, Pollen sent the above remarks to Balfour, covered by a letter in which he raised the issue of reconsidering his instruments for service adoption.[57]

Balfour probably responded by making inquiries that in turn may have provoked certain unknown Admiralty officials who were hostile to Pollen to take action. In January 1916, the Russian government had placed an order for 8 additional Argo range-finders. On 29 February, the Russian naval attache was advised by Rear-Admiral Morgan Singer, the Director of Naval Ordnance, and other Admiralty officials in an interview that Thomas Cooke & Sons were already behind in their deliveries to the Admiralty and that the fulfillment of such an order was thus not likely to be on time, that the price of the Argo range-finder—which was three times that of the comparable Barr & Stroud instrument—was excessive, and that the British government would refuse Thomas Cooke & Sons permission to accept the order.[58] On being informed of this state of affairs by the Russians, Pollen on 29 February 1916 filed an angry protest with Balfour.

Pollen conceded that the Admiralty had a right to insist that they had a priority claim upon the production of the Argo Company's manufacturers. But he disputed the charge of there being serious arrears in delivery on existing orders, and was at a loss to understand how the Admiralty could criticize an instrument that they had never tested. "Whether a given price for any particular improved instrument is exorbitant or not," he went on to observe,

> is a thing that can only be settled by those that know the military value of the improvement, and can therefore put this improvement to a financial test. Our

rangefinder in its present perfected state has been submitted to the fire control experts of several naval Powers, has been ordered by six, has been delivered and paid for at the full price by two. It could not be delivered to the others, because the outbreak of the war made the completion of the orders we had received impossible in the other instances. This rangefinder was delivered to the Russian Government in the beginning of 1914, in the autumn of the same year after war had been declared, and has now been ordered for the third time. I have been informed and believe, that the only reason why an instrument so much more costly than the Barr & Stroud was ordered for experiment was, that the tests that could be made before it went to sea showed conclusively that the superiority of the instrument ought to be overwhelming. That it was ordered in large quantities after it had been tested at sea seems to me to be a final confirmation first, that this superiority was realized when it came to practical tests, and that so shrewd a body of men as those that advise the Russian Government in this matter were satisfied, that this improvement was of a military character that justified the larger price demanded.

After giving a brief account of his relations with the service before the war, Pollen closed with the charge that "it looks now as if, having been compelled by the Admiralty to go abroad, and having established a business in spite of menaces that I need not qualify, an effort is now being made to ruin my Company by traducing me to my customers."[59]

Balfour replied to Pollen on 2 March 1916 with a conciliatory letter, in which he maintained that there had been a misunderstanding and that his inquiries had established that there would be no objection by the Admiralty to the fulfillment of the Russian order by the Argo Company's manufacturer. Pollen thanked Balfour on 3 March 1916 for his "prompt and effective intervention," but apparently believed that further action was necessary. In late April or May 1916, he drafted a detailed account of the Admiralty's attempts in 1913 to bar foreign sales, whose printing and private circulation he must have hoped would clear himself of the charges of reprehensible business conduct before the war. Pollen's untitled paper was still in galley proof,[60] however, when his plans to defend his reputation, and Fisher's hopes for the battle cruiser, were overtaken on 31 May 1916 by the battle of Jutland.

2   The Gun in Battle, 1914-1916

In naval actions fought in 1914 and 1915 that involved firing at long range while steaming at high speed, the gunnery performance of British battle cruisers had been less than satisfactory.

At the battle of the Falkland Islands in December 1914, Sturdee, the British commander, used his speed advantage to keep the range for the most part at between 12,000 and 16,000 yards in order to exploit the superior long-range ballistics of his big-guns. Such distances, however, were much higher than had been the case in standard prewar Battle Practices, and were too great for the 9-foot base range-finders with which the British ships were equipped to measure accurately. In the *Invincible*, and probably the *Inflexible* as well, moreover, the Argo mounting had been placed at the top of the fore-mast,[61] where vibration from the high speed of the ship and funnel smoke rendered it useless, and the keeping of the range through spotting alone was made far more difficult by enemy changes in course and corresponding turns by the British vessels. Finally, neither battle cruiser was fitted with a director, the gunlaying of the *Invincible* was further undermined by mechanical failures in her gun mountings, and armour-piercing projectiles may have failed to detonate because their fuses had not been designed to function when impact was oblique as would occur when ranges were long. Thus although visibility was perfect and much of the engagement took place while the opposing sides were steaming on parallel courses, the percentage of British hits to rounds fired was less than 7 per cent, and the German units sunk only after five hours of shooting.[62]

The battle of Dogger Bank in January 1915 took the form of a chase in which a squadron of five British battle cruisers pursued a fleeing German force of three battle cruisers and one armoured cruiser. This action was fought for the most part at distances of from 16,000 to 18,000 yards, which was again too great for the British 9-foot base range-finders to measure with any degree of accuracy. Only one of the British battle cruisers, the recently commissioned *Tiger*, was equipped with a director, and any advantage that this device might have conferred was probably cancelled by the inexperience of her crew. Funnel and gun smoke made spotting difficult, and thus although the change of range rate was low and constant because courses were nearly parallel and speeds not greatly different, the proportion of hits to rounds fired was even worse than at the Falkland Islands. The effectiveness of British hits with armour-piercing shells was once more probably reduced by their failure to burst properly. In two hours of long-range firing, the British were able to do no more than cripple the armoured cruiser *Blücher* and badly damage the battle cruiser *Seydlitz*, after which the bulk of the German force, except for the *Blücher*, escaped.[63]

In 1915, the maximum range of gunnery practice was increased from 10,000 yards to over 16,000 yards in response to the experience of the Falkland Islands and Dogger Bank.[64] But apart from the fitting of main armament directors to all but two of the Grand Fleet's dreadnoughts,[65] relatively little was done to improve fire control equipment: director sights were modified to follow targets at greater ranges,[66] and the battleships of the 1912 and 1913 programs came into service equipped with 15-foot base range-finders and slightly improved Dreyer Tables,[67] but that was all.

The Royal Navy's thinking on gunnery materiel did not alter for several reasons. In the first place, the battles of the Falkland Islands and Dogger Bank were actions in which the change of range rate was low and unchanging for long periods, during which the deficiencies of the Dreyer tables would not have mattered, and range-finding by spotting the fall of shot, in the absence of effective range-finders, practicable. In the second place, the poor shooting of the *Invincible* class at the Falklands may have been attributed in large part to the fact that they were unsteady gun platforms.[68] Thirdly, the difficulties in gunlaying because of interference from funnel and gun smoke could have been discounted in the belief that the fitting of directors would substantially mitigate if not eliminate this problem. Fourthly, the ineffectiveness of British armour-piercing projectiles does not appear to have been recognized, while the capability of German shells was believed to be low.[69] And finally, the battle cruisers had achieved a complete victory at the Falkland Islands, and their failure to achieve comparable results at the Dogger Bank could be attributed to tactical error rather than technical failings in gunnery.

On the evening of 30 May 1916, the Grand Fleet steamed from its bases at Scapa Flow, Cromarty and Rosyth, upon receiving word from the Admiralty that the German High Seas Fleet was about to conduct a major operation in the North Sea. The main body of the British force was commanded by Jellicoe and, apart from screening or scouting cruisers and destroyers, consisted of 24 dreadnought battleships and 3 battle cruisers. The Battle Cruiser Fleet was commanded by Beatty and again, apart from scouting and flotilla units, consisted of 6 battle cruisers and 4 fast battleships. The German main body was commanded by Admiral Reinhard Scheer, and consisted of 16 dreadnought battleships, supported by 6 pre-dreadnought battleships and screened by cruisers and destroyers, while the scouting force of 5 battle cruisers and attached light cruisers was commanded by Vice-Admiral Franz Hipper. In this account of what was to become known as the battle of Jutland, consideration will be given only to fighting between capital ships. The statistical data—ranges, speeds, courses, timings and hits—have been taken from N. J. M. Campbell's recent and authoritative study of the engagement.[70]

In the late afternoon of 31 May, the light forces of both sides encountered one another, and within an hour and a half the British and German battle cruisers, which had been positioned well in advance of their respective battleship forces, were engaged. For approximately 22 minutes Beatty's 6 battle cruisers fought Hipper's 5 units at ranges of from 14,000 to 21,000 yards, without the assistance of the fast battleships, which had lagged behind after a turn to follow the battle cruisers was not made.[71] Even without the fast battleships, Beatty enjoyed not only a numerical advantage but an even greater theoretical superiority in fire power. The projectile weight of the British broadside of 32 13.5-inch and 12 12-inch guns came to 50,200 pounds, while that of the German broadside of 16 12-inch and 22 11-inch was only 28,846 pounds. During this period, however, the British made at most 6 hits, which inflicted little major damage, while the Germans scored 25, and succeeded in sinking the battle cruiser *Indefatigable*.

The evident superiority of German gunnery during this phase of the battle has commonly been attributed to several factors. The German range-finders were allegedly superior to those used by the British; conditions of light and wind were such that the visibility of the British line from the German ships was better than the view of the German line from the British side; British rules for spotting the initial salvoes were less efficient than those used by the Germans; British fire control personnel had had less practice than their German counterparts; firing instructions on the British side were misunderstood, with the result that the gunners in the German battle cruiser *Derfflinger* were for a time undistracted by return fire; German gunnery was less prone to disruption from damage inflicted by hits because British armour-piercing projectiles did not burst properly; and British range-finding and gunlaying were subject to greater interference from vibration because Beatty chose to steam at 25 knots while the German ships steamed at between 18 and 21 knots.[72]

The question of the change of range rate must also have been a critical factor. During the opening 22 minutes of the engagement, the convergence and divergence of the opposing sides resulted in change of range rates that were high—between 4:00 and 4:10 the average change of range per minute was 350 yards—and changing, and each side made four turns, which caused further variation in the change of range rate. During the first six minutes of the action, moreover, the problem of taking account of the change of rate may have been complicated by the fact that the British ships were not steaming on a straight course, but gradually turning to starboard. These circumstances were unfavorable to British gunnery in particular for several reasons.

In the first place, the rate-plotting mechanisms of the Dreyer tables were incapable of producing accurate estimates of the change of range and change of bearing rates—both of which were needed to calculate the target course and speed by means of the "cross-cut" method—when the change of range and bearing rates were high and changing rapidly.[73] In addition, the manual process of plotting and meaning ranges was so slow that corrections to the clock, whose generated ranges were the ones that were transmitted to the guns, probably lagged significantly behind the actual instantaneous range.

The problem of inaccurate data was compounded by the shortcomings of most of the calculating instruments. The two 12-inch gun units, the *Indefatigable* and *New Zealand*, were fitted with the Dreyer Table Mark I, whose dumaresq/Vickers Clock arrangement was incapable of taking account of a changing change of range rate with any degree of precision. Two of the 13.5-inch gun vessels—the *Lion*, and *Princess Royal*—were fitted with the Dreyer Table Mark III, one—the *Tiger*—with the Dreyer Table Mark IV, both of whose dumaresq/Dreyer-Elphinstone Clock combinations were probably much superior in performance to that of the dumaresq/Vickers Clock but still not entirely satisfactory. Only the *Queen Mary* was equipped with the Dreyer Table Mark II, which incorporated an Argo Clock Mark IV whose variable speed drives and other features had been designed to deal with high and changing change of range rates, and interruptions in the observation of the target, although its effectiveness was undermined by the defects of the system of plotting separate ranges and bearings used in the other marks of the Dreyer Table[74]

The rapid observation and transmission of range observations should have mitigated to some extent the negative effects of defective plotting and calculation. It will be recalled that in so far as rapid observation and transmission of data was concerned, a range-finder on an Argo mounting was far more effective than one that was not. But in the battle cruisers *Indefatigable* and *New Zealand*, the Argo mounting was almost certainly positioned in the forward spotting top as in the *Invincible*,[75] and if so there is reason to believe that at Jutland its accuracy and operation was adversely affected by vibration, as had been the case in the *Invincible* at the Falkland Islands where firing had also taken place at high speed.[76]

The Argo mountings of the 13.5-inch gun armed units were fitted on top of the forward conning tower where they would have been less subject to the continuous effects of ship motion.[77] But at 3:58 p.m., which was ten minutes after the action began, the shock of a heavy caliber shell hit on the *Princess Royal* blew the fuses of the training motor of the Argo mounting and disrupted the range transmission mechanism, and as a consequence it was out of action for between 12 and 15 minutes. During this period, the forward transmitting station of the *Princess Royal* appears to have received only two ranges.[78] A review of the British battle cruiser hitting record during the first 22 minutes of the engagement suggests that the Argo mounting factor—in the case of the two 12-inch gun units with the added complication of the deficiencies of the Dreyer Table Mark I—may have been important. During this period the *Indefatigable, New Zealand*, and *Princess Royal* made no hits.

Beatty's three other battle cruisers scored hits, although not many. If the record of the forward transmitting station of the *Tiger* can be taken as a guide, these vessels were not making more than two range observations a minute, which would not have been good enough to produce a plot that was capable of taking account of change of range rates that were as high as 350 yards a minute and changing continuously. The fire control personnel of the *Lion* and *Tiger*, as a consequence, would have had great difficulty in keeping the clocks of the Dreyer Tables Marks III and IV adjusted to the correct rate. The design of the Argo Clock Mark IV fitted in the *Queen Mary*, on the other hand, made it less dependent upon continuous correction, and thus should have been less affected by the deficiencies of the time-and-range and time-and-bearing plots of the Dreyer Table Mark II. The hitting scores seems to bear this out. Out of the six hits credited to the British battle cruisers during the period under examination, two were made by the *Lion*, one by the *Tiger* and three by the *Queen Mary*.

It remains to be explained why the German battle cruisers made so many more hits. In German battle cruisers, seven range-finders transmitted observations to the central transmitting station, where they could be meaned on a calculating machine (Mittlungs Apparat) or sent on to the gun stations as received. German fire control teams did not plot ranges and were assisted with nothing better than the German equivalent of the dumaresq (Entfernungs Unterschied Peilscheiber) and Vickers Clock. Unlike the arrangements in the Royal Navy, the clock ranges were not transmitted to the guns, the clock acting only as a guide to the range-officer.[79] Although the range-finders do not appear to have been gyroscopically stabilized, the difference in optical design—stereoscopic as opposed to the coincidence system used in the British instruments—may have enabled German operators to take ranges with greater rapidity than their British counterparts.[80] The absence of a plot of the type used by the Royal Navy, moreover, may have enabled the German fire control team to respond more quickly, if not precisely, to changes in the change of range rate.

There was yet a third factor that was probably of some importance. German fire control personnel, unlike those of their opponents, were trained to cope with steep inclination and alterations of course. After Jutland, an Austrian Naval Attaché thus reported that the Germans believed that, although British range-finders had been proved superior to their own,

> in one respect the British seem behindhand as compared with the Germans: namely that they cannot alter range quickly enough and are too dependent on the range clock. The British rely on steady fire at long range, and they adapt their tactics to this and avoid alterations of course and range most assiduously. The Germans, on the contrary, in their firing practices always work with big and rapid alterations of range and exercise firing while turning, so that the gunnery officers consider they have an advantage in this respect.[81]

Taking all factors into account, there is good reason to believe that the German system of fire control was probably more efficient than that of the British under conditions of high and changing change of range rates.

The second phase of what was to become known as "The Run to the South" began at 4:08 p.m. with the coming into action of the 4 fast battleships, and lasted until this force, following the battle cruisers, turned northward at 4:54 p.m. Visibility for the battleships was apparently good until 4:30, and because speeds were nearly equal and the angle of convergence moderate, the change of range rate was well under 200 yards per minute and probably nearly constant. There was little return fire, moreover, because the attention of the German battle cruisers was concentrated on the British battle cruisers. The battleships were also equipped with 15-foot base range-finders, the latest model Dreyer Table, the Mark IV★, and larger guns than the British battle cruisers. Thus although the range was 19,000 yards at the start, straddles and hits were obtained almost immediately.[82] The firing of the battleships was suspended around 4:30 when visibility worsened and the range opened.

Firing between the British battleships and German battle cruisers resumed ten minutes later at 4:40 when courses were practically parallel and speeds equal. The change of range rate, therefore, must have been very low and unchanging, and although the range was apparently over 21,000 yards, one hit was scored on each side. The exchange lasted about 10 minutes, not long after which the British battleships, after sighting the advancing German battleships, turned to the north.

In the meanwhile, Beatty's battle cruisers had engaged the German battle cruisers under rather different conditions. By 4:14, changes in course on both sides and a German increase in speed had placed the opposing lines on sharply converging paths, which between 4:10 and 4:19 gave an average change of range of nearly 600 yards per minute. Between 4:19 and 4:28 both sides altered course several times and the Germans reduced their speed. The change of range rate under these circumstances was unquestionably both high and changing. At 4:26, the *Queen Mary* was sunk by two hits amidships. Firing died away after 4:30 when Beatty turned away, visibility decreased, and both sides were distracted by the prospect of attacks from destroyers. The British battle cruisers turned northward at 4:40 upon learning of the presence of the German battle fleet, the fast battleships, as has already been related, not following suit until 15 minutes later as a result of missing Beatty's order to retire.

The fast battleships made 6 hits between 4:08 and 4:50, while the battle cruisers during this same period scored 5 hits; the Germans, on the other hand, are estimated to have hit the battle cruisers 15 times after 4:08, and the fast battleships once. The change in the change of range rate factor was again probably critical in the engagement between the battle cruisers, the advantage being with the Germans for the reasons given previously. During this phase of the battle, the *Lion* made no hits and the *Tiger* two. It is perhaps significant that no hits were made by the *New Zealand* during the period in question, while 2 of the 5 British battle cruiser hits were made by the previously scoreless *Princess Royal* following the repair of her Argo mounting.[83] In addition, although the *Queen Mary* has been given credit for only one hit on the *Seydlitz*, the gunnery officer of the *Derfflinger* recalled that her shooting was excellent and that his ship received two hits from her sometime after 4:08.[84] In any case, this vessel had the best hitting record of any of the British battle cruisers, a performance that was probably attributable to the Argo Clock Mark IV.

From 4:54 to 6:15, the British battle cruisers and battleships steamed northward towards their own main body at high speed, pursued by the German battle cruisers and battleships. During "The Run to the North," courses were nearly parallel and speeds not greatly different; the range thus changed slowly at a rate that was nearly constant. From 4:57 to shortly after 5:00, the light conditions were such that the German battle cruisers were able to see the British battle cruisers but not be seen themselves, and they were thus able to make 4 hits without being struck in return. At around 5:01 visibility for the British improved for a short time, but no hits were scored. Visibility for both sides then deteriorated sharply, and the British battle cruisers had ceased firing by 5:10. The *Lützow* continued to fire at the British battle cruisers until 5:27, but she did not succeed in hitting.

In the meanwhile, the British fast battleships engaged both the German battle cruisers and battleships from 4:55 to 6:10. Although light conditions favored the Germans, they were adequate for the British, who were thus able to hit more often than the Germans because of the long ranges, low and nearly constant change of range rate, and the excellent ballistics of the British 15-inch gun, which were superior to those of the smaller caliber main battery pieces of their opponents. From 5:41 to 6:10 the British and German battle cruisers again exchanged fire intermittently, visibility being very poor, and during this period both sides obtained one hit.

Periods of clear visibility and good fortune enabled the Germans to obtain hits on units of Beatty's command as they joined up with the British main body. At 6:20, the steering gear of the fast battleship *Warspite* malfunctioned, which caused her to steam in a circle within view of the advancing German battleships. Under intensive fire for some 15 minutes, she sustained 13 hits from heavy caliber projectiles, but suffered no critical damage. The other fast battleships were also fired upon, but were not hit. At around 6:22, the *Princess Royal* was struck twice by projectiles fired by the German battleship *Markgraf*, which caused considerable damage.

Intermittent firing by a few of the British battleships at German battleships began at about 6:17, but effective firing did not take place until 6:30 and then by no more than half of the 24 battleships that made up the main battle line. Visibility, by this time, was poor and firing ranges were, as a consequence, much less than previously—generally under 12,000 yards. Courses were nearly concentric and speeds moderate, and thus the change of range rate was probably low and altering very slowly. Light for the most part favored the British, whose battleships were able to score 9 hits without receiving any in return. The Germans minimized their injuries, however, by turning away into the mist, Jellicoe refusing to follow for fear of the threat posed by German torpedoes and mines.

From 6:20 to almost 6:40, the battle cruisers *Invincible*, *Inflexible* and *Indomitable*, which had been attached to Jellicoe's force, engaged the German battle cruisers on their own. The light initially favored the British, and the ranges were very short—from 8,500 to 11,000 yards. The German battle cruiser *Lützow* received hits that would later cause her to sink, but when the visibility suddenly changed in her favor, she was able to return fire effectively, which resulted in the destruction of the battle cruiser *Invincible* at 6:32. The two sides disengaged within a few minutes, and there was little fighting between 6:40 and 7:00.

The British and German main bodies collided for the last time in an action that was fought between 7:00 and 7:45. This time, the German column of heavy units blundered into the British, who were steaming across their bows and thus able to fire full broadsides while the Germans could reply with only their forward turrets. In response, the German battleships reversed course by turning together while the German battle cruisers covered the retreat by advancing. In the process of executing the turn away, elements of the German battleship line were forced to reduce speed and even go astern in order to maintain formation, while the German battle cruisers for a time steamed on a course that was nearly parallel with that of the British fleet. Many of the British capital ships were able, as a consequence, to fire at targets that were either practically stationary or at a constant range, and in addition while enjoying excellent visibility, which for the Germans, on the other hand, was extremely poor. During the short time that these conditions persisted, the British made 37 hits while being struck only twice, but Jellicoe again declined to pursue, and the Germans thus were able to escape for a second time.

In the fading light between 7:45 and 9:30, the British battle cruisers exchanged fire with the German battle cruisers and battleships at ranges of 11,000 yards or less. Light advantage was with the British, who made 8 hits and were struck only twice. Contact was then lost in the darkness. Fighting during the night did not involve gunnery exchanges between capital ships, and by morning the German fleet had eluded the British, ending the battle.

The gunnery performance of the British battle cruisers has been compared unfavorably with that of the fast battleships.[85] But during "The

Run to the South," the battle cruisers made only one less hit than the fast battleships during the same time span in spite of the fact that the change of range rate conditions under which they fought were far more difficult; the battle cruisers, moreover, were exposed to heavy fire from the German battle cruisers while the fast battleships were not. During "The Run to the North," the far greater number of hits scored by the fast battleships was probably attributable to the fact that their visibility was better and because the long range and low change of range rate enabled them to exploit the superior ballistics of their heavier caliber guns. After 6:15, the light conditions strongly favored the British, ranges were much lower, and change of range conditions were for the most part very easy. Invidious comparisons between the high hitting scores of the slow battleships during this period and small number of hits obtained by the battle cruisers earlier on would also be unfair and misleading.

The destruction of the *Indefatigable, Queen Mary* and *Invincible* nevertheless raised serious questions about British battle cruiser design and fire control methods. Subsequent study has revealed that the losses were probably attributable to the liability of British cordite charges to detonate rather than simply to burn when ignited.[86] But the fact remains that heavier armour protection would have prevented the penetration of the fatal projectiles, while the ability to hit before being hit in return would have made even heavier armour unnecessary.

3 Reaction, Remedy, and Postscript

(a) POLLEN AND FIRE CONTROL, 1916-1925

Convinced that the battle of Jutland vindicated his ideas on gunnery as never before, Pollen scrapped the print written in April in spite of the fact that it had been set in galley proof, and drafted two new memoranda. In the first, which was dated 1 August 1916, he analysed the gunnery aspects of several recent naval battles in general terms, described his fire control system, and reviewed the events surrounding the rejection of his instruments before the war. "It is submitted," Pollen then wrote,

> that the sea actions that have taken place prove conclusively that those Service experts who anticipated (1) that actions would be fought at very great ranges; (2) that ships would be compelled to manoeuvre by the attacks of enemy torpedo crafts, and hence that insuperable difficulties would be introduced in ascertaining rate; (3) that the existing Service rangefinder would not prove sufficiently accurate for long range work, and would give no result at all in conditions of bad visibility; (4) that the Service method of ascertaining the factors that govern change of range, by plotting range and bearing rates, could never possibly give results prompt or accurate enough in the new conditions—and who, holding these views, protested unsuccessfully against the abandonment of the A.C. System, have been amply justified by events. It is equally clear that those who maintained that inferior instruments would be good enough for the British Navy in war, have been shown to have acted under a complete misapprehension.

In these circumstances, it is respectfully suggested that the whole question ought now to be reinvestigated on the two grounds:

(i) That the Service gear does not give the desired results.

(ii) That the only gear designed to meet the conditions that war has shown to be normal—a system developed by successive Boards purely on Service advice, with Service assistance, and ultimately approved as perfect by all Service experts who have seen or worked the instruments—has never yet been tried or reported on, or even seen by the Department [of Naval Ordnance].[87]

Pollen's second memorandum of 7 August 1916 was written after he had received additional information about gunnery during the battle of Jutland. Pollen noted at the outset that he had been informed that range taking had been disrupted by poor light, that guns had been mistakenly laid to fire on targets other than the ones upon which the range–finder was trained, that the fleet had called for a range–finder that was more effective than the Barr & Stroud instrument, that the Battle Cruiser Fleet had "asked that the ships may be fitted with a means of keeping an accurate range on the sights while they are zig-zagging to discompose the enemy's fire control," and that the fast battleships had been provided with additional armour protection, which had reduced their speed. Pollen then argued that modifications to the fast battleships were undesirable because they reduced the Grand Fleet's stock of swift capital ships by nearly half, and unnecessary because the adoption of better fire control equipment would enable British capital ships to hit their targets before the Germans could hit them. He concluded with a description of his instruments, in which he emphasized the ability of his range–finder to measure distances accurately when the light was dim.[88]

Copies of Pollen's first memorandum were sent to admirals Jellicoe, Beatty, Osmond de Beauvoir Brock, Arthur C. Leveson and Hugh Evan-Thomas; Captain Herbert Richmond; and Commander William James. Copies of the second were sent only to Jellicoe and Commander Reginald Plunkett.[89]

Beatty's reply indicated that he was open to suggestion. "I have read your memorandum," he wrote to Pollen on 14 August 1916, "with considerable interest. I agree that an efficient range finder is most desirable and the Argo Clock is undoubtedly superior to the Dreyer Table." Beatty did observe that the Dreyer Table was helm-free, but this mistaken view was probably attributable to the fact that at Jutland rate errors from faulty data were so great as to obscure inaccuracies caused by the inherent short-comings of the service calculating mechanism. He also complained that the "difficulties against taking Ranges with the Range Finder are so great under present conditions that we must learn to do without them," maintained that "the smoke of battle is a difficulty that the finest range finder cannot overcome," and thus expressed some disagreement with Pollen's contention that a knowledge of the rate would result *ipso facto* in a very high proportion of hits.[90]

In a letter to Beatty of 18 August, Pollen observed that the difficulty of battle conditions was a strong argument for better rather than no instruments. "It has always been an axiom," he wrote, that, unless instruments were perfectly accurate, they must be perfectly useless. The thing that has really broken down Service fire control is, that you are fighting at ranges 25 to 50% longer, and speeds far higher, than those for which your fire control was designed. Also you have found that, where you do not get continuous vision of the target—from the smoke of the target's guns and funnels, as well as from the smoke screens and mist—conditions in action are totally different from conditions in battle practice. Here your fire control has broken down because it does not get results *quick* enough, just as at long range it has broken down because not accurate enough. Your range finders and gear might be good enough optically and instrumentally to deal with a target towed at 6 knots at 11,000 yds. and yet give no results at all—as appears to be the case—with a 20 to 25 knot target at 14 to 15,000 yds. when it is periodically obscured by its own smoke.[91]

Jellicoe's response was on the whole dismissive. "I am thoroughly satisfied," he wrote on 18 August,

with the results obtained by the service gear when properly used. The human element can never be eliminated whatever the gear used may be & some ships will always be better than others. My object is to get the whole Fleet up to the standard of the best ships & that ideal is always being aimed at.

Any improvements that can be produced so far as a Range Finder is concerned will be welcome. There is no finality particularly in this respect & I fancy that German Range Finders may be superior to ours. They are generally superior in optical instruments to us. But I certainly do not desire to change our system.

"I am confident," Jellicoe concluded, "that we shall hit the German as soon as he hits us in the future."[92]

"I hope you agree," Pollen wrote to Jellicoe on 22 August, "that if there is no finality in rangefinders there can be none in other gear also," closing with "I sincerely hope you will hit em next time, not only as soon as, but before they hit you!"[93] Pollen wrote again to Jellicoe on 25 August, agreeing that the Germans possessed a better range-finder but disputing the charge that they were better opticians by pointing out that had the Admiralty "given the new Cooke rangefinder a trial, it would have been found to have been as much better than the German rangefinder as the German rangefinder is than Barr & Stroud."[94] On 28 August, Jellicoe informed Pollen that he had "urged upon the Admiralty the desirability of inspecting the rangefinders which are intended for the Russians," but otherwise showed no sign of having been receptive to Pollen's views.[95]

Jellicoe's reaction may be explained by a number of technical factors, which will be discussed in detail further on, but he also had personal and political reasons to turn a blind eye to Pollen's analysis. Jellicoe, it will be remembered, had played a key role in the rejection of the Pollen system and the acceptance of the Dreyer Tables. Criticism of the service gear, he must have realized, would not only inevitably raise questions about his prewar judgement of the fire control question, which he quite naturally would not have welcomed in the wake of the unsatisfactory outcome at Jutland, but in addition endanger the career of Dreyer, a good friend whom he regarded as an efficient subordinate. Dreyer, for his part, could not have been unaware of his vulnerability, and there can be little doubt that the gunnery advice that he offered to his chief was tailored to deny the validity of Pollen's arguments. "I wish I could think that you had any chance of being listened to," Richmond had written to Pollen on 7 August, "but you know as well [as] I do who will have a voice in the reply."[96] Richmond of course meant Dreyer, and his cynicism was in the event fully justified.

On 4 June, Jellicoe had appointed a number of committees to investigate naval materiel in light of experience gained in the battle. Dreyer was placed in charge of those dealing with projectiles and the gunnery of the battle fleet, a separate committee on the gunnery of the battle cruisers being headed by Captain A. E. M. Chatfield.[97] Dreyer's selection to chair the committee on gunnery was questionable on several grounds. Although his claims to expertise in gunnery in general and fire control in particular were very strong, he was the inventor of the service fire control system and as such on the face of it not a disinterested party. Less than three weeks before, moreover, Dreyer had been awarded £5000 by the Admiralty for his services "in connection with Fire Control," which could not have improved any disposition that might have existed to be impartial.[98] And Jellicoe could not have been ignorant of Dreyer's prewar partisanship with regard to Pollen.

Chatfield had been a friend and supporter of Pollen before the war, but his appointment to carry out the investigation of battle cruiser gunnery was no less unfortunate. It would appear that before Jutland, he had assumed the major responsibility for the gunnery efficiency of the battle cruiser fleet,[99] and was thus sensitive to charges that their shooting had been less than satisfactory. Chatfield believed, moreover, that the battle cruisers had made more hits than subsequent research has indicated was the case, and later recalled that he had been "confident our gunnery was superior to theirs under equal conditions."[100] Not long after the battle, Chatfield suggested to Dreyer that the survival of German capital ships in spite of the many hits that he believed must have been made was attributable to faulty armour-piercing projectiles. In August, a Swedish naval officer who had been recently stationed in Berlin informed him that German naval officers had stated that the British shells had been defective; his suspicions confirmed, Chatfield pressed Dreyer to pursue the issue.[101]

There can be little doubt that the defects in British projectile design and manufacture were serious, and contributed to the survival of German warships that might otherwise have been sunk.[102] But the proposition that British shells had failed was attractive to both Chatfield and Dreyer for other reasons as well. In Chatfield's case, it explained how the British battle cruisers could have made hits without achieving any results, thus absolving both himself and the battle cruiser force of blame for inaccurate shooting, while in Dreyer's case, it directed attention away from the shortcomings of the Dreyer Tables. Dreyer may also have realized that the shell failure hypothesis favored Jellicoe, who, it will be recalled, had identified the need for a better armour-piercing projectile before the war and had tried without success to remedy the situation.

The absence of reliable data on the number and timing of hits received by German units in the battle, which would have clearly exposed the shortcomings in battle cruiser gunnery under difficult rate conditions, and the predisposition by the heads of both gunnery committees to emphasize the role played by the shell issue, probably explain why Pollen's analysis of the gunnery lessons of Jutland was rejected. Pollen's second memorandum of 7 August outraged Chatfield, ostensibly on the grounds of security considerations but probably for the imputations regarding battle cruiser gunnery performance as well, and marked "rubbish" by Plunkett, a subordinate who undoubtedly shared the views of his superior, although he had been a strong Pollen supporter before the war.[103] There is no evidence that the Dreyer Tables were at this time seriously criticized, while Jellicoe and Beatty made strong representations to the Admiralty with regard to shell design.[104] In March 1917, Jellicoe, who had become First Sea Lord in December, made Dreyer Director of Naval Ordnance,[105] an appointment that must have convinced Pollen, if he by this time still needed convincing, of the futility of his efforts to gain a reconsideration of his system by the Admiralty.

Pollen may have found some consolation in the fact that by early 1917, American interest in his equipment, which had been sustained by an active correspondence with officers in the US Navy,[106] had begun to increase. In February 1917, Pollen learned that Elmer Sperry, the American inventor, had not yet perfected the plotting system upon which the US Navy had been counting in 1914, that Sperry was considering purchasing the American rights to the Cooke-Pollen range-finder, and that American gunnery officers were still divided on the question of mechanized fire control.[107] America's entry into the war in April 1917 made the resolving of the gunnery question a matter of some urgency, and in May, Pollen was informed that the US Navy's Bureau of Ordnance favored the purchase of a complete set of instruments for trial.[108] Pollen thus decided to work for a confirmed order by visiting the United States, which was to be financed out of the proceeds of lectures on the war given during the trip.[109]

Pollen's tour of the United States lasted from June 1917 through the end of the year. During this period he devoted much of his time to carrying out a semi-private diplomatic campaign to improve cooperation between the United States and Britain in the war, which achieved a great deal.[110] He also succeeded in persuading the US Navy to order a set of his instruments for trials. There can be little doubt that Pollen had made a great impression on American gunnery officers. "Until our interviews with him in Washington," wrote one such person,

> we had no idea in this Fleet that, any so complete solution of the problem had ever been attempted. Results of the very greatest importance may be expected from the forthcoming trial of his instruments, if they function as described by him, and as, apparently they should from their design.[111]

The US Navy also ordered a Dreyer Table Mark V at about this time,[112] but at least one American officer who had been attached to the Grand Fleet was highly skeptical of its value. "We have reason to think," he reported,

> that, in the majority of ships always, and in many cases, in all ships, the Dreyer system of instruments is not, in fact, employed in action. We heard no satisfactory explanation why this system, and not the Pollen System, is employed. In theory, the Pollen System is not only more scientific, but simpler. It seems capable, that is, of a high degree of accuracy which the Dreyer system can, seemingly, never attain.[113]

By March 1918, the Argo instruments—a plotter and clock—were ready for inspection.[114]

On 6 March 1918, Pollen wrote to Sir Eric Geddes, who had become First Lord in July 1917, to invite British naval officers to view the instruments ordered by the US Navy prior to their shipment.[115] Geddes, in the apparent hope of obtaining an impartial evaluation, responded by forming a special committee of officers from the Admiralty and Grand Fleet who had not previously been involved directly with the Argo case,[116] placing Rear-Admiral Edward M. Phillpotts at its head.[117] In the second week of March the committee carried out what could only have been a quick inspection of the Argo Course and Speed Plotter Mark IV, the Argo Clock Mark V (noted in the report as a Mark IV but from its description, a Mark V), a cardboard model of a device that would mean the observations made by several range-finders, and a Pollen–Cooke 15-foot base range-finder.

The committee report, which was submitted to the Admiralty within a few days of the visit to the Argo workshop, maintained that the system of meaning ranges was inferior to the methods then in use, and that the range-finder did not appear to offer any marked advantage over the Barr & Stroud instruments then in service. True-course plotting was criticized on several grounds. The committee argued that true-course plotting would not work if the enemy changed course or speed, that the introduction of the gyro-compass and the Forbes speed log had not made it possible to produce quick and accurate estimates of the firing ship's course and speed upon which the effectiveness of a true-course plot depended, that mechanisms which transmitted range and bearing settings might be mechanically unreliable, and that the plot could be disrupted by a person leaning inadvertently against the paper. The committee also believed that the adoption of what was known as the "straight-line" method of plotting rates would make rate-plotting far more accurate than had previously been the case.[118] The committee was highly impressed, on the other hand, by the Argo Clock.

The committee concluded that "the principles employed in the A.C. method are not considered as suited to service requirements as the present methods in use," but also observed that

> the A. C. system and instruments are the result of great ingenuity and thought, and no pains or expense have been spared in making the instruments as near mechanical perfection as possible to perform the functions required of them, and in this direction they individually possess certain advantages over

service instruments. This is borne out by the experience of the A.C. clocks in use in H.M. service.

The committee then went on to express the view that it was "a matter for regret that the ingenuity and mechanical designing ability displayed in producing these instruments have been lost to the Service . . ." and that "the question is for consideration whether the services of the Inventor and his Staff could be utilized in connection with the design of future fire control instruments."[119]

The committee's report was submitted to Dreyer in his capacity as Director of Naval Ordnance. Dreyer, in his minute of 12 March on the report, expressed his general concurrence, but strongly opposed any suggestion that Harold Isherwood, Pollen's chief designer, be assigned to work in fire control on the grounds that his work on designing mines meant "the Service and the Allied Cause has been getting the fullest advantage of his ingenuity and designing skill" and that, therefore, "to now take him away from Mining design work, would, in my opinion, be a great mistake." Pollen was again accused of having plagiarized the Watkins system, and the Pollen-Cooke range-finder damned with faint praise. "Mr. Pollen," Dreyer then observed,

> no doubt with the very best of intentions, produced a great feeling of unrest in Naval Gunnery Circles when his instruments were on trial, by his whirlwind eloquence and his journalistic efforts.
> I am most strongly of opinion that it would be a grave error to once more put him in touch with the Service at great risk of disturbing the present standardizing Fire Control, methods and machines, in which everyone has complete confidence.

Dreyer included the three prints produced in 1913 (for which see Chapter 6) to support his case.[120]

On 13 March 1918, Pollen wrote to Phillpotts to express his concern with the manner in which the investigation of his gear had been carried out. The shop demonstration, Pollen feared, had not been persuasive because his skeleton staff—which by now included none of the skilled designers—were unable to make the functions of his instruments clear and because of the inherent limitations of what could be accomplished by such an exercise, as opposed to a trial at sea. In addition, Pollen argued that his ignorance of service instruments and methods in a detailed sense prevented him from making "the best points for comparison, and in showing exactly how an alternative method would work."[121] The committee's unfavorable report and Dreyer's minute, however, were accepted by the service members of the board, and the First Lord had little choice but to accept the outcome, which was in effect that no further action would be taken.[122] Pollen's subsequent efforts to change Geddes's mind, which involved an extended correspondence, were to no avail.[123]

In March 1918, the Admiralty, after deliberations that had taken nearly 18 months,[124] had placed an order for 30 Pollen-Cooke 9-foot base range-finders, but only 10 had been completed by the end of the war,[125] and the balance of the contract was cancelled. By this point, moreover, Barr & Stroud appear to have improved their instruments to the point that differences in performance between the products of the two firms may have been greatly reduced if not eliminated.[126] The inadequacy of the Argo Company's production facilities and the availability of alternative instruments of comparable quality may also in part explain the American failure to purchase the Argo plotter and clock in quantity. By 1918, Sperry had more or less perfected his "battle tracer," a helm-free, true-course plotter that differed substantially from the Argo instrument in mechanical design but performed exactly the same functions, while Hannibal Ford had developed a clock that incorporated a differential analyzer. Sperry's well-established instrument company had ample building capacity, while Ford received large orders from the US government that enabled him to create a design and production establishment that within two years dwarfed that of the Argo Company.[127]

The attitude of the Phillpotts committee and the unwillingness of the US Navy to place a production order must also have been affected by the fact that by 1918 the Argo system was unsuitable for deployment without very substantial modification in light of recent war experience. Technical advice from service experts had not been available to Pollen since before the outbreak of war, while during the four years of hostilities the Dreyer Tables had been subjected to extensive detail modification by the gunnery teams of the Grand Fleet, which by taking account of important factors unknown to Pollen tended to disguise the deficiencies that stemmed from fundamental defects in design. Given such circumstances, Pollen's attempts to present his system as a practical alternative to the service gear were almost bound to fail. Dreyer's position, on the other hand, depended on there not being an independent critical examination of his instruments and methods. As Director of Naval Ordnance and, from the spring of 1918, as the Director of Naval Artillery and Torpedoes on the Naval Staff, he was in positions to prevent any such initiative by the Admiralty. An innocuous request for information, however, inadvertently precipitated an investigation of the Dreyer Tables by the gunnery officers of the Grand Fleet that was to have far-reaching consequences.

In the fall of 1918, consideration was being given to the fire control equipment of the battle cruiser approved by the Admiralty some two years before, the *Hood*, which had just been launched. On 9 September 1918, the Admiralty thus asked Admiral Beatty, by now Commander-in-Chief of the Grand Fleet, to forward proposals regarding a certain minor "field" modification that had been made to the Dreyer Tables that might be applied to the Dreyer Table Mark V then being constructed for *Hood*.[128] Inquiry seems to have prompted complaint about several other matters, to which Beatty responded by forming a committee of "experienced officers of the Fleet"[129] who, in consultation with a representative of Elliott's, the manufacturer of the Dreyer Table, evaluated the general design of the existing fire control system. The first and second interim reports of the committee were summarized in a report from Beatty to the Admiralty submitted on 19 November 1918, which stated that the rectification of a number of problems made "a considerable alteration in design" necessary. "Many complaints," the report noted in particular, had been received with regard to the unsatisfactory performance of the clock drive.[130]

Further meetings of the committee were then held to consider "the possibility of standardizing the alterations which are being made by various ships to their Dreyer Tables." In a third interim report, which was submitted to Beatty on 29 January 1919, the committee maintained that the practice of obtaining the target course and speed by the cross-cut method was completely impracticable because "*experience has shown, and it must now be accepted, that it will very seldom, if ever, be possible to obtain the rate of change of range from rangefinders.*" True-course plotting was still considered to be unsatisfactory, and as an alternative the dumaresq was to be set with a change of bearing rate, firing ship course and speed, target bearing, and estimates of the target's course. The target course estimates were either to be measured by a new device that was known as an inclinometer,[131] or based upon aircraft observation. The committee also criticized the arrangements for applying corrections for changes in course, which were apparently highly unsatisfactory when turns were made at high speed, and expressed its preference for straight-line plotting, but noted that its adoption would entail such extensive modifications to the Dreyer Table that its application to existing instruments could not be recommended. There were a host of other criticisms as well.[132]

The final meetings of the committee were concerned with the "future development of fire control tables." In their final report, which was submitted to Beatty on 1 February 1919, the committee observed that in a modern surface action, "observation of fall of shot from the firing ship will always be difficult and uncertain, and frequently impossible, . . . instrumental observations of the enemy from the firing ship will only be obtained intermittently due to smoke screens and varying visibility," and that ". . . own ship and enemy will zigzag to avoid being hit." The committee thus called for the complete redesign of the Dreyer Clock and the adoption of straight-line plotting for ranges and bearings, and an inclination plot, the true-course approach being explicitly rejected. "It is considered," the committee concluded,

> that the process of building up our present fire control table from the original form to the present requirements has resulted in a collection of mechanisms capable of considerable improvement in general arrangement and mechanical detail.
> It appears, therefore, that the time has now arrived to reconsider the general design.
> Generally speaking, our present system necessitates too many operations being carried out by hand. The new table should aim at making as many operations as possible automatic.
> For example:—A combination of all the good points of the Dreyer table, Ford clock,[133] and Argo clock would undoubtedly produce a far more compact and efficient arrangement to meet requirements than our present fire control table. It is recommended that the designs of all these instruments should be reviewed with a view to producing the best obtainable machine.[134]

Beatty fully endorsed the findings of the committee. In his letter to the Admiralty of 7 February 1919, the Commander-in-Chief of the Grand Fleet noted that "the latest pattern of fire control table now existing is in many respects obsolete, based as it is on principles which modern experience has discarded, and the time has arrived when a complete re-design is essential." "The difficulties of putting into effect the recommendations of the Committee," he went on to say,

> both from the technical and commercial points of view, are realized. It is held, however, that the matter is of such importance that every endeavour should be made to surmount these difficulties, and further that financial considerations should not be permitted to stand in the way.
>   . . . .As regards the question of design, it is clear that the highest engineering skill available, together with a clear understanding of the practical requirements, must be brought to bear on the problem.

At the end of his letter, Beatty named a four-man design committee that included Pollen's chief designer, Harold Isherwood. [135]

Impetus for change was probably increased by what the Admiralty learned about American progress in fire control. After a meeting between representatives of the Royal Navy and the Ford Instrument Company on 13 March 1919, Captain H. J. S. Brownrigg, the Director of Naval Artillery and Torpedoes, who had been a member of the Philpotts committee the year before, reported that he and other officers present during the discussions had been "much impressed not only with his [Ford's] inventive capabilities but also with the great rapidity with which ideas are put into effect and with which the finished article is turned out." In his final paragraph, Brownrigg noted that

> the U.S. Bureau of Ordnance in their report which has recently been circulated stated that "some of the best brains in the country" were employed in the solution of Fire Control problems. They appear to have been right and we should do well to follow their example.

In remarks on Brownrigg's report made on 21 March, Captain Henry R. Crooke, the Director of Naval Ordnance, who it will be recalled had been a participant in the evaluation of Pollen's ideas in 1906, raised the issue of past experience with the Argo Company—which he maintained had been "not at all satisfactory or encouraging"—when commenting on the possibility of entering into a secrecy arrangement with a private firm. In response, an older and perhaps by this time wiser Sir Frederick W. Black, still the Director of Contracts, took some pains to defend the behavior of Pollen and his associates. The Argo Company, he observed in his minute of 11 April,

> claimed to have originated their system without suggestion or collaboration of the Admiralty, and therefore, to have full right to exploit it commercially, or to be paid large sums by the Admiralty for refraining from doing so and keeping it secret.

It is, of course, impossible in peace time to acquire or keep secret inventions originated by outsiders quite independently of the Admiralty, except by paying such terms as they may be induced to accept.

Black later warned, with good reason, that the Ford apparatus might infringe valid Argo patents, and then suggested that

it will probably in that event be desirable to give Argo Co., an opportunity of competing for the apparatus required, if their Lordships are prepared to withdraw the decision under which they are debarred from further Admiralty orders.

In a final minute submitted on 8 May 1919, Brownrigg noted that the US Navy had in effect created a secret fire control design section in the form of the Ford Instrument Company, recommended that the Royal Navy should follow suit, and suggested Isherwood's name as one of those whose services should be acquired on a permanent basis, presumably as a member of the proposed Admiralty fire control design team. [136]

In November 1918, Dreyer had resigned as Director of Naval Artillery and Torpedoes to become Chief of Staff to Jellicoe, to whom the War Cabinet had assigned the task of visiting India and the Dominions on a mission to discuss the question of imperial naval defence. Dreyer was immediately preoccupied with the task of collecting papers related to his new job, and in March 1919 left Britain, not returning until February 1920. He was thus distracted or absent during the critical months during which the Grand Fleet and Admiralty gunnery officers formulated requirements and made recommendations regarding fire control. By the time Dreyer was appointed the Director of the Gunnery Division in April 1920, the design process was not only well under way, but political circumstances were also such as to limit severely his powers of interference. [137]

On 1 November 1919, Beatty had become First Sea Lord, and would hold that position until July 1927. Aware by virtue of hard experience of the requirements of war gunnery, informed on the technical aspects of the problem by disinterested expert opinion, knowledgeable about the history of the Pollen case, [138] and in power for a long enough period of time to ensure continuity of policy, Beatty was able to take actions that resulted in the development of a new and far more effective system of fire control. Isherwood and Landstad, formerly Pollen's men, both became members of a permanent Admiralty fire control design establishment, and were largely responsible for working up the plans of what was to become known as the Admiralty Fire Control Table (AFCT) Mark I, which, among other things, incorporated an automatic range plotter and the infinitely variable speed drive of the Argo Clock. [139]

The trials of the new table in 1925 were a complete success, and production models and derivatives were fitted to all new British capital ships and cruisers beginning with the battleships *Nelson* and *Rodney*, and rebuilt units such as the *Warspite, Queen Elizabeth, Valiant,* and *Renown.* The *Barham* and *Malaya,* the "R" class battleships, the battle cruiser *Repulse,* and, perhaps most significantly, the battle cruiser *Hood* soldiered on, however, with late mark Dreyer Tables.[140]

It will be recalled that the Argo system's price of £2,400 (plotter and clock in 1913) had been criticized before the war as being too high, and it is interesting to note, therefore, that the AFCT Mark I cost some £45,000—a striking figure, the effects of inflation notwithstanding.[141] In his remarks of 4 January 1926 on the trials report, Rear-Admiral Sir Frederic Dreyer, by this time Assistant Chief of the Naval Staff, wrote that he was "quite sure that the Policy pursued and the money expended in connection with these experimental Tables are fully justified."[142] Dreyer had good reason to be circumspect in his remarks, for only two months before, a tribunal of the Royal Commission on Awards to Inventors had ordered that Pollen be paid the sum of £30,000 compensation for the plagiarization of the Argo Clock that had occurred in 1911, the fact of which had been exposed in hearings that had taken place in August 1925.[143]

(b)   FISHER, FIRE CONTROL, AND THE BATTLE CRUISER, 1916-1920

Fisher had been troubled by poor shooting at the Falkland Islands and Dogger Bank, but had rationalized his misgivings. The lengthy period required by the battle cruisers at the Falklands to destroy two slower and much weaker opponents was blamed on Sturdee's "dilatory and theatrical tactics."[144] With regard to the Dogger Bank action, Fisher overestimated the damage suffered by the German battle cruisers and was eager to blame bad gunnery on inefficient personnel.[145] His response to the news of Jutland was no less colored by his incomprehension of fire control. "There'll be an outcry," he confided to Captain Thomas E. Crease, his naval assistant, on 3 June 1916,

for ships as heavily armoured as a Spithead fort! *That* will be the red herring! And why didn't Lord Fisher put on more armour? *Hang Lord Fisher!* The 5 fast battle cruisers might have been in this battle with wonderful results! The 18-inch gun! At a mile beyond von Scheer's range![146]

In the margin of a letter from Jellicoe of 15 June, in which the Commander-in-Chief of the Grand Fleet complained of "the inadequacy of the armour protection of our battle cruisers as compared to the German ships," Fisher scrawled, "Never meant to get in enemy's range!"[147]

Fisher remained ignorant of the manner in which defects in British fire control had compromised his vision of the battle cruiser. He continued to express confidence in Dreyer,[148] and suspicions that the fire control of the Grand Fleet had been inferior to that of the German navy—provoked by remarks to that effect made by Philip Watts, the former Director of Naval

Construction—were apparently put aside.[149] In the fall of that year, the old admiral began writing letters to *The Times* to condemn his successors at the Admiralty for their unwillingness to carry out his battle cruiser program. "We are wasting money on half the Navy," he wrote on 2 September 1919, "because it is obsolete already by the immense development of big, fast ships and huge guns . . ."[150] "Our policy," Fisher wrote again on 8 September, "was: Have a big preponderance of speed over your enemy so that you can choose your own distance for fighting; the next, the very biggest gun (a 20 in. gun would have been in the *Incomparable* had I remained at the Admiralty), and so you hit the enemy when he can't reach you, and therefore all his guns might as well be pea-shooters."[151]

On 9 September, Fisher recalled that the battle cruisers had been referred to as "New Testament" ships on their inception in 1905 because "they fulfilled the promise of the "Old Testament" ships"—that is, the dreadnought battleships. The "muddlers" at the Admiralty, he went on to say, did not use the battle cruisers

for the purposes for which they were created. They were diverted to lower uses, but so well conceived were they that they proved their value under conditions for which they were never intended.

"And it was sad that the mission of the battle-cruiser was so totally unappreciated," Fisher then explained,

till the *Invincible* sank Craddock's murderer, von Spee, and all his squadron. Tortoises were apportioned to catch hares. *Millions of tortoises can't catch a hare.* The Almighty arranged the greyhound to catch a hare—the greyhound so largely bigger than the hare as to annihilate it.[152]

In his notes for an autobiography that was then soon to be published, Fisher already had written that "the battle-cruisers were really the battle-ships of the future."[153]

Fisher must have been aware that his views were regarded as extreme by most naval officers. "Mind you," he admitted in his letter to *The Times* of 13 September, "when all these articles are read people will say, 'Here's a lunatic.' " But even if ill informed, isolated, and powerless, Fisher had not lost his faith in himself or his ideas. "Now I will tell you a story," he continued,

about a lunatic. A friend of mine went to see a lunatic asylum where the patients were being treated on a new principle of giving them the utmost latitude to indulge their tastes. The day he went bricklayers were putting

317

up in the spacious grounds some little outbuilding. A bevy of patients had asked for wheelbarrows to trundle about the grounds. They were given them, and my friend met one of them wheeling his barrow upside down. He said to the lunatic, "Ain't you making a mistake? Your barrow ought to be the other way up." "Well, you know, I thought myself I was making a mistake, but when I turned it over the other way they filled it full of bricks!" He was the only sane man among the lunatics. The others were wheeling barrow-loads of bricks for the bricklayers. He used his barrow for his own intended purpose.

"I sometimes think," Fisher then mused, "I am the only sane man. Anyhow I am going to wheel my barrow upside down. I'll see the Admiralty bricks damned first before I wheel them about."[154]

By the end of the year, Fisher may have concluded that recent advances in technology had made all surface capital ships obsolete. Before resigning as First Sea Lord in 1915 he had approved the construction of a new class of high-speed, steam-propelled submarines. In 1916, the Admiralty had ordered the construction of submarines armed with a single 12-inch gun. Examples of both types were completed before the end of the war, and were technically impressive if tactically impracticable.[155] In late 1918 or 1919, Fisher considered proposals by a young submarine commander for a submarine battle cruiser that was to displace 30,000 tons, carry eight 18-inch or 20-inch guns, and steam 30 knots; the vessel was meant to "go into action trimmed down until only her turrets, control towers, periscopes and supports to same are exposed."[156] The old admiral seems to have been impressed. "The greatest possible speed with the biggest practicable gun was," he stated in the second volume of his memoirs, which were published on 8 December 1919, the fifth anniversary of the battle of the Falkland Islands, "up to the time of aircraft the acme of sea fighting. Now, there is only one word—submersible."[157] Fisher died of cancer in July 1920.

On 1 September 1925, H.M.S. *Furious*, once a battle cruiser armed with an 18-inch gun, was recommissioned after complete reconstruction as an aircraft carrier. By the end of the decade, she was joined by *Courageous* and *Glorious*, which were similarly converted. The three carriers retained their high speed and weak protection, and were capable of launching aircraft that carried bombs or torpedoes that were powerful enough to sink any warship at ranges that were far beyond those of even the largest caliber gun. Thus in their final guise, Fisher's last battle cruisers realized his conception of a fast, lightly armoured, and heavily armed warship that was capable of displacing the battleship. As the Japanese and American navies were to prove in the war in the Pacific, the aircraft carrier was indeed the capital ship of the future. Politics and financial limitation, however, disrupted the development of British naval aircraft between 1919 and 1939, reducing the effectiveness of the Royal Navy's aircraft carriers in the Second World War in a manner that was at least reminiscent of the relationship between inadequate fire control and the unsatisfactory performance of the battle cruiser during the First World War. But that is another story.

Notes to Epilogue

1 The most complete account of the events leading to the reappointment of Fisher as First Sea Lord is to be found in Martin Gilbert, *Winston S. Churchill*, vol. 3: *1914-1916—The Challenge of War* (Boston: Houghton Mifflin, 1971), pp. 143-53.

2 Peter Padfield, *Aim Straight: A biography of Admiral Sir Percy Scott* (London: Hodder & Stoughton, 1966), pp. 228-31.

3 Fisher marginalia on Beatty to Fisher, 15 November 1914, and Fisher to Jellicoe, 17 November 1914, in *FGDN*, Vol. 3, pp. 71, 73-4.

4 Admiral Sir Frederic C. Dreyer, *The Sea Heritage: A Study of Maritime Warfare* (London: Museum Press, 1955), p. 91.

5 Fisher to Jellicoe, 23 April 1915, *FGDN*, Vol. 3, p. 202.

6 Great Britain, Admiralty, Technical History Section, *Fire Control in H.M. Ships*. Series: *The Technical History and Index: A Serial History of Technical Problems Dealt with by Admiralty Departments* [henceforward cited as *Fire Control in H.M. Ships*], part 23 (December 1919), pp. 9-10, N.L.M.D.

7 Fisher to Churchill, 10 December 1914, in *FGDN*, Vol. 3, p. 91.

8 Maurice P. Northcott, *Renown and Repulse*, Series: *Ensign*, no.8 (London: Battle of Britain Prints, 1978) pp.1-2, and D. K. Brown, *A Century of Naval Construction* (London: Conway Maritime Press, 1983), p. 112.

9 Fisher to Churchill, 21 December 1914, *FGDN*, Vol. 3, p. 104.

10 Fisher to Jellicoe, 22 December 1914, ibid., p. 106.

11 Fisher to Jellicoe, 23 December 1914, ibid., pp. 107-8.

12 Jellicoe to Fisher, 29 December 1914, F.P. 890a, FISR 1/17, C.C..

13 Fisher to Churchill, 25 December 1914, *FGDN*, Vol 3, pp. 110-11.

14 See Fisher to Rear-Admiral Frederick C. T. Tudor, 27 December 1914, ibid., pp.113-4.

15 For the development schedule of Fisher's battle cruisers, see Brown, *Century of Naval Construction*, p. 112.

16 Churchill note, 28 December 1914, on Fisher to Tudor, 27 December 1914, and Fisher to Jellicoe, 22 January 1915, *FGDN*, Vol. 3, pp. 114, 143-4.

17 Fisher to Jellicoe, 22 January 1914, ibid., pp. 143-4.

18 Fisher to Jellicoe, 23 January 1915, ibid., p. 145.

19 Fisher to Churchill, 25 January 1915, ibid., p.145.

20 The 12-inch guns of an *Invincible* fired a shell that weighed 850 pounds, while the 15-inch guns of the big-gun light cruiser fired a shell that weighed 1,920 pounds. The six gun broadside of an *Invincible* thus came to 5,100 pounds, while the four gun broadside of the big-gun light cruiser amounted to 7,680 pounds. For projectile weights, see Oscar Parkes and Maurice Prendergast (ed.), *Fighting Ships* (London: Sampson Low Marston, 1919), p. 37.

21 R. A. Burt, *British Battleships of World War One* (Annapolis: Naval Institute Press, 1986), p. 303.

22 Fisher to D'Eyncourt, 25 January 1915, DEY/17, D'Eyncourt Papers, N.M.M.

23 Gilbert, *Challenge of War*, pp. 225-7.

24 Mackay, *Fisher of Kilverstone*, pp. 462-4, 472-3.

25 Fisher to Beatty, 8 and 9 February 1915, *FGDN*, Vol. 3, pp. 156-7. For other technical reasons favoring a shallower draught than had previously been the case for British capital ships, which had nothing to do with the requirements of a Baltic naval campaign, see Alan Raven and John Roberts, *British Battleships of World War Two* (London: Arms & Armour Press, 1976), p. 60.

26 For which see below, section 2.

27 Jellicoe to Fisher, quoted in Fisher to Asquith, 28 January 1915, in *FGDN*, Vol. 3, p. 148.
28 Fisher to Jellicoe, 29 January 1915, ibid., pp. 149-50. See also Mackay, *Fisher of Kilverstone*, p. 485.
29 Fisher to Jellicoe, 8 February 1915, *FGDN*, Vol. 3, p. 155.
30 Fisher to Beatty, 8 February 1915, ibid., pp. 156.
31 "Memorandum on the Battle Cruiser Fleet" (5 March 1915), F.P. 4353, FISR 5/26. C.C.
32 Burt, *British Battleships of World War One*, pp. 303-6. For a detailed description of the 18-inch gun, see N. J. M. Campbell, "British Super-Heavy Guns, Part 3," *Warship*, III (London: Conway Maritime Press, 1979), pp. 197-9.
33 Fisher to D'Eyncourt, 5 May 1915, DEY/17, N.M.M., and Lord Fisher, *Records* (New York: George H. Doran, 1920), pp. 200-1, 222-3.
34 Mackay, *Fisher of Kilverstone*, p. 501.
35 Although Fisher and Hadcock continued to discuss the possibility of developing the 20-inch gun, for which see Hadcock to Fisher, 22 November 1915, F.P. 1105, FISR 1/20, C.C.
36 For Fisher and the B.I.R., see John Keeney Gusewelle, "The Board of Invention and Research: A Case Study in the Relations between Academic Science and the Royal Navy in Great Britain During the First World War," unpublished PhD. dissertation, University of California, Irvine, 1971; Roy M. MacLeod and E. Kay Andrews, "Scientific advice in the War at Sea, 1915-1917: the Board of Invention and Research," *The Journal of Contemporary History*, Vol. 6 (1971), pp. 3-40; and John Keeney Gusewelle, "Science and the Admiralty during World War I: The Case of the Board of Invention and Research," in Gerald Jordan (ed.), *Naval Warfare in the Twentieth Century, 1900-1945* (London: Croom Helm, 1977), pp. 105-17.
37 Asquith to Fisher, 22 January 1916, *FGDN*, Vol. 3, p. 292.
38 Fisher to Asquith, 24 January 1916, ibid., p. 292.
39 Fisher to Asquith, 3 February 1916, ibid., pp. 296-300.
40 Beatty to Asquith, 3 February 1916, in A. Temple Patterson (ed.), *The Jellicoe Papers: Selections from the private and official correspondence of Admiral of the Fleet Earl Jellicoe of Scapa*, 2 Vols (London: Navy Records Society, 1966), Vol. 1, pp. 207-10.
41 Raven and Roberts, *British Battleships of World War Two*, pp. 60-2.
42 Jellicoe memorandum quoted in Maurice Northcott, *Hood: Design and Construction*, Series: *Ensign, Special* (London: Bivouac Books, 1975), p. 2.
43 Two of the specifications appear to have been prepared on 1 February 1916, a week before the receipt of Jellicoe's advice, for which see Raven and Roberts, *British Battleships of World War Two*, p. 63.
44 Northcott, *Hood*, pp. 2-3, Raven and Roberts, *British Battleships of World War Two*, pp. 62-3.
45 Fisher to Bartolomé, 18 April 1916, F.P. 4899, FISR 8/33, C.C.
46 Fisher to Jellicoe, 29 April 1916, *FGDN*, Vol. 3, p. 344.
47 Fisher to Jellicoe, 18 May 1916, ibid., Vol. 3, pp. 348-9.
48 Gerard Riley to Pollen, 4 August 1914, P.P.
49 Pollen to Dodge [?], 22 August 1914, and E. C. Tobey to Pollen, 13 February 1917, in P.P. For the development of the Sperry plotter, or "battle tracer" as it was known, see Thomas Parke Hughes, *Elmer Sperry: Inventor and Engineer* (Baltimore: Johns Hopkins, 1971), pp. 230-3.
50 For the Chilean unit taken over in 1914, see Burt, *British Battleships of World War I*, p. 231. For a second Chilean unit that was for the most part incomplete

and not taken over until 1918, see David Brown, *HMS Eagle*, Series: *Warship Profile*, no.35 (Windsor: Profile Publications, 1973), pp. 249-50. For the Brazilian unit, see Alan Vanterpool, "The 'Riachuelo'," *Warship International*, Vol. 6 (Spring, 1969), pp. 140-1, and the corrective letter and drawing by I. A. Sturton in *Warship International*, Vol. 7 (30 September 1970), pp. 205-6.

51 Gerard Riley to Pollen, 4 August 1914, P.P.

52 Reginald Hall draft letter, n.d. but probably 1922, P.P.

53 Pollen to Singer, 16 October 1914; Singer to Pollen, 17 October 1914; Pollen to Singer, 20 October 1914; and Singer to Pollen, 30 October 1914, all in P.P. The Argo electrical rate Clock No. 1 was fitted to transmit to a numerical receiver of the Barr & Stroud type, while the Argo electrical rate Clock No. 2 was equipped to transmit to a follow-the-pointer receiver. The turret instrument cost £1,650, the electrical rate Clock No. 1 £249, and the electrical rate Clock No. 2 £280, in lots of ten. In contrast, a Dreyer Table designed for local control, of which eight were ordered in August 1914, cost £400. For the trials of and orders for the Dreyer local control instrument, see "Local Control in Turret, 'Queen Mary'" (30 July 1914), and "Manufacture of Turret Local Control Instruments" (3 August 1914), *IQ/DNO*, Vol. 3 (1914).

54 Pollen to Riley, 8 September and 15 October 1914, P.P.

55 Pollen to Riley, 8 September 1914, P.P.

56 Pollen's naval business associates had been or would be recalled. Lieutenant George Gipps was assigned to the pre-dreadnought battleship *Triumph* on 7 August 1914, and later killed when that vessel was torpedoed at the Dardanelles in March 1915. Lieutenant Gerard Riley was assigned to the Naval Ordnance Department on 31 October 1914. Harold Isherwood would become a Lieutenant Commander in the Royal Naval Volunteer Reserve in January 1916 (see *Navy List*) and serve as chief designer at the Royal Navy's mining school (for which see Dreyer memorandum, 12 March 1918, in DRYR 2/1, Dreyer Papers, C.C.). For Pollen's wartime activity as a journalist, see "List of Mr. A. H. Pollen's Articles from August, 1914," in PLLN 3/6, Pollen Papers, C.C., and Anthony Pollen, *The Great Gunnery Scandal: The Mystery of Jutland* (London: Collins, 1980), pp. 146-68, 203-25.

57 Copy of letter, author unknown, enclosed with Pollen to Balfour, 1 February 1916, P.P.

58 Russian naval attache to the Admiralty Permanent Secretary, n.d., suggested draft letter that appears to have been written by Pollen, P.P.

59 Pollen to Balfour, 29 February 1916, *CCB*, P.P.

60 For the text of this print, see *PP*, pp. 334-56.

61 For the placement of the Argo mounting in the *Invincible*, see John A. Roberts, *Warship Monographs: Invincible Class* (Greenwich: Conway Maritime Press, 1972), p. 25.

62 For battle cruiser gunnery at the Falklands, see N. J. M. Campbell, *Battlecruisers: The design and development of British and German battlecruisers of the First World War era* (Greenwich: Conway Maritime Press, 1978), p. 9; and V. E. Tarrant, *Battlecruiser Invincible: the history of the first battlecruiser, 1909-16* (Annapolis: Naval Institute Press, 1986), pp. 60-74.

63 Campbell, *Battlecruisers*, pp. 9, 18, 29-32 and 40; for an excellent reassessment of this engagement, see James Goldrick, *The King's Ships Were at Sea: The War in the North Sea, August 1914-February 1915* (Annapolis: Naval Institute Press, 1984), pp. 260-78.

64 Commodore Gustof von Schoultz, *With the British Battle Fleet: War Recollections of a Russian Naval Officer* (London: Hutchinson, 1925), pp. 87-8, and Dreyer, *Sea*

Heritage, p. 95. Battle cruiser firing results at the higher ranges were relatively poor because of inadequate practice, and even Jellicoe was concerned that the Dreyer Tables lacked the capability to deal with the greater distances, for which see Jellicoe to Beatty, 18 November 1915; Beatty to Jellicoe, 21 November 1915; Jellicoe to Beatty, 12 December 1915, and Jellicoe to Beatty, 22 December 1915, in Patterson (ed.), *Jellicoe Papers*, Vol. 1, pp. 187-8, 190-1; and Stephen Roskill, *Admiral of the Fleet Earl Beatty: The Last Naval Hero, An Intimate Biography* (London: Collins, 1980), pp. 131-2.

65 For the wartime fitting of directors, see *Fire Control in H.M. Ships*, p. 10.

66 Peter Padfield, *Guns at Sea* (London: Hugh Evelyn, 1973), p. 264.

67 For the modifications to the later mark Dreyer Tables, see *Fire Control in H.M. Ships*, pp. 26-8.

68 Fred T. Jane (ed.), *Fighting Ships* (London: Sampson, Low Marston, 1914), p. 45.

69 Beatty to Jellicoe, undated, but January 1915 after the battle of Dogger Bank, in Patterson (ed.), *Jellicoe Papers*, Vol.1, p. 131.

70 John Campbell, *Jutland: An Analysis of the Fighting* (Annapolis: Naval Institute Press, 1986).

71 A revisionist analysis of the circumstances surrounding the failure of the fast battleships to turn, which is based on meticulous archival research and a sound understanding of shiphandling and naval procedures, has been carried out by Commander, R.N. ret., Michael Craig Waller, who kindly allowed me to read his yet unpublished work.

72 *FDSF*, Vol. 3 [rev.], pp. 80-5. Campbell, however, has played down the importance of the initial differential in visibility conditions and the firing instructions misunderstanding, for which see *Jutland*, pp. 38-9. On the other hand, Campbell notes that the angle of approach of the British battle cruisers to the German line was such that the turrets were firing across their forward arcs rather than across the broadside [Campbell, *Jutland*, p. 39]. Under these circumstances, gun trunnions would have been canted with respect to the axis of the ship's roll, which would have produced a slight difference in the angle of training of the guns from that indicated by the director sight. This phenomenon, known as "cross-levelling" error, may have resulted in significant mislaying of the guns for deflection. German ships, on the other hand, were firing their armament practically across their broadsides, and would not, therefore, have been afflicted with this problem. For cross-levelling error, see Great Britain, Admiralty, Gunnery Branch, *Progress in Naval Materiel* (July, 1920), pp. 17-18, N.L.M.D.; and for its possible effect on British shooting at Jutland see Hugh Clausen to Anthony Pollen, 6 December 1969, P.P.

73 For the inability of Dreyer Tables to produce an accurate estimate of the change of range rate when the rate was high and changing, see the discussion of the Grand Fleet Dreyer Table Committee Report given in the next section. For the inability of Dreyer Tables to produce an accurate estimate of the change of bearing rate when the rate was high and changing, see *Fire Control in H.M. Ships*, p. 27. According to this monograph, an accurate means of plotting bearings was not available until the development of the Dreyer Table Mark V, which did not enter service in the battleship *Ramillies* until July 1917.

74 In his biography of Percy Scott, Peter Padfield stated that Dreyer discovered that the Dreyer Table in one of the British battle cruisers at Jutland had been partially dismantled, and that, presumably, it had been incapable of operation during the engagement [for which, see Padfield, *Aim Straight*, p. 247n]. For some corroboration of this account, see Pollen to Sir Eric Geddes, 24 January

1918 (draft letter not sent), P.P., and Hugh Clausen to Anthony Pollen, 6 December 1969, P.P. If true, this would seem to indicate that at least one battle cruiser fire control team had concluded that the Dreyer Table was of little value. Dreyer, on the other hand, may have told the story in order to absolve his equipment of blame for the poor shooting of the battle cruisers at Jutland.

75 The positioning of the Argo mounting within the structure of the forward superstructure cannot be verified from either documents or photographs. But it will be recalled that the Admiralty had informed Pollen in 1909 that his mounting would be placed aloft in all ships. In addition, photographs of the *Indefatigable* and *New Zealand* show no range-finder on the forward conning tower as in the 13.5-inch gun battle cruisers, the Argo mounting would not have been placed in any turret because the shock caused by the discharge of the guns would have caused it to malfunction, and the positioning of the mounting in the rear spotting top is doubtful because of the likelihood of interference from smoke. Photographs of the *New Zealand* after the 1917 modifications to her forward control top show what appears to be an Argo mounting positioned on the roof, where it may have been moved when more space was needed within the enclosed structure.

76 Between 3:57 and 4:10, the *New Zealand*'s forward transmitting station recorded 20 ranges while that of the *Tiger* recorded 26, for which see Great Britain, Admiralty, *Battle of Jutland, 30 May to 1 June 1916: Official Dispatches with Appendices* (London: HMSO, 1920), pp. 391, 393-4.

77 "H.M.S. 'Lion': General Details," in DRAX 1/2, Drax Papers, C.C.

78 *Official Dispatches*, pp. 387-8.

79 For German range-finders and fire control in general, see Great Britain, Admiralty War Staff, Intelligence Division, *German Navy; Part IV: Naval Ordnance, Torpedoes, Mines, &c.* (July 1917); Great Britain, Admiralty, Naval Staff, Intelligence Department, *German Gunnery Information Derived from the Interrogation of Prisoners of War* (October 1918); and Great Britain, Admiralty, Naval Staff, Gunnery and Torpedo Division, *Progress in Naval Gunnery, 1914 to 1918* (July, 1919), p. 7, all in N.L.M.D.; Great Britain, Admiralty, Naval Staff, Intelligence Department, *Reports on Interned German Vessels: Gunnery Information*, (February 1919), Adm. 186/240, P.R.O., and Great Britain, Admiralty Naval Staff, Intelligence Division, *Reports on Interned German Vessels: Part V.—Gunnery Materiel* (October 1920), Adm. 186/243, P.R.O.; and Commander Georg von Hase, *Kiel and Jutland* (New York: E. P. Dutton, 1922), pp. 78-83.

80 For a detailed discussion of coincidence and stereoscopic range-finding, see Barr & Stroud, Ltd., "The Principles of Rangefinding," Pamphlet No. 42 (London: by the author, n.d.), pp. 9-32.

81 Austrian Naval Attaché quoted in *FDSF*, Vol. 3 [rev.], pp. 197-8. Marder does not give a reference for this passage.

82 According to Admiral Royer Dick [interviewed by the author in August 1987], who at the battle of Jutland was a midshipman manning the bearing plot of the Dreyer Table in the fast battleship *Barham*, the main difficulty was generating correct bearings, rather than range [for the inherent shortcomings of the Dreyer Table Mark IV★ with regard to plotting bearings, see *Fire Control in H.M. Ships*, p. 27, noted earlier; alternatively, the perception that there was a problem with bearings may have been caused by cross-levelling errors, a phenomenon discussed in note 72]. Dick also recalled that the Argo mounting with a 9-foot base range-finder was positioned in the fore-top of his ship, an arrangement that was probably the case for the other ships in the 5th battle squadron, and the 15-inch gun battleships of the main body as well.

83 H. W. Fawcett and G. W. W. Hooper, ed., *The Fighting at Jutland: The Personal Experiences of Sixty Officers and Men of the British Fleet* (Glasgow: Maclure, Macdonald, n.d., but 1921), p. 20.

84 von Hase, *Kiel and Jutland*, p. 157. These may have been near-misses, which would account for their not being tabulated as hits on the German record upon which Campbell based his invaluable analysis.

85 Sir Julian Corbett to Jellicoe, 3 August 1922, in Patterson (ed.), *The Jellicoe Papers*, Vol. 2, p. 415; Admiral Sir Reginald Bacon, *The Jutland Scandal* (London: Hutchinson, n.d.; 2nd edn. 1925), p. 145–6; *FDSF*, Vol. 3 [rev.], p. 76, and Campbell, *Jutland*, p. 49.

86 Campbell, *Jutland*, pp. 368–78.

87 "Memorandum on Fire Control" (1 August 1916), P.P.

88 "Memorandum II" (7 August 1916), P.P.

89 Lists of the recipients are given on a cover sheet to "Memorandum on Fire Control," P.P.

90 Beatty to Pollen, 14 August 1916, P.P.

91 Pollen to Beatty, 18 August 1916, P.P.

92 Jellicoe to Pollen, 18 August 1916, P.P.

93 Pollen to Jellicoe, 22 August 1916, P.P.

94 Pollen to Jellicoe, 25 August 1916, P.P.

95 Jellicoe to Pollen, 28 August 1916, P.P.

96 Richmond to Pollen, 7 August 1916, P.P.

97 *FDSF*, Vol. 3 [rev.], p. 260.

98 Admiralty Permanent Secretary to Dreyer, 15 May 1916, DRYR 2/1, Dreyer Papers, C.C. Dreyer, it should be noted, made arrangements not to accept the award until the end of the war, with proceeds from the interest during the interim being paid to the Treasury, for which see Dreyer to Commander-in-Chief, H.M. Ships and Vessels, Home Fleets, 18 May 1916, DRYR 2/1, Dreyer Papers, C.C.

99 *FDSF*, Vol. 3 [rev.], p. 84n.

100 Lord Chatfield, *The Navy and Defence: The Autobiography of Admiral of the Fleet Lord Chatfield* (London: William Heinemann, 1942), pp. 141, 151.

101 Ibid., pp. 151–3.

102 Campbell, *Jutland*, p. 386.

103 Roskill, *Last Naval Hero*, p. 193.

104 Chatfield, *Navy and Defence*, p. 154. For Beatty's high opinion of Dreyer at this time, see Roskill, *Earl Beatty*, p. 260. For the Admiralty's initial efforts to come to terms with the shell problem, see Great Britain, Admiralty, Gunnery Branch, *Final Report of the President, Projectile Committee, 1917* (June 1917), N.L.M.D.

105 "Memorandum by Admiral Sir Frederic C. Dreyer, G.B.E., K.C.B." (3 February 1944), DRYR 4/3, Dreyer Papers, C.C.

106 Pollen to Rear-Admiral Bradley Fiske, 27 January 1915; Pollen to Commander Symington, 12 November 1915; Fiske to Pollen, 13 January 1916; Pollen to Fiske, 13 April 1916; Fiske to Pollen, 26 April 1916; Pollen to Lieutenant Gilmor, 17 April 1916; Fiske to Pollen, 2 May 1916; Pollen to Fiske, 9 May 1916; Pollen to Fiske, 17 May 1916; Fiske to Pollen, 7 June 1916; Pollen to Fiske, 3 July 1916; and Symington to Pollen, 13 December 1916; P.P.

107 Extract of a letter sent by E. C. Tobey, apparently a diplomat at the American Embassy in London, to Pollen, acknowledged by Pollen on 13 February 1917, P.P.

108 Pollen to E. C. Tobey, 16 May 1917, with extract of letter from Admiral Earl, Chief of the Bureau of Ordnance, to Tobey, P.P.

109 Tobey to Henry Steven Higgins, 22 May 1917, P.P.

110 For Pollen's efforts to improve Anglo-American relations, see Anthony Pollen, *The Great Gunnery Scandal*, pp. 215-24.

111 Extract quoted in Pollen to Sir Eric Geddes, 24 January 1918, draft letter not sent, P.P. For the backward state of American thinking on fire control prior to Pollen's visit, see Commander (R.N.) R. T. Down to the Admiralty Permanent Secretary, 27 June 1917, report on what had been learned about American gunnery practice during a visit to Washington, D.C., from 6 May to 27 June 1917, in "United States of America; Naval Cooperation; 1918. I," H.S. 1621, Adm. 137/1621, P.R.O.

112 Dreyer minute, "Pollen Fire Control Apparatus" (12 March 1918), DRYR 2/1, Dreyer Papers, C.C.

113 Pollen to Sir Eric Geddes, 24 January 1918, draft letter not sent, P.P. American opinion in 1917 on the question of the Dreyer Table was divided, Admiral Henry T. Mayo, Commander-in-Chief of the Atlantic Fleet being critical while Captain Husband E. Kimmel reporting favorably, for which see Mayo to the Secretary of the Navy (Operations), 11 October 1917, File 8009, and Kimmel to unknown captain, 3 December 1917, photocopies of documents to the author courtesy of Christopher Wright.

114 Pollen to Admiral William Snowden Sims, 27 February 1918, P.P. A range-finder was not included in the order because Pollen could not at this time obtain optical glass in Britain of the required quality, for which see Pollen to Tobey, 17 May 1917, P.P.

115 Pollen to Geddes, 6 March 1918, P.P.

116 Geddes to Pollen, 13 April 1918, P.P. The members of this committee were Rear-Admiral Edward Phillpotts, the Director of Naval Equipment; Captain Cyril Fuller, the Director of the Plans Division, Admiralty Naval Staff; Captain R. M. Colvin, the Assistant Director of the Plans Division; Commander H. J. S. Brownrigg; Commander S. R. Bailey; and Commander J. F. C. Patterson, for which see "Pollen Fire Control System (Report of inspection at York of)," n.d., DRYR 2/1, Dreyer Papers, C.C.

117 Philpotts had become Jellicoe's assistant at the Admiralty in December 1916, and thus was also an associate of Dreyer who became Director of Naval Ordnance not long afterwards. On the other hand, the Rev. Anthony H. Pollen, Arthur's brother, had been the Catholic chaplain on board Philpott's ship, the battleship *Warspite*, during the battle of Jutland. Little can be said, therefore, about any predispositions to favor or disfavor Pollen on the basis of past associations. Anthony Pollen, the younger son of Arthur, however, recalls that his father and Philpotts were friends [information to the author, late summer 1987].

118 In the "straight-line" method, ranges from observing instruments and ranges generated by the clock were plotted to run straight down a narrow strip of paper; if the two range plots ran parallel, this indicated that the rate settings of the clock were correct. If, on the other hand, the plots diverged, this indicated that the rate settings of the clock were incorrect, and that a correction was necessary, the amount of the correction depending upon the angle of divergence. A similar arrangement was suitable for plotting observed and calculated bearings. This system, which was a marked improvement over the original plotting system formulated by Dreyer, was devised by two sub-lieutenants, Alfred J. G. Langley and Lennox A. K. Boswell, for which

see Great Britain, Admiralty, Gunnery Branch, *Reports of the Grand Fleet Dreyer Table Committee, 1918-1919* (September 1919), p. 11, Adm. 186/241, P.R.O.

119 "Pollen Fire Control System (Report of inspection at York of)," n.d., DRYR 2/1, Dreyer Papers, C.C.

120 Dreyer minute, "Pollen Fire Control Apparatus" (12 March 1918), DRYR 2/1, Dreyer Papers, C.C.

121 Pollen to Phillpotts, 13 March 1918, P.P.

122 Dreyer minute, "Pollen Fire Control Apparatus" (12 March 1918) [with comments of the separate members of the Board of Admiralty], DRYR 2/1, Dreyer Papers, C.C.

123 Pollen to Geddes, 5 April 1918; Steel to Pollen, 6 April 1918; Pollen to Geddes, 9 April 1918; Pollen to Steel, 9 April 1918; Geddes to Pollen, 13 April 1918; Pollen to Geddes, 16 April 1918; Steel to Pollen, 21 May 1918; Pollen to Geddes, 28 May 1918; Geddes to Pollen, 30 May 1918; Pollen to Geddes, 31 May 1918; Pollen to Geddes, 6 June 1918; Admiralty Permanent Secretary to Pollen, 18 December 1918; Pollen to the Admiralty Permanent Secretary, 20 December 1918; and Admiralty Permanent Secretary to Pollen, 10 February 1919; all in P.P.

124 For what appears to have been the early stages of the discussions between Pollen and the Admiralty over the possibility of a range-finder order, see Pollen to Masterton Smith, 12 and 17 October 1916, P.P.

125 Staff shortages may have been only part of the problem. On 17 May 1917, Pollen had informed an American contact that he would prefer not to offer his range-finder for a U.S. Navy trial because of the impossibility of getting optical glass in Britain of a quality that was such as to ensure that his instrument would be sufficiently superior to those of Barr & Stroud to justify their greater expense. For the problem of optical glass manufacture in Britain during the First World War, see Roy MacLeod and Kay MacLeod, "War and economic development: government and the optical industry in Britain, 1914-18," in J. M. Winter, ed., *War and Economic Development* (Cambridge: Cambridge University Press, 1975), pp. 165-203.

126 *Fire Control in H.M. Ships*, pp. 32-3, N.L.M.D.

127 Extract quoted in Pollen to Sir Eric Geddes, 24 January 1918, *draft letter not sent*, P.P.; United States of America, US Navy, Bureau of Ordnance, *Navy Ordnance Activities: World War 1917-1918* (Washington, D.C.: Government Printing Office, 1920), pp. 151-9; Vannevar Bush, *Pieces of the Action* (New York: William Morrow, 1970), pp. 183-5; and Hughes, *Sperry*, pp. 158, 232-3 and 284. There can be little doubt that the work of both Sperry and Ford was at least influenced by Pollen. Rear-Admiral Bradley Fiske, with whom Pollen corresponded, was a friend of Sperry. The conception of the Ford Clock was the product of extensive discussions between Ford and US Navy gunnery experts that took place in 1916, which, given Pollen's communications with American naval officers before and during the war, must have been informed by knowledge of Pollen's work. For a detailed technical description of the Ford Clock, see Lt. (j.g.) H.M. Terrill, "Notes on the Theory of the Ford Range Keeper," print issued by the U.S.S. *New Mexico* Gunnery Department, *c*.1919, US National Archives RG38, Entry 178, Box 3, File Folder Conf. 59(65), courtesy of Mr Christopher Wright.

128 Extract from R. R. Scott to Beatty, 9 September 1918, in *Reports of the Grand Fleet Dreyer Table Committee*, p. 4.

129 These were, specifically, the Commander (G) J. F. C. Patterson and staff of the battleship *Barham*; Commander (G) C. B. Prickett and staff of the battle

cruiser *Lion*; Commander (G) T. H. Binney and staff of the battleship *Queen Elizabeth*; and Flag Commander G. C. C. Royle and Lieutenant Commander N. A. Wodehouse of the battleship *Revenge*, for which see ibid., p. 12.

130 Summary of the First and Second Interim Reports, in ibid., pp. 4-5.

131 An inclinometer used measurements of the distance between the firing ship and target, and the length of the observed target image, and the known length of the target, whose identity had to be established, to calculate the inclination—or course—of the target. The instrument was invented by Midshipmen Gerald M. B. Langley and Alfred J. G. Langley in 1916, prototypes were produced in 1917. In 1918, orders were placed with Barr & Stroud, and Elliots, for a trial "Langley Automatic Inclinometer." For the development of the inclinometer, see *Fire Control in H.M. Ships*, pp. 30-1. For the mechanical principles of calculating inclination, see Great Britain, Admiralty, Gunnery Branch, *Handbook for Naval Rangefinders and Inclinometers*, Vol. 2: *Instruments in Capital Ships and Cruisers* (1943), pp. 16-17, N.L.M.D.

132 *Reports of the Grand Fleet Dreyer Table Committee*, pp. 5-12.

133 For the British trials of the Ford clock an example of which was borrowed from an American battleship with the Grand Fleet and mounted in the light cruiser H.M.S. *Cardiff*, see Hugh Clausen to Pollen, 11 November 1969, P.P.

134 Ibid., pp. 14-18.

135 Ibid., pp. 18-19.

136 For the Brownrigg report and accompanying minutes, see "'Ford', Fire Control System: Interviews with representatives of Ford Instrument Coy. of New York," *IQ/DNO* (January 1919-June 1919), N.L.M.D.

137 Dreyer, *The Sea Heritage*, pp. 236-7, 239-61.

138 Pollen to Beatty, 28 June 1920, P.P. It should also be noted that during the war, Beatty may have gone so far as to allow Pollen to examine the Dreyer Table fitted in the *Lion*, for which see Pollen to Beatty, 7 February 1923, P.P.

139 Hugh Clausen, "Invention and the Navy, the Progress from Ideas to Ironmongery," a paper given to the Institute of Patentees and Inventors at the Royal Society of Arts, 30 January 1970, p. 10, P.P. For the AFCT Mark I, see Great Britain, Admiralty, Gunnery Branch, *Handbook for Admiralty Fire Control Table Mark I. (H.M. Ships "Nelson" and "Rodney.")* (September 1927), in Adm. 186/273-4, P.R.O. For the role of naval officers in the design process, see Richard Humble, *Fraser of North Cape: The Life of Admiral of the Fleet Lord Fraser [1888-1981]* (London: Routledge & Kegan Paul, 1983), pp. 80-2.

140 For the fire control equipment of British capital ships after 1918, see Alan Raven and John Roberts, *British Battleships of World War Two*.

141 Rear-Admiral Sir Alfred E. M. Chatfield minute, 5 January 1926, in "Fire Control Table. New Design," p. 6, *IQ/DNO* (July 1923-June 1926), N.L.M.D.

142 Rear-Admiral Sir Frederic Dreyer minute, 4 January 1926, in "Fire Control Table. New Design," p. 6, *IQ/DNO* (July 1923-June 1926), N.L.M.D. The AFCT Mark I, Dreyer later claimed, "was in fact only a rearrangement of my 'Dreyer Table,'" for which see Dreyer, *Sea Heritage*, p. 59.

143 For an account of the hearing of the Argo Company case before the Royal Commission on Awards to Inventors, see Anthony Pollen, *Great Gunnery Scandal*, pp. 130-45.

144 Fisher to Churchill, 18 January 1915, in *FGDN*, Vol. 3, p. 132.

145 Fisher to Beatty, 27 January and 6 February 1915, ibid., pp. 147, 153.

146 Fisher to Crease, 3 June 1916, ibid., Vol. 3, p. 353.

147 Jellicoe to Fisher, 15 June 1916, ibid., p. 356.

148 For Fisher's long-lasting faith in Dreyer, see "Loose notes for autobiographical work," n.d. but probably 1918 or 1919, F.P. 5174, FISR 9/8, C.C.

149 Watts surmised incorrectly that the Germans used the Petravic system of gunlaying (Chapter 5, section 1) at the battle of Jutland, for which see Watts, "Extracts from a Paper on Ships of the British Navy on the Outbreak of War on 4th August 1914 and some Matters of Interest in connection with their Production," read at the Institution of Naval Architects, 9 April 1919, reprinted in *The Further Volume of Lord Fisher's Notes* (31 July 1919), printed for private circulation, pp. 30-1, in F.P. 5463, FISR 10/10, C.C. For Fisher's evident concern with the possibility that the German navy was more advanced than the British in matters of fire control, see Fisher to Captain Thomas E. Crease, 19 April 1919, *FGDN*, Vol. 3, pp. 579-80.

150 Fisher to *The Times* (2 September 1919). For the entire series of letters, see Admiral of the Fleet Lord Fisher, *Lord Fisher on the Navy* (London: Hodder & Stoughton, 1919).

151 Fisher to *The Times* (8 September 1919).

152 Fisher to *The Times* (9 September 1919).

153 "Loose notes," F.P. 5174, FISR 9/8, C.C.

154 Fisher to *The Times* (13 September 1919).

155 John Lambert, "The K Class Steam Submarines," *Warship*, Vol. 2 (London: Conway Maritime Press, 1978), pp. 218-29, and Thomas A. Adams, "The M Class Submarine Monitors," in *Warship*, Vol. 7 (London: Conway Maritime Press, 1983), pp. 25-9.

156 "Submarine or Submersible Battleships," memorandum by unknown young submarine commander passed on to Fisher by Captain S. S. Hall, F.P. 3603, FISR 3/24, and "Specifications for a Submersible Battleship," signed by a R. B. Ramsay, n.d., F.P. 4476, FISR 5/42, C.C. See also proposals for a fully submersible submarine armed with four 12-inch guns in "Specification for Submarine Battleship," n.d., F.P. 3423, FISR 3/22, and "Design No. 745" (diagrammatic sketch), F.P. 4473, FISR 5/41; "Design of Submersible Turret for Pair 12-inch 24 Cal. Guns," Vickers Gun Mounting Department Drawing No. 4524D, n.d., F.P. 4473, FISR 5/40; and "Diagrammatical Sketch of a Submarine Light Cruiser," n.d., F.P. 4475, FISR 5/42, all in C.C.

157 Fisher, *Records*, pp. 212-13. For the dates of publication of Fisher's memoirs, see Richard Hough, *Admiral of the Fleet: The Life of John Fisher* (New York: Macmillan, 1969), p. 357.

Conclusion

In the early 20th century, the British state had the authority to levy taxes on both income and consumption (that is, direct and indirect taxes), possessed a reputation for financial probity that enabled it to borrow at favorable rates of interest, and drew its revenue from an economic base that was the wealthiest in Europe. But the principles of the balanced budget and low income taxes were practically articles of national faith, which together with the commitment to free trade, meant that it was very difficult to increase the spending power of the government in the face of sharply rising social and defence costs. In 1909, virtuoso political leadership enabled the Liberal party to overcome strenuous opposition to extensions of direct taxation, and reinforced by an economic upturn and financial aid from the colonies, allowed Britain to spend much greater amounts on social reform and the navy without recourse to borrowing. For a number of years prior to 1909, however, a condition of moderate to severe financial restriction existed, which had a strong effect on Britain's naval position and the formulation of British naval policy.

British financial difficulties were a key factor in the early stages of the Anglo–German naval rivalry. Germany's capacity to build warships was limited by the imperial government's financial weakness and the heavy spending of the federal states on the army. Germany lacked the cruisers and overseas bases required for an effective surface campaign against British merchant shipping, and in this important respect was a far less dangerous opponent for the Royal Navy than the Franco-Russian alliance. Britain should have been quite capable of mustering the resources to overmatch the German battle fleet, but between 1905 and 1908 both Conservative-Unionist and Liberal financial retrenchment left the Royal Navy with from 10 to 20 per cent less effective buying power each year than had been available in 1904. The threat to Britain's naval supremacy before 1909, therefore, was not only a matter of German naval expansion, but British financial limitation as well.

The years of inadequate government revenue also had certain lasting effects that undermined British naval preparedness even after 1909. Borrowed funds raised by Naval Works Acts passed between 1895 and 1905 had been used to build naval shore facilities that were situated to meet the needs of an anticipated war with France and Russia. The base requirements of a naval war against Germany were far different, but by the time this was recognized after 1905, Parliament was no longer willing to authorize spending on naval works outside of the estimate, more than half of the sums provided by the works vote of the estimate were consumed by the payment of Naval Works Acts annuities, and a compensating increase in

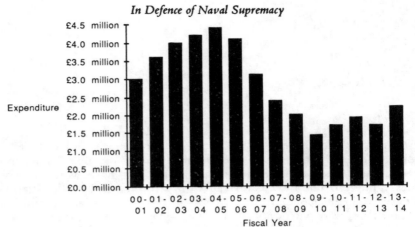

Figure 6   *Effective spending on naval works, 1900–13*

the size of the works vote could not be obtained without cuts in the
shipbuilding vote, which was considered to be unacceptable. Between 1909
and 1913, therefore, effective spending on naval works was less than half
of what it had been between 1901 and 1905, which was probably the main
reason why Britain lacked adequately equipped and defended bases in the
North Sea on the outbreak of war in 1914 (see Figure 6).

And finally, considerations of financial limitation did much to shape
the views of Sir John Fisher, who in turn strongly influenced the
course of British capital ship design. By 1904, Fisher was convinced that
impending reductions in naval expenditure had made the replacement of
the conventional battleship and first-class cruiser by the battle cruiser highly desirable, if not imperative for several reasons. He believed that British
capital ships should be much faster and more powerfully armed than their
enemies, and that these characteristics could only be achieved without
commensurate increases in cost through the sacrifice of heavy armor.
Fisher may also have hoped that because such vessels would be capable
of doing the work of either a battleship or first-class cruiser, or because
coastal defence submarines might reduce or eliminate the need for a battle
fleet, they could be built in smaller numbers, resulting in major savings in
construction costs, manning and maintenance. Fisher was then persuaded
by the success of the *Dreadnought* that the introduction of faster and more
powerfully armed battle cruisers would upset the capital ship programs of
foreign rivals, which would enable Britain to build fewer units of her own
and thus allow her to reduce expenditure even further.

Fisher's approach to capital ship design was a reflection of his conviction that the formulation of an efficient naval policy required the close
integration of strategy, tactics and technology. The fact that Britain needed
a navy that was both affordable and capable of winning decisive victories
prompted his call for the replacement of the battleship and armoured
cruiser by the battle cruiser; the battle cruiser's weak armour protection
made it necessary for it to fight a long-range engagement where it was
less likely to be hit by enemy fire; and the difficulties of having to fire

effectively at long range drove him to favor the all–big–gun system and advanced methods of fire control. "Strategy," Fisher thus had written in 1904, "should govern the types of ships to be designed. Ship design, as dictated by strategy, should govern tactics. Tactics should govern the details of armament."[1] Fisher may have overvalued the tactical and strategic worth of superior speed and long-range gunnery, and undervalued heavy armor protection, but the major breakthrough in fire control that would have made his concept of the battle cruiser at least plausible, if not practicable, and which, in any case, would have substantially increased the capability of both pre–dreadnought and dreadnought battleships as well, was neither technically infeasible nor prohibitively expensive.

Between 1905 and 1912 Arthur Hungerford Pollen developed a wholly original system of fire control, which was designed to use various data to compute the elevation and deflection settings on gunsights in a manner that took account of the relative motion of the firing ship and target, even when the range was changing at a rate that was itself changing or when the firing ship was altering course and speed. In its final form it consisted of a range-finder of special design that was fitted on a gyroscopically-stabilized mounting, a plotting unit, a calculator, and an electrical data transmission system. Pollen's work was guided by three major principles: first, that the requisite rapidity of operation and reliability could only be obtained by the automation of as many functions as was possible; second, that the mathematics of relative motion had to be solved exactly, not approximately; and third, that success in practice could not be achieved without instruments built to high standards of mechanical workmanship.

Pollen was incorrect to believe that the development of his instruments would reduce the difficulty of hitting a moving target from a moving ship to that of hitting a stationary target from a stationary ship. Consistent results with optical range-finders were difficult to achieve, high speed and changing courses resulted in ship motion that interfered with gun-laying even when director firing was employed, and neither rate nor probably true-course plotting by themselves were capable of producing satisfactory results under difficult conditions.[2] It cannot be doubted, however, that full Admiralty cooperation with Pollen's efforts would have resulted in the putting into service of a fire control system that was far superior to that which was actually adopted by the Royal Navy or possessed by foreign fleets. The use of range-finders with longer base lengths and better optics, which were available, together with the gyro-mounting, and the adoption of both automatic rate and true-course plotters—which in effect was what was done after the war—and of the Pollen calculator in its final form, the Argo Clock Mark V, almost certainly would have enabled British ships to hit more often—perhaps even much more often—when range and bearing rates were high and changing.

Admiralty objections to the cost of Pollen's instruments were in large part based on comparisons with other equipment that was mechanically far simpler and less capable, or arose from a failure to recognize the fact that Pollen's prices of necessity had to cover high research and development expenses, and the purchase of manufacturing facilities. It will be remembered that following the war, the Admiralty willingly paid ten times Pollen's charges for a plotting and calculating system that performed the same functions on essentially the same principles, albeit in a much more sophisticated way. In retrospect, his financial demands seem to have been reasonable, considering both the value of his work and the costs of carrying it out. In absolute terms, the expense of equipping the entire fleet with his equipment would have amounted to considerably less than the construction costs of a single dreadnought. And with adequate financial support, the manufacture of Pollen's instruments in the numbers that were required should not have posed insurmountable difficulties.

Pollen possessed several personal attributes that served him well in his career as an inventor. He was, first and foremost, both well-educated and extremely intelligent—not a technician by training, he nevertheless could understand technical problems in their essentials, and then formulate the lines upon which a sound solution could be developed. Pollen was, in addition, a shrewd industrial manager, articulate, confident in his ideals, and tenacious and determined. Thus he had the sense to seek first-class expert advice on a consulting basis and was willing to pay employees wages that were well above standard in order to obtain work of the necessary quality; could argue his case in speech or writing with clarity and force, which won him the support of much of the service and the financial backing of many wealthy businessmen; believed in the power of technology to solve problems and was convinced that important interests of his country would be served by the development of his instruments; and continued to work for years in the face of great adversity.

At the same time, Pollen was not without characteristics that to some extent must have obstructed his efforts. From an artistic and even bohemian background, politically a Liberal, a Catholic in an emphatically Protestant country, and a critical thinker, he was probably ill-suited by nature to work easily with naval officers who were members of what was a culturally and politically conservative, hierarchical, and conforming sub-culture. Pollen, in particular, may have had little understanding of, or if he did sympathy for, the collegial character of the service, and the concomitant closed network of personal relationships that governed so much of service professional as well as social life. Pollen's communications with political leaders, businessmen, and journalists, on the other hand, while of great use on occasion in overcoming opposition, were undoubtedly feared and resented by his service opponents. Pollen was not always able to restrain his facility with the spoken and written word, which was sometimes used to attack his enemies with highly insulting effect. And finally, he was perhaps not as aware as he should have been of the political costs of maintaining visible friendships with Fisher's worst enemies.

The shortcomings of outlook or behavior, to be sure, were not all on one side. The Admiralty was generally distrustful of inventors, and though more open to the adoption of perfected new weapons than is perhaps generally supposed, was as unwilling as other government departments then were to support research and development.[3] Most naval officers, by education and experience, were not equipped to deal with technical issues, and this was especially true of fire control, which involved both mathematical and mechanical matters that were novel, difficult and complicated. Officers of proven high executive capacity—such as Wilson, Bacon, Jellicoe, and Dreyer—probably enjoyed a measure of immunity from criticism for even serious errors made with regard to gunnery machinery because technical competence was not as highly valued or as easily measured as the ability to command. And the close relationship that naturally grew up between officers who served together in the same ship—experience that related Wilson and Jellicoe, Wilson and Dreyer, Bacon and Dreyer, and Jellicoe and Dreyer—fostered strong bonds of loyalty that later on could override other considerations.

There was, in addition, perhaps more to the resentment of Pollen by certain members of the service than simply dislike of civilians. Fire control was regarded as the special preserve of gunnery officers, who had been able to establish themselves as an elite in the late 19th and early 20th century with the onset of the gunnery revolution. Their high standing had been derived in large part from the importance of human marksmanship. Pollen's work, because it greatly increased the role of machines in the carrying out of the aiming of the guns, to a certain extent reduced the significance of human intelligence, training, skill, and the courage that was required to perform complicated tasks while under fire. To gunnery officers such as Dreyer, Pollen's approach thus may not have seemed just mistaken, but because it depreciated their fighting role, threatened their claims to special status in a way that provoked at least a measure of uneasiness if not bad feeling.

The negative effects of Pollen's background and personal shortcomings such as they were, and service attitudes towards technology, misplaced favoritism, xenophobia, and professional insecurity, were much exacerbated by what appears to have been the obstinacy and technical ignorance of Wilson and Bacon, and the zeal and ambition of Dreyer. But even this combination of factors need not have wrecked Pollen's relations with the Royal Navy. Fisher, when properly advised in 1906, had supported Pollen with decisive results, and continued strong leadership in gunnery affairs on his part would undoubtedly have resulted in the inventor receiving the cooperation and funding from the service that was required to perfect his system. Fisher, however, lacked the technical knowledge to make informed decisions on his own, while his past experience with the introduction of new technology—the quick-firing gun, the destroyer, the water-tube boiler, the all-big-gun armament, and turbine propulsion, which had more or less succeeded once the decision to proceed had been made—perhaps caused him to underestimate the difficulty of the fire control problem. In any case, when his close advisors divided on the question of gunnery, he accepted over-optimistic reports of progress from interested parties, and then withdrew.

Fisher's virtual abdication of authority with respect to fire control exposed manifold weaknesses in Admiralty organization. The absence of a properly constituted naval staff meant that centralized direction of gunnery policy ceased to exist. The Ordnance Department, on the other hand, was incapable of effectively formulating or carrying out major policy on its own. On a day to day level, serious clerical understaffing meant that naval officers were overwhelmed with routine paperwork, with the result that the Director of Naval Ordnance and his subordinates had little time to give important policy matters proper consideration, and on occasion the handling of reports and correspondence broke down altogether.[4] In addition, the Ordnance Department lacked a permanent staff of technicians expert in fire control, and its leadership changed every two years because of the practice of rotating officers regularly between shore and sea duty, which made continuity in the execution of policy unlikely.

In the absence of firm direction from the top and consistent direction from the Ordnance Department, Pollen's work was disrupted and delayed by the actions of a powerful service clique. Ogilvy, who alone had the stature to counteract the hostile tide, was eliminated by chance. By the time Pollen was able to put forward a practicable set of instruments, the years of conflict with his opponents had created a history of technical setbacks, administrative disagreement, and personal animosity. His opponents, in the meanwhile, were able to obfuscate the technical issues by offering an alternative, which if derivative and inferior, was nonetheless an improvement on existing instruments. In the end, the Admiralty temporized by adopting elements of both systems, although the gear of Pollen's rival predominated. This action, which was in part a matter of political compromise, put an end to the troubling open division of the service on the gunnery question, but at the cost of equipping the fleet with a less effective system of fire control.

Fisher, in his mistaken belief that the long-range gunnery problem had been solved, did his utmost to secure the replacement of the battleship by the battle cruiser. His case was greatly weakened, however, by the non-existence of a fire control system that was capable of producing hits when the range was long and changing rapidly at a rate that was itself changing, and although his influence was sufficient to perpetuate the construction of battle cruisers in addition to that of battleships, the battle cruiser was never generally accepted as the successor of the battleship. The implementation of Fisher's "battle cruiser only" strategy was made unnecessary by the Lloyd George budgets and colonial aid, which enabled Britain to build capital ships in large numbers, but Fisher succeeded when he was First Sea Lord in gaining approval for an increase in gun caliber in 1909, and even when out of power had a strong effect on Churchill's views that led to a second increase in gun caliber in 1912.

The attempt to build simultaneously large numbers of battleships and battle cruisers that were also much more heavily armed than those of other navies—in effect a conflation of the strategy of numbers and strategy of quality—caused increases in naval spending that strained even the expanded financial resources of the post-1909 Liberal government. Sharply rising naval expenditure during the five years prior to the outbreak of the First World War increased bad feeling between Britain and Germany, giving the naval rivalry an intensity during this later period that it might not otherwise have had. The enormous sums required for new capital ship construction, moreover, consumed a disproportionate amount of the navy estimate, which not only prevented expenditure on North Sea bases, but was also a factor that underlay the Admiralty's decision to reject the Pollen system for a cheaper alternative. And the resulting lack of an effective system of fire control, in combination with the deployment of inadequately protected battle cruisers and the excessive volatility of British ammunition, was to have disastrous consequences at the battle of Jutland.

This work puts forward views about the "Fisher revolution" and the naval policy of the Liberal government, and makes assessments of major naval figures, that differ substantially from those of standard accounts. The battle cruiser *Invincible* rather than the *Dreadnought*, was the centerpiece of Fisher's capital ship program, and his major goal from at least 1905 onwards was the replacement of the battleship by the battle cruiser. The Fisher Admiralty was badly divided over important technical issues and, as a consequence, the capital ship policy of the Admiralty was not based upon a coherent body of strategic, tactical or technical principles, but rather was either inconsistent or the product of compromise. Although Fisher and his circle fought under the banner of technological progressivism, their actions did much to delay the adoption of advanced methods of fire control. Service resistance to change there undoubtedly was in large measure, but shortcomings in Fisher's brand of "personal rule" were also much to blame for major defects in Royal Navy materiel and methods.

Given the success of the Admiralty's strategy of building capital ships that were superior to those of rival navies and the Admiralty's belief that further major changes in capital ship design were in the offing, the Liberal reductions in spending on the navy between 1906 and 1908 were not an unreasonable short-term response to serious financial difficulties. While it is difficult to know with any degree of certainty, it can be argued that the opposition of Lloyd George and Churchill to the Admiralty program of 1909 was more a matter of their need to satisfy Radical constitutents, and tactical considerations with respect to Cabinet politics, than of serious pacific objections to naval expansion. The "Radical" budget of 1909 did as much for the navy as for social reform, and as a piece of naval legislation was comparable to the Naval Defence Act in importance.

Fisher's leadership at the Admiralty was indecisive when it came to the critical gunnery question, and the soundness of his technical judgement on capital ship design is open to considerable question. Although both Jellicoe and Battenberg deserve credit for their early support of the Pollen system and their efforts on the inventor's behalf after the setbacks of 1908, they must also bear much of the blame for the failure from 1912 onwards to subject the fire control question to a thorough and impartial inquiry. Bacon's reputation as a technical progressive requires qualification, and his shortcomings as one of Fisher's main technical advisors needs to be recognized. Wilson's influence on the development of important aspects of British naval gunnery during and after the Fisher regime had serious negative consequences, which must be taken into account when evaluating this officer's record. Beatty's intelligent action at the close of the war and afterwards with regard to fire control enhances his stature as a naval administrator. And the consistent backing given by Beresford and Custance to

Pollen's approach to naval gunnery suggests that there was more to their views on naval policy than has generally been allowed.

Pollen's leading role in the early development of British fire control, and the influence of this work on Admiralty planning in general and Fisher's thinking in particular, made him a figure of major importance in pre-1914 British naval affairs. In addition, his work had considerable significance from the purely technical standpoint. Pollen's use of differential analyzers in the Argo Clock anticipated the efforts of such notable scientists as D. R. Hartree and Vannevar Bush, whose exploitation of differential analyzers in the 1930s has been generally regarded as a landmark in the history of computers.[5] And although Harold Isherwood deserves the highest praise for the actual design of the individual instruments, it was Pollen who subjected the fire control problem to scientific analysis and then formulated the idea of not one invention, but of a family of inventions that were to be capable of dealing with the manifold difficulties posed by aiming large-caliber naval guns accurately when ranges were long and the range and bearing altering at high and varying rates. Pollen may thus be considered not only as an important pioneer in the development of the computer, but in addition as an early practitioner of what was later to become known as systems analysis.

A few general observations will be made in closing about this monograph's three main subjects, British finance, technology and naval policy.

Before 1914, the financial position of the British state was significantly stronger than those of its major European rivals because it was able to raise revenue through substantial increases in direct taxation. French and German governments, in contrast, could not obtain such changes in their own tax structures during this period without incurring what were considered to be unacceptable political costs and, as a consequence, remained dependent to a far greater degree upon inherently less productive indirect taxation. Thus while the naval spending of pre-First World War British governments was occasionally severely restricted by financial considerations, it nevertheless enjoyed greater access to the wealth of society than was the case in France and Germany, Britain's two main rivals, a financial advantage that probably mitigated to a significant degree the negative strategic effects of the late 19th and early 20th century erosion of her industrial lead. By the same token, because National Socialist Germany's expenditure on armaments was uninhibited by the social considerations that had restricted its Wilhelmine predecessor, Britain during the late 1930s was deprived of the financial advantage upon which she had previously depended, which exacerbated the military impact of her industrial decline.

In 1908 and 1909, advocates of stronger naval defence or increased social welfare were bitterly divided because it appeared that greater expenditure on naval construction could only be gained at the expense of domestic programs, or vice versa. In fact, proponents of neither side possessed the political strength to overcome the other, while the state's existing share of national income was yet small enough to admit of very great expansion. Through imaginative and skilled political management, the diverging vectors were resolved to produce a parliamentary constituency that was strong enough to overcome opposition to alterations in tax structure and, as a consequence, the state acquired the additional financial resources that were needed to increase rapidly and simultaneously spending on defence and social welfare. Hawks and doves, in short, while rhetorical opposites, were by no means irreconciliable political forces; their cooperation in Britain and other countries in later years probably explains much about the politics of industrial democracies in the 20th century.[6]

The advent of steam propulsion enabled warships to move more quickly and independently of the wind, while advances in ordnance made it possible to fire projectiles accurately to much greater distances. Higher speeds, the freedom to maneuver, and greater gun range, however, posed the new problem of how to set gunsights to take account of the relative motion of the firing ship and target. Because human judgement was inadequate to the task of solving the relative motion problem under battle conditions, mechanical means of data collection, calculation, and data transmission were essential if fast ships with heavy-caliber ordnance were to be exploited to anything approaching the limits of their capabilities. Fire control equipment was, therefore, a critically important aspect of capital ship design, and its history must be taken into account in order to understand the development of surface naval warfare in the 20th century.

Aspects of the naval fire control story may throw light on the question of lagging British technical development during the late industrial period. H. W. Richardson has observed that under certain conditions, desirable levels of technological innovation cannot be achieved through the operation of market forces and that, therefore, the government should intervene through the bearing of direct costs, the minimization of risk, or changes in institutional environments.[7] In Pollen's case, the Admiralty was extremely reluctant to engage in this kind of activity even when secrecy requirements meant that the inventor was deprived of the support of the market. Such unwillingness was probably characteristic of both the Admiralty and the War Office, and would have been particularly discouraging to small firms, which in industrial economies are an important source of new ideas but often lack the capital to develop them. The defence materiel procurement process in Britain thus may not have played as large a role in the stimulation of technological innovation as in other countries with less tight-fisted and more imaginative bureaucracies, which might to a certain extent explain Britain's comparatively unsatisfactory technical performance during the late 19th and 20th centuries.

The introduction of the dreadnought type capital ship produced an extended controversy in the British press and Parliament over naval strategy, tactics, and technology. Fisher's real views on capital ship design and the development of the Pollen system were of central importance to the dreadnought policy, but because of Fisher's deviousness with regard to his plans for the battle cruiser and fire control secrecy requirements, neither matter became the subject of serious public discussion. If not quite *Hamlet* without the Prince of Denmark, the absence of these two issues meant that the open debate over what was the most important British naval defence decision made in the critical decade before the outbreak of the First World

War did not deal with major concerns of insiders at the Admiralty. Then, as perhaps now, the matters that were the main focus of the popular consideration of a prominent national security question were not those that were most significant to the deliberations of the actual decision-makers.

At certain times before 1914, the explicit goal of Admiralty warship building policy was not only naval security in the event of war, but deterrence. In 1889, the First Lord expressed the hope—in vain as it turned out—that the numbers of new units authorized by the Naval Defence Act would be great enough to persuade rival powers to give up any thought of competing with Britain in naval terms. In 1905, 1909 and 1912, Britain introduced new model capital ships that were much more capable than existing types, partly in the belief that the possession of the technological initiative would at least discourage aggression if not lead to cutbacks in foreign building. The *Dreadnought* was a success with regard to the disruption of German construction, but when the adoption of new model capital ships later on did not have the same effect, more costly units had to be built in large numbers, and as a result financial resources were consumed that might have better been spent on fire control. In having to choose between capital ships with larger guns and more effective fire control, the Admiralty was in effect confronted by the conflicting requirements of deterrence and war fighting; its decision in favor of the former amounted to the putting up of a bold front at the cost of operational capability.

And finally, it may be useful to relate the vicissitudes of British naval policy in the early 20th century to the writing of Carl von Clausewitz. "Everything in war," the great German military philosopher wrote when considering the susceptibility of all military plans to misadventure,

> is very simple, but the simplest thing is difficult. The difficulties accumulate and end by producing a kind of friction that is inconceivable unless one has experienced war. . . . Friction is the only concept that more or less corresponds to the factors that distinguish real war from war on paper. The military machine—the army and everything related to it—is basically very simple and therefore seems easy to manage. But we should bear in mind that none of its components is of one piece: each part is composed of individuals, every one of whom retains his potential of friction. . . . This tremendous friction, which cannot, as in mechanics, be reduced to a few points, is everywhere in contact with chance, and brings about effects that cannot be measured, just because they are largely due to chance.[8]

Fisher believed that the possession of capital ships that were qualitatively far superior to those of rival fleets would, among other things, reduce the play of friction in naval warfare to negligible proportions, and thus would do much to guarantee the Royal Navy success in battle. His efforts to gain the technological initiative through the adoption of new inventions, however, by placing much greater demands on the procurement process, made friction a critical factor on the drawing boards in peace as well as on the oceans in war. In the absence of a well-organized, technically literate, and adequately staffed bureaucracy, fire control research and development generated high levels of friction that factionalized the pre-1914 materiel school, which personalized and politicized the carrying out of policy. The result was the wrecking of Fisher's radical strategy and the production of a seriously flawed weapons system.

In the late 20th century, the exploitation of technological innovation to enhance national security has become commonplace. The strategy of the United States and her allies, in particular, has been to deploy weapons in smaller numbers but of more advanced design than the Soviet Union and associated powers in the attempt to obtain both greater capability and lower expenditure. But while the managerial resources of the western military-industrial establishments are far superior to those that were available to the early 20th century British state, there have been equally great if not greater increases in the complexity of new technology. The propensity, moreover, of individuals and groups of individuals to pursue their own interests at the expense of the institutions and larger society of which they are a part has probably not diminished. The play of friction in the process of arms procurement has thus by no means been eliminated and, as a consequence, the seeking of technological panaceas to strategic dilemmas must still involve considerable risk. With regard to this and other issues previously discussed, the story of Fisher, the battle cruiser and the Pollen system of fire control, may seem not only modern or recent, but contemporary.

Notes to Conclusion

1 *FP*, Vol. 1, p. 28.
2 A definitive answer is difficult to give in the absence of data on the performance of Pollen's final true-course plotter, which may or may not have been practicable. Rate-plotting as put forward by Dreyer before 1914 was definitely not satisfactory and was only somewhat more so after certain modifications that were introduced during the war by others. The incorporation of rate- rather than true-course plotting in the post-war British fire control system does not necessarily signify much. It will be remembered that in the case of the Admiralty Fire Control Table, Mark I, rate-plotting was adopted in conjunction with an inclinometer and aircraft observation, which provided a measurement of the target's course, if not its speed. One post-war objection to the true-course approach was that battle ranges were expected to be as high as 30,000 yards, which would have required a track chart and plotting instrument of prohibitive size [for this objection, see Hugh Clausen to Anthony Pollen, January 19, 1970, to the author courtesy of Anthony Pollen]. And it could be argued that true-course plotting would have worked well in the First World War, but that the Admiralty's unwillingness to adopt it afterward was influenced by the view that future naval engagements would involve much more frequent changes in course and speed on both sides than had previously been the case, under which circumstances a true-course plot might be of less value than a rate-plot. A detailed critical technical analysis of Pollen's true-course plotter and post-war British and American plotting systems might do much to clarify this issue.
3 For the Admiralty's mistrust of civilian inventors particularly in matters that involved the development of an invention, see the memorandum by the Director of Navy Contracts, dated 2 June 1913, in response to a letter from a Mr. J. Gardner to Winston Churchill, dated 5 May 1913, *IQ/DNO*,

Vol. 2, 1913, N.L.M.D. To be fair to the Admiralty, however, it should be noted that an unwillingness to fund scientific or technical research seems to have been characteristic of the British government in general, for which see Arthur Marwick, *Deluge: British Society and the First World War* (New York: Norton, 1970; f.p. 1965), p. 17. For an example of the mishandling of inventors by another government department, the War Office, in the case of the early development of aviation for military purposes, see Alfred M. Gollin, *No Longer an Island: Britain and the Wright Brothers, 1902-1909* (Stanford: Stanford University Press, 1984).

4 For the overwork of the Director of Naval Ordnance because of administrative understaffing, see Jellicoe to Pollen, 25 August 1907, P.P. For the serious paperwork breakdowns in the Naval Ordnance Department, see Director of Naval Ordnance circular memorandum, dated 13 March 1914, in *D.N.O. Standing Orders, 1910-1917*, N.L.M.D.

5 Vannevar Bush, *Pieces of the Action* (New York: WIlliam Morrow, 1970), pp. 181-5; Herman H. Goldstine, *The Computer from Pascal to von Neuman* (Princeton: Princeton University Press, 1972); Simon Lavington, *Early British Computers* (Manchester: Digital, 1980), pp. 4-7; and Larry Owens, "Vannevar Bush and the Differential Analyzer: The Text and Context of an Early Computer," *Technology and Culture*, Vol. 27 (January 1986), pp. 63-95.

6 For a provocative exploration of this thesis, see William K. Domke, Richard C. Eichenberg, and Catherine M. Kelleher, "The Illusion of Choice: Defense and Welfare in Advanced Industrial Democracies, 1948-1978, *The American Political Science Review*, Vol. 77 (March 1983), pp. 19-35.

7 H. W. Richardson, "Chemicals," in Derek H. Aldcroft (ed.), *The Development of British Industry and Foreign Competition, 1875-1914* (London: George Allen & Unwin, 1968), pp. 274-5.

8 Carl von Clausewitz, *On War*, edited and translated by Michael Howard and Peter Paret (Princeton: Princeton University Press, 1976), p. 119.

Appendix

Tables

SOURCES

Financial Tables: Sidney Buxton, *Finance and Politics: An Historical Study, 1789-1885*, 2 vols (New York: Augustus M. Kelley, 1966; first published in 1888); Bernard Mallet, *British Budgets, 1887-88 to 1912-13* (London: Macmillan, 1913); Great Britain, Parliament, *Parliamentary Papers* (Commons), 1914, vol. 50 (*Accounts and Papers*, vol. 1), "Financial Statement (1914-15)," pp. 2-5, and "National Debt," pp. 6-9; ibid., Annual Navy Estimates, 1889-1914; ibid., Annual Navy Appropriation and Dockyard Accounts, 1889-1914; ibid., Imperial Defence, Naval Defence, and Naval Works Acts Accounts; Australia, Parliament, "Estimates of Revenue and Expenditure . . .," in *Papers Presented to Parliament*, 1911-1914; Great Britain, Colonial Office, "Federated Malay States: Financial Report for the Year 1913," Supplement to the "F.M.S. Government Gazette," 31 July 1914; New Zealand, House of Representatives, "Public Accounts," in *Appendix to the Journals of the House of Representatives of New Zealand*, vol. 2, 1911, and vol. 1 for 1912, 1913 and 1914.

Warship Characteristics: Great Britain, Parliament, *Parliamentary Papers* (Commons), Annual Navy Estimates; Robert Gardiner, Roger Chesneau, Eugene M. Kolesnik (eds) [Conway's] *All the World's Fighting Ships, 1860-1905* (London: Conway Maritime Press, 1979) and Robert Gardiner and Randal Gray (eds) [Conway's] *All the World's Fighting Ships, 1906-1921* (London: Conway Maritime Press, 1985).

Admiralty-Argo/Pollen Financial Transactions: Great Britain, Admiralty, *Pollen Aim Correction System: General Grounds of Admiralty Policy and Historical Record of Business Negotiations* (February 1913), p. 21.

Table 1 *British Government Expenditure and Revenue, 1874–75 to 1914–15*

Fiscal Year	Deficit	Surplus	Expenditure	Revenue
1874-75	£ *	£ 593,833	£ 74,328,040	£ 74,921,873
1875-76	*	509,920	76,621,773	77,131,693
1876-77	*	439,809	78,125,227	78,565,036
1877-78	2,640,197	*	82,403,495	79,763,298
1878-79	2,291,817	*	85,407,789	83,115,972
1879-80	2,840,698	*	84,105,754	81,265,056
1880-81	*	933,633	83,107,925	84,041,288
1881-82	*	349,736	85,472,556	85,822,282
1882-83	*	98,178	89,716,278	89,814,456
1883-84	*	205,620	87,879,564	88,085,184
1884-85	1,049,772	*	91,092,882	90,043,110
1885-86	2, 642,543	*	94,343,844	91,701,301
1886-87	*	776,006	92,125,152	92,901,158
1887-88	*	2,378,000	87,424,000	89,802,000
1888-89	*	2,798,940	85,673,872	88,472,812
1889-90	*	3,221,001	86,083,315	89,304,316
1890-91	*	1,756,257	87,732,855	89,489,112
1891-92	*	1,067,000	89,928,000	90,995,000
1892-93	*	20,000	90,375,000	90,395,000
1893-94	169,000	*	91,303,000	91,134,000
1894-95	*	765,000	93,919,000	94,684,000
1895-96	*	4,210,000	97,764,000	101,974,000
1896-97	*	2,473,000	101,477,000	103,950,000
1897-98	*	3,678,000	102,936,000	106,614,000
1898-99	*	186,000	108,150,000	108,336,000
1899-1900	13,883,000	*	133,723,000	119,840,000
1900-01	53,207,000	*	183,592,000	130,385,000
1901-02	52,524,000	*	195,522,000	142,998,000
1902-03	32,932,000	*	184,484,000	151,552,000
1903-04	5,415,000	*	146,961,000	141,546,000
1904-05	*	1,414,000	141,956,000	143,370,000
1905-06	*	3,466,00	140,512,000	143,978,000
1906-07	*	5,399,000	139,415,000	144,814,000
1907-08	*	4,726,000	151,812,000	156,538,000
1908-09	714,000	*	152,292,000	151,578,000
1909-10	26,248,000	*	157,945,000	131,697,000
1910-11	*	31,855,000	171,996,000	203,851,000
1911-12	*	6,455,000	178,545,000	185,090,000
1912-13	*	180,000	188,622,000	188,802,000
1913-14	*	750,000	197,493,000	198,243,000
1914-15*	0	0	209,455,000	209,455,000

*Estimate

Table 2   British National Debt, 1874–75 to 1914–15 (Debt figures are for the level of debt at the start of the fiscal year; debt service figures are the amount paid during the fiscal year)

Fiscal year	I Funded debt	II Terminable annuities	III Unfunded debt	IV Total of columns I, II, & III	V Debt service
1874-75	£ 723,514,005	£ 42,370,351	£ 4,479,600	£ 770,363,956	£ 27,094,479
1875-76	714,797,715	46,378,819	5,239,300	766,415,834	27,443,750
1876-77	713,657,517	43,514,347	11,401,800	768,573,664	27,992,834
1877-78	712,621,355	41,337,225	13,943,800	767,902,380	28,412,750
1878-79	710,843,007	38,685,609	20,603,000	770,131,616	28,644,183
1879-80	709,430,593	35,704,856	25,870,100	771,005,549	28,762,874
1880-81	710,476,359	32,034,785	27,344,900	769,856,044	29,575,264
1881-82	709,078,526	33,321,073	22,077,500	764,477,099	29,665,945
1882-83	709,498,547	31,706,597	18,007,700	759,212,844	29,679,097
1883-84	712,698,994	26,283,175	14,185,400	753,167,569	29,651,526
1884-85	640,631,095	90,238,724	14,110,600	744,980,419	29,548,239
1885-86	640,181,896	85,022,386	14,033,100	739,237,382	23,449,678
1886-87	638,849,694	84,947,890	17,602,800	741,400,384	27,978,023
1887-88	637,637,640	80,394,390	17,517,900	735,549,930	26,566,525
1888-89	609,740,743	76,926,771	17,385,100	704,052,614	28,548,094
1889-90	607,057,811	73,891,623	16,093,322	697,042,756	28,256,079
1890-91	585,959,852	70,336,149	32,252,305	688,548,306	28,999,806
1891-92	579,472,082	66,550,579	36,140,079	682,162,740	27,402,132
1892-93	577,944,665	62,550,043	35,312,994	675,807,702	26,745,629
1893-94	589,533,082	59,056,324	20,748,270	669,337,676	25,782,070
1894-95	587,631,096	55,717,505	21,446,300	664,794,901	26,285,334
1895-96	586,015,919	52,492,709	17,400,300	655,908,928	26,338,745
1896-97	589,146,878	49,183,748	9,975,800	648,306,426	26,045,872
1897-98	587,698,732	45,291,694	8,133,000	641,123,426	25,812,781
1898-99	585,787,624	41,150,011	8,133,000	635,070,635	25,921,123
1899-1900	583,186,305	36,702,267	8,133,000	628,021,572	23,939,315
1900-01	552,606,898	60,190,755	16,133,000	628,930,653	20,788,292
1901-02	551,182,153	60,154,800	78,133,000	689,469,953	25,984,701
1902-03	609,587,248	60,295,402	75,133,000	745,015,650	28,930,255
1903-04	640,085,726	55,560,036	75,133,000	770,778,762	32,185,588
1904-05	637,633,319	51,363,458	73,633,000	762,629,777	31,367,086
1905-06	635,682,863	47,756,246	71,633,000	755,072,109	32,433,925
1906-07	634,047,429	43,459,548	65,713,000	743,219,977	35,936,574
1907-08	631,928,334	40,864,211	56,713,000	729,505,545	38,707,565
1908-09	625,608,890	39,407,575	46,459,400	711,475,865	34,911,999
1909-10	621,838,957	38,009,337	42,839,603	702,687,897	26,368,797
1910-11	614,868,547	35,876,861	62,500,000	713,245,408	29,246,397
1911-12	610,315,194	34,417,265	40,400,000	685,232,459	31,104,783
1912-13	602,200,092	33,044,389	39,500,000	674,744,481	34,858,760
1913-14	593,453,857	31,519,908	36,500,000	661,473,765	.....
1914-15*	586,717,872	29,552,219	35,000,000	651,270,091	.....

*Projected

Table 3   *British Naval Expenditure, 1889–90 to 1914–15*

Fiscal year	I Estimate : net expenditure	II Estimate : net expenditure + appropriations in aid	III Net expenditure + appropriations in aid + spending above estimate	IV Total effective naval spending [III – annuities paid from est.]
1889–90	£ 13,643,968	£ 14,333,416	£ 15,588,502	£ 15,588,502
1890–91	13,910,732	14,807,466	18,061,816	17,997,600
1891–92	14,278,049	15,172,566	18,150,638	18,080,816
1892–93	14,325,948	15,330,856	17,402,741	17,291,833
1893–94	14,306,546	15,297,424	16,327,641	16,174,763
1894–95	17,642,424	18,571,101	18,595,685	18,500,343
1895–96	19,637,238	20,543,278	21,264,377	21,169,035
1896–97	22,271,901	23,190,957	23,886,177	23,790,835
Total 1889–1896	£ 130,016,806	£ 137,247,064	£ 149,277,577	£ 148,593,727
1897–98	£ 20,848,863	£ 21,837,416	£ 22,547,844	£ 22,452,502
1898–99	23,880,875	24,935,358	26,145,598	26,050,256
1899–1900	25,731,220	26,979,944	28,478,842	28,383,500
1900–01	29,998,529	31,169,727	33,302,260	33,206,918
1901–02	30,981,315	32,249,377	34,994,553	34,872,298
1902–03	31,003,977	32,327,715	35,525,731	35,227,836
1903–04	35,709,577	37,242,791	40,503,873	40,001,863
1904–05	36,859,681	38,293,738	41,696,313	41,062,075
Total 1897–1904	£ 235,013,938	£ 245,036,066	£ 263,194,974	£ 261,257,248
1905–06	£ 33,151,841	£ 34,861,442	£ 38,175,045	£ 37,159,234
1906–07	31,472,087	33,262,649	35,693,850	34,599,541
1907–08	31,251,156	32,866,506	33,950,169	32,735,767
1908–09	32,181,309	33,827,490	34,775,752	33,511,720
1909–10	35,734,015	37,385,460	37,385,460	36,059,652
1910–11	40,419,336	42,441,419	43,903,499	42,580,747
1911–12	42,414,257	44,384,340	46,793,789	45,471,037
1912–13	44,933,169	46,822,965	48,742,182	47,419,430
Total 1905–1912	£ 291,557,170	£ 305,852,271	£ 319,419,746	£ 309,537,128
1913–14	£ 48,732,621	£ 50,819,150	£ 52,920,960	£ 51,609,402
1914–15*	51,550,000	53,573,261	54,673,261	53,361,703

*Projected

Table 4 *Naval Spending in Addition to the Navy Estimate, 1889–90 to 1913–14 (Imperial Defence, Naval Defence and Naval Works Acts)*

Fiscal year	I Expenditure above navy estimate	II Annuity paid from estimate	III Net relief to navy estimate (I – II)
1889-90	£ 1,255,086	£ 0	£ 1,255,086
1890-91	3,254,350	64,216	3,190,134
1891-92	2,978,072	69,822	2,908,250
1892-93	2,071,885	110,908	1,960,977
1893-94	1,030,217	152,878	877,339
1894-95	24,584	95,342	-70,758
1895-96	721,099	95,342	625,757
1896-97	695,220	95,342	599,878
Total 1889-1896	£ 12,030,513	£ 683,850	£ 11,346,663
1897-98	£ 710,428	£ 95,342	£ 615,086
1898-99	1,210,240	95,342	1,114,898
1899-1900	1,498,898	95,342	1,403,556
1900-01	2,132,533	95,342	2,037,191
1901-02	2,745,176	122,255	2,622,921
1902-03	3,198,016	297,895	2,900,121
1903-04	3,261,082	502,010	2,759,072
1904-05	3,402,575	634,238	2,768,337
Total 1897-1904	£18,158,948	£ 1,937,766 *	£ 16,221,182
1905-06	£ 3,313,603	£ 1,015,811	£ 2,297,792
1906-07	2,431,201	1,094,309	1,336,892
1907-08	1,083,663	1,214,402	-130,739
1908-09	948,262	1,264,032	-315,770
1909-10	0	1,325,808	-1,325,808
1910-11	0	1,322,752	-1,322,752
1911-12	0	1,322,752	-1,322,752
1912-13	0	1,322,752	-1,322,752
Total 1905-1912	£ 7,776,729	£ 9,882,618	£ -2,105,889
1913-14	£ 0	£ 1,311,558	£ -1,311,558

*During this period, Imperial Defence Act annuity payments of £95,342 per annum were made from 1897–98 through 1900–01. Naval Works Acts annuity payments began in 1901–02 at £122,255 and by 1904–05 had risen to £634,238. Naval Works Acts annuity payments from 1901–02 to 1904–05 totalled £1,556,398. The net relief to the Navy Estimates provided by the Naval Works Acts was thus the total expenditure above the estimate from 1897–98 to 1904–05 [£18,158,948] – spending under the Imperial Defence Act having ended in 1894–95 – minus the Naval Works Acts annuity payments from 1901–02 to 1904–05 [£1,556,398], a sum of £16,602,550.

Table 5 *Contributions of Australia, New Zealand and Malaya, Exclusive of Sums counted as Appropriations in Aid, to British Naval Expenditure, 1905–06 to 1913–14*

Fiscal year	I Australia: naval establish-ment [manning]	II Australia: naval works	III Australia: fleet unit [naval construction]	IV New Zealand and Malaya: naval construction	V Total effective dominion expenditure (I + II + III + IV)
1905–06	£ 0	£ 0	£ 0	£ 0	
1906–07	0	0	0	0	
1907–08	0	0	0	0	
1908–09	0	0	0	0	
1909–10	0	0	0	0	0
1910–11	96,291	26,500	850,000	489,289	1,462,080
1911–12	248,738	40,000	1,515,000	605,711	2,409,449
1912–13	608,955	180,865	604,397	525,000	1,919,217
Total 1905–1912	£ 953,984	£ 247,365	£ 2,969,397	£ 1,620,000	£ 5,790,746
1913–14	£ 1,005,649	£ 123,590	£ 753,537	£ 219,034	£ 2,101,810

Table 6 *Expenditure under Vote 8 (Shipbuilding, Repairs, Maintenance, etc.) and Vote 9 [Naval Armaments] of Navy Estimate, 1889–90 to 1913–14*

Fiscal year	I Vote 8 [shipbuilding, repairs, maintenance, etc.] including appropriations in aid	II Vote 9 [naval armaments] including appropriations in aid	III Vote 8 + Vote 9 (I + II)
1889-90	£ 4,682,600	£ 1,777,401	£ 6,460,001
1890-91	5,230,285	1,446,343	6,676,628
1891-92	5,192,067	1,554,149	6,746,216
1892-93	4,939,994	1,695,618	6,635,612
1893-94	5,041,096	1,316,361	6,357,457
1894-95	7,374,748	1,739,220	9,113,968
1895-96	8,964,474	1,970,080	10,934,554
1896-97	10,529,504	2,686,060	13,215,564
Total 1889-1896	£ 51,954,768	£ 14,185,232	£ 66,140,000
1897-98	£ 8,367,384	£ 2,871,841	£ 11,239,225
1898-99	10,786,629	2,676,174	13,462,803
1899-1900	12,413,239	2,630,614	15,043,853
1900-01	14,789,320	3,622,223	18,411,543
1901-02	15,155,410	3,959,266	19,114,676
1902-03	15,320,888	3,252,152	18,573,040
1903-04	19,153,948	3,206,682	22,360,630
1904-05	18,852,326	3,722,971	22,575,297
Total 1897-1904	£ 114,839,144	£ 25,941,923	£ 140,781,067
1905-06	£ 16,039,125	£ 3,020,308	£ 19,059,433
1906-07	14,749,097	2,909,835	17,658,932
1907-08	14,105,190	2,263,346	16,368,536
1908-09	14,791,662	2,182,991	16,974,653
1909-10	17,209,296	2,574,736	19,784,032
1910-11	21,086,188	2,978,173	24,064,361
1911-12	21,319,267	3,923,303	25,242,570
1912-13	22,907,709	4,511,705	27,419,414
Total 1905-1912	£ 142,207,534	£ 24,364,397	£ 166,571,931
1913-14	£ 24,867,445	£ 4,925,427	£ 29,792,872

Table 7 *Expenditure under Vote 10 [Naval Works] of Navy Estimate, 1889–90 to 1913–14*

	I	II	III	IV	V
Fiscal year	Vote 10 [naval works] including appropriations in aid	Annuities in repayment of naval works acts loans	Vote 10 [naval works] including appropriations in Aid – repayment annuities (I – II)	Expenditure under naval works acts	Effective expenditure on naval works (III + IV)
1889–90	£ 437,316	£ 0	£ 437,316	£ 0	£ 437,316
1890–91	411,563	0	411,563	0	411,563
1891–92	385,762	0	385,762	0	385,762
1892–93	413,739	0	413,739	0	413,739
1893–94	397,149	0	397,149	0	397,149
1894–95	654,675	0	654,675	0	654,675
1895–96	455,402	0	455,402	721,099	1,176,501
1896–97	482,670	0	482,670	695,220	1,177,890
Total 1889–1896	£ 3,638,276	£ 0	£ 3,638,276	£ 1,416,319	£ 5,054,595
1897–98	£ 627,435	£ 0	£ 627,435	£ 710,428	£ 1,337,863
1898–99	748,341	0	748,341	1,210,240	1,958,581
1899–1900	766,573	0	766,573	1,498,898	2,265,471
1900–01	888,593	0	888,593	2,132,533	3,021,126
1901–02	1,004,775	122,255	882,520	2,745,176	3,627,696
1902–03	1,088,816	297,895	790,921	3,198,016	3,988,937
1903–04	1,470,970	502,010	968,960	3,261,082	4,230,042
1904–05	1,584,997	634,238	950,759	3,402,575	4,353,334
Total 1897–1904	£ 8,180,500	£ 1,556,398	£ 6,624,102	£ 18,158,948	£ 24,783,050
1905–06	£ 1,829,272	£ 1,015,811	£ 813,461	£ 3,313,603	£ 4,127,064
1906–07	1,796,897	1,094,309	702,588	2,431,201	3,133,789
1907–08	2,507,925	1,214,402	1,293,523	1,083,663	2,377,186
1908–09	2,215,007	1,264,032	950,975	948,262	1,899,237
1909–10	2,714,451	1,325,808	1,388,643	0	1,388,643
1910–11	3,038,865	1,325,808	1,716,113	0	1,716,113
1911–12	3,240,421	1,322,752	1,917,669	0	1,917,669
1912–13	3,022,297	1,322,752	1,699,545	0	1,699,545
Total 1905–12	£ 20,365,135	£ 9,882,618	£ 10,482,517	£ 7,776,729	£ 18,259,246
1913–14	£ 3,552,896	£ 1,311,558	£ 2,241,338	£ 0	£ 2,241,338

Table 8　*Expenditures on Warship Construction by General Category, 1888–89 to 1913–14 [not including cost of armament]*

Fiscal year	Battleships	Cruisers	Flotilla	Total
1888-89	£　623,500	£　1,163,110	£　959,585	£　2,746,195
1889-90	£　722,945	£　2,140,170	£　530,490	£　3,393,605
1890-91	1,813,605	3,438,878	185,017	5,437,500
1891-92	2,750,096	2,674,106	232,693	5,656,895
1892-93	1,898,246	1,791,859	437,194	4,127,299
1893-94	1,318,398	1,077,042	741,861	3,137,301
1894-95	2,285,049	1,419,841	1,145,848	4,850,738
1895-96	3,372,239	2,092,840	732,911	6,197,990
1896-97	2,678,315	3,419,972	1,506,015	7,604,302
Total 1889-1896	£　16,838,893	£　18,054,708	£　5,512,029	£　40,405,630
1897-98	£　2,166,066	£　2,474,197	£　581,187	£　5,221,450
1898-99	3,406,912	2,814,508	605,692	6,827,112
1899-1900	3,926,203	2,786,579	824,830	7,537,612
1900-01	4,105,749	3,908,132	990,073	9,003,954
1901-02	3,892,866	4,745,138	342,100	8,980,104
1902-03	3,216,036	4,332,514	1,192,224	8,740,774
1903-04	4,373,831	5,876,067	1,127,607	11,377,505
1904-05	4,547,657	5,660,297	1,385,695	11,593,649
Total 1897-1904	£　29,635,320	£　32,597,432	£　7,049,408	£　69,082,160
1905-06	£　4,103,692	£　4,694,079	£　1,184,545	£　9,982,316
1906-07	3,351,935	4,494,685	1,210,887	9,057,507
1907-08	3,723,412	2,873,134	1,363,012	7,959,558
1908-09	4,298,530	1,608,172	1,683,284	7,589,986
1909-10	4,578,805	2,624,681	2,592,747	9,796,233
1910-11	5,884,374	4,348,939	2,882,336	13,115,649
1911-12	6,056,072	3,665,094	2,269,315	11,990,481
1912-13	7,203,164	3,069,600	2,826,449	13,099,213
Total 1905-1912	£　39,199,984	£　27,378,384	£　16,012,575	£　82,590,943
1913-14	£　8,134,959	£　2,865,466	£　2,813,922	£　13,805,285
Including expenditures by Dominions and Malaya, 1910-11 to 1913-14				
1910-11	£　[as above]	£　5,372,017	£　3,050,336	£　14,306,727
1911-12	"	5,027,466	2,353,315	13,436,853
1912-13	"	4,297,500	[as above]	14,327,113
Total 1905-1912	£　[as above]	£　30,991,734	£　16,264,575	£　86,456,293
1913-14	£　8,284,959	£　2,926,236	£　[as above]	£　14,025,117

Table 9   *Expenditures on Cruiser Construction by Type, 1888–89 to 1913–14*
[not including cost of armament]

Fiscal year	First-Class Cruisers	Second-Class Cruisers	Third-Class Cruisers	All Cruisers
1888-89	£ 339,074	£ 411,587	£ 412,449	£ 1,163,110
1889-90	£ 578,060	£ 745,312	£ 816,798	£ 2,140,170
1890-91	1,152,008	1,926,599	360,271	3,438,878
1891-92	1,086,480	1,399,081	188,545	2,674,106
1892-93	887,776	898,125	5,958	1,791,859
1893-94	418,095	658,695	342	1,077,132
1894-95	475,235	941,056	3,550	1,419,841
1895-96	828,047	1,141,206	123,587	2,092,840
1896-97	1,846,607	1,148,792	424,573	3,419,972
Total 1889-1896	£ 7,272,308	£ 8,858,866	£ 1,923,624	£ 18,054,798
1897-98	£ 1,416,127	£ 658,672	£ 399,398	£ 2,474,197
1898-99	1,954,761	428,736	431,011	2,814,508
1899-1900	2,486,473	149,123	150,983	2,786,579
1900-01	3,802,752	71,818	33,562	3,908,132
1901-02	4,484,122	258,748	2,268	4,745,138
1902-03	4,076,702	149,564	106,248	4,332,514
1903-04	4,671,896	130,320	1,073,851	5,876,067
1904-05	4,018,013	99,308	1,542,976	5,660,297
Total 1897-1904	£ 26,910,846	£ 1,946,289	£ 3,740,297	£ 32,597,432
1905-06	£ 4,247,609	£ 31,115	£ 415,355	£ 4,694,079
1906-07	4,494,448	0	237	4,494,685
1907-08	2,692,610	0	180,524	2,873,134
1908-09	1,231,813	106,821	269,538	1,608,172
1909-10	1,074,752	1,152,210	397,719	2,624,681
1910-11	2,556,455	1,388,128	404,356	4,348,939
1911-12	2,436,216	862,484	366,394	3,665,094
1912-13	1,662,513	1,190,404	216,683	3,069,600
Total 1905-1912	£ 20,396,416	£ 4,731,162	£ 2,250,806	£ 27,378,384
1913-14	£ 936,325	£ 1,867,560	£ 52,519	£ 2,856,404
Including expenditures by Dominions, 1910-11 to 1913-14				
1910-11	£ 3,535,033	£ 1,432,628	£ [as above]	£ 5,372,017
1911-12	3,647,638	1,013,434	"	5,027,466
1912-13	2,712,513	1,368,304	"	4,297,500
Total 1905-1912	£ 23,636,416	£ 5,966,996	£ [as above]	£ 30,991,734
1913-14	£ [as above]	£ 1,928,330	£ [as above]	£ 2,917,174

Table 10 *Expenditures on Flotilla Construction by Type, 1889–90 to 1913–14 [not including cost of armament]*

Fiscal year	I Sloops		II Gunboats		III Torpedo Boats and Torpedo Gunboats		IV Destroyers		V Submarines	
1889-90	£	35,485	£	141,631	£	353,380	£	0	£	0
1890-91		266		14,670		170,081		0		0
1891-92		0		0		232,693		0		0
1892-93		0		46		411,271		25,877		0
1893-94		32,866		0		447,077		261,918		0
1894-95		132,754		0		122,787		890,307		0
1895-96		82,005		0		12,171		698,735		0
1896-97		180		0		2,470		1,503,365		0
Total 1889-1896	£	283,290	£	156,347	£	1,751,930	£	3,380,202	£	0
1897-98	£	23,048	£	31,954	£	0	£	526,185	£	0
1898-99		103,972		101,198		0		400,522		0
1899-1900		201,527		65,189		2,126		555,988		0
1900-01		219,481		6,806		55,216		708,570		0
1901-02		168,807		0		42,888		130,243		162
1902-03		125,743		0		145,775		700,253		220,453
1903-04		56,814		0		105,287		726,655		238,851
1904-05		353		0		39,744		1,035,014		310,584
Total 1897-1904	£	899,745	£	205,147	£	391,036	£	4,783,430	£	770,050
1905-06	£	0	£	0	£	0	£	534,193	£	650,352
1906-07		0		0		310,958		469,442		430,487
1907-08		0		0		542,613		471,273		349,126
1908-09		0		0		409,501		740,131		533,652
1909-10		0		0		69,724		2,000,751		522,272
1910-11 *		0		0		12		2,560,472 [2,728,472]		321,852
1911-12 *		0		0		0		1,782,396 [1,866,396]		486,919
1912-13		0		0		0		2,077,536		748,913
Total 1905-1912*	£	0	£	0	£	1,332,808	£	10,636,194 [10,888,194]	£	4,043,573
1913-14	£	0	£	0	£	0	£	2,046,615	£	767,307

*Bracketted figures include Australian units. The exact figures for the Australian vessels were not available, and were extrapolated from accounts for comparable British vessels. Uncertainty as to when payment was made mean that the figures given are very approximate.

Table 11 *Expenditure on Fuel; Ammunition; Reconstruction, Major Repairs, and Refits; and Minor Repairs and Maintenance, 1889–90 to 1913–14*

Fiscal year	I Fuel for warships	II Ammunition	III Reconstruc- tion, major Repairs, and refits	IV Minor repairs and maintenance	V Total ship overhead (I + II + III + IV)
1889-90	£ 494,333	£ 660,000	£ 460,503	£ 358,400	£ 1,973,236
1890-91	520,938	560,729	404,435	382,735	1,868,837
1891-92	517,892	477,000	278,840	851,027	2,124,759
1892-93	435,509	461,000	411,856	919,205	2,227,570
1893-94	468,077	506,000	313,172	949,172	2,236,421
1894-95	546,912	462,000	281,953	956,715	2,247,580
1895-96	506,577	661,420	383,928	930,910	2,482,835
1896-97	617,546	1,010,200	303,201	1,717,303	3,648,250
Total 1889-1896	£ 4,107,784	£ 4,798,349	£ 2,837,888	£ 7,065,467	£18,809,488
1897-98	£ 807,398	£ 1,098,300	£ 469,554	£ 1,996,831	£ 4,372,083
1898-99	973,561	1,206,700	458,563	2,128,724	4,767,548
1899-1900	1,144,855	1,128,850	582,733	2,570,509	5,426,947
1900-01	1,721,970	1,379,900	666,287	3,292,418	7,060,575
1901-02	1,626,142	2,082,600	774,548	1,948,735	6,432,025
1902-03	1,599,135	1,619,500	1,377,180	2,009,565	6,605,380
1903-04	1,835,514	1,435,700	2,258,987	2,207,782	7,737,983
1904-05	1,806,220	1,560,000	1,525,913	1,992,827	6,884,960
Total 1897-1904	£11,514,795	£11,511,550	£ 8,113,765	£18,147,391	£49,287,501
1905-06	£ 1,299,394	£ 1,185,000	£ 781,649	£ 1,851,696	£ 5,117,739
1906-07	1,397,892	1,172,000	618,910	2,575,012	5,763,814
1907-08	1,468,629	875,000	1,000,234	2,607,667	5,951,530
1908-09	1,754,162	700,000	893,514	3,042,557	6,390,233
1909-10	1,748,264	770,000	801,634	3,107,614	6,427,512
1910-11	1,991,064	800,000	940,278	3,820,353	7,551,695
1911-12	2,458,663	1,210,000	727,420	3,092,975	7,489,058
1912-13	2,458,663	1,480,000	1,099,270	3,480,829	8,518,762
Total 1905-1912	£14,576,731	£ 8,192,000	£ 6,862,909	£23,578,703	£53,210,343
1913-14*	£ 2,610,500	£ 1,638,160	£ 936,683	£ 2,293,071	£ 7,478,414

Table 12 *Expenditure on Active Naval Personnel System, 1889–90 to 1913–14 – Vote 1 [Wages, etc. of Officers], Vote 2 [Victualling and Clothing], Vote 13 [Half Pay, etc.], and Vote 14 [Naval, etc., Pensions]*

Fiscal year	I Vote 1 [Wages] including appropriations in aid	II Vote 2 [Victualling] including appropriations in aid	III Vote 13 [Half Pay] including appropriations in aid	IV Vote 14 [Pensions] including appropriations in aid
1889-90	£ 3,259,064	£ 1,254,202	£ 799,152	£ 921,810
1890-91	3,415,980	1,345,743	789,712	937,676
1891-92	3,525,839	1,483,095	785,501	957,310
1892-93	3,658,746	1,537,310	780,392	967,910
1893-94	3,753,456	1,636,193	777,442	996,987
1894-95	3,950,338	1,649,839	775,749	1,020,149
1895-96	4,189,322	1,739,243	762,143	1,040,212
1896-97	4,503,381	1,706,350	757,744	1,060,991
Total 1889-1896	£ 30,256,126	£ 12,351,975	£ 6,227,835	£ 7,903,045
1897-98	£ 4,730,166	£ 1,788,223	£ 763,525	£ 1,085,247
1898-99	5,053,146	2,166,594	782,972	1,109,299
1899-1900	5,331,457	2,297,078	786,105	1,127,805
1900-01	5,632,158	2,365,060	781,979	1,146,504
1901-02	5,916,636	2,393,288	786,799	1,168,323
1902-03	6,199,227	2,524,909	793,897	1,189,266
1903-04	6,489,466	2,887,352	803,806	1,210,679
1904-05	6,892,617	2,947,215	814,670	1,234,205
Total 1897-1904	£ 46,244,873	£ 19,369,719	£ 6,313,753	£ 9,271,328
1905-06	£ 6,975,495	£ 2,641,124	£ 845,925	£ 1,249,193
1906-07	7,199,128	2,341,742	853,593	1,295,881
1907-08	7,146,759	2,529,095	871,001	1,340,670
1908-09	7,291,767	2,935,832	881,639	1,359,535
1909-10	7,386,054	2,991,531	910,106	1,394,852
1910-11	7,517,040	3,139,148	921,767	1,444,494
1911-12	7,679,478	3,381,080	955,533	1,490,169
1912-13	7,893,434	3,545,707	991,349	1,545,119
Total, 1905-1912	£ 59,089,155	£ 23,505,259	£ 7,230,913	£ 11,119,913
1913-14	£ 8,405,971	£ 3,790,696	£ 1,006,861	£ 1,587,251

Table 13 *Expenditure on Active Naval Personnel System and Naval Reserve, 1889–90 to 1913–14 – Total Votes 1, 2, 13, 14 (from Table 12) and Vote 7 [Naval Reserve]*

Fiscal Year	I Votes 1, 2, 13 and 14, including appropriations in aid	II Vote 7 [Reserve] including appropriations in aid	III Total Votes 1, 2, 7, 13 and 14 (I + II)	IV Votes 1, 2, 13 and 14, percentage of total (I percentage of III)
1889–90	£ 6,234,228	£ 140,083	£ 6,374,311	% 97.8
1890–91	6,489,111	151,264	6,640,375	97.7
1891–92	6,751,745	160,792	6,912,539	97.7
1892–93	6,944,358	172,102	7,116,460	97.6
1893–94	7,164,078	179,042	7,343,120	97.6
1894–95	7,396,075	192,111	7,588,186	97.5
1895–96	7,730,920	203,967	7,934,887	97.4
1896–97	8,028,466	206,202	8,234,668	97.5
Total 1889–1896	£56,738,981	£ 1,405,563	£58,144,546	% 97.6
1897–98	£ 8,367,161	£ 227,708	£ 8,594,869	% 97.4
1898–99	9,112,011	243,429	9,355,440	97.4
1899–1900	9,542,445	228,869	9,771,314	97.7
1900–01	9,925,701	221,481	10,147,182	97.8
1901–02	10,265,046	246,462	10,511,508	97.7
1902–03	10,707,299	264,312	10,971,611	97.6
1903–04	11,391,303	292,296	11,683,599	97.5
1904–05	11,888,707	386,388	12,275,095	96.9
Total 1897–1904	£81,199,673	£ 2,110,945	£83,310,618	% 97.5
1905–06	£ 11,711,737	£ 300,650	£ 12,012,387	% 97.5
1906–07	11,690,344	357,495	12,047,839	97.
1907–08	11,887,525	359,649	12,247,174	97.1
1908–09	12,468,773	374,288	12,843,061	97.1
1909–10	12,682,543	373,140	13,055,683	97.1
1910–11	13,022,449	391,869	13,414,318	97.1
1911–12	13,506,260	397,329	13,903,589	97.1
1912–13	13,975,609	415,088	14,390,697	97.1
Total 1905–1912	£100,945,240	£ 2,969,508	£103,914,748	% 97.1
1913–14	£ 14,790,779	£ 444,392	£ 15,235,171	% 97.1

Table 14 *Proportions of Total Naval Expenditure spent on Manning, Works and Materiel, 1889–90 to 1913–14*

Fiscal year	I Manning: Votes 1, 2, 7, 13, 14	II Works: Vote 10 and Naval Works Acts	III Materiel: Votes 8, 9, Imperial and Naval Defence Acts	IV Balance: other Votes
1889–90	% 40.1	% 2.8	% 49.5	% 7.6
1890–91	36.8	2.3	55.	5.9
1891–92	38.1	2.1	53.6	6.2
1892–93	40.9	2.4	50.	6.7
1893–94	45.	2.4	45.2	7.4
1894–95	40.8	3.5	49.1	6.6
1895–96	37.3	5.5	51.	6.2
1896–97	34.5	4.9	55.3	5.3
Average 1889–1896	% 39.2	% 3.2	% 51.1	% 6.5
1897–98	% 38.1	% 5.9	% 49.8	% 6.2
1898–99	35.8	7.5	51.5	5.2
1899–1900	34.3	8.	52.8	4.9
1900–01	30.5	9.1	55.3	5.1
1901–02	30.	10.7	54.6	4.7
1902–03	30.9	12.1	52.3	4.7
1903–04	28.8	11.7	55.2	4.3
1904–05	29.4	12.	54.1	4.5
Average 1897–1904	% 32.2	% 9.6	% 53.2	% 5.0
1905–06	% 31.5	% 13.5	% 50.	% 5.
1906–07	33.8	11.8	49.5	4.9
1907–08	36.1	10.6	48.2	5.1
1908–09	36.9	9.1	48.8	5.2
1909–10	34.4	7.3	52.9	5.4
1910–11	30.8	7.	57.9	4.3
1911–12	30.2	7.	58.5	4.3
1912–13	30.8	6.6	58.6	4.
Average 1905–1912	% 33.1	% 9.1	% 53.	% 4.8
1913–14	% 30.7	% 6.9	% 58.1	% 4.3

Table 15 *Proportions of State Expenditure devoted to Spending on Defence, 1889–90 to 1912–13 (not including colonial spending)*

Fiscal year	I Army: gross expenditure	II Navy: gross expenditure	III Total defence spending (I + II)	IV Navy % of total defence spending	V Defence % of total state spending
1889-90	£ 17,651,116	£ 15,588,502	£ 33,239,618	% 46.9	% 38.6
1890-91	18,586,423	18,061,816	36,648,239	49.3	41.8
1891-92	18,299,479	18,150,638	36,450,117	49.8	40.5
1892-93	18,367,413	17,402,741	35,770,154	48.7	39.6
1893-94	18,722,467	16,327,641	35,050,108	46.6	38.4
1894-95	18,524,501	18,595,685	37,120,186	50.1	39.5
1895-96	19,090,114	21,264,377	40,354,491	52.7	41.3
1896-97	18,613,307	23,886,177	42,499,484	56.2	41.9
Total •1889-1896	£147,687,820	£149,277,577	£297,132,397	% 50.2	% 40.2
1897-98	£ 20,347,522	£ 22,547,844	£ 42,895,366	% 52.6	% 41.7
1898-99	21,043,796	26,145,598	47,189,394	55.4	43.6
1899-1900	44,281,605	28,478,842	72,760,447	39.1	54.4
1900-01	92,629,316	33,302,260	125,931,576	26.4	68.6
1901-02	94,410,361	34,994,553	129,404,914	27.	66.2
1902-03	70,525,821	35,525,731	106,051,552	33.5	57.5
1903-04	39,991,480	40,503,873	80,495,353	50.3	54.8
1904-05	31,961,864	41,696,313	73,658,177	56.6	51.9
Total 1897-1904	£415,191,765	£263,195,014	£678,386,779	% 38.8	% 54.8
1905-06	£ 29,766,279	£ 38,175,045	£ 67,941,324	% 56.2	% 48.4
1906-07	29,062,401	35,693,850	64,756,251	55.1	46.5
1907-08	27,449,894	33,950,169	61,400,063	55.3	40.4
1908-09	27,071,355	34,775,752	61,847,107	56.2	40.6
1909-10	27,412,029	38,711,268	66,123,297	58.5	41.9
1910-11	27,742,994	42,441,419	70,184,413	60.5	40.8
1911-12	27,877,428	44,384,340	72,261,768	61.4	40.5
1912-13	28,202,000	46,822,965	75,024,965	62.4	39.8
Total 1905-1912	£224,584,380	£314,954,808	£539,539,188	% 58.2	% 42.4

Table 16 Characteristics of British Battleships, 1889–1913

Program	Class	Number built	Displacement (tons)	Speed (knots)	Average cost per ship including armament
Naval Defence Act	Royal Sovereign	8	14,150	15.5	£ 923,023
	Centurion	2	10,500	17.0	620,252
1892–3	Renown	1	12,350	17.5	£ 746,247
1893–94	Majestic	2	14,560	16.0	£ 962,373
Spencer Prog.	Majestic	7	14,560	16.0	£ 962,373
1896–97	Canopus	5	13,150	18.0	£ 910,078
1897–98	Canopus	1	13,150	18.0	£ 910,078
	Formidable	3	14,500	18.0	1,091,492
1898–99	London	3	14,500	18.0	£ 1,117,195
	Duncan	4	13,270	19.0	1,084,844
1899–1900	Duncan	2	13,270	19.0	£ 1,084,844
1900–01	Queen	2	14,150	18.0	£ 1,215,896
1901–02	King Edward VII	3	15,585	18.5	£ 1,455,770
1902–03	King Edward VII	2	15,585	18.5	£ 1,455,770
1903–04	King Edward VII	3	15,585	18.5	£ 1,455,770
	Swiftsure	2	11,800	19.0	939,072
1904–05	Lord Nelson	2	16,090	18.0	£ 1,652,693
1905–06	Dreadnought	1	17,900	21.0	£ 1,813,100
1906–07	Bellerophon	3	18,600	20.75	£ 1,728,608
1907–08	St. Vincent	3	19,250	21.0	£ 1,698,012
1908–09	Neptune	1	19,900	21.0	£ 1,536,769
1909–10	Colossus	2	20,000	21.0	£ 1,666,807
	Orion	4	22,500	21.0	1,895,225
1910–11	King George V	4	23,000	21.0	£ 1,951,999
1911–12	Iron Duke	4	23,000	21.25	£ 2,042,871
1912–13	Queen Elizabeth	4	27,500	24.0	£ 2,685,799
Malaya	Queen Elizabeth	1	27,500	24.0	£ 2,685,799
1913–14	Royal Sovereign	5	27,500	20.4	£ 2,642,236

Table 17   Characteristics of British First-Class Cruisers, 1889–1911

Program	Class	Number built	Displacement (tons)	Speed (knots)	Average cost per ship including armament
Naval Defence Act	Edgar	9	7,350	18.0	£ 398,220
1893–94	Powerful	2	14,200	22.0	£ 744,227
Spencer Prog.	Diadem	8	11,000	20.25	£ 581,805
1897–98	Cressy	6	12,000	21.0	£ 791,263
1898–99	Drake Kent	4 4	14,150 9,800	23.0 23.0	£ 1,043,655 756,457
1899–1900	Kent	2	9,800	23.0	£ 756,457
1900–01	Kent	4	9,800	23.0	£ 756,457
1901–02	Devonshire	6	10,850	22.0	£ 880,494
1902–03	Duke of Edinburgh	2	13,550	23.0	£ 1,197,550
1903–04	Warrior	4	13,550	23.0	£ 1,204,310
1904–05	Minotaur	3	14,600	23.0	£ 1,415,073
1905–06	Invincible	3	17,250	25.0	£ 1,752,768
1906–07	*	*	*	*	*
1907–08	*	*	*	*	*
1908–09	Indefatigable	1	18,500	25.0	£ 1,536,769
1909–10	Lion	2	26,270	27.0	£ 2,089,283
Dominions	Indefatigable	2	18,500	25.0	£ 1,536,769
1910–11	Lion	1	26,270	27.0	£ 2,089,283
1911–12	Tiger	1	28,430	28.0	£ 2,593,100

Table 18 *Dreadnought Battleship and Battlecruiser Construction – Great Britain, Germany and the United States, 1905–1914*

Fiscal year [April–March]	Great Britain			Germany			United States			Germany + U.S.A.		
	L.D.	Lcd.	Cpl.	L.D.	Lcd.	Cpl.	L.D.	Lcd.	Cpl.	L.D.	Lcd.	Cpl.
1905–06*	3[5]	1	0	0	0	0	0	0	0	0	0	0
1906–07	5	3	1	0	0	0	2	0	0	2	0	0
1907–08	1	5	1	5	1	0	2	0	0	7	1	0
1908–09	3	3	5	5	4	0	2	4	0	7	8	0
1909–10	3	2	4	2	3	2	2	0	2	4	3	4
1910–11	10	6	3	5	5	3	0	3	2	5	8	5
1911–12	2	8	4	4	3	4	2	1	2	6	4	6
1912–13	7	3	7	2	2	5	2	2	2	4	4	7
1913–14	6	5	5	3	5	3	2	1	1	5	6	4

Calendar year	Great Britain			Germany			United States			Germany + U.S.A.		
	L.D.	Lcd.	Cpl.	L.D.	Lcd.	Cpl.	L.D.	Lcd.	Cpl.	L.D.	Lcd.	Cpl.
1905*	1[3]	0	0	0	0	0	0	0	0	0	0	0
1906	4	3	1	0	0	0	2	0	0	2	0	0
1907	4	6	0	4	0	0	2	0	0	6	0	0
1908	1	2	5	5	4	0	0	3	0	5	7	0
1909	6	3	4	2	4	2	2	1	0	4	5	2
1910	6	4	2	5	2	3	2	2	4	7	4	7
1911	5	8	4	4	5	4	2	2	2	6	7	6
1912	7	5	8	3	2	5	2	2	2	5	4	7
1913	6	5	5	3	5	3	1	0	0	4	5	3
1914	6	3	5	1	1	5	1	2	2	2	3	7

*Bracketted figure includes the 2 semi-dreadnoughts of the *Lord Nelson* class.

Table 19 *Cumulative Dreadnought Battleship and Battlecruiser Starts – Great Britain, Germany and the United States, 1905–1914*

Fiscal year [April-March]	Britain *	Germany	U.S.A.	Germany + U.S.A.	Germany + U.S.A. + 10 %	Germany + 60 %
1905-06	3 [5]	0	0	0	0	0
1906-07	8 [10]	0	2	2	2.2	0
1907-08	9 [11]	5	4	9	9.9	8.0
1908-09	12 [14]	10	6	16	17.2	16.0
1909-10	15 [17]	12	8	20	20.2	19.2
1910-11	25 [27]	17	8	25	27.5	27.2
1911-12	27 [29]	21	10	31	34.1	33.6
1912-13	34 [36]	23	12	35	38.5	36.8
1913-14	40 [42]	26	14	40	44.0	41.6

Calendar year	Britain *	Germany	U.S.A.	Germany + U.S.A.	Germany + U.S.A. + 10 %	Germany + 60 %
1905	1 [3]	0	0	0	0	0
1906	5 [7]	0	2	2	2.2	0
1907	9 [11]	4	4	8	8.8	6.4
1908	10 [12]	9	4	13	14.3	14.4
1909	16 [18]	11	6	17	18.7	17.6
1910	22 [24]	16	8	24	26.4	25.6
1911	27 [29]	20	10	30	33.0	32.0
1912	34 [36]	23	12	35	38.5	36.8
1913	40 [42]	26	13	39	42.9	41.6

*Bracketted figures include the 2 semi-dreadnoughts of the *Lord Nelson* class.

Table 20 *Cumulative Dreadnought Battleship and Battlecruiser Launches –
Great Britain, Germany and the United States, 1905–1914*

Fiscal year [April-March]	Britain *	Germany	U.S.A.	Germany + U.S.A.	Germany + U.S.A. + 10 %	Germany + 60 %
1905-06	1	0	0	0	0	0
1906-07	2 [4]	0	0	0	0	0
1907-08	7 [9]	1	0	1	1.1	1.6
1908-09	10 [12]	5	4	9	9.9	8.0
1909-10	12 [14]	8	4	12	13.2	12.8
1910-11	18 [20]	13	7	20	22.0	20.8
1911-12	26 [28]	16	8	24	26.4	25.6
1912-13	29 [31]	18	10	28	30.8	28.8
1913-14	34 [36]	23	11	34	37.4	36.8

Calendar year	Britain *	Germany	U.S.A.	Germany + U.S.A.	Germany + U.S.A. + 10 %	Germany + 60 %
1905	0 [0]	0	0	0	0	0
1906	1 [3]	0	0	0	0	0
1907	7 [9]	0	0	0	0	0
1908	9 [11]	4	3	7	7.7	6.4
1909	12 [14]	8	4	12	13.2	12.8
1910	16 [18]	10	6	16	17.6	16.0
1911	24 [26]	15	8	23	25.3	24.0
1912	29 [31]	17	10	27	29.7	27.2
1913	34 [36]	22	10	32	35.2	35.2

Table 21 *Cumulative Dreadnought Battleship and Battlecruiser Completions –*
Great Britain, Germany and the United States, 1905–1914

Fiscal year [April-March]	Britain *	Germany	U.S.A.	Germany + U.S.A.	Germany + U.S.A. + 10 %	Germany + 60 %
1905-06	0	0	0	0	0	0
1906-07	1	0	0	0	0	0
1907-08	2	0	0	0	0	0
1908-09	5 [7]	0	0	0	0	0
1909-10	9 [11]	2	2	4	4.4	3.2
1910-11	12 [14]	5	4	9	9.9	8.0
1911-12	16 [18]	9	6	15	16.5	14.4
1912-13	23 [25]	14	8	22	24.2	22.4
1913-14	28 [30]	17	9	26	28.6	27.2

Calendar year	Britain *	Germany	U.S.A.	Germany + U.S.A.	Germany + U.S.A. + 10 %	Germany + 60 %
1905	0 [0]	0	0	0	0	0
1906	1 [0]	0	0	0	0	0
1907	0 [0]	0	0	0	0	0
1908	4 [6]	0	0	0	0	0
1909	8 [10]	2	0	2	2.2	3.2
1910	10 [12]	5	4	9	9.9	8.0
1911	14 [16]	9	6	15	16.5	14.4
1912	22 [24]	14	8	22	24.2	22.4
1913	27 [29]	17	8	25	27.5	27.2

Table 22 *Active and Reserve Naval Manning Levels, 1889–90 to 1913–14*

Fiscal year	I Active naval personnel	II Reserve naval personnel	III Total active and reserve (I + II)	IV Active % of total (I % of III)
1889–90	65,400	20,118	85,518	76.5
1890–91	68,800	21,159	89,959	76.5
1891–92	71,000	21,445	92,445	76.8
1892–93	74,100	23,430	97,530	76.
1893–94	76,700	24,010	100,710	76.2
1894–95	83,400	24,570	107,970	77.2
1895–96	88,850	25,100	113,950	77.
1896–97	93,750	25,800	119,550	78.4
Total 1889–1896	622,000	185,632	807,632	77.
1897–98	100,050	27,000	127,050	78.7
1898–99	106,390	27,600	133,990	79.4
1899–1900	110,640	28,650	139,290	79.4
1900–01	114,880	28,700	143,580	80.0
1901–02	118,625	28,650	147,275	80.5
1902–03	122,500	27,780	150,280	81.5
1903–04	127,100	28,550	155,650	81.7
1904–05	131,100	33,505	164,605	79.6
Total 1897–1904	931,285	230,435	1,161,720	80.2
1905–06	129,000	31,805	160,805	80.2
1906–07	129,000	27,450	156,450	82.5
1907–08	128,000	27,036	155,036	82.6
1908–09	128,000	23,484	151,484	84.5
1909–10	128,000	22,069	150,069	85.3
1910–11	131,000	20,335	151,335	86.6
1911–12	134,000	17,789	151,789	88.3
1912–13	136,000	18,412	154,412	88.1
Total 1905–1912	1,043,000	188,380	1,231,380	84.7
1913–14	136,417	28,764	165,181	82.6

Table 23 *Admiralty – Argo/Pollen Financial Transactions, 1905–1913*

Calendar year	Equipment purchased by Admiralty	Payment
1905	Two-observer range-finding system and manual plotting table with accessories [Jupiter trials]	£ 5,300
1906	Range-finder mounting, transmission system and automatic plotting table [Ariadne trials]	£ 6,500
1908	For services rendered and for secrecy to November 1909	£ 11,500
1909	Range-finder mounting, transmission system, automatic plotting table and Argo Clock Mark I [Natal trials]	£ 7,660
1910	Extension of secrecy through 1912	£ 2,160
1910	45 Range-finder mountings at £1,350 each (with tools and accessories ordered later but excluding the cost of gyroscopes, afterwards cancelled)	£ 60,750
1911	Modifications to Natal plotting table	£ 210
1912	Spare parts and miscellaneous gear for the mounting order	£ 6,975
1912	Rate plotter [Orion]	£ 580
1912	Drawings, etc.	£ 200
1912	6 Argo Clocks Mark IV at £2,133 each	£ 12,798
1913	Installation of Argo Clocks, £150 each	£ 900
TOTAL		£115,533

List of Sources

All sources have been cited in the notes. For consolidated lists of the major published works on British naval history in the late 19th and early 20th century, see the relevant chapters by Ruddock F. Mackay and Arthur J. Marder in Robin Higham (ed.), *A Guide to the Sources of British Military History* (Berkeley and Los Angeles: University of California Press, 1971) and the author in Gerald Jordan (ed.), *British Military History; a Guide to the Recent Literature; a Supplement to Higham's Guide to the Sources of British Military History* (New York: Garland, 1988). A consolidated list of manuscripts, printed government papers, and contemporary and current newspapers and periodicals examined by the author is given below.

A Manuscript Collections

The following collections were consulted during research in England carried out from November 1977 to August 1979, May to June 1982, October to December 1983, August 1986, and August 1987:

1 INDIVIDUALS:

H. O. Arnold-Forster (British Library, London)
Herbert Henry Asquith, First Earl of Oxford (Bodleian Library, Oxford)
Arthur James Balfour, First Earl of Balfour (British Library, London)
Admiral of the Fleet Sir David Beatty, First Earl Beatty (N.M.M.)
Admiral Lord Charles William de la Poer Beresford (N.M.M.)
Admiral Sir Cyprian Arthur George Bridge (N.M.M.)
Admiral of the Fleet Alfred Ernle Montacute Chatfield (N.M.M.)
Hugh Clausen (C.C.)
Vice-Admiral Arthur Craig-Waller (N.L.M.D.)
Captain Thomas E. Crease (N.L.M.D.)
Admiral Sir Reginald Neville Custance (C.C.)
Vice-Admiral Kenneth Gilbert Balmain Dewar (N.M.M.)
Admiral Sir Frederic Charles Dreyer (C.C.)
Sir Eustace Henry William Tennyson-D'Eyncourt (N.M.M.)
Admiral of the Fleet Sir John Arbuthnot Fisher (C.C.)
George Gipps (P.P. and N.M.M.)
Sir William Graham Greene (N.M.M.)
Admiral Sir William Reginald Hall (C.C.)
Admiral Sir Frederick Tower Hamilton (N.M.M.)
Maurice Pascal Alers Hankey (C.C.)

Vice-Admiral J. E. T. Harper (C.C.)
Admiral Sir William Hannam Henderson (N.M.M.)
Rear-Admiral Sir Horace Lambert Alexander Hood (C.C.)
Archibald Hurd (C.C.)
Admiral of the Fleet Sir John Rushworth Jellicoe (British Library, London)
Admiral Osbert Charles Gresham Leveson-Gower (N.M.M.)
Admiral Sir Arthur Henry Limpus (N.M.M.)
Reginald McKenna (C.C.)
Admiral of the Fleet Sir Charles Edward Madden (N.M.M.)
Edward Marjoribanks, Second Baron Tweedmouth (N.L.M.D.)
Admiral of the Fleet Sir William Henry May (N.M.M.)
Louis Alexander Mountbatten (Battenberg), First Marquess of Milford Haven (I.W.M.)
Admiral of the Fleet Sir Gerard Uctred Noel (N.M.M.)
Admiral Sir Geoffrey Oliver (C.C.)
William Waldegrave Palmer, Second Earl of Selborne (Bodleian Library, Oxford)
Admiral Sir Reginald Aylmer Ranfurly Plunkett-Ernle-Erle-Drax (C.C.)
Arthur Hungerford Pollen (Anthony Pollen, London, and C.C.)
Vice-Admiral Sir Arthur Francis Pridham (C.C.)
Admiral Sir Herbert Richmond (N.M.M.)
Admiral Sir Edmond John Warre Slade (N.M.M.)
Sir William Thomson, First Baron Kelvin of Largs (Cambridge University Library, Cambridge)
Henry G. Thursfield (N.M.M.)
Sir James Richard Thursfield (N.M.M.)
Admiral of the Fleet Sir Rosslyn Erskine Wemyss (C.C.)
Arnold White (N.M.M.)

Note

Collected papers of the following individuals do not exist

Admiral Sir Reginald Hugh Spencer Bacon
Admiral Sir Percy Moreton Scott
Admiral of the Fleet Sir Arthur Knyvet Wilson

2 INSTITUTIONS AND ORGANIZATIONS:

Admiralty (P.R.O.)
Battle Cruiser Squadron (Drax Papers, C.C.)
Cabinet (P.R.O.)
Committee of Imperial Defence (P.R.O.)
Grand Fleet (N.L.M.D., P.R.O.)
Home Fleet [General Orders] (Drax Papers, C.C.)
Mediterranean Fleet (Fisher Papers, C.C.)
Department of the Controller of the Navy [Ship's Books/Ship's Covers] (P.R.O./N.M.M.)

Naval Intelligence Department [Reports] (N.L.M.D.)
Department of the Director of Naval Ordnance (N.L.M.D., N.M.M., P.R.O.)
Naval Staff, Gunnery Division (N.L.M.D.)
Patent Office (P.O.L.)

B   Printed Government Sources

Australia, Parliament, *Papers Presented to Parliament*, 1911–1914
Great Britain, Admiralty, *Navy Lists*, 1889–1914
Great Britain, Colonial Office, "Federated Malay States: Financial Report for the Year 1913," Supplement to the "F.M.S. Government Gazette," July 31, 1914
Great Britain, Laws, Statutes, etc., Various Acts,1888–1914
Great Britain, Parliament, *Parliamentary Debates*, 1888–1914
Great Britain, Parliament, *Parliamentary Papers*, 1888–1914
New Zealand, House of Representatives, *Appendix to the Journals of the House of Representatives of New Zealand*, 1911–1914

C   Contemporary Newspapers, Periodicals, and Annuals

Army and Navy Gazette
Blackwood's Edinburgh Magazine
Fighting Ships [Jane's]
Fleet and Naval Year Book
Journal of the Royal United Services Institution
National Review
Naval Annual
Naval and Military Record
Naval Review
Navy League Annual
Nineteenth Century and After
Times [London]
Transactions of the Institution of Naval Architects
United Service Magazine

D   Current Periodicals

American Historical Review
Annals of the History of Computing
Historical Research
Economic History Review
English Historical Review
History
Historical Journal

International History Review
International Security
Journal of Contemporary History
Journal of Modern History
Journal of Oriental Studies
Journal of the Royal Naval Scientific Service
Journal of Strategic Studies
Mariner's Mirror
Military Affairs
Naval History
Naval War College Review
Papers of the Peace Science Society (International)
Stanford Research Institute Journal
Technology and Culture
United States Naval Institute Proceedings
Warship
Warship International

Index